TENTH EDITION

Principles and Practices of Teaching Reading

Arthur W. Heilman
The Pennsylvania State University
Professor Emeritus

Timothy R. Blair
University of Central Florida

William H. Rupley
Texas A&M University

Merrill
Prentice Hall

Upper Saddle River, New Jersey
Columbus, Ohio

Library of Congress Cataloging-in-Publication Data

Heilman, Arthur W.
    Principles and practices of teaching reading / Arthur W. Heilman, Timothy R. Blair,
William H. Rupley.—10th ed.
      p. cm.
    Includes bibliographical references and index.
    ISBN 0-13-042083-2
    1. Reading (Elementary) I. Blair, Timothy R. II. Rupley, William H. III. Title.

LB1573 .H325 2002
372.4—dc21

2001030323

Vice President and Publisher: Jeffery W. Johnston
Editor: Linda Ashe Montgomery
Editorial Assistant: Evelyn Olson
Production Editor: Linda Hillis Bayma
Production Coordination: Amy Gehl, Carlisle Publishers Services
Photo Coordinator: Sandy Lenahan
Design Coordinator: Diane C. Lorenzo
Cover Designer: Rod Harris
Cover photo: Image Bank
Production Manager: Pamela D. Bennett
Director of Marketing: Kevin Flanagan
Marketing Manager: Krista Groshong
Marketing Coordinator: Barbara Koontz

This book was set in New Baskerville by Carlisle Communications, Ltd. It was printed and bound by R.R. Donnelley &
Sons Company. The cover was printed by The Lehigh Press, Inc.

Photo Credits: Timothy R. Blair, p. 424; Scott Cunningham/Merrill, pp. 4, 30, 72, 90, 244, 255, 312, 412, 457, 494, 522; Laima
Druskis/PH College, p. 300; KS Studios/Merrill, pp. 148, 552; Anthony Magnacca/Merrill, pp. 20, 56, 76, 206, 369, 378, 385,
448, 503, 511, 513, 538; William H. Rupley, pp. 16, 61, 96; Barbara Schwartz/Merrill, pp. 22, 36, 102, 113, 153, 282, 417, 454;
Anne Vega/Merrill, pp. 43, 47, 132, 151, 166, 227, 309, 391, 415, 485, 497; Tom Watson/Merrill, p. 528.

Pearson Education Ltd., *London*
Pearson Education Australia Pty. Limited, *Sydney*
Pearson Education Singapore Pte. Ltd.
Pearson Education North Asia Ltd., *Hong Kong*
Pearson Education Canada, Ltd., *Toronto*
Pearson Educación de Mexico, S.A. de C.V.
Pearson Education—Japan, *Tokyo*
Pearson Education Malaysia Pte. Ltd.
Pearson Education, *Upper Saddle River, New Jersey*

Merrill
Prentice Hall

10 9 8 7 6 5 4 3 2 1
ISBN 0-13-042083-2

To our wonderful wives, Jeanné and Agnes,

for their patience, continued understanding, and love

Preface

A knowledgeable, thinking, and caring teacher of reading is a key variable in whether or not children will be successful in learning to read. The tenth edition of *Principles and Practices of Teaching Reading* continues to be based on this assertion. Recent research on successful reading programs has again highlighted the important role of the teacher and has identified instructional variables that promote student learning. Those variables of teacher beliefs, attitudes, knowledge, and behaviors that contribute to student achievement in reading form the hallmarks of this book.

This edition of *Principles and Practices of Teaching Reading* continues to reflect the importance of teaching children to read by presenting new topics and expanding other significant literacy topics. The major focus of the text is to present, in a reader-friendly format, the implementation of a comprehensive and balanced viewpoint in teaching children to become literate. One of the long-standing hallmarks of the text continues to be a blending of both concise syntheses of up-to-date research findings and practical strategies, activities, and lesson plans for illustrative purposes. The many practical examples, games, lesson plans, and activities provide concrete ideas for the classroom. In addition, each chapter has field-based assignments and portfolio entries.

Significant changes in this edition include:

- An extensively revised discussion of balanced reading programs stressing the importance and necessity of combining research-based skills and strategies with fine literature;
- Summaries of major findings from the National Reading Research Center, CIERA, and the National Reading Panel;
- A revised chapter on emergent literacy;
- Expanded coverage of interactive strategies to promote reading comprehension;
- A revised chapter on literature-based reading by Donna Norton, author of the classic textbook on children's literature, *Through the Eyes of a Child;*
- Expanded coverage for meeting the needs of diverse learners;
- Updated flashback features, which provide a valuable historical perspective on teaching reading;

- Updated "Inclusion Strategies" sections that provide modifications of various topics when working with children with special needs in regular classrooms; and

- For professors, a new Instructor's Manual that includes test questions, discussion questions, and blackline transparency masters.

Acknowledgments

Writing a book is certainly a team effort. We thank our many students, public school teachers, and colleagues for their insights into and suggestions for several parts of this revision. Finally, we would like to extend our appreciation to the staff at Merrill/ Prentice Hall, especially Linda Montgomery and Linda Bayma, and Amy Gehl of Carlisle Publishers Services for their help and expert guidance throughout the preparation of this book.

DISCOVER
THE **Companion Website**
Accompanying This Book

THE PRENTICE HALL COMPANION WEBSITE
A Virtual Learning Environment

Technology is a constantly growing and changing aspect of our field that is creating a need for content and resources. To address this emerging need, Prentice Hall has developed an online learning environment for students and professors alike—Companion Websites—to support our textbooks.

In creating a Companion Website, our goal is to build on and enhance what the textbook already offers. For this reason, the content for each user-friendly website is organized by topic and provides the professor and student with a variety of meaningful resources. Common features of a Companion Website include:

For the Professor–

Every Companion Website integrates **Syllabus Manager™**, an online syllabus creation and management utility.

- **Syllabus Manager™** provides you, the instructor, with an easy, step-by-step process to create and revise syllabi, with direct links into Companion Website and other online content without having to learn HTML.

- Students may log on to your syllabus during any study session. All they need to know is the web address for the Companion Website and the password you've assigned to your syllabus.

- After you have created a syllabus using **Syllabus Manager™**, students may enter the syllabus for their course section from any point in the Companion Website.

- Clicking on a date, the student is shown the list of activities for the assignment. The activities for each assignment are linked directly to actual content, saving time for students.

- Adding assignments consists of clicking on the desired due date, then filling in the details of the assignment—name of the assignment, instructions, and whether it is a one-time or repeating assignment.

- In addition, links to other activities can be created easily. If the activity is online, a URL can be entered in the space provided, and it will be linked automatically in the final syllabus.

- Your completed syllabus is hosted on our servers, allowing convenient updates from any computer on the Internet. Changes you make to your syllabus are immediately available to your students at their next logon.

For the Student–

- **Topic Overviews**—outline key concepts in topic areas

- **Strategies**—these websites provide suggestions and information on how to implement instructional strategies and activities for specific topics

- **Web Links**—a wide range of websites that allow the students to access current information on everything from rationales for specific types of instruction, to research on related topics, to compilations of useful articles and more

- **Electronic Bluebook**—send homework or essays directly to your instructor's email with this paperless form

- **Message Board**—serves as a virtual bulletin board to post—or respond to—questions or comments to/from a national audience

- **Chat**—real-time chat with anyone who is using the text anywhere in the country—ideal for discussion and study groups, class projects, etc.

To take advantage of these and other resources, please visit the *Principles and Practices of Teaching Reading*, Tenth Edition, Companion Website at

www.prenhall.com/heilman

Contents

Note: Every effort has been made to provide accurate and current Internet information in this book. However, the Internet and information posted on it are constantly changing, so it is inevitable that some of the Internet addresses listed in this textbook will change.

Principles and Practices of Teaching Reading

I

Foundations of Literacy Instruction

CHAPTERS

Overview

Children's growth and development in literacy depend on their having knowledgeable, caring, and thoughtful teachers; and helping students learn to read and write is an exciting, rewarding, and honorable responsibility. Thus, the first part of this text focuses on the overwhelming importance of the teacher in a successful literacy program, as well as specific characteristics of successful teachers, the nature of the reading process, guiding principles of a balanced literacy program, and language—the core from which effective literacy instruction emanates.

Integrating Principles of Teaching Reading

Individual principles of reading instruction, which will be presented in Chapter 1, will serve as fundamental guiding ideas throughout this text. The first four chapters will reinforce the following principles:

- Reading and writing are language processes.
- Reading is a meaningful, active, constructive, and strategic process.
- Reading and writing are developmental processes.
- Teachers must strive for a balanced literacy program to teach all students to read and write independently.
- Teachers of literacy must forge partnerships with the home and community to promote reading growth.
- The key to successful literacy instruction is the teacher.

CHAPTER 1

Principles of Reading Instruction

Chapter Outline

For the Reader

As you prepare to become an effective teacher of reading, it is important that you understand your enormous influence on whether students will learn, the features of quality reading instruction, and the process of reading itself. Reading is a basic communication skill and a primary means of learning in our society. You most likely are a competent reader, one who gives little thought to how you read and how you get meaning from what you read.

Reading is a complex process. It depends on a variety of factors, such as the reader's experiential and conceptual background, word recognition strategies, reasoning ability, purpose for reading, environment, motivation, and text complexity. These features of reading influence our attempts to construct meaning from what we read. This chapter presents some basic aspects of the reading process and sets forth principles to help guide you at all grade levels of reading instruction.

Key Ideas

- Reading is interaction with language that has been coded into print.
- The result of reading is construction of meaning.
- Reading is a language process.
- Learning to read is a developmental process.
- Many methods can be used to teach reading effectively.
- Instruction must be tailored to the needs of each student.
- Teachers must strive for a balanced literacy program.

A MESSAGE TO TEACHERS-IN-TRAINING

The ability to teach reading successfully has always been of paramount importance. This book is based on the premise that you will have a profound influence on how well your students learn to read. Teaching is a major challenge and a complex process. As you will learn throughout this text (especially in Chapter 2), research has helped us make tremendous advances in determining how effective reading teachers teach. As a teacher-in-training, you should be aware that how you promote **literacy*,** the ability to read and write proficiently, in the classroom will have a profound effect on your students' lives. The ability to read—that uniquely human process that results from a multitude of factors—is truly a magical phenomenon. It can open the minds of children to new worlds, emotions, insights, and imaginative ideas; information of all types; and exciting, creative pursuits. It can also help them further their education and career opportunities and increase the quality of their lives through personal enjoyment. This is exactly why being a teacher of literacy is such a challenging, exciting, and rewarding experience.

The process of reading is the major vehicle for teaching and learning in our schools. Quoting from the joint position statement titled "Learning to Read and Write: Developmentally Appropriate Practices for Young Children" adopted in 1998 by the International Reading Association (IRA) and the National Association for the Education of Young children (NAEYC), the authors stated:

> Learning to read and write is critical to a child's success in school and later in life. One of the best predictors of whether a child will function competently in school and go on to contribute actively in our increasingly literate society is the level to which the child progresses in reading and writing. (p. 196)

Unfortunately, not all children experience the rewards and joys of literacy, and you will need to customize your instruction to suit students' varying strengths and weaknesses and to suit an intended instructional goal. If all reading instruction were the same for all students in each grade, teaching reading would be easy. One thing that makes teaching so rewarding and challenging, however, is the fact that children are different. They differ in a multitude of ways: in intelligence, background knowledge, language background, social awareness, thinking abilities, creativity, and interests, to name a few. Learning to read is a complex process that is affected by a host of factors, many of which are under your control and some of which are not. Your knowledge and expertise can help you make a difference in children's lives. You will have much influence in guiding children to develop their language abilities to the fullest; your involvement is both indispensable and a privilege. Historian Henry Adams articulated it best: "Teachers affect eternity; they never know where their influence will end."

THE READING PROCESS

Do you sometimes "read" without thinking of or understanding some of the writer's message? We all have experiences in which we "read" material but are thinking of other things. You may still be able to "read" aloud from your high school French,

---

*Words appearing in boldface in the text are defined in the Glossary.

Latin, or Spanish textbook, but can you understand or comprehend all of what you read? The true reading process is a dynamic one, requiring active, meaningful communication between the author and the reader. This text defines **reading** as the active process of constructing meaning from written text in relation to the experiences and knowledge of the reader.

The major goal of reading instruction is to foster in students the ability to interact with and to understand printed language. Reading is an internal, mental process that cannot be observed or studied directly. Many investigators relate reading to thinking and argue that the two are inseparable in understanding printed language. In a much-quoted study of reading comprehension, Thorndike (1917) defined *reading* as "thinking":

> The reading of a paragraph involves the same sort of organization and analysis as does thinking. It includes learning, reflection, judgment, analysis, synthesis, problem-solving behavior, selection, inference, organization, comparison of data, determination of relationships, and critical evaluation of what is read. It also includes attention, association, abstraction, generalization, comprehension, concentration, and deduction.

Reading once was thought to be a passive process: It was supposed to consist of a hierarchical list of word-identification and comprehension skills that, once mastered, would enable one to comprehend what one was reading. Instruction emphasized the identification and pronunciation of words, called **decoding** skills, because they were the most easily taught. Today, however, if teachers accept the idea that a major aspect of reading is comprehension, then they must put into proper perspective both major facets of reading: decoding words rapidly and accurately, and combining information from the text with existing knowledge to construct meaning. The following examples illustrate the importance of these two aspects as well as the basic features of reading; anyone who reads English will have no trouble with decoding or intonation:

> Some squares do not have four sides.

> Thomas Jefferson was a friend of tyranny.

Reading these sentences demands reader interaction, as does all written material. The reader must relate existing knowledge to the ideas that the text represents and use this knowledge to make sense of that text.

A person reading "Some squares do not have four sides" might react in any number of ways: "This is a misprint—it should say, 'All squares have four sides.' No, maybe that's not the kind of square that is meant; Reginald Philbut is a square, and he doesn't have four sides. No, that's not what it means. What is the author talking about? Well, no matter. I don't see how he can say that some squares do not have four sides. Maybe this is a trick statement. I had better read more to see if I can figure out what this statement means."

The last sentence illustrates how we use existing knowledge to make sense of what we read. The reader is using knowledge both about squares as geometric figures and about squares in a figurative sense (representing a conservative individual). In addition, the reader is employing a strategic approach by using such knowledge

Oe characteristic of American education is the commitment to the concept of universal education. Evidence of this commitment is seen in our compulsory school attendance laws. Massachusetts was the first state to enact a compulsory school attendance law in 1852. In the 1800s, only a small percentage of students completed high school.

From *Abraham Lincoln: The Boy, The Man* by Lloyd Ostendorf. Springfield, IL: Hamann The Printer, Inc. 1962.

UPDATE

Today, 70 to 90% of students complete the 12th grade. Additionally, schools' populations are becoming increasingly culturally diverse. According to a recent report from the National Assessment of Educational Progress (NAEP) (1992), students are doing well in acquiring basic knowledge, but few students are learning to use this knowledge effectively in thinking and reasoning. Thus, teachers of reading today are being encouraged to promote comprehension of ideas requiring higher cognitive thinking. The authors of *Becoming a Nation of Readers* (Anderson, Hiebert, Scott, & Wilkinson, 1985) stated, "Discussions before reading and discussions and questioning after reading should motivate children's higher level thinking, with an emphasis on making connections with their prior knowledge of the topic" (p. 58).

These last sentences put the two essentials of reading—automatic decoding and comprehension—in proper perspective. Fluent reading demands rapid and accurate decoding of printed words, but mere decoding of words is not reading until it evokes the meaning or meanings that those words represent.

about text to realize that this may be a trick statement or that further reading may help explain the sentence. This reader is thus exercising the thinking abilities Thorndike described.

In the second example, a reader who knows little of Thomas Jefferson might reason, "Well, it's good to be apprised of this man's character. I'll be suspicious of everything he says or writes, particularly about government and people's rights." However, anyone who knows much about Jefferson might react by saying, "How ridiculous! Who is writing this stuff? Where was this book published? I had better read more; this might be a misprint. Didn't Jefferson say, 'I have sworn eternal hostility to every form of tyranny over the mind of man'?"

UNDERLYING THEORIES

Our understanding of how children learn to read has greatly improved in the last two decades. This greater understanding of the reading process has emerged primarily from the field of cognitive psychology (Pearson & Stephens, 1994; Samuels & Kamil, 1984). While word identification is crucial, today's concept of the reading process stresses the process of meaning construction.

Two theoretical models, supported by an abundance of research, have helped shape our understanding of the reading process: the schema and interactive theories of reading. Harris and Hodges (1995) define schema theory as "a view that comprehension depends on integrating new knowledge with a network of prior knowledge" (p. 227). A central component of this theory relates to the interrelated and interdependent relationship between text comprehension and the reader's background knowledge. As students read, they use past experiences to interact with new information presented in the text. Thus, as readers process printed words, they construct meaning from them based both on the words and on background knowledge. This background knowledge, called **experiential** and conceptual background, is defined as a reader's experiences that are both concrete and abstract (knowledge), as well as the reader's reasoning abilities in using this knowledge. For example, in reading about how to grow vegetables, readers integrate knowledge about gardening and related experiences with new information. They process the text to formulate hypotheses that make sense in light of existing background knowledge.

Directly related to schema theory is the **interactive theory of reading,** which holds that reading is an active process in which, to comprehend text, students interact with a multitude of factors related to themselves, the text being read, and the context in which reading occurs. Figure 1.1 depicts the interactive nature of reading by grouping significant factors under the headings of Reader, Text, and Context. Central to the interactive theory (Rumelhart, 1985) is the reader's use of prior knowledge and various strategies to interact with text. In this sense, the reader is an active participant interacting with the text by applying specific strategies to construct meaning. The term *strategic reader* reflects the view that readers consciously apply strategies to enhance their understanding of ideas.

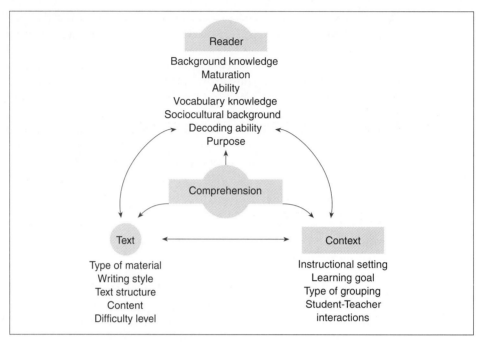

Figure 1.1   Interactive reading factors.

WHAT CONSTITUTES A BALANCED LITERACY PROGRAM?

Before moving on to the stages of reading development, principles of teaching reading, and then specific reading approaches and strategies, it is helpful to have an overall view of a balanced literacy program in terms of its major content strands and major program areas. A **balanced literacy program** is one that uses a variety of teaching approaches, strategies, and materials to teach students what they need to know. The emphasis is on the word *variety* because children are different in so many ways that one approach or strategy will not work equally well with every child. If all literacy instruction could be the same for all students in each grade, teaching literacy would be easy. The complexity of teaching is quickly realized when one tries to "differentiate" one's instruction according to student needs and the instructional goal. Blair-Larsen and Williams (1999) state "Subscribing to the balanced view of reading instruction enables teachers to base instruction on the needs of individual students rather than limit their classroom reading instruction to a current trend or to a single focus or approach" (p. 3). Literacy teachers must use different approaches and strategies to meet the varied needs of students. Spiegel (1999) addressed this very aspect of balanced reading instruction in stating, "A balanced approach requires and enables a teacher to reflect on what he or she is doing and to modify instruction daily on the needs of each individual learner" (p. 13). Most literacy programs cover the following content strands: word recognition, word meaning, comprehension, reading study

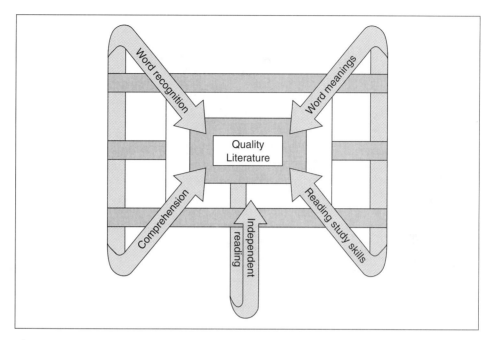

Figure 1.2   Major content strands of a balanced elementary school literacy program.

skills, independent or recreational reading, and literature. Each strand is fostered through instruction and an abundance of practice in meaningful text. The strands are analogous to braiding hair or weaving a basket, with each strand woven together in a continuum. The strands must be woven correctly to achieve the desired result. In most literacy programs today, such skills, strategies, and understandings are being developed increasingly through the reading of quality literature. (See Figure 1.2.)

It is also helpful to understand the major program areas of a complete, balanced literacy program. Regardless of grade level, the literacy curriculum includes experience in each of the following five program areas: developmental reading, application-transfer, independent or recreational reading, content reading, and functional reading.

Developmental reading involves sequential development of reading skills and strategies. Students also need interesting, varied practice with new material (application-transfer) if they are to master reading. In the recreational component, students apply their reading skills and strategies to a variety of literary forms to expand their interests and develop lifelong reading habits. The content reading component includes systematic instruction in reading study skills and comprehension strategies so that students are able to understand content material. Finally, the functional reading component includes experiences in which students apply their reading strategies in practical situations: For example, they receive instruction and practice in filling out job and loan applications, using telephone books, and reading magazines and newspapers. Figure 1.3 provides a view of the major program areas of a balanced literacy curriculum, along with the purposes of each and materials used to implement their instructional goals.

COMPONENTS	PURPOSES	MATERIALS
Developmental reading	Systematic learning of word identification, word meanings, comprehension, content skills, and strategies. Development of proficient, strategic readers who comprehend written language.	Literature-based, basal-reader, language-experience, and content-area programs.
Application-transfer	Reading experiences designed to help students master skills and strategies taught in the main program component and to enhance the transfer of reading skills to other reading situations.	Various types of literature, high-interest/low-vocabulary readers, supplemental basal-reader programs, games, audiovisual aids, workbooks, teacher-made materials, newspapers, magazines, and content texts.
Recreational reading	Literary experiences to which students apply their reading abilities to expand their knowledge of a variety of subjects and become lifelong readers.	Various types of literature, paperback books, and book clubs.
Content reading	Specific learning of skills and strategies to use in content areas.	Various types of literature, encyclopedias, card catalogs, almanacs, atlases, maps, charts, graphs, tables, diagrams, and content texts.
Functional reading	Instruction in how to use reading to gain basic, practical information needed in everyday activities.	Telephone books, newspapers, catalogs, driver's manuals, job and loan applications, and magazines.

Figure 1.3   Program components of a balanced literacy program.

WHAT ARE THE STAGES OF READING DEVELOPMENT?

It is often said that reading programs never rise above the quality of instruction found within them. Teachers must understand students as learners and must view learning to read as a developmental process. Several reading authorities have offered considerable support for the developmental view of reading. Important reading behaviors identified by Clay (1979), Stanovich (1986), and Chall (1996) focus on well-developed decoding strategies and understanding of meaning.

Jeanne Chall's comprehensive reading development stages from preschool through grade 8 are discussed later in this chapter, in relation to the principle that reading and writing are developmental processes. Her proposed reading stages (shown in Figure 1.4) illustrate the major qualitative reading abilities, as well as the relationship of reading to listening comprehension. It is important to understand that these stages may overlap and are not fixed. That is, a first grader could be in Stage 3 and a sixth grader could be in Stage 1. The characteristics associated with each stage should be viewed as representative. They should serve as guidelines for understanding the curriculum and planning quality reading instruction.

PRINCIPLES OF READING INSTRUCTION

Sound instructional principles tend to be learner oriented. They can be applied consistently to children who have noticeably different learning capacities, interests, and experiences. While learning to read is a complicated process, you already know many effective learning principles from your study of educational psychology. Learning to read depends on the same learning principles as do other cognitive skills, such as past experiential and conceptual backgrounds, purposes for learning, learner motivation, task difficulty, and instructional quality. You must integrate these principles with your specific knowledge of developing reading abilities.

Principles of teaching reading should evolve from the best knowledge available in general psychology, educational psychology, curriculum planning, studies in child growth and development, reading research, and from child guidance and psychological clinics. In formulating principles, it is necessary to consider all facets of human growth and development, including intellectual, physiological, psychological, and emotional aspects. As such, the principles discussed in this section can serve as guidelines for teacher behavior. You may question whether some of these principles are absolutely valid. Such questioning is healthy, especially if it stimulates the formulation of rational alternatives.

1. Reading and writing are language processes.

Teachers must understand the relationships between reading and writing and children's oral language. Children's oral language reflects their experiences with objects, ideas, relationships, and their interactions with their world. Much has been written about what children bring to school and the role of the school in building on each child's abilities. Teachers should help children transfer the language background that they bring to school directly to their reading and writing (Snow, Burns, & Griffin, 1998).

Recent studies have shown that experiences that promote success in reading occur long before a child begins formal schooling (Hiebert, Pearson, Taylor, Richardson, & Paris, 1998). For example, before starting school, many children can recognize letters of the alphabet, write their names, identify brand names, use books properly, and retell all or parts of favorite stories. Many children also exhibit knowledge of

1 STAGE DESIGNATION	2 GRADE RANGE (AGE)	3 MAJOR QUALITATIVE CHARACTERISTICS AND MASTERIES BY END OF STAGE	4 HOW ACQUIRED	5 RELATIONSHIP OF READING TO LISTENING
Stage 0: Prereading, "pseudo-reading"	Preschool (ages 6 months–6 years)	Child "pretends" to read, retells story when looking at pages of book previously read to him/her; names letters of alphabet; recognizes some signs; prints own name; plays with books, pencils, and paper.	Being read to by an adult (or older child) who responds to and warmly appreciates the child's interest in books and reading; being provided with books, paper, pencils, blocks, and letters.	Most can understand the children's picture books and stories read to them. They understand thousands of words they hear by age 6 but can read few if any of them.
Stage 1: Initial reading and decoding	Grade 1 & beginning grade 2 (ages 6 & 7)	Child learns relation between letters and sounds and between printed and spoken words; child is able to read simple text containing high-frequency words and phonically regular words; uses skill and insight to "sound out" new one-syllable words.	Direct instruction in letter-sound relations (phonics) and practice in their use. Reading of simple stories using words with phonic elements taught and words of high frequency. Being read to on a level above what child can read independently to develop more advanced language patterns, knowledge of new words, and ideas.	The level of difficulty of language read by the child is much below the language understood when heard. At the end of Stage 1, most children can understand up to 4,000 or more words when heard but can read only about 600.

Figure 1.4 Stages of reading development: An outline of the major qualitative characteristics and how they are acquired.

1 STAGE DESIGNATION	2 GRADE RANGE (AGE)	3 MAJOR QUALITATIVE CHARACTERISTICS AND MASTERIES BY END OF STAGE	4 HOW ACQUIRED	5 RELATIONSHIP OF READING TO LISTENING
Stage 2: Confirmation and fluency	Grades 2 & 3 (ages 7 & 8)	Child reads simple familiar stories and selections with increasing fluency. This is done by consolidating the basic decoding elements, sight vocabulary, and meaning context in the reading of familiar stories and selections.	Direct instruction in advanced decoding skills; wide reading (with instruction and independently) of familiar, interesting materials which help promote fluent reading. Being read to at levels above their own independent reading level to develop language, vocabulary, and concepts.	At the end of Stage 2, about 3,000 words can be read and understood and about 9,000 are known when heard. Listening is still more effective than reading.
Stage 3: Reading for learning the new Phase A Phase B	Grades 4–8 (ages 9–13) Intermediate, 4–6 Junior high school, 7–9	Reading is used to learn new ideas, to gain new knowledge, to experience new feelings, to learn new attitudes; generally from one viewpoint.	Reading and study of textbooks, reference works, trade books, magazines, and magazines that contain new ideas and values, unfamiliar vocabulary and syntax; systematic study of words and reacting to the text through discussion, answering questions, writing, etc. Reading of increasingly more complex fiction, biography, nonfiction, and the like.	At beginning of Stage 3, listening comprehension of the same material is still more effective than reading comprehension. By the end of Stage 3, reading and listening are about equal; for those who read very well, reading may be more efficient.

Figure 1.4 (continued)

Source: From Jeanne S. Chall, *Stages of Reading Development,* 2nd edition, ©1996. Reprinted with permission of Wadsworth, an imprint of the Wadsworth Group, a division of Thompson Learning. Fax 800-730-2215.

The meanings acquired from reading are closely related to our experiential and conceptual backgrounds.

written language and its purpose to communicate. They may scribble (write) letters and stories and read their compositions to others, make up spellings, and create letterlike forms. In addition, children often demonstrate an understanding of stories and use stories to bring meaning to their play. These behaviors indicate an understanding of language that can form the foundation for effective literacy instruction. Anderson, Hiebert, Scott and Wilkinson (1985) highlight the importance of oral language facility to the reading process:

> Reading instruction builds especially on oral language. If this foundation is weak, progress in reading will be slow and uncertain. Children must have at least a basic vocabulary, a reasonable range of knowledge about the world around them and the ability to talk about their knowledge. These abilities form the basis for comprehending text. (p. 30)

The relationship of oral language development is crucial to reading, as are the other language processes. The language arts—listening, speaking, reading, and writing—are the tools of communication. All of the language arts are interrelated;

growth in one reinforces and facilitates growth in the others. While it may be convenient to discuss the language arts separately, they are inextricably intertwined. A primary method by which to promote all the language processes is through their integration in reading quality literacy selections.

2. Reading is a meaningful, active, constructive, and strategic process.

Reading is comprehension and good readers are good comprehenders (Snow et al., 1998). Reading is an active process of constructing meaning by making connections between our existing knowledge to the knowledge presented in a book or text. The product of "making these connections" or interacting with printed language should be comprehension. Readers must be active; that is, they must use all available resources to construct meaning and make sense of the text. Reading involves the interaction of several factors, including textual factors, background knowledge, and the social setting in which reading occurs. In addition, the effective reader applies various reading strategies at the right time and in the right doses for understanding: The student becomes a strategic, or flexible, reader. Flexible readers choose from a variety of strategies to fulfill their purposes in comprehending text.

3. Reading and writing are developmental processes.

If teachers accept that reading and writing are the construction of meaning (comprehension), then there is no such thing as mastery of literacy ability; rather, it is a constantly evolving process. Individuals' experiential and conceptual backgrounds continue to grow. As one's background knowledge grows, so does one's ability to interact with text and acquire new information; therefore, literacy capabilities are constantly expanding. Reflecting the belief that reading is a developmental process whereby children move through various stages in an orderly and predictable manner, many authors have proposed that each child moves through various stages of reading development. While the stages are not entirely separate, they do provide teachers with an overall view of development and how their students' growth and their instruction fit into the big picture. Chall (1996) views reading development as a sequence of stages (see Figure 1.4). Stage 0 (preschool) focuses on learning to recognize and identify letters; Stage 1 (grade 1 and beginning of grade 2) emphasizes decoding or word-pronunciation abilities and comprehension of simple stories; Stage 2 (grades 2 and 3) centers on making decoding abilities automatic and increasing comprehension; and Stage 3 (grades 4–8) encourages comprehension in a variety of different texts, including content-area books and complex fiction.

4. Teachers must capitalize on student diversity and plan appropriate instruction for the wide range of individual differences in the classroom.

Today, more than ever before, our classrooms are multiracial, multicultural, and multiethnic. Many classrooms today each contain students representing more than a dozen languages and a great diversity of ethnic and racial backgrounds. Providing children with a balanced literacy program requires teachers to understand diversity and to develop a teaching style that both respects and capitalizes on the strengths of all children. Successful teachers value and accept a student's culture, community, language, and past experiences (Diller, 1999). Many students speak a dialect other than mainstream English and many are learning English as a second language. In both cases, to be successful, teachers of reading must know their students' backgrounds, must employ additional knowledge and skills in their teaching, and must monitor their instructional decisions in the classroom.

With the national movement in our schools toward inclusion and inclusive schooling, teachers also must provide for the needs of exceptional children in the regular classroom literacy program. Inclusion is predicated on the belief that all students, including those traditionally classified as mildly, moderately, and severely disabled, should be educated with their peers in neighborhood schools. Exceptional children often need different literacy instruction from that which is found in most classrooms (Sears, Carpenter, & Burnstein, 1994). Specialized services required to help these children meet their literacy needs are provided and coordinated in the classroom by the special education teacher and the regular classroom teacher. As a result of the inclusive movement, strategies for delivering instruction such as the consulting teacher model, collaborative consultation, computer instruction, and parents as teachers are among those now being recommended (David, 1991). To meet the needs of all students, literacy teachers need to recognize and appreciate student diversity, believe that all students can and will learn, and provide excellent, personalized instruction to all children (Allington, 1995).

5. Teachers must strive for a balanced literacy program to teach all students to read and write independently.

Because children are different in a multitude of ways, including the manner in which they become mature, strategic readers, teachers need to use a variety of approaches to successfully teach literacy. Speaking to this point, Spiegel (1994) states:

> Theorists and researchers may make pronouncements that a particular way is "the" way. But there is no one way to develop literacy, through a particular approach or through certain materials. And there never will be. The path through authors, texts, and contexts will vary for each reader. Therefore literacy teachers must strive to find the balance for each child. Fortunately many literacy educators understand this, and in spite of mandates from above or outside, modify the curriculum each day based on what their learners really need.

Effective teachers do not attempt to mold each child to a particular curriculum or approach. Students respond differently in a variety of areas, including responses to different types of instruction (direct and indirect); commercial and personalized, learner-centered programs; motivational strategies (intrinsic versus extrinsic); and instructional materials (published readers, literature books, computers, magazines, games, and so forth). A formula for balanced reading instruction for all students, regardless of age, grade, interests, needs, learning style, and learning rate is incompatible with our knowledge of students and learning. What is compatible with it, however, is the development of a self-monitoring, reflective attitude or disposition that generates useful information about the students, the reading process, the classroom environment, and possible teaching approaches and strategies to accomplish one's goals. Teachers who engage in a process of monitoring their own teaching become more confident in their abilities and are able to provide the balanced literacy instruction students need. Effective teachers teach children what they need to know by modifying and adjusting their curricula to meet their students' learning needs: "A balanced curriculum of the integrated language arts begins with an affirmation that different learners need different approaches to help them become proficient readers and writers" (Smith, 1996, p. 2). A balanced literacy approach that combines the best of all worlds is the most effective way to meet the needs of all the diverse learners in a classroom and ensure that students develop independence in their reading.

Developing independence in reading requires the acquisition of methods for identifying words, interaction with the text, and construction of meaning. It is essential that a balanced approach to reading be achieved using both a skill development program and a focus on fine literature. Whether using cues about analyzing spelling to help with pronunciation, looking at the structural parts of a word, or considering the context in which the word appears, one must develop facility in identifying (i.e., decoding) printed word forms. Fox (2000) speaks to the importance of providing a balanced instructional program in word identification, or decoding: "Overrelying on any one cue is inefficient, time-consuming, and likely to result in poor comprehension. Good readers know this and hence balance syntactic, semantic, and letter and sound cues with the type of text they are reading, the reading environment, their own reasons for reading, and their background knowledge" (p. 13). These cues are best taught and practiced in conjunction with sentences and/or whole texts, not in isolation. Students then learn to decode in the context of real reading, which involves the whole reading process. This principle is not in conflict with the principle that students must see reading as an active, meaning-making process. Research has shown the close relationship between decoding ability and total reading performance (Fox, 2000). Once students can decode words at an automatic level, they can spend more time and energy on comprehension.

A balanced literacy program also relates to reading and writing in the content areas. Successful learning in content areas depends on students' application of reading study skills, comprehension strategies, and writing ability. A literacy program is not complete without adequate attention to content areas, and success in the regular literacy program does not automatically guarantee success in the content areas (Richardson & Morgan, 2000). Many students experience difficulties in these areas that are further compounded when they are not taught to become independent learners. If we truly believe in the educational principle of independent learning, we must devote more time to teaching the skills and strategies needed in the content areas. For students to be independent learners, we must teach them how to pursue the ever-increasing amount of knowledge in nearly all fields. In other words, they must learn how to learn.

The effective literacy program integrates the entire curriculum across all content areas around reading, writing, listening, and speaking activities.

6. Literature should be an integral part of literacy instruction throughout the entire school curriculum.

The time has passed when literature was thought to be an add-on or separate entity reserved only for the recreational or independent reading program. Quality literature of all types should be an integral part of the daily language arts program and should be fused into content subjects (Buchoff, 1995; Buss & Karnowski, 2000). Entire works of quality literature or authentic texts can be the main vehicle for learning the language processes and achieving various instructional goals; learning basic vocabulary and how to decode knowledge; developing comprehension strategies, content reading skills and strategies, and inferential and critical-thinking abilities; and promoting a joy of reading.

7. Successful literacy instruction depends on the ongoing assessment of each student's reading strengths and weaknesses.

The teacher's ability to assess students' needs lies at the heart of effective instruction (Barrentine, 1999). Effective reading teachers make instructional decisions based on assessment information. **Assessment** is defined as "the procedures used by teachers to identify students' strengths and weaknesses in planning and executing instruction to meet the students' needs." A key to correctly assessing students' progress in reading is to obtain information from multiple sources, both formal and informal. Kleitzien (1996) reported on the characteristics of nationally recognized elementary schools in the U.S. Department of Education's Blue Ribbon Schools recognition program. The schools that have been recognized utilize a variety of assessment tools ranging from teacher-made tests to basal program assessments to anecdotal records to portfolios to standardized tests. Teachers should ensure that the assessment process permeates all aspects of instruction, from making initial placement decisions to adjusting daily instruction based upon yesterday's lesson.

8. Teachers must be able to create, manage, and maintain a classroom environment conducive to learning.

Teaching children what they need to know while advancing their literacy abilities is a tall order. While classroom management is less important with a small group of students, you most likely will be responsible for a class of 20 to 30 students. Moreover, many school systems now organize the early grades into primary blocks, which group students from different age and grade levels. Studies on teaching reading have clearly shown that effective teachers are proficient in classroom organization and management (Evertson, Emmer & Worsham, 2000). Proper planning, managing of group instruction, and monitoring of student progress can help teachers deal with a broad range of student abilities.

Motivation is an important feature of both acquiring literacy and associating value with literacy (Gambrell, Palmer, Codling, & Mazzoni, 1996). Students who read and write both for school and for enjoyment become better readers and writers because the more students read and write, the better readers and writers they become. Classroom teachers have a direct influence on promoting motivation through their selection and implementation of instructional activities based on student need (Benton, Belk, & Holifield, 1994). Teachers who use strategies that promote high levels of student engagement and provide a wide range of meaningful literacy activities encourage the development of positive attitudes toward literacy. In sharing motivational strategies utilized by expert literacy teachers, Turner and Paris (1995) emphasize that classroom activities directly affect student motivation. They found that teachers who promote children's motivation for literacy do so "by molding literacy instruction to the needs, interests, and skills of their students" (p. 672).

9. Teachers of literacy must forge partnerships with the home and community to promote reading growth.

Without a doubt, teachers alone cannot do a complete job of educating students. Teachers must have a cooperative relationship with parents and the community as a whole to have a successful literacy program. The role of school libraries can play a significant role in involving parents and students in literacy activities after

The key to successful literacy instruction is the teacher.

regular school hours (Alvermann, DeGroff, Green, & Young, 1996). Parents—children's first teachers—are in a unique position to provide meaningful literacy experiences for their children. Faires, Nichols, and Rickelman (2000) investigated the effects of parental training and involvement in teaching reading lessons to first graders. Following specific, structured training sessions centered on the Reading Recovery model, parents taught home lessons developed by the classroom teacher. Results indicated that "students who received extra help from their parents significantly increased their reading level when compared to the students who did not receive additional help at home" (p. 210). In *Becoming a Nation of Readers* (Anderson et al., 1985), the National Institute of Education's Commission on Reading recommended two timeless ways that parents can help their children:

- Parents should read to preschool children and informally teach them about reading and writing. Reading to children, discussing stories and experiences with them, and—with a light touch—helping them learn letters and words are practices that are consistently associated with eventual success in reading.

1. Reading and writing are language processes.
2. Reading is a meaningful, active, constructive, and strategic process.
3. Reading and writing are developmental processes.
4. Teachers must capitalize on student diversity and plan appropriate instruction for the wide range of individual differences in the classroom.
5. Teachers must strive for a balanced literacy program to teach all students to read and write independently.
6. Literature should be an integral part of literacy instruction throughout the entire school curriculum.
7. Successful literacy instruction depends on the ongoing assessment of each student's reading strengths and weaknesses.
8. Teachers must be able to create, manage, and maintain a classroom environment conducive to learning.
9. Teachers of literacy must forge partnerships with the home and community to promote reading growth.
10. The key to successful literacy instruction is the teacher.

Figure 1.5 Principles of reading instruction.

- Parents should support school-aged children's continued growth as readers. Parents of children who become successful readers monitor their children's progress in school, become involved in school programs, support homework, buy their children books or take them to libraries, encourage reading as a free-time activity, and place reasonable limits on such activities as TV viewing. (p. 117)

Parents can contribute a great deal to every stage of reading development. As teachers, we need to communicate with parents what we know about reading development, how we teach reading, and, specifically, how parents can help (Snow, 1999).

10. The key to successful literacy instruction is the teacher.

Successful instruction and learning do not happen by accident. Observation of effective teachers and examination of current research (Neuman & Roskos, 1998; Pressley, Rankin, & Yokoi, 1996; Blair, 1984) make it clear that the classroom teacher has a tremendous influence on whether children are successful in learning to read. Results of research do not indicate that any particular literacy method or material is best for all children; rather, the teacher is one of the major variables that determine the effectiveness of reading instruction. The instructional practices of effective reading teachers are clustered in the following four areas: ongoing assessment of students' literacy development, structure and direction of students' learning, provision of opportunities to practice and apply skills in meaningful contexts, and maintenance of a high level of student involvement in learning (Rupley & Blair, 1988).

Figure 1.5 summarizes the 10 principles of reading instruction.

SUMMARY

The ability to read is a uniquely human process that can open new worlds to children. Teaching students to read is an exciting, rewarding, and honorable responsibility. Effective teachers of reading are knowledgeable, skillful, exciting, and caring. This first chapter discussed the reading process, an overview of the reading curriculum, principles of teaching reading, and stages of reading development.

Reading is defined as "an active process of constructing meaning from written text in relation to the reader's experiences and knowledge." Reading is a complex process; our knowledge of it recently has been reshaped primarily by research on schema theory and by viewing reading as an interactive process. We now know that reading is an active, dynamic, and strategic process whereby readers use cues from themselves, the text, and the context in which the reading occurs to construct meaning.

An overview of a balanced literacy curriculum was presented. The major content strands of the elementary school curriculum for all grade levels—word recognition, word meaning, comprehension, reading study skills, independent or recreational reading, and literature—were covered. A balanced literacy program includes the program areas of developmental reading, application-transfer, independent or recreational reading, content reading, and functional reading. Chall's stages of reading development were presented with the qualitative characteristics of preschool through eighth grade.

To synthesize understanding of major concepts and provide a foundation for the rest of the text, principles for teaching reading were presented with brief explanations of each. Key elements of the principles include the importance of the teacher to student learning and the integration of reading development with the other language arts using quality literature.

YOUR POINT OF VIEW

Discussion Questions

1. In your opinion, which of the principles of teaching reading are the most important for improving the quality of reading instruction? Provide a rationale for your choices.
2. Refer to Chall's stages of reading development (Figure 1.4) and reread the category "How Acquired" for each stage. What features would a reading instructional program need in order to develop the reading abilities associated with each stage?

Take a Stand For or Against

1. A teacher's definition or concept of reading will, in the final analysis, have little impact on practices used in teaching students to read.
2. A child's problems in learning to read can usually be attributed to one factor.

Field-Based Assignments

1. In the classroom you are visiting, ask the teacher if you can shadow or work individually for a day with a child who is experiencing extreme difficulties in reading. Keep in mind that it is extremely beneficial to acquire sensitivity to a frustrated reader at any grade level. Be as helpful as you can with the student and informally ask some of the following questions:

   What are your favorite subjects in school?

   Do you like to read?

   How can I help you become a better reader? In what areas do you feel you need help?

   What kind of stories do you like to read?

   Do you have time to read at home? Do you read at home?

   As you reflect on your time working with this student, ask yourself the following questions and share your perceptions with your peers:

   How did you feel about helping a problem reader?

   Did the student appear confident in completing activities during the day?

   What could you do to help this youngster improve?

   What sensitivities should a classroom teacher possess to meet the needs of children who are experiencing difficulties in reading?

2. Meeting the needs of children with a wide range of individual differences demands the very best from reading teachers. For instance, in a first-grade class, the teacher can expect the range of reading ability to span from readiness to the third- or fourth-grade level. In the third grade, the span can include first- through sixth-grade reading levels, and in the sixth grade, it can include second-grade through high school ability levels. Added to this factor, the many differences in the areas of emotional and social maturity, psychological well-being, personal interests, preferred learning styles, and language facility make teaching a tremendous challenge. Ask as many classroom teachers as you can the following question: "How do you handle the many differences among your students in the teaching of reading?" Take notes and categorize your responses in the areas of teaching methods, grouping plans, and instructional materials. Compare your findings with those of your peers and create a master list of ways for teaching to meet individual needs. Remember, teachers of reading must realize that capitalizing on differences is an indispensable aspect of their profession. How successful one is in differentiating instruction will be seen in how much children progress in their reading and writing.

Accommodating student differences

Teaching Methods	Grouping Plans	Instructional Materials
_____	_____	_____
_____	_____	_____
_____	_____	_____

Portfolio Entry

Because attitude guides practice, one of the first steps in becoming an effective reading teacher is to examine your own attitudes about reading. Taking into account what was discussed in this first chapter and your own reading habits, write a one-page entry entitled "Energetic reading." Include in your discussion answers to the following questions:

What do you think it means to be an energetic reader?

Are you an energetic reader?

What books have you read in the past two months?

Who are your favorite authors?

What magazines do you regularly read?

What do you think teachers can do to promote this quality of energetic reading?

What are some factors that can thwart the development of this desirable trait?

BIBLIOGRAPHY

Allington, R. L. (1995). Literacy lessons in the elementary schools: Yesterday, today, and tomorrow. In R. L. Allington & S. A. Walmsley (Eds.), *No quick fix: Rethinking literacy programs in America's schools* (pp. 1–15). New York: Teachers College Press and Newark, DE: International Reading Association.

Alvermann, D., DeGroff, L., Green, C., & Young, J. (1996). A dialogue about libraries and parents. *NRRC News: A Newsletter of the National Reading Research Center.* Athens, GA: NRRC, University of Georgia.

Anderson, R. C., Hiebert, E. H., Scott, J. A., & Wilkinson, I. A. G. (1985). *Becoming a nation of readers: The report of the Commission on Reading.* Washington, DC: The National Institute of Education.

Barrentine, S. J. (Ed.). (1999). *Reading assessment: Principles and practices for elementary teachers.* Newark, DE: International Reading Association.

Benton, G., Belk, J., & Holifield, S. (1994). Increased student motivation through paired reading. *Balanced Reading Instruction, 1,* 16–20.

Blair, T. R. (1984). Teacher effectiveness: The know-how to improve student learning. *The Reading Teacher, 38,* 138–141.

Blair-Larsen, S. M., & Williams, K. A. (Eds.). (1999). *The balanced reading program.* Newark, DE: International Reading Association.

Buchoff, R. (1995). Family stories. *The Reading Teacher, 49,* 230–233.

Buss, K., & Karnowski, L. (2000). *Reading and writing literary genres.* Newark, DE: International Reading Association.

Chall, J. S. (1996). *Stages of reading development* (2nd ed.). New York: Harcourt Brace.

Clay, M. M. (1979). *The patterning of complex behavior.* Auckland, New Zealand: Heinemann Educational Books.

David, J. L. (1991). Synthesis of research on school-based management. *Educational Leadership, 46*(8), 45–53.

Diller, D. (1999). Opening the dialogue: Using culture as a tool in teaching young African American children. *The Reading Teacher, 52,* 820–828.

Evertson, C., Emmer, E. T., & Worsham, M. E. (2000). *Classroom management for elementary teachers* (5th ed.). Boston: Allyn & Bacon.

Faires, J., Nichols, W. D., & Rickelman, R. J. (2000). Effects of parental involvement in developing competent readers in first grade. *Reading Psychology, 21,* 195–215.

Fox, B. J. (2000). *Word identification strategies.* (2nd ed.). Upper Saddle River, NJ: Merrill/Prentice Hall.

Gambrell, L. B., Palmer, B. M., Codling, R. M., & Mazzoni, S. A. (1996). Assessing motivation to read. *The Reading Teacher, 49,* 518–533.

Harris, T. L., & Hodges, R. E. (Eds.). (1995). *The literacy dictionary.* Newark, DE: International Reading Association.

Hiebert, E. H., Pearson, P. D., Taylor, B. M., Richardson, V., & Paris, S. G. (1998). *Every child a reader: Applying reading research in the classroom.* Center for the Improvement of Early Reading Achievement (CIERA). Ann Arbor, MI: University of Michigan School of Education.

Kleitzien, S. B. (1996). Reading programs in nationally recognized elementary schools. *Reading Research and Instruction, 35,* 260–274.

Learning to read and write: Developmentally appropriate practices for young children (1998). Joint position of the International Reading Association (IRA) and the National Association for the Education of Young Children (NAEYC). *The Reading Teacher, 52,* 193–216.

National Assessment of Educational Progress. (1992). *Executive summary of the NAEP 1992 Reading Report Card for the Nation and the States* (ISBN 01-16-041942-5). Washington, DC: U.S. Government Printing Office.

Neuman, S. B., & Roskos, K. A. (Eds.). (1998). *Children achieving: Best practices in early literacy.* Newark, DE: International Reading Association.

Pearson, P. D., & Stephens, D. (1994). Learning about literacy: A 30-year journey. In R. B. Rudell, M. R. Rudell, & H. Singer (Eds.), *Theoretical models and processes of reading* (4th ed., pp. 22–42). Newark, DE: International Reading Association.

Pressley, M., Rankin, J., & Yokoi, L. (1996). A survey of instructional practices of outstanding primary-level literacy teachers. *Elementary School Journal, 96,* 363–364.

Richardson, J. S., & Morgan, R. F. (2000). *Reading to learn in the content areas* (4th ed.). Belmont, CA: Wadsworth.

Rumelhart, D. E. (1985). Toward an interactive model of reading. In R. B. Ruddell & H. Singer (Eds.), *Theoretical models and processes of reading.* Newark, DE: International Reading Association.

Rupley, W. H., & Blair, T. R. (1988). *Teaching reading: Diagnosis, direct instruction, and practice* (2nd ed.). Upper Saddle River, NJ: Merrill/Prentice Hall.

Samuels, S. J., & Kamil, M. L. (1984). Models of the reading process. In P. D. Pearson (Ed.), *Handbook of reading research*. New York: Longman.

Sears, S., Carpenter, C., & Burnstein, N. (1994). Meaningful reading instruction for learners with special needs. *The Reading Teacher, 8,* 632–637.

Smith, C. B. (1996). How to get information from your child's school. *The ERIC Parent Reader*. Bloomington, IN: ERIC/Family Literacy Center, Indiana University.

Snow, C. E. (1999, May). *Why the home is so important in learning to read*. Paper presented at the George Graham Lecture in Reading, Charlottesville, VA.

Snow, C. E., Burns, M. S., & Griffin, P. (Eds.). (1998). *Preventing reading difficulties in young children*. Washington, DC: National Academy Press.

Spiegel, D. L. (1994). Finding the balance in literacy development for all children. *Balanced Reading Instruction, 1,* 6–11.

Spiegel, D. L. (1999). The perspective of the balanced approach. In S. M. Larsen & K. A. Williams (Eds.), *The balanced reading program*. Newark, DE: International Reading Association.

Stanovich, K. E. (1986). Matthew effects in reading: Some consequences of individual differences in the acquisition of literacy. *Reading Research Quarterly, 21,* 360–406.

Thorndike, E. L. (1917). Reading as reasoning: A study of mistakes in paragraph reading. *Journal of Educational Research, 8,* 323–332.

Turner, J. C., & Paris, S. G. (1995). How literacy tasks influence children's motivation for literacy. *The Reading Teacher, 48,* 662–675.

2

Teacher Effectiveness in a Balanced Literacy Program

Chapter Outline

For the Reader

Teachers' tremendous influence upon learning has been documented and emphasized for years. Specific instructional behaviors that have the greatest impact on learning have not been at issue until relatively recently, however. General qualities, such as mental health and enthusiasm, are certainly important, but what specifically sets apart effective teachers of literacy from those who are less effective?

If you have had experience teaching, you realize the tremendous responsibilities that teachers have in the classroom. If you are preparing to become a teacher, the realities and complexities of working with 25 to 35 students in a teaching situation may (justifiably) seem overwhelming. Every day, teachers are responsible for covering certain material, ensuring learning, minimizing discipline problems, and maintaining a pleasant atmosphere for learning. You may ask, "What exactly does an effective teacher of literacy do?"

"Where should I place my efforts so that the classroom experience is rewarding and profitable for both me and my students?"

The overall objective of this text is to provide you with the essential knowledge, concepts, and skills of an effective teacher of literacy. This chapter synthesizes teacher characteristics that make a difference in teaching.

Key Ideas

- Studies of teacher effectiveness have pointed out a number of characteristics related to student learning.

- The six areas of importance to competent reading instruction are (1) assessment, (2) explicit/direct instruction, (3) opportunity to learn, (4) student attention to learning tasks, (5) teacher expectations, and (6) classroom management.

- Guidelines for effective literacy instruction must be applied differently in each classroom and depend upon a host of variables, including students' needs, material content, grade level, and learning objectives.

- Teaching is a decision-making process, and the judgments teachers make are the keys to the success or failure of literacy programs.

- Effective teachers of literacy continually reshape teaching decisions, depending on each student's progress.

HISTORICAL OVERVIEW

It is generally accepted that the teacher plays a major role in determining the effectiveness of a literacy program. Recognition of this significant role is not new. Over the past 70 years, a number of major studies have demonstrated the importance of the teacher to student learning. Gates (1937) found that although mental age is correlated with beginning reading success, the type of teaching and the teacher's expertise and effectiveness are equally important. In her 3-year study, Jeanne Chall (1967) concluded that even more than the instructional materials, the teacher generally determines students' attitudes toward learning to read.

The importance of the teacher to student learning was apparent in a major investigation that compared different reading instructional methods at the first-grade level (Dykstra, 1967). The study noted wide differences in reading achievement among classes and school systems that were using similar instructional methods. The differences underscore the importance of the teacher's role in reading instruction.

These early studies on effective teaching yielded little specific information about exactly what teachers do in the classroom that makes them effective, however. Being a good, decent individual who is interested in students is clearly insufficient. As John Pescosolido (1980) stated, "Just being a 'nice' person doesn't a teacher of reading make, but a nice person doing some important things in terms of the reading process results in good teaching and good learning."

In a synthesis of the findings on teacher effectiveness in reading, Blair (1984) concluded that the effective teacher of reading is characterized by exhibiting the following traits:

- Provides adequate instructional time to teach reading and ensures students are engaged in learning.
- Diagnoses students' strengths and weaknesses and teaches to students' needs.
- Teaches basic reading skills using the explicit/direct approach.
- Provides independent practice of targeted reading skills to ensure transfer of skills to actual reading situations.
- Uses predominantly group instruction to increase student time-on-task.
- Believes one's teaching will make a difference and expects students to be successful.
- Manages the classroom efficiently to minimize wasted time.

Reading success depends largely on the type and quality of instruction. After analyzing successful exemplary reading programs, Duffy (1999) stated "I am convinced that the teacher is more important and has greater impact than any single, fixed, reading program, method, or approach" (p. 492).

MAJOR EFFORTS: CONVERGING EVIDENCE

Across the United States, a growing consensus of key elements in a balanced literacy program is being reached. In this consensus, the focus is on the teacher. The quality of the instruction students receive is a major factor in their reading success. The

International Reading Association (IRA) (2000) issued its position statement on "Excellent Reading Teachers." The statement listed the following research-based qualities of excellent classroom teachers:

1. They understand reading and writing development, and believe all children can learn to read and write.
2. They continually assess children's individual progress and relate reading instruction to children's previous experiences.
3. They know a variety of ways to teach reading, when to use each method, and how to combine the methods into an effective instructional program.
4. They offer a variety of materials and texts for children to read.
5. They use flexible grouping strategies to tailor instruction to individual students.
6. They are good reading "coaches" (that is, they provide help strategically).

Baumann and Duffy (1997) of the National Reading Research Center (NRRC) summarized the key ideas that were instrumental in fostering motivated, lifelong learners. Following are the key ideas for preschool and elementary school reading gleaned from 5 years of conducting research on fostering reading growth.

- Reading skills and strategies can be taught effectively and efficiently when instruction is systematic and integrated with quality children's literature.
- Phonics is one important component of a beginning reading program and should be taught explicitly within the context of authentic reading and writing activities.
- Motivation to read and reading ability are synergistic, mutually reinforcing phenomena.
- Literacy learning occurs both at school and home, and connections between home and school enhance children's learning in both environments.
- Thinking and talking about books promote children's critical understanding of what they read. (pp. 5–6)

Two National Research and Development Centers of the Office of Educational Research and Improvement have addressed the qualities of effective teaching and effective school programs. Pressley, Allington, Wharton-McDonald, Collins Block, and Morrow (1998) reported findings from the National Research Center on English Learning & Achievement (CELA). Successful first-grade literacy teachers:

- Emphasized reading, writing, and literature
- Worked to make the classroom a positive, reinforcing, cooperative environment
- Taught literacy skills explicitly, in context
- Demonstrated excellent classroom management skills
- Set high but realistic expectations and consistently encouraged students to try more challenging tasks
- Provided long uninterrupted periods for successful reading and writing experiences
- Made strong connections across the curriculum
- Fostered student self-regulation

Hiebert, Pearson, Taylor, Richardson, and Paris (1998) of the Center for the Improvement of Early Reading Achievement (CIERA) reported on qualities of effective schools and teachers. Included in the center's 10 principles for "Improving the Reading Achievement of America's Children" are the following research-based conclusions:

- Focused and well-designed reading programs in the early primary grades increase levels of reading achievement (on both comprehension and word recognition measures). These programs include several well-articulated characteristics:
  (a) systematic phonics instruction, (b) frequent opportunity to read lots of texts of appropriate difficulty, and (c) frequent opportunity to write (and spell) lots of texts of their own.
- Effective reading teachers have high expectations of students and are deliberate about instruction of reading skills and strategies. Effective teachers are aware of the strengths and needs of their students, using various assessment tools to monitor their students' growth in reading skills and strategies.
- For early success in reading to result in high levels of literacy, children in the late primary and middle grades must continue to receive instruction in strategies that will allow them to negotiate the vocabulary and comprehension demands of different kinds of texts, especially science and social studies texts. Middle-schoolers benefit from instruction on strategies to monitor reading for understanding. Further, daily opportunities to read are significantly related to reading achievement. (Bingham, 1998)

Additionally, CIERA researchers Taylor, Pearson, Clark, and Walpole (1999) examined both school and teacher factors that were associated with student achievement in the primary grades (K–3). Significant school factors included collaboration across grade levels, systematic and continuous assessment linked to instruction, early reading interventions for students falling behind, innovative staff development programs, collaboration between special teachers and the classroom, and parent collaboration and communication. Teacher factors related to student growth included communication with the home, classroom activities that maintained high levels of student engagement, large amount of small-group instruction, allocation of time for independent reading, and word recognition (especially phonics) instruction coupled with coaching or assisting students to apply their skills while reading.

CHARACTERISTICS OF EFFECTIVE LITERACY INSTRUCTION

The areas that appear to be of primary importance in competent literacy instruction include the following:

Assessing students' literacy strengths and weaknesses.

Structuring literacy activities around an explicit/direct instructional format.

Providing students with opportunities to learn and apply skills and strategies in authentic literacy tasks.

Ensuring that students attend to the learning tasks.

Believing in one's teaching abilities and expecting students to be successful.

Maintaining effective classroom control. (Blair & Rupley, 2000)

Assessing Students' Reading

The ability to teach students what they need to know requires that teachers of literacy continually use a blend of formal and informal measures to identify students' strengths and weaknesses in interacting with text (Barrentine, 1999). Without the teacher's pervasive concern for knowing and responding to students' needs, literacy instruction can be irrelevant and mindless drudgery for all concerned. This pervasive concern about assessment can be related to Chall's stages of reading development (see Chapter 1). Teachers should provide instruction that reflects the students' level of reading development.

Teachers' use of reading assessment and its effects on reading achievement have been part of many research investigations that span more than 40 years. Pescosolido (1962) appraised the effects of a variety of teacher factors on achievement and found that a major factor associated with high levels of reading achievement was the teacher's ability to judge accurately students' attitudes toward reading. Blair (1975) found that teachers who secured and used supplementary materials, provided differentiated instruction, kept records of student progress, and arranged conferences about student progress were effective in improving student reading skills. The results of this study also revealed significant differences in class-achievement scores for teachers who exerted more effort on the job. Finally, Rupley (1977) found that effective teachers of reading used more ongoing assessment than did less effective teachers.

More recently, assessment has been increasingly emphasized. External assessment of procedures, such as standardized tests, typically focuses on students' basic skills in reading and writing and provides little information for instructional decision making. Today's teachers of literacy realize that testing is only one small part of assessment and that literacy is the ability to use reading and writing as tools for learning, thinking, and problem solving.

Effective teachers of literacy rely on a variety of assessment tools, including informal tests, interviews, observations, samples of students' work, portfolios, and students' judgments of their own performance (Henk & Melnick, 1992). Such assessment procedures give teachers information about their students and help them make informed instructional decisions to maximize their teaching effectiveness.

Using assessment as an integral part of effective instruction involves several provisions. First, effective literacy teachers employ informal, ongoing assessment procedures rather than relying on infrequently administered standardized tests. Second, their procedures aim to determine appropriate instructional practices rather than simply students' grade-level placement. Third, effective teachers use

The key to interactive instruction is the active communication and interaction between teacher and student.

ongoing assessment to evaluate student outcomes regularly in relation to actual classroom instruction. Effective teachers of literacy use a variety of assessment techniques to adjust instruction frequently so that students' chances of success in instructional tasks are increased.

The fact that effective teachers assess students' literacy more frequently using a variety of procedures than do less effective teachers should be carefully analyzed. By itself, assessment has no beneficial effects. Therefore, one cannot expect students' literacy achievement to improve simply by increasing the frequency of assessment. Yet effective teachers of reading and writing expend considerable effort in developing and using ongoing assessment. It is how they incorporate this information into their instruction that probably determines students' reading achievement (Taylor et al., 1999).

Another plausible explanation is that effective teachers select instructional strategies appropriate to the desired student outcomes in relation to the students' existing literacy capabilities. Instructional tasks that are too difficult for students limit their chances of successful learning. Teachers who pace their instruction by progressing in small, closely related steps to maximize students' success in literacy activities increase students' chances of success. Ongoing assessment that focuses on students' literacy strengths and weaknesses enables teachers to identify instructional procedures that increase success.

Effective teachers of literacy, then, employ a variety of ongoing, informal assessment procedures to

- adjust instruction in terms of its impact on students' learning.
- identify instructional activities and tasks that maximize student success.
- select instructional strategies appropriate to desired literacy outcomes in relation to students' existing reading capabilities.
- pace reading instruction by progressing in small, related steps to maximize students' success rates.

Explicit/Direct Instruction

Effective teachers of reading teach students what they need to know. Although it seems simplistic and obvious, teachers of literacy "teach"; that is, students do not become independent learners through maturation alone. **Explicit/direct instruction** means imparting new information to students through meaningful teacher–student interactions and teacher guidance of student learning. The key to explicit/direct instruction is the active communication and interaction between teacher and student. This style of teaching can be direct or indirect, well structured or less structured in nature (Hancock, 1999). The type of learning to be accomplished determines the degree of directness or structure. The majority of learning objectives in teaching literacy can be classified as either skills or strategies. Both types of learning are important for success in literacy; however, they require different lesson-presentation methods. **Skills** involve lower-level cognitive processing, are specific in nature, and "are more or less automatic routines" (Dole, Duffy, Roehler, & Pearson, 1991). Examples of literacy skills include the various decoding methods used in phonics, structural analysis, and context analysis; specific comprehension skills such as recognizing sequential development, fact versus opinion, and a stated main idea; reading study skills such as using an index and interpreting a bar graph; and writing skills such as capitalization, punctuation, and spelling. **Strategies** require higher-level cognitive processing, are less specific in nature than skills and "emphasize intentional and deliberate plans under the control of the reader" (Dole et al., 1991). Examples of cognitive strategies applied to literacy include making predictions, summarizing a story, reacting critically to what is read, inferring main ideas, and editing a piece of writing.

Each type of learning requires a different degree of directness and control by the teacher (see Figure 2.1). As shown, skill learning requires more control and direction by the teacher than does strategy learning, which requires less teacher directness and is more under the control of students. However, teaching is neither wholly direct nor indirect—on a continuum, a given teaching lesson is only more or less direct than another. Interactive teaching of both skills and strategies is important, and both types of lessons should be included in a teacher's repertoire.

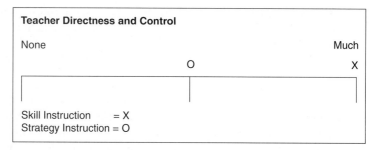

Figure 2.1 Skill versus strategy learning: Teacher directness and control.

1. **Review**
   Review homework
   Review relevant previous learning
   Review prerequisite skills and knowledge for the lesson
2. **Presentation**
   State lesson goals or provide outline
   Present new material in small steps
   Model procedures
   Provide positive and negative examples
   Use clear language
   Check for student understanding
   Avoid digressions
3. **Guided Practice**
   Spend more time on guided practice
   High frequency of questions
   All students respond and receive feedback
   High success rate
   Continue practice until students are fluent
4. **Corrections and Feedback**
   Provide process feedback when answers are correct but hesitant
   Provide sustaining feedback, clues, or reteaching when answers are incorrect
   Reteach material when necessary
5. **Independent Practice**
   Students receive overview and/or help during initial steps
   Practice continues until students are automatic (where relevant)
   Teacher provides active supervision (where possible)
   Routines are used to provide help for slower students
6. **Weekly and Monthly Reviews**

Figure 2.2 Functions for teaching well-structured tasks.

Source: From B. Rosenshine and R. Stevens (1995), Functions for Teaching Well-structured Tasks. In B. Rosenshine, "Advances in Research in Education," *Journal of Educational Research,* May/June, Vol. 88, No. 5. Reprinted by permission of the author.

Skill learning

Skill learning is particularly suitable to the **explicit/direct instruction** approach. Summarizing the literature on the teaching procedures for direct instruction, Rosenshine and Stevens (1986, 1995) delineated six instructional functions for teaching well-structured objectives (see Figure 2.2). Teachers who use these procedures consistently see higher-than-average achievement among their students.

At the heart of the explicit/direct instruction method are explicit explanations, modeling, and guided practice. Explicit explanations can include defining a reading skill, modeling or demonstrating its use in an actual reading situation, and thinking aloud with students about what the skill is and how it is used (i.e., showing how to apply it in context) (Blair & Rupley, 1988). Effective teachers provide varied, meaningful practice to ensure mastery and transfer of a skill to other meaningful reading situations (Rupley & Blair, 1988). Directly controlled by the teacher, this practice is characterized by varying degrees of teacher–student interaction. In this process, the teacher acts as a mediator. Based on Vygotsky's theoretical work (1962), **mediated instruction** involves providing guidance to a student in learning a particular skill. During practice, the amount of guidance is great at the beginning; it then declines to little or none. Similar to mediated instruction is "coaching" students. CIERA researchers Taylor et al. (1999) reported on qualities of effective primary-grade teachers. One quality was that most teachers taught phonics in isolation but coached students or provided help to students as they attempted to use various phonics skills in real reading situations.

Guiding student learning is certainly not new; it has been an effective teaching strategy for years. The renewed interest today is the result of new research on the teaching–learning process and the social environment of the classroom.

Figure 2.3 depicts this gradual shift of responsibility for the application of a reading skill from the teacher to the student.

Strategy learning

Teaching students strategies or strategic reading behaviors with which to interact with and comprehend text requires a different style of interactive teaching. Most strategies require higher-level thinking, as opposed to skills, which are more factual, or literal, and amenable to specific learning objectives. Strategies are behaviors a reader applies before, during, and after reading to construct and understand the author's message. Examples of strategies include the abilities to preview a selection, ask questions to understand and clarify ideas while reading, summarize a passage, and react critically to what was read. Referring again to Figure 2.1, it is important to note that teaching students strategies requires a different style of explicit/direct instruction from that used to teach skills. The emphasis is on helping students understand the "when" and "why" of utilizing various strategies. Teaching a strategy still requires teachers to explain, inform, model, or demonstrate what they want students to know, but it is not a strict step-by-step procedure under complete control of the teacher, as it is for skill instruction. Teaching cognitive strategies also follows the gradual shift of

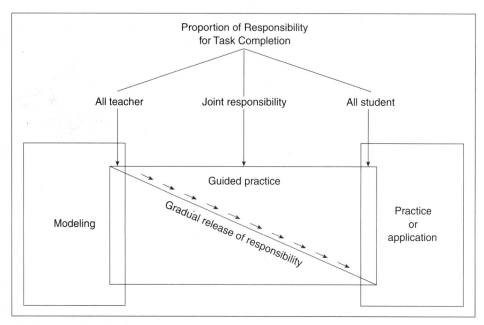

Figure 2.3   The gradual-release-of-responsibility model of instruction.
Source: After Campione, 1981. Reprinted with permission from P. D. Pearson and M. C. Gallagher, *The Instruction of Reading Comprehension* (Urbana, IL: University of Illinois, Center for the Study of Reading, October 1983), p. 732.

control and responsibility for the learning and application of a reading strategy from the teacher to the student (Figure 2.3). Rosenshine and Meister (1992, 1995) describe the teaching of cognitive strategies as including the following steps:

1. Present the new cognitive strategy.
2. Regulate difficulty during guided practice.
3. Provide varying contexts for student practice.
4. Provide feedback.
5. Increase student responsibility.
6. Provide independent practice. (p. 27)

Central to teaching strategies is the use of instructional procedures called **scaffolds** to aid students while they learn the strategy. A definition of *scaffolds* is provided by Rosenshine and Meister (1992, 1995):

> Scaffolds are forms of support provided by the teacher (or another student) to help students bridge the gap between their current abilities and the intended goal. . . . Instead of providing explicit steps, one supports, or scaffolds, the students as they learn the skill. (p. 26)

Scaffolds can be general aids such as modeling or demonstrating a strategy, or they can be specific aids used to teach a strategy. For example, in teaching the strategy of generating questions, a teacher may use the scaffold of teaching students to use reporters' questions *(Who? What? Where? When? Why? and How?)* as they think about what they read. In teaching any cognitive strategy, the teacher acts more as a facilitator than a director in helping students learn to interact critically with text.

The importance of giving analytical consideration to classroom structure and direct teaching as means for improving literacy teaching effectiveness seems clear. The literacy program should not be regimented and inflexible. Structure and direct instruction depend on the desired reading outcomes and the grade level. Analyzing how these variables influence students' reading and making changes when necessary enhance teacher effectiveness.

Effective teachers of literacy, then, utilize an interactive style of teaching to

- maximize student involvement in tasks or academic activities related specifically to lesson content and desired outcomes.
- control student behavior using task-related comments rather than criticizing or scolding.
- monitor and guide the direction of learning.
- vary the degree of structure in relation to desired behavioral objectives; less structure and less-direct instruction are employed for strategy or creative outcomes, and more structure and control are used for skill outcomes.
- utilize a pattern of instruction at the primary level that allows students to contact the teacher, work in small groups, and use a variety of materials.
- utilize a pattern of instruction at the intermediate level that allows for larger instructional groups, more discussion at higher cognitive levels, less teacher direction, and greater student-initiated learning.

Opportunity to Learn

Opportunity to learn refers to whether students have been taught the skills relevant to the areas for which they are assessed. Teachers who specify literacy behaviors to be achieved prior to teaching and who teach content relevant to these outcomes often have students who achieve at a higher reading level than do teachers who do not (Rupley, Wise, & Logan, 1986).

Opportunity to learn is a variable associated with explicit/direct instruction. Teachers could employ structure and direct instruction, but if the instruction does not relate to an assessed learning task or a valued outcome, then students have not had an opportunity to learn the product. For example, students who do well in learning isolated reading skills as a result of intensive instruction but who do poorly in actual reading may lack the opportunity to learn how to apply such skills in actual reading tasks. Allington reported that low-achieving readers receive different instructional emphases than high-achieving students (Allington 1983). Low-achieving students spent more time on worksheets rather than whole-text reading and on word recognition rather than comprehension activities.

Providing students with opportunities to apply their reading and writing skills in meaningful content areas appears to be extremely important; however, teachers must be sure to use materials that students can handle. The more time students spend on actual reading in which they can be highly successful, the more they probably will learn; while the more they are involved in actual reading tasks that limit success, the less likely they will be to enhance their learning.

Practice activities in reading are of the utmost importance. Such activities are best designed around three areas: (1) planning for practice, (2) delivering effective practice, and (3) evaluating the effectiveness of practice assignments.

When planning for practice, teachers should ask:
- Is the intended practice related to the students' needs?
- Is the level of the materials appropriate and interesting?
- Is the content of the practice within the students' experiential background?
- Are different ways of practice provided to meet students' needs and maintain their interest?
- Is the amount of practice appropriate for the instructional period?
- Are directions and examples provided to students to ensure understanding (i.e., are they clear)?
- Is it necessary to vary the type of practice in one class period (having students work on two or three different types of materials relating to one aspect of reading), or will one practice activity be sufficient?

When delivering practice, teachers should ask:
- Are several exercises completed with the students before they work on their own?
- How will the students' progress during practice sessions be monitored?
- Do individual students know how to get help if I am working with another student?
- What should students do if they finish an activity early?
- Do the students understand how the practice activity relates to reading in meaningful text?

When evaluating the effectiveness of practice assignments, teachers should ask:
- Did the practice accomplish its goal?
- What are the students' patterns of correct and incorrect responses?
- How will the results of this practice session modify the next practice activity? (Rupley & Blair, 1987)

Opportunity to learn is not equal to coverage of materials and topics. Opportunity to learn, ongoing assessment, structure, and direct instruction are related. The reading instruction that is offered must relate to assessment data, desired outcomes, instructional format, and application in actual reading tasks. Opportunity to learn should reflect the desired learning outcomes, not simply cover the content.

Effective teachers of reading, then, attend to students' opportunity to learn and apply skills in actual reading situations to

Students helping other students is an effective learning strategy.

- ensure that instruction focuses on desired and valued reading outcomes.
- guard against isolated reading skills and strategies becoming ends in themselves rather than means to effective reading comprehension.
- provide for application of reading skills and strategies in silent reading tasks that ensure maximum student success.
- ensure that students understand how to apply their reading skills and strategies for reading enjoyment.

Attention to Learning Tasks

Students' attention to learning tasks and engagement in pertinent learning materials logically fall under the direct supervision of the teacher. The historic *Beginning Teacher Evaluation Study, Phase II* (McDonald, 1976) provided clear support for the importance of maintaining a reasonably high level of student involvement. Appropriate reading materials alone are not sufficient to maximize achievement. Effective teachers not only use appropriate materials but also attend to actively engaging students in learning from the materials. Simply requiring that all students complete similar learning tasks does not ensure maximum attention, because students approach various learning tasks with varying interest, capabilities, and understanding. Effective literacy teachers take these factors into account as they attempt to engage students in meaningful reading instruction.

Inclusion Strategies

The Importance of Additional Practice and Cooperative Learning Opportunities

The direct instruction approach works especially well for those reading skills and abilities that are specific in nature. This teaching approach is effective with all children. Still, each step in this approach should be modified to meet student needs and the topic at hand. An abundance of meaningful practice is necessary for all students in mastering the lesson objective in this approach. As you work with exceptional students in the regular classroom, it is helpful to know and be prepared to provide additional supervised and independent practice a few days after a lesson is finished. Many exceptional students will need a great deal of meaningful practice after the point at which you would normally judge that students have mastered the reading skill. This is not a reflection on your teaching but a reminder of the reality that different students need different amounts of practice.

Such practice needs to occur at an appropriate level of difficulty and be accomplished with a variety of materials. Additional practice can be supplied through supplemental textbooks, newspapers, magazines, commercial learning kits, literature books, teacher-made materials, games, computers, and various realia (real objects such as maps and word cards). Also, both teacher-supervised and independent practice can be accomplished in a variety of settings, especially in cooperative learning groups. Cooperative learning promotes more active learning, with students talking and working together rather than listening passively to the teacher. As with any type of cooperative grouping, this arrangement won't be successful without careful preparation and skillful application on your part. Requirements for cooperative grouping include the following:

1. Organizing students heterogeneously in small groups.
2. Explaining the lesson objective and the criteria for success for the entire group.
3. Reviewing the desired communication behaviors needed (e.g., listening to others, allowing everyone to participate, helping one another).
4. Monitoring the progress of each group and helping each group as students work on the assigned activities.
5. Evaluating the group's efforts and assigning a group grade for the entire activity.

Academic engaged time, or **time on task,** refers to the classroom time when students are actually attending to the work at hand. Classrooms in which students are actively engaged in learning for a large proportion of the time demonstrate higher achievement in reading and writing than do classrooms in which students are not so engaged. Engagement is the key; merely completing reading and writing activities is not synonymous with learning.

Researchers have modified the definition of *time on task* to include students' success rate while working productively. Fisher, Marliave, and Filby (1979) label this concept **academic learning time (ALT).** They define the term as "the amount of time a student spends engaged in an academic task he/she performs with high success" (p. 52). A high success rate is considered to be above 80%. Allocated time, student engagement, and student success rate define academic learning time. Collectively, academic learning time occurs when a student has the time or opportunity to learn, is actively engaged with the task at hand, and is succeeding at the task.

Recently, CIERA researchers Taylor et al. (1999) studied quality time and reported that effective teachers in grades K–3 maintained students on task and engaged 96% of the time while students of less effective teachers were on task and engaged an average of 63%. The type of grouping utilized in reading is related to student engagement. Students with the most effective teachers spent considerably more time in small-group instruction per day in reading as compared with students of the least-effective teachers (48 minutes versus 25 minutes).

Effective teachers of literacy, then, help maximize students' focus on learning tasks by

- allocating more time to reading instruction.
- keeping students actively engaged in learning during the instructional period.
- providing academic feedback to students about their work to increase attention to tasks and amount of engaged time.
- setting purposes for learning.
- presenting an overview of what is to be learned.
- using examples and illustrations to relate new learning to what has been presented previously and to help students understand how to apply what they are learning.
- monitoring students' involvement to ensure a high success rate.

Promoting reading comprehension

Comprehension development has been the major focus in the literacy field since the mid-1970s. Our understanding of the reading process and the ways teachers can foster reading comprehension have greatly increased in the last 20 years (Watts & Cerra, 1996). The overall goal of reading instruction is the development of active readers who can both understand printed language and strategically monitor their own reading performance. All the best intentions and instruction are lost if students cannot comprehend successfully, are unable to regulate and monitor their reading, and do not choose to read for various purposes on their own. Central to this development of active, strategic readers is the important role of the classroom teacher. Only through the teacher's careful and expert planning, teaching, and guidance will students grow into mature, independent readers (Kincade, 1996). Pivotal to the development of reading comprehension are the instructional strategies used by the classroom teacher and the way in which instructional time is utilized during the day. Fielding and Pearson (1994) summarized the significant research on comprehension strategies that promote increased student learning. A consensus is building in the literacy field that a successful comprehension program includes the following components:

1. direct teaching of comprehension skills and strategies spanning different cognitive levels in both narrative and expository text
2. use of peer and cooperative learning in the classroom
3. provision of a multitude of opportunities for students to interact with their peers and teachers about what they are reading
4. allotment of large amounts of time for actual text reading (Fielding and Pearson, 1994)

The key point is how much classroom time is utilized for these areas. Unfortunately, past investigations paint a discouraging picture concerning the amount of time devoted to actual text reading in elementary classrooms. In *Becoming a Nation of Readers,* Anderson, Hiebert, Scott, & Wilkinson (1985) reported that students spend only a small amount of time in classrooms actually reading whole texts. Rosenshine (1979) reported that in some elementary classes, students spend 50 to 70% of their time completing seatwork assignments.

While there are no definitive data on the optimal time allocations to actual text reading, direct teaching, and discussion/interaction periods during reading class, Fielding and Pearson recommend that, "of the time set aside for reading instruction, students should have more time to read than the combined total allocated for learning about reading and talking or writing about what has been read" (p. 63). While common sense supports the importance of allocating sufficient classroom time to actual text reading and discussion of what has been read to promote reading comprehension, even more importantly, classroom research indicates the value of providing students with extensive practice with real reading. In a recent summary of some of the most important instructional advancements in the last 30 years, Rosenshine (1995) highlighted research in the following areas:

- cognitive processing (most notably, the importance of knowledge structure and developing student background knowledge)
- teacher-effectiveness literature (especially the need for direct teaching for well-structured skills)
- cognitive strategies (their importance and procedures for teaching them to students).

In all three areas, an important instructional implication for teachers is to provide an abundance of extensive practice through independent reading so that students develop and refine their knowledge structure, master specific skills, and develop the facility to use cognitive strategies. Aside from direct teaching, practice, practice, and more practice in real texts is needed to help students learn.

Effective teachers monitor students' involvement to ensure a high success rate.

Thus, a major challenge for teachers is to monitor the amount of classroom time devoted to instruction, actual text reading, and writing or talking about what was read. Preliminary findings seem to indicate that classroom time may not be used as wisely as one might believe or wish. In an elementary school classroom-time study by Blair, Turner, and Schaudt (1995), the findings were the antithesis of the Fielding and Pearson recommendations referred to in the preceding paragraph. The Blair et al. study found that teachers only allocated a little over one third of classroom time to actual text reading (the rest of the time was devoted to instruction and discussion). With classroom time being such an important yet limited commodity and comprehension being the ultimate goal of literacy programs, it is crucial that teachers monitor how classroom time is spent.

Teacher Expectations

The most pervasive conclusion of school and teacher effectiveness studies was that teachers of reading profoundly influence how much students learn. This influence stems from both classroom actions and belief systems. Effective literacy programs have teachers who believe in themselves and expect their students to succeed in learning (Johnson, Livingston, Schwartz, & Slate, 2000). Simply put, students learn more if you hold high academic expectations for them. Thus, expectations for students may bias teachers' actions: If students perform according to what is expected of them, expectations can become self-fulfilling prophecies.

Having different expectations for different students is natural as long as the expectations reflect diagnostic data (such as achievement scores, specific strengths and weaknesses in comprehension, and motivational concerns) rather than socioeconomic status, gender, race, or ethnic background. Good and Brophy (1987) showed that students for whom teachers have low expectations may

receive less instruction.

be expected to do less work.

receive less frequent praise.

be called on less often.

receive less time to respond to questions.

be asked predominantly factual questions.

be seated farther from their teachers.

receive less eye contact.

be smiled at less often.

be criticized more frequently for incorrect responses.

receive less help.

It is fortunate that some students are not as affected by low teacher expectations as others are. However, it is important to realize the potential impact that expectations can have on students.

In addition to holding high, realistic expectations for students and communicating them, effective teachers have a strong sense of efficacy, or the expectation that their efforts will result in valued outcomes (Fuller, Wood, Rapoport, & Dornbush, 1982). In effect, teachers with a high sense of efficacy say, "I know I can teach these students!" These teachers believe in themselves and believe that investing substantial effort in their work will raise student achievement.

Being aware of the power of expectations and translating this awareness into sound instruction takes effort. That effort involves

- ensuring that reading instruction is based on diagnostic data.
- communicating goals and expectations to students.
- ensuring that all students participate in the reading lesson.
- classroom management.

Classroom Management

Directly related to student achievement in reading is the teacher's classroom management ability. Without the ability to manage complex interactions, a teacher's best intentions and instructional techniques are ineffective. Researchers have shown that teachers of high-achieving students in reading are good classroom managers (Evertson, Emmer, & Worsham, 2000). Effective classroom management creates and maintains an atmosphere conducive for learning. Managerial skills include planning for instruction, developing routines to manage group interactions, devising monitoring procedures, and responding to off-task behavior (Blair & Jones, 1998). Chapter 12 covers classroom management in detail and discusses specific techniques and strategies for the teacher of reading and writing.

Effective teachers of reading, then, manage the classroom to

- ensure conditions that are conducive to student learning.
- plan meaningful reading activities.
- manage group instruction.
- monitor student progress throughout the reading period.
- respond appropriately to student misbehavior.

DECISION MAKING IN READING INSTRUCTION

While the literature on effective teaching has yielded specific guidelines for teaching reading, the guidelines apply differently to each classroom depending upon a host of variables, including student needs, material content, grade level, and learning objectives. This realization underscores the notion of effective teachers of reading as decision makers: Teaching is a decision-making process, and teachers' judgments are the keys to the success or failure of reading programs.

To teach students what they need to know, teachers must base their decisions about planning and instruction on assessment information (as opposed to race, gender, socioeconomic status, ethnic background, or personal characteristics). Studies of teacher planning have reported that many teachers focus on instructional activities when making decisions (Stern & Shavelson, 1983). This contradicts the traditional thinking that teachers should focus on specific objectives in making decisions. A focus on activities should not be interpreted to exclude objectives in the planning process, however. Student characteristics should help shape reading and writing activities into meaningful experiences.

Figure 2.4 outlines the decision-making process for planning and actual teaching (interactive decision making). As shown, instructional implementation depends on decisions made both before and during teaching. Planning decisions center on the ability to modify and adapt the major reading activity to meet learning needs. Students' instructional levels, strengths, weaknesses, and personal qualities will factor

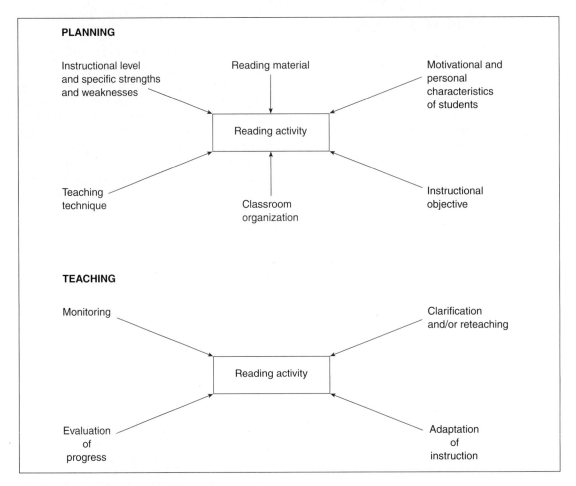

Figure 2.4   Interactive decision making.

into these decisions. The teacher's learning objectives (e.g., basic word identification or critical thinking), teaching techniques (e.g., directed reading activity, language experience approach, explicit/direct instruction, or reciprocal teaching), and grouping or classroom organization will also influence decisions.

Planning instruction, however, does not mean the end of decision making. Effective teachers modify their instruction based on student responses: either mastery of material, which requires no modification, or difficulty, which requires further explanation or reteaching. The goal should be to progress at a speed that maintains student involvement and achieves instructional goals.

Figure 2.5 summarizes six areas of effective instruction. Attention to these areas should enable teachers to better determine and improve the effectiveness of their reading instruction.

Assessment

Focus: Students' reading strengths and weaknesses

Features: Ongoing—combining both informal and standardized measures of reading outcomes related directly to instructional goals. Data are used to plan appropriate classroom structure and instruction.

Guiding questions:
- Are the students placed on their instructional level of reading materials (that is, not too difficult and not too easy)?
- Are you continually using informal observational techniques and diagnostic tests to detect strengths and weaknesses in word identification and comprehension?
- Is the instruction based on a diagnosis of student needs?
- Are you adjusting your instruction according to students' progress?

Explicit/Direct Instruction

Focus: Instructional organization and process

Features: Stated purposes for learning in terms of academic skills. Explicit/Direct instruction emphasizes the importance of the teacher in learning. It provides a focus on the product for identifying and conceptualizing instruction. Such instruction is differentiated by grade level and type of task.

Guiding questions:
- Do you vary the amount of structure in your class depending on student characteristics, grade level, and objectives?
- Do you allow for less structure when teaching more complex tasks (for example, do you solicit emotional responses to a story or judgments of the desirability or acceptability of a character's behaviors)?
- Do you devise more structured lessons when teaching basic reading skills (such as word identification and comprehension)?
- Do you give your students appropriate feedback?

Opportunity to Learn

Focus: Instruction aimed at measurable and desired reading outcomes; application of skills in actual reading tasks

Features: Matching the instruction to desired outcomes and teaching content relevant to these. Opportunity to learn maximizes students' understanding of the purposes for learning skills and of applying these skills to actual reading situations.

Guiding questions:
- Do you allow sufficient instructional time to teach what your students need to know?
- Do you allow time for your students to practice their reading skills in actual reading situations?
- Do you plan ways to monitor student practice of targeted reading skills?
- Are your students practicing their reading skills in materials that will ensure a high degree of success?

Attention to Learning Tasks

Focus: Maintaining a high level of student involvement in learning

Features: Maximizing students' involvement and attention to learning. Attention to the learning tasks looks at students' needs, based on diagnostic data. It involves students in instruction at a moderate level of difficulty, monitors their engagement in the instruction, and maximizes attention to learning by focusing on tasks related directly to desired outcomes.

Guiding questions:
- Do you clearly communicate the specific purposes of each lesson to your students?
- Do you plan your instruction to ensure a high percentage of academic engaged time?
- Do you design seatwork assignments to ensure student involvement?
- Do you use a reward system with students to reinforce specific positive behaviors?

Classroom Management

Focus: Creating, managing, and maintaining a classroom environment conducive to learning

Features: Preparation of materials and activities prior to actual teaching to prevent management difficulties. During instruction, successful managers grasp the total classroom situation, monitor students' work, and respond appropriately to student misbehavior.

Guiding questions:
- Do you prepare materials in advance and distribute them at appropriate times?
- Do you select and apply appropriate group management techniques to manage student misbehavior?
- Do you monitor student progress by responding quickly and appropriately to student responses to material?

Teacher Expectations

Focus: Believing one's students can learn and communicating this expectation to them

Features: Ensuring that instruction is based on diagnostic information. Teachers convince students that they will be successful in the classroom.

Guiding questions:
- Are your instructional decisions based on diagnostic data?
- Are all students involved in the reading class?
- Do you communicate to your students that they will be successful in your reading class?
- Are you exhibiting a positive attitude toward teaching and continually striving to learn and to grow?

Figure 2.5 Summary of effective teacher practices.

SUMMARY

Time and time again, research has demonstrated the importance of the teacher in effective literacy instruction. Admittedly, we still have much to learn about what makes an effective teacher. However, a great deal of the available information warrants careful consideration. We know, for example, that teachers who include provisions for ongoing assessment, explicit/direct instruction, opportunity to learn, attention to learning tasks, accurate expectations, and efficient classroom management are more effective than teachers who do not include provisions for these practices.

All teachers of literacy can benefit from knowing about the practices of competent teachers. Teacher-effectiveness research identifies some characteristics associated with effective teaching of literacy. Teachers of literacy should sort out and analyze these characteristics in terms of their own capabilities and classrooms.

YOUR POINT OF VIEW

Discussion Questions

1. What reasons account for the different characteristics of effective primary-grade teachers versus effective intermediate-grade teachers?
2. What are the implications of explicit/direct instruction for the teaching of critical-thinking skills?

Take a Stand For or Against

1. Opportunity to learn is the most powerful variable in education.
2. Small-group explicit/direct instruction is more beneficial than large-group explicit/direct instruction.

Field-Based Assignments

1. Successful reading teachers work hard for their success and know where to put their time and effort to make a difference. As you are beginning to study what effective reading teachers do, interview at least one classroom teacher in the school you are visiting to find out what that teacher thinks constitutes effectiveness in teaching literacy at that teacher's grade level. Use the following questions as a guide in interviewing (add others if you wish) and share your results with your classmates and professor.

    What do you think are the characteristics of effective reading teachers?

    How do you plan for teaching an entire class in reading?

    What types of assessments do you make on your students' literacy abilities?

    What teaching methods do you use in teaching reading?

    What do you think are the perennial problems of teaching in today's schools?

2. As discussed in this chapter, effective teaching and learning is context specific. This means that effective teaching behaviors need to be applied differently depending on the grade level taught, the instructional goal of the lesson, and the characteristics of your students. As you will recall, the degree of structure and control a teacher has in a lesson will vary depending upon the instructional goal. Different degrees of teacher control and structure are necessary for achieving different instructional goals. Make notes of the types of activities completed during the reading/language arts periods in the school you are visiting for 2 or 3 days and respond to the following questions:

> In what types of activities did the teacher exercise the most control?
>
> In what types of activities did the teacher exhibit less control?
>
> What type of grouping was used for highly teacher-controlled activities as opposed to those activities that were less controlled and more open?
>
> Looking back over the 2 or 3 days, do you think the control of the different learning activities varied in relation to the instructional goals? Did this seem to make a difference in terms of student learning?

Portfolio Entry

The statement, "It's the teacher who is the single-most significant factor in determining whether or not children will be successful in learning to read," is a popular pronouncement repeated by many educators. With this in mind, write a one-page response to one of the following in your teaching portfolio:

- Reflecting on your past teachers, do you remember having a teacher who particularly motivated you to read and learn on your own? If so, discuss the qualities of this person and the influence this teacher had on your life.
- "Good reading teachers are born teachers." Do you agree or disagree with this statement? Why?

BIBLIOGRAPHY

Allington, R. L. (1983). The reading instruction provided readers of different reading abilities. *Elementary School Journal, 83*, 549–559.

Anderson, R. C., Hiebert, E. H., Scott, J. A., & Wilkinson, I. A. G. (1985). *Becoming a nation of readers: The report of the Commission on Reading.* Washington, DC: The National Institute of Education.

Barrentine, S. J. (Ed.) (1999). *Reading assessment: Principles and practices for elementary teachers.* Newark, DE: International Reading Association.

Baumann, J. F., & Duffy, A. M. (1997). *Engaged reading for pleasure and learning: A report from the National Reading Research Center.* Athens, GA: National Reading Research Center.

Bingham, C. S. (1998). *Improving reading.* Greensboro, NC: SouthEastern Regional Vision for Education (SERVE).

Blair, T. R. (1975). *Relationship of teacher effort and student achievement in reading.* Unpublished doctoral dissertation, University of Illinois, Urbana.

Blair, T. R. (1984). Teacher effectiveness: The know-how to improve student learning. *The Reading Teacher, 38,* 138–141.

Blair, T. R., & Jones, D. L. (1998). *Preparing for student teaching in a pluralistic classroom.* Boston: Allyn & Bacon.

Blair, T. R., & Rupley, W. H. (1988). Practice and application in the teaching of reading. *The Reading Teacher, 41,* 536–539.

Blair, T. R., & Rupley, W. H. (2000). *Assessing instructional emphases in a balanced reading program.* Keynote address, Balanced Reading Special Interest Group. Indianapolis, IN: International Reading Association Annual Convention.

Blair, T. R., Turner, E. C., & Schaudt, B. A. (1995, October). *Classroom time allocation: Actual text reading and discussion time.* Paper presented at the College Reading Association Annual Conference, Clearwater, FL.

Chall, J. S. (1967). *Learning to read: The great debate.* New York: McGraw-Hill.

Dole, J. A., Duffy, G. G., Roehler, L. R., & Pearson, P. D. (1991). Moving from the old to the new: Research on reading comprehension instruction. *Review of Educational Research, 61,* 239–264.

Duffy, A. M. (1999). Characteristics of exemplary first-grade literacy instruction. *The Reading Teacher, 52,* 462–479.

Dykstra, R. (1967). *Continuation of the coordination center for first-grade reading instruction programs* (Final Report). Washington, DC: U.S. Department of Health, Education, and Welfare. Office of Education, Bureau of Research.

Evertson, C., Emmer, E. T., & Worsham, M. E. (2000). *Classroom management for elementary teachers* (5th ed.). Boston: Allyn & Bacon.

Fielding, L. G., & Pearson, P. D. (1994). Reading comprehension: What works. *Educational Leadership, 51,* 62–68.

Fisher, C., Marliave, R., & Filby, N. (1979). Improving teaching by increasing academic learning time. *Educational Leadership, 39,* 52–54.

Fuller, B., Wood, K., Rapoport, T., & Dornbush, S. (1982). The organizational content of individual efficacy. *Review of Educational Research, 52,* 7–30.

Gates, A. I. (1937). The necessary age for beginning reading. *Elementary School Journal, 37,* 497–508.

Good, T. L., & Brophy, J. E. (1987). *Looking in classrooms* (4th ed.). New York: Harper & Row.

Hancock, J. (Ed.). (1999). *The explicit teaching of reading.* Newark, DE: International Reading Association.

Henk, W., & Melnick, S. (1992). The initial development of a scale to measure "perception of self as reader." In C. K. Kinzer & D. Leu (Eds.), *Literacy research, theory, and practice: Views from many perspectives* (pp. 111–118). Chicago: National Reading Conference.

Hiebert, E. H., Pearson, P. D., Taylor, B. M., Richardson, V., & Paris, S. G. (1998). *Every child a reader: Applying reading research in the classroom.* Center for the Improvement of Early Reading achievement (CIERA). Ann Arbor, MI: University of Michigan School of Education.

International Reading Association. (2000). *Position statement on excellent reading teachers.* Newark, DE: International Reading Association.

Johnson, J. P., Livingston, M., Schwartz, R. A., & Slate, J. R. (2000). What makes a good elementary school? A critical examination. *Journal of Educational Research, 93,* 339–348.

Kincade, K. M. (1996). Improving reading comprehension through strategy instruction. *Reading Psychology, 17,* 273–81.

McDonald, F. J. (1976). *Summary report: Beginning teacher evaluation study: Phase II, 1973–74.* (Final Report: Vol. 1). Princeton, NJ: Educational Testing Service.

Pescosolido, J. D. (1962). *The identification and appraisal of certain major factors in the teaching of reading.* Unpublished doctoral dissertation, University of Connecticut, Storrs.

Pescosolido, J. D. (1980). Letter to author.

Pressley, M., Allington, R., Wharton-McDonald, R., Collins Block, C., & Morrow, L. M. (1998). *The nature of effective first-grade literacy instruction.* The National Research Center on English Learning & Achievement. Albany, NY: University of Albany.

Rosenshine, B. (1979). Content time and direct instruction. In P. Peterson & H. Walberg (Eds.), *Research on teaching: Concepts, findings and implications* (pp. 28–56). Berkeley, CA: McCutchan.

Rosenshine, B. (1995). Advances in research on instruction. *Journal of Educational Research, 88,* 262–268.

Rosenshine, B., & Meister, C. (1995). Scaffolds for teaching higher-order cognitive strategies. In A. C. Ornstein (Ed.), *Teaching: Theory into practice.* Boston: Allyn & Bacon.

Rosenshine, B., & Stevens, R. (1995). Functions for teaching well-structured tasks. *Journal of Educational Research,* 88, 262–268.

Rosenshine, B. V., & Meister, C. (1992). The use of scaffolds for teaching higher-level cognitive strategies. *Educational Leadership,* 49, 26–33.

Rosenshine, B. V., & Stevens, R. (1986). Teaching functions. In M. C. Wittrock (Ed.), *Handbook of research on teaching* (3rd ed.), pp. 376–391. Upper Saddle River, NJ: Merrill/Prentice Hall.

Rupley, W. H. (1977). Stability of teacher effect on pupils' reading achievement gain over a two-year period and its relation to instructional emphases. In P. D. Pearson (Ed.), *Reading: Theory, research and practice* (pp. 69–72). Clemson, SC: National Reading Conference.

Rupley, W. H., & Blair, T. R. (1987). Assignment and supervision of reading seatwork: Looking in on 12 primary grade teachers. *The Reading Teacher, 40,* 391–393.

Rupley, W. H., & Blair, T. R. (1988). *Teaching reading: Diagnosis, direct instruction, and practice* (2nd ed.). Upper Saddle River, NJ: Merrill/Prentice Hall.

Rupley, W. H., Wise, B. S., & Logan, J. W. (1986). Research in effective teaching: An overview of its development. In J. V. Hoffman (Ed.), *Effective teaching of reading: Research and practice.* Newark, DE: International Reading Association.

Stern, P., & Shavelson, R. J. (1983). Reading teachers' judgments, plans, and decision making. *The Reading Teacher, 37,* 280–286.

Taylor, B. M., Pearson, P. D., Clark, K., & Walpole, S. (1999). *Beating the odds in teaching all children to read: Lessons from effective schools and exemplary teachers.* Center for the Improvement of Early Reading Achievement (CIERA) (Rep. No. 2-006). Ann Arbor, MI: University of Michigan School of Education.

Vygotsky, L. (1962). *Thought and language.* Cambridge, MA: M.I.T. Press.

Watts, S. M. & Cerra, K. K. (1996). Can you teach reading comprehension with children's books? Fostering reader response and developing comprehension strategies. *Balanced Reading Instruction, III,* 1–7.

CHAPTER **3**

Language:
The Key to Literacy

Chapter Outline

For the Reader

Language is a powerful means through which we learn, develop and expand our interests, communicate with others, and communicate with ourselves (National Council of Teachers of English, 1996). Language continually shapes our views of the world and ourselves. Whether it is a child saying "cookie," a scientist explaining a new theory, an author writing a book, or a student reading a CD-ROM encyclopedia entry, the central purpose of language is communication of meaning. Reading is based on language, as are listening, speaking, and writing. Language cuts across every goal and function of the school. Everything that is taught in the school passes through a communication process before students learn it. Purposes for language use in the schools include (1) obtaining and communicating information through the use of a variety of text sources, (2) responding to creating and interpreting literary texts, (3) learning and reflecting, and (4) solving problems and thinking critically (Standards for the English Language Arts, 1996).

Key Ideas

- Reading and writing are related to all language functions found in the elementary school curriculum.

- Learning to read and write is related to, and built upon, children's past language experiences.

- Reading and writing instruction should be a natural outgrowth of students' past language experiences and language development.

- Learning to read and write are developmental processes related to continued language development.

- Teaching reading and writing should build logically and systematically on students' language capabilities.

LANGUAGE AND READING AND WRITING

Reading is a language process requiring the understanding of and the interaction with written language. Language provides a bridge that enables ideas, information, and data to pass between parent and child, teacher and student, and student and peer. Reading has a unique relationship with language. Because we acquire or refine most of our concepts and reasoning capabilities through the use of language, reading enables us to go beyond what we can see or manipulate. In a broad sense, reading frees the mind from direct experiences. There are, however, differences between spoken and written language. Spoken language is different in form from written language. As noted by Jeannette Veatch (1996), "One does not read spoken language easily. One reads written language as it was intended" (p. 513).

Recognizing Words

Written language involves the learner in solving two codes. One is accessing the text or print by understanding the relationship between the orthography (the writing system) and the phonemes (speech units represented by the writing system). This understanding permits the reader to recognize, decode, or approximate the pronunciation of words not recognized as whole words. Reading research has documented the importance of children understanding the relationship between letters and letter combinations and the sounds they represent (Rupley & Willson, 2000); however, how best to facilitate this development in reading instruction is an ongoing debate. Children who are emerging readers and writers need to know the relationship between their own speech sounds and how these are represented in print. Some children find this difficult because they are not aware of how words and sounds in their speech are marked or that they are distinct units (Dickinson, Wolf, & Stotsky, 1999). Children entering school have rarely been asked to think about language and the terms associated with describing their learning-to-read feature of language. For example, concepts such as words, sounds, letters, and so forth that teachers use to teach reading are representations of language that children may be lacking. A critical component of effective reading instruction is making sure that children connect their language with the language they are to read. Classroom-based research (Juel & Minden-Cupp, 2000) indicates that teachers who model language features of reading such as segmenting words into chunks (*b–at*) and identifying letter-sound relationships help children to connect print with their oral language. According to the research, when the children had learned many letter-sound relationships, the teachers provided modeling about how to combine known letter-sounds with texts that made sense.

A major part of recognizing words for beginning readers is called **phonemic awareness.** Phonemic awareness is the ability to hear the sequence of sounds that make up spoken words. This ability should be a key component of word study in beginning reading instruction and it begins before children can master the relationship between letters and letter combinations (graphemes) and the sounds they represent (phonemes) (Teale & Yokota, 2000).

Constructing Meaning

Constructing meaning is the second important code. Readers interact with writers so that there is communication between the two. Writers of books, notes, lists, directions, and so forth are using language to communicate with a reader. Interaction between the text and reader depends on the reader's experiential and conceptual background, purposes for reading, and setting, as well as the text content. This interaction involves a strategic approach that requires knowledge of language structures, comprehension monitoring, and understanding meaning. Such interaction is language-related, but it goes beyond the reader's oral language background, because much of this interaction involves reading and writing experiences that support and extend all language capabilities.

Oral Language and Reading

One view of the relationship between oral and written language is that in the beginning stages of reading development, children depend on their oral language abilities for comprehension. That is, emerging readers' comprehension of print is linked closely to their spoken language capabilities and experiences with print. For example, a young child who frequently plays computer games will often learn to recognize words such as *exit, open,* and *close,* because of their importance in operating a computer and playing computer games. At this early stage of learning about words, called the *logographic* stage, children learn words as wholes. These words are often embedded in logos in print within children's environment, as the word *McDonald's* is embedded in golden arches. As children's reading becomes more automatic and proficient, their dependence on spoken language abilities in comprehending print generally disappears, and print is comprehended in terms of its structural and meaning features. This capability is reflected in stage 2 of Chall's (1996) reading stages, in which children begin to become more proficient in using letter-sound relationships in their reading. Samuels (1988) has attributed this increased proficiency to word recognition becoming more automatic; that is, it requires less attention to sounding out words and more attention to comprehension.

Research supports the idea that students undergo developmental shifts in the degree of importance of oral language in their comprehension of text. Young children often depend more on their oral language skills, while older students, who are more proficient in reading, depend more on their experience with reading and writing. Emergent readers who are learning about orthographic features and acquiring word-recognition skills are also developing an understanding of how print functions, the nature of stories, and other important components of literacy that will enhance their comprehension. As they build experience with print, emergent readers rely less upon the speech code representation and focus more on meaning.

This phenomenon suggests a reciprocal relationship between literacy and oral-language development. Students' language awareness depends heavily on their literacy experiences, which help them to understand language features, such as syntax and semantics, and to develop and expand their vocabularies. Direct experiences with reading and writing enhance and facilitate the development of language awareness, which enhances and facilitates literacy and reasoning development (Stahl, 1999). Language awareness, which includes knowledge about phonemes, words, sentences, story structure, and communication of meaning, evolves primarily through a variety of direct experiences with print in both reading and writing situations.

Balanced Reading Instruction That Builds on Oral Language

Reading for meaning is in many ways closer to children's previous experiences with language than is associating visual symbols with the sounds they typically represent. Prior to reading instruction, children have spent several years listening to and speaking meaningful language. Most children begin school with a speaking vocabulary of approximately 8,000 words and are capable of using language to express themselves. However, they use this language within familiar contextual settings and focus on communication with others. The process and the demands of literacy are based on **decontextualized language use,** which requires the development of language awareness. Decontextualized language has three characteristics that are more closely associated with written language than with oral language:

1. Information must be conveyed that is new to the hearer.
2. Background knowledge necessary for the hearer to interpret the message needs to be provided.
3. The information must be communicated through words and syntax, not by relying on intonation and extra-linguistic resources such as gestures. (Dickinson, Wolf, & Stotsky, 1999, p. 372)

Contextualized Language

Children have a variety of experiences with oral language and literacy when they come to preschool, kindergarten, and first-grade classrooms. Some may have been read to from birth and had many experiences with writing and a variety of other literacy activities. Other children may have had minimal experiences with literacy activities (Harp & Brewer, 2000). Children's experiences with oral language and print enhance their development of decontextualized language capabilities. As children learn to recognize print by associating logos (e.g., McDonald's, Captain Crunch, Nike, etc.) with it, engage in pretend and real writing activities, understand the features of books (page, top, bottom, front, back, etc.), and so forth they begin to develop decontextualized language capabilities.

Because children learning to read and write rely heavily on their language backgrounds and their early experiences with literacy, they can experience difficulties when they are asked to do something that does not build on their existing capabili-

Children have a wide variety of experiences with language when they come to school.

ties. Failure to build on children's existing language capabilities may result in their failure to see that they are really involved in a language process. The materials and methods used for reading and writing instruction often divorce the act of reading from language involvement by emphasizing letter-sound relationships, the mechanics of writing, and other isolated skills that fail to stress the language-meaning features of print. Lack of balanced reading instruction may or may not be deliberate. Our concern is how the learner perceives what is going on. Phonics, for example, can provide motivation only for a limited time—it is not a self-sustaining activity. Only direct involvement in actual reading and writing will help children develop literacy capabilities that complement and extend their language development.

Billy ⑮
Sept. 15, 1999
Puggles is a very nice guinea pig
because she never bites anyone
she's really not much trouble
because y you never have to
take her for a walk
around the block. she's a
vegetarian. and her favoritte
food is crisp, crunchy celery.
you don't ever have to feed
her more than 1 cup since
Puggles only eats
once a day.

Figure 3.1   An illustration of how children's experiences both in and out of school build the foundation for their writing development.

Teachers who are teaching and facilitating reading are aware of experiences and growth that children undergo before they enter school. Many children already have had language experiences that form a solid foundation for their experiences with reading. Children whose parents read to them often and who have been engaged in literacy experiences will begin to make connections between print and oral language, recognize some words as whole words, know the features of a book, relate pictures to text, develop emerging understanding about writing, and understand many other relationships between oral and written language. Children who have not had opportunities to engage in informal reading activities may not yet do so. Figure 3.1 provides an example of how language experiences outside of school and those in school contribute to children's writing.

As noted earlier, whether or not teachers build on children's oral language skills will influence the degree of their students' benefits from literacy activities. Students are not likely to be able to read language that is significantly different from their speaking and listening capabilities, nor are they likely to be able to write better than they can speak. Oral-language capabilities provide the foundation for literacy development at the beginning stages and at each stage that follows. Teachers of reading should view children's experiences both in and out of school as bound together with language and communication: All involve developing and extending concepts. Children build comprehension capabilities in reading and expression capabilities in writing on these concepts (Tompkins, 1998).

STRUCTURE OF LANGUAGE

Language instruction has its own distinct terminology. Teachers of literacy will frequently encounter these terms in their readings about literacy instruction, as well as in many of the instructional materials and reading programs used to teach literacy.

Terms Associated with Phonology

Phoneme: the smallest unit of sound within a language. When the word *top* is pronounced, three phonemes are utilized: /t/ , /o/, /p/.

Grapheme: a written symbol (letter or letter combination) used to represent a sound in a language. The word *top* has three graphemes representing three phonemes. The word *chop* has three graphemes representing three phonemes (*ch* is a consonant digraph representing one sound).

Grapheme-Phoneme Relationship: the sound(s) represented by a letter or a letter combination. Also referred to as *letter-sound correspondence.*

Phonics: different approaches and strategies designed to teach the orthographic (written) code of language and the relationships between spelling patterns and the speech sounds represented by the spelling patterns.

Terms Associated with Meaning Features of Language

Semantics: describes the meaning relationships among words. Semantic acquisition refers to how children acquire vocabulary and how they begin to acquire semantic systems that are based on simple vocabulary acquisition.

Morpheme: the smallest unit of meaningful language. Morphemes can be one of two types: free or bound. A free morpheme functions independently in larger language units. For example, *dog* is a free morpheme composed of three phonemes. A bound morpheme must be used with another morpheme. Bound morphemes include affixes and inflectional endings. If *s* is added to *dog* to form a plural, the *s* in *dogs* is a bound morpheme, and therefore the word *dogs* contains two morphemes.

Terms Associated with Structural Features of Language

Syntax: describes the patterns found within a language (the grammar of the language). Syntax includes the various patterns in which words can be strung together. It also includes the ways in which words function in different language patterns, as illustrated by the following example.

Light the fire. (verb)

She saw the *light.* (noun)

He danced *lightly* across the ring and threw a *light* punch. (adverb, adjective)

Research has supported the idea that children need to learn about the relationships between word spellings and pronunciations to become successful readers (Adams, 1990; Chall, 1996; Stahl, 1999). As one teaches these relationships, many of the language-development characteristics and features presented earlier in this chapter must be taken into consideration. However, reading instruction can overemphasize words as individual units. Overemphasizing words inhibits the development of abilities in using syntax and semantic features to arrive at meaning. Furthermore, it does not reflect the purpose of phonics, which is to develop automatic word recognition so children can devote their attention to comprehension. Understanding the importance of language in teaching literacy is essential to developing a quality instructional program.

LANGUAGE VARIATIONS

Children acquire the language to which they are exposed—generally that of their parents, which reflects the parents' geographic region (Goldfield & Snow, 1999). Although most languages share some common features (e.g., syntactic, semantic, and phonetic features), variations occur even among speakers of a common language. Dialects, for example, differ from region to region. Another important variation influencing children's literacy acquisition occurs when they are learning to read and write in English but have a first language (e.g., Spanish, Vietnamese, or Navajo) other than English.

Culturally and Linguistically Diverse Learners

Culturally and linguistically diverse learners are children whose culture as well as language or dialect differ from those of the school. The number of linguistically diverse learners in American classrooms is growing.

Dialects, in a broad sense, are the ways that people speak in different parts of a country or in specific cultures. The components of a dialect are pronunciation, grammar, and vocabulary. Generally speaking, phonological divergences of dialects are differences in speech sounds within words; thus, a grapheme (written letter symbol) may represent different phonemes (speech sounds) in different dialects. Grammatical and syntactical divergences of dialects are differences in inflectional changes, verb forms, verb auxiliaries, and the structures of phrases and sentences.

Linguistically diverse (bilingual and non-English-speaking) students who lack competency in the language of the classroom do not enter the school setting from a linguistic void. These students have mastered a language and its systems of significant speech sounds, grammatical structures, and meaningful vocabulary. Linguistically diverse children often face the expectation that they will read and comprehend English with competency as part of their school curriculum. Many factors, however, inhibit rapid acquisition of English as a second language, while others facilitate linguistically diverse students in becoming bilingual in their first language and in English. For example, linguistic components such as phonology, syntax, and semantics make learning English difficult. *Phonology* refers to the inventory of meaningful speech sounds used to form grammatical structures in a particular language system. Vietnamese children who are learning English as a second language, for example, have never heard in their native language the sounds /s/, /es/, /t/ , and /d/ at the end of a word. Some languages follow a different syntax from that of English. Spanish, for example, contains no possessive forms of nouns (e.g., *my dad's car*), so children who are native Spanish speakers sometimes experience difficulties with such language structures in English. The semantics of other languages are also different. A Navajo speaker learning English would perceive the concept of the word *rough* as a series of many attributes, each having different labels depending on the texture of the object.

Reading development is linked to students' strengths and weaknesses in their oral language capabilities (listening and speaking). Many linguistically diverse students might experience greater success in literacy development if their primary language formed the basis for their learning. Children's primary language can provide a support system for learning English and can enhance the growth of their self-confidence.

THE READING AND WRITING CONNECTION

The connection between reading and writing should be apparent, although each is often treated separately. As with listening, speaking, and reading, the purpose of writing is to communicate meaning. Students who understand that others can read their writing and that they can read the writing of others realize the communicative concept of reading and are likely to understand that reading is constructing meaning, not just sounding out words.

Some of the key strategies that successful readers and writers use have been summarized by Larry Lewin (1992). He points out that good readers and writers routinely and knowingly use the following strategies.

1. Prepare by
   - tapping their existing knowledge background for a topic before they read and write.
   - determining their purpose(s) for reading and writing.
   - predicting how what they are reading or what they are to write will turn out.
   - self-selecting topics they want to read about or write about.
2. Compose a first draft by
   - monitoring their own understanding of their text and the text of others.
   - monitoring their own reactions to text.
   - relating new information in their reading and writing to what they already know (see Figure 3.2).

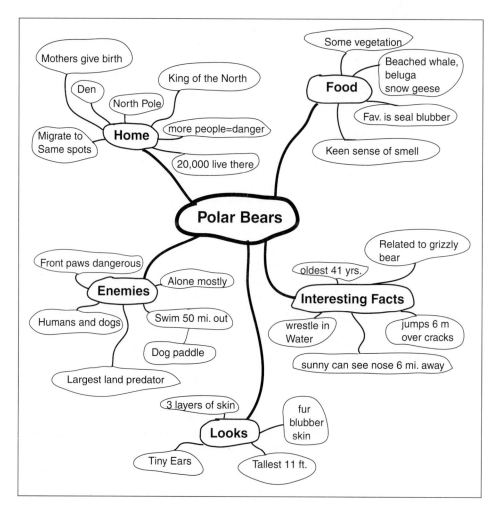

Figure 3.2   An example of a child's preparation for writing a story about polar bears.
Source: Matt Rupley

- expanding their vocabulary both during and after a first reading and a first draft of writing.
- knowing where to get help and assistance when either the reading or writing breaks down.
- distinguishing in their reading and writing the important from the less important ideas.
3. Repair by
- reconsidering the first meaning that they construct in their reading and writing.
- repairing their text to improve its meaning by rereading or rewriting.
- appreciating an author's craft and working to expand and enhance their own writing craft (see Figure 3.3).

Polar Bears

The animal I am studying is the polar bear. The polar bear is the largest land predator on the earth. It has three layers of protection which are fur, blubber, and skin. The tallest one ever recorded was eleven feet, standing on it's hind legs. Compared to it's body the polar bear has tiny ears.

The polar bear lives at the North Pole. They are the king of the North. They migrate and go to the same spots each time. About 20,000 polar bears live there. They dig their own dens, where the mothers will give birth to their cubs. With more people moving there polar bears may be in danger.

The polar bear's favorite food is seal blubber. Polar bears have a keen sense of smell. They can smell twenty miles away. Some of the foods they eat are snow geese, beached white whales, and beluga. Polar bears may eat some vegetation.

The polar bears only enemies are human and dogs. They are not hunted a lot, which lets them live long. Their front paws are dangerous weapons. The polar bear can swim fifty miles out to sea. They swim by dog paddling. They like to wrestle with each other in the water. However, they spend most of their time alone.

Some interesting facts about the polar bear include that the oldest one recorded was 41 years old. The Polar Bear can jump six meters over cracks in the ice. If it is sunny you can see the polar bears nose six miles away. Did you know the polar bear was related to the grizzly bear?

Now you know some interesting things about the polar bear. Thank you for reading my research report.

Figure 3.3 A polished piece of writing that is intended to be shared with classmates.

4. Share by
   - communicating to others their reactions to their own and others' writing.
   - applying their newly acquired information to future reading and writing tasks.

Students' experiential and conceptual backgrounds are important in both comprehending text when reading and composing comprehensive text when writing. Students write best about things of which they have background knowledge. Likewise, they read with best comprehension about things that are in their experiential and conceptual backgrounds. One of the most important features of reading and writing is that they both enhance children's language resources, particularly their oral language capabilities.

Several important observations (Stahl, Osborn, & Lehr, 1999) that support the integrated role that writing plays in the development of children's reading capabilities include the following:

Inclusion Strategies

Meeting Students' Literacy Needs

Many factors influence student reading, such as knowledge of letter-sound relationships, knowledge of language functions and structure, and background knowledge of the text being read. Also, as students progress through school, their reading capabilities increase as they learn more about language through literacy activities and expand their experiential and conceptual knowledge. Writing development seems to follow a similar pattern. Students with superior language capabilities are often better able than students with less-developed abilities to organize their writing and to produce text that is more coherent and longer.

A classroom environment that nurtures language development is important for all students to experience growth in their literacy capabilities. For those exceptional students included in the classroom, modification of existing structure and language demands may be necessary. Children who do not have well-developed language skills can benefit from explicit language instruction. For example, young children in kindergarten or first grade who lag behind in their language development can often benefit from instruction that targets the lexicon (word meaning). The focus of such instruction would be on verbs, which are the key to grammar, and would include formal syntax training as an accompanying feature (Rice, 1996).

An additional feature that is appropriate for all children is a language environment within the classroom that invites children to engage in reasoning about language. Paired reading and writing can create situations in which students who are lagging behind their age-peers can work with younger children on reading and writing. Support is provided for each child, and each gets valuable practice and literacy opportunities. The result is a community of language users who have much to talk about and much to share through listening, reading, and writing.

1. Children often include in their writing the syntactic patterns, themes, and content of the materials they read.
2. Children learn through writing that the purpose of text is to be understood.
3. Children learn that different readers respond to the same text differently. They come to realize that meaning is a result of an interaction between the author and the reader.
4. Children realize that to write clearly and communicate well with readers, their writing must have an underlying organization and may require the use of other sources to maximize communication.
5. Children learn that reading is about thinking and reasoning. This is perhaps their most important understanding.

Interactive Features of Reading and Writing in Constructing Meaning

The connections between reading and writing suggest that teachers should integrate reading and writing throughout instructional programs. The key strategies noted in the previous section of this chapter are those that teachers can develop, nurture, and polish by combining reading and writing in the classroom to better develop children's literacy. Shanahan (1988) developed seven instructional principles based on the reading-writing relationship. Each of these principles, which are discussed in the following paragraphs, illustrates how to combine reading and writing in the classroom.

Teach both reading and writing

Although many individuals argue that reading and writing are similar in terms of the skills, strategies, and cognitive processes they involve, Shanahan (1988) does not consider them to be all that similar, suggesting that children need opportunities to be taught both. Students do not become writers only through reading instruction, nor do they become readers only through writing instruction. Students need both reading and writing opportunities so that each skill can enhance the development of the other.

Introduce reading and writing from the earliest grades

Teachers who create literate environments in their classrooms don't treat literacy as a subject having a specific scheduled period. Language is an integral part of the learning environment, and reading and writing opportunities should abound throughout each day. Teachers should work to infuse reading and writing instruction in the study of literature and content-area subjects (Wood, 2001). Writing and reading activities can vary in purpose, requirements, and audience for both literature texts and content-area texts. A valuable guide for helping teachers accomplish the infusion of literacy throughout the curriculum is presented in Table 3.1. The examples shown can be easily expanded and modified to meet the needs of individual children.

Reflect the developmental nature of the reading and writing relationship in instruction

Tierney (1992) suggests that reading and writing are developmental processes and that different abilities are dominant at different points in development. Shanahan (1988) notes that in the beginning stages of reading, spelling and word recognition are dominant. These findings coincide with Chall's (1996) research on stages of reading development and with Adams's (1990) analysis of beginning reading development. With more-capable readers, the connection between reading and writing focuses on comprehension, vocabulary, and organization. What students learn at different points in their reading and writing development can have important implications for instruction.

Reading and writing can be integrated at developmental stages by using writing activities that are appropriate for students' levels of reading and oral-language development. Teachers can use multiple types of materials in teaching students to read,

Table 3.1

Guidelines for infusing literacy throughout the curriculum

WRITING	PURPOSE	REQUIREMENTS	AUDIENCE
1. Weather and temperature charts	Compare conditions over a nine-month period.	Thermometer to take temperature. Observe clouds at same time of day. Accuracy.	Science class.
2. Personal letters	Exchange accounts of experiences with friend.	Interesting personal information. Informal writing level.	A friend who knows me.
3. Invitations	Inform and invite audience to a program, party, etc.	What, who, why, when, where. (Proofreading is important.)	Parents, neighbors, friends.
4. Puppet plays	Entertain.	Original story that entertains. Puppets.	Class, parents, other invited guests.
5. Diaries	Record daily experiences and feelings.	Short notes on things important to me.	Me.
6. News stories	Inform about news, events, sports, etc.	Accuracy—who, what, when, where. Clear, brief reporting. (Editing and proofreading are important.)	Whole school. If city paper, large unknown audience that wants information.
7. Forms	Obtain social security card, driver's license. Send for information.	Accurate information, clear handwriting. (Proofreading is important.)	People who don't know me. Government.
8. Imaginative	Entertain, enjoy.	Fresh ideas, imagination, feelings.	Class. If published, a large, unknown audience.
9. Autobiographies	Tell others about myself. Compile class book.	Facts about myself, feelings, wishes. (Proofreading is important.)	Class and parents. If published, a large, unknown audience.
10. Book reports	Report author, title information, summary, and personal reactions.	Careful reading and writing for summary. (Proofreading is important.)	Class. If book review in a paper, people who might want to read the book.

Table 3.1			
Guidelines for infusing literacy throughout the curriculum (continued)			
WRITING	**PURPOSE**	**REQUIREMENTS**	**AUDIENCE**
11. Reports and projects in social studies, science, etc.	Share new facts and information.	Research from several sources, data, main ideas, and details. Accuracy of facts, best order for ideas. (Proofreading is important.)	Class. If journal or magazine article, people wanting that information.
12. Biographies	Report knowledge about well-known person.	Research from several sources. Comparisons of information. Accuracy. (Proofreading is important.)	Class. If published, a large, unknown audience.
13. Editorials	Persuade someone to my viewpoint.	Knowledge of ways to persuade and use facts. Rewriting to clearly persuade.	People who read the newspaper. Some will agree with the writer, some will disagree.
14. Minutes for meetings	Keep a record of what happened.	Accurate listening and reading.	Class, group, or organization.

Source: From *The Effective Teaching of Language Arts* (5th ed., pp. 466–467) by D. Norton, 1997, Upper Saddle River, NJ: Merrill/Prentice Hall. Copyright 1997 by Pearson Education. Reprinted by permission of Pearson Education, Inc., Upper Saddle River, NJ 07458.

write about, synthesize, evaluate, or analyze text. Writing activities that encourage children to use new words can reinforce vocabulary development. Writing activities for young learners should focus on real-life experiences to ensure that students' language structure and text reflect their background knowledge. Writing activities can also replace, supplement, or enhance many of the independent practice and application activities recommended in reading instructional materials.

Make the reading and writing connection explicit

Teaching a particular reading or writing skill does not guarantee that it will transfer to actual applications. Students need explicit/direct instruction in reading and writing as well as close supervision by the teacher for learning to occur. They also need to understand when to use a skill or strategy. Lessons in reading and writing should therefore complement each other. In other words, when appropriate, what students learn in reading should be transferred for use in writing, and vice versa. Reading and writing instruction can be simultaneous, showing students the specific purpose of and the relationships between the two subjects. Students learn much about the

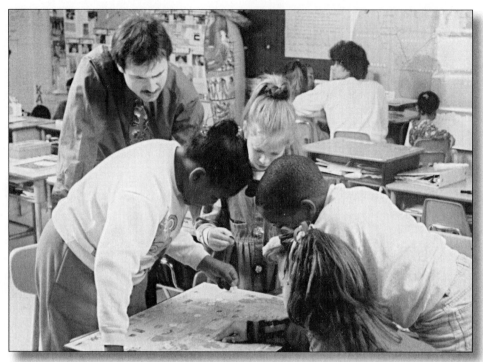

Teachers can use a variety of activities to stimulate students' writing.

nature and structure of writing through instruction in the grammar, process writing patterns, and expository writing patterns of stories and through other reading instruction that focuses on text processing. Learning these aspects of reading enables students to better use them in writing and thus develop more mature writing styles. Younger students often pattern their writing after books they have read or listened to. Schell (1993) points out a classic example of this: After reading *Brown Bear* by Bill Martin, children modeled the story language in their writing (Brown dog, brown dog, what do you see? I see a fat cat looking at me.). Literary aspects, such as characterization, irony, foreshadowing, dialogue, and sarcasm, that teachers focus on in their reading programs also are modeled for students to use in their own writing.

Emphasize product and process knowledge in instruction

Shanahan (1988) urges teachers to be aware of the differences between product knowledge and process knowledge. Product knowledge is substantive (vocabulary and word knowledge), while process knowledge is related to reasoning ability. The latter is concerned with strategies and procedures for solving problems and carrying out complex activities. Readers and writers both must monitor themselves to make sure the text makes sense and must use strategies to aid comprehension.

Reading and writing instruction that focuses on vocabulary knowledge and relates text to students' background knowledge can expand product knowledge. Most teachers do a good job of teaching in this area. The process aspect of reading and writing, however, requires a focus on the how and why. In process instruction, students discuss how they preview text, how they predict outcomes and events, how they come up with ideas about text they have read or stories they have written, how and why they choose to revise their thinking about text, and why they edit text. Awareness of the many processes that reading and writing share benefits both reading and writing acquisition and development.

Emphasize communication

Reading and writing are communication processes; readers and writers are concerned with meaning. This text emphasizes that language is communication of meaning and that reading must be recognized as a language process. Highlighting the communication function of language capitalizes upon the essentials of language growth: people to talk to, read about, and write to, and things to read and write about that are meaningful to students.

Teach reading and writing in a meaningful context

The different functions of children's language (see Figure 3.4) can be used strategically for teaching reading and writing in a meaningful context. Teachers can explore and develop these functions by integrating reading and writing. They can have students write explanations of text, rewrite text, prepare lists, write directions, write and evaluate advertising aimed at encouraging consumer use, write and edit a class newspaper, write books and stories for other classes and students, keep minutes of group meetings, plan schedules, and so forth. The central point for teachers to consider is that students must have opportunities to integrate reading and writing in a variety of literacy experiences.

CONSIDERATIONS FOR A LANGUAGE-RICH CLASSROOM ENVIRONMENT

When considering how to create a language-rich environment in the classroom, a teacher should ensure two important qualities. One is a classroom environment that encourages and supports literacy development. The second is the incorporation of language-rich environmental features and activities into reading and writing instruction.

Sulzby and Barnhart (1992) describe what a literacy-rich environment generally is like:

> Materials are at children's reach and there is sufficient time during the day for children to interact with those materials. Reading and writing tend to become less visible as separate activities and become more deeply embedded in other aspects of classroom life. (p. 125)

Instrumental Language—The teacher can:

1. Be accessible and responsive to children's requests, but teach independence by having children state their requests effectively.
2. Encourage the use of instrumental language with other children, helping them to expand their own language through providing help and direction to peers.
3. Analyze advertising, propaganda, etc., to help children become aware of how language can be used by people to get what they want.

Regulatory Language—The teacher can:

1. Create situations that let children be "in charge" of small and large groups.
2. Find instances in which regulatory language is used inappropriately to teach appropriate regulatory language or the alternative, instrumental language.
3. Attempt to use less regulatory language as a teacher.

Interactional Language—The teacher can:

1. Create situations that require children to share work areas or materials and talk about how they are to do it.
2. Find ways of having small group (especially pairs or trios) discussions in a variety of subject areas. Through these discussions, students not only learn the subject matter more thoroughly, they practice communication.
3. Let students work together to plan field trips, social events, and classroom and school projects.
4. Whenever possible, mix children of different ages, sexes, and races in work groups or discussion groups.
5. Have informal social times and, as a teacher, engage in some talk that is not "all business."

Personal Language—The teacher can:

1. Use personal language to give permission to children to share personal thoughts and opinions.
2. Be willing to listen and talk personally during transition times: for example, when children are coming in in the morning. Converse with children while on cafeteria or playground duty.
3. Provide some comfortable, attractive areas in the classroom where students can talk quietly.
4. Encourage parents and family members to visit and participate in classrooms.
5. Read stories or books that prompt a very personal response from students.

Figure 3.4   Instructional strategies to promote language functions.

Reading and writing are infused into the daily instructional activities and experiences of the children so that they become a natural and integral part of learning. Pinnell (1996) has conceptualized different ways for teachers to consider how children's language functions (see Figure 3.4). Knowledge of such functions can form the basis for using instructional strategies and materials to infuse literacy into children's classroom experiences. Language-rich classroom environments have features that encourage students to interact with language; that is, they have things to talk about, read about, and write about.

Imaginative Language—The teacher can:

1. Create situations that naturally elicit spontaneous dramatic play; for example, house corner, dress up, blocks for younger children, and drama and role-playing for older children.
2. Read stories and books which feed the imagination and which are a stimulus for art, drama, and discussion.
3. Provide time for children to talk in groups and/or with partners before they begin their writing or imaginative topics.
4. Encourage "play" with language—the sounds of words and the images they convey.

Heuristic Language—The teacher can:

1. Structure classroom experiences so that interest and curiosity are aroused.
2. Create real problems for children to solve.
3. Put children in pairs or work groups for problem-solving activities.
4. Use heuristic language to stimulate such language in children. Saying "I wonder why" often prompts children to do the same. (This should, however, not be contrived; it should be an honest problem.)
5. Try projects which require study on the part of the entire class, including the teacher. Find some questions that no one knows the answer to.

Informative Language—The teacher can:

1. Plan activities which require children to observe carefully and objectively and then to summarize and draw conclusions from their observations (field trips are a good opportunity).
2. Require children to keep records of events over periods of time and then to look back at their records and draw conclusions; for example, keeping records on classroom pets.
3. Use questioning techniques to elicit more complex forms of information giving.
4. Instead of having tedious classroom reports, have children give their reports to small groups and encourage feedback and discussion of those reports.

Figure 3.4 (continued)

Source: From G. S. Pinnell, "Ways to Look at the Functions of Children's Language." In B. Power & R. Hubbard (Eds.), *Language Development: A Reader for Teachers* (pp. 152–153), 1996, Upper Saddle River, NJ: Merrill/Prentice Hall. Copyright 1996 by Pearson Education. Reprinted by permission of Pearson Education, Inc., Upper Saddle River, NJ 07458.

Classroom Centers

Centers to promote literacy development can be set up in the classroom. Such centers can focus on reading, writing, and oral language. A writing center could provide children with access to such things as a typewriter, a computer, pencils, pens, markers, lined and unlined paper, notepads, staplers, scissors, and other materials that encourage students to write and share their writing with others. To stimulate students' imagination and motivation to write, many teachers also include in their writing centers old magazines, pictures, artifacts, coupons, catalogs, stamp pads, and other objects they have collected.

Any classroom arrangement that brings students together to talk and listen to one another can promote language development.

A reading center is more than just a library with a collection of books. It is an area in the classroom that invites children to read. A large collection of reading materials could include books on a variety of topics and aimed at several different reading levels—including big books, read-along books, audiotaped books, rebus books, and picture books—along with catalogs, magazines, stories written by children in the class, newspapers, and travel brochures. A variety of reading materials for all grade levels is recommended for each classroom (our college students still get excited when they read children's books, as do many fifth and sixth graders). Furniture for the reading center can range from easy chairs to an old bathtub, as long as it is comfortable and inviting to students.

Centers to promote oral language (speaking and listening) are not as well defined as writing and reading centers; however, any classroom arrangement that brings students together to talk and listen to one another can promote oral-language development. Many of the suggestions presented in Figure 3.4 can be the focus of a permanent or temporary center in the classroom. For example, a drama center stocked with old clothes, hats, shoes, puppets, and other materials can be used to stimulate role-playing and dramatic play that result in spontaneous interaction. A garden or plant center where students gather to watch and care for plants will create interest and stimulate their curiosity. This type of project can help students begin to better understand heuristic language as the teacher encourages them to interact with each other by asking questions that begin with "I wonder why."

How teachers use their activity centers to promote literacy depends on what functions the centers serve and how much direct instruction the teachers provide. Pinnell's instructional strategies to promote language functions (Figure 3.4) can serve as guidelines to help determine the functions and purposes of the centers and plan appropriate learning activities.

In addition to using centers to promote reading and writing development, teachers can display examples of students' writing; encourage them to write stories to take home; label objects in the classroom (e.g., This is the door. Here is our light switch.); write dictated lists and schedules; place notepads, paper, and writing tools in activity centers; establish pen pals for students; set up a classroom post office; write class newspapers; encourage diary and journal writing; and establish an interactive web site on the Internet.

Reading Activities and Instructional Opportunities in a Language-rich Environment

Incorporating a classroom's language-rich features into reading and writing instruction capitalizes on the benefits of such an environment. Suggestions for integrating and promoting language development in literacy instruction appear throughout this book; expanded discussions are found in chapters dealing with emergent literacy, comprehension, meaning vocabulary, and instructional materials and programs.

Reading aloud to students of all ages has several benefits and has been frequently cited (Adams, 1990) as a major factor contributing to reading and writing development. First, it can help students understand that the purpose of reading is to communicate meaning. Students often cry, laugh, and express other emotions when listening to stories read to them. Such reactions indicate that they comprehend what they hear.

Second, reading aloud to students can foster a desire to read and can help students associate value with reading. Most students look forward to the teacher's reading aloud to them daily. Later, children may read many of the books and magazines from which the teacher reads.

Third, reading aloud to students can enable the teacher to take advantage of teaching moments. Teaching moments are situations that arise during a school day when the teacher can reinforce, reintroduce, or illustrate something that has been taught previously. For example, if a lesson about different meanings of words preceded reading aloud to children, and what is being read aloud has some multiple-meaning words, the teacher can point this out and illustrate the lesson concept with examples from the selection being read.

Students in the lower grades often benefit from hearing the same books read aloud to them several times. When these books are then made available for students to read independently, these frequently become the books they enjoy reading the most. In addition to reading books, students enjoy hearing poetry, limericks, and song lyrics. Students at all grade levels enjoy being read to, and teachers at all grade levels should be encouraged to make reading aloud part of their daily instruction.

Reading aloud to students gives them the opportunity to see the relationships among reading, writing, speaking, and listening. It is one way to enable them to connect, through the use of language, old learning with new learning. Encouraging students to discuss and ask questions about what is read aloud to them engages them in the reading and language relationship. Questions broaden their experiences and reinforce the concept that reading is a communication process. Therefore, questions that encourage children to express their feelings about their favorite parts of a story, the author's language, the characters, and possible upcoming events in the story are more beneficial than questions about literal information. Reading written materials aloud to students helps them acquire and develop language skills and creates an enjoyable experience for both teacher and students.

Shared reading is similar to reading aloud, except that in shared reading students see the text as the teacher reads aloud to them. Students are invited to read along and the focus is still on enjoyment of the story. Big books, which are large books with enlarged print and pictures that students in group settings can easily see, are frequently used in the early grades for shared reading. The language of most big books is repetitive and predictable, which helps the students to read along easily.

Although shared reading is typically associated with kindergarten and first grade, it can be used successfully at all grade levels. One benefit of shared reading is that it is a way to immerse students in language-rich activities regardless of their grade level or reading capabilities. An additional benefit is that shared reading can allow students to apply their reading skills in meaningful reading situations. For example, the teacher can point out beginning letters and letter combinations and encourage students to respond to the sounds represented, direct students' attention to common phonograms (e.g., *tion, at,* and *et*) found in words within the context of the story, ask students to predict what the next word might be within the syntax of the story, and ask students to predict what events might happen next in the story.

Paired reading is a modification of shared reading. In this version, one student reads aloud as another follows along. Students can take turns reading and following along as they read text. Paired reading is often employed with a less-capable reader following along as a more-capable reader reads the story aloud. This technique enables the students to support each other in their reading of text and provides valuable practice time for both students. The less-capable reader should also be given opportunities to read as the more-capable reader follows

Reading teachers have long recognized reading aloud to children as a means to promote students' interest in reading. In years past, elementary school teachers, predominantly in the early grades, recognized that their students benefited greatly from listening to good literature. Some of the direct benefits of reading aloud to students that these teachers realized were gaining an appreciation of life's possibilities, helping to satisfy basic needs vicariously, nurturing young minds, motivating wide interests, and providing an escape into the world of fantasy and imagination.

The Country School by Winslow Homer, The St. Louis Art Museum.

UPDATE

Today, teachers view with even more importance the practice of reading aloud to children both in the early and the upper grades. Reading aloud is considered not just a worthwhile activity that is added on to the curriculum, but rather an integral component in the literacy program. By reading aloud to young students, the teacher is helping them develop important concepts about literacy such as that print communicates meaning and that stories follow a structure. Reading aloud to older students can provide such benefits as introducing them to classic literature, illustrating literary features, and motivating them to read recreationally.

along. Paired reading is an enjoyable activity for older students who help younger students with their reading. For example, a fifth grader might do paired reading with a second grader.

Reader theater and modifications of it are other ways that teachers can encourage students to work cooperatively and focus on oral language, listening, reading, and writing. Reader theater is usually described in terms of children reading literature by performing the parts of characters. Students can perform stories, pieces of literature, picture books, plays, narrative poems, and other types of children's literature. Modifications can include children reading all or parts of a literary text and then turning it into a script to be acted out. Students collaborate with each other on the interpretation of their reading, what to act out, how to act it out, and how to bring everything together for a performance. Students benefit from working cooperatively, using creative writing and interpretation, and being motivated to read literature.

Independent reading is the cornerstone of successful reading instruction, because students need opportunities to practice and apply their reading skills to meaningful text. In independent reading, the teacher acts as facilitator and role model, providing students with a wide range of readily available reading material, encouraging them to read, and initiating informal discussions with them about their reading. Time should be set aside daily for students at all grade levels to read independently. Teachers should also read during this time to provide students with a model that demonstrates the value and enjoyment of reading. The practice and application of their reading capabilities make students better readers, expand their vocabularies, enhance their reasoning capabilities, and associate value with reading.

Writing Activities and Instructional Opportunities in a Language-rich Environment

A language-rich classroom environment gives students opportunities to participate in a variety of writing activities. Examples of such opportunities include displays throughout the classroom of writing by both teacher and students, notecards and notepads placed in activity areas (e.g., library, block center, drama center, and science center), story starters (beginnings that students devise based on their experiences and that the teacher uses to illustrate how stories are written), and discussions with students about what their attempts at writing (e.g., scribbles, invented spellings, letter strings, text for artwork, first drafts, and final drafts) mean to them.

Teachers can integrate reading and writing at developmental stages by using writing activities appropriate to students' level of reading and oral-language development. Teachers can use multiple texts for students to read, write about, synthesize, evaluate, or analyze. Vocabulary can be reinforced through activities that encourage students to use the vocabulary words in their writing. Such writing activities should focus on real-life experiences to ensure that the language structure and text reflect the students' background knowledge. An excellent way to integrate reading and writing is encouraging students to each keep a reading log. A **reading log** (see Figure 3.5) involves short-term writing activities that can support student discussion or reflection about what they have read. In addition, writing activities can replace or supplement many of the independent practice and application activities recommended in instructional reading materials.

Practical activities such as making lists (e.g., of birthdays, attendance, or library books) can help students understand organizing, categorizing, and alphabetizing. Most students have some knowledge of list making because they see their parents and teachers doing it. Other practical activities similar to making lists include writing labels for items in the classroom, writing instructions for the care of plants and animals, and writing out job responsibilities. These activities are similar to the instructional strategies used to promote informative language presented in Figure 3.4.

Although students enjoy writing lists and similar tasks, such activities do not focus on the communicative features of printed language to the extent that diary and journal writing do. Diary writing is personal writing that students can easily read because it is based on their own experiences and concepts. Students can record classroom and personal events in their diaries. Figure 3.6 provides an example of a kindergartner's diary entry, written early in the school year, about a trip to Galveston, Texas (Rose Marie went on a ferry boat and on the ferry boat, she saw dolphins). Another approach is to keep a classroom diary for the whole class, with all members participating by dictating to the teacher their experiences with birthday parties, field trips, special occasions, and so forth.

Journal writing encourages students to share their feelings, noting important events in their lives. Such writing is intended for the teacher to read, and therefore students must communicate with a reader. In **response journals,** the teacher both reads and responds to the students' journals. The teacher's written responses provide students with a model of writing and reinforce the connection between reading and writing. Note and letter writing can be used to connect a writer with one or more readers. Classroom pen pals, teachers, parents, brothers, sisters, and other people familiar to students can be the audience to whom students write notes and letters. Because the writer and reader share many common experiences in this type of communication, the writer need not communicate as completely as in other types of writing for the reader to construct meaning.

Writing notes and letters to less-familiar people offers an opportunity to communicate with new audiences. Students can write notes and letters to their favorite authors, to national and community leaders, and to pen pals. The World Wide Web enables children today to correspond with people from all over the world. The responses that their letters generate provide students with further opportunities to understand the communicative features of literacy.

PICTURES

Every time I read, I end up with some kind of picture in my head about the story. I can draw in my log and share my picture with the group. When I draw a picture, I need to write a little about why I drew it so that I can remember where the picture came from, what made me think about it, and why I wanted to draw it.

CHARACTER PROFILE

Think about a character I really liked (or really didn't like, or thought was interesting). The map can show what I think the character looked like, things the character did, how the character went with other characters, what made this character interesting, and anything else that I think is important!

AUTHOR'S CRAFTS AND SPECIAL TRICKS

Sometimes authors use special words, paint pictures in my mind with words, make me wish I could write like they do, use funny language, write dialogue that is really good, and many other things. In my log, I can write examples of special things the author wrote in the story.

POINT OF VIEW

Sometimes as I read about a character I think that the author did not consider other points or ideas. In my log, I can write about a character's point of view that the author did not address.

ME & THE BOOK

Sometimes what I read about a character or an event makes me think of things in my own life. I can write in my log and tell about what the character or the event or other ideas make me think about from my own life.

SEQUENCES

Sometimes events in the book might be important to remember the order they happened. I can make a sequence chart explaining why I thought it would be important to remember.

SPECIAL STORY PART

Mark the page number so I can remember where to find it. Write the first few words, then ". . ." and the last few words so I can remember what I want to share. Then write about why I thought it was interesting or special.

WONDERFUL WORDS

Find some really wonderful words—words that are new to me, or crazy, descriptive, ones I might want to use in my own writing, ones that are confusing, or whatever. Write down the word or words and share them with my group. I'll write a short note about why I picked the word and the group number where I found the word so that I can find it again.

BOOK/CHAPTER CRITIQUE

Sometimes when I'm reading, I think to myself. "This is absolutely GREAT!!!" Other times I think to myself, "If I were the author, I sure would do this differently." I can write about things the author did really well, and things he or she might want to do better.

INTERPRETATION

When I read, I think about what the author is saying to me, what he or she hopes that I'll take away from the story. I can write down my interpretation in my reading log and share what I'm thinking with the rest of my group. I need to listen to others' interpretations to see if they have similar, the same, or different ideas.

Figure 3.5 An example of features of a reading log.

Source: From *Creating an Integrated Approach to Literacy Instruction* by T. E. Raphael & E. H. Hiebert, © 1996. Reprinted with permission of Wadsworth, an imprint of the Wadsworth Group, a division of Thomson Learning. Fax 800-730-2215.

Figure 3.6 An example of a kindergartner's journal writing early in the school year.

One of the important features of promoting numerous and varied opportunities for classroom writing is that the teacher demonstrates models of the writing process. Routman (1995) identified several ways that teachers can model writing. Many of these are presented and further discussed throughout this book; a few also are presented in the following list to illustrate how teachers can model the writing process for their students. A key feature of these modeling activities is that the teacher writes in front of the students and talks about the process involved in writing the message, story, outline, or whatever he or she is writing. Such think-aloud behavior helps students to reason about the act of writing as a means of communication.

- Many teachers write their daily schedules and classroom events on the chalkboard so that students know what will be occurring during the day. Rather than writing this information before students arrive, however, teachers can capitalize on this opportunity to model writing by doing so in front of students and talking with students about the process. For example, writing "Today is Bryan's birthday. He is 7 years old today." could announce the birthday of a classmate to students. The teacher could discuss with the class why certain words are capitalized, why certain punctuation is used, and so forth. It is best to write information in paragraph form rather than just listing events. The teacher can then ask questions that encourage students to figure out the structure of the writing as well as its conventions.
- Brainstorming about writing topics as a class enables the teacher to focus on students' interests and to model features of the writing process (see Figure 3.7). Students can generate topics, which the teacher lists, and the teacher can demonstrate how to elaborate upon the topics and write a first draft. Students then can participate in topic elaboration as well as writing and revising the first draft. The teacher can use this first draft to again model for students how to revise and polish their writing. Whole-class and small-group rewriting and revising can help further model the writing process. Teachers can select examples of writing that students have generated together or can use examples of their own writing for modeling. The teacher can direct students to focus on word choice, descriptions, topic choice, and other features by questions such as "Is there another word that would work better here? I like the way this describes . . . How could you expand this section so the reader knows exactly what you mean?"

Modeling for students what is involved in the writing process—ranging from capitalization to communication of ideas—helps them better understand how writing functions. Many of the language functions presented in Figure 3.4 can form the basis for writing activities and help teachers focus on what to model for their students.

O.L.S.C.17

Hi I'm Rose Marie Rupley. I invented the Oobleck Lander Spacecraft. This is why I made it out of certain things.

It needs an aluminum shell and engine because Oobleck sinks other objects depending on the size and weight. Aluminum is very light but is very sturdy. It needs the propeller because the sky is green on planet Oobleck and you cannot see anything. The propeller will clear a path and allowing light through. It needs a satellite to send observations of the planet such as what life is on it, what the planet looks like, and how the landing went. The boosters, wings, and controls are major parts of getting there because without the boosters or the wings it could not steer or move, and without the controls it would not work. The observation windows are for observing the planet. The Oobleck boat is a boat that has the ability to move through the Oobleck with a high powered motor. It's made to collect samples of the Oobleck and life forms. The foam and breaks are major things in landing because Oobleck doesn't absorb into the foam so the Oobleck cannot sink the craft and without breaks you could never land on the planet. The escape pod is for emergencies only! It's designed to hold up to 750 pounds or five people. The fuel pipes are to feed the boosters but most of the fuel comes from the solar powered ray absorber.

This is Dr. Rose Marie Rupley, a major crewmember and inventor of the Oobleck craft assures you that this craft will work and make history!

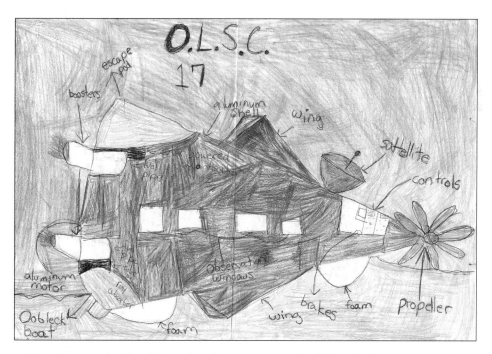

Figure 3.7 An example of writing related to a content area (science) that integrates background knowledge with learning.

SUMMARY

Literacy instruction must include a sense of involvement with language. A language-rich classroom environment is essential to promoting literacy growth. Such an environment does not treat reading and writing as separate subjects, but rather emphasizes them in all aspects of classroom life. A language-rich environment in the classroom should have two important components. First, it should encourage and support literacy development. Second, it should incorporate language-rich features and activities into reading and writing instruction.

Building on students' existing language capabilities is the key to effective literacy instruction. Reading is a language process related to all language functions in the elementary school curriculum. Students' language awareness depends on literacy experiences, which help them to understand language features such as syntax and semantics, develop and expand their vocabularies, and refine and extend their knowledge of text. Literacy builds a bridge of understanding between oral language and reading and writing. Reading, as a language process, frees the mind from direct experiences.

Oral-language capabilities contribute to students' literacy development. In the beginning stages of learning to read and write, their comprehension of print is linked closely to their spoken language. This important linkage should be reflected in instruction, which should be based on oral-language development. Culturally and linguistically diverse learners also need instruction that broadens and enriches both their language and informational backgrounds to encourage their success in literacy.

It is generally accepted that reading and writing are interrelated. Both reading and writing compose meaning, which involves interaction between an individual's experiential and conceptual backgrounds and the text. Although reading and writing are similar in many respects, each must be taught, and students need many varied opportunities to engage in reading and writing activities.

YOUR POINT OF VIEW

Discussion Questions

1. How does student development in speaking, listening, and writing affect reading development?
2. Why is it important for teachers to understand the language and literacy needs of diverse learners?

Take a Stand For or Against

1. The processes of learning to speak and learning to read are basically the same.
2. A language-rich classroom environment allows the teacher simply to guide students' literacy acquisition, and little or no instruction is necessary.

Field-Based Assignments

1. Children's literacy capabilities vary within classrooms and in relation to literacy tasks. For example, a child writing in a journal may on one occasion write only one or two phrases or sentences and on another occasion write several sentences. In the school in which you are working, examine several journal entries of several different students. Note variations within and among the journals for such characteristics as (1) length, (2) spelling patterns, (3) topics, (4) creativity, (5) whether pictures are drawn to accompany writing, and (6) features of editing and revising. Interview some of the children about what they wrote, have them read their writing aloud to you, and discuss with them how they selected topics to write about.

2. The importance of a language-rich classroom environment was a focal point of this chapter. Visit several classrooms and note how language is represented in the classrooms. Some examples to look for include reading centers, written directions and examples, displays of children's writing, big books, classroom libraries, reading and writing materials, activity centers, and so forth.

Portfolio Entry

Using the information you gained from noting how language is promoted within various classrooms, list how you would utilize this information in your own classroom. You may wish to draw or use photographs of the language-promotion features of the classrooms you visited.

BIBLIOGRAPHY

Adams, M. J. (1990). *Beginning to read: Thinking and learning about print.* Cambridge, MA: M.I.T. Press.

Chall, J. S. (1996). *Stages of reading development* (2nd ed.). New York: Harcourt Brace.

Dickinson, D., Wolf, M., & Stotsky, S. (1999). Words move: The interwoven development of oral and written language. In J. Berko (Ed.), *The development of language* (4th ed.), (pp. 369–420). Upper Saddle River, NJ: Merrill/Prentice Hall.

Goldfield, B. A., & Snow, C. E. (1999). Individual differences in language acquisition. In J. Berko (Ed.), *The development of language* (4th ed.) (pp. 299–324). Upper Saddle River, NJ: Merrill/Prentice Hall.

Harp, B., & Brewer, J. A. (2000). Assessing reading and writing in the early years. In D. S. Strickland & L. M. Morrow (Eds.), *Beginning reading and writing.* New York: Teachers College Press.

Juel, C., & Minden-Cupp, C. (2000). One down and 80,000 to go: Word recognition instruction in the primary grades. *The Reading Teacher, 53,* 332–334.

Lewin, L. (1992). Integrating reading and writing strategies using an alternating teacher-led/student-selected instructional pattern. *The Reading Teacher, 45,* 586–591.

National Council of Teachers of English. (1996). *Standards for the English language arts.* Urbana, IL: Author.

Norton, D. E. (1997). *The effective teaching of language arts.* (5th ed.). Upper Saddle River, NJ: Merrill/Prentice Hall.

Pinnell, G. S. (1996). Ways to look at the functions of children's language. In B. M. Power & R. S. Hubbard (Eds.), *Language development: A reader for teachers* (pp. 146–154). Upper Saddle River, NJ: Merrill/Prentice Hall.

Raphael, T. E., & E. H. Hiebert, (1996). *Creating an Integrated Approach to Literacy Instruction* (p. 34). New York: Holt, Rinehart, & Winston, Inc.

Rice, M. L. (1996). Children's language acquisition. In B. M. Power & R. S. Hubbard (Eds.), *Language development: A reader for teachers* (pp. 3–12). Upper Saddle River, NJ: Merrill/Prentice Hall.

Routman, R. (1995). *Invitations: Changing as teachers and learners K–12.* Portsmouth, NH: Heinemann.

Rupley, W. H., & Willson, V. L. (2000). Content, domain, and word knowledge: Relationship to children's reading comprehension. *Journal of Reading and Writing,* 419–432.

Samuels, S. J. (1988). Decoding and automaticity: Helping poor readers become automatic at word recognition. *The Reading Teacher, 41,* 636–647.

Schell, L. (1993). Letter to the author.

Shanahan, T. (1988). The reading-writing relationship: Seven instructional principles. *The Reading Teacher, 45,* 636–647.

Stahl, L. A. (1999). Saying the "p" word: Nine guidelines for exemplary phonics instruction. In R. Robinson, M. McKenna, & J. Wedman (Eds.), *Issues and trends in literacy education* (pp. 52–61). Boston, MA: Allyn & Bacon.

Stahl, L. A., Osborn, J., & Lehr, F. (1999). Beginning to read: Thinking and learning about print. In R. Robinson, M. McKenna, & J. Wedman (Eds.), *Issues and trends in literacy education* (pp. 176–185). Boston, MA: Allyn & Bacon.

Sulzby, E., & Barnhart, J. (1992). The development of academic competence: All our children emerge as writers and readers. In J. W. Irwin & M. A. Doyle (Eds.), *Reading/writing connections: Learning from research* (pp. 120–144). Newark, DE: International Reading Association.

Teale, W. H., & Yokota, J. (2000). Beginning reading and writing: Perspectives on instruction. In D. S. Strickland & L. M. Morrow (Eds.), *Beginning reading and writing.* New York: Teachers College Press.

Tierney, R. J. (1992). Ongoing research and new directions. In J. W. Irwin & M. A. Doyle (Eds.), *Reading/writing connections: Learning from research* (pp. 246–259). Newark, DE: International Reading Association.

Tompkins, G. E. (1998). *Language arts: Content and teaching strategies.* (4th ed.) Upper Saddle River, NJ: Merrill/Prentice Hall.

Veatch, J. (1996). From the vantage of retirement. *The Reading Teacher, 49,* 510–517.

Wood, K. D. (2001). *Literacy strategies across the subject areas.* Boston: Allyn & Bacon.

Emergent Literacy

Chapter Outline

For the Reader

Long before children start school, reading and writing are a major part of their lives. Before the age of 6 months, children often are given alphabet blocks, books with print, picture books, mobiles with words and letters hanging from them, and so forth. Parents and older brothers or sisters interact with young children by reading books, pointing out signs, and playing "school." These early experiences with literacy form the foundation for later reading and writing development.

Can you recall your first experiences with literacy? You probably had a variety of literacy experiences prior to beginning school—children in our society generally do. You may have had books read to you. You probably saw adults making lists and writing notes and letters. You encountered print in your everyday activities through trips to places such as McDonald's, Kmart, Sears, and Kroger. You could recognize the brand names of your favorite cereals, soft drinks, and toys. You may have also experienced print through educational television programs, such as *Sesame Street, Mr. Rogers' Neighborhood, Reading Rainbow,* and other programs with a rich reading and writing format. Furthermore, you may have begun at a young age to explore writing through scribbles, writing letters, and drawing, as well as asking others to write lists, stories, and titles for your art.

In addition to such direct experiences with print, children begin to develop an awareness of stories and story structure, and this is often reflected in their play and make-believe activities. Children's literacy experiences vary according to their home backgrounds and opportunities for language interaction with adults. These early experiences are the beginnings of reading and writing, which form the foundation for the lifelong process of learning to read and write (Teale & Sulzby, 1999).

Key Ideas

- Emergent literacy is a concept that applies to all young children.
- Children's early literacy experiences vary according to their home backgrounds and opportunities for language interaction with adults. These early experiences are the beginnings of reading and writing.
- Classrooms that are rich and varied in language opportunities contribute to and nurture children's emergent literacy development.
- Through exposure to print, children begin to establish concepts about print, experiment with its use, and develop understandings about what it means and how it functions.
- Parents reading aloud to their children contributes significantly to children's experiential and conceptual backgrounds for developing concepts about print, understanding relationships between oral and written language, and developing phonemic awareness.

- Experiences with environmental print help children understand both the forms and functions of print, develop a sight vocabulary, recognize letters and letter names, and develop knowledge of visual details.
- Children must understand the following about print before acquiring conventional literacy: (1) print is meaningful, (2) specific language is used to talk about language, and (3) letters and letter combinations represent speech sounds.
- Emerging and beginning literacy stages are broad and lay the foundation for ongoing literacy development in a developmentally appropriate way.
- In planning an emergent literacy and beginning reading program, teachers should capitalize upon what they know about effective teaching, children, learning, and language development.
- Explicit instructional activities in the early literacy program should not be discrete, isolated skills lessons, but should be woven into literature-based instruction.
- Assessment in the literacy program helps teachers adjust their instruction to address students' literacy needs.

THE CONCEPT OF EMERGENT LITERACY

Emergent literacy has been defined in a variety of ways; however, features common to most definitions are that (1) emergent literacy is the reading and writing behaviors of children that occur before and develop into conventional literacy, (2) emergent literacy is developmental, and (3) it is a concept that can be applied to all children. As noted by Sulzby and Barnhart (1992):

> All children are becoming literate—all are emerging as writers and readers. It is clear that some children come from backgrounds in which they have been included in literacy events from birth forward as a matter of course. Other children have had few such experiences. In our research and that of other researchers we note that the kinds of [literacy] behaviors we describe . . . are shown by children from low- as well as middle- and high-income families and by children from all the ethnic and cultural backgrounds that have been studied. (pp. 122–123)

Characteristics of Emergent Literacy

Teale and Sulzby (1999) have painted a word portrait of young children as literacy learners. Important characteristics of their portrait include the following.

1. Almost all children in our society begin to exhibit understandings and learnings about reading and writing early in their lives. Most children, by the age of 2 or 3, can identify signs (e.g., McDonald's, Taco Bell), labels (e.g., favorite cereals, candy bars), and logos (e.g., Nike, Disney). Children are playing and using writing, and even though their writing attempts may look like scribbles, they reflect characteristics of the writing system (see Figure 4.1). Exactly when children's literacy learning begins is difficult to establish; what is clear is that it occurs long before they enter kindergarten or first grade.

2. Literacy learnings and understandings develop from direct experiences in which reading and writing are integral experiences directed toward the accomplishment of some goal. That is, the purpose is not to read something or to write something, but reading and writing are used to reach a goal. For example, children see others who are reading recipes to help them cook, television guides to determine what is on television, directions to help them assemble a toy or model, books for enjoyment or information, and so forth. Such experiences communicate to children that reading and writing are not ends in themselves, but a functional means to accomplish a variety of purposes.

3. The development of reading and writing in young children happens together and each is related to the other. Oral language development enhances literacy development and literacy development contributes to young children's continued oral language development. Children who are read to and given opportunities to experiment with writing grow in their understanding of how print functions. They increase their vocabulary, better understand story structure, and can recognize the difference between written and oral language.

4. Children's learning about literacy is best brought about by their active participation in multiple opportunities for reading and writing. A classroom environment that is rich in print and varied in providing students many different ways to engage in reading and writing will enhance young children's emergent literacy development.

Variations in Children's Literacy Experiences

Although all children are emerging in their reading and writing development, children will have had varying literacy experiences before beginning school. Reading materials in the home and the role of literacy in the home are two factors that directly influence children's literacy experiences. For example, children who have access to a variety of books, have parents who read aloud to them (or, in many instances, have older siblings who read aloud to them), see others write notes, make lists, and write letters, and who are exposed to print in their community are likely to exhibit understandings and behaviors of emergent literacy.

Contributing to variations in children's level of emergent literacy development are gender and school experiences. Teachers have always known that girls typically outpace boys in early literacy development. Beach and Robinson (1992) examined the knowledge and understanding of print that children brought to their first school experience and how these changed as a function of grade level and gender. The researchers administered several emergent literacy tasks to preschool through third-grade children. The results indicated the following.

1. Preschool children had some knowledge and understanding of written language when they came to school. For example, they recognized logos, realized that logos conveyed a message, and wrote using scribbles or letterlike forms. Many of the preschoolers could write at least the first letter of their names (see Figure 4.1) and respond to their own writing by telling what they had written.

2. Kindergarten children showed more knowledge about print and its meaning than did preschoolers. They were a little better in reading environmental print, and most of them knew that they read print in a book. All of them could write their names and were using many letters in their writing.

3. First graders attended more to the actual print than did pre-first-grade children. All of them knew that it is the print that is read in a story. Many of them knew the terminology used to talk about print (e.g., *words, letters, sounds*) and wrote stories using letters. Approximately two thirds of them were reading conventionally.

4. Finally, second- and third-grade children knew the concepts associated with print, used conventional and invented spellings in their writing, and were reading and rereading their writing in a conventional manner.

Beach and Robinson (1992) also found differences between boys and girls in some of their emergent literacy behavior. Girls did better than boys on the tasks that were most like school literacy tasks (e.g., reading a book, noting errors in word and letter order) in first grade, but differences narrowed in second grade and disappeared in third grade. Girls also outperformed boys in writing and rereading their writing until second grade, when there was no difference. Boys scored higher when preschool and kindergarten boys and girls were compared on environmental print-in-context tasks. In other words, when given tasks from their everyday environment, pre-first-grade boys outperformed pre-first-grade girls. Pre-first-grade and first-grade girls excelled in written language that was more decontextualized from real life.

In summarizing the implications of their findings for classroom literacy instruction, Beach and Robinson noted the following:

> Both boys and girls should be provided with opportunities to interact with written language that requires both problem solving behaviors and lesson learning behaviors. Activities to foster problem solving behaviors would include reading and writing materials in play areas such as home centers or dramatic play areas such as hospital, restaurant, or post office centers as well as including functional print as part of everyday literacy routines. Activities to foster lesson learning behaviors would include structured literacy experiences around books, responses to books, language experience stories, the opportunity to read books independently or with friends, and the opportunity to not only observe an adult or literate "expert" write but also to experiment with writing and reading as well. (p. 16)

Early in their lives, children are exposed to environmental print. They see it in stores, on signs, on television, in restaurants, and in their homes. They are exposed in varying degrees to print in books, magazines, newspapers, and to adults who write lists, letters, notes, and other messages. Through this exposure to print, children begin to establish concepts about print, experiment with its use, and develop understandings about what it means and how it functions. The emerging literacy behaviors that children typically demonstrate in varying degrees are associated with their interactions with print (e.g., storybooks, writing opportunities, and art and play activities) and their environment. Through such experiences, children begin to develop concepts about print and what it means to read and write.

ACQUIRING CONCEPTS ABOUT PRINT: HOME–SCHOOL CONNECTIONS

The experiences that children have with print and the concepts that relate to these experiences contribute significantly to their emergent literacy. As discussed in earlier chapters, reading is an active process in which readers interact with a multitude of factors related to themselves, the text, and the context in which reading occurs to construct meaning. Meaning depends upon the reader's experiential and conceptual backgrounds. Knowledge that children's backgrounds develop through trips with their parents, playing with friends, watching television, using computers, and so forth forms a basis for language on which teachers can build meaningful literacy experiences.

Children's literacy learning before going to school can have a tremendous beneficial influence on their beginning reading and writing development. Establishment of and maintenance of home–school connections that promote parent and

Through exposure to print, children begin to understand the concept of literacy.

family involvement will provide varied opportunities for enhancing children's literacy growth. Initiatives to promote home–school relationships can be designed in one of two ways (Tracey, 2000). In the first method, information comes from the school to the parents and is a one-way flow of information. Programs intended to work with parents to support their children's literacy development are typically those in which the school provides information through newsletters, back-to-school activities, and other means. Another way to develop and nurture home–school connections is through two-way communication, which emphasizes a collaborative effort between families and school. Both forms of communication can enhance children's reading and writing development.

Activities that the school and teacher can do that are based on either one-way, collaborative, or both forms of communication with parents include:

1. Stressing the importance of being in an environment that promotes and enables literacy activities to occur. Back-to-school nights, newsletters, workshops, parent–teacher meetings, and flyers that stress the importance of children having a quiet place to read, a collection of their own books, an

abundance of writing materials, and other features of a print-rich environment. The school can support books in the home by letting children borrow books from the school library and classroom literacy centers (Morrow, 2000), and by providing read-along audiotapes (the teacher tapes the book) to accompany books that children have been reading in class to provide meaningful practice. Also, CD-ROM talking books are available for use at home.

2. Encouraging and supporting shared literacy experiences through ideas such as those recommended by Tracy (2000):
   - getting your children to talk about what you are reading to them
   - helping the child understand the story by encouraging the child to describe the story in the child's own words
   - praising your children when they ask a good question or make interesting comments about a book
   - relating the book to your life by talking about interesting things the book reminds you of that really happened
   - asking questions that begin with why and how
   - waiting for answers by allowing your child time to think of a good answer
   - pointing to the words as you read with younger children
   - taking turns reading with older children
   - choosing books carefully that are not too easy or too difficult
   - having fun and making reading together an enjoyable experience

3. Using parents in collaborative communication models that emphasize acquiring information from parents to enhance the quality of beginning reading and writing instruction. Collaborative procedures could include:
   - forming classes where parents write to their children (journals, photo albums, letters, memory books, etc.)
   - acquiring from parents perceptions about their children's reading and writing development (strategies can include interviews, parent questionnaires such as Figure 4.9, and home journal entries about literacy activities)
   - encouraging parent participation in the classroom literacy program (reading books aloud, supervising classroom centers, telling stories about themselves, modeling the use of reading and writing, etc.)
   - involving community leaders in recruiting and encouraging parents in the community to actively participate in their children's literacy development

As noted in *Becoming a Nation of Readers* (Anderson, Hiebert, Scott, & Wilkinson, 1985), how significant adults interact with children about their experiences influences children's understandings and knowledge. Interactions in which significant adults talk about their experiences with children helps children develop concepts and vocabulary. Although a background of experiences and oral language emerges from such interactions and helps establish a basis for success in reading, the abilities essential for reading rely more on written language experiences: parents and adults reading to children, children's experiences with environmental print, and children's art and play activities.

The value of parents participating in their children's literacy development supports the language-development concepts and phonemic-awareness concepts of emergent literacy. Essentially, parents contribute significantly to children's experiential and conceptual backgrounds for establishing ideas about print, understanding relationships between oral and written language, and developing phonemic awareness.

Reading aloud to children has many direct benefits that contribute to their emerging literacy. They may learn that print is read left to right, what a page is, where to begin reading on a page, that pages are read top to bottom, differences between pictures and print, what constitutes a word, and how oral language is represented in written form, among other things. Listing these benefits does not imply that parents and adults who read to children make a conscious effort to "teach" such concepts. Children acquire much of this understanding indirectly through parents' modeling and informal discussions. When parents ask questions such as "What do you think will happen next?" "How big do you think gigantic is?" and "Where does this story take place?" they are helping children develop concepts related to lifelong reading strategies and understandings. In addition, when parents make comments about the words and illustrations an author has used in a story, they are helping their children to understand the communicative aspects of print.

Environmental Print

Children acquire background knowledge for literacy through interaction with print in their environment. **Environmental print** is print in the environment that is encountered in meaningful settings. Examples of such print are labels and signs on objects (e.g., McDonald's restaurants, Coke and Pepsi cans, Kmart bags, and Crest toothpaste tubes), signs (e.g., *Stop, Yield,* and *Post Oak Mall*), and functional print (e.g., telephone books, newspapers, catalogs, TV guides, lists, and menus).

Experiences with environmental print help children understand both the forms and functions of print, build a sight vocabulary, recognize letters and letter names, and develop knowledge of visual details. Environmental print knowledge will vary in relation to children's opportunities to interact with it. For example, in some rural communities, children may not have eaten at a McDonald's, may never have shopped at WalMart, and may not have access to a public television station. This does not imply that these children have a deficit in environmental print experiences, it simply means that their experiences are different from those of many other children and must be accommodated in instruction.

Parents and adults who point out and talk about print in the child's environment are facilitating the development of print concepts. For example, parents facilitate the development of print concepts when they respond to questions such as "Is that McDonald's?" by saying, "Yes, look at the sign. It starts with a big golden *M* and says 'McDonald's.'" When parents point out the Dairy Queen sign and comment, "We are at Dairy Queen," they are helping to build their child's understanding of print and promoting the child's understanding of how print functions. Similar examples of parents and children interacting with environmental print are using the

Yellow Pages together; talking about the pictures and text in menus; reading the newspaper comics; noting traffic signs; reading labels when shopping for food; using and talking about computer activities, games, and operations; and so forth. Such interactions help children realize that language in our society can direct, inform, and entertain us.

Art and Play Activities

Children's art and play activities are also important features related to their experiential and conceptual backgrounds for literacy development. Experiences with art, paper, and pencils are related to children's early reading and writing development. Drawings and scribbles are early forms of writing. Although these are not perceived as conventional writing, children use these forms to tell a story or represent an event.

For example, after going to see the circus, 3-year-old Rose Marie drew a series of pictures about her experience. She then asked her mother to write the words *balloons*, *clowns*, *elephants*, *lions*, and *cotton candy* under the appropriate pictures. Rose Marie then simulated reading by looking at each picture as she told a story to her mother. Rose Marie proudly announced, "I can read!" Later in the day, she was making wiggly lines beneath each of the circus pictures and said "I'm writing a story for Matthew," who is her 1-year-old brother. Rose Marie's pretend writing was linear, and she moved from left to right as she "wrote" her circus story. She also, as do many children, used some individual letters in her writing and put in some dots. When asked to read her story the next day, she was consistent in her rereading: It was almost identical to her reading of it on the day she wrote it.

When Matt, a 4-year-old, drew the picture shown in Figure 4.1, he proudly announced that it represented his mommy and daddy, then a short time later he returned to his parents saying, "I wrote a story. See, it says 'Mommy' and 'Daddy.' " Matt could easily differentiate the picture from what he had written and pointed to each word as he read it. Even days later, when he passed by his picture on the refrigerator, he would proudly say, "Mommy and Daddy and Matt," as he pointed to each of the words he had written. What is also notable about what Matt as a 4-year-old represented is a transfer of his understanding of the letter *M* in his name to the beginning letter in the word *Mommy*. Phonemically, he used invented spelling to represent the word *and* and represented knowledge of language structure in using the word *and*. In addition, he wrote in a left-to-right fashion, and he used predominantly uppercase letters, which is a reflection of his interaction with print in his environment (Goodman, 1996).

Opportunities for young children to draw and experiment with paper and pencil establish background knowledge for later reading and writing tasks that are more instructional in nature. Children often request that their artwork be labeled or titled, that their names be written on it, and that a story about it be written. Such requests show that they are beginning to acquire many of the print concepts associated with emerging literacy and are connecting oral language with literacy.

Figure 4.1   An example of a 4-year-old's incorporation of picture and print.

Print Concepts Associated with Decontextualized Language

Understanding how print functions in decontextualized language is central to acquiring literacy abilities that go beyond language in familiar contextual settings. Many of the literacy experiences children have before formal schooling determine how well they understand features of decontextualized language. Such experiences are related to storybook reading: for example, knowing that stories have structure, reading from left to right and top to bottom, and knowing the differences between print and pictures. These concepts about print often develop more slowly than others, but they are essential to acquiring conventional literacy capabilities.

Print Is Meaningful

Although most young children can tell the difference between print and pictures and can distinguish print from other graphic symbols, an essential understanding for continued literacy growth is the concept that print represents meaningful language. While some children understand the meaning features of print when they come to school, others do not see any connections among oral language, reading, and writing. Children will not benefit from literacy activities that do not reflect their speaking and listening capabilities. Teachers who provide opportunities for children to focus on the concepts that (1) print represents a message and (2) this message must be as sensible as spoken language will enhance the development of the concept that print is meaningful.

Language Used to Talk About and Teach Literacy

Adults often take for granted that young children understand what reading is, including the left-to-right progression of print, the meanings of basic language terms used in teaching literacy, the relationship of our writing system to features of oral language, and the basic **functions of written language,** which are to inform, to entertain, and to direct. For example, the term *word* is essential in most beginning reading instruction. The teacher may tell children that they will look at words, learn how to figure out words, spell words, think about words, write words, and so forth. Before beginning school, few children have been asked to think about written words and the language used to talk about written words. There is a major gap between understanding of language and understanding of the language we use to talk about language (e.g., *word, sentence, letters, paragraph*). Furthermore, children's concepts about print are developmental (Miller, 2000; Sulzby & Barnhart, 1992). Children develop the concept of *word* over many varied and meaningful written language experiences. They are influenced by attention to environmental print, attention to visual details of print, phonemic awareness, and decoding ability.

Emergence of concepts about print directly reflects early literacy experience in the child's environment. Parents and others who read to children and provide a literacy-based environment contribute significantly to knowledge of the function and form of written language. However, children's conceptual understanding of reading and writing instructional terminology and the functions of print are not simply the result of defining the terms and discussing the functions of print. Rather, a language-based literacy program emphasizing oral and written activities best helps children refine and apply their emerging abilities in these areas. Activities should expose

Parents and others who read to children contribute significantly to their knowledge of the function of written language.

children to print in the form of oral reading, environmental print, various arts forms (e.g., music and art), writing, shared-book experiences, meaningful language usage, and play activities.

Phonemic Awareness

Several researchers (Busink, 1997; Rupley, Rodriquez, Mergen, & Willson, in press; Snow, Burns, & Griffith, 1998) have advanced the idea that phonemic awareness is necessary for learning to decode. That is, children who are aware that speech is composed of a sequence of sounds get off to a more successful start in beginning reading and beginning spelling instruction. Phonemic awareness is developmental and, therefore, children in beginning literacy programs will vary in their abilities to use it to decode words. We believe that phonemic awareness is essential for success in beginning reading and writing, and teachers will have to provide activities to promote children's further development and refinement of it.

As noted throughout this text, children must be able to recognize words and use their background knowledge to construct meaning. They can accomplish this in three major ways. First is visual memory (recognizing whole words), second is letter-sound correspondence (phonics), and third is context (semantics and syntax). Ma-

I want a pocit nife and a
Nickelodeon pog maker.
I wand a new sega jinus and a
super soceer x p55. I want a ant farm
and a miny trampileen. I want a
treder box and a moke kir grole hark
daves modersicel.

Figure 4.2 A first grader's journal entry about what he wants for Christmas.

ture readers use all three of these, depending on the text they are reading. Beginning readers, however, need to develop automatic decoding skills (Chall, 1996; Stahl, 1999), which are facilitated by **phonemic awareness,** or understanding that words are made up of sounds.

Children acquire phonemic awareness through exposure to books that make language sing and something fun to play with. For example, nursery rhymes, Dr. Seuss books (e.g., *Hop on Pop, The Cat in the Hat,* and *Green Eggs and Ham*), toy books, "I can read" books, and interactive computer books are excellent sources for helping children develop phonemic awareness. Some children may acquire the ability to recognize letters by name before they develop phonemic awareness; however, phonemic awareness is necessary if they are to figure out the relationship between phonemes and words (Cunningham, 1999).

Two important areas related directly to phonemic awareness and literacy development are onsets and rimes, and invented spelling. Knowledge of syllables, which are the units of pronunciation in the English language, is enhanced when onsets and rimes are used for word recognition. (An *onset* is all the letters in a word before a vowel; a *rime* is the vowel and the letters that follow.) It appears that at the onset–rime level, children are better able to retain parts and wholes of words that assist them in word recognition (Moustafa, 1995). As illustrated in Figure 4.2, which depicts a first grader's journal entry about what he wants for Christmas, and Figure 4.3, which shows a 4-year-old's Easter card, invented spelling helps children practice and refine their understanding about symbol and sound relationships. Teachers have noted that children who use invented spelling often write more, use more complete thoughts, reflect more on their writing, and often say words aloud and listen to how the words sound as they represent these sounds with letters.

Phonemic awareness facilitates beginning reading development. The feature of phonemic awareness that promotes children's beginning reading development is the ability to understand that spoken words can be segmented into sounds. The concept of emergent literacy suggests that phonemic awareness further supports reading development as children interact more with print through reading and writing activities and develop word recognition capabilities.

Figure 4.3   A 4-year-old's Easter card.

INSTRUCTIONAL FEATURES OF EARLY LITERACY AND BEGINNING LITERACY PROGRAMS

There are general areas of the literacy curriculum that apply to various grade levels. These areas include developmental reading, application-transfer, independent or recreational reading, content reading, writing, and functional reading. Early and beginning literacy programs form a foundation for the literacy curriculum and include all of the significant components found at higher grade levels, such as word recognition, vocabulary, comprehension, study skills, independent reading, writing, literature, and so forth. The early and beginning reading stage is not narrow, but rather is broad; for literacy to develop later, the early literacy instructional program should lay the foundation in a developmentally appropriate way. Children in a beginning literacy program have widely varying reading and writing abilities. As noted in Chall's stages (1996), Sulzby's research (1991), and Adams's (1990) summary of research on reading acquisition, some children enter kindergarten and first grade already reading and writing conventionally, while others may have limited understanding about and experiences with literacy. Instruction at the appropriate level is important for kindergarten and first-grade children, because it lays the foundation for future literacy growth.

In planning an emergent literacy and beginning reading program, teachers should capitalize on their knowledge of effective teaching and children's learning and language development. To maximize the probability that children will learn to read and write, teachers should do the following:

- Design activities around a language arts base (listening, speaking, reading, and writing) to build on and extend the language backgrounds of children. A language-rich classroom provides the environment in which such activities flourish and nurture children's literacy growth.
- Develop in children the concept that literacy is communication and that constructing meaning is essential.
- Teach and expand children's vocabularies through the use of both oral and written contexts.
- Provide children varied opportunities to read and to be involved with meaningful reading and writing activities, including reading literature, writing stories, participating in creative dramatics, and sharing books orally.
- In an integrated fashion, teach essential reading terminology (e.g., *word, letter, sound,* and *sentence*) and concepts (e.g., left-to-right progression, page, and letter names)
- Stimulate and support interest in reading by reading aloud a variety of stories that capture children's interest.
- Incorporate the arts (e.g., music and drama) as well as drawing, cutting, and pasting to increase motivation and foster language growth.
- Prepare activities to foster and teach listening skills associated with literacy.
- Set short-term goals based on assessment results that build on children's strengths and that they can readily achieve.
- Give children tasks that they understand and can complete with a high degree of success.
- Give responsibility to all children, not just those who are already confident.
- Select goals for your program according to children's needs, not according to what a commercially prepared program states.

Language-Based Reading and Writing Instruction

Children who lack literacy-related experiences benefit from language-based initial literacy instruction. Such instruction includes numerous opportunities to experience and interact with print. For example, teachers should use a variety of writing activities, read books aloud, use shared reading, use storytelling, label objects in the room, use music and play, and use read-along books. They also should make predictable books, big books, learning and play centers, catalogs, and magazines available to children. The appropriate beginning point is a language-rich classroom environment that helps children acquire and refine basic concepts that are emerging in their literacy knowledge.

The instructional activities discussed in the following sections can encourage, support, and extend students' learning in beginning reading. Many of the activities appropriate for early literacy instruction, such as oral reading, storytelling, journal writing, and language and learning centers, are important instructional components of beginning literacy instruction.

Play and Learning Centers

Teachers are an important part of classroom play and learning centers. Morrow (2000) notes that adult guidance in using various materials during playtime in learning centers results in children participating in more literacy activities. Teachers guide students in the use of literacy materials by reminding them to perform tasks specific to the play area (e.g., fill out forms for prescriptions, fill out forms for patients, and read to pets in a veterinarian's office play area). Adults also modeled behaviors for children by participating in play with them. The role of the teacher in using classroom play centers is extremely important in guiding and modeling literacy behavior that children can emulate. Morrow (2000) recommends that when selecting a setting for dramatic play areas, teachers choose those that relate to a theme being studied in the classroom that literacy materials can further enrich. The following themes and literacy materials can be used for dramatic play areas:

- Fast-food restaurant, Chinese restaurant, seafood restaurant, ice cream store, or bakery. Literacy materials could include menus, order pads, cash registers, specials of the day, recipes, and lists of flavors or products.
- A newspaper office with writing paper, telephones, computers, directories, maps, typewriters, and areas that focus on sports, travel, general news, and weather.
- A supermarket or local grocery store could include cans of food, cereal boxes, packaged foods, cash registers, shopping receipts, coupons, checkbooks, newspaper ads, and telephones.

Teachers can develop other play and learning centers focusing on situations familiar to all children, such as the local discount store, pet store, post office, and so forth. Teachers should make literacy props available in all of their play centers. Literacy props could include telephone books, cookbooks, food coupons, and grocery store ads in a kitchen play center; calendars, appointment books, signs, magazines, and assorted business forms in an office play center; and library book return cards, children's books, stamps and ink pads, bookmarks, and sign in/sign out sheets in a library play center.

Reading and Writing Centers

In addition to using thematic centers to support literacy activities, teachers should include reading centers and writing centers in their classrooms. Such centers can be for use by large groups, small groups, or individual students. Examples of how such centers can function (Labbo, Murray, & Phillips, 1996) include the following:

- **Rug-time center.** Students and teacher can meet to discuss a story they read together, plan a thematic unit, sing songs, share teacher- and student-authored stories, and so forth. A key feature of the rug-time center is that it can serve as a starting or jumping-off place for other center activities.
- **Computer writing center.** Children are offered a free choice to use the computer either individually or in collaboration to write stories, make lists, write letters, or write stories for pieces of art they made. The word-processing use of the computer writing center can be enhanced by encouraging children to simply experiment with language and composition. Children who have difficulty writing by hand may be more expressive and experimental with language when using the computer. For example, Figure 4.4 shows a child's lengthy response, written on a computer, to a choral reading of "Five Little Monkeys Jumping on the Bed." She first drew the picture and then wrote the story later at the computer writing center (Labbo et al., 1996).
- **Computer center for skills practice and reinforcement.** Such a center can be based on the abundance of computer software available for the practice and reinforcement of reading and writing skills. In addition to commercial software, the World Wide Web has many sites that deal with reading and writing. For example, children can write letters to children in other states and countries, communicate with public and private agencies, and interact with children's authors and magazine publishers. The purpose of these computer activities is to provide opportunities for children to practice and apply their reading and writing skills to meaningful text and at a level appropriate to their individual needs.
- **Listening library center.** This should be an inviting area furnished with pillows, carpet squares, and child-sized chairs in a corner or in the back of the classroom where children go to listen to tape-recorded books. Children can read the books and listen to the accompanying tape recording. Teachers can use commercially prepared, adult-prepared, or older-student-prepared tapes.
- **Art and making-things center.** Here, children can express themselves in ways that go beyond typing or writing in their journals. Such a center can extend and enrich children's understanding and reasoning about concepts and ideas. Children can illustrate events in stories that have been read to them or that they have written, they can infer ideas and characters through art, and they can compare and contrast their art with that of illustrators in the books they read.

One Child's Response to the Topic "Beds"

my bed Has mace mas on it my bed
Has 2 plos on is it is vare bec
sam tis my brair sies wath me in
my bed I Hav to dals won is namd
jenny and won is namd badea my mom
fasis cad bracfast for me

(My bed has Mickey Mouse on it. My bed has two pillows on
it. It is very big. Sam is my brother sleep with me in my bed.
I have two dolls. One is named Jenny and one is named
Baby. My mom fixes good breakfast for me.)

Figure 4.4   A child's computer-typed response to a choral reading of "Five Little
Monkeys Jumping on the Bed."
Source: From D. Labbo, B. Murray, & M. Phillips, "Writing to Read: From Inheritance to
Innovation and Invitation," *The Reading Teacher, 49,* (1996), p. 318. Reprinted with permission
of the authors and the International Reading Association. Copyright by the International
Reading Association. All rights reserved.

Thematic Units for Writing and Reading Activities

For writing and reading to be an integral part of early literacy instruction, children
need a wide range of experiences and activities to motivate them to read and write.
Thematic units built around play centers can be expanded to thematic units that create an environment that promotes children's reading and writing.

Isom and Casteel (1991) described the success of two kindergarten teachers in promoting reading and writing by designing their yearly program around central themes. The teachers focused on the following three goals to build their literacy environment.

Create an environment around a topic

The teachers created a spectacular display for their topical unit to get children motivated. For example, the teachers made the outside of their classroom look like the front of a barn when they used a farm unit. They made their classroom into a jungle when the theme was jungles. For the jungle theme, paper vines, monkeys, a life-sized tiger, and a life-sized gorilla were used.

Provide for language and concept development

The teachers used oral reading, discussion, questioning, art projects, and individual inquiry to facilitate children's language and concept development. They used a variety of books, pictures, tapes, and models about the jungle.

Provide for group and individual writing

As a result of daily classroom discussions and activities, children produced group-dictated stories that were often followed by individually dictated stories and illustrations. Children also were stimulated to write at the classroom writing center, which contained blank books in the shape of the theme. They also dictated big-book stories and illustrated them. Children shared their writing with each other so much that their books became worn with use.

Some teachers build units to promote reading and writing development by using cereal boxes. The outsides of cereal boxes contain environmental print that appeals to all young children. Kettering and Graybill (1991) used the boxes to connect home and school in a way that demonstrated to children that reading is purposeful and relevant to everyday life. They used cereal boxes for developing literacy with graphs by having children place their favorite cereal boxes in columns on the floor and then asking questions about which cereal most students liked, how many more Fruit Loop boxes there were than Cheerios boxes, and of which cereal there were the fewest boxes. Later, they had the children make bar graphs that represented students' favorite cereals.

Cereal boxes were also used in a study of nutrition by having children graph the grains from which the cereals were made using columns for corn, oats, wheat, and rice. Stories such as *The Little Red Hen* were used to help children understand how grain is made into food. Other stories, such as *The Terrible Eater* and *What a Good Lunch,* were also employed in the unit on nutrition.

Writing activities included listing cereals by grain, writing ads for favorite cereals, designing new boxes, describing how to make breakfast, creating new cereals, and so forth. Children's writing was then combined into classroom books, displayed around the classroom, and shared with parents.

Writing and reading activities based around thematic units both create experiences for children to write about and motivate them to participate in reading and writing activities. Teachers can create a classroom environment in which writing and reading emerge as a consequence of students' interest and active participation.

Literature, Book, and Writing Activities

Early reading instruction can use children's literature in a variety of ways. Tape recorders can be used to tape children's books, and commercially taped books and stories also are available. Talking books that have been taped commercially can introduce youngsters to the content of children's literature or help them gain experiences with it. Books taped by the teacher should be read in a normal manner, with the children following along in the book as they listen to the recorded text. Without this instruction to follow along, children often simply listen to the stories, which defeats the purpose of taping the book: to help them connect what they hear with the print that represents language. Teacher-prepared tapes also are better for developing literature appreciation than commercially prepared tapes are. Children can help select the books to be taped if they are given brief overviews of the books.

Computer software

Computer software is also available for introducing and teaching literacy at the beginning reading level. New software programs are becoming available daily. A highly motivating feature of much of this software is that it is interactive. Children become actively involved in hearing, reading, and seeing the animation of the story. Some software allows children to select different events or endings for stories. Other software enables children to select animated characters and settings for stories that they write. Children can be introduced to the worlds of dinosaurs, underwater life, space travel, and other exciting places and events. They can see the pictorial representation of the print, they can hear the print read aloud, and they can see the print. We have been in kindergarten and first-grade classrooms in which children have drawn animals and events that they experienced through interactive computer software; these drawings are often labeled, written about, sequenced, talked about, and used as a focal point for language development.

One of the resources becoming more readily available to teachers of beginning reading and writing is CD-ROM talking books. These books are interactive and use multimedia features that may include animation, sound effects, music, and modeled fluent reading (Labbo, 2000). Because CD-ROM books are interactive, they have the potential to provide children with additional opportunities to become actively engaged with stories. The following suggestions for what young children can do with talking books are offered by Labbo (2000):

- Listen to the story.
- Read along with the story.
- Echo read the story.
- Read it first, then listen to it.
- Read it with a partner in digital Readers' Theatre.
- Look for letters and words that you know.
- Find words with the same sounds.
- Find rhyming words.

- Read along in a book copy of the CD-ROM book.
- Tell how one screen fits with other screens.
- Tell how the special effects fit the story.
- Tell about similar stories you have read.

Students will require teacher scaffolding to ensure that they will benefit from the suggestions. Teachers should model in whole class or small groups the purposes, outcomes, and strategies for using the CD-ROM talking books features. Such modeling can focus on how to click on features of the software for specific purposes, such as the pronunciation of a word, how to animate a character, passages to reread, and so forth.

Assistance needs to be available for the children to support their engagement with digital stories. Teachers, parents, aides, older students, and capable peers need to stand beside the children when they are in the computer center to offer assistance in using each of the strategies. As children use the strategies and develop competence in their use, then the software may provide adequate scaffolding.

Management of the children's time and use of the computer center should be as important as it is in other classroom activities. Management strategies would include setting reasonable time limits that enable children to successfully complete the chosen activity, making appropriate assignments from the suggestions to support children's varying literacy needs, and setting clear expectations for sharing in production of outcomes for the activities.

Computers can be used with emergent readers and writers in a variety of ways to meet their needs (Eisenwine & Hunt, 2000). For example, Hyperstudio can be used to

1. Help children learn one-to-one correspondence, which is the oral and written representation of words, by making individual talking books that have enlarged primary font. Children click on each word as a finger points to the word and it is read aloud by the computer.
2. Assist children in getting meaning by using animation and music (*I can walk*— a man is walking along to music).
3. Teach informational text with talking books that are coordinated with teaching units, such as Spiders and Turtles. Clips from other software sources can be imported to illustrate the content.
4. Create big books and use a shared keyboard concept to retell stories and create new stories. Simpletext will enable the children to write their stories and then have the computer read them aloud in a variety of voices.
5. Engage in independent reading and use special effects and graphics. KidPix, a software program, is intended to enable children to write independently.

Predictable books

A **predictable book** is one in which students can grasp easily what the author is going to say next. A basic feature of predictable books is much repetition of content and language. Generally, the pictures in predictable books closely match the text. Other basic characteristics of predictable books are strong rhythm and rhyme, repeated language patterns, logical sequence, supportive illustrations, and traditional story structure. These characteristics allow predictable books to be used in a variety of ways to support emergent literacy. Examples of support include identifying rhyming words, making sounds associated with animal characters, talking as the characters might talk, dramatizing how the characters might act, making picture dictionaries for items presented in the stories, creating murals and clay figures, identifying and classifying characters by similar and different traits, and writing different endings. Such activities with predictable books help create a language-based instructional program that enhances literacy development. The content and language repetition coupled with the pictures help children begin to feel and act like readers early in their reading development. Predictable books also help children to use prediction strategies as they read. This frees them from focusing on individual words as they read and allows them to devote their attention to meaning and making sense of the text. Procedures for using predictable books include the following:

- Discuss the book cover with the children by focusing on the illustrations, which may reflect the characters, the setting, and primary events. Point out and discuss the title: what a title is, how a title is related to the story, and what might be a good title for a book based on the cover illustrations. Praise the children for correct title predictions and point to each word in the title as it is read aloud. Ask the children to make predictions about the story and write these predictions down for later discussion.
- Turn to the front inside page and point out the title, author, publisher, and dedication, if one is given. Direct the children to recall their predictions about the story and begin reading to them, pointing to each word as you read it.
- Read the entire story aloud. After you read the story, read the predictions that students made earlier about the story. Encourage individual children to share their interpretations of the story and relate them to their predictions.
- Stories can be reread as often as desired by the children. A variety of strategies can be used in rereading predictable books. Choral reading, in which all of the children read the story in unison as the teacher points to the words, can be used when children feel comfortable with the story. Echo reading, in which the teacher reads a part of the story, which the children repeat, echoing what was read, also can be used. After multiple readings of the same story, children often can be encouraged to begin reading along with the parts they know.

Once children begin to experience success with teacher direction, they can begin to read predictable books on their own. Teachers must be willing to accept approximations of story language and to support students' attempts to complete reading of predictable books. They also must provide ample opportunities for children to model and transfer their prediction strategies to other reading activities, such as shared and paired reading.

Wordless picture books

The story in a wordless picture book is told by the sequence of detailed pictures. The story is often repetitive, and children "read" the story by interpreting the pictures.

Teachers can create a classroom environment in which literacy emerges as a consequence of students' interest and active participation.

Wordless picture books can be used to reinforce and extend concepts associated with emergent literacy. Dialogue balloons can be added for characters, and students can dictate to the teacher what the story characters may be saying; story text can be dictated and written strips attached to appropriate pages; and children can draw their own pictures to either change the ending or extend the story.

Writing is easily integrated into the use of wordless picture books because they provide children the opportunity to write or dictate their individual interpretations of a story. Their dictations can be written by the teacher, an older student, a parent volunteer, or a teacher's aide. Children's stories can be bound into big books, shape books, or regular-sized books to be read and reread by the students.

Big books

Big books have large pictures and print that children in group settings can easily see. The stories often use predictable, repetitive language and focus on content that is appealing to young children. Big books are used frequently in shared-reading settings, where the teacher is supportive because the children and the teacher read the story aloud together (Eldredge, Reutzel, & Hollingsworth, 1996). Because the language is repetitive, teachers can let children finish reading parts of sentences and phrases. Teachers point to the words as they read with feeling and expression (modeling reading fluency). Using big books helps children to develop an appreciation for reading, make connections between print and oral language, understand directionality of print (reading left to right and top to bottom), predict words and events, and see relationships between graphemes and phonemes in meaningful context.

Introducing and using big books is an exciting and enjoyable experience for both the teacher and the children. The following procedures can be useful to teachers as they begin to use big books:

- Because big books are cumbersome to hold, it is recommended that the teacher use an easel to hold the book open. The use of an easel allows the teacher to point to important print features and pictures as the book is read aloud. A pointer is important to have when drawing children's attention to print and pictures because use of the hand often obscures part of the page. Writing materials (e.g., flip chart or chalkboard) should be handy to record children's responses.
- Children's involvement with big books is heightened when the teacher is enthusiastic about both the content of the books and the children's responses. Discussion can focus on the book's cover, title, inside cover page, and illustrations. Children can be asked to predict titles, events, sequence, and so forth. The predictions can then be written for later discussion as the book is read aloud by the teacher, chorally by the students, or with echo reading.

We have observed wide variation in the effective use of big books in kindergarten and first-grade classrooms. Some teachers working with children who have limited literacy experiences focus on helping them understand the features of books, such as the front and back, pages, left-to-right and top-to-bottom progression, title, author, and words. During shared reading, these teachers emphasize each of these features without interfering with appreciation and enjoyment of the story. They often have children come up and turn to their favorite page, indicate where the top of the page is, show where they would begin reading, and so forth. Big books are also placed in the reading center, where children can use them individually or with each other. We have often observed children playing "school" by using big books to read to two or three other children, modeling many of the things that their teacher emphasized during reading of the big book.

Teachers can purchase big books through commercial publishers or make their own. Many of the large, paperback picture books that can be purchased inexpensively at discount stores can be used to construct big books: Teachers buy two copies of the book, cut out and paste the pictures on tagboard, and write the story text beneath the appropriate pictures using large print. Books selected for use in making big books should reflect children's interests and background knowledge. Other ideas for making big books include using song lyrics, old calendars, and children's drawings.

Big books also can be made from cereal boxes and used either with a thematic unit on nutrition or in shared reading. Box fronts from children's favorite cereals can be glued to large sheets of tagboard, with large print used to write predictable text: "Trix, the cereal that the rabbit loves to munch." "Fruit Loops, the cereal where colors come in a bunch." and "Cheerios, the cereal that you can eat for lunch." Children can construct other types of big books by dictating group-experience stories about their favorite cereals.

Big books are available for subjects such as science and social studies. These books are excellent for introducing new concepts and vocabulary. Children can help the teacher create big books in content areas that relate to direct experiences they have had, both in and out of the classroom. Using shared experiences, children dictate to the teacher how they want their experiences to be represented in print. They can draw their own pictures to represent their experiences, or the teacher can help select appropriate illustrations, such as photographs or magazine pictures. Language-experience activities also can result in the construction of big books, shared experience charts, or individual student books. For example, one kindergarten class created a big book about the rabbit, mice, and gerbil that were kept as pets in the classroom. The children dictated information about the size of the animals, their living conditions, and the types of food they ate. The teacher recorded the children's dictations in large print and used photographs taken with an instant camera to illustrate the text. This activity preceded a visit by a veterinarian who specialized in exotic animals. After the veterinarian's visit, the children dictated additional information to add to their *Care and Feeding of Animals* big book. The children made a similar big book for a unit on farm animals.

Interactive writing activities

Interactive writing has features that support and extend emergent reading capabilities acquired through the use of predictable books, wordless books, big books, and shared reading (see Figure 4.5). Interactive writing has two important features (Button, Johnson, & Furgerson, 1996). First, children are active in the writing process. That is, they are holding the pencil and doing the writing. Second, the teacher plays an active role through questioning and direct instruction to focus children's attention on the conventions of print (e.g., spacing, capital letters, punctuation).

Button et al. note that interactive writing is a valuable part of an emergent literacy program because

> it provides so many opportunities to teach directly about language conventions, sense of story, types of writing, and concepts about print. These teaching moments do not follow a specified sequence but evolve from the teacher's understanding of the students' needs. . . . Too often teachers feel they must choose between using holistic literacy experiences and teaching basic skills. In interactive writing sessions, teachers do both at the same time. (p. 454)

Poetry in the Literacy Program

Literature in the early reading program should include poetry, and the best way to introduce it is to read it aloud. Many other activities can further acquaint children with poetry, including writing, creative dramatics, art, reading, and language awareness activities.

Interactive Writing Expectations and Guidelines in Primary Classrooms over a School Year

Beginning of the year ———————————→   Later in the year ————————————→

Establish Routine
Negotiate simple text (a label)
Construction of text may be completed in one day
  (news)
Repeat orally word or line to be written

The teacher will
Model hearing sounds in words
Model sound-symbol relationships
Support letter recognition (using alphabet chart
  or chart listing class members' names)
Model and question for Concepts About Print
  (CAP): spacing, left-to-right directionality, top-
  to-bottom directionality, word-by-word match-
  ing during shared reading
Link words to be written with names of children in
  the class

The teacher may
Write more of the text
Write challenging parts of words/text
Assist with letter formation

Routine Established
Negotiate a more complex text
Construction of text continues over several days
Count the words to be written before starting
  to write

Students will
Hear dominant sounds in words
Represent sounds with symbols (letters)
Write letters without copy
Have control of core words
Begin linking known words to unknown words
Leave spaces between words
Use familiar chunks (*-ed, -ing*)
Control word-by-word matching during shared
  reading
Punctuate sentences on the run
Write text with little support
Make generalizations about print

Figure 4.5   Interactive writing expectations and guidelines in primary classrooms over a school year.
Source: From K. Button, M. Johnson, & P. Furgerson, "Interactive Writing in a Primary Classroom," *The Reading Teacher, 49* (1996), p. 450. Reprinted with permission of the authors and the International Reading Association. Copyright by the International Reading Association. All rights reserved.

Children enjoy listening to poetry that is predictable, and they will often join in reading it aloud with the teacher. For example, one child named Billy had a favorite poem about a frog; after the teacher read it to him several times, he took much delight in reading it to himself and to his friends. What made the poem so appealing to him was the repetition of the line "Hop, hop, hop," which made up about seven stanzas of the poem.

Poems can be read to children as they listen with their eyes closed to the melody of the poem. Children can be encouraged to form mental images of the contents and discuss their perceptions of the melody and mental images. By rereading the same poem with a different language melody each time, teachers can help children begin to appreciate and understand poetry's language features.

Teachers can use language activities to have children compose poems individually or in groups. An excellent poetry form for introducing such activities is the haiku.

Colorful pictorial materials such as paintings, photographs, and drawings can stimulate children to form the word pictures for a haiku. A haiku is a 17-syllable pattern in three lines, with five syllables in the first and third lines and seven syllables in the second line. A picture of a dancing bear inspired one child, Donald, to dictate the following haiku to his teacher, who assisted him with identifying words to fit the haiku pattern. This assistance is important; the teacher can help children identify words by discussing features of the picture with them and offering word possibilities.

The brown dancing bear,
Dancing around in his cage,
Dancing on his toes.

Pictures that children draw can be used to stimulate poetry writing. One girl, Janet, drew a picture of some ghosts for a Halloween activity and dictated the following poem to her teacher.

Ghosts are floating in the air,
Floating, floating, floating.
Look out there's a monster
over there.

Other poetry-writing experiences can relate to music and art activities. For example, a kindergarten class composed the six lines of the following poem with guidance from their teacher.

Music, music in the air.
Music, music everywhere.
We went skipping,
sliding,
jumping,
running,
bouncing,
hopping,
dancing,
Round and round the room.

Poetry can be used to encourage students' reading and writing. In addition, children can learn concepts associated with phonemic awareness using the context of poems to focus on spelling patterns and the sounds represented. For example, a teacher could use the "Hop, hop, hop" part of the poem that so intrigued Billy to teach the sounds the letters *op* represent in words such as *stop, flop, mop,* and *pop*. Children could then use these words to generate more stanzas for the poem, replace words in the poem, and write new poems.

Reading Aloud and Telling Stories

We emphasize the importance of reading aloud to children to encourage all teachers to make it an integral part of their daily literacy program. Children need to understand early in their literacy development that the purpose of print is to communicate. Reading stories and other written materials that captivate their minds and stimulate their interest in reading helps youngsters conceptualize written language and the basic features of written text. Specifically, the daily oral sharing of books is important for emerging literacy development. Children learn basic concepts from this practice, including story language, expectations for story characters, and storytelling. In essence, they learn to talk like a book. Also, reading aloud to them expands their vocabularies and background knowledge and is an enjoyable experience.

Storytelling is another important practice that can help children understand the relationships between oral language and literacy. All children love to hear a well-told story. Sources that teachers can use for identifying stories to tell include family traditions or events, parts of favorite books that appeal to children, stories about traditional holidays or made-up holidays, and characters familiar to the children. Norton (1999) emphasizes the importance of careful planning for telling a story. She encourages teachers to prepare for storytelling by (1) planning a brief introduction that relates the story to the children, (2) relating the story incidents in the intended sequence and being spontaneous, (3) making characters come alive by effective use of voice, gestures, and posture, (4) using interesting speech patterns to represent characters and mood, and (5) using verbal, mechanical, or musical sounds to accompany the telling of the story.

Teachers can use several variations in telling stories. They can tell the story and stop at appropriate places to ask children to predict what will happen next. They can also stop and ask children questions about their feelings or about why certain events might have happened in the story. Sometimes, interrupting a story diminishes youngsters' interest in it; on other occasions, however, discussions during a story heighten their interest. Teachers should monitor children's interest closely and adjust discussion during storytelling to maintain a high level of interest.

Another variation of storytelling is to have children illustrate a story that has just been told. This requires them to relate the story directly to their comprehension of language. Teachers can promote discussion of the pictures by the children and write their comments at the bottom of each of their picture pages. For example, Rose Marie, a kindergartner who lives close to Houston, Texas, drew a picture and wrote her reactions to a story told to her class about winter in Indiana (see Figure 4.6). Her teacher could use the drawing to discuss major story events, sequence, and character traits, and as a prompt if Rose Marie wishes to retell her story.

A third variation is to start a story and direct children to add to it. As each child makes a contribution, the teacher writes the response on a flip chart for everyone to see. This reinforces the relationship between oral and written language, and it also

Figure 4.6 Rose Marie's representation of and written reaction to a story told to her kindergarten class about winter in Indiana.

illustrates the concepts associated with literacy language such as words, letters, sentences, and communication of meaning. Interactive writing strategies can also be used as the children write their own contributions for discussion.

In still another variation of storytelling, children can dramatize stories told to them. This can be integrated into the concept of readers' theater, whereby children create a script for a book or part of a book. Students can write the script individually, in pairs, or in small groups. Once the script is written, the writers and other children can dramatize it. Dramatizing stories helps youngsters develop understanding of story parts. In preparing the script, children must translate the story parts into an integrated whole. Dramatization also reinforces the communicative function of print by helping the teacher better understand students' comprehension of stories that are told to them and read to them.

EXPLICIT/DIRECT INSTRUCTIONAL ACTIVITIES

The majority of the activities presented so far place the teacher in the role of facilitator and promoter of literacy activities for children. However, some areas of early literacy programs do require explicit/direct instruction. Facilitating acquisition and development of listening capabilities, auditory discrimination, visual discrimination, phonics, comprehension, and vocabulary requires explicit instruction. These are not taught as discrete, separate activities that resemble isolated skills lessons, but are woven into literature-based activities. Instruction in these areas still aims to develop capabilities within the context of meaningful text and language, but the teacher's role is more central in initiating, guiding, and directing students' learning.

Guided Reading

Guided reading uses a teacher explicit/direct approach to guide children in their reading and comprehending of text; however, the discussion of what they read is student-centered. Guided reading matches children with books that are appropriate to their reading needs. The books are challenging and familiar to the students and they are used to teach specific reading strategies that the students can choose and apply in context. It is the teacher role to provide needed scaffolding, employ ongoing assessment strategies, and use text selections that continue to enable children to expand their reading development and use of reading strategies. The basic features of guided reading are:

- **Assessing students' reading capabilities and grouping by their instructional reading levels.** Groups can be formed by using a variety of assessment procedures. For example, teachers can use informal reading inventories, running records, observations, and placement assessment tools that accompany basal reading series. It is a crucial feature of guided reading that teachers know each student's reading level and reading strategies so groups that are similar in these two areas can be formed. Groups may range in size from four to six students and are flexible, that is, students are moved in and out of groups based on the teacher's ongoing assessment of their needs.

- **Using leveled texts for reading.** Teachers need to know the reading level of many books and be familiar with the content. Many basal series provide leveled texts for use in guided reading instruction. In addition, Fawson and Reutzel (2000) have provided levels for all of the children's stories in the five most used basal reading series (Harcourt Brace, Silver Burdett Ginn, Houghton Mifflin, Scott Foresman, and Scholastic) at the kindergarten, first-, and second-grade levels. They leveled the stories A through L, which is a text gradient that ranges in difficulty from early kindergarten reading to grade 2 (see Appendix A). Additional leveled texts would be necessary for using guided reading with children reading at grade 3 and above.

- **Presenting book introductions.** The teacher prepares and presents a book introduction to the group of students that is aimed at motivating them, activating their background knowledge for both content and strategy use, and introducing either difficult or new concepts. Introductions can focus on (a) a presentation of the title and asking students to make predictions about the story content; (b) a walk through the book looking at illustrations, discussing language usage, predicting events, connecting with background knowledge, introducing either new or difficult concepts, pointing out and discussing vocabulary words, and posing and answering questions; (c) an identification of questions to be answered through reading the story. For example, questions can relate what students have read to what they are going to read, focus on how and why, and require synthesis of the text into the big ideas. The purpose of the book introduction is to engage children in a discussion about the story, bring up questions for them to answer, point out information in the text, and establish purposes and expectations for reading.

- **Reading independently.** The students read the story or a selected part of the story independently (silently or whisper read) while the teacher serves as a facilitator. Students are encouraged to ask for help in applying problem-solving strategies when needed. While the students are reading the teacher observes their reading behaviors to confirm strategy use. Prompts and cues are given to help the students apply their problem-solving strategies. Students who experience difficulties are provided assistance as needed. Assistance can focus either on the word level (Does that make sense? Does that sound like a word you know? What sound do you see in the word?), the meaning level (Does that sound like language? What are the important things that happened early in the story? Why do you think this happened?), or both. An important role for the teacher during this time is the ongoing assessment of individual readers and the recording of observations.

- **Checking comprehension and use of problem-solving strategies.** When the children have read the story the teacher focuses on comprehension and application of the problem-solving strategies. The students are encouraged to make responses about the story to each other. The teacher may ask students to reread selected parts of the story to assess fluency (word recognition, rate, and intonation), point out parts of the story to support their discussion of problem solving, and reread the story to themselves or to a partner. Additional after-reading activities may be used to provide for extension and application of the students' responding to the text. Such activities could include journal writing, drama, art, storytelling, and additional reading.

Guided reading is intended to facilitate children in becoming competent readers at a level appropriate to their abilities. It focuses on fluency, word recognition, silent reading, and application of reading strategies. Guided reading uses many of the features associated with effective reading instruction, such as scaffolding, ongoing assessment, grouping to meet individual needs, application of word recognition strategies in meaningful texts, and focusing on comprehension. A concern related to using guided reading is whether or not a basal reading program can fit into it in a meaningful manner. Use of the text leveling presented in Appendix A in conjunction with many of the supplementary leveled books provided with many basal reading series should enable teachers to incorporate guided reading into their balanced literacy instruction.

Listening Capabilities

In developing listening skills, one deals with a much broader area than simple auditory discrimination of speech sounds. Listening is involved in all facets of the curriculum. Listening is required for following directions, developing and expanding concepts, maintaining discipline, planning curricular activities, and the like. Listening also is closely related to many literacy behaviors, such as developing auditory memory and processing language presented orally in stories and discussions. Therefore, what is required in the classroom is a variety of listening situations in which students can be engaged.

Providing students with direct listening instruction can make them better listeners. Children can be taught to focus on the speaker, predict while listening, form images of what they hear, think of questions, take notes, draw pictures, and select strategies appropriate to what the listening situation demands. Meaningful listening instruction can be developed around the following steps (Brent & Anderson, 1993):

- **Identify the needed skill or strategy.** Through observation, teachers can identify listening needs. They can help students to activate their background knowledge of what "good listening" is in relation to a specific activity. For example, if during sharing time, students appear not to be listening, the teacher can have them identify future ways to show that they are listening during sharing time. Additional listening strategies, such as blocking out distractions or taking one-word notes, might need to be added based on children's needs.

- **Teach the lesson.** Listening instruction is integrated into daily teaching activities. During shared reading, listening strategies can be integrated with the reading and discussing of the book. Teachers may choose to be more explicit in listening instruction and focus their lessons on individual listening strategies.
- **Supervise practice and debriefing.** At the ends of lessons, teachers can engage students in discussions about how they were effective listeners (e.g., how taking notes helped or how distractions were blocked out) and how strategies vary in relation to the purposes of listening. In addition, students may keep individual portfolio logs of how they use listening strategies and how they are becoming better listeners.
- **Review skills and strategies previously taught.** Listening strategies that have been taught need to be reviewed and extended into other listening situations. Teachers can help children use these strategies by alerting them before the strategies will be needed for a listening situation.
- **Select strategies for specific situations.** The ultimate goal of teaching listening skills is for students to analyze listening situations and adjust their listening strategies automatically. This can be accomplished by encouraging students to predict what listening strategies they will need for different listening situations and by rewarding and reinforcing appropriate use of the strategies.

Many learning activities in school depend on listening—listening to stories, listening to the teacher, and listening to other students. Following are a few activities to involve children in listening to and interpreting language. They call upon the learner to attend to, process, retain, and respond to language stimuli.

Riddles

Most youngsters are intrigued by riddles. They enjoy both telling and listening to riddles, and they often come up with many variations of the same riddle. Both factual and nonsense riddles are appropriate to use in developing children's listening capabilities. In addition, children often come away from an activity that uses riddles motivated to write their own riddles and sometimes even to construct a book of riddles. For example, one youngster named Sharon brought home her book of riddles, which consisted of seven pages. Each page was a variation of one riddle that her teacher had used to encourage listening: "Why did the hippopotamus cross the road?" (Answer: It was the chicken's day off.) Examples of riddles that Sharon had written include "Why did the cat cross the road?" "Why did the giraffe cross the road?" and "Why did the bug cross the road?" Of course, each riddle had the same answer: "It was the chicken's day off." The teacher had written this and several other riddles on the chalkboard; Sharon had copied the text and asked her teacher to help her write each of the different animal words. She also had drawn a picture for each variation of the riddle. Her parents knew that she must have been listening, because she also asked them several other riddles: "What chases the moon away every morning?" (the sun); "What goes away when you stand up?" (your lap); and "What holds up trains?" (train robbers). The classroom activity clearly had promoted careful listening by Sharon and had motivated her to create, write, and read her own riddles.

Teachers can write short, descriptive passages on the chalkboard—about objects, characters from a story, shared experiences, or events from stories—then direct students to listen carefully, read a passage to them, and ask them to draw a picture of what is being described. As the teacher reads the passage aloud, the teacher should direct students to focus on the written text as well as the spoken words. Two examples of this kind of activity follow.

> I wanted to catch a lot of fish.
> I stuck my tail through a hole in the ice.
> I didn't catch any fish.
> I now have a short tail.
> Who am I?

> I grow outdoors.
> In the summer I am full of leaves.
> Sometimes I have baby birds living in me.
> In the fall I am full of colors.
> What am I?

Not only does listening to these descriptions help children develop listening skills, but also, children can discuss what clues were the most important in helping them figure out what was being described.

Telling and reading stories

The activities described earlier for storytelling and reading aloud are also excellent ways to encourage listening in a meaningful context. Before telling or reading stories, the teacher can plant the ideas that good listening is the key to enjoyment of the story and that print is meaningful.

Visual Discrimination

By the time children come to school, they have had thousands of experiences in seeing and noting likenesses and differences. They are capable of fairly high-order visual discrimination, in many cases based on relatively small clues. **Visual discrimination** is the ability to see similarities and differences. For example, at the age of 3 years, most children can identify and claim their own tricycles from a group, and identify common trademarks on the basis of size, color, shape, and function. They can sort a group of objects by size and shape without much difficulty based on visual discrimination. They can identify and click on the correct icon when playing their favorite computer games.

We have found from working in many primary classrooms that one of the most effective ways to help children develop the ability to visually differentiate letters and words is through wide exposure to meaningful text. Furthermore, as children begin to recognize whole words, they become better able to visually discriminate words that are spelled differently. Many times teachers must point out the features of words to facilitate development of visual discrimination. They can do this using meaningful text—big books, predictable books, library books, and children's writing, for example. An example of this practice was observed recently in a kindergarten classroom. Jason had checked out *The Whole Book of Wheels* from the school library. His teacher asked him which two words in the title start with the same letter. Jason did not respond. The teacher rephrased her question: "Show me the two words that start with the letter *W*." Jason immediately pointed to *Whole* and *Wheels*. This example illustrates the importance of integrating visual-discrimination activities into a literacy program rather than treating them separately as skill lessons that may not be meaningful for children.

Phonemic Awareness

The importance of phonemic awareness was discussed in Chapter 3, where it was noted that it is an important precursor to acquiring conventional reading capabilities. Stahl (1999) points out that in learning to read, children need to view words in terms of the sounds they represent. By understanding that spoken words contain phonemes (sounds), children can learn the relationship between letters and the sounds they represent.

Many children come to school playing language games with rhyming words. Rhyming words are an excellent starting point for teaching and reinforcing phonemic awareness. However, for rhyming activities to be effective, teachers must ensure that children understand the concept of rhyming words. Examples of activities using rhyming words are presented next.

Instructional Activities

Rhyming Color Names.   Review some familiar color names with children (e.g., red, blue, green, orange, black, white, yellow, and brown). Write the color names on the chalkboard and direct students to listen carefully to the ending sounds in the two words you will pronounce. Ask students to think about which color word rhymes with (has the same ending sound as) the two words pronounced. Model one or two examples for them before calling on students to give a response.

<u>Said</u> and <u>Fred</u> rhyme with? (red)
<u>Down</u> and <u>frown</u> rhyme with? (brown)
<u>Night</u> and <u>bright</u> rhyme with? (white)

Rhyming Lines and Jingles.   Jingles and rhyming lines can demonstrate intonation and rhyming elements. These involve longer language units that also provide experiences for auditory memory. The following example uses number words and asks children to discriminate the word that is stressed and complete the statement with a number word that rhymes with that word. Follow the same procedures used for the color-name activity.

I saw a number on the door
The number that I saw was _____. (four)

The door led into a den
The snakes I counted numbered _____. (ten)

I left the room and I did see
A boy who said his age was _____. (three)

To keep this rhyming game alive
We have to say the number _____. (five)

Many rhyming and jingle activities are similar to those that Griffith and Olson (1992) proposed for developing children's phonemic awareness. In addition to such activities, they recommend that teachers read books that play on language (e.g., those that use alliteration, repetition of vowel sounds within words, and rhymes), provide writing opportunities that allow children to use invented spellings, and draw boxes around sounds represented by letters in written words (e.g., [d] [u] [ck]).

Visual and Auditory Integration

Visual and auditory integration is combining visual and auditory capabilities with print. It usually occurs after children have learned to recognize letters and some words. A series of instructional activities can build on students' reading and writing experiences to help youngsters acquire these capabilities.

Once children have developed phonemic awareness and visual discrimination of letters and words, teachers can use words from big books, predictable books, children's writing, and environmental print to teach visual and auditory integration. The earlier example of Billy's fascination with the poem that repeated the phrase "Hop, hop, hop" in several stanzas suggests ways to teach auditory and visual integration.

- The word *hop* can be used to illustrate how the words *stop, pop, mop, flop,* and others require children to visually discriminate between the different beginning letters, hear the sounds represented, and integrate both to determine that *hop* and *pop* are different words.
- Using different endings can reinforce visual and auditory integration (e.g., *hop— hot* and *pop—pot*). Changing words and inserting them into text can prompt a discussion of changes in meaning and whether or not the language makes sense.

Phonics

Phonics is teaching reading in a manner that stresses symbol-sound relationships (Harris & Hodges, 1995). The focus here is on presenting some instructional guidelines that do not treat phonics as an isolated skill, but rather weave it into classroom literacy activities. Combining what is presented here with the variety of activities presented in Chapter 5 can help teachers develop a selection of activities that match their students' needs.

Literature and literacy activities that are happening in the classroom can provide materials for teaching phonics. These sources can furnish words to illustrate phonic generalization: The words are taken out of text and then placed back in the text to illustrate application of phonics in reading. This still allows for the systematic study of words in terms of their graphemic and phonemic features (letters and sounds typically represented); however, phonics is integrated into the literacy program, not isolated from it.

Stahl (1999) identified some guidelines for phonics instruction that can apply in literature-based classrooms and classrooms using a basal text as the core text:

- Phonics instruction builds on children's phonemic awareness.
- Phonics instruction is clear and direct. By using words familiar to students from their reading and writing activities, (see Figure 4.7) teachers can illustrate letter-sound relationships in a more meaningful fashion. It is recommended that teachers present a written word, such as *bear,* and stress that it starts with the letter *b* and represents the sound /b/. Or, teachers can present the letter *b,* then show words that begin with the sound that letter represents. Following these activities, children practice reading other words beginning with the letter *b.*
- Phonics is an integral part of the reading program, not a dominant feature of instruction. Teachers can use text that students have read or written to teach a high-utility phonic element (e.g., a beginning consonant digraph, such as *sh*). Written examples of words from the text can be applied to help in reading another text containing several examples of the phonic element.
- Phonics should focus on reading words, not learning rules. Children can be shown multiple examples of the application of a rule to illustrate a particular spelling pattern, but they should not be required to memorize or recite the rule.
- Phonics instruction may include the use of onsets and rimes. An **onset** is the part of a syllable before the vowel. A **rime** is the part of a syllable from the vowel onward. Approximately 500 words can be derived from the following rimes:

-ack	-ain	-ake	-all	-ame	-and
-ank	-ap	-ash	-at	-ate	-aw
-ay	-eat	-ell	-est	-ice	-ick
-ide	-ight	-ill	-in	-ine	-ing
-ink	-ip	-ir	-ock	-oke	-op
-or	-ore	-uck	-ug	-ump	-unk

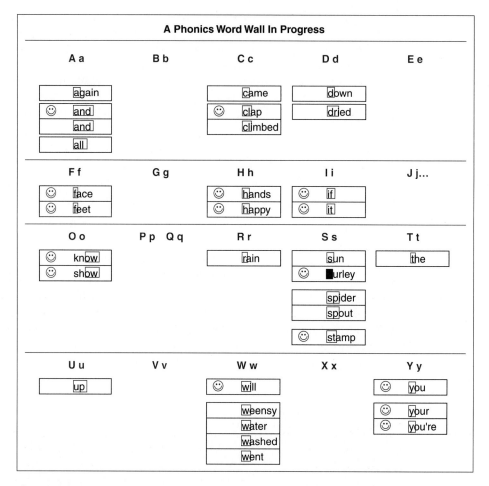

Figure 4.7   An example of using familiar words to teach phonics in beginning literacy instruction.

Source: Reprinted by permission of the publisher from Strickland & Morrow, *Beginning Reading and Writing* (New York: Teachers College Press, © 2000 by Teachers College, Columbia University. All rights reserved.), p. 128.

Children can be taught to compare unknown words with known words and then ask themselves if their predictions or identifications of unknown words make sense in the story. Again, familiar literacy activities can supply words to highlight the use of onsets and rimes. For example, if students know the words *clap* and *duck*, then they can figure out the word *cluck* using their knowledge of onsets and rimes.

- Phonics instruction may include invented spelling practice. Although invented spelling is no substitute for direct phonics instruction, practice with invented spelling does improve children's awareness of phonemes and reinforces the meaning-making concepts of both reading and writing.

- Phonics instructions is intended to develop in children the ability to use independent word-recognition strategies, focusing on the internal structure of words. Phonics makes children aware of orthographic patterns in words and helps them use this knowledge to recognize words. The ability to recognize orthographic letter patterns makes children efficient in identifying words.

Phonics instruction should develop automaticity in word recognition. Children who can automatically recognize words spend less time decoding the text and more time on comprehension. Automatic word recognition comes about through practice in reading words. This is the purpose of Chall's (1996) second stage of reading development, when children develop fluency in reading. Continuing to use meaningful literacy activities that allow children to apply their knowledge of phonics provides them with the practice needed to improve both their word recognition capabilities and comprehension.

A classroom environment that supports children's acquisition of phonic knowledge will provide for application of phonic generalizations. Phonic charts (see Figure 4.7) that students and teacher develop cooperatively can be displayed for the students' reference when reading. Words that illustrate particular letter–sound relationships on the charts can come from children's writing, predictable books, big books, and literature-based reading series. For example, teachers can develop large classroom charts such as the following using onsets and rimes.

	ake
bake	*shake*
rake	*lake*
make	*cake*

Teachers can make such charts for individual students or for the whole class. Those used with individual students can be bound into a booklet that the child refers to when reading and writing. Children can add their own words to those listed as they encounter words that fit the spelling pattern. The teacher also can add more words as they are found in children's reading and writing.

Another medium that can be used to develop children's phonic knowledge is big books. Children can make and add to their own phonic big books, which can be made available for the whole class to use. For example, after Mrs. Smalling's first grade went on a field trip to the zoo, each child selected an animal, drew a picture of it, and then drew pictures representing words that began with the same letter as the animal's name. One child, Shawn, drew pictures of a bear, a boat, a bottle, a box, a ball, Batman, and the Batmobile. Mrs. Smalling then printed the names of three of the objects beneath them and asked Shawn to print the beginning letter for the remaining objects. He printed the letter *b* and, with the teacher's help, then printed the rest of the words. Mrs. Smalling assembled all of the children's products into a big book that not only represented their trip to the zoo, but also served as a support for phonic knowledge and application.

We observed a first-grade teacher present part of a 60-minute video on the human body to her class. She used only that portion of the video (a section about the skeletal

Meeting Students' Emergent Literacy Needs by Building Background Knowledge

Helping children increase their background knowledge is essential in promoting vocabulary development and comprehension of text. Children cannot understand things about which they have no prior knowledge, whether it be language structure, words that represent ideas, or the content of what they are reading. This inclusion strategies feature presents an example of how teachers can use visuals to better prepare children for literacy activities by expanding their background and vocabulary knowledge.

Visual materials are excellent ways to expand and refine concepts associated with children's background knowledge and literacy. For example, a picture of an eroded hillside is much more effective in fixing the concept of erosion than is a definition of the word.

The same picture can be used at different levels for teaching words and meanings. Imagine a picture available to almost every teacher: a downtown scene in an average-sized city. It shows a bus, a boy on a bicycle, various storefronts and offices, a police officer directing traffic, a fire hydrant, and a bank. Without going into more detail, we might build a hierarchy of concepts for children. The degree of teacher direction will vary according to students' existing capabilities.

"Point out the police officer."

"Where is the police officer standing?"

"Yes, he is really standing where two streets cross—what is that called?"

"That's an intersection." (The students' capabilities and interest will determine whether or not the teacher further explains the term *intersection*.)

"How many kinds of travel or transportation do we see?"

"Some people are walking."

"Some are riding in a bus. It is a city bus."

"How do we know that it is a city bus?"

"There are lots of cars."

"Do you see any boats?"

"Why do you think there aren't any boats?"

Inclusion Strategies

Meeting Students' Emergent Literacy Needs by Building Background Knowledge (continued)

The teacher points to a building with a symbol on it for the phone company and asks, "What is this building?"

"It must be the telephone office."

"How do we know that?"

"It has a sign for the phone company."

"What is this building?"

"McDonald's!"

"How do we know?"

"It has a McDonald's sign."

The teacher negotiates a discussion with the children about concepts related to background knowledge, vocabulary, and language. The picture we have visualized could be used in a variety of ways. Through its use the teacher can stress concepts and direct children to notice any of the following:

- Details
- Symbols standing for things
- Many different names for the same thing (e.g., *McDonald's, restaurant,* and *fast-food restaurant*)
- The same word having different meanings according to usage (e.g., *meter* for *parking meter, gas meter,* or *electric meter*)

The value of visuals is their wealth of detail and their ability to convey conceptual information in a concrete manner (e.g., seeing a picture of a longhorn steer). What children can see stays in their minds, so it can be referred to and recalled by children after a discussion has progressed to other things.

system) that was appropriate to her unit of instruction. Days later, when the class was studying insects, one of her students, Heather, asked where a ladybug's skeleton was. As the teacher began to explain the ectoskeleton of insects, she made many references to the video about the human skeletal system that the children had seen. Every child appeared to understand as they talked about the skeletal system of insects and humans.

Children can begin to understand relationships among speaking, reading, and writing by creating stories from pictures.

Building Background Knowledge and Fostering Reading Comprehension

Throughout the book we have encouraged teachers to create and provide a wide range of reading and writing opportunities for their students. Reading and writing are processes aimed at communication of meaning, and children in the beginning literacy program benefit from exposure to a wide range of texts. A classroom with a wide range of texts that are read aloud, used for teaching reading and writing, and available for students' use will provide for development of both decoding and comprehending capabilities. Background knowledge will be expanded and the children's abilities to construct meaning will be fostered.

Gambrell and Dromsky (2000) endorse the creation of a classroom environment that supports wide and varied opportunities to read that encourage children to make personal connection with the text. They encourage the use of several comprehension strategies with beginning readers and writers. Among the strategies they recommend that teachers use are K-W-L (see Chapter 10), retellings (see Chapter

7), and text frames (see Chapter 7). They also developed a set of guidelines that apply across a range of comprehension strategies and techniques for teaching comprehension in the beginning literacy program.

1. Focus on teaching only one strategy at a time. Make sure that children are able to use the strategy with a high success rate in applying it to appropriate materials.
2. Use scaffolding to support students' construction of meaning. Model the application of the strategy in appropriate reading materials.
3. Use explicit/direct teaching and concrete examples of when and where to use strategies.
4. Provide an abundance of opportunities for practice in use of the strategies.
5. Allow students opportunities to select their reading materials for practice. Self-selection enhances motivation and increases the likelihood that the texts are meaningful for the students.
6. Encourage students to engage in discussing, reading, and sharing both narrative and informational texts.

Marie Clay (1991) sees much value in introducing new storybooks to young readers. Storybook introduction ensures that children have a "successful first reading early in the lesson before the teacher develops lesson activities" (p. 264). New storybooks also activate children's existing background knowledge and introduce new knowledge. Existing concepts are extended for both the storybook's content and its language (see Figure 4.8). The following steps are used to introduce new storybooks:

- The teacher uses illustrations to encourage students to respond to the storybook and relates the story to other stories they have read.
- The teacher gets students to discuss experiences related to the new story and then identifies areas that may confuse students. The teacher can then clear up these areas of confusion.
- The teacher sketches out the plot or the sequence of events up to the climax. The purpose is to create an overview of the story structure that will provide a framework for the children's anticipation of what will come later.
- The teacher stimulates children to relate personal experiences or other stories they have read to the theme or topic of the new story. Such a discussion identifies and clears up conceptual problems related to the plot.
- The teacher uses novel language features (e.g., an unusual name, unfamiliar syntax, or multiple-meaning words) in talking about the story. The discussion of the story deliberately focuses on these features.
- The teacher uses a particularly difficult or new sentence pattern two or three times and may have the students repeat it. This provides them with a language model (to help build background knowledge) that they can use in reading the text. Clay notes that this "is not memorizing the lines of the book but rather readying the mind and ear to grapple with novelty." (p. 267)

Example 1: Introducing a Student to *The Great Big Enormous Turnip*

Setting the topic, theme, and characters
Teacher: Let's look at our new book. This story is about a big turnip, isn't it? *The Great Big Enormous Turnip.*

Prompting constructive activity
Teacher: Let's see what happened. Here's a little old man and he's . . . (Pausing) What's he doing?
Child: He's telling it to grow.
Teacher: And then what's he trying to do?
Child: Pull it out.
Teacher: Pull it out! Can he pull it out?
Child: (Shakes his head.)
Teacher: No! Who does he ask to help him?
Child: The little old woman.

Increasing accessibility or presenting new knowledge
Teacher: (Turning the page) They're asking the granddaughter to help, aren't they?

Accepting a partially correct response
Teacher: Who do they ask next?
Child: The dog.
Teacher: The black dog, that's right.

Providing a model (of anticipating the outcome)
Teacher: And does it come up? Does it? I think it might. And they all . . . (turns the page). Oh, no, not yet! Who do they have to ask?

Example 2: Introducing a Student to *Trug and Leaf*

The teacher clearly thought this story might be difficult for this child to understand, but for some good reason she selected it at this stage of the child's progress.

Setting the topic, title, and characters
Teacher: I've got another book about Trug for you. It's about Trug and Leaf this time and poor Leaf is ill.

Figure 4.8   Examples of storybook introduction.

ASSESSING EMERGENT LITERACY

Many commercially prepared tests are available for use in early literacy programs; however, many of these tests do not provide teachers with information they need to make informed decisions about their instruction. Furthermore, assessment results obtained from such tests often focus on comparing a child's performance with that of other children and thus provide little diagnostic infor-

Probing to find out what the child knows
Teacher: Do you know what it means when you are ill?
Child: (No response)
Teacher: It means you are sick, and Trug's going to try to look after her. Look, she's in bed.

Asking the child to work with new knowledge
Teacher: Trug's going to get some water for her. What do you think water might start with?
Child: *W.*
Teacher: I bet you can show what word says *water.*

Accepting partially correct response
Teacher: That word does start with *w.* It says *will.*

Tightening the criteria of acceptability
Teacher: Can you find another?
Child: (Locates *water.*)
Teacher: That's got *w,* hasn't it? Right, he's going to get some water.

Prompting constructive activity (to understand the plot)
Teacher: He's trying to carry it in his hands. Is that working? It drips on the mud, doesn't it? That's
             not much good. Look, it's still dripping! Has he got any water left? I wonder, how he is go-
             ing to get the water? What does he see? What can he use?
Child: The egg.
Teacher: Where has the baby bird come from?
Child: The egg.
Teacher: He's come out of the egg, hasn't he? What's Trug going to do with the egg?
Child: Put water in it?

Providing a model (of reflecting on the story)
Teacher: He had a good idea, didn't he? And he can take the water to Leaf. She might get better now
             that she's got a drink of water, mightn't she? Do you think so? Because she's ill, isn't she?

Figure 4.8   (continued)
Source: From M. Clay, "Introducing a New Storybook to Young Readers," *The Reading Teacher, 45* (December 1991), pp. 268–269. Reprinted with permission of the author and the International Reading Association. Copyright by the International Reading Association. All rights reserved.

mation for the teacher. Assessment in the literacy program should help teachers adjust their instruction to address students' needs. If, for example, a teacher discovers that some children can recognize environmental print but have had limited experiences with actual storybooks, then the teacher could use opportunities to build on the students' environmental print knowledge in exposing them to storybook reading.

Assessment of children's early literacy experiences is important in an effective reading and writing program. Assessment should focus on the experiential and conceptual areas associated with success in beginning literacy, such as language, concepts of print, the language of instruction, and phonemic awareness. In her presentation of the stages of reading development (see Chapter 1), Chall (1996) identified many of the early literacy behaviors that children acquire before beginning first grade. These emerging literacy behaviors provide the foundation for children to move toward acquiring traditional literacy. Behaviors that are acquired in early literacy learning include (1) knowing that books are for reading, (2) understanding that certain words begin with certain sounds, (3) aurally discriminating rhyming words, (4) recognizing some environmental print, (5) pretending to read by retelling stories while looking at the pages, (6) playing with and knowing the uses of books, pencils, and paper, and (7) engaging in early writing attempts.

The most useful and valuable assessments of early literacy are obtained with the use of observational, informal techniques that focus on children's experiences with print. The purpose of informal assessment is to adjust instruction based on the results. Teachers must evaluate carefully the appropriateness of their instruction in light of students' progress. Each teaching situation is also an assessment situation.

Information from Parents

Home background plays a significant role in children's emerging literacy. Several home factors that contribute to children's early literacy development include parents reading to children, children's observation of parents reading, children's reading and pretending to read to their parents, and books' availability to children (books are bought for children and trips are made to the library).

Obtaining information from parents about children's home backgrounds is extremely important. Such information can indicate students' level of emergent literacy. Many teachers ask parents to complete questionnaires about their children. While some teachers may wish to develop parent questionnaires that parallel their individual instructional programs, Figure 4.9 provides a useful example. This questionnaire has been used successfully by several school districts.

The questions in Figure 4.9 are representative of the kind of information teachers may wish to gather about their students; of course, questions may be added or deleted. Valuable information gathered from parent questionnaires can be used in adjusting literacy instruction. For example, knowing the names of the children in a child's family and information about them enables the teacher to engage the child in meaningful oral language and literacy activities by talking, reading, and writing about things that are familiar to the child. The teacher also can use information about children's special abilities and interests to encourage their participation in literacy situations based on familiar settings and information.

Observing Children's Literacy Behaviors

Teachers can become excellent observers of children and can record their observations through note taking. Classroom observation should focus on major instructional areas and should reflect the literacy program's goals. Benchmarks of

Child's Name: _____

Parent's Name: _____

Language(s) Spoken in the Home: _____

Names and Ages of Brothers and Sisters: _____
_____

Family Trips, Interests, and Hobbies: _____
_____
_____

Child's Special Abilities and Interests (Hobbies, Sports, Music, etc.): _____
_____
_____
_____

> Please respond to the list of questions and statements below. Please write in your responses where requested.

1. Does your child enjoy being read to? _____

2. Does your child have a favorite book? _____

3. Does your child ever pretend to read the favorite book to others? _____

4. Does your child ever demonstrate the following behaviors with reading situations? Please place a check mark next to the behaviors you have observed._____

    a. Turn the pages of a book from front to back? _____

    b. Point to where you or he/she is reading? _____

    c. Read along when read aloud to? _____

    d. Show you where to begin reading? _____

    e. Point to words he/she knows in the stories? _____

    f. Tell you what he/she thinks will happen in stories? _____

    g. Name the characters pictured in stories? _____

    h. Know how to recognize some words, such as store names (for example, McDonald's, Kmart, and Kroger), brand names (for example, of cereals, toys, and clothing), and his/her name? _____

continued

Figure 4.9 Home information questionnaire on emerging literacy.

Please list some of the words your child can recognize/read: _____

_____

i. Know the functions of lists, television guides, phone books, catalogs, and newspapers? _____

_____

j. Scribble and tell you what he/she is writing? _____

k. Write letters in his/her scribbles? _____

l. Write some words, such as his/her name, family members' names, and common words (for example, *is, the,* and *and*)? _____

m. Know some of the letters of the alphabet by sight? _____

If so, which ones? _____

n. Know some of the sounds represented by letters? _____

o. Try to sound out words? _____

p. Know what words can rhyme and rhyme words? _____

5. Is your child already reading? If so, please list some of the books, magazines, and other materials that he/she reads. _____

_____

_____

_____

6. Please list any information about your child's reading and writing that would be of interest to his/her teacher. _____

_____

_____

_____

_____

_____

_____

Figure 4.9   (continued)

emerging literacy, such as the broad categories presented in Figure 4.10, can form the basis for observation. In addition to these broad categories, teachers can focus on such major concepts as book awareness, comprehension, readinglike behavior, directionality, print and word awareness, and use of cuing systems. Observation and note taking should be based on the literacy curriculum of the

Broad Categories	Brief Explanation of Categories
1. Attending to Pictures, Not Forming Stories	The child is "reading" by looking at the storybook's pictures. The child's speech is *just* about the picture in view; the child is not "weaving a story" across the pages. (Subcategories are "labelling and commenting" and "following the action.")
2. Attending to Pictures, Forming ORAL Stories	The child is "reading" by looking at the storybook's pictures. The child's speech weaves a story across the pages, but the wording and the intonation are like those of someone telling a story, either like a conversation about the pictures or like a fully recited story, in which the listener can see the pictures (and often *must* see them to understand the child's story). (Subcategories are "dialogic storytelling" and "monologic storytelling.")
3. Attending to Pictures, Reading and Storytelling Mixed	This category for the simplified version was originally the first subcategory of category 4. It fits between categories 2 and 4 and is easier to understand if it is treated separately. The child is "reading" by looking at the storybook's pictures. The child's speech fluctuates between sounding like a storyteller, with oral intonation, and sounding like a reader, with reading intonation. To fit this category, the majority of the reading attempt must show fluctuations between storytelling and reading.
4. Attending to Pictures, Forming *WRITTEN* Stories	The child is "reading" by looking at the storybook's pictures. The child's speech sounds as if the child is reading, both in the wording and intonation. The listener does not need to look at the pictures (or rarely does) in order to understand the story. If the listener closes his/her eyes, most of the time he or she would think the child is reading from print. (Subcategories are "reading similar to original story," and "reading verbatim like story.")
5. Attending to Print	There are four subcategories of attending to print. Only the final one is what is typically called "real reading." In the others the child is exploring the print by such strategies as refusing to read based on print-related reasons, or using only some of the aspects of print. (Subcategories are "refusing to read based on print awareness," "reading aspectually," "reading with strategies imbalanced," and "reading independently" or "conventional reading.")

Figure 4.10 Simplified version of the Sulzby storybook-reading classification scheme.

Source: From E. Sulzby, "Assessment of Emergent Literacy: Storybook Reading," *The Reading Teacher, 44* (March 1991), p. 500. Reprinted with the permission of the author and the International Reading Association. Copyright by the International Reading Association. All rights reserved.

Note: Sulzby no longer uses the simplified version to train teachers; she uses the full 11-point scale. The simplified version is, however, useful as a synopsis of the full scale.

school and of the teacher's classroom. It should be objective, not judgmental. In essence, effective note taking is creating a snapshot of children exhibiting strengths and weaknesses in relation to a given literacy task. Information from observations can be used to develop appropriate instructional activities that build on children's existing capabilities.

Classification Scheme for Assessment of Emergent Reading and Writing

A simple assessment strategy that can be used with children's favorite storybooks was developed by Elizabeth Sulzby (1991). She recommends that for classroom use, teachers select storybooks with characters and plots that children have responded to enthusiastically over repeated readings.

To conduct a formal assessment, the teacher should select a quiet place in the classroom and request of the child, "Read your book to me." For informal assessment, the teacher can eavesdrop while one child reads to another child or to a group of children. To prompt the child's reading, the teacher can use encouragement such as "It doesn't have to be like grown-up reading—just do it your own way." If this is unsuccessful, the teacher can read with or to the child, pausing for the child to complete sentences or phrases. After completing a few pages of reading with the child, the teacher can again ask the child to read: "It's your turn now. Please read to me." During the reading, the child should hold the book and turn the pages.

Teachers can evaluate students' reading and writing using the classification scheme presented in Figure 4.10, making notes as the child reads. Sulzby (1991) believes that "the classification scheme is a direct measure of emergent reading and of initial conventional reading. It can be extended into the early conventional period by using other assessment strategies such as informal reading inventories and running records" (p. 499). She also notes that it has been found to be successful in assessing emergent reading and writing behaviors of children from middle- and low-income families of both Anglo and Hispanic backgrounds.

Results from the storybook-reading classification scheme can be used to plan appropriate reading and writing instruction. For example, if a child is attending to pictures and forming oral stories, the teacher can begin to provide more literacy activities that focus on reading and storylike language. Opportunities for the child to hear others read (e.g., the teacher's oral reading, taped books, paired reading, and shared reading) can be used to promote continued development of early literacy.

Language-Based Assessment Techniques

In addition to the assessment strategies just noted, other language-based procedures can be used successfully to assess children's early literacy development. Coupled with observation of students' engagement in both formal and informal literacy opportunities—such as during instruction and during the time they spend at language-based centers—these other techniques can provide a wealth of assessment information. They include the following:

- Hand the child a book and observe how the child holds it. Does the child turn the book so the cover is right-side up? Does the child turn the pages? Ask the child to point out or tell where the story begins, how to turn the pages, where to begin reading on a page, and what words, letters, and sentences are.

- Tell a short story and include parts that do not fit in with the story. Ask the child to tell you what is wrong with the story. A child who understands the concept that oral language must make sense will usually respond by indicating that he or she doesn't understand the story or that it is silly.
- Engage in discussions that help the child expand and refine the child's use of language. For example, if a child says "That's nice," the teacher can respond by saying, "You mean a gold watch is nice?" or "Why do you think my watch is nice?"
- Provide a sentence strip and ask the child to cut off a word, a letter, two words, the beginning word, the ending word, and so forth. This will give you some indication of the child's knowledge about ordinal and spatial features of print, such as word boundaries, as well as the child's understanding of beginning and ending words within the context of written sentences.
- Tell short, unfinished stories appropriate to the child's experiential and conceptual background and direct the child to complete the stories orally. Evaluate whether the child's endings relate to the beginnings of the stories. Also evaluate whether the child is attempting to provide endings that make sense.
- Present the child with a hypothetical situation in which a new student who doesn't know anything about reading and writing is coming into your classroom. Direct the child to share with you what he or she would tell this student about reading and writing.
- Provide the child with writing opportunities and note the child's attempts to communicate meaning. Note how the child uses invented spellings (e.g., *brthda* for *birthday* and *kresms* or *krms* for *Christmas*). The focus should be on attempts to construct meaning rather than sentence structure, correct spelling, grammar, and word usage.

Using Assessment Information

How teachers use information from their observations and informal assessments will depend on their instructional literacy program. As noted earlier, however, the purpose of assessment is to adjust instruction to address students' needs. Chall's stages of reading and Sulzby's storybook-reading classification scheme can provide help in interpreting assessment information and planning appropriate instruction. One way to use this assessment information is to consider how children's literacy capabilities are growing and changing. By looking at students' strengths, teachers can begin to consider the demands of subsequent learning and how these strengths can be used to meet the demands. For example, if a child in first grade has had limited experiences with print in the home and the environment, then the expectation that this child will succeed in conventional literacy activities will lead to failure. Instead, providing the child with abundant opportunities to engage in print activities associated with emergent literacy and offering literacy instruction that builds on these will prompt literacy growth.

SUMMARY

Emergent literacy is the reading and writing behaviors of children that precede and develop into conventional literacy. While all children experience emergent literacy, children's experiences before beginning school vary. Such variations may result from parents' reading aloud to them, opportunities to interact with environmental print, and experiences with art and play activities.

Before acquiring conventional literacy capabilities, children must (1) know that print represents a message and that this message must be as sensible as spoken language, (2) understand the concepts represented by the language used to talk about print, and (3) develop phonemic awareness, which is an awareness of sounds in spoken words. Children learn these concepts through a variety of written-language experiences, which suggests that a language-based literacy program best helps children refine and apply their emerging abilities in these three areas.

The literacy program in the early grades lays the foundation for later development. In planning an emergent and beginning reading program, teachers should take into account what they know about children, effective teaching, learning, and language development. The appropriate beginning point is a language-based classroom to help children acquire and refine basic concepts that are emerging in their literacy knowledge. Such an environment includes play and learning centers, thematic units for reading and writing, big books, predictable books, poetry, storytelling, and reading aloud.

Some areas of early literacy programs, however, do require explicit/direct instruction. Facilitating children's acquisition and development of listening capabilities, phonemic awareness, visual discrimination, background knowledge, vocabulary, and phonics requires explicit instruction. These are not taught as discrete, separate activities that resemble isolated skills lessons, but rather are woven into the literature-based activities taking place in a language-rich classroom.

Assessment of children's early literacy experiences is important in an effective reading and writing program. Assessment should focus on the experiential and conceptual areas associated with success in beginning literacy: language development, concepts about print, the language of instruction, and phonemic awareness. Teachers can use several assessment techniques. Information from parents, observation, and classification schemes are informal procedures that focus on growth and change in children's literacy capabilities.

YOUR POINT OF VIEW

Discussion Questions

1. Refer to the section Thematic Units for Writing and Reading Activities and discuss the important concepts that would bind together a unit on nutrition.
2. Assume that you have worked closely with a group of 6-year-olds who learned to read before entering school. Discuss the literacy capabilities you think they would possess and the types of instruction that would be appropriate for their continued literacy development.

Take a Stand For or Against

1. First graders don't need instruction in phonics because they will learn for themselves how to use letter-sound relationships to figure out unknown words.
2. Combining reading and writing instruction is too difficult to accomplish in the classroom, and if youngsters can read, they will also learn to write.

Field-Based Assignments

1. Big books, predictable books, toy books, shape books, read-along books, and computer books should be in abundance in kindergarten and first-grade classrooms. Visit a kindergarten and first-grade classroom in your school and examine the books and literacy materials used to support children's emergent literacy. Interview some of the children by asking them such questions as "Which is your favorite book?" "Why is that your favorite?" and "Can you tell me what it says on this page?" Either tape-record or write down the children's responses for sharing and discussion with your classmates.
2. Learning centers that promote the role of literacy are one important way to engage young children in meaningful reading and writing activities. Plan a learning center based on the features discussed in this chapter and set it up in your classroom. Observe how children interact in their use of language when playing in your center. Based on your observations of how children interact in your center, make appropriate modifications, adding more text materials, removing inappropriate materials, integrating writing to a greater extent and so forth.

Portfolio Entry

Using the assessment strategies recommended in this chapter, gather information about several children and record it in your portfolio. Alternative means for gathering information include interviewing students, photographing them in various literacy activities, and either attaching the outcomes of the activities with the photos or recording the children's comments about the activities. Reflect on what the information could mean for you in terms of your own emergent literacy instruction.

BIBLIOGRAPHY

Adams, M. J. (1990). *Beginning to read: Thinking and learning about print.* Cambridge, MA: MIT Press.

Anderson, R. C., Hiebert, E. H., Scott, J. A., & Wilkinson, I. A. G. (1985). *Becoming a nation of readers: The report of the Commission on Reading.* Washington, DC: The National Institute of Education.

Beach, S. A., & Robinson, R. J. (1992). Gender and grade level differences in the development of concepts about print. *Reading Psychology, 12,* 309–328.

Brent, R., & Anderson, P. (1993). Developing children's classroom listening strategies. *The Reading Teacher, 47,* 122–126.

Busink, R. (1997). Reading and phonological awareness: What we have learned and how we can use it. *Reading Research and Instruction, 36,* 199–215.

Button, K., Johnson, M. J., & Furgerson, P. (1996). Interactive writing in a primary classroom. *The Reading Teacher, 49,* 446–454.

Chall, J. S. (1996). *Stages of reading development* (2nd ed.). New York: McGraw-Hill.

Clay, M. M. (1991). Introducing a new storybook to young readers. *The Reading Teacher, 45,* 264–273.

Cunningham, P. M. (1999). What kind of phonics instruction will we have? In R. Robinson, M. McKenna, & J. Wedman (Eds.), *Issues and trends in literacy instruction* (pp. 76–90). Boston, MA: Allyn & Bacon.

Eisenwine, M. J., & Hunt, D. A. (2000). Using a computer in literacy groups with emergent readers. *The Reading Teacher, 53,* 456–458.

Eldredge, J. L., Reutzel, R. D., & Hollingsworth, P. M. (1996). Comparing the effectiveness of two oral reading practices: Round-robin reading and the shared book experience. *Journal of Literacy Research, 28,* 201–225.

Fawson, P. C., & Reutzel, R. D. (2000). But I only have a basal: Implementing guided reading in the early grades. *The Reading Teacher, 54,* 84–97.

Gambrell, L. B., & Dromsky, A. (2000). Fostering reading comprehension. In D. S. Strickland & L. M. Morrow (Eds.), *Beginning reading and writing* (pp. 143–153). New York: Teachers College Press.

Goodman, K. S. (1996). Acquiring literacy is natural: Who skilled cock robin? In R. Robinson, M. McKenna, & J. Wedman (Eds.), *Issues and trends in literacy instruction* (pp. 65–70). Boston, MA: Allyn & Bacon.

Griffith, P. L., & Olson, M. W. (1992). Phonemic awareness helps beginning readers break the code. *The Reading Teacher, 45,* 516–525.

Harris, T. L., & Hodges, R. E. (1995). *The literacy dictionary: The vocabulary of reading and writing.* Newark, DE: The International Reading Association.

Isom, B. A., & Casteel, C. P. (1991). Creating a writing-rich environment in the preschool classroom. *The Reading Teacher, 44,* 520–521.

Kettering, L., & Graybill, N. (1991). Cereal boxes foster emergent literacy. *The Reading Teacher, 44,* 522–523.

Labbo, L. D. (2000). 12 things young children can do with a talking book in a classroom computer center. *The Reading Teacher, 53,* 542–546.

Labbo, L. D., Murray, B. A., & Phillips, M. (1996). Writing to read: From inheritance to innovation and invitation. *The Reading Teacher, 49,* 314–323.

Miller, W. (2000). *Strategies for developing emergent literacy.* Boston, MA: McGraw-Hill.

Morrow, L. M. (2000). Organizing and managing a language arts block. In D. S. Strickland & L. M. Morrow (Eds.), *Beginning reading and writing* (pp. 83–98). New York: Teachers College Press.

Moustafa, M. (1995). Children's productive phonological recording. *Reading Research Quarterly, 30,* 464–476.

Moustafa, M. (2000). Phonics instruction. In D. S. Strickland & L. M. Morrow (Eds.), *Beginning reading and writing* (pp. 121–123). New York: Teachers College Press.

Norton, D. (1999). *Through the eyes of a child: An introduction to children's literature* (5th ed.). Upper Saddle River, NJ: Merrill/Prentice Hall.

Rupley, W. H., Rodriquez, M., Mergen, S., & Willson, V. L. (in press). Effects of structural features on word recognition development of Hispanic and non-Hispanic second readers. *Reading and Writing: An Interdisciplinary Journal.*

Snow, C. E., Burns, M. S., & Griffith, P. (Eds.). (1998). *Preventing reading difficulties in young children.* Washington, DC: National Academy Press.

Stahl, L. A. (1999). Saying the "p" word: Nine guidelines for exemplary phonics instruction. In R. Robinson, M. McKenna, & J. Wedman (Eds.), *Issues and trends in literacy instruction* (pp. 52–61). Boston, MA: Allyn & Bacon.

Strickland, D. S., & Morrow, L. M. (Eds.). (2000). *Beginning reading and writing.* New York: Teachers College Press.

Sulzby, E. (1991). Assessment of emergent literacy: Storybook reading. *The Reading Teacher, 44,* 498–500.

Sulzby, E., & Barnhart, J. (1992). The development of academic competence: All our children emerge as writers and readers. In J. W. Irwin & M. A. Doyle (Eds.), *Reading and writing connections: Learning from research* (pp. 120–144). Newark, DE: International Reading Association.

Teale, W. H., & Sulzby, E. (1999). Emergent literacy: New perspectives. In R. Robinson, M. McKenna, & J. Wedman (Eds.), *Issues and trends in literacy instruction* (pp. 139–143). Boston, MA: Allyn & Bacon.

Tracey, D. H. (2000). Enhancing literacy growth through home-school connections. In D. S. Strickland & L. M. Morrow (Eds.), *Beginning reading and writing* (pp. 46–57). New York: Teachers College Press.

Teaching Students to Become Strategic Readers

Overview

Just as a fine orchestra studies and practices interrelated parts of a performance with the ultimate goal of putting the parts together in splendid fashion, the teaching of literacy involves a host of interrelated understandings that must be studied and practiced and ultimately combined in an efficient and effective "performance." An effective literacy program stresses the instruction and application of the essential strategies, skills, and abilities that produce strategic readers and writers. The ability to interact successfully with text demands the simultaneous use of several tools in our language. Chapters in this part will focus on the role of word pronunciation and vocabulary growth and the development of strategies to comprehend written ideas.

Integrating Principles of Teaching Reading

The following principles, presented in Chapter 1, will be reinforced in this part:

- Reading and writing are language processes.
- Reading is a meaningful, active, constructive, and strategic process.
- Reading and writing are developmental processes.
- Teachers must strive for a balanced literacy program to teach all students to read and write independently.
- The key to successful literacy instruction is the teacher.

5

Word Identification

Chapter Outline

For the Reader

The core of an effective literacy program is the instruction and application of skills and strategies that produce good readers. This assertion applies equally at all grade levels, with specific instruction dependent upon student learning needs. Regardless of the instructional materials utilized, research suggests that good literacy programs include emphasis on word identification, comprehension, writing, and reading study skills and strategies. Because learning to read is a long-term, developmental process, building a solid foundation in the essential reading abilities should be a goal of every education program. This chapter focuses on developing the various word-identification skills and strategies that skilled readers need.

Key Ideas

- Students need a variety of word-identification skills and strategies to arrive at the meaning of what they read.

- Basic sight vocabulary, phonics, structural analysis, and contextual analysis are word-identification skills and strategies that children should learn so that they can comprehend written language.

- Students must have opportunities to apply word-identification skills and strategies in meaningful authentic reading situations.

- Students need to develop flexibility in identifying words so that they can use all available cue systems to arrive at meaning.

- Each student needs to develop and continually expand a basic sight vocabulary.

- The major purpose of teaching word-identification skills and strategies is to provide tools for deriving meaning from reading.

- Word-identification skills and strategies are best taught through explicit/direct instruction.

WORD-IDENTIFICATION STRATEGIES

Learning to read involves the interrelationship of two broad areas: word identification and comprehension. **Word identification** is the process of decoding written symbols. Research has indicated that good readers are superior in identifying words (Snow, Burns, & Griffin, 1998). Comprehension involves understanding and interacting with the ideas expressed in text (or decoded text). Obviously, the ability to identify words is necessary for comprehension. Speaking to the importance of word identification in acquiring vocabulary and world knowledge and subsequently independent reading, Juel and Minden-Cupp (2000) stated:

> We know that children who learn to read early on read considerably more than their peers who are still struggling to decode, and through reading they learn things that increase their text comprehension. . . . Thus, the critical question is how can teachers help children gain enough skill to successfully enter this world so that, in a sense, children can read enough to become their own teachers? (p. 332)

To become proficient in identifying words, readers must employ a variety of word identification strategies. Beginning readers must continually expand their sight vocabularies. A **sight vocabulary** is made up of words that are recognized instantly. Many of these words are not spelled the way they sound (e.g., *to, know,* and *they*); these irregular words are taught using the **whole-word approach. Phonics** instruction consists of teaching letter-sound relationships to provide an approximate pronunciation, whereby the sound elicits a meaningful association of the word meaning in the text. Phonics is important because English is an alphabetic language in which there are consistent relationships between letters and sounds (even though all the letter-sound correspondences are not always predictable). Instruction in **structural analysis** looks at visual patterns and meaning that change as a result of adding inflectional endings (e.g., *-s, -ed, -ing,* and *-ly*), prefixes (e.g., *ex-* and *pre-*), and suffixes (e.g., *-ment* and *-ous*) and combining root words to form compounds (e.g., *sidewalk* and *playground*). Instruction in **contextual analysis** helps students figure out meanings of words by how they are used in the context of the text. Knowing words on sight, applying letter-sound relationships, recognizing word parts, and using context clues are important parts of decoding, that is arriving at the pronunciation of a word, given the printed letter representations (Fox, 2000).

When fostering word-identification skills, remember the following:

- Students who receive planned and explicit instruction on word-identification skills and strategies in small-group settings are better able to use the alphabetic code than students who do not receive such instruction. This instruction should guide students to develop a flexible, problem-solving attitude toward identifying words using the available cue systems—whole-word recognition, phonics, structural analysis, and context.
- Good readers are good decoders. Yet, word-identification instruction is not reading; it is providing tools to help understand the meaning of written language. Instruction must provide opportunities for students to apply their

Students must develop flexibility in identifying words so that they can use all available cue systems to determine meaning.

word-identification skills in meaningful or authentic reading situations (Duffy-Hester, 1999).
- While accuracy is important in identifying words, it is important to further develop **fluency** or the ability to decode a word with relative ease with no hesitation. This ability to be fluent is also called **automaticity** of word identification. Fluency is developed through an abundance of practice in real reading situations. Being a fluent reader allows the reader to focus on understanding ideas while reading, not pronouncing each individual word.

Integration in Authentic Reading Situations

With automatic decoding of printed symbols a goal of reading instruction and a prerequisite for students to be able to devote a large percentage of their attention to processing meaning, an important consideration is how word-identification or decoding skills (i.e., whole-word recognition, phonics, structural analysis, and context) are taught and practiced in our schools. Chapter 2 discussed the explicit/direct instructional approach and its effectiveness in teaching reading skills. The actual teaching and guided practice of a particular skill precedes independent practice of it. Meaningful practice should be provided to ensure transfer of a new skill to a variety of situations. This stage—independent practice—signals a change in instructional practice. With our new understandings of the reading process, particularly its interactive nature, the emphasis for independent practice has switched from a reliance on isolated worksheets to integrating independent practice in more authentic reading situations. Hiebert (1994) defined authentic literacy tasks as "ones in which reading and writing serve a function for children, activities such as enjoying a book or communicating an idea in a composition" (p. 391). Workbooks, computer software, and other types of practice materials (including games) are still used, but their use is supported through story content to ensure that students can apply the skill in recreational or independent reading.

In addition to explicit instruction with an abundance of practice in authentic situations, it is important that teachers monitor and help students apply new word-identification skills. Supporting this notion of monitoring and giving help in real reading situations to ensure proper learning and transfer of a new skill or strategy is recent research from CIERA. Taylor, Pearson, Clark, and Walpole (1999) identified effective practices of primary-grade teachers. Important practices not only included explicit teaching of phonics in small groups, but also the nature of the practice was unique. The researchers stated that "what really set the teachers in the most effective schools apart from their counterparts was their use of coaching children in how to apply the word identification skills they were learning in phonics while they were reading everyday texts" (p. 158). Effective instruction includes careful attention to both teaching and practice.

FIVE MAJOR INSTRUCTIONAL TASKS

In mastering the reading process, five instructional tasks represent the major thrust of beginning reading instruction. These instructional tasks help students to do the following:

1. Understand that reading is a language process.
2. Develop and expand sight vocabulary.
3. Learn to associate visual symbols with speech sounds.
4. Achieve fluency or automaticity in decoding.
5. Realize that reading is always a meaning-making process and that printed word symbols represent language.

Some instructional materials and activities overlook or give undue emphasis to one or two tasks. Students can learn much of what is taught through such an instructional approach, but in doing so they run the risk of developing attitudes and

Students must have opportunities to apply word-identification skills and strategies in meaningful, authentic reading situations.

habits harmful to the concept of reading. Beginning reading instruction that overemphasizes the mechanics and ignores comprehension is not meaningful.

Too much emphasis on word-identification skills can be detrimental. Students may develop a set of behaviors that neglects one or more aspects of the reading process. This may result in habits that handicap the reader in later development. For instance, a student may develop a habit of sounding out every word she encounters in reading. This means the student will be sounding out the same word the 10th, 20th, or even the 50th time she sees it in reading. The student has learned that reading is sounding out words, and this becomes a goal in all reading situations. On the other hand, overemphasis on learning whole words rather than other word-identification techniques forces the student to make fine visual discriminations when minimal sounding techniques would have made the task much easier. Knowledge of whole words combined with context and minimal sounding clues are more efficient than using one technique alone.

The premise underlying this discussion is that major instructional tasks are inseparable parts of one total instructional process. Students should learn to use all of the cue systems in written language—whole-word recognition, phonics, structure, and context—in learning to read and in achieving fluency in word identification. Thus, the major task of reading instruction is to blend these instructional components properly.

One thing that makes reading instruction complicated is that no blueprint spells out precisely where and how much instructional time and effort teachers should devote to each cue system. Second, no blueprint tells us which instructional techniques work best with individual learners. Understanding individual differences among learners offers the answers to these questions.

SIGHT VOCABULARY

Students increase their sight vocabulary directly through instructional procedures, independent reading, and activities, and indirectly through television, road signs, bulletin boards, carton labels, and the like. Obviously, the most important source of learning is meaningful reading situations, such as those provided by charts, teacher-written stories, predictable books, big books, and easy-to-read trade books. A skill of such significance to the total reading process should be taught effectively. Following are several justifications for learning words as wholes:

- A child who knows a number of words as whole words can better understand, see, and hear similarities among these known words and new words. Having a large sight vocabulary is invaluable in helping identify other words.
- When words are recognized instantly, analysis is minimal. The reader can focus on reading for meaning.
- Numerous high-frequency words (e.g., *was, the,* and *those*) should be learned as units simply because students see them over and over in any reading situation and they contribute significantly to using syntax as a means of getting meaning from reading.

There is a difference between learning certain frequently used words and learning to rely extensively on one word-identification strategy in beginning reading, whether that strategy is whole words, phonic analysis, or context. The normal pattern of learning dictates that the student develop a sight vocabulary or learn some words as wholes through the whole-word approach.

The normal student's experience with reading results in a constantly growing stock of words recognized as wholes. The student establishes automatic stimulus-response patterns for dozens of frequently used words, such as *that, with, be, are, and, was, it, the, in, to, than, you, they, said, when,* and *can.* A number of these structure words and other frequently used words must be learned to the point at which recognizing them is automatic (Samuels, 1994).

The most popular list of high-frequency sight words is the 220-service-word Dolch list. Developed by Edward Dolch (1948) more than 50 years ago, this list includes a high percentage of irregularly spelled words found in beginning reading materials. Palmer (1986) tested whether the Dolch list applies to today's reading materials. Her findings agree with previous studies, which concluded that the Dolch list remains relevant. The Dolch words constituted 60% of the vocabulary in four of five basal series passages analyzed. Other common words in a student's sight vocabulary include words of personal interest, words in content areas, and words in reading and language arts books from preschool.

The whole-word approach focuses on learning words as wholes rather than through any form of analysis. Irregular words (i.e., those not spelled the way they sound) are best taught through this approach in meaningful context. The most common words taught by this approach include basic service words, words of personal interest to students, words that appear regularly in students' first readers, and content-area words, such as geographical, scientific, and mathematical terms. However, regular words (i.e., those spelled the way they sound) can also be learned through this approach. This is especially true when teaching new words as a way of building background knowledge before reading. As will be discussed later in the chapter, teaching new words as whole words in conjunction with teaching a story is a main avenue for word learning. The following is a step-by-step procedure detailing the teaching of a word through the whole-word approach.

- Present the word visually (e.g., on a posterboard or chalkboard) and pronounce the word.
- Pronounce the word for the student again, making sure the student is looking at the word at the time you say the word.
- Use the word in written context familiar to the student. Ask the student to make up a sentence containing the word and write the sentence on the board. Ask the student to discuss the meaning of the sentence.
- Present the word again visually and ask the student to pronounce it.
- Provide an abundance of meaningful practice in authentic reading situations (e.g., experience stories, big books, and writing).

A major avenue for teaching whole words is the Guided Reading Plan for a story. A main component in the prereading step is building vocabulary. Most vocabulary words are taught through the whole-word approach. The practice component of the whole-word approach is built into this instructional method through the ensuing story to be read and the variety of practice activities associated with most reading programs. The activities systematically present, integrate, and repeat new vocabulary words in a variety of authentic reading situations. If a teacher is using trade books for instruction without an accompanying teacher's guide, the teacher must select the key vocabulary to be taught and design appropriate independent practice. Words selected for emphasis should be those that contribute to understanding the story to enable students to recognize, understand, and use the words.

Teachers can include the teaching of whole words in the literacy program in innumerable ways, including the following:

- In conjunction with literature (narrative and expository)
- Language-experience stories
- Reading aloud using big books and predictable books
- Written activities including using the typewriter and computer, writing diaries and journals, and writing creative stories and poems
- Oral-language activities and games
- Development of scrapbooks
- Various games and puzzles
- Reading of newspapers and magazines
- Reading aloud to students
- Independent reading
- Word walls with new sight words

Regardless of the means used to develop sight vocabulary, the application must be meaning-based, relating new vocabulary to prior knowledge and experience.

Names

One of the first printed words a child learns is his or her name. The practice of learning names in printed form provides the basis for teaching letter-sound relationships. Children also can begin to recognize names of common objects in the classroom that are labeled.

Instructional Activities

Reading Children's Names.   Tape each child's first name on the front of his or her desk. Use other words with it so that each name is within a meaningful context. Doing this will more likely result in processing print as it is related to comprehension.

Mary sits here.	Mike sits here.
Sarah sits here.	Sandy sits here.

Children learn the names of other children in meaningful context just as they learn the words in a sentence. Children also learn very quickly to recognize a number of names in printed form. Use chalkboard announcements involving students' names.

Hand out books   Water the plants
John and Helen   Jean and Billy

Labeling Objects. Print naming words in short phrases on separate oaktag cards to make naming labels and attach them to objects in the room.

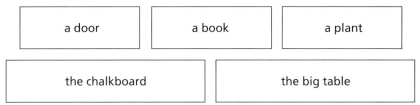

a door	a book	a plant

the chalkboard	the big table

Collect a number of pictures that depict objects or animals within the range of the children's experiential and conceptual backgrounds (photographs of the school and community are appropriate). Paste the pictures on cardboard and print the naming words in short phrases beneath them. Use these to generate language-experience stories.

a cat   a cow   a horse   a house

To add the kinesthetic mode to the words, duplicate a page of drawings and leave space for children to copy the names from models displayed on the chalk-tray. In the first experience, outline the printed words with dots. Have each child mark over the dots and "write" the words.

Later exercises may omit the dotted outlines. Have each child copy from the printed models on the chalktray, chalkboard, or bulletin board.

Writing Short Stories. As children begin to recognize many words, provide many opportunities for them to apply this skill in context. Write short, meaningful sentences that relate directly to the names of the children and objects in the classroom. Children are more likely to succeed because the concepts represented are meaningful to them. Combine the sentences to construct a story.

<u>Our Class</u>

John and Helen hand out books.

Jean and Billy water the plants.

Mary, Mike, and Sarah sit at the big table.

A plant, a book, and a door are in the room.

Develop similar application activities for objects and animal names. Read a short phrase and direct students to select from a list the words that make sense in the sentence. Write the words in the spaces and call on students to read each sentence. If several choices make sense, ask about the meaning of each word selected.

On his farm there is _____ _____ .

In the woods lives _____ _____ .

Sandy went to the farm in _____ _____ .

At the farm she saw _____ _____ .

a cat   a cow   a bear   a horse   a car

Language-experience stories enhance sight vocabulary in meaningful context (Heilman, 2002). Stimulate students to dictate group-experience stories by posing questions that encourage them to use words introduced in teacher-directed instruction. For example, ask "What do we do at school? What is in our classroom? What do we know about a cat, a cow, and a horse?" to stimulate students to compose stories that make meaningful application of sight-word instruction.

Picture Dictionaries

A picture dictionary is excellent for developing word meanings as well as a multitude of other skills, such as letter sounds and letter names.

Instructional Activities

Making a Picture Dictionary.   Secure a number of small pictures from workbooks, magazines, and the like. Have one page devoted to each letter of the alphabet. Let the students paste pictures of animals whose names begin with each letter on the appropriate pages. Then print a picture-naming word beneath each picture. (Note the use of **a** or **some** with the words to focus attention on them.) A partial **M-m** page follows.

a man

some milk

a mule

a monkey

a mop

some meat

Using a Picture Dictionary. Use the picture dictionary in determining other words that make sense in the sentences and stories. For example, ask students to find two words in their picture dictionaries that have the long **a** sound. Use examples and illustrations to model for students how to use the dictionary to identify and select words for their writing activities.

Reporters' Questions

Instruction on and practice with reporter's questions *(Who? What? Where? When? Why?* and *How?)* help children learn some important terms used in reading instructions and in following directions. Each experience with these important words helps students learn them as sight words.

Instructional Activity

Using Reporters' Questions. Write the words **who, what, where, when, why,** and **how** on the chalkboard. Say the words (making sure each student is thinking about the word as it is pronounced), and point to each word as you say it. Use the chalkboard, an overhead projector, or duplicated materials to present materials similar to the following.

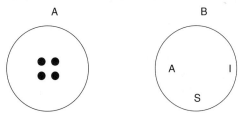

Direct students' attention to the written context for each of the materials. Encourage discussion and write their responses next to each question.

Circle A

<u>How</u> many dots?	There are four dots.
<u>How</u> did you learn this?	We counted them.
<u>When</u> did you count them?	Just now!
<u>What</u> color are the dots?	They are black.
<u>Where</u> is the circle?	Around the dots!
<u>Why</u> is the circle around the dots?	So we could ask <u>how,</u> <u>what, when, where,</u> and <u>why</u> questions.

Circle B

<u>Where</u> are the letters?

<u>How</u> many letters are there?

<u>What</u> are the letters?

<u>What</u> is around the letters?

<u>Why</u> is it around the letters?

Position Words

The importance of teaching the meanings of certain crucial terms used in reading helps avoid unnecessary instructional problems. Students must understand the position words *in, on, above, below, over, under,* and the like.

Instructional Activity

Using Position Words.   Use a format similar to the following circle-square-table. Prepare cards on oaktag and put them on the chalktray or tape them on the chalkboard so all can see. Provide each participating student with three or four word cards. Each card should have the same position word printed on both sides. As children hold up the requested card, check for accuracy.

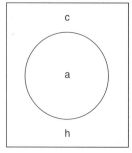
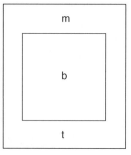
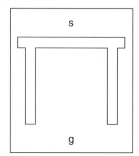

Read the following directions:

Hold up the word **in.** (pause) What letter is in the circle?

Hold up the word **over.** (pause) What letter is over the square?

Hold up the word **on.** (pause) What letter is on the table?

Continue using all of the word cards issued to the children. Each can be used more than once if desired—for example—**in** the circle, **in** the square, and **under** the circle, square, and table.

Words Often Confused

Students need varied and interesting practice on confusing words commonly found in their reading materials. This practice should help them recognize the words at sight.

 Instructional Activities

Presenting Individual Words.   Use the chalkboard, an overhead projector, or duplicated materials consisting of words frequently confused in early reading. Present these words in pairs and direct students' attention to the differences in letter combinations. Following are several examples.

their	every	when	four	which
there	very	were	for	with

Presenting Words in Sentences.   Present words in meaningful context, underlining the frequently used words. Paying heed to the underlined words, read the sentences in unison with the class or a group. Focus discussion on the meaning features of the words.

Their house is over there.

Everyone said it was very cold.

When were they taken there?

These sell four for a dollar.

Which boy will go with you?

Using Words in Meaningful Context.   Prepare a short text that contains blank spaces. Write the two words that will complete the sense of the context. Ask students to write the correct word in each blank space. You may have to read the sentences aloud for many of the students. Discuss both the meaning features and graphic features of their word choices.

(to, two)   1. The _____ boys were going _____ the store.

(for, four)   2. These boxes sell _____ _____ a dollar.

(think, thank)	3.	I _____ you should _____ him for it.
(very, every)	4.	_____ teacher was _____ busy.
(you, your)	5.	Have _____ had _____ dinner?

Scrambled Sentences

Practice in assembling scrambled sentences helps students acquire a basic sight vocabulary and a knowledge of terms used in reading instruction (such as *period* and *question mark*). Understanding basic sentence structure also aids in comprehension.

Instructional Activity

Arranging Words into Sentences.   On separate cards, print individual words from sentences used previously on the chalkboard. Present them in scrambled order, then ask students to arrange the words in proper order. Follow each sentence with a card bearing the proper punctuation. This is one of many ways to repeat frequently used words.

today	Tuesday	is	?	!	.

play	we	together

Classification

Classifying words is a good way to introduce and practice sight vocabulary. It is also a beginning step toward successful comprehension. Classifying interesting and concrete terms can motivate students to succeed.

Instructional Activities

Classifying Words.   Write classification words on the board and underline them. Point to each word and read it. Ask students to repeat each word after you pronounce it. On oaktag or cardboard, print each of the other words to be used in the exercise. Hold up one card at a time and call on a student to pronounce the word and to tell under which heading the word belongs.

animals	clothing	food	school
a dog	a hat	my milk	a book
a cat	the shoes	my cookies	a desk
a cow	a dress	my pie	the paper

As a variation, place a number of appropriate words in a box at the bottom of the page. Ask students to copy the words under the correct heading. They can work individually or in small groups. Focus discussion on why words were grouped together.

Using Classifications in Context. Develop further categories. Have students complete short sentences by selecting the words that make sense in context. See the following for an example.

Animals	Animal Sounds	Animal Homes
a dog	moos	the farm
a cow	barks	the house
a cat	oinks	the woods
a bear	meows	

_____ _____ barks.

_____ _____ is the home of a cow.

A dog _____.

On _____ _____ a cow moos.

A cat meows in _____ _____.

PHONICS

Importance of Phonic Instruction

Overwhelming research support exists for giving phonics a prominent role in a successful reading program (Hiebert, Pearson, Taylor, Richardson, & Paris, 1998; Snow et al., 1998). Emphasizing the importance of sounds in our language and of knowing sound–symbol relationships in becoming a skillful reader, Adams and Henry (1997) stated, "Research has now taught us that people's knowledge of phonology—of the pronunciations of words—is the nexus of the reading system" (p. 427). The International

Inclusion Strategies

Kinesthetic-Tactile Reinforcement of Sight Words

All students learning the various word identification skills need additional practice to ensure mastery. Many exceptional students profit from a more multisensory approach to learning. Besides the many authentic tasks (e.g., applying a new skill in reading or writing a story), games, cooperative activities, computer software, commercial skills books, and various kits for practicing word-identification skills, teachers may develop a kinesthetic-tactile (movement-touching) technique or game for reinforcement as part of a lesson. This technique enables the reader to use four sensory modalities in the process of learning words. For example, you might obtain a cookie sheet and a small amount of white sand. After teaching certain vocabulary words through the whole-word approach, you can have a student spell the word in the sand as he or she is saying it. After the student prints the word in the sand, it can be retraced several times as it is pronounced. This provides a multisensory approach as the student uses the kinesthetic and tactile modes of learning in addition to the auditory-visual modes. The student sees the word (visual), hears the word (auditory), traces the word with a finger (kinesthetic), and feels the word as it is traced (tactile). As the teacher, you can easily shake the cookie sheet to smooth out the sand for the next student. A variation of this multisensory technique is to use cut-out letters made of sandpaper. Students can spell words and trace each word with an increased tactile sensory input.

Reading Association (1997) released a position statement on phonics. The statement, "The Role of Phonics in Reading Instruction," lists three basic assertions:

- The teaching of phonics is an important aspect of beginning reading instruction.
- Classroom teachers in the primary grades do value and do teach phonics as part of their programs.
- Phonics instruction, to be effective in promoting independence in reading, must be embedded in the context of a total reading/language arts program.

Likewise, the National Reading Panel (2000) released a major report on scientific research-based reading instruction. The panel found that successful readers must be taught phonemic awareness skills, phonic skills, reading fluency, and comprehension. In addition, CIERA (1998) put forth 10 research-based principles for improving children's reading achievement. Two of the 10 principles highlighted letter-name knowledge and phonemic awareness as the most powerful predictors of success in reading and systematic or explicit word-identification instruction and practice as part of successful primary-level instruction.

Phonic instruction consists of teaching letter-sound relationships so that the learner can identify new words in print. Because English is alphabetic in that written words represent a collection of speech sounds, phonic instruction is crucial in helping beginning readers understand how our language works (Adams & Henry, 1997;

Samuels, 1994). Beginning readers inevitably encounter many words they do not recognize. By applying knowledge of letter-sound relationships in combination with available context clues and understanding that printed language must make sense, students can better comprehend what they read. Most likely, a written word that puzzles a student is one he or she has spoken or heard many times, so applying letter-sound relationships determines the pronunciation or yields an approximate pronunciation.

A purpose of phonic instruction is to teach the beginning reader that printed letters and letter combinations represent speech sounds heard in words. The sounds heard in words are quite different from sounds heard in isolation. In the sentence "The cat ran after the mice," the written word *cat* blends three phonemes just as they are in the oral word. But readers should not produce three syllables: *kuh-ah-tuh* (cat). Phonics instruction should teach the learner to blend the sounds that the printed letters represent when encountering a new word. Blending permits a child to determine whether or not the word is in his or her speaking or listening vocabulary and whether it makes sense in context. Phonic instruction should teach the learner to use all available cue systems in combination with letter-sound relationships to identify words and comprehend written text, giving primary attention to word meanings and comprehension. Too much emphasis on using letter-sound relationships to identify isolated words will cause the learner to think these relationships constitute reading. Phonic instruction should stress that reading is a meaning-making process and provide extensive practice in authentic tasks.

Tasks in Phonics

Phonics involves a series of tasks taken together. Phonics teaching materials include a number of techniques common to all approaches. They may differ in the sequence in which skills are introduced, the emphasis on learning rules, the number of steps taught, and the degree of phonic instruction included in beginning reading. The major phonics tasks include the following:

- Discriminating speech sounds in words
- Using written letters to represent the speech sounds
- Using the sound represented by a letter or letters in a known word to unlock the pronunciation of unknown words in which these particular letters occur
- Identifying sounds of consonants in initial and final positions
- Blending consonants
- Identifying special consonant digraphs (such as *th, ch, she,* and *wh*)
- Discerning short and long vowel sounds
- Distinguishing double vowels, vowel digraphs, and diphthongs
- Identifying vowels followed by *r*
- Identifying the effect of a final *e*
- Discerning the sounds of *y*.

All of the preceding tasks are not equally important in learning to read, and each should not receive the same amount of instructional time. They are simply the framework, because some include many specific elements.

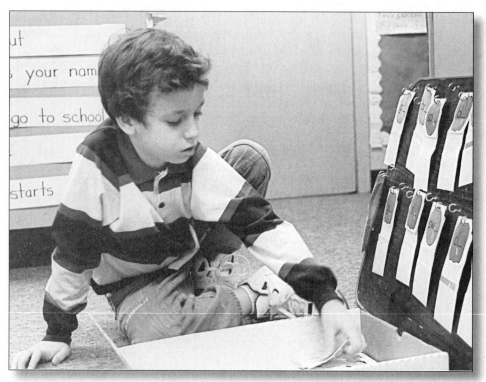

Phonic instruction improves children's ability to identify words.

A necessary prerequisite for and at the same time a powerful predictor of success in beginning reading is **phonemic awareness** (Snow et al., 1998). Richgels, Poremba, and McGee (1996) define this term and discuss its importance:

> Phonemic awareness is *conscious* attention to phonemes, which are the units of sound that speakers and listeners *unconsciously* combine and contrast to produce and perceive words in spoken language. For example, in English, the phonemes /d/, /i/, and /p/ are combined to make the word *dip,* and the /d/ and /t/ phonemes are contrasted when distinguishing the words *dip* and *tip.* Children must go beyond such unconscious use of phonemes when they learn to read and write. Conscious attention to phonemes is involved when they isolate sounds in words during invented spelling or use the sounds associated with letters to identify words and recognize word families. (p. 633)

Direct instruction lessons and activities that focus on phonemes, including adding and subtracting new sounds to words, blending phonemes into words, separating phonemes within words, and analyzing words by sounds in meaningful and authentic materials, promote this ability. In addition, this phonemic awareness instruction needs to be structured and planned (Yopp & Yopp, 2000).

The actual learning of phonics as it relates to reading usually begins early in the preschool years. The child learns the sound of a word like *mommy* and can easily differentiate it from similar-sounding words. He may have a pet kitty and a playmate Kathy. The child can differentiate if asked "Where is Kathy?" even though the kitty is also present.

Phonic instruction begins when an adult talks with an infant, thus providing the child with a model. A child who associates sounds with objects and does not confuse words that are very similar—such as *mommy, money, monkey,* and *maybe*—is mastering auditory discrimination, which is important for phonic analysis in the reading process. The later tasks in learning phonics depend on mastery of this basic language function. Beginning reading instruction in the school should build on the child's previous language experiences. In reading, students must discriminate among written word symbols and learn that these symbols represent the speech sounds of words they speak and understand.

Phonic Instruction

While a variety of specific techniques can help students learn the relationships between letters and speech sounds, the main approach is the analytic (or implicit) approach. Regardless of the approach, however, teachers should remember that (1) an important goal of phonic instruction is the approximate, not exact, pronunciation of words, (2) letter-sound correspondences are best communicated through direct/ explicit instruction, and (3) phonic instruction should include an abundance of practice in contextual reading situations.

The last two points highlight the importance of mastering automatic word-identification skills. Without explicit instruction and meaningful practice to the point of overlearning and automaticity, students are less likely to understand and interact with the ideas in the text.

Juel and Minden-Cupp (2000) conducted research on the characteristics of successful first-grade classrooms. Children entering first grade with low reading skills achieved the greatest success with the implementation of the following four practices:

1. Teachers modeled word recognition strategies by (a) chunking of words into component units such as syllables, onset/rimes, or finding little words in big ones; (b) sounding and blending individual phonemes; and (c) considering known letter-sounds and what makes contextual sense.
2. Children were encouraged to finger point to words as text was read.
3. Children used manipulable materials to actively compare and contrast words (e.g., pocket charts for sorting picture cards by sound and word cards by spelling pattern).
4. Instruction groups were small with lesson plans designed to meet the specific needs of each child within that group. (p. 334)

Teaching Methods

There are a multitude of teaching techniques in the area of phonics. Basically, instruction can be termed analytic or synthetic.

Analytic phonics teaches letter-sound relationship by referring to words already known to identify a particular phonic element. This approach begins by having students learn a certain number of words by the whole-word approach, after which they examine the relationships that exist among the phonic elements. Using this approach, there are two basic ways of teaching a skill lesson: *inductive,* in which the teacher begins by giving examples illustrating a generalization and guiding the children to a conclusion; and *deductive,* in which children are told the generalization and then asked for examples to verify it.

Examples of the inductive approach include the following:

- It is assumed that children know the words (e.g., *ball, bat,* and *bundle*) or the words are taught through the whole-word approach.
- The teacher asks the children what is alike about the words and leads the children to discover that the words contain the letter *b,* which represents the /b/ sound.
- Other words with the sound of /b/ are solicited.
- Words used are presented in written context.
- Practice exercises are given using the words in context.

Examples of the deductive approach include the following:

- The words (e.g., *ball, bat,* and *bundle*) are listed on the board. The words are in the children's listening–speaking vocabulary).
- The teacher tells the children that all the words begin with the letter *b* and represents the /b/ sound as in *big.*
- Other words are solicited with the sound of /b/.
- Words are presented in written context.
- Practice exercises are given using the words in context.

The inductive approach is generally preferred over the deductive approach, although this decision rests with the teacher, as some children respond better to the deductive method.

Synthetic phonics begins with direct instruction of phonic elements, beginning with letters of the alphabet, followed by syllables, then monosyllabic words through polysyllabic words, then phrases, and finally whole sentences. Once children learn the sounds represented by the letters, they blend the parts of the words together to form a known word. Synthetic phonics includes the following three variations of sound blending: (1) letter by letter *(b-a-t),* (2) the initial consonant is sounded and the rest of the word is added as a word family *(b-at),* and (3) the initial consonant and vowel are sounded together and the final consonant is added *(ba-t).*

The analytic approach to phonics is more widely used today. Keep in mind, however, that the difference between analytic and synthetic is one of initial emphasis (whole-word versus letter-sounds first). Emphasis must be evaluated in terms of successful teacher implementation of a particular method and learner preference. Auditory blending is a crucial skill in the analytic approach, as well as in the synthetic approach, because a youngster must be able to divide an unknown word into syllables or structural elements, attempt pronunciation of the smaller units, and, finally, blend the units together. Certainly both approaches can be effective. Baer (1999) recommends using both synthetic and analytic approaches to phonics instruction.

Another approach to identifying words that has received considerable attention is to teach word patterns called word families, phonograms, rhyming parts, or onset–rimes (Treiman, 1985). This focus is different from giving attention to individual letters and sounds or patterns of letters. With onset-rimes, the consonant sound /s/ that comes before the vowel sound in a syllable is the onset and the vowel sound and consonants coming after it are referred to as rime. The rime or phonogram is the part of a one-syllable word that begins with a vowel. For example, the underlined parts of the following words are phonograms or rimes: cake, hat, flag, law, park, and rain. When teaching phonograms or word families to students, an effective technique is to apply consonant substitution until the students can identify the unfamiliar word. For example, by showing the known words *cake* and *make,* the students can figure out the pronunciation of the unknown word *wake.* In this technique, the teacher does not have to directly teach the sounds of the vowels as the word family or phonogram will naturally indicate the appropriate sound.

Explicit/Direct Teaching of Phonics

The most beneficial teaching method of phonics (whether you use an analytic or synthetic approach) is explicit/direct instruction. As stated in Chapter 2, skills are best taught and learned through the explicit/direct instructional approach. In this approach, the teacher gives direct, step-by-step explanations of a particular skill or strategy. Viewing this approach from an interactive viewpoint in the reading process, it also emphasizes the "when" and "why" of using various skills and strategies. The process of explicit/direct instruction includes the following steps:

Stage one: planning

1. Area of needed reading instruction
2. Intended learning outcome
3. Past learning

Stage two: teaching

4. Building background
5. Teacher-directed instruction, modeling, and guided practice
6. Independent student practice
7. Ongoing diagnosis
8. Modifying instruction (Rupley & Blair, 1988)

In the planning stage, the teacher (1) selects the desired area of reading instruction appropriate to students' needs, (2) identifies specific learning outcomes and appropriate instructional features reflecting assessment information, and (3) determines areas of related past learning from assessment information. The first phase in teaching a skill or strategy is to review past learnings with students and to motivate them to participate in the lesson. The second phase is to explain formally, model, and/or demonstrate the goal of the lesson for students. Easy, concrete examples based on students' experiential backgrounds are most suitable for the actual instructional activities. This phase also includes guided or supervised practice of the particular skill or strategy. At this point, the teacher walks the students through an individual or group activity to make sure they all understand the skill or strategy and when and why they are to use it. In the next phase, independent practice, students are expected to complete an activity on their own to apply the skill and strategy in a real reading or authentic situation. Next, ongoing diagnosis focuses on assessing students' progress to ensure mastery of the intended goal. Last, in the modifying instruction phase, the teacher responds to his or her own monitoring of instruction and ongoing assessment procedures. Figure 5.1 provides an example of an explicit/direct instruction lesson on a word-identification skill.

• Area of Needed Reading Instruction

Understanding of the vowel diphthongs *oi* and *oy*.

• Intended Learning Outcome

Given a series of words containing the vowel combinations *oi* and *oy,* students will be able to pronounce the words correctly.

• Past Learning

Students know the vowel sounds (long and short).
Students know vowel principles.

• Building Background

Review with students the vowel principle that helps them pronounce the words *heat* and *boat.* Remind students that when you discussed this principle, you reminded them that it did not hold true all of the time. Tell them that today they will learn two vowel combinations that do not follow the double vowel principle.

• Teacher-directed Instruction, Modeling, and Guided Practice

On the board write two lists of known words that contain the *oi* and *oy* vowel combination. For example:

oil	toy
soil	boy
boil	joy

Figure 5.1   Explicit/Direct instruction lesson.

Ask students to pronounce the words. Next ask: How many vowels are there in each word? What usually happens when there are two vowels together in a word? Do you hear the sound of the first vowel in *oil* and *toy?* Tell students that *oi* and *oy* are special vowel combinations that usually stand for the sound heard at the beginning of *oil.* Isolate the sound of *oi* for students. Solicit other words that have this sound. Lead students to the conclusion that *oi* and *oy* represent the vowel sound found in the word *oil.* Present a new list of real and nonsense words containing the vowel combinations *oi* and *oy.* Make sure they can pronounce the words correctly.

• Independent Student Practice

Write the following words on the chalkboard and ask students to fill in the sentence blanks with the correct words. After they finish, read the sentences aloud to check mastery of *oi* and *oy* combinations.

soil	enjoy
boy	moisture
coin	toy
noise	poison

The plastic airplane was his favorite _____.

The _____ is dry and needs to be watered.

The insects were killed with _____.

That 1923 dime is a rare _____.

I hope you will _____ the picnic.

The _____ in the air caused rain.

The _____ in the yellow shirt threw the ball.

The neighbors next door make a lot of _____.

• Ongoing Diagnosis

Read with each student individually during the silent reading section of a directed reading activity. Note the student's application of the vowel combination of *oy* and *oi* and decide if further direct instruction and/or practice is necessary.

• Modifying Instruction

The independent student practice can be simplified by using pictures representing the words that students are to select to complete the sentences. Write the naming words beneath each picture to emphasize the written text that represents the pictures. Another modification is to write a choice of words beneath the blank and have students select the one that makes sense to complete the sentence. For example:

The plastic airplane was his favorite _____.

toy   enjoy   soil

This can be made easier by giving the students only two words from which to select.

The difficulty level can be increased by providing several choices that make sense in each sentence; have students identify all words that would meaningfully complete the sentences.

Figure 5.1   (continued)

Source: From *Teaching Reading: Diagnosis, Direct Instruction, and Practice,* Second Edition, by W. H. Rupley & T. R. Blair, 1990, Upper Saddle River, NJ: Merrill/Prentice Hall. Copyright 1990 by Pearson Education. Reprinted by permission of Pearson Education, Inc., Upper Saddle River, NJ 07458.

The following instructional activities can be used to supplement a literacy program based on students' interaction with meaningful language. Reading and writing activities based on real-life experiences are invaluable.

Consonant sounds

Some instructional materials used in beginning literacy advocate that the teaching of the letter-sounds start with consonants because one of the most important clues to the sounds of vowels comes from consonants that follow vowels. A consonant-vowel-consonant pattern usually results in a short vowel sound, as in *cat, den,* and *can.* The same is true if the vowel is followed by two consonants (e.g., *cattle, dentist,* and *canvas*). Starting from the premise that children have learned to recognize a few words at sight—which for illustrative purposes we will assume include the words *be, back,* and *ball*—they are ready to associate the sound of /b/ in these words with the written symbol *b.*

Instructional Activities

Introducing Initial Consonants.   Print an uppercase **B** on the chalkboard and say, "Today we will learn all about the letter **B.** Next to the uppercase **B,** I will print a lowercase **b.** This uppercase **B** is also called a capital **B.** Now I am going to write   Bb
some words that begin with lowercase **b.**"

Write **be, back,** and **ball** on the chalkboard. Point to each word   be
and pronounce it. Stress the initial sound of **b** without distorting it. Di-   back
rect students to look at each word as it is pronounced. Ask, "Who can
give us another word that begins with the sound heard in the words?"   ball
Answer, "Yes, **bear, boat,** and **big.** We write **Bobby** with a capital **B**   bear
because it is somebody's name."
    When a number of examples have been given, ask, "What sound do   boat
we hear at the beginning of each of these words?" Continue, "That's
right, they all begin with the sound of *b*—*be, back, ball, bear, boat, big,*   big
and *Bobby.*" Point to each word as it is pronounced. Note that in no in-   Bobby
stance were the children asked to sound the letter *b* in isolation.

Applying Initial Consonants.   To provide for immediate meaningful application of the sound represented by the letter *b* and ways that initial consonants combined with context can provide clues for word identification, write sentences such as the following on the board.

B_____ put the b_____ in the water.
We will b_____ coming b_____ to class after lunch.

Announce, "You all have done well telling me words that begin with the **b** sound. Look carefully at each word on the board as I say it. Each word begins with the letter **b** and the sound of **b.** I am going to read a sentence for you two times that has two words missing. The missing words begin with the letter **b** and the **b** sound." Point to the blanks and the letter **b.** "Listen and watch carefully as I read this sentence one time." Point to the first sentence and move your hand left to right under the words as you read each sentence to the children. "Now, I want each of you to listen and watch carefully as I read the sentence again. Tell me which of the words from our list makes sense in the context." Point to the list and read aloud each word as you point. Read each sentence, asking a student for a word from the list that makes sense in each blank. Write each response in the appropriate blank.

Engage all students in instruction by asking them if the word choices sound like something they would say. Ask if they could draw a picture of what is happening. Tell them why their choices are either correct (make sense) or incorrect.

Both of the preceding activities for teaching letter-sound association possess features of effective reading instruction. Specifically, these features include the following:

- Relating new learnings (letter-sound association) to past learnings (sight words).
- Asking literal-level questions such as, "Who can give other words beginning with the sound represented by *b?*" and "Does the sentence make sense?"
- Using direct instruction.
- Moving in small, related instructional steps.
- Providing for immediate application of skills in meaningful reading situations.
- Rewarding students' efforts and thinking, not just the correctness of responses.

In addition to the group work just described, you can begin to make the transition to student use and application by giving each child an opportunity to practice and apply the concept. Applications can be done in the group setting by using meaningful text that is similar to the earlier examples. Read the text several times as students follow along. Have them select and discuss their word choices for each blank. Monitor their performance closely to ensure that they are successful.

Most of these kinds of activities provide no opportunity to apply auditory discrimination skills in meaningful context and are intended to be supplementary. Application is extremely important, and the teacher must provide for it.

Instructional Activities

Identifying Objects. In a row of pictures such as the following, ask each student to mark the objects whose names begin with the same sound as the name of the object in the picture on the extreme left.

Matching Pictures and Words.   Show the picture of an object and follow it by four words, none of which names the picture but one or more of which begin with the same sound as the name of the pictured object. Ask students to draw a circle around the boxes or words that begin with the same sound. For example:

	house	baby	cup	bath

Show a picture of a familiar object along with the word represented by the object in the picture. The example shown here is a bell. Let the children see the letter **b** and hear the sound **b** represents. Then ask them to mark all the other words in a supplied list that begin with the same sound.

bell

be   play
lake   boat
book

Identifying Sounds in Words.   Show a series of boxes, each containing three words. Pronounce one of the words and direct students to underline the word pronounced. They need not know all of the words as sight words, provided they are familiar with the initial sound of each. In the following example, you could pronounce the italicized words.

1	2	3	4	5
call	*tell*	hill	*may*	hat
bank	sell	fill	pay	show
play	fell	*bill*	say	*bat*

Matching Words.   In columns, present words, some of which begin with the same sound and the same letter. Ask students to draw a line from the word in column A to the word in column B that begins with the same sound. For example:

A	**B**		**A**	**B**
me	be		big	did
ball	said		dog	but
sail	make		car	call

An important skill to learn is substituting known letter-sounds in unknown words. Assume the children know the words *take* and *make*, then they encounter the unknown word *rake*. They should be able to combine the *r* sound that they know from words like *run, rain,* and *ride* with the sound of *ake* in *take*. By this process, they unlock the new word (Yopp, 1992).

In beginning reading, it is common to teach a number of monosyllabic words containing frequently used phonograms. Practically all workbooks use these word families to teach new words. Work on the substitution of initial consonants parallels early levels of most basal series. Moving through early levels, the child sees words such as *came, fame, same, name,* and *game* and words containing other common phonograms. Each of these words contains a familiar, often recurring, phonogram. Students should not receive isolated drills on these word endings. Nevertheless, students can understand a number of important words independently when they know some sight words containing commonly used letter combinations and can substitute initial letter-sounds.

Instructional Activities

Using Pictures to Teach Letter-Sound Combinations. Use pictures in teaching letter-sound substitutions. The pictures should present words that are part of students' experiential and conceptual backgrounds. In the following examples, some children may perceive the hen as a chicken. Direct students to name the picture, listen to the first sound in the picture name, and write the letter that represents this sound in the blank. Do the first two with them to make sure they understand what they are to do.

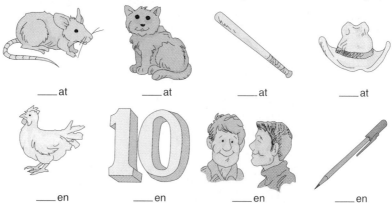

    ___at   ___at   ___at   ___at

    ___en   ___en   ___en   ___en

Applying Letter-Sound Substitution Skills in Meaningful Sentence Context. By applying such skills in context, students begin to understand that phonics is a tool for getting meaning. You can use sentences such as the following in a group setting to allow students to apply their skills. Such instruction builds on past learnings to enhance students' chances of success. Note that many of the words used for learning the sound represented by **b** are found in these sentences.

Bobby has a _____ pet _____ .

fat	cat
bat	hat
hat	mat

The _____ will be back at _____ o'clock.

pen	ten
men	hen
ten	pen

Bill took his _____, _____, and _____ to the baseball game.

hat	ball	cat
rat	fall	bat
fat	call	sat

Some teachers prefer to teach a particular consonant sound at the ends of words at the same time that they deal with it as an initial sound. Other teachers work through the initial sounds and then work on single consonant sounds at the ends of words. Either procedure teaches students to notice visually and aurally the final consonants in short words. They know words such as **men, log, pen, bold,** and **leg** and the sounds of letters, including **t.** They are then asked to substitute at the end of these words the sound presented by **t** to get **met, lot, pet, bolt,** and **let.**

Simple consonant blends

To avoid confusion in dealing with many words that children will discover early in the literacy process, you must focus their attention on more than the initial consonant. Consonant blends fall into two classes: simple two-letter consonant blends, and a smaller group of three-letter blends.

The 24 two- and three-letter simple blends may be divided into three major groups on the basis of a common letter:

1. Those that begin with *s: sc, sk, sm, sn, sp, st, sw,* and *str*
2. Those that conclude with *l: bl, cl, fl, gl, pl, sl,* and *spl*
3. Those that conclude with *r: br, cr, dr, fr, gr, pr, tr, scr, spr,* and *str*

The preceding groups are not intended to suggest a particular order in which blends should be taught. A logical sequence would probably be determined by the vocabulary found in the instructional materials actually used in beginning reading.

Teachers and early readers differ according to when they deal with blends, which they teach/learn first, and how rapidly they cover the blends. Most materials suggest teaching initial blends before blends and special consonant sounds at the ends of words (as in *rest, nest, best, bark,* and *mark*). Although teaching consonant blends can take numerous approaches, the objectives of all methods are to lead the student to:

- See the printed letters involved.
- Understand that in every instance the letter sounds combine into a blended sound.
- Discriminate auditorily among the sounds of individual letters and blends, as in *dug, rug, drug* and *sold, cold, scold.*

Any procedure for teaching initial consonant sounds can help teach each of the different consonant blends.

Instructional Activities

Identifying Blends in Object Names. Secure a number of pictures of familiar objects whose names begin with a blend. Show the pictures one at a time and have students write or say the blended letters. (They are not to simply name the picture.) Examples are **skate, train, bridge, plate, grapes, sled, frog, clock, star, blanket, snake, store, plow, clown, swing,** and **school.**

Adding Letters. In step 1, list words on the chalkboard that begin with **p** to which **s** can be added as a first letter to form the blend **sp.** Pronounce these words with students.

In step 2, write the **sp**-blend word to the right of each original word. Have students note the visual pattern of **sp** at the beginning of each word. Guide them in pronouncing the two words in each pair in rapid succession and in noting the blended sound in the second word in each pair (such as **pot—spot, pin—spin,** and **pill—spill**).

Step 1	Step 2
pot	spot
pin	spin
pill	spill
peak	speak
pool	spool
poke	spoke
park	spark

Following is a variation of the previous activity. Instruct the students to add a letter such as **c, g, p** or **t** in front of each of the letter groups to pronounce a consonant blend. Circle the letters that blend.

_____ reat	_____ roud	_____ rain	_____ rop
_____ reek	_____ rail	_____ rice	_____ ruly
_____ rint	_____ reen	_____ row	_____ rize
_____ rip	_____ rack	_____ ree	_____ rand

Identifying Blends in Sentences. Prepare and duplicate sentences containing a number of blends. Have students underline each blend. For example:

The black crow flew away from the tree.
Pretty bright flowers grew near the bridge.
What is the price of the green dress in the store window?
We will rest when we reach the coast about dusk.

Use Reading Clues in Teaching Initial Blends. Instruct the students, "Write the blend that spells the word that fits the clue" Examples:

We use our _____ _____ain to think.

Apples and pears are _____ _____uits we eat.

We put our nose to a rose to _____ _____ell it.

A _____ _____amp is needed to mail a letter.

Consonant digraphs

A digraph is a combination of two letters that when pronounced result in one speech sound. This sound is not a simple blend of the two letters. Some digraphs have more than one sound (e.g., *ch* = *k* in *character*, *sh* in *chiffon*, and *ch* in *church*). The techniques used in teaching consonants and simple blends and the activities for teaching *ch* and *sh* that follow apply in teaching other digraphs.

Instructional Activities

Identifying Digraphs.   Place words beginning with **ch** on the board and direct students' attention to these initial letters. Pronounce each word, making sure students listen to the sound of **ch** in each word and look at the word at the same time you pronounce it. When pronouncing each word, emphasize but do not distort the **ch** sound.

    Have students pronounce each word as you point to it. Point to words randomly to encourage maximum attention. Ask students to provide other words that begin with the **ch** sound heard in **chair, child,** and **chance.** Write these on the board beneath the original words.

chair
child
chance
chick
chill
chose

Contrasting Single Consonants and Digraphs.   Contrast single initial consonant sounds and initial digraph sounds in words. Write the words shown in column A on the chalkboard and pronounce these words with students. Next, write the words in column B, pointing out the visual pattern **sh** at the beginning of each word. Have students pronounce each pair of words (such as **hip—ship**) to contrast the differential initial sounds. Use the procedure outlined earlier with other words that begin with **s** or **sh.** As students contrast the initial sound in each pair of words, they note the visual pattern (**s—sh**) and hear the initial sounds these letters represent.

    Use reading clues to introduce and teach initial digraphs. Read the clue and then ask students to spell the word by using one of the digraphs provided in parentheses. Discuss how the letters chosen determine the meaning of a word in context.

A	B
hip	ship
hop	shop
hot	shot
hark	shark
hare	share
harp	sharp
sell	shell
sort	short
sip	ship
save	shave
self	shelf
sock	shock

used in bread _____ _____eat (wh, ch)   not open _____ _____ut (th, sh)
find on seashore _____ _____ell (sh, th)   largest in ocean _____ _____ale (th, wh)
can sit on it _____ _____air (sh, ch)   not fat _____ _____in (wh, th)
never do it! _____ _____eat (th, ch)   sun can do it _____ _____ine (wh, sh)
use your head _____ _____ink (sh, th)   must be round _____ _____eel(wh, th)

Supplying Digraphs.   Read the clue, then ask students to spell the word by adding a digraph. Examples:

Part of your leg that rhymes with chin: _____ _____in
Doesn't cost much: _____ _____eap

At a later time, you may need to teach that *ch* = *k* as in *chorus, chemistry, chrome,* and *character,* and that *ch* = *sh* as in *chauffeur, chamois, chef,* and *Chicago.* Other frequently seen digraphs include *sh, wh, th, gh, ng,* and *ph.* The sounds of these letter combinations are as follows:

- *Sh* is the sound heard in *shoe, shop, shell, short, wish,* and *fish.*
- *Wh* sounds like *hw* in *when—hw*en, *wheel—hw*eel, and *which—hw*ich. When *wh* is followed by *o,* the *w* is silent as in *whole—h*ole, *whose—h*ooz and *whom—h*oom.
- *Th* has two sounds. When voiced, it sounds like *th* in *th*em, *th*ere, *th*ey, and wi*th.* Voiceless, it sounds like *th* in *th*in, *th*ree, *th*row, and wid*th.*
- *Gh* can have the sound of *f* in lau*gh,* tou*gh,* and cou*gh.* It can be silent as in ni*gh*t, bou*gh,* ei*gh*t, and thou*gh*t.
- *Ng* sounds as in sa*ng,* wi*ng,* so*ng,* and ru*ng.*
- *Ph* usually sounds as *f* in *ph*one, ne*ph*ew, and gra*ph.*

Vowel sounds

Difficulties exist in teaching vowel phoneme–grapheme relationships because numerous vowel phonemes exist, but only a limited number of letters and letter combinations represent these phonemes. However, a majority of these difficulties are easily taken care of as students learn the various vowel generalizations and use this knowledge in their reading and writing. The teacher should provide guidance, and most students learn phonic analysis more quickly with guidance that leads to insights. Requiring rote memorization of a myriad of generalizations hinders some students' understanding of the relationships between the generalizations and their reading. Children may become so preoccupied with learning the generalizations that they miss the application. On the other hand, verbalizing a generalization often helps learning.

Short vowel sounds

Techniques for teaching letter-sound relationships are unlimited. Each illustration presented deals with only one vowel-letter sound, because all of the other vowel sounds can be taught in the same manner, simply by changing the stimulus words. Practically any lesson can be presented using the chalkboard, an overhead projector, language-experience stories, recipes, big books, and so forth. The following activities illustrate the importance of teaching students to blend sounds represented by letters and letter combinations without distortion. Blending is an extremely important, yet often neglected, area in many reading programs.

Instructional Activities

Visual and Auditory Association Illustrated Using Short e.   Select a few easy words that have been used previously and contain the vowel pattern being taught. Write these words in a column and pronounce each word with students. Have them note the vowel letter in the middle of the word and emphasize the sound it represents, for example, the **e** in **met, set,** and **pet.**

The following material may constitute different presentations on different days. Column A contains a pattern of CVC words, column B contains mixed patterns, and column C contains longer words. The sounds represented by these vowels in CVC words are highly regular. This allows you to structure learning around tasks in which students can experience success. Once students have learned such CVC pattern words, you can introduce the other CVC patterns that are less regular.

A	B	C
met	leg	desk
set	men	bell
pet	bed	dress
bet	pep	sled
let	wet	best
jet	hen	help

Experiencing great success with one pattern of CVC words should enable students to succeed with mixed patterns. Instruction can then focus on longer words. Thus, you build instruction in small, related steps.

For the following activity, instruct the students, "In the blank, write a word that makes sense in each sentence. Choose the word from the right-hand column."

I like to _____ a cat.	met
Bobby _____ me that he could ring the bell.	set
Bill _____ me sail the ship.	let
	bet
	pet

The _____ let me play in the big boat.	leg
The cat fell off of the boat and got _____.	men
Bob took a nap in _____.	bed
	hen
	wet
Bill had to _____ Bobby pull the _____ up the hill.	desk
They are _____ pals and like to play in the snow.	bell
Mary put her book on her _____ at school.	sled
	best
	help

Provide opportunities for application of each skill in meaningful context for each area of instruction. Use meaningful examples appropriate to children's needs and capabilities and build on previous learning.

Instructional Activities

Contrasting Short Vowel Sounds in Words. In step 1, write a column of identical initial and final consonants, leaving a blank space for adding a vowel letter. In step 2, insert a vowel letter to complete the first word, and then in step 3, call on a student to name the word. Continue using a different vowel letter for each blank space. In step 4, when the column is complete, have students read the words in rapid succession to contrast the vowel sounds. In step 5, present the words in meaningful context, omitting the vowel letter. Call on each student to provide a vowel for the word that makes sense in the sentence.

Step 1	b____g	Step 2	(i)	Step 3	big
	b____g	(insert	(e)	(children	beg
	b____g	vowel)	(u)	name	bug
	b____g		(a)	word)	bag

Step 4
(pronounce the
series of words
in rapid succession)

Step 5   Mark has a b____g pet.
Mark has a b____g for a pet.
Mark has a b____g b____g in a b____g.
A dog will b____g for food.

Other stimulus patterns are b**u**d, b**a**d, and b**e**d; p**a**n, p**u**n, p**i**n, and p**e**n; p**a**t, p**e**t, p**i**t, and p**o**t; and h**u**t, h**i**t, h**o**t, and h**a**t.

Working with Final Phonograms. Use pictures in teaching final phonograms. Have students name the picture, then blend the initial letter (shown beneath the picture) with each of the phonograms at the right of the picture. Focus students' attention first on naming the picture and then selecting the final phonogram. Finally, have the students write the correct letter pattern in the blank spaces to complete the word. If they experience difficulties, have them say each phonogram (such as /at/, /ot/, and

/ut/) and then blend the initial letter (/c/) with each. Again, be sure that students can recognize each picture and name it. The pictures of the well and the cot may not be in all students' experiential and conceptual backgrounds.

c _ _	p _ _	t _ _
at	en	op
ot	an	ip
ut	in	ap

w _ _ _	d _ _ _	l _ _ _
ill	ock	ack
all	uck	ock
ell	eck	ick

Long vowel sounds

Generalizations covering vowel letter-sound relationships are numerous; however, many of these do not apply to a large number of letter patterns. Therefore, separate teaching procedures are cited for two adjacent vowels (*ea, ai, ee,* and *oa* patterns) and final *e* words.

Two adjacent vowels representing a single sound are referred to as vowel digraphs (f*ee*t, b*oa*t, s*ai*l, m*ea*n). One of the more widely quoted generalizations relates to vowel digraphs: "When two vowels come together the first vowel usually represents a long sound and the second is not sounded, or when two vowels come together, the first vowel does the talking, the second goes walking." Two-vowel combinations have about as many exceptions to this rule as instances in which it applies. For the specific vowel combinations of *ee, oa, ea,* and *ai,* it holds much more frequently.

Instructional Activities

Contrasting Single-Double Vowel Patterns. Prepare lists of words in which column A has a single vowel (m**e**t) and column B is identical except for an added vowel (m**ea**t).

Ask students to read the first word under column A and listen for the short vowel sound. Then ask them to read the first word under column B, note the two-vowel pattern, and listen for the long vowel sound. As a final step, have them read each pair in rapid succession to note the contrasting vowel sound (such as m**e**t–m**ea**t and l**e**d–l**ea**d).

A	B		A	B		A	B
e	ea		a	ai		e	ee
met	meat		man	main		fed	feed
led	lead		lad	laid		met	meet

men	mean	pal	pail	pep	peep
bed	bead	ran	rain	bet	beet
stem	steam	bat	bait	wed	weed
set	seat	plan	plain	step	steep

Prepare similar word lists using the **o—oa, e—ea,** and **a—ai** patterns.

Provide opportunities for application by using sentences such as the following. Focus on selecting words that make sense in the sentence:

The _____ ate _____ for dinner.
    (man, main)   (meat, met)
Bobby put the _____ in the _____.
          (bait, bat)   (pal, pail)
The _____ had to _____ on the _____.
    (men, mean)   (step, steep)   (weed, wed)

Instructional Activities

The Effect of Final e.   Write a column of CVC words on the chalkboard, each of which contains the medial vowel **a** (step 1). As you pronounce these words, have students tell which vowel sound they hear in the word **(a).** Explain that you will change each word by adding the letter **e** at the end.

Step 1	Step 2
can	cane
hat	hate
mad	made
pal	pale
rat	rate
plan	plane

Print the words shown in step 2. As you pronounce these words, have students note the **a_____e** pattern and tell the vowel sound they hear in each of the words **(ā).**

Have students explain what vowel sound they hear in words with two vowels when one is a final **e.** Restate their explanations: "In many short words showing two vowels, a final **e** is not sounded while the first vowel has its long sound." Introduce the following word pairs for other final **e** series: **bit—bite, pin—pine, hid—hide, kit—kite, rid—ride, slid—slide, not—note, hop—hope, rod—rode,** and **rob—robe.**

Prepare an exercise for either chalkboard presentation or independent seat-work. List CVC words, some of which can be changed to another word by adding a final **e.** Have students read the stimulus word and determine if adding the letter **e** makes a known word. Make sure they ask themselves if the word they are making sounds like a word they have heard before. Make sure each child understands the task by completing some examples in a group. Name the word (if an oral exercise) or ask students to write the word in the space provided. For example, if the word can be changed into another word by adding a final **e,** write the new word on the line provided. If adding an **e** does not make a word, leave the line blank.

can _____   hid _____

rat _____   sob ___*___

top _____*_____	mad _____
plan _____	bit _____
kit _____	not _____
hop _____	tap _____
cat _____*_____	rob _____
cut _____	big* _____
*spaces left blank	

Long vowel sounds at the end of short words

Two generalizations cover single vowels at the end of words: "If a word has only one vowel that ends the word, the vowel sound usually is long" and "If a word has no other vowel and ends with *y*, the letter *y* serves as a vowel and is pronounced as long *i*." These generalizations apply in a limited number of high-frequency words and can be taught at the chalkboard, using columns of words. Utilize activities similar to those discussed throughout the earlier sections.

be	by	try	go
me	my	sky	no
he	cry	fly	so
we	why	fry	ho
she	dry	shy	yo-yo

Vowels affected by particular consonants

The long and short vowel sounds are by far the most important vowel clues in helping determine the pronunciation of words. In addition, other vowel patterns should be explained, even though they may be of less importance in phonic analysis. When a vowel precedes *r*, the sound of that vowel is affected by the *r*. Usually a blend results, which is neither the long nor the short sound of the vowel (as in *car, curl, fir, for,* and *park*). When the vowel *a* is followed by *l* or *w*, the resulting sound is a blend (as in *yawn, tall, awful, talcum, awning,* and *ball*).

Although a number of words contain a vowel followed by *r*, it is debatable whether this particular letter-sound combination causes beginning readers much trouble. That is, if children master the long and short vowel relationships, they are not likely to experience serious trouble with vowels followed by *r*. Undoubtedly, many successful readers are unaware of the difference between the vowel sounds in the words *can* and *car*.

Diphthongs

Diphthongs are two adjacent vowels, each of which is sounded, such as the *ou* in *house*, *oi* in *oil*, *oy* in *boy*, *ow* in *how* (but not the *ow* in *blow, grow,* or *throw,* where the sound is long *o*). Teaching diphthongs is probably not of major importance in the total phonics program. A number of words that are learned as sight words contain these sounds, and certain words can serve as keys to help students hear the sounds (such as *house, oil, boy,* and *how*).

Summary of vowel generalizations

The following generalizations govern vowel pronunciation:

- A single vowel followed by a consonant in a word or syllable usually has the short sound (as in *can* or *cancel*).
- A single vowel that concludes a word or syllable usually has the long sound (as in *me, ti-ger,* and *lo-co-mo-tive*).
- In the vowel digraphs *oa, ea, ee, ai,* and *ay,* the first vowel is usually long and the second is silent (as in *coat, reap, head, wait,* and *play*). The digraphs *oo, au,* and *ew* form a single sound that is not the long sound of the first vowel (as in *food, good, haul,* and *few*).
- In words containing two vowels, one of which is final *e,* the final *e* is usually silent and the preceding vowel is long.
- Single vowels followed by *r* usually result in a blended sound (as in *fir, car, burn,* and *fur*). The vowel *a* followed by *l* or *w* usually results in a blended sound (as in *yawn, tall, claw,* and *awful*).
- The letter *y* at the end of words containing no other vowel has the letter sound of *i* (as in *my, try, sky,* and *shy*).
- Diphthongs are two-vowel combinations in which both vowels contribute to the speech sound (as in *house, boy,* and *cow*).

Word Sorts

A highly successful technique for increasing word-identification abilities is to encourage students individually and in small groups to learn words by arranging them in a word sort. A **word sort** is a method of sorting word cards (or picture cards) into various categories. The categories can be on the basis of similar word meanings or word characteristics (such as letter patterns). If teachers establish the categories to be sorted, it is called a closed sort; if the students establish the categories, it is labeled an open sort. This method is usually most successful as a natural extension of students keeping a word bank of new and personal words from their reading stories and from various instructional activities. Manila file folders or boxes are easy to use as storage areas for word sorts. Through interaction with their peers, students not only have multiple opportunities to see and hear the words by sorting them into categories, but also as a result they are able to commit the words sorted to an automatic or mastery level. The following is the procedure for a short-vowel word sort developed by Bear, Invernizzi, Templeton, and Johnston (2000):

1. Make a collection of word cards to model the sort on a tabletop, pocket chart, or overhead projector.

2. Model the sort with a group of students. Begin by laying down a well-known word as a header for each vowel. Read each word and isolate the vowel by saying something like this: "Here is the word *cap*. Listen, *cap, ap, a*. We will listen for other words that have the same vowel sound in the middle." Repeat for each category.

3. Pick up a new word such as *fast* and say something like this: "I am going to put this word under *cap*. Listen, *cap, fast*." Continue to model one or two words in each category, reading each new word and comparing it to the header.

4. Invite students to try sorting next. Correct any errors made during the first sort. The final sort might look something like this:

cap	*pig*	*hot*
fast	ship	stop
camp	fish	lock
hat	sit	shop
mad	hill	job
trap	him	not

5. After all the words have been sorted, lead a discussion to focus your students' attention on the common features in each word: "How are the words in each column alike?"

6. Reread the words in each column and then lead the students in sorting a second time. Any mistakes should be left until the end and checked by reading down the columns.

7. Students should be given their own set of words to sort at their seats, with partners, or for homework.

8. Appropriate follow-up routines include buddy sorting, writing sorts, word hunts, games, and so on. Since it is easy to simply sort the words visually by attending to the vowel letters, the buddy sort described in Chapter 4 is particularly important as a follow-up activity. Model this sound sort first in the group and then let partners work together. One partner reads each word aloud while the other partner indicates where it goes without seeing the word.*

DEVELOPING FLUENCY

The ability to understand and react to ideas expressed in writing is the essence of reading. However, this is only possible if students can first decode words; that is, if students can accurately pronounce and interpret written symbols. Successful readers are superior in decoding or word identification. The key idea is that successful readers are not just good decoders but that they do it quickly. This ability to decode words quickly or automatically with little conscious effort is known as automaticity or fluency (Samuels, 1997). By being automatic in identifying words, the reader is allowed more time to think about and react to the meaning of what they are read-

*Words Their Way: Word Study for Phonics, Vocabulary, and Spelling Instruction, 2/e (p. 158) by Bear/ Invernizzi et al., © 2000. Reprinted by permission of Prentice-Hall, Inc., Upper Saddle River, NJ.

ing. In other words, the reader can devote almost total attention to the comprehension process. Without automaticity or fluency, the student must devote considerable time and effort in figuring out unfamiliar, individual words and simply cannot devote their undivided attention to the meaning of the whole text. How does a student show fluency? A student shows fluency by reading orally with expression and with comprehension. The direct implication for reading teachers is twofold: (1) accuracy in decoding or word identification is achieved by directly or explicitly teaching skills and strategies to students and (2) interesting and varied practice in a variety of contexts must be provided to develop fluent reading.

PRACTICAL TECHNIQUES FOR DEVELOPING AUTOMATICITY OR FLUENCY

In addition to the initial teaching of a decoding ability, interesting and varied practice is necessary to achieve automaticity or fluency. Listed below are three practical strategies for promoting automaticity or fluency with your students.

Repeated Readings

This highly successful method simply requires a student to reread a section of text several times until a high degree of fluency is achieved—whether it is a part of a story, a content-area book, magazine, or newspaper article. The rationale for this method is that many students never have the opportunity to develop their reading fluency and repeated readings allow students to experience this feeling (which allows students more time to think about and comprehend what they are reading). The following suggested steps are provided by Samuels (1997) for using this method:

1. Select passages from 50 to 200 words from stories students are reading.
2. Read the passage to them, followed by the students reading the passage several times until the passage is read fluently (you may want to tape-record the first and last oral reading so the students can hear the difference).
3. Discuss with students how athletes develop their skills by practicing basic movements over and over until they become automatic and how repeated reading is similar in terms of practice.
4. Students can time themselves when reading a passage and make a graph showing improvement in reading times.

Phrase Reading

Phrase reading is an excellent strategy for promoting students' ability to read in idea units, to understand what they read, and to increase automaticity in word learning. Furthermore, phrase reading is helpful in reducing word-by-word reading, which is a major roadblock to successful silent reading. It is a good idea for students to practice reading in phrases by pausing slightly between each phrase. The basic steps in using phrase reading are:

- Select reading material that is on the student's easy or independent reading level.
- On a one-to-one basis, ask the student to read one paragraph or page aloud and tape-record this reading.
- Model for the student reading the paragraph or page in a word-by-word fashion and in meaningful phrases.
- Using a pencil (you may want to reproduce the text for ease of marking), divide the first two sentences into meaningful phrases; another method is to reproduce the reading material by typing it in phrases in a vertical column.
- Divide the rest of the sentences into meaningful phrases with both you and the student explaining how a sentence should be divided.
- Have the student read the text aloud in meaningful phrases two or three times; you may want to read the phrases aloud together with the student.
- Tape the last oral reading and compare the tape with the initial reading of the text.
- Discuss with the student the benefits of reading sentences in meaningful phrases as opposed to word-by-word reading.

Readers Theatre

Readers theatre (Sloyer, 1982) is an interpretative activity in which students practice and read a script aloud for others. Students bring characters to life through their intonation and inflection and at the same time increase their fluency and comprehension. The steps for using readers theatre are as follows:

1. Choose a narrative text on the student's instructional or independent reading level.
2. Read and discuss the story with the students.
3. Devise a script cooperatively with the students and choose parts.
4. Have students practice their script by themselves and with their peers to promote fluency of oral reading.
5. Rehearse the script as a group.
6. Perform the play script in front of the class or small group.
7. Review the performance with the students noting how well the performance went and discussing the key ideas in the story.

STRUCTURAL ANALYSIS

Structural-analysis instruction helps students identify words whose visual patterns change as a result of adding:

- Inflectional endings (such as *-s, -ed, -ing,* and *-ly*).

- Prefixes (such as *pre-, ex-,* and *un-*).
- Suffixes (such as *-able, -ment,* and *-ness*).
- Root-to-root compounds (such as *sidewalk, playground,* and *basketball*).

Structural-analysis skills allow students to focus on larger units of letter patterns within known words (Rupley & Blair, 1988). Obviously, use of some of these techniques relies on previous learning. For instance, a child who uses structural analysis in unlocking words with inflectional endings must recognize the root word (such as *help*) as a familiar unit or be able to sound out the root word, solve the ending (such as *-ing*), and blend the two *(helping)*. Later, this type of analysis should not be necessary, because the student perceives the word *helping* as one familiar unit.

In applying structural-analysis skills to solve unknown words, children do better if they recognize parts of words that they have studied. Instruction thus should build on what students have already mastered in reading. By building on students' prior learning, you can increase their attention to new learning, increase their chances of success with new learning, and diagnose their progress from one learning outcome to the next.

An important concept in structural analysis is syllabication. A syllable is a vowel or group of letters containing a vowel that is pronounced as a unit. Students' ability to determine the basic units of pronunciation (that is, syllables) supports effective word learning. **Syllabication** is included under structural analysis because it is the division of a word into its basic units of pronunciation. Phonic generalizations are applied to letters only after this division.

Students usually learn a number of one-syllable root words before they try to understand polysyllabic words. As they encounter long words, they learn that most prefixes and suffixes and some inflectional endings constitute syllables. During early experience with high-frequency affixes, students break words into parts and then combine the parts into the whole, such as *re-read-ing, pre-heat-ed, bi-week-ly,* and *dis-ap-pear-ance*. After many experiences, children reduce their reliance on this type of analysis and blend the parts into the whole more smoothly.

A series of pictures may help students develop the ability to combine syllables into words. The pictures presented should be familiar to students. They should either listen to the teacher's pronunciation of the picture's name or pronounce it themselves and indicate the number of syllables heard. Students may also clap out the number of syllables in words that the teacher pronounces.

A knowledge of vowel behavior within words is a major aid in breaking words into syllables, but the sounds of vowels and letter combinations are not as consistent as those of prefixes and suffixes. Nevertheless, many generalizations are useful. Although the following examples are not words, the letter combinations can be broken into syllables: *comration, ragmotex, obsebong,* and *fasnotel*. The likely syllabication is *com-ra-tion, rag-mo-tex, ob-se-bong,* and *fas-no-tel*. Most fluent readers would pronounce these nonsense words in substantially the same way. These readers probably would not recite rules to themselves before pronouncing these words, but they probably would be subconsciously influenced by rules they had learned.

Instructional Activities

Generalizing Two Consonants Between Vowels.   When you teach generalizations applicable to syllabication, provide a number of examples. Then lead students to see for themselves what happens. Out of this experience, they can develop rules. Starting with the question, "What usually happens when two consonants come between vowels?" place a number of words on the board. For example:

af ter	win dow	rab bit	let ter
gar den	can dy	din ner	sum mer
fas ter	pen cil	lit tle	cot ton

Work toward the generalization "When two consonants come between vowels, the syllable division comes between the consonants" or "One consonant goes with each vowel." Point out that this rule does not always hold, but that it is the best guess to make when trying to pronounce an unknown word. In the case of double consonants, there are few exceptions to the rule.

Generalizing One Consonant Between Vowels.   To teach what happens when one consonant comes between two vowels, place a list of known sight words on the board. For example:

be gin	fe ver	to tal	de cide
o ver	di rect	ti ger	me ter
fa tal	mo ment	pu pil	ho tel

Inflectional Endings

Inflectional endings include -s, -es, -ed, and -ing for verbs, -er and -est for adjectives and adverbs, and -ly for adverbs. Note that inflectional endings depend on context. Therefore, be sure to provide application exercises when you teach inflectional endings.

Instructional Activities

Adding -s, -ed, or -ing to Words.   Instruct students, "In the space provided, add **-s, -ed,** or **-ing** to the known word. Write each new word in the column, then read the words." Note that word endings are important features of syntax. Using one or two words with the new word being formed can heighten students' attention to syntax.

Known Word	-s	-ed	-ing
play	He _____	I _____	I am _____
look	He _____	I _____	She is _____
call	She _____	She _____	He is _____

flap	She	It _____	It is _____
wait	He	He _____	I am _____
rain	It	It _____	It is _____
work	She	I _____	They are _____

Adding -er, -est, or -ly to Words.   Instruct students, "In the space provided, add **-er, -est,** or **-ly** to the stimulus word. Then read each word."

Known Word	-er	-est	-ly
warm	_____	_____	_____
great	_____	_____	_____
high	_____	_____	_____
soft	_____	_____	_____
kind	_____	_____	_____

Using s Endings.   Present the known words **look, call, clap,** and **play,** and review them when **s** is added to the end. Do this on the chalkboard and direct students' attention to the written words.

A	B
I look	He looks
I call	He calls
I clap	She claps
I play	She plays

Direct them to look at sentences as you read each one aloud, pausing briefly when coming to a blank space, then reading the rest of the sentence. Using the words from list B, have the students orally give you a word that makes sense for each sentence. For example:

Bobby _____ in the yard.

The robin _____ his wings to fly.

The dog by the door _____ mean.

Bill _____ his dog to come in at night.

Choosing -er, -est, or -ly Endings.   Write clues using words that can take **-er, -est,** or **-ly** inflectional endings. Provide blanks at the right of the clues for the new words formed. Instruct students, "Read the clue. In the blank to the right, write a new word, adding the proper inflectional ending to the underlined word. The new word must fit the clue." For example:

Ending: **-er, -est, -ly**

Clue	New Word
1. sweeter than all others	_____
2. taller than all others	_____

3. in a quick manner   _____

4. works more hard than Bill   _____

5. in a quiet way   _____

6. with swift action   _____

Choosing -s Endings.   Provide application by using activities such as the following. Ask students to select the word that makes sense in each sentence.

play   1. He _____ ball with us.

plays   2. I _____ ball with him.

        3. They will _____ ball with us after school.

        4. She _____ a game with a bat and a ball.

work   1. Dad _____ at home on Saturday.

works   2. Mother _____ at school on Monday.

        3. Jan has to _____ at the game.

        4. The horse _____ on the farm.

Choosing -s, -er, -est, or -ly Endings.   Use sentences such as the following to provide further application of inflectional endings in meaningful context. Activities should build on what students have learned. Encourage them to think about whether their choices make sense in the sentences.

1. I like to _____ in the yard on _____ days.
          (play, plays)   (warm, warmer, warmest)

2. Today is the _____ day of the year.
      (warm, warmer, warmest)

3. This doll _____ like the _____ one in the store.
       (look, looks)   (soft, softest, softly)

Choosing Degrees of Comparison.   Use additional activities to point out how inflectional endings describe degrees of comparison. For example:

1. Mark is _____ than John. He is at the
       (high, higher, highest)
   _____ point on the ladder.
  (high, higher, highest)

2. This fur is the _____ fur of all.
       (soft, softer, softest)

3. Jane is a _____ person. She is _____ than
       (kind, kinder, kindest)   (kind, kinder, kindest)
  Fred, Bill, or Bob. She is the _____ person I know.
        (kind, kinder, kindest)

4. The _____ time I ever had was at the circus.

    (great, greater, greatest)

Prefixes and Suffixes

Prefixes are added at the beginnings of words to produce new words. Examples of prefixes include *pre-, ex-, un-, in-, dis-,* and *re-.* Suffixes are added at the ends of words to produce new words. Examples include *-able, -ment, -ness, -er, -or, -ful,* and *-ish.*

Instructional Activities

Adding Prefixes and Suffixes.   Using root words that take prefixes and suffixes, provide lists such as the following. Instruct the students, "In each blank space, add a prefix or suffix to make a word. For prefixes, use **in-, dis-,** or **re-.** For suffixes, use **-ment, -able,** or **-ness.**"

_____ agree	_____ disagree	_____ agree
_____ direct	_____ indirect	_____ direct
_____ fill	_____ refill	_____ fill

Choosing Suffixes.   Write clues using words that can take suffixes. Instruct students, "Read the clue. In the blank to the right, write a new word, adding the proper suffix to the underlined word. The new word must fit the clue." For example:

Suffixes: **-or, -less, -ful**

Clue	New Word
1. one who visits	_____
2. to be of help	_____
3. without end	_____
4. one who invents	_____
5. with hope	_____
6. without hope	_____
7. able to harm	_____
8. one who sails	_____

Suffixes: **-able, -ness, -ish, -er**

Clue	New Word
9. something that looks like	_____
10. can be washed	_____
11. one who paints	_____
12. having a fever	_____
13. thinking only of oneself	_____

14. being idle   _____
15. can be adjusted   _____
16. can be fixed   _____
17. one who fixes   _____
18. looking green   _____
19. someone who sings   _____
20. something that you can sing   _____

Upon completion of the clue activities, have students use the new words formed from the clues in their own sentences or stories. Write some of these on the chalkboard and use them for class discussion. As a group, discuss the meaning of the stories or sentences. Example sentences for clues 1 through 3 follow.

Uncle Frank was a <u>visitor</u> at our house.
The apple is the <u>sweetest</u> of all the apples we picked.
Our teacher is very <u>helpful.</u>
The road was <u>endless.</u>

Choosing Prefixes and Suffixes.   To help students apply their knowledge of prefixes and suffixes, use activities such as the following. Ask students to select the prefix or suffix to complete the underlined word so that the sentence makes sense.

1. I _agree_ with Dan that we should buy a dog.
2. I _____agree_____ with Dan that we should name the dog Spike.
   (in-, dis-, re-)
3. Dan and I are in _____disagree_____ about the name for our dog.
   (-ment, -able, -ness)
4. I guess I am a _____disagree_____ person.
   (-able, -ment, -ness)

1. Joe drank all of the water in the bottle.
2. He will _____fill_____ the bottle with water.
   (re-, in-, dis-)
3. The bottle is _____fill_____.
   (re-, in-, dis-) (-ment, -able, -ness)

Compound Words

Compound words are formed by combining root words. Examples include *sidewalk, playground,* and *basketball.*

Instructional Activities

Using the Same Word in a Number of Compound Words. Write three compound words for each group of words. To maximize success, begin with two words to combine. Then, as students experience success, increase the number of combinations. For example:

air	plane		_____	
book	case		_____	
door	way		_____	

air	plane	craft	port
_____		_____	_____
book	case	keeper	worm
_____		_____	_____
door	way	bell	mat
_____		_____	_____

Combining Words to Make Compounds. Present lists of words that students can combine to form meaningful compound words. For example:

A	B
shoe _____	ball
sun _____	light
basket _____	maker

Choosing Compound Words. Write three words in a row, only one of which is a compound. Tell students, "Each line contains one compound word. Underline the compound word and write it in the blank space at the end of the line." For example:

children	dancing	fireplace _____
someone	beaches	crawling _____
alike	mousetrap	puzzle _____
downpour	happily	permitted _____
autumn	mistake	handbag _____

Using Compounds in Sentences. Write sentences, leaving a blank for students to fill in a compound word. Instruct them, "Complete each sentence by writing a compound word in the blank space." Provide practice in a group setting to make sure each student understands the task. For example:

A player can hit a home run in a game of _____.

The teacher wrote on the _____ with a piece of chalk.

The front window in a car is the _____.

The mail carrier puts mail in our _____.

In addition to providing sentences, encourage students to suggest their own sentences that include compound words. If they have difficulty, provide them with a written list of compound words to use. Either write the sentences on the chalkboard or have students write them on a sheet of paper. Discuss each sentence and its meaning. Use the activity to write group-composed stories.

CONTEXTUAL ANALYSIS

Students can use contextual clues only when they can recognize or sound out most of the words in a sentence. Phonics is only one of many skills that can aid reading for meaning. For instance, when a student does not know the meaning of a word, arriving at its exact pronunciation through phonic analysis will not help. The following sentence contains an unknown symbol:

The man was attacked by a marbohem.

Everyone reading this page can sound out *mar-bo-hem*, but no one knows what attacked the man, since *marbohem* does not convey meaning to the reader. If other words are substituted for *marbohem*, some readers may still have trouble with the meaning, even though they can analyze the speech sounds in the words. For example:

The man was attacked by a pecarry.

The man was attacked by a freebooter.

The man was attacked by an iconoclast.

The man was attacked by a fusilier.

The man was attacked by a hypochondriac.

Contextual clues can help explain unknown words if the reader demands meaning. Using context plus a minimal amount of letter analysis of the beginning of the words is far better than context alone. This combination of clues is also better than intensively analyzing each word while ignoring the contextual setting of the unknown word.

In the following sentence the blank line represents an unknown word:

The boy waved good-bye as the train left the _____.

Even with a blank line substituting, most readers have no problem supplying the correct word. The task is even simpler with the first letter supplied:

The boy waved good-bye as the train left the s _____.

Other reading situations present more difficult problems, for example:

The girl waved good-bye to her _____.

Here, a number of possible word choices make sense: *friend, mother, sister, teacher, brother, parents, family, playmate, aunt, cousin, uncle,* and so forth. Select any word that makes sense and insert only its first letter in the blank space. Note how that initial letter eliminates many of the words that were possibilities.

The importance of combining skills becomes more obvious in larger contexts. In the first version of the following story, it is possible to get the sense of the story even if one is not sure of the identity of a number of the missing words.

> John and his cousin _____ started on their fishing trip. John said, "I have my trusty _____ pole, a _____ full of lunch, and a can of _____." After walking a long time, John said, "Not far from here there is a _____ across the stream. We can sit on the _____ and fish." When they started fishing, John said, "I'm not going to _____ from this _____ until I catch a _____ _____." Finally _____ said, "I am tired of sitting on the _____. I am going to take a walk along the _____." _____ had walked only a short way when he lost his _____ and fell into the stream. The water was not very deep, and he waded out. "Hey," said John, "You're lucky. You won't have to take a _____ when we get home."

This next version inserts the initial letter in each unknown word, which in all cases happens to be the letter *b*.

> John and his cousin B_____ started out on their fishing trip. John said, "I have my trusty b_____ pole, a b_____ full of lunch, and a can of b_____." After walking a long time, John said, "Not far from here there is a b_____ across the stream. We can sit on the b_____ and fish." When they started fishing, John said, "I'm not going to b_____ from this b_____ until I catch a b_____ b_____." Finally B_____ said, "I am tired of sitting on the b_____. I am going to take a walk along the b_____." B_____ had walked only a short way when he lost his b_____ and fell into the stream. The water was not very deep, and he waded out. "Hey," said John, "You're lucky. You won't have to take a b_____ when we get home."

(Words in order of their omission are **Bob, bamboo, bag, bait, bridge, bridge, budge, bridge, big bass, Bob, bridge, bank, Bob, balance,** and **bath.**)

Learning to read is very complicated. From the beginning, the learner who is attempting to identify unfamiliar words should look for and accept help from all available clues. The simultaneous use of all options helps simplify beginning reading. Occasionally, phonics is the only key to meaning that a student can utilize. More often than not, however, all of the word-identification skills—basic sight vocabulary, phonics, structural analysis, and contextual analysis—can be used together. Phonics should be used only when needed.

The two broad kinds of context clues are syntactic and semantic. The value of context clues lies not only in their ability to identify words by themselves but also in their ready application to whole-word learning, phonics, and structural analysis. As with the other decoding skills, students' ability to use context clues should be developed through both direct and informal instruction, with an abundance of practice in real reading situations. As we know, word learning is related to comprehension. Whether students are developing sight vocabularies or using phonics or structural analysis, they must have interesting, varied, and realistic practice with words in context. The use of context not only reflects the natural reading process, but also allows students to focus on meaning to aid them in determining whether the words make sense in context.

Syntactic Clues

The ordering of words in a sentence is syntax. Using an example presented earlier (The girl waved good-bye to her _____), knowledge of language helps us to determine that a person, place, or thing fits in the blank. This knowledge allows us to eliminate possibilities that do not make sense in this sentence.

When used in combination with phonics and structural analysis, **syntactic clues** enable students to figure out the meanings of unknown words. Syntactic clues include the following:

- *Structure words.* Noun markers (such as *my, this,* and *any*), verb markers (such as *am, are,* and *is*), clause markers (such as *now, if,* and *before*), and question indicators (such as *why, who,* and *which*) signal what is coming next. For example:
  - He took *my* brother to the game.
  - He *is* going to the game.
  - My brother will go to the game *if* he is home.
  - *Who* is going to the game?

- *Phrases.* A phrase may describe or refine a word. For example:
  - The boy *with the brown hair* is Mike.
  - The game *between the Reds and the Cubs* is sold out.

- *Language grammar.* Meaning patterns in language can indicate where certain words fit.
For example:
  - He took my *brother* (noun) to the game.
  - He *took* (verb) my brother to the game.
  - He took my brother to the game in a big, *shiny* (adjective) car.

- *Appositives.* An appositive is a word or words that explain the previous word. For example:
  - Jones, *the quarterback,* was injured on the first play.
  - Jubilation, *great excitement,* filled the stadium when the home team won.

Semantic Clues

Semantics refers to the reader's knowledge of word meanings and the reader's conceptual and experiential backgrounds in relation to comprehending what is read.

Although syntactic clues can help explain word meaning by allowing readers to limit their choices of meaning for unknown words, semantic clues provide them with more clues to word meaning.

If a related sentence or sentences either precede or follow a sentence, the additional contextual information can help indicate the meaning. Suppose that "The girl waved good-bye to her _____" is followed by "He waved back and wiped tears from his eyes as the train began to move." In this example, the word *he* tells you that the unknown word refers to a male.

A reader who makes the connection between the male referent and the initial letter pattern or patterns of an unknown word and the sounds represented can even better determine meaning. In "The girl waved good-bye to her f_____. He waved back and wiped tears from his eyes as the train began to move," the letter *f* further narrows down the possibilities.

Johnson and Pearson (1984) classified the major kinds of **semantic clues** available to readers. A modified listing of their categories follows. Again, recognize that for semantic clues to be used efficiently, the referent for the unknown word must be in the readers' experiential and conceptual backgrounds.

- *Definitions or explanations.* Difficult words that students encounter in their reading are often defined within the text. Words such as *is, are,* and *means* signal explanations.
  Herbivores are animals *that feed on green plants.*

- *Synonyms and antonyms.* In addition to using the unknown word, writers often use synonyms or antonyms.
  The *robust* rabbit loved to visit the garden. He was so *fat* he could hardly squeeze through the fence.

- *Figurative language.* Meanings of unknown words can be obtained from metaphors and similes used in relation to preceding and following text.
  It was raining *cats and dogs.* Several cars stalled in the flooded streets.

- *Summary statements.* Based on connected story information, the meaning of an unknown word may become known.
  Mark used to be a *stellar* basketball player. He could make shots from anywhere on the court. The crowd always cheered when their star player was introduced.

Contextual-Analysis Instruction

Ensuring application of word-identification skills in meaningful context allows students to develop an awareness of context for word meaning. Rather than repeating all of the earlier activities, following are a few examples.

Bobby put the b_____ in the water.

Bobby has a pet _____.

We use our _____ _____ ain (br) to think.

Clue: Used in bread: _____ eat.

(ch, wh)

Mark wants to learn how to _____.

(sale, sail)

Bill has a ball and a bat. The bat and ball c_____ in a set.

Dad will paint Bill's n_____ on the bat and ball in green paint.

Oil comes from _____ wells.

The _____ time I ever had was at the circus.

If you can wash something, then it is _____ able.

Joe drank all of the water in the bottle. Joe will re_____ the bottle with

water. The bottle is _____ fill _____.

A player hit a home run in the game of _____.

The front window in a car is the _____.

Dictionary Instruction

Using the dictionary is another important word-identification skill associated with reading instruction. The three major goals in dictionary instruction are (1) finding a particular word, (2) determining its pronunciation, and (3) selecting the correct meaning of the word in the context in which it is used.

Dictionary skills are often neglected, even though teachers acknowledge the value of these skills. This neglect may stem from a teacher's feeling of inadequacy about certain relatively difficult facets of dictionary use, such as diacritical markings or pronunciation keys. On the other hand, the teaching may fall short when dictionary skills are considered something extra rather than as an intrinsic part of literacy instruction.

Both teachers and pupils should use the dictionary as a source for word meanings, not as a form of rote drill or a penalty for making certain errors (Lehr, 1980). Certain knowledge is essential for successful use of the dictionary. This knowledge includes the following:

- Being aware of alphabetical order.
- Understanding that letters and combinations of letters have different sounds in different situations and that some letters are silent.
- Knowing that *y* at the end of most words is changed to *i* before adding *es* for plurals.
- Recognizing root words and the various inflected and derived forms of root words.
- Realizing that a word can have many different meanings.

Skill in using the dictionary paves the way for greater independence in reading because it does the following:

- Unlocks the sounds or pronunciations of words.
- Discloses new meanings of words that may be known in only one or a limited number of connotations.
- Confirms the spelling of a word when the reader can only approximate its correct spelling.
- Expands vocabulary through mastery of inflected and derived forms.

Teachers must refine and expand these skills as students move upward through the grades. The success that students feel and the utility they derive from dictionary usage can be most important factors in how they react to the dictionary as a tool for helping in all facets of communication. Students must realize that dictionary skills are needed throughout life; failure to master these skills can negatively influence their attitudes and learning development for many years to come.

Dictionary usage involves a number of developmental tasks. Educators generally agree on these tasks and the order in which they should be presented. The tasks include the following:

- Recognizing and differentiating letters.
- Associating letter names with letter symbols.
- Learning the letters of the alphabet in order.
- Arranging a number of words in alphabetical order by their initial letters.
- Extending the last skill to the second and third letters of words, eventually working through all letters of a word, if necessary.
- Developing facility in rapid, effective use of the dictionary, that is, knowing where letters (such as *h, p,* and *v*) fall in the dictionary, and opening the dictionary as near as possible to the word being studied.
- Developing the ability to use accent marks in arriving at word pronunciations.
- Learning to interpret the phonetic spellings used in the dictionary.
- Using the pronunciation key that appears on each double page of most dictionaries.
- Working out different pronunciations and meanings of words that are spelled alike.
- Determining which is the preferred pronunciation when several are given.
- Selecting the meaning that fits the context.
- Using the guide words found at the top of each page to tell at a glance if the page contains the word being sought.
- Using special sections of a dictionary intelligently (such as geographical terms and names, biographical data, and foreign words and phrases).

Although particular skills are characteristically taught at given grade levels, the individual student's skills should determine what is taught. Fortunately, dictionaries are available at all difficulty levels, from simple picture dictionaries to massive unabridged editions. The individual student's needs and abilities should dictate what type of dictionary to study.

SUMMARY

To become independent readers, students must learn to use a variety of word-identification skills and strategies. Sight vocabulary, phonics, structural analysis, and contextual analysis are the basic word-identification skills that enable readers to comprehend what they read. Competent and flexible readers do not rely heavily on any one skill; they use various clues in combination. In teaching word identification skills, remember the following principles:

- Students' language background should form the basis for word-identification instruction. Small, related instructional steps increase the likelihood that students will attend to the instruction and succeed. The teacher should closely monitor each student's progress.
- Explicit instruction should build on what children know and are successful with.
- Opportunities to apply word-identification skills in meaningful contexts should be part of all word-identification instruction.
- Contextual analysis should be integrated with all other word-identification instruction. By combining sight vocabulary, phonics, and structural analysis with context, children maximize their changes of determining meaning.
- Word-identification skills can be taught in a number of ways. Any technique that proves successful for a child is justifiable, provided that it does not inhibit later growth and the instructional approach is reasonably economical in time and effort expended.
- Students should not be taught to rely heavily on any one word-identification technique. Overemphasis on phonics causes children to sound out the same words hundreds of times and attempt to sound out words that do not lend themselves to letter-sound analysis, such as *once, knight, freight, some, one, eight, love, know, head, move, none, have,* and *laugh.*
- Students require varying amounts of instruction while they are learning word-identification skills. Assessment that reveals what a child knows and does not know is essential for good instruction. In the final analysis, the optimum amount of word-identification instruction for each individual is the minimum that he or she needs to become an independent reader.

YOUR POINT OF VIEW

Discussion Questions

1. Early reading instruction inevitably causes children to develop a mindset relative to reading. What reading mindset might children develop when they receive no opportunities to apply word-identification skills in meaningful contexts?
2. Is it possible to teach children to rely too much on any word-identification technique? Does learning to read involve the simultaneous application of all word-identification skills? Is each a part of a unitary process called reading?

3. How do mature readers differ from beginning readers in their use of word-identification strategies?
4. What is the optimum amount of any type of word-identification instruction?
5. What role does ongoing assessment play in word-identification instruction?

Take a Stand For or Against

1. The spelling patterns found in the English language constitute a major obstacle in learning to read English.
2. Teaching sight words, letter-sound analysis, and contextual analysis at the same time inevitably leads to confusion.
3. Since a student must learn word-identification skills before becoming an independent reader, these skills should be taught before reading for meaning is stressed.

Field-Based Assignments

1. Prepare a written lesson plan on a word identification skill and if possible teach the lesson to a small group of your peers or to actual children in the classroom you are visiting. Use the lesson format for explicit/direct instruction as described and illustrated in this chapter. Following the teaching of your lesson, respond to the following questions.

Did students understand the lesson objective?

Did students need additional explanation and practice?

Do I need to reteach a part of the lesson?

What did I learn today that would be of help in tomorrow's lesson?

2. Work individually with a student experiencing difficulties in decoding. Read a short story with the student, taking turns reading out loud. Note how the student decodes words as well as specific word-identification strengths and weaknesses. Prepare a short summary of your student's decoding abilities and list as many authentic practice opportunities or tasks to ensure mastery as you can (these practice activities would accompany your direct instruction lessons on the targeted areas). Use the following as a guide.

Reading level of material

Word-identification strengths

Specific areas needing improvement

Listing of possible authentic reading tasks or activities to ensure mastery

Portfolio Entry

Because of the widespread interest in both teaching students to decode words and using fine literature in the teaching of reading, a balanced literacy approach combining both emphases is being recommended by many experts. In your opinion, what are the possible negative effects of favoring one aspect over the other in the teaching of reading? Write a one-page reaction to this question.

BIBLIOGRAPHY

Adams, M. J. (1990). *Beginning to read: Thinking and learning about print.* Cambridge, MA: MIT Press.

Adams, M. J. (1994). Modeling the connections between word recognition and reading. In R. B. Rudell, M. R. Rudell, & H. Singer (Eds.), *Theoretical models and processes of reading* (4th ed., pp. 838–863). Newark, DE: International Reading Association.

Adams, M. J., & Henry, M. K. (1997). Myths and realities about words and literacy. *School Psychology Review, 26,* 425–436.

Baer, G. T. (1999). *Self-paced phonics* (2nd ed.). Upper Saddle River, NJ: Merrill/Prentice Hall.

Bear, D. R., Invernizzi, M., Templeton, S., & Johnston, F. (2000). *Words their way: Word study for phonics, vocabulary, and spelling instruction* (2nd ed.). Upper Saddle River, NJ: Merrill/Prentice Hall.

Dolch, E. W. (1948). *Problems in reading.* Champaign, IL: Garrard Press.

Duffy-Hester, A. M. (1999). Teaching struggling readers in elementary school classrooms: A review of classroom reading programs and principles for instruction. *The Reading Teacher, 52,* 480–495.

Fox, B. J. (2000). *Word identification strategies: Phonics from a new perspective* (2nd ed.). Upper Saddle River, NJ: Merrill/Prentice Hall.

Harris, T. L., & Hodges, R. E. (1995). *The literacy dictionary.* Newark, DE: International Reading Association.

Heilman, A. W. (2002). *Phonics in proper perspective* (9th ed.). Upper Saddle River, NJ: Merrill/Prentice Hall.

Hiebert, E. H. (1994). Becoming literate through authentic tasks: Evidence and adaptations. In R. B. Rudell, M. R. Rudell, & H. Singer (Eds.), *Theoretical models and processes of reading* (4th ed., pp. 391–411). Newark, DE: International Reading Association.

Hiebert, E. H., Pearson, P. D., Taylor, B. M., Richardson, V., & Paris, S. G. (1998). *Every child a reader: Applying reading research in the classroom.* Center for the Improvement of Early Reading Achievement (CIERA). Ann Arbor, MI: University of Michigan School of Education.

Johnson, D. D., & Pearson, P. D. (1984). *Teaching reading vocabulary* (2nd ed.). New York: Holt, Rinehart & Winston.

Juel, C., & Minden-Cupp, C. (2000). One down and 80,000 to go: Word recognition instruction in the primary grades. Center for the Improvement of Early Reading Achievement. *The Reading Teacher, 53,* 332–335.

Lehr, F. (1980). ERIC/RCS: Content reading instruction in the elementary school. *The Reading Teacher, 33,* 888–891.

National Reading Panel. (2000). National Reading Panel releases report on research-based approaches to reading instruction. Press release, http://www.nationalreadingpanel.org/Documents/pr_finalreport.htm.

Palmer, B. C. (1986). Is the Dolch list of 220 sight words still relevant? *Reading Improvement, 23,* 227–230.

Richgels, D. J., Poremba, K. J., & McGee, L. M. (1996). Kindergartners talk about print: Phonemic awareness in meaningful contexts. *The Reading Teacher, 49,* 632–642.

The Role of Phonics in Reading Instruction. (1997). A position statement of the International Reading Association, Newark, DE.

Rupley, W. H., & Blair, T. R. (1988). *Teaching reading: Diagnosis, direct instruction, and practice* (2nd ed.). Upper Saddle River, NJ: Merrill/Prentice Hall.

Samuels, S. J. (1997). The method of repeated readings. *The Reading Teacher, 50,* 376–381.

Samuels, S. J. (1994). Word recognition. In R. B. Rudell, M. R. Rudell, & H. Singer (Eds.), *Theoretical models and processes of reading* (4th ed., pp. 816–837). Newark, DE: International Reading Association.

Samuels, S. J. (1979). The method of repeated readings. *The Reading Teacher, 32,* 403–408.

Sloyer, S. (1982). *Readers theatre: Story dramatization in the classroom.* Urbana, IL: National Council of Teachers of English.

Snow, C. E., Burns, S., & Griffin, P. (1998). *Preventing reading difficulties in young children: Report of the Committee on the Prevention of Reading Difficulties in Young Children.* Washington, DC: National Academy Press.

Taylor, B. M., Pearson, P. D., Clark, K., & Walpole, S. (1999). Effective schools/accomplished teachers. *The Reading Teacher, 53,* 156–159.

Treiman, R. (1985). Onsets and rimes as units of spoken syllables: Evidence from children. *Journal of Experimental Psychology, 39,* 161–181.

Yopp, H. K. (1992). Developing phonemic awareness in young children. *The Reading Teacher, 45,* 696–707.

Yopp, H. K., & Yopp, R. H. (2000). Supporting phonemic awareness development in the classroom. *The Reading Teacher, 54,* 130–143.

6

Meaning Vocabulary

Chapter Outline

For the Reader

The relationship between vocabulary knowledge and reading comprehension is a strong one (Thompson, 1999). Vocabulary emphasis should be a major component of every reading program. Meaning vocabulary can be thought of as hooks for background knowledge, concepts about the world, integration of new learning with what is known, and representation of abstract understandings. Thus, the broader our vocabularies, the better able we are to interact with and understand text.

As you read this book, you probably encounter words that are either new to you or different in meaning from those with which you are familiar. You may figure out the meanings of these words by using context, series or a dictionary, or by asking someone. Yet questions about how best to teach and expand vocabulary are varied and much depends on the capabilities and interests of your students.

The importance of vocabulary in reading has long been a major concern of researchers. Some researchers believe that vocabulary cannot be directly taught because students encounter so many new words in their reading (Nagy & Herman, 1996). Other researchers believe that vocabulary instruction helps foster vocabulary development (Goerss, Beck, & McKeown, 1999) and that direct instruction can improve reading performance.

This chapter recognizes both viewpoints. It advocates explicit/direct instruction, wide reading, and language-building activities to reinforce and extend students' meaning vocabularies.

Key Ideas

- Associating experiences and concepts with words contributes significantly to children's vocabulary development.

- Vocabulary is a major component contributing to reading comprehension.

- Vocabulary evolution comes about through a rich and varied exposure to words in all forms of language interaction.

- Effective vocabulary instruction helps students establish relationships between words and meaning in a personal manner.

- Providing varied opportunities to encounter and use new words is a key component in promoting vocabulary growth.

- Engaging students in active discussion of new words is critical to promoting vocabulary growth.

- Semantic-features analysis can help students understand relationships among words and associate their background knowledge with new words.

VOCABULARY KNOWLEDGE AND READING

Students' word recognition capabilities, vocabulary growth, and comprehension development are essential parts of a balanced reading and writing program. Reading instruction that focuses on the growth of children's vocabulary results in enhancing their abilities to infer meanings and to better comprehend what they read (Rupley, Logan, & Nichols, 1999). Daneman (1991) clearly presented the relationship between vocabulary and reading comprehension and the mutual benefits that they share in promoting children's reading development. Vocabulary is partially an outcome of a reader's comprehension skills, and reading comprehension is partially an outcome of a reader's vocabulary knowledge. As students' vocabulary grows their ability to comprehend what they read grows also; furthermore, as their comprehension capabilities grow so do their abilities to learn the meaning of new words from context.

The words that readers know represent the concepts and information available to them to comprehend and understand what they read. Vocabulary knowledge supports the reader's text processing and interaction with the author, which in turn promote the formation and validation of concepts and new learning. The vocabulary and experiences of the author and the reader are woven together to form the fabric of learning, confirming, reasoning, experiencing, enjoying, and imagining.

Language Development and Word Meanings

The groundwork of word-meaning development is the continuous development of language ability. Readers and writers share meanings. We acquire meanings for words through direct experiences with people, places, objects, and events that create and refine meaning vocabulary. Vocabulary is also acquired through vicarious experiences, including interactive technology, pictures, films, filmstrips, reading, and writing (Blachowicz & Fisher, 1996).

Increasing one's vocabulary is much more than learning names to associate with experiences. Vocabulary knowledge closely reflects children's breadth of real-life and vicarious experiences. Students cannot comprehend and understand well without some knowledge of the concepts that are represented by the print. As noted by Rupley, Logan, and Nichols (1999), "Vocabulary is a shared component of reading and writing—it helps the author and the reader to comprehend through the shared meanings of words" (p. 337).

Vocabulary Growth

Students' knowledge of words can range from a simple level to a complex level. Word knowledge can be viewed as a "continuum from no knowledge, to a general sense, such as knowing that mendacious has a negative connotation; to narrow, context-bound knowledge; to having knowledge but not being able to access it quickly; to rich decontextualized knowledge of a word meaning" (Beck & McKeown, 1991, p. 272). A form of simple-level work knowledge is definitional. **Definitional knowledge** is word knowledge based upon a definition, such as coming from a dictonary, thesaurus, glossary, word bank, or other individuals. Often, however, definitions do not help a reader understand the contribution of an unknown word to meaning. To comprehend, a reader needs some idea not only of a word's meaning, but also of the ways the meaning contributes to the cohesiveness of the ideas or information represented. The simple level of word knowledge may also be contextual.

Contextual knowledge is word meaning derived from context, which can include a sentence, a passage, a discussion, or a picture (Watts, 1995). However, contextual clues have limitations, because using them requires some knowledge of the context and how the meaning of the words combine to facilitate author and reader interaction. Often using either sentences or short paragraphs as context for determining a word's meaning is inadequate because there is too little information for children to use their background knowledge to know or to infer the meaning of a word. Knowing a word at a simple level helps readers construct some meaning for what they read. However, as new words are encountered more frequently in text, frameworks and relationships are established that contribute to refining, extending, changing, and adding to children's meaning vocabularies.

Both definitional and contextual features of vocabulary instruction can be part of an effective program, but in isolation, they have limited potential in increasing students' word knowledge. However, combining definitional and contextual approaches does help students develop a meaning vocabulary.

Able readers integrate information as they read to construct meaning. If context is not enough to figure out the meaning of an unknown word, skilled readers use their language knowledge and word knowledge to help them infer meaning. However, knowing a word in its fullest sense goes beyond simply being able to define the word or get some gist of it from the context. Associating experiences and concepts with words contributes significantly to comprehension.

Vocabulary and Concept Development

Readers' experiential and conceptual backgrounds are extremely important in vocabulary development. Background experiences enable readers to develop, expand, and refine the concepts that words represent. Vocabulary knowledge is developmental and is related to background experiences. Tennyson and Cocchiarella (1986) note two phases in the learning of concepts. The first phase is the formation of concepts in relation to attributes (which they refer to as prototypes), making connections with existing concepts. The second phase is using procedural knowledge, which is "the classification skills of generalizing to and discriminating between newly encountered instances of associated concepts" (p. 44). In phase 1, individuals may undergeneralize or overgeneralize as a result of their limited experiences with the concept. This is often evident in young children when, for example, they call all large animals in a pasture "cows" and all liquids for drinking "milk" or "juice." In phase 2, individuals can distinguish between cows and horses and among various liquids for drinking. Vocabulary expands when the student has numerous opportunities to encounter new words and examples that are representative of the word in rich contextual settings. Individuals do not use restricted definitions of words as they engage in literacy activities, but construct meaning in terms of word meanings for the concepts that represent their background knowledge.

EXPLICIT VOCABULARY INSTRUCTION

Teaching vocabulary versus incidental learning of words through wide reading should not be viewed as competing philosophies. Many students may not benefit from incidental learning of word meanings, but do benefit from explicit instruction. Much of the criticism leveled at vocabulary teaching concerns practices in which students are not actively involved in the personal discussion of words, such as defining words using a dictionary and writing sentences for those words. Moreover, the numerous words that students learn through incidental activities call into question the effectiveness of teaching vocabulary. Any instructional practice must be called into question that fails to teach words so that students encounter the words in meaningful text and fails to immerse the students in vocabulary-rich activities. Teaching vocabulary within the context of real books and teaching words that are functionally important within a particular content area can promote vocabulary development (Zechmeister, Chronis, Cull, D'Anna, & Healy, 1995).

Vocabulary emphasis should include explicit instruction and appropriate practice in specific skills along with broad reading opportunities and other language activities. Vocabulary instruction is most effective when it relates new words or derivations of words to existing vocabulary and background knowledge. For example, Mary is a first grader who thinks that all animals are pets. She will have a difficult time with the concepts of farm animals and zoo animals. Sending her to a dictionary, listing words on the chalkboard, or telling her would be ineffective in teaching the vocabulary words associated with milk cows, farm life, or zoo animals.

Inclusion Strategies

Expanding Children's Meaning Vocabularies

Vocabulary emphasis should include explicit instruction and appropriate practice in specific skills along with the opportunity for wide reading, writing, and other language activities. We are not recommending that practice activities be unrelated to authentic reading and writing opportunities. Rather, some students—particularly those having difficulty in literacy learning—need to practice vocabulary. As noted earlier, context does not guarantee word learning, because students must be able to recognize enough of the words to construct meaning and to use context effectively as a clue to word meaning. Wide reading and writing will provide students with many opportunities to learn new words in contextual settings; however, direct teaching of vocabulary has a place.

1. Choose words for vocabulary instruction that come from contextual reading (literary and content texts) to be done in the classroom.
2. Use direct vocabulary instruction to take advantage of the many forms (such as mental pictures, kinesthetic associations, smells, and tastes) used to store word knowledge. These forms can assist children in using independent strategies for learning and retaining the meanings of words.
3. Build a conceptual base for word learning. Use analogies, language features, characteristics, sets (e.g., a horse is an animal), and relationships to known words (such as associating newspapers, magazines, and catalogs as information sources that can be read or looked at selectively) to trigger students' background knowledge of concepts and to relate new words to that which is known.
4. Provide many varied opportunities for students to engage in language-based activities (e.g., recreational reading, writing, field trips, interactive software, and creative dramatics). These should be the primary means of vocabulary learning. Teachers foster the learning of new words that are not taught directly by providing opportunities for students to use new words in the classroom in their speaking, listening, reading, and writing.
5. Generate learning of new words by helping students develop strategies associated with structural features of words (combining roots and adding prefixes and suffixes). (Blachowicz & Fisher, 1996)

Imagine the possible comprehension problems Mary might experience when encountering such words as *Hereford, hedgehog,* or *grizzly bear.*

Concept Wheel/Circle

The concept wheel/circle presented in Figure 6.1 is an instructional procedure that builds on students' background knowledge and stimulates brainstorming and

Figure 6.1   A concept wheel for the word *migrate*.

Source: From W. H. Rupley, J. W. Logan, and W. D. Nichols, "Vocabulary Instruction in a Balanced Reading Program," *The Reading Teacher, 52* (1999), p. 339. Reprinted with permission of the authors and the International Reading Association. Copyright by the International Reading Association. All rights reserved.

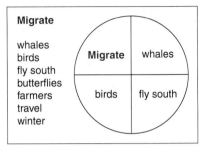

discussion. A new word is visually represented in a way that illustrates the connection between existing conceptual knowledge and the new word. For example, the word *migrate* could be introduced in a way that emphasizes its relation to the study of animals. Students could brainstorm and discuss words that come to mind for *migrate.* The teacher would guide the discussion in a manner that helps students to conceptualize both the word and its varied meanings (meanings could range from birds flying south for the winter, whales swimming from one part of the ocean to another, people traveling from one city to another, and so forth). When the discussion is ended, the teacher lists words that appropriately fit with *migrate* on the chalkboard or overhead. Each student can be directed to look in a textbook (in this case science) at the use of the word (*migrate*) in context, listen to a glossary definition read by the teacher, and then select three words from the list to help in remembering the word (*migrate*). Gwen wrote the words *whale, birds,* and *fly* in her concept wheel.

The concept wheel can be used in alternative ways as well. Students can be given a wheel without the vocabulary word and brainstorm and discuss what would be an appropriate word for the concepts. Teachers can use a wheel that is partially completed with words and have students suggest other words. Also, completed wheels can be used to have students identify the content area wheel and discuss what they know about the concepts represented.

Semantic Mapping

Semantic mapping incorporates many of the guidelines for vocabulary teaching and enables students to enlarge their vocabularies, understand relationships between existing and new concepts, perceive multiple meanings of words, and learn actively. Semantic mapping structures information categorically so that students can more readily see relationships between new words and concepts and their existing background knowledge.

Semantic mapping can be used for preteaching vital concepts and information for content area text before students read. Upon completion of the semantic map, the teacher discusses with the students how the new vocabulary words relate to words that they already know. Students thus understand better the content of the topic they will cover or the story they will read. Figure 6.2 presents an example of a semantic map for the topic of solar energy and illustrates how teaching certain words prior to

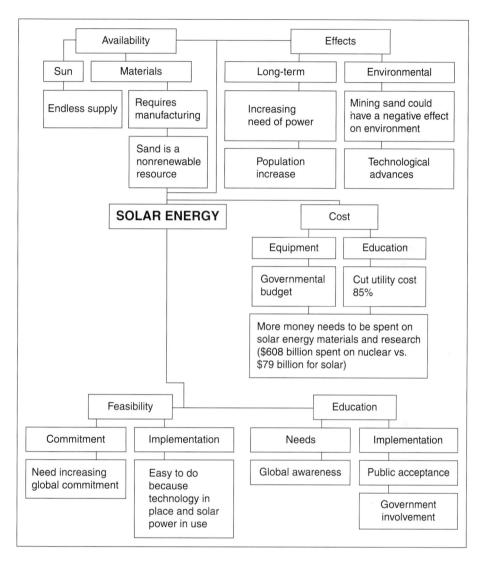

Figure 6.2 A semantic word map for solar energy.
Source: From W. H. Rupley, J. W. Logan, and W. D. Nichols, "Vocabulary Instruction in a Balanced Reading Program," *The Reading Teacher, 52* (1999), p. 342. Reprinted with permission of the authors and the International Reading Association. Copyright by the International Reading Association. All rights reserved.

reading can help students activate their background knowledge, relate existing knowledge to new concepts, and understand how new words and concepts are related. Teachers should invite class discussion by relating students' past reading and direct experiences to the semantic map. In discussing the semantic map, students must think about the relationships between the target word and their experiences.

The procedure for developing a semantic map for vocabulary instruction includes the following:

- Selecting a word that is central to a topic or story.
- Writing the central word on the chalkboard or a chart.
- Brainstorming words related to the central theme or topic and writing these words.
- Grouping the words into categories and labeling these categories.
- Noting additional words essential to the topic and placing these additional words in the appropriate categories.

Concept of Definition

A variation of semantic mapping is a procedure that Schwartz and Raphael (1985) devised to help students acquire a concept of definition. They recommend direct instruction considering three questions about a concept being studied: (1) What is it? (2) What is it like? and (3) What are some examples? The procedure is for students in grades 4 and above. Conducted over several instructional periods, its basic features include introduction and refinement of the strategy, further refinement, and writing a definition.

Introducing the strategy

Introduce students to the idea that they can develop a new strategy to aid them in the reading process. Focus on what they will learn, why it is important, and what they will be doing. Following the general introduction, introduce the word map (see Figure 6.3) and organize familiar information in terms of the three questions.

Modeling the procedures

Assist students in organizing the information by modeling for them using think-alouds. Then have students complete independent activities, mapping given words and a word of their choice. After mapping, have the students use the information to verbalize a definition with the class.

Refining the strategy

Following the introduction, give the students sentences that provide at least one class (What is it?), three properties (What is it like?), and three examples. Examine the sentences with the students and mark (check, circle, or underline) the types of information necessary to map the information. Following this mapping, have students supply oral or written definitions for the given concepts. Assist them to realize that they need not always identify three properties or three examples; they may use fewer or more in understanding the word.

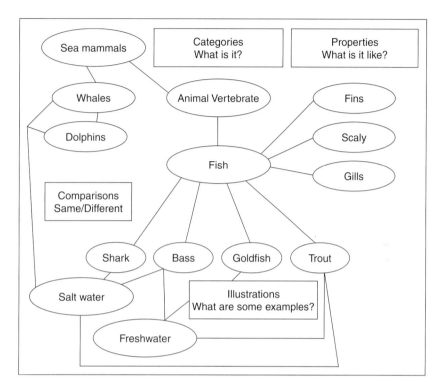

Figure 6.3 A concept of definition word map.

Source: From W. H. Rupley, J. W. Logan, and W. D. Nichols, "Vocabulary Instruction in a Balanced Reading Program," *The Reading Teacher, 52* (1999), p. 343. Reprinted with permission of the authors and the International Reading Association. Copyright by the International Reading Association. All rights reserved.

Further refining the concept

Use context that is less complete and inspire students to use sources of word meanings (such as dictionaries, encyclopedias, and textbooks) to complete their word maps. Invite them to discuss the concepts, using their background knowledge and the other sources of information.

Writing a definition

Use all of the mapping components without using a map. This is an internalization. Ask the students to evaluate the completeness of given definitions. If definitions are incomplete, have the students write whatever additional information they feel is needed.

Providing students with direct instruction in vocabulary can lead to helping them acquire strategies for learning new words and understanding the relationships among words. This procedure aids teachers in affording students opportunities to discuss new concepts, and discussion appears to be a key in promoting active thinking about words.

Webbing

Webbing is a method that graphically illustrates how to meaningfully associate word meanings and enables students to make connections between what they know about words and how words are related. Webbing makes it possible for students to see the relationship between words and concepts that they have already read or experienced. To help promote concept acquisition and vocabulary knowledge, teachers can leave the center word blank. Students can begin to understand the relationship of words in the web by choosing and discussing words that might complete the center word. The web in Figure 6.4 was done with the teacher directing the students to think of words that could be associated with electricity. As noted in the web, their responses ranged from Thomas Edison to Santa Claus and from generators to lightning. Webbing can be used to introduce a lesson to determine students' vocabulary and concept knowledge, to summarize a lesson that reflects what students have learned, and as a follow-up activity in which students can expand and create their own webs. Cells can be linked by a variety of relationships, such as synonyms, antonyms, expanded concepts, connotations, and preciseness.

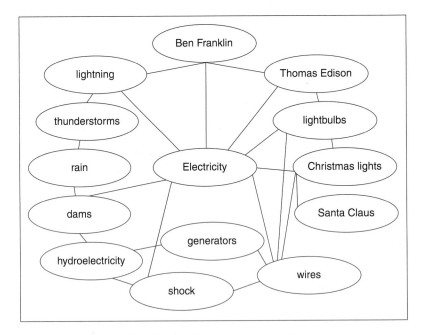

Figure 6.4   A semantic web of words describing electricity.

Source: From W. H. Rupley, J. W. Logan, and W. D. Nichols, "Vocabulary Instruction in a Balanced Reading Program," *The Reading Teacher, 52* (1999), p. 344. Reprinted with permission of the authors and the International Reading Association. Copyright by the International Reading Association. All rights reserved.

Webbing can also be used to help children develop their vocabulary for frequently occurring words found in both their reading and writing. Laframboise (2000) discusses the use of Said Webs, which is an instructional strategy for teaching "tired words" (e.g., happy, mad, sad, glad, big, good, cry, laugh, and so forth), or words that are frequently overused. She feels that children often encounter alternatives for tired words in their reading, but these do not become part of their vocabulary. The webbing method that she recommends has three purposes: (1) relating new and unknown words to known words to increase familiarity, (2) providing deeper and more meaningful processing of alternative words, and (3) encouraging students to independently explore new words for both their reading and writing activities.

The instructional steps for Said Webs have many of the basic features of webbing. Each of the steps is presented as follows, and a constructed web is illustrated in Figure 6.5.

1. The class spends a few minutes brainstorming words that are related to *said* (see the Brainstorm word lists for webs). This list is called a start list and is intended to establish a core of words that will be used during the next steps in the strategy.
2. The class as a group identifies and marks the words on the start list that they agree are the most common.

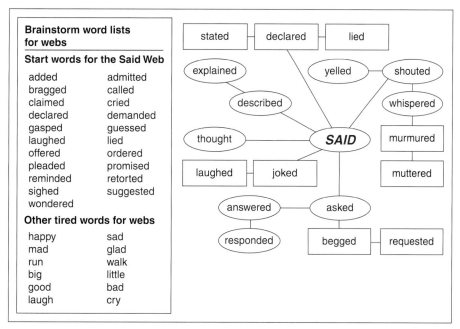

Figure 6.5 Start list and Said Web with words added during small-group construction of web.

Source: From K. L. Laframboise, "Said Webs: Remedy for Tired Words," *The Reading Teacher, 53* (April 2000), p. 541. Reprinted with permission of the author and the International Reading Association. Copyright by the International Reading Association. All rights reserved.

3. Heterogeneous groups of four to five students are formed and provided with three different color markers and chart paper. Students in each of the groups will use the markers to create webs with the words from the start list. The teacher directs the students to use the circled words, as the words for the first level of the web students should categorize all of the words on the start list. Words that are either synonyms or antonyms should be shown in that relationship (see Figure 6.5 for words such as *asked—answered—responded*). Children in the groups discuss and agree on the meanings of the words and can use resources to support their discussions.

4. Students continue to work in groups and as individual students think of words that are not on the start list, these words are added to the web with a different color marker (note the black rectangle words in Figure 6.5).

5. Charts are then displayed around the room so that students in each group can gather around them, read and study the words, and add to the webs. Each group uses its third color marker to add words to a web as they move from one web to the next. All the groups move from web to web until they are back to their own web, where they can add words that they learned from reading the other webs.

6. Students now react to the new words that have been added to their webs by asking questions such as: "Why is this word in this group?" "What does this word mean?" and "Where else could this word(s) go?"

7. Charts are then displayed and a single combined web is created. This final web remains displayed in the classroom for children to refer to during their reading and writing activities. New words can be added to the web as children come across them in their literacy activities.

Semantic-Features Analysis

Semantic-features analysis can help students understand relationships among words and relate their background knowledge to the new words. Figure 6.6 is an example. Semantic-features analysis is most appropriate for words related by class or common features.

To analyze, list several familiar words that are related (such as *algae eater, angelfish, black molly,* and so forth) on the chalkboard or a chart. Guide the students to discuss features associated with the words listed. As the students suggest features, write them across the top of the board or chart, creating a matrix that the students can complete in terms of present ($+$), absent ($-$), and sometimes (0). As the students broaden and define their concepts, the teacher adds words and features to the list and analyzes them. Semantic-features analysis can be used with narrative reading materials to analyze characters, settings, plots, and so forth. It is also effective in the content areas when introducing new topics, reviewing topics, and integrating topics across different content areas. The arrays can be developed and enlarged as students' knowledge backgrounds expand.

| Types of fish | | Features | | | | | | | |
	Location			Size			Behavior		
	Bottom	Middle	Top	Small	Middle	Large	Peaceful	Aggressive	Violent
Algae Eater									
Angelfish									
Black Molly									
Dwarf Gourami									
Goldfish									
Guppy									
Neon Tetra									
Piranha									
Siamese Fighting									
Zebra-fish									

Figure 6.6 A semantic-features analysis.

Source: W. H. Rupley, J. W. Logan, and W. D. Nichols, "Vocabulary Instruction in a Balanced Reading Program," *The Reading Teacher, 52* (1999), p. 345. Reprinted with permission of the authors and the International Reading Association. Copyright by the International Reading Association. All rights reserved.

Teaching Relationships Among Words

To help students understand the relationships among given words, use words that differ in degree (such as *tiny, minute,* and *small*) and ask students to discuss them and generate other words that fit the examples. An assortment of procedures can teach relationships among words. A good source for choosing words for this activity is shared-literature study (Iwicki, 1992). By building connections between "old" vocabulary words and words found in their new books, students begin to understand relationships among words they encounter in reading. Students are not just asked to supply words that fit the example but rather to describe how the word fits in the stories they have read. For example, Matthew just finished reading *The Last Dinosaur* and used *enormous* to describe the size of the dinosaur. His teacher asked Matthew if he thought that Paul Bunyan could be described as enormous, too. Matthew responded by saying, "Yes. Because he was enormous and he was a giant, bigger than anyone else."

Such discussion and activities that relate new words and concepts to past readings and discuss them in relation to authentic text are helping to expand students' vocabularies meaningfully.

Instructional Activities

Understanding Relationships Among Words.   Give students several words that are related and ask them to identify others appropriate to the given words. The words supplied by the students can be similar or opposite in meaning and should be based on their reading of stories and books, as noted earlier.

Similar meanings can include:

big, huge, . . . (giant, grand, jumbo)
small, tiny, . . . (minute, wee, miniature)

Opposite meanings can include:

big, huge, . . . (small, tiny, minute)
shout, yell, . . . (whisper, soft, quiet)

Combinations of meaning can include:

big, small, . . . (giant, little, enormous)
shout, whisper, . . . (yell, soft, quiet)

Ask students to provide context and write their context sentence for each of the words. After the students understand the relationships between the words, have them provide additional words that retain similar meaning in the sentences. The following example is based on a story the children had read that focused on the concepts associated with big and small:

In the story, *Our Little Wonder,* Rich and Robbie got a pet tiger kitten. It was so _____ that they could hold it in their hands. They thought about the mother tiger and wondered how such a little thing could grow up to be so _____.

Students can supply words that relate to other stories they have read about size. For example, Donald might use the word **jumbo** to describe the mother cat, while Matthew might choose the word **giant** to describe her. Teachers can direct students to think about words that are the opposite of those supplied for either sentence. Words such as **minute, tiny, little,** and so forth could be used to complete the first sentence.

Develop additional activities around the concept of related words. For example, write the word **release** on the board. Ask the students to discuss words that are related in meaning and list them on the board. Then, ask students to discuss words that are different in meaning and list them. Have them discuss why they listed a word in a particular column. For example:

Related	**Different**
free	grasp
dismiss	hold
	clutch
	capture
	keep

Use sentences to illustrate the different meanings. Note the changes in meaning for the words substituted for **release.** Again encourage students to use their knowledge of stories they have read to construct sentences for the words and write the sentences on the board. Discuss with them how the meaning changes depending on which word is used in the sentence.

> John decided to <u>free</u> the bird.
> John decided to <u>grasp</u> the bird.
> John decided to <u>capture</u> the bird.
> John decided to <u>keep</u> the bird.

Compare related words for sentence comprehension. Invite the students to read sets of sentences and determine if they have similar meanings. Have them write **S** on the line to indicate that sentences communicate similar meanings, and have them write **D** to show that they have different meanings. Complete one or two examples with the students to make sure that they understand the task and will succeed at it.

_____ 1. Bill took his dog for a ride in the car.
_____   Bill took his dog for a ride in the park.
_____ 2. The park is not far from Bill's house.
_____   The park is close to Bill's house.
_____ 3. The park has an enormous field where Bill's dog can play.
_____   The park has a minute area where Bill's dog can play.

Word-Association Vocabulary Instruction

Word-association vocabulary instruction enables students to learn the meanings of several connected words. Students can add new words to their existing vocabulary and understand relationships between the concepts that words represent.

This approach can be followed in teaching synonyms, antonyms, context clues, roots, prefixes, suffixes, and concept classifications (such as animals, size, actions, and story themes). Word-association strategy applies to all school subjects. Following are a few suggested activities to help promote meaningful vocabulary growth.

Instructional Activities

Associating Words with Known Concepts in Context.   Keep an accurate list of new words that students encounter and learn. Words that contain the same root, prefix, or suffix, and words in concept classifications can form the basis for expanding meaning vocabularies. Teach new words by relating them to similar words the students already know.

In content areas, such as mathematics, relate new words to known concepts in meaningful context, using examples in the students' background knowledge. For example, students connect concepts through reading and writing of connected vocabulary (see Figure 6.7).

In interest areas, such as basketball, connect new words to the concept in a meaningful context. For example, connect **court, score, second, scoreboard, bounce, shot, shoot, dribble, foul, rebound, time out,** and **rim.**

Using Categories for Classification of Words.   Connect new words to words and concepts already known by the students for new word categories. For example, using **basketball,** illustrate word relationships with the same roots, prefixes, and suffixes.

Roots	Prefixes	Suffixes
basket**ball**	**re**bound	dribbl**ing,** dribbl**ed**
base**ball**	**re**take	jump**ing,** jump**ed**
foot**ball**	**re**make	scor**ing,** scor**ed**

Classify words that students know from their reading of literature and basal stories in terms of similar properties and introduce new words that relate to the known properties. For example, a thematic unit on farm life might use the following:

Animals	Farm Animals	Pets	Animal Sounds	Animal Sizes
pig	pig	—	pig—oink, grunt	enormous pig
cow	cow	—	cow—moo, low	huge cow
sheep	sheep	—	sheep—baa, bleat	large sheep
goat	goat	—	goat—baa, bleat	big goat
cat	cat	cat	cat—meow, hiss	small cat
dog	dog	dog	dog—bark, growl	tiny dog, little dog, great dog

Figure 6.7 Example of a student's connecting concepts through comparison and contrast or represented by vocabulary.

Instructional Activities

Structural Analysis.   Generate instructional activities for the area of structural analysis. Teach affixes (prefixes, suffixes, and inflection endings) to help students relate the new to what they know. Using word families (derivations of known words, such as **depend—dependable, undependable, dependent,** and **independent**) can enhance understanding of the meaning relationships among derived words within a family and promote independent word learning.

Introduce prefixes and their effects on meaning by presenting sentences containing prefixes. Focus students' attention on what happens to the meaning of a known word when a specific prefix is used. Once the students understand the task, have them read the rest of a given story or use one that they have read and select the words that make sense in context. The following story illustrates the use of the prefix **un-:**

Jason set off walking to town and on the way he met a kind man. The name of this kind man was Farmer John. Farmer John was kind to everyone, even Jack, who was never friendly or kind to anyone. Jason had never met anyone who was as unkind and unfriendly as Jack. Jason helped Farmer John load his wagon with hay. Jason and Farmer John took the wagon to town to sell the hay.

Farmer John's _____ friend went with them. Jason had
          (kind, unkind)

to walk beside the wagon. He thought that it was _____
                                                                                         (fair, unfair)

that he had to walk and Farmer John and his _____
                                                                              (kind, unkind)

friend rode in the wagon. Jason knew that the _____
                                                                             (kind, unkind)

Jack would not help them _____ the wagon when they got to town.
                                            (load, unload)

When students express an interest in word building using roots, prefixes, and suffixes, construct activities to extend their understanding of word families and the effect that affixes have on word meaning. To build words, read the definition for a word that you already know (it is important that students have meaning for the base word). Then think about what you know about the prefixes and suffixes. Give short definitions to make new words. Do one or two examples with students to make sure that they will be able to do the task. For example:

depend: to rely on (clues: **in-, un-, -able, -ent**)

depend_____: trustworthy, reliable

_____depend_____: not trustworthy, not reliable

_____depend_____: self-reliant, doing things oneself

depend_____: relying on someone else, unable to do things oneself

agree: to consent to (clues: **dis-, -able, -ment**)

____agree_____: a quarrel or argument

agree_____: pleasing, pleasant

____agree_____: not pleasing, unpleasant

agree_____: a contract or an understanding

Provide opportunities for students to apply different prefixes in meaningful context. Progress from sentences to longer passages to ensure a high degree of success. Depending on students' needs, the teacher can introduce the activity with sentences and then proceed to using connected text from stories that the children have read.

Bob isn't able to go to the football game with me.

Bob is _____ to go to the football game with me.
   (able, unable)

The teacher said to read the story again.

The teacher said to _____ the story.
            (read, reread)

Susan gave Billy a glass of milk. Billy drank all of it and asked for more.

Susan _____ his glass and said, "This is all of the milk."
   (filled, refilled)

Billy yelled, "It's _____ that Donald got three glasses of milk
            (fair, unfair)

and I got just two."

Donald said, "It's _____ of you to yell at Susan."
            (kind, unkind)

Susan _____, "You are a(n) _____ person, Billy,
   (agreed, disagreed)   (kind, unkind)

when you yell at me."

Contextual Approaches

Often, a single sentence has inadequate context for students to use their prior knowledge to comprehend the meaning of a word. Consider the following sentence: *Fennecs were crouched behind several small bushes waiting for any type of prey to come along the path to the water hole.* Are fennecs people or animals?

Most likely, you must guess what a fennec is because the sentence does not provide enough information to allow you to use your background knowledge. If they know fennecs are animals, readers can use their knowledge of animals. If they know fennecs are wild animals, readers can use their knowledge of wild animals. Knowing that they are wild, fawn-colored animals with large ears may help readers form an even better understanding of fennecs. Furthermore, readers who are aware that fennecs are African foxes can use their knowledge of foxes to make sense of the sentence. Sufficient natural context is often essential in teaching word meaning.

Now consider this next sentence: *Randy's eyes became as large as silver dollars as the physician's assistant approached him with the sphygmomanometer.* The context helps to some degree to understand the context of the event (perhaps a doctor's office), that Randy is experiencing some kind of emotion (perhaps fear or excitement), and that the *sphygmomanometer* is a thing (perhaps an instrument). However, none of this context is helpful in getting the gist of the word or construction of meaning until one reads further: *She asked him to roll up his sleeve so she could take his blood pressure. Wrapping the wide band tightly around his upper arm, she commented "This new* sphygmomanometer *is so much more accurate in taking a patient's blood pressure than the old one we used to have."*

Skilled readers integrate information as they read to construct meaning. If context is not enough to explain an unknown word, skilled readers may use their knowledge of prefixes, suffixes, and root words to determine the meaning. They perform these operations so rapidly and automatically that they are not aware of them. If they cannot determine the meaning of a word, they may reason that it is not important to know the word and continue reading the text.

Knowledge of what skilled readers do when encountering unknown words has direct implications for teachers. In learning to use context, students must understand how their knowledge of content can help them determine meanings of unknown words. However, context does not always provide total understanding, and often it may mislead students.

Modeling Application/Contribution of Context to Word Meaning

Contextual analysis is best taught by guided practice in which the teacher models the procedure, uses familiar written examples, and provides scaffolding as children become proficient in using contextual analysis. **Modeling** means that the teacher thinks out loud, talking through the processes used in the application of structural analysis, thus providing instruction in strategies to use in real reading situations and supporting students' attempts to apply their knowledge through the use of scaffolds. Class discussions with students about how they derive word meanings from context, and what they do if context does not work, help them understand the strengths and limitations of the process.

An illustration of modeling the use of context clues follows. Assume that we read a sentence containing an unknown word: "Jack was sure his _____ would let him go." This is the opening line of a story, and the author has yet to unfold the plot or background. Many words might complete the idea when this is all we know. Is Jack being held prisoner? The word could be *captors.* Is he thinking of getting permission? The word might be *mother, father, friends,* or *teacher.*

If we note something about the unknown word, we may get a valuable clue. For instance, in "Jack was sure his p _____ would let him go," *mother, father, teacher,*

Discussions with students about how they derive word meanings help them to develop strategies.

and *friends* can be eliminated because of the initial letter clue, but several possibilities remain, such as *pal, playmates,* and *parents.*

When the sentence does not provide contextual clues, we can read further to see if additional text provides the information. As we read on, we discover the context: "Mother and father both agreed that they would let Jack go to the game." Thinking about the unknown word in the earlier sentence leads us to recognize it as *parents,* because the latter sentence refers to *mother* and *father,* who are parents.

Rarely does a sentence alone provide sufficient context to unlock the meaning of unknown words: For example, "Although their *sojourn* was brief, it was enjoyable," "It was a *moot* point and the judge did not allow it," and "Most teachers today use an *eclectic* approach for teaching reading." If we consider the context supplied both before and after an unknown word, the meaning is more likely to be revealed.

Suppose a child is reading early in a passage the following: "*It's my _____,*" *said Donald.* The child encounters a number of word-meaning possibilities that would make sense in context—my *idea, turn, opinion* or a possession such as *bike, bat, ball,* or *saxophone.* As the child considers the following context, the recognition of the unknown word falls into place. *The boys searched everywhere, but they did not find the lost puppy. "I hope Zach doesn't get hit by a car," said Billy. Donald was very worried. He had been thinking all afternoon about not closing the gate when he went to play ball. The puppy must have gotten out when he left the gate open. "It's my fault," said Donald. Then he told Billy about leaving the gate open.* Such examples can help students better use contextual analysis to get meaning from unknown words.

Different Meanings for the Same Word

Some words have more than one meaning. Such words are called **polysemous words.** In early language development, students master the concrete levels of understanding before the abstract. Students may know such words as *aid, blue, mine, broadcast,* and *fence,* and they can know several meanings for each word and still not be familiar with many others.

Students probably will have no difficulties with the following meanings for the word *air:*

My daddy puts <u>air</u> in the tires.
We hang our clothes outside to <u>air</u> them.
We breathe <u>air</u>.

The same students, however, may be confused by the following meanings:

Mrs. Jones is disliked because she puts on <u>airs</u>.
She was asked to <u>air</u> her view.
That was an <u>air</u> ball.

Students may understand what *blue* means in "The boy had a blue coat" but not be familiar with "The boy felt *blue* when his aunt left." They may understand "Grandfather rode the *horse*" but not "The coach warned the boys not to *horse* around," "That's a *horse* of a different color," or "The mayor accused the council of beating a dead *horse.*"

The relationships of words to each other and the subtle meanings that the same word conveys depend upon the context in which a word appears and the reader's background knowledge. Ample reading and language-based experiences broaden children's acquisition of meaning vocabularies.

Instructional Activities

Following are several activities for promoting students' interest in vocabulary development. While they all illustrate the importance of context in defining words, please note that context ranges from the highly concrete, such as labeling naming objects and pictures, to more abstract activities associated with guided writing activities.

Deriving Word Meanings Through Use in Context.   Learning meanings and multiple words for the same object can be fascinating and highly motivating for young children. Many primary-grade classrooms that we visit have words written in context and displayed throughout the classroom. For example, the door in one classroom was labeled in the following manner:

This is the <u>doorway</u> to our room.
This is the <u>entry</u> to our room.
This is the <u>entrance</u> to our room.
This is the <u>gateway</u> to our room.
This is the <u>portal</u> to our room.

Another classroom had a picture of a giant that reached from ceiling to floor. Listed alongside the giant were words in context, which the children had written. They obviously were intrigued by the word **enormous:**

This giant is <u>huge</u>.
This giant is as <u>huge</u> as a tree.
This giant is <u>jumbo</u>.
This giant is as <u>jumbo</u> as an elephant.
This giant is <u>enormous</u>.
This giant has <u>enormous</u> hands as big as a desk.
This giant has <u>enormous</u> ears as big as my kite.
This giant has <u>enormous</u> eyes as big as my head.

Other words and sentences written by the children to describe the giant included **immense, tremendous, massive,** and **stupendous.** The context of the picture and the sentence strips initially provided by the teacher were excellent stimuli for children to engage in a self-motivated study of words in context.

Different teachers help students realize that many words have several meanings according to how they are used. Many teachers we have observed illustrate this concept with simple words (such as **can, stick, run,** and **set**). As you ask for different usages, write the students' responses on the board or a chart. At the same time, attempt to fix the various meanings by using other words and concepts from stories the students have read and their experiential/conceptual backgrounds. For example:

I <u>can</u> spell my name. (<u>Can</u> means "able.")
Mother is going to <u>can</u> some peaches. (<u>Can</u> means "to preserve.")

Use some other examples for the word **can,** depending upon students' background knowledge:

<u>Can</u> it Joe. (<u>Can</u> means "stop talking.")
If you are late one more time, the boss will <u>can</u> you. (<u>Can</u> means "to dismiss from a job.")
Why don't you trade in that old tin <u>can</u> and get a new car? (<u>Can</u> means "a battered old car.")

Billy ⑮ Oct. 17, 1994
The fish reminds me of   It feels like a cement wall
a baracada swimming in the   that has already dried up.
ocean. It reminds me of a   It feels bumpy like tree
gold fish swimming quickly   bark when it's picked off.
in the salt water. It looks   When dropped it sounds like
like an oupside down vase.   a domino falling from
It looks like a space ship   the sky. The fish sounds
going up to outer space.   like ice hockey players
It smels like cheese on a   playing a game on the ice.
sandwich with mustard.   It tastes like dried up cheadide
It smels like fresh pizza   cheese. It tastes like the fish
when it's scarfed down.   filled sea.

Figure 6.8   An example of an activity to encourage development of descriptive vocabulary.

After several group activities stressing different meanings, not simply different sentences, present written activities. Give students several words to illustrate different usages by using a word map.

This activity can provide information about students' background knowledge, writing capabilities, and ability to generalize word meanings. Furthermore, it is highly motivating; it can promote interest in expanding word knowledge through writing activities, as illustrated in Figure 6.8.

Homonyms

The relationships between homonyms are not so apparent as are those between words that are similar or opposite in meaning. **Homonyms** are words that sound exactly alike but are spelled differently. Many common homonyms look very much alike (such as *their—there, see—sea, hear—here,* and *course—coarse*), so young readers can have problems with both whole-word recognition and meanings.

Instructional Activities

Using Contextual Analysis with Homonyms.   Context plays an important role for homonyms because it provides information for comprehension.

Use the Cloze-maze technique for instructional activities. Give students written sentences appropriate to their language backgrounds and ask them to identify the words that make sense in the sentences. For example:

The _____ made the grass shine in the sunlight.
  (do, dew)

Mother had to _____ the apples at the store.
    (way, weigh)

The softball team that _____ the game was from our town.
      (one, won)

I went down to the _____ to look for some fish.
    (sea, see)

Working with homonyms can be enjoyable and motivating for students. It can help them understand the influence that context has on word meaning. It also can help them use context to understand the contributions that words make to meaning. Once students have grasped the concept of homonyms, point out other examples in their reading of authentic text and focus discussion on how the context provides them with a strategy for determining the meaning of the word.

LANGUAGE-BASED APPROACHES

Providing varied reading, writing, and language-based activities can contribute significantly to vocabulary development. Language-based activities help develop automaticity in word recognition strategies using word knowledge and activate experiential and conceptual backgrounds to construct meaning.

Independent Reading Programs

Teachers can use numerous techniques to promote independent reading. The essential point is to allocate time for students to read on their own. Ways to promote independent reading include bookselling sessions, class book fairs, reading aloud to students on a regular basis, creating a book corner in the classroom, using children's literature, and having free-reading sessions daily.

Providing students time to read independently is crucial to motivating them to read for pleasure. A particular time set aside each day for silent reading of self-selected materials by students and teacher is sustained silent reading (SSR), or uninterrupted sustained silent reading (USSR). This activity should stress enjoyment of reading materials, so students should not be required to report on this reading. SSR can stimulate students' independent reading, but just allowing time to read is not enough. Students need access to a variety of reading materials. The materials can include literature books, magazines, newspapers, and travel brochures. Some students may need help in locating interesting reading materials, and others may need direction in terms of their responsibilities during the reading period. Teacher guidance and assistance are extremely important in the beginning reading program.

In the beginning reading program, teachers can motivate independent reading in a variety of ways. One way is to use audiotape recorders to tape children's books.

Students can help select the books to be taped if they are given a brief overview of each book before it is recorded. When taping, teachers should read relatively slowly to ensure that students can make the connection between what they hear and the print that represents the language.

Once a book has been taped, students can listen to it and follow along in the text at a listening center. The teacher should help students understand what they are to do and get them started. Without proper instruction, they may just listen to the stories.

Commercially taped books and stories, videocassettes, and CD-ROMs are also readily available (Jongsma, 2000). Talking books and closed-caption videocassettes can introduce students to content or the experience of literature.

Predictable books help students begin to use prediction strategies as they read. This frees them from focusing on individual words. In predictable books, students can easily grasp what the author is going to say next. Such books contain much repetition of content and language structure.

Additional ways to encourage reading in the early grades include the use of big books, poetry, storytelling, reading aloud to students, learning and play centers, and creative dramatics. These techniques can help promote a language-rich classroom that motivates young students to engage in literacy.

Broad reading is an integral part of the application phase of the reading program, and it is one of the basic characteristics of effective reading instruction. Opportunities for independent reading provide means for expanding vocabulary knowledge, refining and building experiential and conceptual backgrounds, and developing an interest in reading.

Poetry Writing

Writing activities can motivate students to become more actively engaged in learning new words and internalizing the meanings of words. Donna Norton (1997) has identified several ways that teachers can provide rich opportunities for students to use their developing vocabularies. Among the ways she suggests to expand vocabulary knowledge are poetry writing and individualized dictionaries.

Writing poetry is an excellent means to encourage students to expand their vocabularies. Several different forms of poetry stress various types of vocabulary. For example, haiku can be used to expand students' meaning vocabularies. Teacher assistance is important in writing haikus; it enables the teacher to present a variety of words for the same poem.

The brown dancing bear,

Dancing around in his cage,

Dancing on his toes.

The teacher could help the student find other words for *dancing* and encourage her to think of her own. Words such as *gliding, prancing, swaying,* and *skipping* could replace *dancing.* The images that the different words convey can be discussed with the child, and she can illustrate them with pictures.

Noah Webster's blue-backed *Speller* was one of the most widely used texts for beginning reading instruction between 1780 and the early 1800s. The *Speller* did not contain as much religious material for reading as earlier readers did and children could better relate to the reading content because of the inclusion of content that was appealing to them. Furthermore, the language and content were more appropriate to their background knowledge than that found in earlier reading instructional materials.

Spelling Book. 139

book, dŏve, fu̶ll, u̶se, can, chaise, gem, thin, thou,

No. 146.—CXLVI.

THE DOG.

This dog is the mastiff. He is active, strong, and used as a watch dog. He has a large head and pendent ears. He is not very apt to bite; but he will sometimes take down a man and hold him down. Three mastiffs once had a combat with a lion; and the lion was compelled to save himself by flight.

THE STAG.

The stag is the male of the red deer. He is a mild and harmless animal, bearing a noble attire of horns, which are shed and renewed every year. His form is light and elegant, and he runs with great rapidity. The female is called a hind; and the fawn or young deer, when his horns appear, is called a pricket or brocket.

UPDATE

Just as Noah Webster recognized in the 1700s, teachers today realize that children need wide and varied opportunities to read text with which they can associate their experiences to expand their concepts and vocabulary. Meaning vocabulary can be thought of as the hooks on which we hang ideas and construct meaning for our reading and writing. It is through our meaning vocabulary that we represent our world, both its concrete and its abstract features.

Another form of poetry that stresses descriptive words and action words is cinquains. Norton (1992) notes that students should first listen to or read numerous cinquains. Then the teacher should discuss the structure of cinquains and illustrate them for students. Following these activities, students can write their own poems. The structure of cinquains is as follows:

Line 1:   A single word for a title.

Line 2:   Two words to describe the title.

Line 3:   Three words to express action.

Line 4:   Four words to express feeling.

Line 5:   The title again, or a word like the title.

Norton recommends that teachers and students draw a diagram for the cinquain:

title

describe title

action, action, action

feeling about the title

title

Cinquains can be written in groups or by individual students and can be about characters from their reading to experiment with descriptive and action words. Norton (1992) presented the following examples of students' cinquains for books that they had read. After reading *The Story of Ferdinand,* a group of second graders wrote this cinquain:

Ferdinand

Happy, strong

Sitting, smelling, growing

Loves to smell flowers

Independent (p. 68)

A sixth-grade class wrote the following after reading *Johnny Tremain:*

Johnny

Brave, patriotic

Daring, delivering, riding

Made a strong commitment

Apprentice (p. 69)

Another form of poetry that encourages students to use contrasting words is diamante. The requirements for each line of diamante are as follows:

Line 1:   Noun

Line 2:   Two adjectives

Line 3:   Three participles

Line 4:   Four nouns or phrases

Line 5:   Three participles noting change

Line 6:   Two adjectives

Line 7:   Contrasting noun

Norton (1992) recommends that the diamante be illustrated to denote the structure and that the teacher discuss the structure, illustrate the terms, and read several written examples. Again, she urges the use of a written diagram to help students recall the form of the diamante:

noun

describing, describing

action, action, action

transition nouns or phrases

action, action, action

describing, describing

noun

A fourth-grade class produced the following diamante (Norton, 1992) after reading *The Velveteen Rabbit:*

Toy

Stuffed, velveteen

Sitting, lying, riding

Love made him real

Walking, running, leaping

Real, furry

Rabbit (p. 70)

Writing: Journals, Diaries, and Response Journals

Additional writing forms that can promote and encourage the development of students' meaning vocabularies are journal writing, diary writing, and response-journal writing (see Figure 6.9). Because journal writing is intended for the teacher to read, it provides an excellent opportunity for the teacher to use response-journal writing to further students' vocabulary. Students can select their own topics or teachers can provide students with ideas for journal writing. Topics and ideas can focus on characters, settings, events, and language features (words chosen by authors). Teachers can respond in writing and subtly introduce words that relate to what students have written.

For example, Matthew wrote in his journal, "I really liked reading *The Marble Cake Cat* because the cat kept looking for a home where he could be just a cat

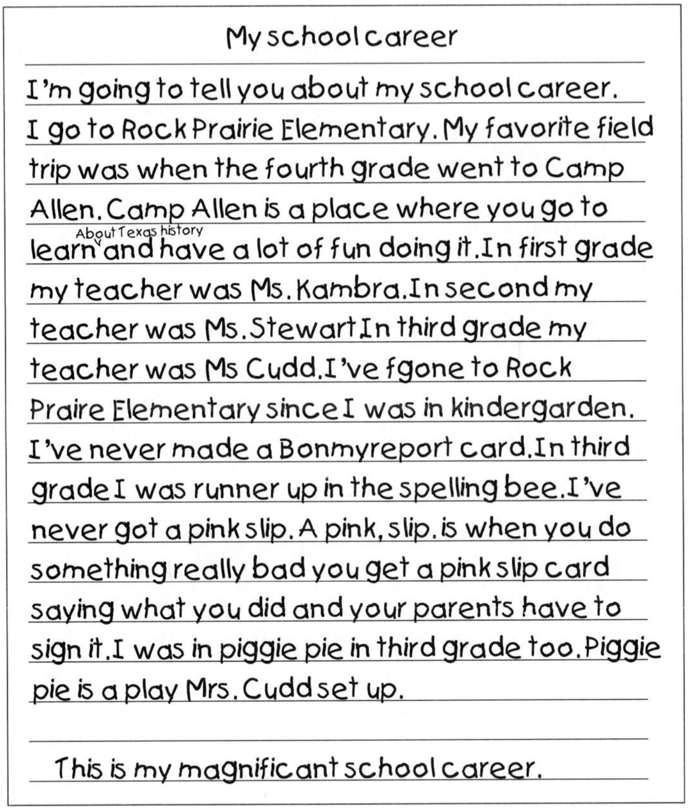

> ## My school career
>
> I'm going to tell you about my school career.
> I go to Rock Prairie Elementary. My favorite field
> trip was when the fourth grade went to Camp
> Allen. Camp Allen is a place where you go to
> learn About Texas history and have a lot of fun doing it. In first grade
> my teacher was Ms. Kambra. In second my
> teacher was Ms. Stewart In third grade my
> teacher was Ms Cudd. I've fgone to Rock
> Praire Elementary since I was in kindergarden.
> I've never made a Bonmyreport card. In third
> grade I was runner up in the spelling bee. I've
> never got a pink slip. A pink, slip. is when you do
> something really bad you get a pink slip card
> saying what you did and your parents have to
> sign it. I was in piggie pie in third grade too. Piggie
> pie is a play Mrs. Cudd set up.
>
> This is my magnificant school career.

Figure 6.9   An example of a student's writing in which words are defined in rich context.

Source: Rose Marie Rupley

and Tommy liked him and treated him just the way a cat likes to be treated." Mrs. Hansen responded to Matthew's journal entry by writing, "Matthew, *The Marble Cake Cat* is one of my favorite books. He was really a unique cat, one of a kind, but all he wanted was to be treated like a cat. You and I liked the book and it sounds like it's one of your favorite books, too." The word *unique* appears throughout this book and is most likely a word that Matthew is beginning to associate meaning with. Mrs. Hansen took the opportunity to reinforce the meaning of the word and made a mental note to emphasize its use in her language interaction with Matthew.

Student-Compiled Dictionaries

Teachers have long used student-compiled dictionaries to help children develop their meaning vocabularies. Dictionaries can vary from picture versions for emerging readers to content-area versions with graphs, examples, and written definitions for upper elementary students. These can take the form of paper-and-pencil versions to those developed on the computer. Lower-elementary-grade children can compile individual dictionaries for significant events in their lives that teachers can capitalize upon to further vocabulary growth.

For example, Billy's kindergarten teacher read a story to the class about a man who sells balloons. Billy drew a picture of his family as a "balloon family." He described his picture to his teacher in terms of the size of the balloons: "The biggest one is daddy. The littlest one is Matthew. The bigger one is mommy." His teacher wrote the words *littlest, biggest,* and *bigger* under the appropriate balloon family member. Billy added this page of artwork to his picture dictionary and was well on his way to understanding the graphic representation and meanings associated with the words *biggest, bigger,* and *littlest.*

Entries for individual dictionaries can come from stories that the children read, from discussion of topics in science, social studies, and math, from listening to stories read to them, and from field trips. The students can select their own words to include in the dictionaries or teachers can choose words that they believe are important to developing concepts.

Instructional Activities

Using a Semantic Map. Following the completion of a semantic map, have the students write stories or plays to represent the concepts and words used in the map. Using the outline of the semantic map shown in Figure 6.2, encourage students to write a story about traveling in snow, riding in an airplane, being a weather forecaster, or traveling across the United States. Discuss the words and concepts in the semantic map, and provide assistance as the students write their stories.

Using Word Maps. Using a word map (see Figure 6.3), ask students to write several definitions for a given word or concept. Have them exchange definitions, then have each student try to identify the word that is defined. Use word maps as the framework for a story. Develop several related word maps (such as for dog, park, and games), and have the students integrate the concepts represented in the maps in a story that they write.

Using Webs. Have the students use webs to organize and develop the stories and reports that they write. For example, if a student wants to write about a trip to the zoo, assist the student in developing a web of experiences to organize the information. If another student wants to write about space flight, help the student develop a web to organize this information. Figure 6.10 shows a story web that a third-grade student developed for a story about bats. Figure 6.11 is the story he wrote.

Using Semantic-features Analysis. Basing writing activities around a semantic-features analysis, such as that shown in Figure 6.6, have the students write riddles such as the following and exchange them with each other:

"You can find me almost everywhere. I am read for enjoyment, information, and current events. Who am I?"

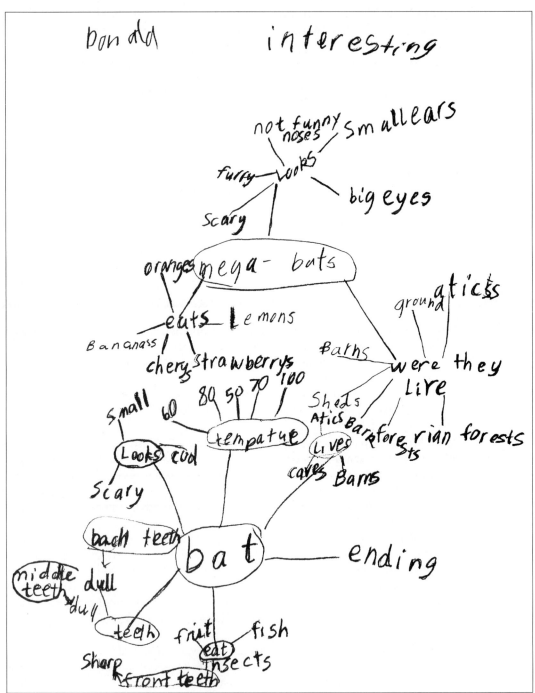

Figure 6.10 A story web about bats prepared by a third grader.

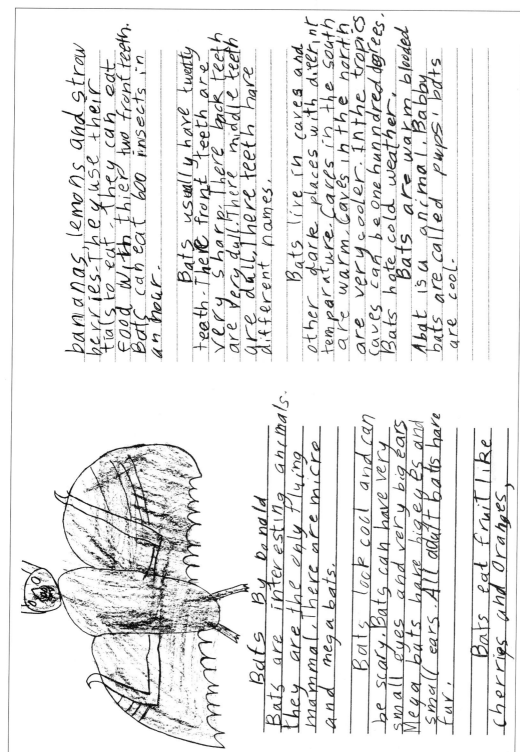

bananas, lemons and straw
berries. They use their
tials to eat. They can eat
food with thier two front teeth.
Bats can eat 600 insects in
an hour.

Bats usally have twenty
teeth. Their front teeth are
very sharp. There back teeth
are very dull. There middle teeth
are dull. There teeth have
different names.

Bats live in caves and
other dark places with diffrent
temparature. Caves in the south
are warm. Caves in the north
are very cooler. In the tropics
caves can be one hunnderd degrees.
Bats hate cold weather.

Bats are warm blooded
Abat is a animal. Babby
bats are called pups. Bats
are cool.

Bats By bonald
Bats are interesting animals.
they are the only flying
mammal. There are micre
and mega bats.

Bats look cool and can
be scary. Bats can have very
small eyes and very big ears
Mega bats have big eyes and
small ears. All adult bats have
fur.

Bats eat fruit like
cherries and oranges,

Figure 6.11   The story about bats that was organized and written in relation to the story web the third grader prepared.

239

"I warm the earth, help plants grow, and help you start your day. Who am I?"

"I have four legs, you can see me in a zoo, and I always have my trunk with me. Who am I?"

Have students use their analyses for content area subjects to help them organize and write reports.

Word Derivation.   Studying words of recent origin can motivate both word learning and writing. English is a living language, and as such it is always growing and changing. Introduce students to recently coined words. Then place the words in categories, using semantic maps, webs, and semantic-features analysis.

Following are some newly coined words. Have the students work in small teams, relying on their own knowledge and on materials available in the classroom and library.

rapper	desktop	in-line skates
SCUD missile	cellular telephone	ergonomics
fax	CD	Netscape

In the process of placing words in categories, students may discover that some categories are too broad, such as science or technology, because they cut across almost every heading. Have the students analyze words such as **ergonomics** for insights into the logic of coining new words.

Working on a unit devoted to new words in English leads to an understanding of how language works and develops. Motivation is high during such study, particularly among students who have become overdrilled on reading skills instruction. Many writing experiences can grow out of the study of newly coined words. For example, have students coin their own words and write definitions for them. Examples include the following:

rewhisperment	freezerator	unfreezable
uncar	peddlemobile	cyberiffic
diseating	pickerupper	CD-ROMERATOR

Not only can children write definitions, but they can also write stories using their coined words, draw pictures, write advertisements to sell a new product, and so forth. Students can keep their own dictionaries of newly coined words to share with classmates.

Using a language-based approach can encourage students to incorporate new words into their writing. Have the students develop word banks for the words they encounter in their oral language, reading, and writing. Words selected for their word banks have special meaning for the students. Words can be grouped in terms of activities (such as field trips, films, and guest speakers) and integrated into writing activities and reading activities.

SUMMARY

As students expand their experiential and conceptual backgrounds, they expand and refine their knowledge of words. Meaning vocabulary is a major factor in reading comprehension. The words that readers know represent the concepts and information that they have available to help them construct meaning for what they read. Readers who know a word in its fullest sense can associate experiences and concepts with the word. Students' vocabulary knowledge is developmental.

Researchers disagree about the effectiveness of direct vocabulary instruction. Some argue that students encounter far too many words in their reading for direct instruction to be beneficial and that wide reading and a variety of quality language activities promote vocabulary growth most effectively. Others believe that direct vocabulary instruction can increase vocabulary knowledge. This position supports teaching words that are usable, that generate the learning of other new words, and that are keys to understanding given text.

We support a position that recognizes both wide reading and explicit vocabulary instruction to (1) relate new words to background knowledge, (2) provide opportunities to encounter and learn new words, and (3) focus on words that have utility in learning new concepts. Procedures for teaching vocabulary include semantic mapping, word mapping, webbing, and semantic-features analysis. To enhance vocabulary learning, engage students in discussions about the words they are learning from their reading of literary and content texts.

YOUR POINT OF VIEW

Discussion Questions

1. You have been given the responsibility to develop the concept "university or college life" for a group of incoming students. Develop a semantic map that would indicate what it is like to attend your university or college. Share your semantic map with your classmates and discuss the concepts represented.
2. Assume that you are teaching the three states of matter (gas, solid, and liquid) to a group of fourth graders. Contrast having the students look up words such as *fluid, molten, solid, gaseous, evaporation,* and *condensation* and writing definitions that relate the students' existing knowledge to new words and concepts. Discuss some procedures for teaching new words and concepts that might be more effective than writing definitions and sentences for the new words.

Take a Stand For or Against

1. Teachers are wasting their time teaching new words to students.
2. Engaging students in discussions about new words promotes learning of these words.

Field-Based Assignments

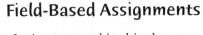

1. As was noted in this chapter, semantic mapping incorporates many of the guidelines for vocabulary teaching and enables students to enlarge their vocabularies, understand relationships between existing and new concepts, perceive multiple meanings of words, and learn actively. Semantic mapping structures information categorically so that students can more readily see relationships between new words and concepts and their existing background knowledge.

   Identify a topic in a content area in which children with whom you are working have appropriate interest and background knowledge. Begin to develop a semantic map for the topic by following these guidelines:

   • Select a word that is central to a topic or story.
   • Write the central word on the chalkboard or a chart.
   • Brainstorm a list of words related to the central theme or topic and write these words.
   • Group the words into categories and label these categories.

   Focus your discussion on relating students' past reading and direct experiences to the semantic map. In examining the semantic map, students must think about the relationships between the target word and their experiences.

2. Identify one or two words in a dictionary that you think your students will not know the meaning of (such as *heinous, hiatus, sojourn, moot,* or *redoubtable*). Present a written dictionary definition and direct the students to give you a sentence using one of the words. Write each sentence on the chalkboard. Examine the limitations of using only a dictionary to understand new words by focusing on the students' use of the unknown words in their sentences.

Portfolio Entry

Collect some examples of students' webs and stories they have written in relation to the webs. Discuss with the students why they selected specific words to represent the concept or idea that is central to their web. For example, talking with the student who developed the web and story about bats in this chapter might lead you to ask questions such as, How did he know this information? What are descriptive words in comparison with action words? and What new words did he learn? Reflect on what the students share with you in terms of teaching meaning vocabulary in your own reading instructional program.

BIBLIOGRAPHY

Beck, I., & McKeown, M. (1991). Conditions of vocabulary acquisition. In R. Barr, M. Kamil, P. Mosenthal, & P. Pearson (Eds.), *Handbook of reading research* (Vol. 2, pp. 789–814). White Plains, NY: Longman.

Blachowicz, C., & Fisher, P. (1996). *Teaching vocabulary in all classrooms.* Upper Saddle River, NJ: Merrill/Prentice Hall.

Daneman, M. (1991). Individual differences in reading skills. In R. Barr, M. Kamil, P. Mosenthal, & P. Pearson (Eds.), *Handbook of reading research* (Vol. 2, pp. 512–538). White Plains, NY: Longman.

Goerss, B. L., Beck, I. L., & McKeown, M. G. (1999). Increasing remedial students' ability to derive word meaning from context. *Reading Psychology, 20,* 151–175.

Iwicki, A. L. (1992). Vocabulary connections. *The Reading Teacher, 45,* 736.

Jongsma, K. (2000). Vocabulary and comprehension strategy development. *The Reading Teacher, 53,* 310–312.

Laframboise, K. L. (2000). Said webs: Remedy for tired words. *The Reading Teacher, 53,* 540–542.

Nagy, W., & Herman, P. (1996). Incidental vs. instructional approaches to increasing reading vocabulary. In R. Robinson, M. McKenna, & J. Wedman (Eds.), *Issues and trends in literacy education* (pp. 257–268). Boston: Allyn & Bacon.

Norton, D. (1992). *The impact of literature-based reading.* Upper Saddle River, NJ: Merrill/Prentice Hall.

Norton, D. (1997). *The effective teaching of language arts* (5th ed.). Upper Saddle River, NJ: Merrill/Prentice Hall.

Rupley, W. H., Logan, J. W., & Nichols, W. D. (1999). Vocabulary instruction in a balanced reading program. *The Reading Teacher, 52,* 338–347.

Schwartz, R. M., & Raphael, T. E. (1985). Concept of definition: A key to improving students' vocabulary. *The Reading Teacher, 39,* 198–205.

Tennyson, R., & Cocchiarella, M. (1986). An empirically based instructional design theory for teaching concepts. *Review of Educational Research, 56,* 40–71.

Thompson, R. A. (1999). Balancing vocabulary instruction with teacher-directed and student-centered activities. In S. Blair-Larson & K. Williams (Eds.), *The balanced reading program* (pp. 24–36). Newark, DE: International Reading Association.

Watts, S. M. (1995). Vocabulary instruction during reading lessons in six classrooms. *Journal of Reading Behavior, 27,* 399–424.

Zechmeister, E. B., Chronis, A. M., Cull, W. L., D'Anna, C. A., & Healy, N. A. (1995). Growth of a functionally important lexicon. *Journal of Reading Behavior, 27,* 201–212.

7

Comprehension

Chapter Outline

For the Reader

Can you recall having read something, thinking that you comprehended it, but being frustrated when asked to demonstrate your understanding on an exam? It was not that you didn't comprehend. Instead, your purpose for reading, your perception of important information, your level of understanding, or your background knowledge differed from the expectations of the person who wrote the exam. We have all read material that was beyond our background knowledge, and as a result, we just couldn't make sense of it.

The reading process is dynamic, requiring active, meaningful communication between the author and the reader. Reading without meaning is unsatisfying and inconsequential. As a teacher of reading, a paramount feature of your reading program should be to further students' comprehension abilities. This chapter examines the comprehension process and the factors that affect it. It recommends teaching strategies for improving comprehension. No other topic is more important in establishing a literate society.

Key Ideas

- Students' background knowledge of the content and the language functions of reading affect comprehension.

- Reading instruction should be comprehension based.

- Quality instruction can enhance and develop reading comprehension.

- Effective questioning and teacher response are crucial to promoting reading, comprehension, and understanding.

- Explicit/direct comprehension instruction emphasizes students' understanding the when and why of comprehension strategies.

- The curriculum of comprehension instruction should focus on teaching students strategies to help them determine importance, summarize information, draw inferences, generate their own questions, and monitor their understanding of what they read.

- Connecting reading and writing is a foremost feature of comprehension instruction that assists students in developing strategies for reading and interpreting text.

- Comprehension depends on a variety of factors, including background knowledge, text content, the context in which reading occurs, sociocultural background, purposes for reading, and the reader's motivation and strategies.

CONCEPTUALIZATIONS OF READING COMPREHENSION

Although we cannot observe comprehension directly, numerous research studies, theories, and models provide probable explanations about its components and development. Most of these explanations view reading comprehension as a number of interdependent skills and abilities.

Chapter 1 presented an interactive conceptualization of the reading process. The interactive view of reading has come about as a result of researchers and teachers reconceptualizing what reading comprehension is and focusing on cognitively based views of reading.

The Interactive View

The cognitively based view of reading comprehension emphasizes both the interactive nature of reading and the reader's role in constructing meaning (Dole, Brown, & Trathen, 1996). The interactive view recognizes the roles of both the reader and the written text in reading comprehension. It depends neither on only what the reader brings to the text nor on only what is written on the page. Essentially, readers simultaneously use many different areas of background knowledge as they read, ranging from print features (such as letters, word parts, and words) to facts to strategies (Rupley & Willson, 1996). The interactive view of reading considers the importance of both written text and background knowledge in comprehension of print. We believe it is most applicable to reading instruction. Tierney and Pearson's (1994) view of reading comprehension reflects much of the current understanding of the process:

> A reader's background knowledge, including purposes, has an overriding influence upon the reader's development of meaning, and reading comprehension involves the activation, focusing, maintaining, and refining of ideas toward developing interpretations that are plausible, interconnected, and complete. In addition, there is a sense in which the reader's comprehension involves two other facets: the reader knowing (either tacitly or consciously) that his or her interpretations for a text are plausible, interconnected, and completely make sense, and, ideally, the reader's evaluation of the transfer value of any acquired understanding. (p. 501)

We can view background knowledge as an individual's experiential and conceptual backgrounds for (1) written text (word recognition, concept of print, understanding of word order, and understanding of word meanings), as well as for (2) the content of what is being read and for (3) how text is organized (Alexander & Murphy, 1996). Background knowledge has been noted as being crucial to reading comprehension and is theorized to give text consistent with background knowledge a storage advantage over incidental information during reading and understanding of text.

Schema Theory

A concept directly related to the interactive view of reading comprehension has had a major impact on both reading research and instruction. This concept is **schema theory,** which describes how knowledge is represented and how new knowledge is integrated with prior knowledge (Harris & Hodges, 1995). Anderson (1994) described the essential features of schema theory in relation to reading:

> According to schema theory, reading involves more or less simultaneous analysis at many different levels. The levels include graphophonemic, morphemic, semantic, syntactic, pragmatic, and interpretive. This means that analysis does not proceed in a strict order from the visual information in letters to the overall interpretation of a text. (p. 473)

A powerful feature of schema theory is that it helps explain how new learning is integrated with an individual's existing knowledge. It explains how we learn, modify, and use information we acquire through our experiences.

A major concept of schema theory is that our experiences and knowledge are organized by meaning (as in a thesaurus) rather than by word (as in a dictionary). For example, we have **schemata** (plural of *schema*) for places (e.g., grocery store,

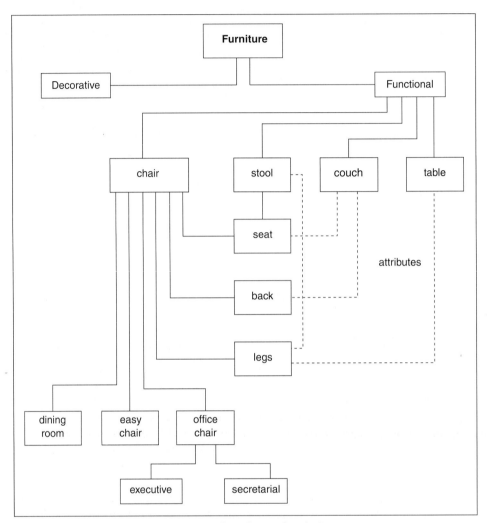

Figure 7.1   A partial representation of a schema for chair.

Source: Reprinted with permission from B. Taylor, L. A. Harris, and P. D. Pearson, *Reading Difficulties: Instruction and Assessment,* Second Edition (New York: McGraw Hill, 1995), p. 13.

home, and school), events (football game, political convention, and wedding), roles (parent, teacher, and student), emotions (love, hate, and fear), and language concepts (story, menu, and sentence structure).

Figure 7.1 illustrates the semantic features of schemata. It is a partial semantic network for *chair,* and it shows how *chair* is a schema as well as a member of other classes related to each other (functional furniture).

An adaptation of Taylor, Harris, and Pearson's (1995) description of this semantic network will help explain the nature of schemata. An important feature of this theory is that it refers to the attributes of a schema as slots. **Slots** (e.g., *seat, back,*

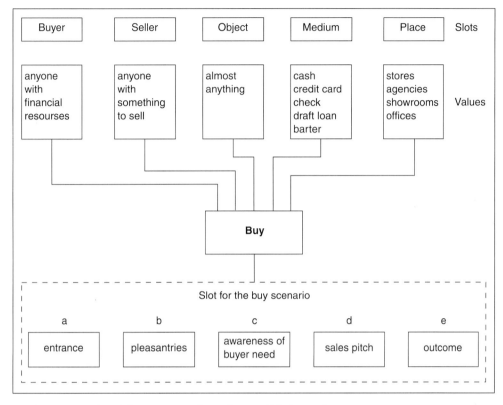

Figure 7.2 Partial representation of a possible buy schema.
Source: Reprinted with permission from B. Taylor, L. A. Harris, and P. D. Pearson, *Reading Difficulties: Instruction and Assessment,* Second Edition (New York: McGraw Hill, 1995), p. 14.

and *legs*) must be filled or recognized for an individual to activate a schema and recognize *chair.* The chair schema illustrates both an upward and downward organization. The upward organization shows the relationship of chair to functional furniture. The downward organization points out the different types or examples of chairs to fill a slot.

Schemata are considered to be abstract in nature. That is, they do not represent fixed concepts (e.g., specific events, objects, or emotions), but idealized concepts, which in fact may not even exist (Taylor, Harris, & Pearson, 1995). Anderson (1994) indicates differences between schemata for concepts versus for actions and events. Schemata for concepts and for actions and events differ mainly in the ways their slots are filled. Action and event schemata have episodic or sequential dimensions.

Figure 7.2 is a schema for an action—buying something. Slots for a *buy* schema may be selected. For example, the buyer and medium slots could be anyone from a small child with one dollar to a tycoon with millions of dollars. The possible slots for a *buy* scenario are episodes generally associated with buying something. How the slots in the buy schema are filled (a child with one dollar or a tycoon with millions) influences how the episodic slots are filled for the scenario. Taylor et al. (1995) note:

> There is a great deal of cross-referencing among schemata. For example, if a buy schema is selected and the buyer is a criminal, then the separate schema for criminal is called up and added to the buy schema. The values (actors) that fill variable slots (roles) in one schema are themselves schemata in other parts of a person's semantically organized memory. (p. 13)

Schemata are considered to be incomplete; that is, empty slots are always waiting to be filled as a result of new experiences. Consider a group of first graders preparing to play a game of basketball. They meet on the basketball court and choose two teams. These children have only a partial schema for the game of basketball. When a teacher assists them in getting the game started by demonstrating a tip-off, a slot for their schema of basketball is filled. However, they fill additional empty slots (e.g., what constitutes a foul, how to keep score, and when to end a game) as they more fully develop a basketball schema.

In fact, readers may change, elaborate on, or discard a schema as they proceed through text. Readers comprehend by using existing knowledge, which can change when they encounter new information. Although changes in schemata happen slowly, they can be considered new learning. New learning may result from modifying an existing schema or from creating a new one.

How schemata influence comprehension

Schema theory helps to explain how readers use prior knowledge to comprehend and learn from text. Students' reading comprehension or lack of comprehension can be based on teachers' noting whether or not students are engaging their schemata before, during, and after reading. Rumelhart (1984) suggests several features of schemata that may influence comprehension:

- Students may not have the necessary schemata in relation to the content of the text. They may lack schemata for such topics as world politics, world economics, and farm life. As a result, students have no way to hypothesize about text content.
- Students may have appropriate schemata for text content but lack schemata for the language of the text; therefore, they cannot access schemata for understanding the content. For example, "The magistrate chastised the assembly of onlookers for the brouhaha that erupted when the verdict was rendered" is more easily understood when written as "The judge scolded the people in the courtroom for the disruption that took place when he gave his decision."
- Students may have well-developed schemata for the content and language, but the author may not have provided enough clues to suggest them. In such instances, students need assistance in filling in the gaps.

- Students may find their schemata activated and perceive meaning; however, their meaning may be different from that intended by the author. Students who often think that they know more than the author in their reading of text are most likely to demonstrate such comprehension.

How social and cultural factors affect schemata

Schema theory highlights the importance of readers constructing meaning as they process text. In addition to helping to change the concept of reading comprehension to enhance instruction, schema theory has helped explain the effects of sociocultural variations on reading. Research conducted by Steffensen, Joag-Dev, and Anderson (1979) shows that readers from distinctly different cultures give differing interpretations of reading materials deemed culturally sensitive. Individuals who read materials related directly to their culture spend less time reading and recall more information.

Similar results were reported by Erwin (1991), who found that when elementary students were read a passage containing cultural information for which they had background knowledge, they could successfully answer questions without instruction. When hearing a story containing unfamiliar cultural information, however, they had extreme difficulty answering questions about the story. Even when the teacher added direct instruction to help the children build some knowledge of the different culture, they still had trouble both answering questions and discussing the content of what they read and studied.

An analysis of research (Anderson, 1994) supports the idea that reading material with identifiable cultural content directly influences an individual's comprehension. When the reader's culture and the text's cultural content are mismatched, the reader constructs different meaning. Linguistically and culturally diverse students may be unfairly evaluated if the teacher focuses on how closely their comprehension matches the text of what they are required to read. If the materials used for reading instruction contain culturally loaded content, students may not have the appropriate schemata to construct meaning that even approximates the author's intent.

The interactive view of comprehension is that readers construct meaning in relation to their background knowledge and the text. Knowing that they use this knowledge to interpret problems that characters in stories encounter can help teachers to acquire a better understanding of children's cultural knowledge. Teachers can help children develop a more global understanding and appreciation of cultures by studying a variety of stories from different cultures (Leavell & Ramos-Machail, 2000). However, because children will often have inaccurate or incomplete cultural and historical information about the content and events of stories, teachers must frequently be critical participants in literature discussions. Research has shown that children need to have a depth of cultural experiences through books, themes, and characters (Lehr & Thompson, 2000). Readers' responses to multicultural books at an early stage of discussion typically focus on literal remarks and broad leaps into interpretive statements. Interpretation of multicultural books is a later development in their conversations and discussions and comes about by teachers knowing when to become either an active or passive participant in children's discussion of a variety of cultures.

Implications of schema theory for teaching reading comprehension

Schema theory can help teachers develop better strategies to enhance reading comprehension. Several important considerations include the following:

- Make sure that the materials students are asked to read are within their experiential and conceptual backgrounds in terms of content and language.
- Help students activate their background knowledge prior to reading. Providing students with specific information to activate and build their background may be most beneficial when the goal of instruction is comprehension of a given text. Mapping strategies similar to those used in vocabulary instruction, discussions, student- and teacher-identified reading purposes, study guides, and prereading questions can help readers activate their prior knowledge relevant to the reading task.
- Help students develop background knowledge for materials that contain new information. Field trips, films, filmstrips, pictures, guest speakers, and so forth can help students build background knowledge to construct meaning for new information. Discussing new vocabulary, exploring the relationships among new and known concepts, and directly experiencing new ideas help build background knowledge to which new information can be related. These activities are of major importance in the content areas of science and social studies, for which the suggestions in the teachers' manuals often are not extensive and the previous text read by the students is by itself insufficient to build background for text containing new information (McKeown, Beck, Sinatra, & Loxterman, 1992).
- Demonstrate for students how to use strategies for constructing meaning. That is, if students are to understand information in what they read, model how to do this, using familiar materials. If they are to go beyond what is found in the materials, think aloud (model this) for them, relating the text to their background knowledge.
- Monitor students' performances closely to determine whether they have an appropriate schema but fail to activate it or whether they lack a schema to construct meaning. This requires that teachers know their students well. Teachers must be sensitive to sociocultural factors that impede students' comprehension of the cultural aspects of reading matter.

In schema theory, readers build connections between old knowledge and new knowledge through repeated interactions with content. These interactions result in hypotheses that the readers confirm or reject in relation to the text and their background knowledge. Comprehension is the synthesis of these hypotheses that results in constructing meaning.

Metacognition

In addition to using background knowledge to construct meaning, readers must monitor their comprehension and know when the process is breaking down. This monitoring of comprehension is **metacognition.** Good readers are aware of how they construct meaning and can apply corrective strategies when they are not comprehending. Metacognition requires knowing how to achieve the goal that has not been accomplished and knowing when a goal has been reached. Readers therefore must have the ability to monitor their comprehension. Good readers know when they have achieved their purposes for reading, when they understand and do not understand what they are reading, and how to correct and regulate their comprehension of text.

Teachers should help students become aware of what they are doing and why they are doing it. In addition, teachers should model how to check, monitor, and test hypotheses. Metacognitive training makes students aware of what good readers do when reading for meaning. It enables them to employ strategies to monitor their own reading and focus on comprehension.

A cognitive view of reading comprehension based on an interactive model has direct implications for classroom reading-comprehension instruction. Decoding and comprehension are both essential elements of a literacy instructional program. Teaching strategies for constructing meaning from text, monitoring comprehension, and providing opportunities to apply metacognitive strategies to learning are major features of teaching literacy.

WHAT TO TEACH

Early research in reading comprehension viewed it as a set of skills that students were to master. Learning each skill was assumed to result in a synthesis of skills: reading comprehension. Today, we realize that many factors influence comprehension and that a list of skills should not determine comprehension instruction. New views of reading comprehension recognize it as an interactive, cognitive process. Readers use their background knowledge, text information and cues, and the context in which they are reading to construct meaning. Comprehension instruction based on the cognitive view focuses on teaching strategies that students can use as they read text; these strategies should be adaptable to any text they read.

Determining Importance

The majority of reading comprehension in school requires students to determine the author-dictated importance of what they read rather than what they as readers perceive to be important. How good readers do this has been investigated; the findings suggest that (1) good readers use their background knowledge to access and evaluate what they are reading, (2) good readers use their knowledge of the author's bias, goals, and intentions to sort out what is important from what is unimportant in what they are reading, and (3) good readers are knowledgeable about text structure, which helps them identify and organize important information in what they read. Dole, Duffy, Roehler, and Pearson (1991) note, "In summary, the ability to separate the important from the unimportant leads to effective comprehension, and the ability to accomplish this task seems readily amenable to instruction" (p. 244).

Summarizing Information

Readers who can effectively summarize information can also sort through large pieces of text, distinguish important from unimportant ideas, and bring the ideas together so that the new text represents the original. The ability to summarize appears to be developmental (Rupley & Willson, 1997). Young children can successfully summarize the plot of simple stories, but they appear to have more difficulty summarizing more complex tasks such as determining how story sections contribute to the story's theme.

Drawing Inferences

Inference provides the foundation for reading comprehension. Readers use inferences to fill in gaps, to relate their background knowledge to the text, and to make sense of what they read. A large amount of research supports teaching inference from the beginning of reading instruction.

Generating Questions

Students who learn and have opportunities to generate their own questions prior to reading have improved comprehension compared with students who answer teacher-asked questions. Kindergarten through fifth-grade children are capable of asking predictive questions to set their own purposes for reading. Teachers must provide examples and structure on how to generate questions, however.

Monitoring Comprehension

As we noted earlier, comprehension monitoring (metacognition) is another important factor associated with good readers. "Comprehension monitoring and fix-it strategies appear to be important for developing expertise in reading comprehension. It is not only that good readers monitor; it is also that their monitoring appears to be the key to restoring lost comprehension" (Dole et al., 1991, p. 248). Expert readers typically monitor their comprehension at an unconscious level as they continuously search for and construct meaning as they read.

Quality instruction can enhance and develop reading comprehension.

QUESTIONING STRATEGIES TO PROMOTE COMPREHENSION AND UNDERSTANDING

Teacher-identified questions are the most common method of comprehension instruction. Such questions are important for focusing students' learning on building understanding of a particular text content. Teachers must carefully identify questions that enable students to establish meaningful purpose for reading and to understand the text in an integrated fashion. Teacher-identified questions should help students attend to the important features of a story, not trivial information that may misdirect their thinking. In addition, teacher questions should help students relate their backgrounds to story content, develop strategies for interacting with text, and learn to understand written language.

Literal Questions

Both literal and inferential questions are important in teaching reading. **Literal questions** focus on explicitly stated information and require the reader to recall or recognize such information. Effective literal questions should help students to build comprehension of the total story (summarizing information). "What did John see in the woods?" is an important question if the fact that he found an unusual set of footprints leads him to spend a summer in the woods searching for a creature. However, a question such as "What is the dog's name?" is trivial if the answer does not contribute to students' understanding of the story.

Prereading questions, such as those often suggested in a basal reader series, should encourage students to focus their attention on the text information related to the desired understanding. If the students are to know the content of what they read, then teacher-identified prereading literal-level questions are important.

Inferential Questions

Inferential questions require students to fill in information by using their background knowledge to deduce meaning as they read. A question such as "Why do you think so?" is an inferential question that should activate background knowledge appropriate for a story. "What do you think will happen?" can stimulate students to make predictions about story content before reading.

Asking both literal and inferential questions before reading a story can help students set purposes for reading, activate their background knowledge, and predict story information. Questions can come from the teacher, the students, or both. Again, it is important to remember that teacher-identified questions typically focus on knowledge of the text content.

Activating students' backgrounds

How questions are asked can either limit students' inquiry or expand it. For example, asking students, "Did you think about the story before you read?" does not promote activation of their background knowledge. However, asking, "What do you already know about this story and what do you think will happen?" will better assist students in understanding how they can use their background knowledge to understand what they read. The following comprehension-questioning strategy (Nessel, 1987) illustrates how teachers can engage students in better understanding of what they read and uses both teacher and student questions to activate students' experiential and conceptual backgrounds:

1. Identify one or two major turning points in the story.
2. Stop the reading at these points and ask, "What do you think will happen?" Encourage differences of opinion.
3. Have students give support for their predictions by asking, "Why do you think so?" or "What have you experienced that makes you think so?"
4. As students read further in the story, ask them to evaluate their original predictions in light of what they have read. Ask, "Do you still think that will happen or have you changed your mind?" Ask them to give reasons for retaining or changing their predictions. Ask, "Why do you want to keep (change) your prediction? What did you read that helped you decide?"
5. Design follow-up activities to encourage reflection on story content and language, to elicit creative responses (such as enacting, writing, and drawing), and to improve the students' ability to both make and justify predictions.

This strategy for teacher questioning focuses on the students' background for the story, not just their related experiences. It provides the students many opportunities to share information and to add to their existing knowledge base. Discussions also help students develop and refine their metacognitive abilities as they keep, change, and discard earlier predictions about a story. Students' predictions and supporting arguments provide insights into their ability to connect prior knowledge with story content to make sense of what they read.

Helping Students Develop Comprehension Strategies (Question-and-Answer Relationships)

Teaching question-and-answer relationships (QAR) facilitates students' story comprehension by providing them with a strategy for reading and answering questions (Raphael, 1986). Use of QAR with young students has been shown to be effective in helping them to determine whether a question can be answered with background knowledge alone or in combination with information in the text.

QAR identifies two basic sources of information for answering questions: in the book and in the reader's head (see Figure 7.3). Raphael (1986) notes that most students can make this distinction after discussions using a short text and one or two related questions as examples. To introduce the relationships, present the sample text on an overhead projector or chart, read the text, and then ask the first question. This question should be one that has an answer in the book. As the students respond to the question, locate the information in the text rather than focusing on the accuracy of the responses.

The second question should require an "in-my-head" response. Focus on the source of the answer in addition to its appropriateness. Once students understand the differences between *in the book* and *in my head* (Raphael notes that this takes minutes for upper-grade students and several weeks for early primary students), focus on developing each type. You should try to expand only one of the categories at a time.

Developing the in-the-book category includes helping students to realize when the answer to a question is either (1) explicitly stated in the text in one or two sentences or (2) explicitly stated in the text but requires putting together information from several parts. Raphael suggests that teachers refer to the synthesis of explicit text as putting it together. This instruction stresses strategies for locating information.

Expand the think-and-search category (see Figure 7.3) when working with upper-elementary and middle-school students by including strategies for identifying information in terms of text structure. Knowledge of text structure can help students understand how text information is organized and how such knowledge helps them locate information to answer questions.

Once students are competent in the in-the-book QARs, expand the "in-my-head" component. The two categories for this component are (1) author and you, and (2) on my own. The primary distinction between these two is whether or not the student needs to read the text for a question to make sense. If the answer requires interaction of the text and the student's background, then the question is related to

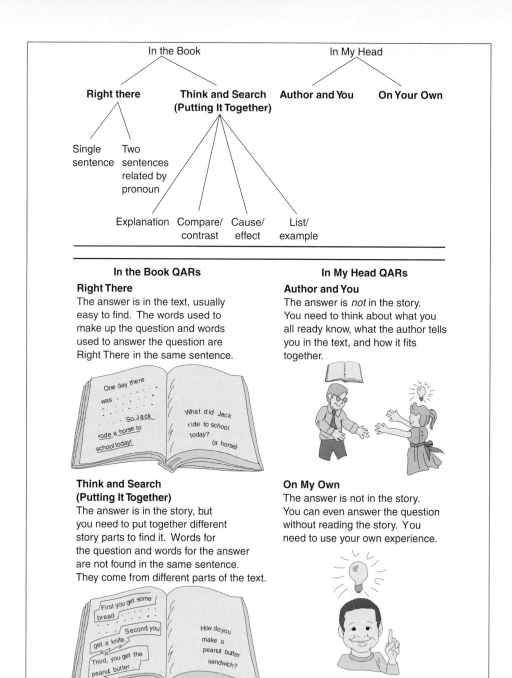

Figure 7.3 Relationships among the four types of question-and-answer relationships and ways to explain them.

Source: From T. Raphael, "Teaching Question-Answer Relationships, Revisited," *The Reading Teacher, 39* (May 1986), pp. 517 and 519. Reprinted with permission of the author and the International Reading Association. Copyright by the International Reading Association. All rights reserved.

the author-and-you component. If the response to a question depends only on the student's background knowledge, then it is the on-my-own component. For example, if students are asked to answer a question such as, "Why did Sally run home and change her clothes?" it is important for them to know that Sally was playing in the sand pit even though her mother had told her never to play in such a dangerous area. This information—coupled with the reader's knowledge that by changing clothes Sally might be able to prevent her mother from knowing where she had been—provides an answer for the question. An on-your-own question might be "How do you feel when your mother punishes you for misbehaving?" which the reader can respond to without reading or understanding the story.

A valuable feature of QAR that we have observed is that teachers use it as a framework for their comprehension instruction. Teachers we have observed and worked with have used it to identify the types of questions that are most important for guiding students in the reading of a story. On-my-own questions are one means that they use to activate students' background knowledge and stimulate students to think about how it relates to a given story prior to reading. On-my-own and author-and-you questions help teachers extend and encourage student interaction with the text and promote their drawing inferences.

Teacher Responses/Wait-Time

Although the quality of questions is important, the teacher's responses to students' answers are equally important. To develop students' thinking and to improve the quality and quantity of class discussions, teachers should be aware of their reactions to student responses.

For example, allowing students enough time to organize information and think about a response to a question has many positive benefits. Waiting for approximately three to four seconds after asking a question, with no further comment, can result in the following:

- The length of response increases.
- The number of unsolicited but appropriate responses increases.
- Failure to respond decreases.
- Confidence in responses increases.
- Student-to-student comparisons of information increases.
- Evidence-inference statements increase.
- The frequency of student questions increases.

The benefits of wait-time indicate that it is a powerful yet simple strategy to enhance students' interactions with questions posed by the teacher. Increasing wait-time benefits all students, shifts the responsibility for the dialogue to them, and encourages speculative and reasoning responses. Essentially, wait-time gives students the chance to activate their background knowledge and to relate their experiences to the questions asked. This is an important point for teachers to consider, especially when asking inferential questions.

Inclusion Strategies

Enhancing Student Participation in Responding to Questions

Positive teacher comments to student discussions and responses such as, "You were thinking very well to come up with that idea," "Can you tell us more?" and "You are off to a good start" will encourage students to go beyond single-answer responses and become more reflective about what they read. In addition, restating questions that use prompts and cues will help maximize students' likelihood of responding successfully in discussions focused on what they have read. For example, after reading about leopard frogs in a science unit, a student is asked to respond to the question "Why do leopard frogs hibernate during the winter months?" If the student cannot respond, the teacher could use the following techniques:

- Rephrase the question—"Leopard frogs are reptiles. What have we learned about reptiles that causes them to hibernate in the winter?" (Student does not respond.)
- "Let me name some reptiles that hibernate that we have already read about—snakes, lizards, and turtles. Each of these reptiles hibernates in the winter just like the leopard frog. Why do these reptiles hibernate?" (Student does not respond.)
- "During the hot months of summer, reptiles like to sun themselves in areas warmed by the sun. The body temperatures of reptiles depend on how warm it is around them. What happens in winter that would cause a leopard frog to hibernate?" (Student responds and elaborates on his response.)

The strategy of rephrasing questions built on background knowledge helps students to make cognitive connections between that which they have learned and how it relates to that which they are learning. In the example just provided, the teacher could have told the student why leopard frogs hibernate in the winter if the student had not built connections to prior knowledge. Telling the student why should be done in a friendly and knowledgeable manner, followed by asking the student to elaborate on the teacher's response. Teachers should avoid going to another student for a response because it often demeans the capabilities of the student who did not respond to the initial question.

Responding to students

Coupled with wait-time, responding effectively to students' answers and comments encourages them to make predictions, elaborate on the text content, and draw inferences. A teacher's response may involve asking questions that encourage students to clarify and expand their responses, redirecting students' thinking and strategy, or monitoring students' strategies to correct and provide alternatives. The teacher's response can also provide insights about how students derived an answer and can promote interaction among students about how an answer was derived. When students share their strategies with each other, it shifts the focus from getting a right answer to how the answer was derived.

EXPLICIT/DIRECT COMPREHENSION INSTRUCTION

Enabling students to interact with and construct meaning for text is the goal of literacy instruction. The concept of reading comprehension has been expanded to include background knowledge, text structure, flexible use of knowledge, reader habits, fluency, automatic word recognition, automatic word knowledge, and the orchestration of skills that support each other in a variety of ways. Such an expanded belief of comprehension should stimulate teachers to perceive themselves as people who assist students in developing understandings about text content, using strategies to understand the text, and learning how the process of reading functions.

Rethinking Explicit/Direct Instruction

Direct instruction once was thought of as the teacher directing and managing all aspects of students' learning, which included what they read, when they read it, and how they thought about it. An interactive view of literacy instruction often refers to direct instruction as explicit instruction. Explicit instruction emphasizes students' understanding the when and why of comprehension strategies. The importance of explicit/direct instruction was brought out in Smagorinsky and Smith's (1992) review of research addressing how best to facilitate students' literacy understandings. They argued that the job of teachers of literature is "determining what kinds of literature students need to know how to read, identifying strategies necessary for reading them, and designing instruction to teach the strategies" (p. 295).

Regardless of what it is called, explicit/direct instruction has some important features. Among the more important instructional features are modeling, gradually turning over the responsibility of learning to students, and ultimately enabling students to apply the strategies independently.

Modeling

Modeling is an effective way that teachers can help students understand reading strategies and how to apply them. It is most effective when it is applied to reading content rather than being done as an isolated, infrequently used skill-instruction activity. As its name implies, **modeling** is demonstrating for the students how to do learning tasks. As Dole et al. (1991) and Duffy and Roehler (1991) noted, modeling varies in relation to how much information is explicitly provided. For example, in classrooms with many opportunities for students to read books independently, the teachers' modeling is the reading of books themselves, thinking aloud about how they select books to read, guiding students through thinking aloud about literacy features (e.g., foreshadowing, flashbacks, and alliteration), and talking with students about their favorite authors.

Explicit types of modeling are talk-alouds and think-alouds. Both of these involve teacher discussion and teacher-student interaction. An important feature of **talk-alouds** is the teacher demonstrating the strategies while discussing the steps in the process.

Think-alouds often discuss the steps used in a strategy, but they also include a description of the reasoning that readers use when performing the task. Think-alouds are intended to help students "get inside the teacher's mind" and begin to understand what strategies they can use when doing similar tasks. An example of a think-aloud illustrates how teachers can use them in their literacy instruction:

> I want to show you what I look at when I come across a word I don't know the meaning of. I'll talk out loud to show you how I figure it out. Then I will help you do this. reading "The cocoa steamed fragrantly." Hmm, I've heard that word *fragrantly* before, but I don't really know what it means here. I know one of the words right before it though—*steamed*—I watched a pot of boiling water once and there was steam coming from it. That was hot so this must have something to do with the cocoa being hot. OK, the pan of hot cocoa is steaming on the stove; that means steam coming up and out, but that still doesn't explain what fragrantly means. Let me think again about the hot cocoa on the stove and try to use what I already know about cocoa as a clue. Hot cocoa bubbles, steams and smells! Hot cocoa smells good. [reading] "The cocoa steamed fragrantly." That means it smelled good! [addressing the students] Thinking about what I already knew about hot cocoa helped me figure out what the word meant. (Duffy & Roehler, 1991, pp. 869–870)

The purpose of modeling is to teach students strategic reasoning. When teachers attempt to explain how they think, however, they tend to do it in a step-by-step manner that can oversimplify the process of strategic reasoning. Herrmann (1992) recommends two ways that teachers can better use modeling of strategic processing in their classrooms. First, select short passages from several texts that contain unfamiliar content. Talk out loud and tape-record the process used to construct meaning as the passages are read. Listen to the recordings to identify the thinking used to construct meaning for the passages. Revise and refine this initial modeling attempt. By practicing this type of modeling before teaching, teachers can avoid oversimplification of strategic reasoning.

A second way to use modeling effectively is to encourage students to think aloud about the strategies they use when reading. Encouraging students to talk about their thinking when solving a reading comprehension problem or engaging in a reading comprehension process helps other students verify or reject the strategies that they use. In addition, students often synthesize cognitive processing strategies so that they are generalizing or using a more integrated process than that demonstrated by the teacher. The result is that the teacher can begin to see how students are generalizing about what they are learning and developing automaticity in its application.

Gradually turning over the responsibility of learning to students is another important feature of explicit/direct instruction. Instruction in an area of reading comprehension (see Figure 7.4) can begin as a series of connected lessons that move from students' understanding what they are to learn (modeling that learning), to application of the learning in real text with teacher support, then to students applying the learning independently. In earlier instructional phases, the teacher offers more guidance (scaffolding). The teacher adjusts instruction based on the use of ongoing assessment to determine instruction appropriate to students' needs.

- **Area of Needed Reading Instruction**

Reinforcement of the ability to make inferences.

- **Intended Learning Outcome**

Students will complete an open-ended story by writing inferences to complete the story.

- **Past Learning**

Students are aware of and have had some practice in drawing inferences from short passages and sentences.

- **Building Background**

Review the concept of drawing inferences from reading material by writing on the chalkboard key concepts that students need to remember when they think about inferences. For example, write that inferences are used when the purpose for reading requires students to anticipate outcomes, make generalizations, and draw conclusions.

Give students some quick verbal situations in which they must make inferences and ask different students to tell you whether the purpose for reading was to anticipate an outcome, make a generalization, or draw a conclusion.

- **Explicit Instructions**

Write several open-ended statements and questions on the chalkboard and have the class read each one silently. For example, give students a headline from a news article and ask them to infer or predict what the article is about.

Write students' responses on the chalkboard and discuss why each one inferred what they did.

Next, list open-ended story starters on the chalkboard and have each student respond. Instruct students that they are to write the outcome of the story starter. Then instruct students to list the events that caused the final outcome.

Story starting examples can include:

It was a cold, snowy morning in the mountains. Jim had lost all his camping gear and food to the grizzly bears last night. He prepared to turn back when suddenly he heard . . .

Jerry had one more lap of the car race to go. He was neck and neck with the other lead car. As they began the last lap of the race, Jerry . . .

- **Independent Student Practice**

Hand out a story starter similar to the ones in the teacher-directed instructional activity. For example:

The hot July summer was making it hard to live in New York City. Several teenage youths were standing on the street corner near the jewelry store when suddenly . . .

Discuss the inferences that could be included in this story and list them on the chalkboard. Distribute an additional story starter and allow ample time for students to write an ending.

continued

Figure 7.4 Direct instruction example for teaching reading comprehension.

• **Ongoing Diagnosis**

Teacher evaluation of the inferences made in students' written responses.

    Discuss and share written responses to the story starter with the group. Students who are experiencing difficulty with this activity can be grouped together for additional instruction. Give them written passages and short stories and guide them in making inferences.

• **Modifying Instruction**

The difficulty level for this activity can be easily varied. Easier tasks can focus on events that are extremely familiar to students: holidays, games, television programs, and so forth. More difficult tasks can be based on longer passages and more abstract concepts.

Figure 7.4   (continued)

Source: From *Teaching Reading: Diagnosis, Direct Instruction, and Practice,* Second Edition, by W. H. Rupley & T. R. Blair, 1990, Upper Saddle River, NJ: Merrill/Prentice Hall. Copyright 1990 by Pearson Education. Reprinted by permission of Pearson Education, Inc., Upper Saddle River, NJ 07458.

Scaffolding

Scaffolding is teacher support that enables students to do comprehension activities that by themselves would be too difficult. This support for learning can be gradually taken down and ultimately removed as students become capable of performing the activity, strategy, or behavior on their own. Scaffolding allows teachers to transfer the responsibility for learning to students gradually and still provide expert guidance. Pearson and Fielding (1991) discuss the role of scaffolding in comprehension instruction:

> In scaffolded instruction, the teacher determines the difference between what students can accomplish independently and what they can accomplish with just more expert guidance, and then designs instruction that provides just enough scaffolding for them to be able to participate in tasks that currently are beyond their reach. When scaffolded instruction operates according to plan, two things happen: first, the tasks and texts of the moment gradually come more and more under the learner's control; and second, more difficult tasks and texts become appropriate bases for further teacher-student interaction. (p. 849)

Explicit/direct instruction is an important feature of a program to help students become better readers. Explicit or direct instruction is active, reflective teaching in which the teacher recognizes that reading is an interactive process and that students can be effectively taught to become strategic in their comprehension of text.

Effective Explicit/Direct Comprehension Instruction Guidelines

Although instructional methods used depend on students' capabilities, the text being read, the purposes for reading, and the context in which reading occurs, teachers can provide effective instruction by concentrating their efforts in the following ways:

- Designing reading programs that allow students to develop meaning vocabulary by using concept-acquisition strategies based on the students' background knowledge.
- Concentrating on improved questioning abilities that include appropriate questions, appropriate feedback to students' responses, and instructional methods (such as reciprocal teaching) that encourage students to develop thinking and reasoning strategies.
- Providing explicit/direct instruction that is appropriate to the type of learning (ranging from knowledge to strategies) and students' background.
- Focusing instruction on strategies for reading comprehension rather than skill acquisition, using modeling and scaffolding to enhance students' success in learning, and applying these strategies in authentic texts.
- Helping students establish purposes for reading that encourage them to engage actively in a variety of reading that includes both literary and informational texts.
- Giving students varied opportunities to assume their own responsibility for learning through application of reading-comprehension strategies in a variety of texts.

Example of Explicit/Direct Comprehension Instruction

Explicit/direct instruction will help students interact with and understand written language. Figure 7.4 is an example of a explicit/direct comprehension lesson. Teachers' editions of basal readers contain a variety of lessons and suggestions on teaching such lessons that both beginning and experienced teachers can use. Teachers may need to modify such lessons, however, to include modeling, moving students toward independent application in a variety of texts, and scaffolding. The attributes of the following lesson components (see Figure 7.4) foster students' abilities to construct meaning and develop strategies for what they read:

1. *Using past learning.* This component focuses on determining students' existing experiential and conceptual backgrounds in relation to the focus of instruction. The teacher bases assessment on what the students already know and that they need to relate to and understand the text used for instruction and practice application of comprehension strategies.
2. *Building background.* After determining what existing knowledge to activate, focus on how to do this in the lesson. Utilize students' existing schemata. Model, explain, and demonstrate the lesson objective; review examples for application in meaningful context; and provide purposes for learning by assisting students in asking questions and making predictions about the text and strategies they will use.
3. *Modeling, explaining, and demonstrating.* This component involves making sure students understand the tasks and how they are to apply their strategies to reading. Use materials familiar to the students and focus on explicit strategies and flexibility in the application of strategies.

4. *Practice in application of strategy.* Students can do this either independently or in small groups that the teacher monitors closely to provide appropriate scaffolding. Encourage students to monitor their own application of the comprehension task and relate its application to similar text and comprehension tasks. This will assist them in assuming more of the responsibility for their own learning.

5. *Ongoing assessment.* Based upon students' performances in both group and independent activities, assess their learning. Focus on their application of comprehension strategies in other comprehension tasks. Students' responses provide teachers with information about what students do and do not understand. This information is valuable in determining what instruction is needed to assure students' learning.

6. *Modifying instruction.* Based on ongoing learning assessment, the teacher modifies instruction. You may need to provide scaffolding for some students in the initial instruction of a comprehension strategy by simplifying the task. However, because an important feature of scaffolding is to enable students to perform comprehension tasks that are beyond their existing capabilities, some tasks may need to be extended and reinforced with more difficult activities, which in a sense stretch the students' capabilities and learning.

Determining What Is Important

Because determining what is important (the main ideas or central problems) is a major feature of comprehension instruction in elementary reading programs, teachers should use instructional procedures that promote this ability. Students benefit when teachers help them use their background knowledge to understand the story line of narrative text, recognize relationships among information presented in informational text, and apply reading strategies appropriate to the desired comprehension outcomes. This highlights the importance of enhancing students' comprehension by helping them determine what is important in what they read. Some basic guidelines for teaching students to determine what is important in text include the following:

1. *Build on students' background knowledge for both content and strategies for reading.* Use concrete examples from previous text the students have read to illustrate and model how they determined what was important in these texts. List students' responses for them to review and use as guides for reading new texts. A major feature of this guideline is that the teacher is never introducing totally new information or concepts, but always building on what the students already know.

2. *Organize the students' background and strategy knowledge.* Simply activating background and strategy knowledge is insufficient if these do not enhance understanding of the text content and what strategies work best in reading the

text. Help students organize what they know that is directly applicable to what they are going to read and how they should best read it. For example, do they need to know genre, setting, main ideas, and so forth? Will they be looking for information that is right there, dispersed throughout the text, or combined with their knowledge and the author's knowledge (QAR)?

3. *Model the process for students.* Use examples within the students' background knowledge to model the strategies that best meet the desired purposes for reading and determining what is important. Two strategies for modeling are (1) recall and compare ("This reminds me of . . .") and (2) predict and justify ("This will probably happen because of that."). For example, using familiar texts, help students recall and compare the three little pigs' wanting to build a house with Little Red Riding Hood's wanting to visit her grandmother. Assisting students in inferring from other events in such familiar stories enables them to understand that numerous possibilities may exist, but they must make sense in the story. That is, they are credible in relation to important text events and information. For transfer and application, teacher guidance and scaffolding are important features of this step. Help students evaluate their story problems and redirect their thinking if necessary. You may have to use additional examples and illustrations within students' background knowledge.

4. *Use ongoing assessment and supporting transfer and application.* As students become more proficient in their application of their learning of text, concepts, and strategies, this learning can serve as a foundation for expanding their knowledge. Transfer to similar text may require maximum teacher scaffolding to help students build connections between their new learnings and similar text.

5. *Refine and expand students' strategies.* Students can equate what is important in text in numerous ways, such as by the category of problem, the variety of solutions, and multiple but related problems. Instruct vocabulary in relation to story problems. Concepts connected with vivid vocabulary can be used to classify characters (e.g., as *dauntless, intrepid, collaborative, domineering, spineless,* or *dependable*) and build relationships among character traits, problems, and solutions. Through examination of setting and its effect on story problems, continue to expand students' knowledge, concepts, and strategies.

Modifying Explicit/Direct Reading Instructional Activities

Many of the recommendations for teaching stories found in commercial reading series are based on directed reading activities (DRAs). The basic features of DRAs associated with commercial reading series are (1) introduction of identified vocabulary, (2) introduction of the story, (3) silent reading of the story, (4) questions about and discussion of the story, (5) skill activities with workbooks and

You probably read *Weekly Reader* or a similiar type of school weekly news magazine when you were in elementary school. These news magazines have been an important feature of many teachers' reading programs for several years. Such news magazines provide students with opportunities to apply reading skills to reading materials dealing with timely topics or current events.

MY WEEKLY READER

CURRENT EVENTS — COMMUNITY LIFE — GEOGRAPHY — HELPFUL SEATWORK — BIOGRAPHY — HEALTH — NATURE STUDY

Vol. I   SEPTEMBER 21, 1928   No. I

Two Poor Boys Who Made Good Are Now Running for the Highest Office in the World!

Issued weekly, from September to June, except Thanksgiving and Christmas weeks, by American Education Press, Inc., 40 South Third Street, Columbus, Ohio, and 1123 Broadway, New York, N. Y. Yearly subscription 75c a year. Special rates to schools.

A QUAKER BOY

A LITTLE boy sat in Quaker meeting. He had been there an hour. He began wiggling and wiggling, and whispered to his father, "Dost thou think meeting will be over soon?" After

church, he was punished, for Quakers were very, very strict.

That was in Iowa, about fifty years ago. The boy was Herbert Hoover. Today we are talking of making him President. Herbert was born in a small cottage. Next to it was his father's blacksmith shop.

Herbert went to Oklahoma to visit his Uncle Laban. His three were the only white children in town. All the rest were Indian boys and girls.

Such fun as he had playing with the Indian boys! They taught him how to build Indian fires; how to trap rabbits and squirrels, and how to catch fish.

When Herbert was nine, his mother took a very bad cold and died. The Hoover children were orphans now.

Herbert went to live on a nearby farm with his Uncle Allan. Here he fed the pigs, hoed the garden, and helped milk the cows. He went to the country school every day. Quakers were very strict about school, too. They thought that learning was next in importance to religion.

A LITTLE NEWSBOY

F IFTY-FIVE years ago, a baby boy was born in New York City. It was on the East Side, near the river, where

Special permission granted by *Weekly Reader,* published by Xerox Education Publications, © 1928, Xerox Corp.

Weekly Reader was and still is a popular type of reading material found in elementary classrooms. Along with various newspapers, magazines, catalogs, and quality literature, these materials represent the "real reading" component of a complete literacy program. This component emphasizes the application of literacy capabilities in meaningful reading situations. Several of the more recent magazines for elementary age children are *Time Magazine for Kids, Kids' Discover, Sports Illustrated for Kids,* and *Zillions: Consumer Reports for Kids.*

worksheets, and (6) enrichment activities. Teachers may wish to modify this organization to meet the needs of their students. Modification can be accomplished in the following ways:

- *Using enrichment activities before reading the story.* In one classroom we visited, the teacher used the enrichment activity about how shadows change in relation to the position of the light source before children read the story "Bear's Shadow" in their readers. Understanding why Bear did what he did to try to lose his shadow is a concept central to understanding the story. Using enrichment and extension activities prior to reading can activate students' background knowledge for the important information and concepts in the story they are going to read.
- *Focusing on skill and strategy application both before and after reading.* Associating these specifically to a story before students read it and discussing examples of applying the skills and strategies after reading provide students with concrete examples for application. This enables students to apply the skills and strategies to the text rather than to isolated examples.
- *Presenting and discussing comprehension questions before reading.* This enables students to use their background knowledge to predict content and establish purposes for reading.
- *Classifying and discussing vocabulary after reading the story.* This often results in teachers being better informed of students' acquisition of information and expansion of concepts related to vocabulary knowledge that is specific to a given piece of literature or a specific informational text.

Anticipation Guides

Anticipation guides are intended to assist students in integrating new knowledge and concepts with their existing background knowledge. Generally, an anticipation guide incorporates a series of statements given to the students before reading a selection. The students agree or disagree with each statement and share their reasoning with each other. Anticipation guides are intended to stimulate students' thinking, inquisitiveness, and attention for the text that they will read. As a result of their reading the text, students will verify their beliefs, modify or refine their beliefs, and analyze their beliefs in light of new information. Figure 7.5 is an example of an anticipation guide for fifth graders studying colonization (Merkley, 1997). As noted in the figure, students are provided with explicit statements about which they are to agree or disagree prior to reading the text.

Developing Fluency

Fluency is the reader's ability to orally project the "natural pitch, stress, and juncture of the spoken word in written text, automatically and at a natural rate" (Richards, 2000, p. 534). Oral reading fluency is a critical component in helping children to

---

AG for Fifth Graders Studying Early U.S. Colonization

Part A

Prereading directions: Carefully read statements 1–4. Under the "You" heading, put a check (✓) in the Agree column if you mostly agree. Put a check (✓) in the Disagree column if you mostly disagree. Be ready to explain why you checked as you did.

    You
Agree   Disagree

    1. The main reason people move to a new location is for better paying jobs.
    2. Strangers to an area are welcomed by people already living in that area.
    3. Available transportation is a major concern when choosing a new place to live.
    4. If given enough time, a new location always turns out to be a better place to live than the old location.

(Group and/or class discussion)

Part B

Purpose for reading: Now read pages 117–121 about immigration to the New World from England in the 1600s. When you finish p. 121, mark under the "Colonist" heading how you think a colonist would respond to each statement. Be sure to have proof from the text, pp. 117–121, to support why you think the colonist would agree or disagree.

    Colonist
Agree   Disagree

    1. The main reason people move to a new location is for better paying jobs.
    2. Strangers to an area are welcomed by people already living in that area.
    3. Available transportation is a major concern when choosing a new place to live.
    4. If given enough time, a new location always turns out to be a better place to live than the old location.

(Group and/or class discussion)

Figure 7.5   Example of an anticipation guide for a fifth-grade unit on U.S. colonization.

Source: From D. Merkley, "Modified Anticipation Guides," *The Reading Teacher, 50* (December 1996/January 1997), pp. 365–368. Reprinted with permission of the author and the International Reading Association. Copyright by the International Reading Association. All rights reserved.

construct meaning for the variety of text that they will read. Automatic word recognition, reading rate, and reading with feeling and expression are the three important components of reading fluency that lead to comprehending and enjoying reading. Fluency is an important part of becoming a successful reader. It is an important element of beginning reading instruction and for older struggling readers as well. Students need regular opportunities to read easy materials—materials at their independent level—to enhance and develop their reading fluency (Ivey & Broaddus, 2000).

Teachers have a variety of methods available for developing fluency in beginning and older struggling readers. Several methods have been discussed by Richards (2000) and include modeling, repeated readings, paired oral reading, and Oral Recitation Lessons. These methods can be accomplished in the following ways:

- Modeling can be done by a variety of individuals, including the teacher, older students who can model for younger students, and parents. Various classroom activities such as daily oral reading of a variety of texts, shared reading, and guided reading provide teachers with opportunities to model reading fluency.
- Repeated reading is a method in which students read and reread a short passage (independent level) until they reach a high level of word recognition accuracy and speed. Repeated reading is intended to develop automatic word recognition, which then allows the reader to focus on comprehension. Teachers can use explicit/direct instruction to model the repeated reading fluency and the whole class practices the process. Students can then individually practice reading fluency in an identified area of the classroom that is used for oral reading.

Shared reading and guided reading are instructional procedures that use repeated reading and enable the teacher to support all three components of reading fluency: automatic word recognition, reading rate, and reading with feeling and expression. Shared reading is an interactive process where the students participate in making predictions, rereading, segmenting and blending sounds, and comprehending. Guided reading has the component of rereading selected texts to support predicting and question answering. Rereading of familiar text where the focus is on semantic and syntactic features, word recognition features (phonemic awareness and graphophonic cueing system), and comprehension is done with teacher support and modeling and aids in the development of reading fluency (Short, Kane, & Peeling, 2000).

Readers Theater scripts provide students with familiar, independent-level texts that can be read by various individuals in a rehearsed fashion that establishes both reading fluency and comprehension. Numerous opportunities are provided for reading with feeling and expressions and for teacher and student modeling of reading fluency.

- Paired oral readings place the students in pairs where they take turns reading familiar texts aloud to each other. One student is a reader and the other student is a listener who provides feedback to the reader about reading fluency. Teacher modeling and supervised practice should be an introductory component of using paired oral readings. The teacher should model how to hold the book so both reader and listener can see it, how to sit shoulder to shoulder, how to make predictions about the story based on title and illustrations, and how to read and how to listen to provide feedback. The modeling of reading fluency and providing feedback are the important components. The teacher should model having reading difficulty and show how the partner could help in a constructive fashion. Such modeling should be done over several days to assure that students can begin to apply the process independently. Once students are paired the teacher should provide scaffolding when needed to support students' use of the process. Paired oral readings can be used as a part of the individual practice component of repeated reading.

- Oral Recitation Lessons are teacher-directed/explicit instructions in which the teacher uses selected text and (1) reads it aloud, (2) introduces the text, focusing on comprehension, (3) discusses the feelings and expressions represented in the text, (4) asks students to practice oral reading of the text as both a group and individually, and (5) asks students to read parts of the text for an audience. Features of a text that the teacher could use to focus on the feelings and expressions include distinguishing the difference in pitch or loudness of the voice to indicate questions or statements, knowing the character's emotions as represented in the text, recognizing text elements and features (all capital letters representing strong feelings), and using appropriate pausing and phrasing with longer parts of the text.

There are several important points that teachers should consider when focusing on reading fluency (Richards, 2000). First, text chosen for reading should be easy and familiar to the children—at an independent level without much teacher guidance or an instructional level with more teacher support and direction. Second, texts chosen for developing reading fluency should match the children's language patterns. Texts such as rhyming patterns, repeating refrains, predictable structures, and summarizing portions promote a more natural, fluent reading. Third, reading fluency instruction is important and should lead students to become more capable in recognizing words, using and developing knowledge of language features (syntax and semantics), and comprehending what they read.

STORY SCHEMA

A **story schema** is a set of expectations about how stories are usually organized (Gordon & Braun, 1983). An internal organization of story knowledge enables readers to process print by retaining story information in memory until it makes sense and adding more information as they read. A reader's story schema also is important in recalling what is read. Features of a story schema can include setting, theme, plot, and resolution.

Setting

The story setting may contain both major and minor settings. Major settings include time, place, character, and state. Time may be either implied (e.g., "Sally looked out her window") or stated (e.g., "One clear and bright summer morning"). Time may also be represented by "Once upon a time" or "Long, long ago," both of which are characteristic of fables and fairy tales. Place, too, may be either implied (e.g., "Everyone sat down to breakfast") or stated (e.g., "Mark went to visit Aunt Jane's farm"). Major and minor characters are typically identified by name (e.g., Mark, Aunt Jane, or Frank), occupation (e.g., bellhop, police officer, or teacher), or relationships (e.g., friend, mother, or neighbor). State refers to what is occurring. Ongoing states found in different stories include a party at which children are playing games; wishes and superstitions; and fishing, camping, and hiking. Minor settings include the same elements as major settings and develop the story. For example, the major setting time may be summer, but a minor setting time may be one day. The major location may be Aunt Jane's farm, but a minor location may be an old barn on another farm. The major character may be Frank, the hired hand, but a minor character may be Aunt Jane. The ongoing state for the major setting may be new experiences on the farm, but a minor state may be new friendships.

Theme

Theme can be either the goal of the main character or the author's message. For example, Billy's wanting his friends to have a good time at his birthday party is a goal of the main character and is a story theme.

Plot

Story plot contains five subparts that together represent an episode. First, the starter event begins the episode. It may be an action by a character or an occurrence (e.g., Billy opening his birthday gifts). Second, the character has an inner response—feelings, thoughts, goals, or plans (e.g., Billy was disappointed when he didn't get a new bicycle for his birthday). Third, action is how the story character plans to achieve his or her goal (e.g., Billy planned to work at odd jobs and save his money for a bicycle). Fourth, what happens is the outcome of the character's actions (e.g., Billy found only a few odd jobs and couldn't save enough money to buy a new bicycle). Fifth, reaction is a response to an outcome or earlier action (e.g., Billy decided to buy a used bicycle and fix it up). Episodes are tied together by relationships (e.g., Billy got a used bicycle and then began to fix it up or Billy spent all his money on a used bicycle and his parents gave him the money to fix it up).

Resolution

Resolution can be thought of as the main character achieving his or her goal or the moral of a story. For Billy and his bicycle, the resolution could be that he finally got a bicycle, which he was very proud of buying himself. A possible moral could be that a person who is willing to work hard for something can achieve his or her goal.

Figure 7.6 is a story told by a 4-year-old boy to his teacher and it clearly indicates that he has a concept of setting. His story begins with "Once upon a time." In addition, it is apparent that he has a well-established setting, theme, and plot in his story. However, he has limited use of resolution or bringing his story to a cohesive conclusion. Although the previous discussion of story structure represents the ideal, most children, such as this 4-year-old, recognize and incorporate story structure in their literary experiences. Knowledge of story structure may help students to utilize their inferential capabilities as they read and to construct meaning for story parts that are not well developed.

Once upon a time there was a kid named Matt. He was walking through the woods. And then he saw a bunch of woodpeckers. And then he tried to catch one. And then he actually caught a baby. And then he saw the woodpecker crying. So and then the woodpecker actually lost his mommy. Then there was a kitten. And then they seemed like saying something to the bird and human. He saw a hole that a snake fits in. And well he seemed like he was going back and going into the woods. Then he saw a little girl named Suzanne. And then there was a kid named Donald. And standing with Donald, was a kid named Bobby, who was older than any of them. And he said: Why are you so far into the woods. We are going to pick berries and we just got to this place. The end.

Figure 7.6   This story illustrates children's knowledge of story grammar or schema and its emerging characteristics as their literacy capabilities grow.

Guidelines for Teaching Story Structure

Following are some basic guidelines for teaching story structure.

1. Use well-formed stories to introduce both the structure and the terminology of story grammar. Demonstrate and model for students the features of story schemata using the stories as concrete examples. Connect the information to their experiential and conceptual background knowledge.
2. Initiate and illustrate reading purposes. Activate students' background knowledge in relation to the story content and concepts and to guide their thinking by referring to well-known examples.
3. Distinguish the story structure before identifying the content. Initially, examine and discuss the structural features to enable the students to perceive the permanence of the structure. Only the content of the stories changes.
4. When students are able to connect story structure with specific story content, ask story-specific questions. Questions should match the attributes of the story structure being dealt with. Comprehension of explicit story information should be the focus of the story. Following students' ability to note features of story structure with explicit-directed instruction, begin to focus more on inferential questions.
5. Introduce stories that don't adhere to ideal story structure to ensure that students realize that not all stories follow the same structure, which supports the earlier guideline for explicit-directed instruction, proceeding from the simple to the complex.

Story Mapping

Story mapping focuses on the structure rather than the specific content of stories. It provides students with a conceptual means for seeing how the contents of stories fit their structure. Story mapping assists readers in remembering the story elements. A feature of story mapping is to provide students with a framework to guide them either in comprehension of text or in the composition of text. Developing and using story mapping strategies is not difficult and many of the strategies can be used with varying lengths of texts (excerpts to books), differing story elements, and for both reading and writing. Teachers can use story frames with all grade levels and texts. Important instructional considerations involve providing students with appropriate modeling in completing the frames, stimulating discussions about story contents as frames are completed, continuing to provide concrete examples and guidance as students begin to independently complete story frames, and encouraging students to share and discuss their individual reading and writing maps.

An example of story maps (Staal, 2000) can be found in Figures 7.7 and 7.8. Story faces are maps that provide students with a recognizable object upon which they can map a story. Story faces are easily adaptable to a variety of story structures. For example, a happy resolution would be represented by a smiling face and a sad resolution would be represented by a frowning face. There are other flexible features of using story face maps that include the number of events varying in relation to those in the story, the features of the setting varying in relation to descriptors, and the number of character traits varying in terms of those represented in the story.

Through the use of story maps, students begin to use their knowledge of story structure to organize and learn story information. Students exhibit more interaction with each other as they discuss their story maps and ask questions about stories. Perhaps one of the most important advantages of story maps is that students perceive stories as wholes, made up of important and recurring parts.

VISUAL DISPLAYS OF TEXTS

Visual displays of story information can be used to teach reading-comprehension strategies and assist students in understanding text content. Webbing is a visual display that can help demonstrate the features of story structure and help students understand the relationships among text elements (e.g., characters, plot, setting, and reaction) Norton (1997) concluded from the results of a 3-year study with literature webbing that it is one of the most effective ways to teach the important characteristics of a story. Figure 7.9 presents an example of a web for "Three Billy Goats Gruff."

Discussion Webs

The discussion web incorporates all of the language arts—listening, speaking, reading, and writing. It can be used as either a prereading or prewriting activity and as a postreading activity. In addition, the discussion web promotes the use of cooperative learning groups. Figure 7.10 is an example of a discussion web based on "Jack and the Beanstalk."

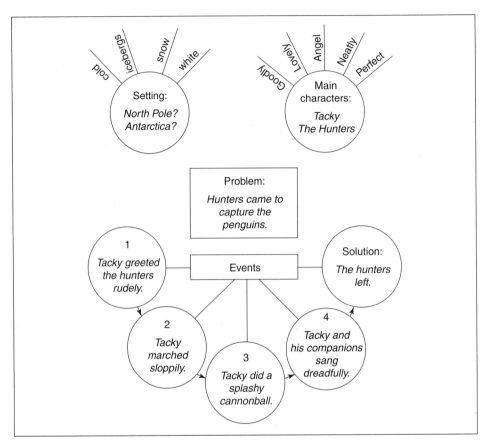

Figure 7.7   A happy face story map.

Source: From L. A. Staal, "Teaching Ideas: The Story Face: An adaption of story mapping that incorporates visualization and discovery learning to enhance reading and writing," *The Reading Teacher, 54* (September 2000), pp. 26–31. Reprinted with permission of the author and the International Reading Association. All rights reserved.

Teachers and students go through five steps in completing a discussion web (Alvermann, 1991):

1. Prepare students to read the selection by activating their background knowledge, establishing purposes for reading, and discussing new vocabulary and concepts.

2. Upon completion of their reading, introduce the discussion web with a question ("Was it all right for Jack to bring home things from the giant's castle?"). Students work in pairs and discuss the pros and cons associated with the question by writing key words in the no and yes columns. Although students need not write a response for each line in the columns, they should be encouraged to give an equal number of responses.

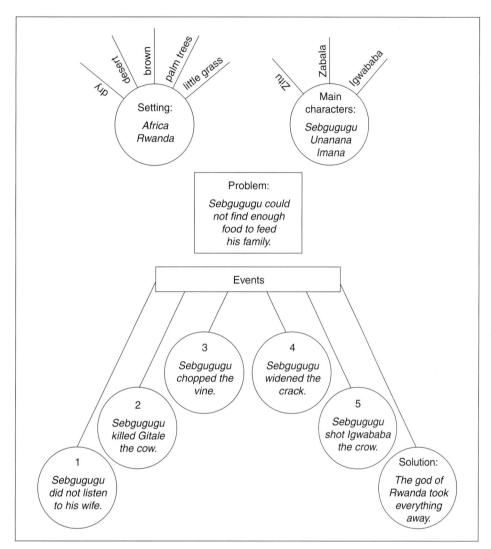

Figure 7.8 A sad face story map.

Source: From L. A. Staal, "Teaching Ideas: The Story Face: An adaption of story mapping that incorporates visualization and discovery learning to enhance reading and writing," *The Reading Teacher, 54* (September 2000), pp. 26–31. Reprinted with permission of the author and the International Reading Association. All rights reserved.

3. After students have had sufficient time to write their responses, they are paired with another set of partners, and the four students compare their responses. The focus of this step is for the group to reach a consensus; however, individuals may disagree with the conclusion.

4. When each group of four students has reached a conclusion, the teacher or group appoints a group spokesperson. Each group then has approximately 3

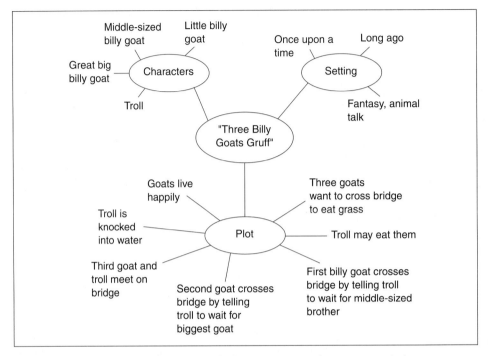

Figure 7.9   An example of a story web that represents characters and plot development in chronological order.

Source: From *The Effective Teaching of Language Arts* (5th ed.) by D. Norton, 1997, Upper Saddle River, NJ: Merrill/Prentice Hall. Copyright 1997 by Pearson Education. Reprinted by permission of Pearson Education, Inc., Upper Saddle River, NJ 07458.

minutes to discuss which of all the reasons given most supports the group's conclusion. Each group should select only one reason to ensure that all spokespersons will have at least one new reason to present. Spokespersons report for each group as part of a whole-class discussion.

5. Individual students write answers to the discussion web question, including their own ideas as well as those expressed by other students. These individual responses are displayed in the classroom so other students can read them.

Elementary teachers can use the discussion web with a variety of students and content areas. It can serve as an alternative to end-of-story questions found in reading series and is appropriate for small groups as well as the whole class. Use of the discussion web has resulted in many students frequently constructing their own questions for the web.

RECIPROCAL TEACHING

A strategy to help students establish purposes for reading and increase their interactions with the teacher and each other is called reciprocal teaching (Brown 1988).

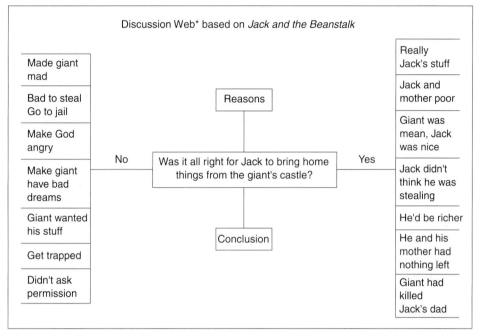

*Adapted from Duthie, J. (1986). The History and Social Science Teacher, 21, 232-236.

Figure 7.10   A discussion web based on "Jack and the Beanstalk."
Source: From D. Alvermann, "The Discussion Web: A Graphic Aid for Learning Across the Curriculum," *The Reading Teacher,* 45 (1991), p. 95. Reprinted with permission of the author and the International Reading Association. Copyright by the International Reading Association. All rights reserved.

Reciprocal teaching has two major features: (1) instruction and rehearsal of questioning, summarizing, predicting, and clarifying, and (2) use of scaffolding dialogue from both the teacher and the students as a means for learning questioning, summarizing, predicting, and clarifying (Rosenshine & Meister, 1994). Reciprocal teaching has been used primarily for teaching in the content areas, but it can be used to teach the structure of narrative text as well.

Essentially, with this strategy the teacher and students take turns in assuming the teacher's role. The goal of reciprocal teaching is gradually transferring to the student the responsibility for thinking while reading. Briefly, the procedure involves four basic steps: (1) predicting, which requires students to activate their background knowledge to predict what they will find in a given text; (2) questioning, in which students learn to determine what a good question is, how to ask questions, and how to read to answer questions; (3) summarizing, or identifying the important content in a passage; and (4) clarifying, which requires students to address reasons that text might be difficult to understand (such as vocabulary, new concepts, and author style).

Reciprocal teaching with narrative text should focus on the features of story schemata, purposes for reading, and comprehension. Predicting should consider the resolution. Questioning should identify important information with which to establish purposes for reading. Summarizing should deal with plot. Finally, clarifying should identify which strategies to employ to construct meaning. The purpose of associating the interactive procedure with story schemata is to teach another strategy to construct meaning. In introducing and developing the concepts associated with story schemata, model the strategy and demonstrate with familiar examples.

LITERATURE CIRCLES

Literature circles consist of small groups of students who are reading books with a similar theme and discussing their reading with each other. Comprehension is central to the discussion; however, the goals of literature circles are for students to meaningfully listen and interact with each other about what they have read. Through their use of inquiry and critique, students engage in *grand conversations* (Martinez-Roldain & Lopez-Robertson, 2000), which is the central intent of the literature circle—to talk about what they have read in their own insightful manner.

The purposes that literature circles serve for students and their components for literacy instruction have been explored by Brabham and Villaume (2000) and are presented below:

- *The importance of literature circles.* Literature circles advance students' abilities to develop inquiry and insights as they address text-level problems in a variety of ways, debate with the author, evaluate the content of the text and the writing style of the author, and in summary construct active and personal meanings.

  The teacher provides scaffolds, which are the conversations and interactions used to temporarily support the students' development of inquiry and critique. These scaffolds are aimed at students taking over the responsibility for discussion and interpretation of what they read.

  Teachers will need to recognize that procedural questions and answers are still important, but they function only as the starting points for building students' conversational skills so they can talk about texts in enlightening, personal, reflective, and explorative ways.

- *Grouping students in literature circles.* The most frequently recommended number of students in literature circles ranges from four to six. However, a group as large as the whole class or only two students can be used to engage students in conversations about what they read. The important consideration for grouping is how the number of students impacts their opportunities to make enlightened, thoughtful, reflective, and exploratory responses to each other's contributions.

- *Texts that should be used.* There are two major concerns related to the texts used in literature circles. First, the quality of the text must connect with critical issues and background experiences of the reader to stimulate responses that encourage participation in discussions (grand conversations). Second, student selection of texts is a feature of many literature circles and the type of text may include novels, picture books, informational books, poetry, and magazine and newspaper articles. The texts that are used will be determined by the availability of multiple copies and curriculum learning outcomes.

- *Student preparation for literature circles.* Scaffolds are an integral part of preparing students for participation in literature circles. A variety of scaffolds can be used ranging from teacher developed to student developed to a combination of both. For example, teachers may model different discussion roles, provide guiding questions for reading, and develop story maps. Students may note words for vocabulary enrichment, use sticky sheets to record comments, use a reading log, and identify questions and ideas to guide their reading. As noted by Brabham and Villaume (2000), " . . . scaffolds are important because they help students and teachers move toward 'grander' conversations; however, they are intended to be updated periodically to match evolving needs and insights of readers. . . . scaffolds should be eliminated when students and teachers have internalized them and no longer require their support." (p. 280)

ORAL LANGUAGE, READERS' THEATER, AND VISUAL ARTS

Students can demonstrate understanding of what they read using drama, readers' theater, oral-language activities, visual arts, and writing. These methods can also be used as means for instruction. Throughout this chapter and other chapters in this book, we have discussed the importance of oral language in literacy development. Furthermore, in our presentation of modeling, one of the essential features was encouraging students to talk aloud about the strategies they used to construct meaning for text.

Oral-Language Interactions

Opportunities for oral-language interaction in the classroom need to be realistic and not based on situations contrived by the teacher. One example of a good opportunity is the discussion web, which gives students an opportunity to interact and learn from each other. Such interaction facilitates comprehension, understanding of text, and the recognition that individuals can have differing interpretations of text.

Additional ways to stimulate oral interaction among students are to group them together to complete projects (e.g., in science and social studies), share their reactions to books they have read, discuss features of language in books they have read (e.g., most interesting parts, most exciting parts, and confusing parts), and work cooperatively in writing activities (e.g., plays, poems, stories, and articles). Such activities can be used effectively at all grade levels and can encourage students to talk about and share what they are learning with others.

Readers' Theater

Readers' theater does not depend on students' actions to convey meaning, but involves using the voices and emphasizing the meaning-bearing cadences of language to make the print come alive (Hoyt, 1992). Teachers can use either published scripts

Integrating reading and writing enhances students' reading comprehension.

or the students' reading selections for readers' theater. However, using students' reading selections shifts the focus to their responses to literature and integrates features of story schemata, writing, and classroom discussion. Integrating such features reinforces and provides an opportunity to apply past learning.

Teachers can use several variations with readers' theater. They can have only one student at a time reading the part of each character, have several students take turns reading the same part and discuss the variations in their readings, use choral reading of parts, or read parts together in small groups. Hoyt (1992) argues that reading parts chorally or together in small groups gives all students a role, which encourages repeated reading for fluency.

Modeling and scaffolding are important components of readers' theater. The teacher can model reading the various parts with feeling and illustrate how variations in language communicate meaning. Teachers can use think-alouds to model how they decided to read certain parts with anger, excitement, disappointment, and so forth. Scaffolding is important to ensure that students who have difficulty have background knowledge to relate to the story content and characters. Repeatedly practicing the story with teacher assistance can help students become more confident in presenting the story to an audience.

Visual Arts

Visual arts such as drawing and painting offer students a way to express their understanding of text that doesn't require oral or written language expression. A pictorial representation of a story requires students to use both the affective and cognitive domains; they must think about the story as a whole in selecting what to represent visually. Although a visual representation may seem like a simple task, Hoyt (1992) notes that it requires a lot of evaluation, analysis, and summarization.

Hoyt (1992) recommends a visual arts activity, called sketch to stretch, that teachers can use to facilitate students' comprehension. After students have read some text (story, poem, or nonfiction), they have a limited time to create a sketch about what they learned, what they were thinking, what they liked, and so forth. The teacher also creates a sketch on the chalkboard, easel, or overhead projector. The time limit encourages students to create a general impression of the text rather than many details. The sketches serve as a focal point for discussion as students clarify, reflect, and consider relationships before verbally discussing their learning.

Visual arts activities should not take the place of actual time spent in reading and writing; however, they can provide teachers with alternative means for assessing and teaching reading comprehension. As stated by Hoyt (1992), Visual arts "can be a powerful vehicle for learning that deserves a place in the reading program" (p. 584).

THE READING AND WRITING CONNECTION

Many of the instructional strategies discussed in this chapter can serve to integrate reading and writing and to enhance reading comprehension. Several additional strategies follow. The use of these strategies can help students develop and refine both their reading and writing capabilities.

Probable Passages

The probable-passages strategy (Wood, 2001) can illustrate the similarities between processes used in constructing meaning for both reading and writing. This strategy depends on a story schema that uses the story features of setting, character(s), problem(s), solution(s) to the problem(s), and ending. The steps in developing a probable passage include preparation, prereading, reading, and postreading.

Preparation

Analyze the story selection to identify the significant concepts and vocabulary. Present these words visually along with the story features (the features may need modification to correspond to the structure of the story to be read). Present an incomplete story frame on the chalkboard to use both before and after reading. In this incomplete story frame, incorporate the story features (e.g., "This story takes place in _____ and has a character who wants _____.").

Prereading

Read the list of significant concepts and vocabulary and direct students to construct a story line mentally. After the students have mentally developed a story line, have them determine where to place each of the key words in the story frame. They should realize that some words may fit in more than one feature and that they can use words from their background knowledge that are logical choices. Have the students justify their responses, requiring them to verbalize their versions of the probable passage.

Upon completion and discussion of the story features, have students use this information to develop a probable passage. Write in the information for the story frame and guide students' responses by asking such questions as "How can we make that idea fit here?" "Can we reword this sentence to better communicate an idea?" and "Can we shorten this and still make it say the same thing?"

Reading

Upon completion and discussion of the story frame, have the students either read or listen to the story.

Postreading

Have students modify the story frame after reading to represent the actual story events more accurately.

The probable-passages strategy integrates reading and writing. It also activates students' background knowledge prior to reading. It provides a structure for students to use in making predictions, reinforces the features of story schemata, and engages all students in writing text both before and after reading.

Thinking and Writing About What Students Read

The importance of questioning and reading comprehension were discussed earlier in this chapter. Teacher- and student-identified questions were both cited as means to promote active engagement with text and purposes for reading. Questions also can be an integral part of a literacy program that encourages students to think about what they are reading. Teachers are often caught in a dilemma when making the transition from reading instruction based solely on a basal reader series to a literature-based reading program. Angeletti (1992) shares her experiences in making such a transition and how she used question cards to help her students think about and respond to what they read in their own books. One of the major features of her instruction was encouraging students to write about the books they were reading by writing questions on cards to stimulate higher-order thinking. The basic elements of her instruction follow:

1. Question cards were used to encourage students to state opinions (see Figure 7.11). The teacher modeled the cards' use during oral reading of the book to students. Students asked questions of the teacher, who modeled the role of the reader.

Comparison and contrast card 1

Choose two characters from one story. Do the characters look alike? How are they alike? How are they different? What problems do the two characters have that are the same? How are the feelings of the characters different?

Comparison and contrast card 2

Choose two stories. Were the places alike? How were the stories the same? How were they different? How were the story endings different? Which story did you like better? Why? Which character did you like better? Why?

Opinions

What did you like about the main character? What did the character do that made you like him or her? What did you think about the ending? Was anything surprising to you in the story? What was it? Why were you surprised?

Inference

Look at the pictures and at the title. What do you know about the story before you begin to read it? Read the story. Think about the ending. If the story had continued, what might have happened? Why?

Drawing conclusions

Draw a picture of your favorite character. Tell as much as you can about what kind of person your character is. Tell things he or she did in the story. Is this a nice person? Why or why not? Would you like to have this person for a friend? Why or why not?

Characters

As you read a story you learn about the characters by what they say and do. Choose a character from your story. What kind of person is your character? Do you like him or her? Why? How would they act if you were with him or her?

continued

Figure 7.11 Examples of question card.

Author's style

Every writer has his or her own style of writing. When we learn the author's style, we know what to expect from that writer. We often know whether books written by a particular author will be easy picture books or chapter books. We know what kind of characters are typical of the writer—animals that talk, or people like us. We might know whether there will be a happy ending. We know whether we would enjoy reading another book by the same author. Choose an author whose style you know and tell what you know about the author's style of writing. Give examples from books you have read by that author.

Author's purpose

Sometimes authors write a story to teach you something. Sometimes they tell a story about something that happened to them. Sometimes they just want to entertain you. Or, they may have another reason for writing. Tell in one sentence why the author wrote the story you read. Then tell how you knew the author's reason for writing the story.

Type of literature

Tell what kind of book you are reading. Look for clues that let you know. If it is fantasy fiction, for example, there may be animals that talk, or magic things may happen. If it is realistic fiction, there may be real people in the story, and the story could have happened, but the author made it up, perhaps using ideas from his or her own life. If you find rhyming words, short lines, and writing that makes every word count, you are reading poetry. Or you may be reading facts from a book like an encyclopedia. If so, the book is factual. Think about what section of the library you would go to in order to find the book. Then put your book into one group and tell what clues let you know which type of book it is.

Figure 7.11   (continued)

Source: From S. R. Angeletti, "Encouraging Students to Think About What They Read," *The Reading Teacher, 45* (1992), pp. 295–296. Reprinted with permission of the author and the International Reading Association. Copyright by the International Reading Association. All rights reserved.

2. Practice opportunities were provided for the whole class as students asked the questions of readers who wanted to share the book they were reading. Angeletti recommends that the teacher provide guided practice opportunities for a long period to ensure that all students will succeed in the next steps.

3. Small-group practice was used with student-formed groups of two to five students. The groups used the cards as questioning guides. Through practice students became aware of books other students were reading, talked with each other about their books, and planned for other books they would read and talk about together.

4. Students' written responses to the question cards became a major focus of the instruction. Angeletti (1992) noted that students' writing moved from simple retelling to elaboration about what they read that included inferences, conclusions, and characters' motives.

The program was extremely successful with first, second, and fifth graders. Writing revealed that students at all ability levels learned to choose their own questions and write responses that reflected understanding and appreciation of the books they had read. Students were in control of their own learning as a result of the modeling and scaffolding that the teacher provided in the early stages of instruction.

Matt Rupley

How I get ready for school in the morning

First, I get out of my feather soft bed. Sometimes I just sit there and think about school. Once, when I was getting up I fell of the bed because the blanket had slipped off.

After I am out of bed I turn on my milk snake old bright purple tube light so he stays warm and cozy. I've had for about six years. In the mornings I like sitting there looking at him because he has so many different colors.

Next, I go and eat breakfast. I absolutely love crunchy waffle crisps with icy milk. "Yum." Just thinking about it makes me hungry. On Monday my mom makes absolutely, unbelievably delicious and smooth pancakes. I devour at least two of the delicious pancakes.

After that I usually go do my hair in my bathroom, unless we are in a rush. Once when I was doing my hair I accidentally mistake shampoo for gel. If we are in a rush I go put on my Nike shoes, and brush my teeth with an electric toothbrush so they stay clean.

It's seven thirty-five, so I better speed it up. Then, I make my feather bed very neatly and open my blinds. I also pick up dirty cloths and any toys off the carpet floor in my bedroom. I double check to make sure my snake's light is on. Now, I get my backpack that hangs from the chair and I pack my Eastwood backpack neatly. Then, I turn off my computer, Kenwood radio, closet light by shutting the door, and my bathroom light. Now, I shut the door and kennel my Rottwhiler, Alexa. Next, I hope into my parent's 2000 suburban, speed to school and hurry to class. Now you know how I get ready for school in the morning.

Figure 7.12 An example of a student writing a description of how he begins his day. He will share this with his classmates who will compare and contrast each of their writings about how they begin their day.

Developing the Reader-Writer Relationship

Other procedures can make students aware of the reader-writer relationship in constructing meaning. Following are several examples that emphasize the reading-writing connection in comprehension (also see Figure 7.13).

- Have students rewrite stories and text to be appropriate for students at a lower grade level.
- To establish real purposes for writing, have students write to authors, companies, classmates, and so forth. Let them interact in small groups to evaluate the communication features of their writing (see Figure 7.12). When their writing is not clear, ask such questions as the following:
  - What do you want the reader to know or do?
  - How can this say the same thing in a shorter manner?
  - What did you mean to say here?
  - Who do you want to be able to read this?
  - Can you come up with a way to help me better understand what you want to say?

- Give students objects or puzzles and direct them to write directions or descriptions for these. Have them exchange the written directions or descriptions with other students who attempt to draw the object or puzzle.
- Provide stories that have no endings. Have students read the stories and write appropriate endings for them.
- Point out and illustrate examples of literary elements, such as foreshadowing, flashbacks, anticlimax, and so forth. Have students write examples of each and exchange them with each other for sharing.
- Give students examples of poorly formed stories to revise and rewrite in small groups. Have them discuss why they revised certain parts.

The preceding are just a few ways to connect reading and writing and to enhance reading comprehension. The key common element of these activities is their emphasis on communicating meaning.

COMPREHENSION ACTIVITIES

Figure 7.13 provides activities that are intended to help reinforce comprehension skills and strategies. Note that these activities are only supplemental and that explicit/direct instruction using the features of teaching comprehension strategies is recommended.

■ **SEQUENCE OF EVENTS**

■ Ask students to bring in their favorite comic strips from the newspaper. Collect these for several days. Cut the comic strips into individual frames and place in envelopes. Give these to students and allow them to arrange the pieces to tell a story. Variations of this can integrate reading and writing: (1) delete a frame and have students infer what is missing and write a description for it, (2) delete the ending frame and have students infer and write an ending for the strip, and (3) remove some of the balloons of dialogue and have students infer appropriate dialogue.

■ Prepare short stories in which the sentences are out of order. Students are to rearrange the sentences in an order that makes sense.

Example: (1) The strange man walked to the door and knocked.
(2) He was invited into the house.
(3) The small dog barked when he heard the sound at the door.
(4) The lady walked to the door and opened it.
(5) The man hummed to himself as he waited for the door to open.

■ Variations of this can be used for students to predict what happens next, write an ending, and construct sequence maps.

Figure 7.13   Suggested activities for reinforcing and applying comprehension strategies and skills.

■ STORY DETAIL

- Mount a detailed picture on a piece of cardboard. In an accompanying envelope, provide students with three-by-five cards on which individual paragraphs about the picture have been typed and numbered. Students are to read the paragraphs and determine which one provides such things as the (1) most detailed description, (2) enough information for someone who knows a lot about what the picture represents, (3) not enough information to understand the picture, and so forth. This activity can help students realize the importance of their background knowledge in relation to reading for details.
- Provide students with a series of paragraphs in each of which a nonsense phrase or two has been inserted. Students read each paragraph and detect the absurd phrase, which can help identify students who are too reader-based in their reading. Students can replace the nonsense phrase with one that makes sense for the content of the paragraph, which requires them to activate their own background knowledge in relation to the meaning of the text.
- Have students read several paragraphs each describing a different character. Have students select the character they like best and list the words from both the text and their own experiences that describe the character. Students can read their list to the class to see if classmates can identify the character. Encourage students to discuss why they used certain words to describe the character(s).

■ CAUSE OR EFFECT

- Prepare or select several paragraphs which describe several events that result in the occurrence of a final event. Ask the students to determine what happened to cause the final event. (This is an excellent introductory activity for story schema, and instruction can progress to longer paragraphs and stories.)

    Example: Charlie left for work late one morning because the alarm clock didn't ring. Being late caused him to hurry and he slipped on the sidewalk and twisted his ankle. At work he spilled his coffee on some very important papers and the boss was angry. Charlie was caught in the rain and his new shirt faded on his pants. When Charlie got home he kicked the cat.

    Question: What happened that made Charlie kick the cat? Encourage students to discuss and elaborate upon their answers for the question. As students respond, their ideas can be charted on a story map or story frame, which can be used to introduce the concept of story structure.

- Select or prepare several short paragraphs in which there is a final act. Ask the students to explain and discuss why the act occurred.

    Example: Jack slipped out of the house and ran to his favorite climbing tree. As he neared the top, a branch broke and he fell to the ground.

    Question: What happened to make Jack fall?

This activity can help students realize how to identify important literal text information in relation to an outcome. Ask the question or questions before students read to direct their attention to important text information.

Figure 7.13 (continued)

■ Find or make up several reasoning statements for the students and have them give the answers. Discuss with the students how they reached a conclusion and any statements about which they disagree. Encourage them to discuss what would have to change in the given statements to make their answers not be true.

Example: If there are clouds in the sky it may rain;
If there are not clouds in the sky it will not rain.
It is raining;
therefore, there are clouds in the sky.

A variation of this is to have students develop their own reasoning statements and exchange them with classmates who construct an answer.

■ **INFERENCE**

■ Proverbs can be identified for which students determine the different meanings that can be inferred. The fact that proverbs are brief and to the point permits different interpretations, which relate directly to individuals' background knowledge.

Examples: Don't put off till tomorrow what you can do today.
A journey of a thousand miles begins with a single step.
He who hesitates is lost.
Procrastination is the thief of time.
Without starting you will arrive nowhere.
He who is not ready today, will be less so tomorrow.
Make hay while the sun shines.

Getting students to speculate about meaning can also be introduced and practiced with other smaller language units: quotations, nonfactual statements, and analogies.

Examples: It is the good reader that makes a good book.
Character is what you are when no one is watching.
You must have a good memory to be a successful liar.
People are lonely because they build walls instead of bridges.

Students can discuss and interact about the various interpretations for such quotations.

Examples: Good people are more miserable than other people.

Students can discuss why they agree or disagree with such a statement. They can write their own nonfactual types of statements and present them to the class for discussion.

Examples: Shoe is to foot as glove is to _____.
Glove is to hand as shoe is to _____.
_____ is to foot as _____ is to hand.

Students can discuss their choices for completing the analogies, and the teacher can emphasize that differences are due to the inferences students make in relation to their background knowledge.

Figure 7.13 (continued)

These activities with smaller units of language are not intended to replace the reading of text; their primary purpose is to introduce a concept or strategy (reflecting the instructional guideline that instruction proceed from simple to complex). As students discuss and provide reasons for their inferences, insights into reading are developed. Soon the students begin to see that in the final analysis these words take on the meaning that each reader gives them.

- Begin reading a story to the class but stop before completing it. Provide students with several possible endings and discuss why each ending would or would not be an appropriate ending for the story.

- Select or prepare several paragraphs for students. For each paragraph, provide three or four questions which are not answered directly in the text. Before reading the paragraphs provide students with brief information about the content and have them predict what it is about, what happens, where it takes place, and so forth. Record their predictions on the board and have them read the paragraphs. After reading a paragraph ask the questions you prepared and discuss students' predictions with their responses to the questions.

  Example: Henry flinched as he touched his swollen eye. He was mad at himself for not being more careful yesterday during the team's first game. The first game of the season, and Henry stepped right in front of the first pitch.
  (a) What happened to Henry?
  (b) What game was he playing?
  (c) What do you think happened after he got hit?

■ INFERRING CONCLUSIONS

- Give each student a slip of paper on which is written a job title and the characteristics of that job. Each describes to the class the characteristics of that job.

  Example: I get up early. I wear overalls. I drive a tractor. I milk cows.
  Job: A farmer.

Guide students to discuss the key features of the description that were most important in identifying the job. Have them explain why some features are more important than others.

- Have students participate in a class activity involving riddles. In these riddles only a few facts are given and students must ask yes or no questions to obtain information to infer an answer for the riddle.

  Example: There lying in an open field with a pack on his back. The question is, What can you determine about this situation?

■ INFERRING MAIN IDEA

- Have students write short news articles about world, local, or class events and then select titles for the articles which would be appropriate for newspaper headlines. Students read their headlines to the class and the class predicts what the article is about. The author of the headline and article can provide feedback (warm or cold) about students' predictions of main idea.

Figure 7.13   (continued)

- Provide students with short stories and articles. Students read the text and then represent the important information with a summary drawing. The drawings are presented to the class and the students compare and contrast the drawings and discuss why there are variations. Discussion should focus on the fact that students used different background knowledge in reading and representing story information. Have students explain why they did or did not include certain information in their pictures.

■ MOOD

- Provide students with large pieces of drawing paper and make available crayons. Play an instrumental record for three to five minutes while students listen. Turn off the record player and direct students to draw anything they feel like. At the end of an appropriate time, ask students to write how they feel on the back of their drawings. As students share their drawings with the class, the class tries to determine how the artist was

■ FACT AND OPINION

- Students collect and bring to class several advertisements from magazines and newspapers. In small groups have students select advertisements to discuss with the class. Analyze the advertisements to determine their validity.

- After discussing with students the kinds of articles found in newspapers, have them bring to class two or three of each type discussed. Have students distinguish between articles that describe actual events and those that are the writer's ideas.

  Example: Report on a local bank robbery versus editorial about litterbugs.

- Show students a short film or part of a film in which an incident takes place (an automobile accident, bank robbery, scene in a supermarket, etc.) Ask students to write about what they have seen. Discuss what they have written and then replay the film looking for things they have written about. Compare their descriptions with what actually happens in the film.

■ AUTHOR PURPOSE

- Provide students with several types of books and articles (comics, cookbooks, science texts, fiction, history). Have them classify the books and articles as to why they were written.

- Divide students into several small groups. Working together, each group prepares a short story to be read to the class. After hearing the story, members of the class try to determine the reason why the group wrote the story.

- Provide students with several sets of paragraphs. In each set there are two paragraphs with the same main theme. One of the paragraphs in the set is written so as to provide the reader with factual information about the theme and the other tells a humorous story about the theme. Have the students read the paragraphs in each set and tell why each was written.

  Example: The theme might be raccoons. One paragraph gives facts about the raccoon and the other tells of humorous incidents when a raccoon gets into a camper's tent.

Figure 7.13   (continued)

Source: From Edward C. Turner, "Improving Comprehension Practice and Application Activities" (University of Florida, Gainesville), by permission of the author. (2001)

SUMMARY

Teachers must provide varied opportunities for students to learn comprehension strategies and to apply these strategies in familiar and meaningful reading materials. For any instructional activity to teach reading comprehension, teachers must follow some important guidelines. Pearson and Fielding (1991) offer some essential guidelines for teachers:

1. The strategy must be instructionally relevant.
2. Instruction should proceed from simple to complex.
3. An analysis of instruction and transfer tasks should provide evidence of where breakdowns occur.
4. Explicit/direct instruction should explain when and how to use the strategies.
5. The teacher should use modeling, scaffolding, and feedback during class discussions and during or following independent work.
6. A variety of passages and authentic text should be used to facilitate students' assuming responsibility for application to new situations.
7. Monitoring procedures should be inherent parts of comprehension instruction.

The guidelines for comprehension instruction reflect what research has told us about quality reading instruction and development of reading strategies. These guidelines can be adapted to fit most reading instructional programs.

Instructional strategies can help students develop processes for comprehension. Teachers should combine these strategies, which include explicit/direct instruction, metacognition, story structure, questioning, activation of students' schemata, purposes for reading, and wide and varied opportunities to read books and authentic texts.

YOUR POINT OF VIEW

Discussion Questions

1. Why do you think that it is more effective to teach students reading strategies for comprehension than reading-comprehension skills?
2. Assume that you are going to introduce a unit on the water cycle to a group of third-grade students. What background knowledge might you want to activate before the students read an opening introduction on the water cycle?

Take a Stand For or Against

1. Reading comprehension cannot be taught.
2. Integrating reading and writing has only a minimal effect on students' reading comprehension because reading and writing are different processes.

Field-Based Assignments

1. Collect several samples of children's writing and analyze their writing in terms of story schemata or story grammar. Look for features that may vary such as setting, theme, resolution, and so forth. Discuss with the students variations in features of their writing, for example, why they may have a more elaborate theme for one piece of writing than another, or why the characters are described in more detail in one piece of writing versus another piece, or why one piece has clear and logical resolution in comparison with another piece of writing that doesn't.

2. Select two of the comprehension activities presented in this chapter and use them for instructing a small group of youngsters. Apply the guidelines for teacher-directed/explicit instruction in teaching the activities.

Portfolio Entry

Collect various samples of students' comprehension such as answers to questions, writing responses, and discussion performance about stories read. Reflect on how these samples provide you with different insights and understandings about students' comprehension of what they read.

BIBLIOGRAPHY

Alexander, P. A., & Murphey, P. K. (1996). The research base for APA's learner-centered psychological principles. In N. Lambert & B. McCombs (Eds.), *Issues in school reform: A sampler of psychological perspectives on learner-centered schools* (in press).

Alvermann, D. E. (1991). The discussion web: A graphic aid for learning across the curriculum. *The Reading Teacher, 45,* 92–99.

Anderson, R. C. (1994). Role of the reader's schema in comprehension, learning, and memory. In R. Ruddell, M. Ruddell, & H. Singer (Eds.), *Theoretical models and processes of reading* (4th ed., pp. 469–482). Newark, DE: International Reading Association.

Angeletti, S. R. (1992). Encouraging students to think about what they read. *The Reading Teacher, 45,* 288–297.

Brabham, E. G., & Villaume, S. K. (2000). Continuing conversations about literacy circles. *The Reading Teacher, 54,* 68–78.

Brown, A. L. (1988). *Interactive learning environments.* Paper presented at University of Illinois Conference on Reading Comprehension, Urbana, IL.

Dole, J. A., Brown, K. J., & Trathen, W. (1996). The effects of strategy instruction on the comprehension performance of at-risk students. *Reading Research Quarterly, 31,* 62–85.

Dole, J. A., Duffy, G. G., Roehler, L. R., & Pearson, P. D. (1991). Moving from the old to the new: Research on reading comprehension instruction. *Review of Educational Research, 61,* 239–264.

Duffy, G. G., & Roehler, L. R. (1991). Teachers' instructional actions. In R. Barr, M. Kamil, P. Mosenthal, & P. Pearson (Eds.), *Handbook of reading research* (Vol. 2, pp. 861–884). White Plains, NY: Longman.

Erwin, B. (1991). The relationship between background experience and students' comprehension: A cross cultural study. *Reading Psychology, 12,* 43–62.

Gordon, C. J., & Braun, C. (1983). Using story schema as an aid to reading and writing. *The Reading Teacher, 2,* 116–121.

Harris, T. L., & Hodges, R. E. (1995). *The literacy dictionary: The vocabulary of reading and writing.* Newark, DE: International Reading Association.

Herrmann, B. A. (1992). Teaching and assessing strategic reasoning: Dealing with the dilemmas. *The Reading Teacher, 45,* 428–437.

Hoyt, L. (1992). Many ways of knowing: Using drama, oral interactions, and the visual arts to enhance reading comprehension. *The Reading Teacher, 45,* 580–585.

Ivey, G., & Broaddus, K. (2000). Tailoring the fit: Reading instruction and middle school readers. *The Reading Teacher, 54,* 256–258.

Leavell, J. A., & Ramos-Machail, N. (2000). Leyendas (legends): Connecting reading cross-culturally. *The Reading Teacher, 54,* 256–258.

Lehr, S., & Thompson, D. L. (2000). The dynamic nature of response: Children reading and responding to *Maniac Magee* and *The Friendship. The Reading Teacher, 54,* 480–499.

Martinez-Roldain, C. M., & Lopez-Robertson, J. M. (2000). Initiating literature circles in a first-grade bilingual classroom. *The Reading Teacher, 53,* 270–291.

McKeown, M. G., Beck, I. L., Sinatra, G. M., & Loxterman, J. A. (1992). The contribution of prior knowledge and coherent text to comprehension. *Reading Research Quarterly, 27,* 78–93.

Merkley, D. (1997). Modified Anticipation Guides. *The Reading Teacher, 50,* 365–368.

Nessel, D. (1987). The new face of comprehension instruction: A closer look at questions. *The Reading Teacher, 40,* 604–606.

Norton, D. E. (1997). *The effective teaching of language arts* (5th ed.). Upper Saddle River, NJ: Merrill/Prentice Hall.

Pearson, P. D., & Fielding, L. (1991). Comprehension instruction. In R. Barr, M. Kamil, P. Mosenthal, & P. Pearson (Eds.), *Handbook of reading research* (Vol. 2, pp. 815–860). White Plains, NY: Longman.

Raphael, T. (1986). Teaching question-answer relationships, revisited. *The Reading Teacher, 39,* 516–522.

Richards, M. (2000). Be a good detective: Solve the case of oral reading fluency. *The Reading Teacher, 53,* 534–539.

Rosenshine, B., & Meister, C. (1994). Reciprocal teaching: A review of the research. *Review of Educational Research, 64,* 479–530.

Rumelhart, D. E. (1984). Understanding understanding. In J. Flood (Ed.), *Understanding reading comprehension* (pp. 86–94). Newark, DE: International Reading Association.

Rupley, W. H., & Blair, T. R. (1988). *Teaching reading: Diagnosis, direct instruction, and practice* (2nd ed.). Upper Saddle River, NJ: Merrill/Prentice Hall.

Rupley, W. H., & Willson, V. L. (1996). Content domain and word knowledge: Relationship to comprehension of narrative and expository text. *Reading and Writing: An Interdisciplinary Journal, 8,* 419–432.

Rupley, W. H., & Willson, V. L. (1997). The relationship of reading comprehension to components of word recognition: Support for developmental shifts. *Journal of Research and Development in Education, 30,* 255–260.

Short, R. A., Kane, M., & Peeling, T. (2000). Retooling the reading lesson: Matching the right tools to the job. *The Reading Teacher, 54,* 284–301.

Smagorinsky, P., & Smith, M. W. (1992). The nature of knowledge in composition and literacy understanding: The question of specificity. *Review of Educational Research, 62,* 279–306.

Staal, L. A. (2000). Teaching ideas: The story face: An adaption of story mapping that incorporates visualization and discovery learning to enhance reading and writing. *The Reading Teacher, 54,* 26–31.

Steffensen, M. S., Joag-Dev, C., & Anderson, R. C. (1979). A cross-cultural perspective on reading comprehension. *Reading Research Quarterly, 15,* 10–29.

Taylor, B., Harris, L. A., & Pearson, P. D. (1995). *Reading difficulties: Instruction and assessment* (2nd ed.). New York: McGraw Hill.

Tierney, R., & Pearson, P. D. (1994). Learning to learn from text: A framework for improving classroom practices. In R. Ruddell, M. Ruddell, & H. Singer (Eds.), *Theoretical models and processes of reading* (4th ed., pp. 496–513). Newark, DE: International Reading Association.

Wood, K. D. (2001). *Literacy strategies across the subject areas.* Boston, MA: Allyn & Bacon.

Implementing a Literacy Program

CHAPTERS

Overview

Designing and implementing appropriate literacy opportunities based on students' needs is a tall order for classroom teachers. If all literacy instruction could be the same for all students in each grade, teaching would be easy. The complexity of teaching reading becomes obvious to teachers when they try to differentiate their instruction according to student needs. This part of the text focuses on topics essential for successful elementary school literacy programs. The chapters in this part cover various instructional approaches, procedures, and materials for teaching reading; content-area reading; assessment of students' literacy abilities; classroom management and organization; and the provision of appropriate literacy instruction for children with diverse abilities. Our growing understanding of literacy development and of effective teaching has increased our appreciation of the subtleties and complexities in the learning process. The content in these chapters will furnish important information to help you provide a comprehensive and balanced literacy approach for your students.

Integrating Principles of Teaching Reading

The following principles, presented in earlier chapters, will be reinforced in this part:

- Reading is a meaningful, active, constructive, and strategic process.
- Reading and writing are developmental processes.
- Teachers must capitalize on student diversity and plan appropriate instruction for the wide range of individual differences in the classroom.
- Teachers must strive for a balanced literacy program to teach all students to read and write independently.
- Literature should be an integral part of literacy instruction throughout the entire school curriculum.
- Successful literacy instruction depends on the ongoing assessment of each student's reading strengths and weaknesses.
- Teachers must be able to create, manage, and maintain a classroom environment conducive to learning.
- Teachers of literacy must forge partnerships with the home and community to promote reading growth.
- The key to successful literacy instruction is the teacher.

CHAPTER **8**

Instructional Approaches
for Teaching Literacy

Chapter Outline

For the Reader

Because children are different in a multitude of ways, there has never been and never will be one single literacy approach that succeeds equally with all children. Effective teachers know there are many possible ways to teach reading successfully and strive to combine the best of different approaches to match their instruction to meet their students' learning needs. Effective teachers ask themselves the question "How can I use the best of various approaches to help my students become strategic readers?" Chapter 4 discussed emergent literacy and implementation of the whole-language philosophy. This chapter continues the discussion of how students learn literacy. Basal reader materials are popular and are fully explained in this chapter. Supplemental materials and instructional procedures for teaching literacy also are presented in this chapter as well as in Chapters 6, 7, and 13.

Key Ideas

- The successful use of materials and instructional approaches depends on the classroom teacher.

- Effective teachers use a combination of reading approaches to provide a balanced program to meet the needs of their students.

- Quality literature and real-life literacy experiences should be incorporated into the literacy program at all levels.

KNOWING MULTIPLE WAYS TO TEACH FOR A BALANCED APPROACH

Background Knowledge

Since students are different in a variety of ways, teachers of reading need multiple methods to teach successfully. Effective teachers of reading know and use a variety of instructional approaches and techniques to involve their students in learning and to teach students what they need to know. Alan E. Farstrup, Executive Director of the International Reading Association, emphasized the importance of knowing multiple ways to teach reading by stating "that a strong research base supports the position that multiple methods must be available to support the varying needs of individual learners" (Farstrup, 1999).

Because children are different there has never been and never will be one reading approach that succeeds with all children. Also, all students do not respond equally to a particular approach; thus, teachers need to know multiple ways to teach students to read. This very topic has been of extreme interest to the International Reading Association (IRA) and the association recently released an official position statement on "Using Multiple Methods of Beginning Reading Instruction." The sum and substance of the association's position is stated as follows:

> There is no single method or single combination of methods that can successfully teach all children to read. Therefore, teachers must have a strong knowledge of multiple methods for teaching reading and a strong knowledge of children in their care so that they can create the appropriate balance of methods needed for the children they teach. (International Reading Association, 1999)

BASAL READERS

Elementary schools rely heavily on basal reader programs. As stated in *Becoming a Nation of Readers* (Anderson, Hiebert, Scott, & Wilkinson, 1985), "The observation that basal programs 'drive' reading instruction is not to be taken lightly. These programs strongly influence how reading is taught in American schools and what students read" (p. 35).

The two major reading approaches used in today's classrooms are commercially published basal reader series and literature-based reading programs. Different materials and instructional procedures for teaching literacy are based on different philosophies regarding how children learn and different interpretations of literacy processes (see Figure 8.1). However, all philosophies overlap each other to a certain degree, borrowing various procedures, strategies, and materials. Both of these major approaches encompass many types of materials and other supplemental approaches. The most popular supplemental reading approaches are (1) various phonic programs, (2) the language-experience approach, and (3) computer-based approaches. Figure 8.2 summarizes the major and supplemental approaches for teaching literacy. This chapter focuses on the basal reader, language-experience ap-

Literacy Approaches	Assumptions and Characteristics
1. Basal reader materials	• Students learn best with a structured, eclectic method. • Includes provisions for explicit teaching of word identification, word meanings, comprehension, study skills, and literature appreciation.
2. Literature-based reading materials	• Students learn best with literature as the main vehicle for reading instruction. • Integrates reading skills and strategies with literature selections.

Figure 8.1 Assumptions and characteristics of major approaches for teaching literacy.

proach, and technological materials and procedures. Chapter 9 is devoted entirely to literature-based instruction. While each of these approaches is discussed separately, it must be emphasized that this treatment is for the sake of presentation. Effective reading teachers integrate features associated with different philosophies and materials to match the needs of their students.

Since there is not one miracle approach to teaching reading, it is imperative for teachers to know a variety of approaches and multiple ways to teach a particular learning objective. Reading teachers do not have to make either or choices among different reading approaches and reading techniques. In reality, different reading approaches and techniques are not implemented in isolation but are integrated to achieve desired results. Each approach has its advantages and each needs to be supplemented with parts of another. In addition to the various approaches to literacy, teachers use a variety of supplemental materials in the classroom—ranging from teacher-made multisensory materials to educational games, to newspapers, magazines, environmental print, and CD-ROM software, to commercial kits, and to enrichment books.

The following powerful yet simplistic statement guides effective teachers: Teach students what they need to know. There are many approaches, materials, and techniques to teach the components of reading growth effectively. Successful reading teachers use the best of all of them to teach their children what they need to know. A balanced approach to reading combines the best of all approaches and techniques to meet the needs of children (Spiegel, 1998). Discussing the importance of promoting a balanced program using multiple methods of teaching reading, Cathy M. Roller, Director of Research and Policy for the International Reading Association, states:

> For every method studied, some children learned to read very well while others had great difficulty. Therefore, we cannot end the reading wars by prescribing a single method. If all children are to learn to read, we must have well-trained teachers who are familiar with a wide range of methodologies, who are knowledgeable about children's reading development, who have access to a wide range of reading materials, and who are able to teach children using a combination of methods that meets the needs of the children in their care. (Roller, 1999)

Major Approaches	Advantages
Published Basal Reader Programs: The basal reader is a systematic, coordinated, and sequential anthology of literature stories and related materials designed to teach reading. The basal reader attempts to sequentially and explicitly develop word identification, vocabulary, comprehension, and content-reading skills and strategies through narrative and expository text, and to promote writing and recreational reading as well.	1. Provides carefully planned presentation and development of vocabulary, word identification, comprehension, and content-reading skills and strategies. 2. Provides, in teachers' manuals, good suggestions to use in teaching a story. 3. Fosters integrated development and reinforcement of reading skills and strategies in whole stories. 4. Exposes students to a variety of literary forms. 5. Provides a multitude of materials for a variety of practice and for capitalizing on students' learning styles; materials include student readers, workbooks, picture and vocabulary cards, reading games, supplemental activities, computer software programs coordinated with stories, and recreational reading kits.
Literature-Based Approach: The literature-based reading approach is a coordinated program using all types of literature as the catalyst in teaching children to read. Children are guided to an understanding, enjoyment, and appreciation of literature. Reading skills and strategies are taught through the reading of fine literature and language arts activities.	1. Allows for the development and practice of language processes and strategies in quality literary material as opposed to sterile workbooks and other commercial kits and activities. 2. Promotes a joy of reading and an appreciation of all types of literature. 3. Uses literature as a means to improve reading vocabulary. 4. Integrates reading with listening, speaking, and writing. 5. Creates a desire to use and to refine language.

Supplemental Approaches

Phonic Programs: Numerous phonic programs are available that provide explicit attention to letter–sound correspondences and factors that affect them. Such programs include a variety of formats—games, cooperative activities, computer software, charts, sentence strips, and authentic practice materials (i.e., paragraphs and whole stories).

Language-Experience Approach (LEA): The language-experience approach is a language-arts approach to the teaching of reading using the child's own language. LEA presents reading as a natural extension of speaking. The most common activity is the dictation of a child's experiences to the teacher. The teacher writes down the child's story on a poster board (called an *experience chart*). These stories are then used to teach specific reading skills.

Computer-Based Programs: Numerous computer-based literacy programs are in existence with new programs developed almost daily. Computer-based software includes drill and practice exercises, tutorial dialogues, learning games, books, creative writing, and CD-ROM interactive literature programs employing hypermedia (using text, graphics, video, and audio).

Figure 8.2 Reading approaches.

More recently, Snow, Burns, and Griffin (1998) in their influential book *Preventing Reading Difficulties in Young Children* concurred and stated:

> Basal programs are used in the majority of first-grade classrooms in the United States and thus have substantial influence on both classroom practice and teacher development. In view of this, guidelines and procedures for aligning their instructional goals and methods with research are urgently needed, as are policies for requiring empirical evaluation of their instructional efficacy. (p. 207)

It is paramount that teachers of reading adjust basal materials to meet the needs of their students.

Design and Content

Each basal reader program differs in its rationale, sequence of skills and strategies, story content, instructional recommendations, and supplemental materials. However, most basals set meaning as the paramount goal from the outset. Also, as mentioned in Chapter 1, most basals cover the major content strands of the elementary school reading curriculum—decoding, comprehension, word meanings, reading-study skills, literature, and independent reading—in their own particular way.

Through a series of books of increasing difficulty (a separate book for each level), **basal readers** are designed to bring children to a high degree of reading proficiency. Each level functions as a prerequisite for success at the next level. The focus of basal programs is to develop the reader's competence in vocabulary, word identification, word meanings, comprehension, and study skills through fine literature.

Scott Foresman *Reading* (2000) is a basal reader series for grades K–6. This is a literature-driven program that provides an integrated, balanced approach to literacy. This basal reader program covers all the major content strands in a balanced elementary school curriculum and the major program areas of a complete, balanced reading program, as outlined in Chapter 1. All instruction and classroom activities focus on children's literature (both fiction and nonfiction) and are organized around themes geared directly to students' interests. The major components of the program are listed as follows:

- Accountability
    - Assessment Handbook
    - Unit and End-of-Year Skills Test
    - Skills Assessment
    - Unit and End-of-Year Benchmark Tests
    - Placement Test
    - Individual Reading Inventory

- Literature
    - Pupil Editions
    - Big Books

Little Big Books
Leveled Readers
Oral Language Flip Chart
Read-Aloud Books
Trade Book Library

- Phonics
  Phonics Readers
  Phonics Take-Home Readers
  Phonics Workbook
  Decodable Readers
  Phonemic Awareness & Phonics Manipulatives Kit
  Scott Foresman Phonics System Handbook
  Phonics Sourcebook
  Phonics Songs and Rhymes Flip Charts

- Skills and Strategies
  Practice Book
  Teacher's Resource Book
  Reading Success Kit
  Daily Word Routine Flip Charts
  Writing Process Transparencies

- Management
  Teacher's Editions
  Classroom Routines Kit
  Teacher's Resource Planner CD-ROMs
  Adding English/ESL Support*

In addition, the Scott Foresman program provides teachers with classroom routines, which are research-based management and teaching methods in the areas of instruction (e.g., comprehension and phonic routines), environment (e.g., sign-in and library routines), student (e.g., technology and independent reading workstation routines), and school/home (e.g., technology and independent reading workstation routines), and school/home (e.g., home communication routines).

To promote strategic reading through fine literature, the teacher's edition provides an integrated lesson plan for each story that models our understanding of the constructive nature of reading, involving prereading, during-reading, and postreading development. The teaching of each story in this basal program is presented in a three-part process involving "Prepare and Read," "Guide Comprehension," and "Practice, Apply & Extend."

---

*Overview, Scott Foresman *Reading*, p. 24. Reprinted by permission of Scott Foresman. All rights reserved.

All basal programs include a tremendous number of materials for both teacher and students. For teachers, programs may include the following:

- a teacher's edition for each level, giving detailed lesson plans for each story in the student's book; a complete listing of strategies and skills for developing reading, writing, listening, and speaking processes at each level; and assessment procedures
- detailed descriptions of supplemental literary libraries and recommendations for literacy development in various content areas
- various instructional supplements for application of strategies and skills
- prepared pictures of characters, teaching charts, posters, transparencies, and word cards for specific stories
- various films, filmstrips, recordings, videos, videodiscs, audiocassettes, compact discs, and CD-ROM storybooks and practice activities
- teacher's edition of student workbooks
- a management system, including an informal reading inventory or placement test, criterion-referenced pretests and posttests for each level, phonic inventories, alternative assessments for both reading and writing, portfolio assessment, and various record-keeping devices

For students, basal programs may include the following:

- a student book for each level
- a workbook for each level
- literature libraries including high-interest/low-vocabulary paperback books
- readiness posters and big books
- writing portfolios
- computer software programs
- supplemental games and activities to practice the skills and strategies being taught

Advantages of Basal Series

Although the abundance of materials in basal programs can be overwhelming, the crucial point to remember is that they do not guarantee an exciting and worthwhile program. An effective teacher of reading must orchestrate the materials based on learner needs. Some of the advantages of using a basal series include the following:

- Basal readers contain an anthology of different genres of literature.
- Books are sequenced in increasing difficulty to provide systematic instruction from the emergent literacy phase through the upper elementary grades.
- Graded materials permit teacher flexibility in dealing with individual differences.
- Teacher's guides are available for each book or level. These provide suggestions for a step-by-step teaching program.

- If used properly, basal reader series deal with all phases of the reading program, guarding against overemphasis of some aspects and neglect of others.
- Basal series introduce practice of new skills and strategies in a logical sequence.
- Review is provided.
- Vocabulary is controlled to prevent frustration for beginning readers.
- Prepared materials allow teachers to save time.
- Formal and informal assessments that the series provides reflect the materials that teachers will use.
- Basal programs provide an overall management system for coordinating the elementary school reading program.

Wiggins (1994) cites further advantages of basal programs:

> First, most classroom teachers are comfortable with the basal reader format. . . . Second, a basal program provides consistency as students move from one grade level to the next. . . . Third, a basal reading series provides specific activities designed to teach, reteach, and reinforce the requisite skills and strategies, as well as a consistent and concrete means by which to monitor the success of instruction. (p. 453)

Today's Newer Basals

The last two decades have seen dramatic changes in how we view and teach the reading process in the classroom. With the rise in interest in the study of comprehension, a shift in attention to how we process and retrieve information with corresponding comprehension strategies has taken center stage. This is in contrast to teaching techniques focusing on the isolated instruction of both word identification and comprehension skills. A second change has occurred with more serious attempts at the merging of the teaching of reading with the other language arts, especially the renewed close relationship between reading and writing. A third major change has been the growing emphasis on fine literature in all literacy approaches. Inclusion of this essential element has spurred a more holistic, integrated approach to the teaching of the language processes.

Have the newer basal programs changed to reflect these dramatic shifts in the teaching of literacy? After years of being criticized for not changing significant aspects of their programs, recent research by the National Reading Research Center (Hoffman & McCarthey, 1995) concluded that the newer basals are indeed different from the old ones, reflecting major changes in the literacy field. The researchers examined both the old and new student texts and teacher's manuals of five current basal programs at the first-grade level. The researchers' conclusions follow:

> In summary, our analysis suggests that at the first-grade level the new pupil texts were different from the old: They offered reduced vocabulary control, minimal adaptations, more diversity of genre, more engaging literary quality, more predictable text, and increased decoding demands.

Quality literature should be an integral part of the literacy program.

The newer teacher's editions were different from the old in underlying instructional design, replacing a directed reading model with a shared reading model. Vocabulary was introduced more in the context of the stories in the new teacher's editions; fewer comprehension questions were offered, with a greater attempt to include more higher-level questions. The high degree of focus on skills and isolated skills instruction had decreased from the old to the new. Although skills were still prevalent, they tended to be slightly more integrated. Assessment tools had been broadened considerably from a testing-only mentality to a portfolio approach. The tone of the manuals was less prescriptive than the old, moving in the direction of a "teacher-as decision-maker" model. (p. 73)

Most basals today feature the following characteristics:

- Integrated language arts are emphasized not only during reading instruction but also in the content areas.
- Quality literature is viewed as the driving force in the elementary school reading program, with thematic units designed to facilitate student learning and appreciation.
- Reading and writing are linked specifically as mutually supportive processes.
- Appealing, high-quality literature is carefully selected for both the regular basal readers and supplemental libraries.

- Quality literature is emphasized for independent or recreational reading.
- Multicultural focus is increased.
- Lesson recommendations reflect the idea that reading is an interactive, constructive, and strategic process. Lessons give explicit attention to teaching decoding skills and strategies and comprehension strategies. Instruction includes use of authentic literature and prior knowledge in story preparation. Thinking and problem-solving abilities are taught through literature.
- Cooperative and partner grouping is encouraged.
- Assessment is viewed as ongoing and is linked directly to instruction using a variety of informal and formal measures.
- A real partnership is fostered between the school's elementary reading program and the home.

Economy of teacher time is a major factor in the widespread use of basal series. No teacher would ever have the time to match the meticulous planning that goes into a good basal series. Prepared materials leave teachers more time to develop supplementary exercises as needed. Teachers still must prepare these exercises for certain students, because the basal program cannot meet all individual needs; however, preparing supplementary lessons for a few is easier than building the entire program.

Teacher's Editions

One of the advantages of using a good basal series is the teacher's edition. These editions contain a variety of instructional procedures, lesson plans, and rationales for using certain materials and instructional procedures. Beginning teachers can benefit from becoming familiar with the rationales and concrete suggestions that basal readers contain. Experienced teachers might find the detail of these manuals a bit tedious, but they know that they can take what is offered and adapt it in light of their own experience and their students' learning needs. A teacher's edition is beneficial only if teachers use it properly, however. Teachers should not be awed by these impressive volumes, nor should they follow them word for word—that is not teaching. Teachers should know their students' learning needs better than any teacher's guide. Remember, basal materials work best for a knowledgeable, flexible teacher. Use the suggestions when they match your students' learning needs, and supplement and adapt suggestions at all other times. Teachers should view manuals as a compilation of suggestions that they can use, modify, or discard (Durkin, 1993).

Practice Materials

Basal reader series generally contain a variety of practice supplements. The educational value of using workbooks has been debated for years. It is true that workbook exercises can deteriorate into nothing more than busy work, yet, with proper, teacher-directed instruction, students can use workbooks for meaningful practice.

Properly used, workbooks can have considerable educational value. Because they deal with a wide variety of skills, some exercises will likely provide needed and meaningful practice in essential literacy skill areas. Workbooks also can serve as ongoing diagnostic instruments, because they identify individuals who do not understand a particular reading strategy or skill. A study of miscues will show the alert teacher where to provide further instruction. Workbook exercises are brief—usually one page—which makes them especially appealing to students with short attention spans.

Workbooks, like all other instructional media, are neither all good nor all bad. How the teacher uses workbooks determines whether they contribute to a quality instructional program. Osborn (1984) identified important guidelines for workbook tasks. Carefully consider these guidelines for using workbooks and worksheets that accompany basal reading series:

- Workbook activities should match the instruction and learning taking place in the unit or lesson.
- Some workbook tasks should provide systematic, cumulative, and meaningful review of what students have been taught.
- Workbooks should match the most important learning taking place in the reading program. Activities of lesser importance should be voluntary.
- Workbooks should provide relevant tasks for students in need of extra practice.
- Both the vocabulary and concept features of workbook tasks should be within students' experiential and conceptual backgrounds and should relate to the rest of the program.
- The language features of a workbook page should be consistent with those in the instructional lesson and the rest of the workbook.
- Instructions for completion of a workbook activity should be clear and easy to follow. Teachers should direct one or two practice examples to ensure that students understand the tasks.
- Page layout should combine attractiveness and utility.
- Content should be sufficient to ensure that students are learning and not just being exposed to something.
- Discrimination activities should follow a sufficient number of tasks to provide practice in the components of the discriminations.
- Content of workbook activities should be accurate and precise to ensure that it presents neither incorrect information nor incorrect generalizations.
- Some workbook tasks should be fun.
- The manner in which students respond should be consistent from workbook task to workbook task.

Prereading experiences with live objects are excellent motivators in preparing to read a story.

- Response modes should match normal reading and writing as closely as possible.
- Cute and nonfunctional workbook activities, which may be time consuming (i.e., busy work), should be avoided.
- Workbook assignments should include teacher discussions about their purposes and their relationships to reading.

Guided Reading

An integral part of the teacher's edition of a basal reader is a systematic description of how to teach a reading and/or writing lesson. The ultimate purpose of each lesson in a basal reader is to teach the strategies needed to read and write independently, comprehending and learning from both. Thus, each lesson is a vehicle for increasing youngsters' literacy abilities. The traditional plan for teaching a story is commonly referred to as a **directed reading activity** (DRA). The DRA provides a framework for systematic and sequential growth of reading and language abilities. Although each basal series has its own concept of the DRA, most contain the following components:

- readiness, including prior knowledge, previewing, key vocabulary and concepts, purpose-setting questions (either teacher set or student set, or both), and student predictions about the content of the selection
- silent reading
- comprehension development
- purposeful oral reading
- skill and strategy development, including word identification or decoding, comprehension, study, and vocabulary
- enrichment, including creative assignments related to the story

Similar in nature to the DRA is the **directed reading-thinking activity** (DRTA) (Stauffer, 1975). The three overall stages of the DRTA are readiness, active reading, and reaction to the story. This instructional procedure focuses on reading as a thinking process. Students are encouraged to predict; form a purpose for reading; read to verify, reject, or modify that purpose; then continue that process.

There is no set way to teach a reading lesson. Modern basal reader programs follow a similar instructional format to directed reading and directed reading-thinking activities focusing on teaching strategies before, during, and after reading. Teacher's manual recommendations may be modified, expanded, deleted, or reordered according to students' existing abilities. Reflecting our growing knowledge of the interactive and constructive nature of reading comprehension, newer basals present lessons in a guided reading plan format. Our summary view of the steps in teaching a story are step 1, "Prereading," step 2, "Reading" and step 3, "Postreading." The components of each step are as follows:

Guided Reading Plan

Prereading
- Review prior knowledge.
- Build background information.
- Develop interest in the story and motivation to read by relating the story to the students' own lives.
- Develop new vocabulary and concepts.
- Ask students to make predictions regarding the story.
- Provide students with a purpose (s) for reading.

Reading
- Encourage students as they read to use various checking strategies—confirm their predictions, answer purpose-setting questions, reflect on ideas presented, reread to understand a point, summarize difficult ideas, question oneself about key vocabulary, and slow their reading rate to understand ideas (or speed up when appropriate).

Postreading
- Answer purpose-setting questions.
- Discuss the outcome of prereading predictions.

- Summarize the story with the students, making connections between new and old understandings.
- Answer questions on different cognitive levels to develop an understanding of the story.
- Reflect on the ideas with classmates and teacher.
- Reread portions of the story orally, having a specific purpose in mind.
- Explicitly teach students a new word-identification and/or comprehension skill or strategy related to the story (this explicit instruction may occur in the prereading phase).
- Ensure that students have multiple opportunities to apply the new skill or strategy in authentic practice situations and assist or coach students during this practice time.
- Develop other language-arts abilities related to the story such as writing skills, spelling, and grammar.
- Develop skills and strategies to be used in content or cross-curricular areas.
- Complete creative literature activities related to the story.

The teacher acts as the key in guided reading by selecting activities appropriate to students' needs. No teacher's manual can make reading meaningful and enjoyable. A thinking teacher who views the lesson plans in a manual as guides and not mandates is more likely to provide effective reading instruction. Figure 8.3 provides a guided reading plan for a grade 3 basal story from Scott Foresman's reading program.

A Critical View

Critics have attacked basal readers through the years. They have alleged basals to be inferior because of boring content, cultural bias, absence of literary merit, and unrealistic and repetitive language. Responding to these and other criticisms, authors and publishers have made significant changes in basals to reflect current reading research and teacher effectiveness studies (Hoffman et al., 1998).

Other critics have attacked basal readers for the ways that teachers use them. Research by Durkin (1984) provides some insights into the use of basals in teaching reading. These findings are applicable today. Durkin observed 16 teachers during their reading instruction to better determine how they used basal manuals. She observed first-, third-, and fifth-grade classes. Her findings are not very encouraging; however, if teachers become aware of them, perhaps it will help them improve the quality of basal reading instruction. Following is a summary and discussion of her findings.

Introduction and presentation of new vocabulary words

Most basal manuals suggest introducing new words in written context and illustrating them in familiar, written sentences. Few of the teachers followed this recommendation and rarely did they give any attention to teaching and practicing new vocabulary words.

Theme **The Whole Wide World**
Theme Question *How can we learn about and care for the world?*
Topic **Birds**

Begin the Week

Nights of the Pufflings

by Bruce McMillan

pages 216–230

Genre: Narrative Nonfiction

The children of a town in Iceland help a colony of pufflings on their first flight.

TARGET SKILL

**Comprehension:
Main Idea/Supporting Details**

Narrative nonfiction such as *Nights of the Pufflings* helps students learn to differentiate main idea from supporting details.

Bruce McMillan won the Blue Ribbon Award for *Nights of the Pufflings*, which was named an Outstanding Science Trade Book and an American Library Association Notable Children's Book.

READING ACROSS TEXTS

"Saving the Whooping Crane"

from Peeping in the Shell

by Faith McNulty

pages 232–235

Genre: Expository Nonfiction

The article is about the efforts made in the United States to save the whooping crane. This links *Nights of the Pufflings* to science studies.

Nights of the Pufflings

Saving the Whooping Crane

214a *Nights of the Pufflings* • Begin the Week

Figure 8.3

Source: From Teacher's Edition, Scott Foresman *Reading, Imagine That!* Series, Grade 3, Vol. One, pp. 214a–d, 214–231, 235a–235l. Copyright © 2000. Used with permission.

Leveled Readers

The River Rescue by B. G. Hennessy **70A**
Dad takes Rosa and Roberto for a peaceful day on
the river. `easy` Suggestions for use on p. 136g

Big and Small, Homes for All
by Joanne Mattern **70B**
Some are big, some are small. Birds build all kinds of
nests. `average` Suggestions for use on p. 136g

The Whole Wide World: Collected Readings **2C**
A collection of readings and projects to help students
develop the theme. `challenge` Suggestion for use
on p. 136g

Meeting Individual Needs

Intervention

Leveled Readers
Leveled Readers A and B offer
support for readers working 1 to 2
grade levels below. Leveled Reader C
offers extensions for students reading
on or above grade level. Complete
lesson plans are available in the
Leveled Reader Resource Guide.

Phonics Reader

Additional practice for vowel digraph *ow;* and
vowel diphthong *ow*

Growing Up in Colonial Times by Linda Lott **10**
Although colonial children had many responsibil-
ities, they found time to have fun and be kids!
Suggestions for use on pp. 136f and 235h

Trade Book Library

Theme-related trade books for self-selected reading

Spring by Ron Hirschi
Nature comes to life in this photo essay of the
awakening of spring. `average`

Wild Babies by Seymour Simon
Discover the world of animal babies and see how
they are raised in a variety of ways.
`average/challenge`

From Seed to Plant by Gail Gibbons
How a plant grows is told in simple, easy-to-
understand language. Suggestions for use on p. 235b

Technology

- **Selection Audio CD 6/Tape 11**
- **Phonics Songs and Rhymes Audio
  CD 1/Tape 5**
- **Background-Building
  Audio CD 2/Tape 5**
- **www.sfreading.com** `www`
- **Scott Foresman Internet Guide**
- **Teacher's Resource Planner
  CD-ROM**
- **The Know Zone™**

Self-Selected Reading and Read Aloud

More Books
by Bruce McMillan

My Horse of the North
(Scholastic, 1997) A young girl
trains her horse and practices for
the annual sheep round-up in this
photo essay. `average`

*Penguins at Home: Gentoos of
Antarctica* (Houghton Mifflin, 1993)
The Southern gentoo penguins
raise their young in the snow, ice,
and rocks of Antarctica.
`average`

Books on the Topic

*Project Puffin: How We Brought
Puffins Back to Egg Rock*
by Stephen Kress
(Tilbury House, 1997) Describes a
wildlife scientist's successful quest
to restore puffins to a former
habitat. `challenge`

The Puffins Are Back!
by Gail Gibbons
(HarperCollins, 1991) Describes the
puffins living off the coast of
Maine. `easy`

A Book to Read Aloud

*Puffin's Homecoming: The Story
of an Atlantic Puffin* by Darice
Bailer (Smithsonian Soundprints,
1994) An Atlantic puffin returns to
the place he was born to mate and
raise chicks.

Figure 8.3 (continued)

316

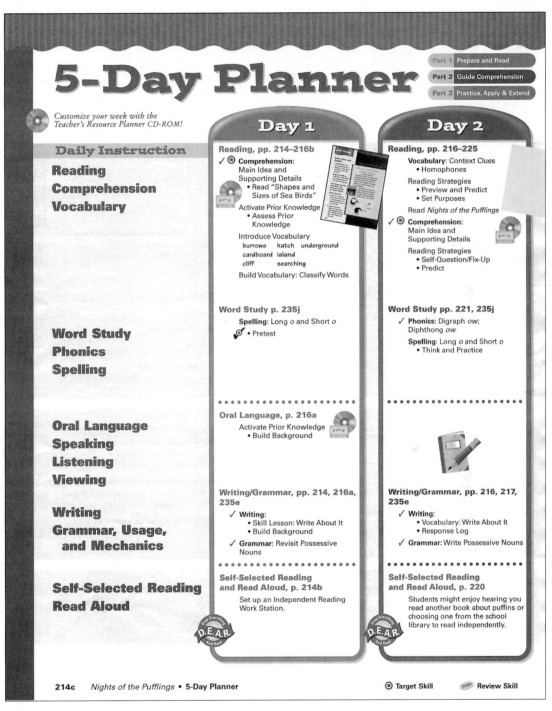

5-Day Planner

Part 1 Prepare and Read
Part 2 Guide Comprehension
Part 3 Practice, Apply & Extend

Customize your week with the Teacher's Resource Planner CD-ROM!

Daily Instruction

Reading
Comprehension
Vocabulary

Day 1

Reading, pp. 214–216b

✓ ◉ **Comprehension:**
Main Idea and Supporting Details
 • Read "Shapes and Sizes of Sea Birds"

Activate Prior Knowledge
 • Assess Prior Knowledge

Introduce Vocabulary
burrows   hatch   underground
cardboard   island
cliff   searching

Build Vocabulary: Classify Words

Day 2

Reading, pp. 216–225

Vocabulary: Context Clues
 • Homophones

Reading Strategies
 • Preview and Predict
 • Set Purposes

Read *Nights of the Pufflings*

✓ ◉ **Comprehension:**
Main Idea and Supporting Details

Reading Strategies
 • Self-Question/Fix-Up
 • Predict

Word Study
Phonics
Spelling

Day 1

Word Study p. 235j

Spelling: Long *o* and Short *o*
 • Pretest

Day 2

Word Study pp. 221, 235j

✓ **Phonics:** Digraph *ow*; Diphthong *ow*

Spelling: Long *o* and Short *o*
 • Think and Practice

Oral Language
Speaking
Listening
Viewing

Day 1

Oral Language, p. 216a

Activate Prior Knowledge
 • Build Background

Writing
Grammar, Usage, and Mechanics

Day 1

Writing/Grammar, pp. 214, 216a, 235e

✓ **Writing:**
 • Skill Lesson: Write About It
 • Build Background

✓ **Grammar:** Revisit Possessive Nouns

Day 2

Writing/Grammar, pp. 216, 217, 235e

✓ **Writing:**
 • Vocabulary: Write About It
 • Response Log

✓ **Grammar:** Write Possessive Nouns

Self-Selected Reading
Read Aloud

Day 1

Self-Selected Reading and Read Aloud, p. 214b

Set up an Independent Reading Work Station.

D.E.A.R. Drop Everything and Read

Day 2

Self-Selected Reading and Read Aloud, p. 220

Students might enjoy hearing you read another book about puffins or choosing one from the school library to read independently.

D.E.A.R. Drop Everything and Read

214c   *Nights of the Pufflings* • 5-Day Planner

◉ **Target Skill**   **Review Skill**

Figure 8.3 (continued)

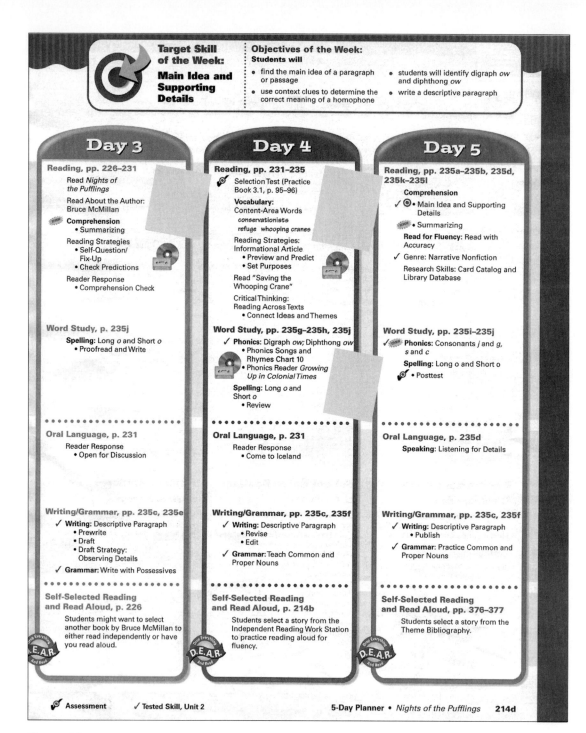

Target Skill of the Week:

Main Idea and Supporting Details

Objectives of the Week:
Students will

- find the main idea of a paragraph or passage
- use context clues to determine the correct meaning of a homophone
- students will identify digraph *ow* and diphthong *ow*
- write a descriptive paragraph

Day 3

Reading, pp. 226–231

Read *Nights of the Pufflings*

Read About the Author: Bruce McMillan

Comprehension
- Summarizing

Reading Strategies
- Self-Question/ Fix-Up
- Check Predictions

Reader Response
- Comprehension Check

Word Study, p. 235j

Spelling: Long *o* and Short *o*
- Proofread and Write

Oral Language, p. 231

Reader Response
- Open for Discussion

Writing/Grammar, pp. 235c, 235e

✓ **Writing:** Descriptive Paragraph
- Prewrite
- Draft
- Draft Strategy: Observing Details

✓ **Grammar:** Write with Possessives

Self-Selected Reading and Read Aloud, p. 226

Students might want to select another book by Bruce McMillan to either read independently or have you read aloud.

Day 4

Reading, pp. 231–235

Selection Test (Practice Book 3.1, p. 95–96)

Vocabulary:
Content-Area Words
conservationists
refuge whooping cranes

Reading Strategies: Informational Article
- Preview and Predict
- Set Purposes

Read "Saving the Whooping Crane"

Critical Thinking: Reading Across Texts
- Connect Ideas and Themes

Word Study, pp. 235g–235h, 235j

✓ **Phonics:** Digraph *ow;* Diphthong *ow*
- Phonics Songs and Rhymes Chart 10
- Phonics Reader *Growing Up in Colonial Times*

Spelling: Long *o* and Short *o*
- Review

Oral Language, p. 231

Reader Response
- Come to Iceland

Writing/Grammar, pp. 235c, 235f

✓ **Writing:** Descriptive Paragraph
- Revise
- Edit

✓ **Grammar:** Teach Common and Proper Nouns

Self-Selected Reading and Read Aloud, p. 214b

Students select a story from the Independent Reading Work Station to practice reading aloud for fluency.

Day 5

Reading, pp. 235a–235b, 235d, 235k–235l

Comprehension
✓ • Main Idea and Supporting Details

• Summarizing

Read for Fluency: Read with Accuracy

✓ Genre: Narrative Nonfiction

Research Skills: Card Catalog and Library Database

Word Study, pp. 235i–235j

✓ **Phonics:** Consonants *j* and *g, s* and *c*

Spelling: Long *o* and Short *o*
- Posttest

Oral Language, p. 235d

Speaking: Listening for Details

Writing/Grammar, pp. 235c, 235f

✓ **Writing:** Descriptive Paragraph
- Publish

✓ **Grammar:** Practice Common and Proper Nouns

Self-Selected Reading and Read Aloud, pp. 376–377

Students select a story from the Theme Bibliography.

D.E.A.R.

Assessment   ✓ Tested Skill, Unit 2   5-Day Planner • *Nights of the Pufflings*   **214d**

Figure 8.3 (continued)

Comprehension

Main Idea and Supporting Details

Seabirds are all slender but come in different sizes. The size helps to identify the different kinds of sea birds.

Objectives

Students will

- find the main idea of a paragraph or passage
- learn that supporting details are facts and bits of information that tell more about the main idea

SKILLS TRACE
Main Idea and Supporting Details

Introduce/Teach	Review/Reteach
TE: 3.1 83	TE: 3.1 89b, 143, 161b, **214–215**, 219 223, 235a
	PB: 3.1 27, 57, 91, 93
Skills Test, Unit 2	

See page136i for a correlation of the skills taught in this unit to national achievement tests.

Introduce

On the board write a simple main idea, such as *There are many different kinds of pets.* Invite volunteers to tell about different kinds of pets. Turn their ideas into sentences and write them as a paragraph under the main idea. Then help students to identify the topic (pets), main idea (there are many kinds of pets), and supporting details (types of pets).

Teach and Practice

Read with students the definition of main idea and supporting details on page 214 before they start reading "Shapes and Sizes of Sea Birds."

For more practice with main idea and supporting details, use Practice Book 3.1, page 91.

214   *Nights of the Pufflings* • **Comprehension**

Meeting Diverse Needs
Intervention

While reading, students can listen to "Shapes and Sizes of Sea Birds" on audiotape or CD.

Then help students begin Practice Book 3.1, page 91 by guiding them in completing the second row in the table.

Selection Audio CD 6/Tape 11, Side 1

**Main Idea and Details About
"Shapes and Sizes of Sea Birds"**

Paragraph	Main Idea	Supporting Details
Paragraph 1	Sea birds' bodies have different shapes, but all are streamlined.	Albatrosses, penguins and pelicans are stout. Terns and petrels are slender.
Paragraph 2	Sea birds vary a lot in size.	The least storm petrel is 13 cm (5 in.) long. The largest albatross has a wingspan of more than 360 cm (12ft.).

Figure 8.3 (continued)

Sea birds' bills are different. One can easily recognize a pelican by its large bill. A puffin's bill is colorful and shaped like a triangle.

Close and Assess

Help students summarize the information in the passage. Ask:

What did you learn about sea birds? What did you find out about sea birds that you did not know before?

Discuss with students their answers to Write About It. Do students understand that the main idea of a passage is the most important idea about a topic? Can they point out supporting details?

Answers to Write About It

1. The main ideas are in paragraph 1, last sentence; paragraph 2, first sentence; and paragraph 3, first sentence.

2. Supporting details could include any of the sentences except the ones listed in question 1.

Ongoing Assessment

Main Idea and Supporting Details

If... students cannot identify the main idea of each paragraph in the selection,	**then...** help them to identify the topic of each paragraph. Use the Main Idea and Supporting Detail questions in **Guiding Comprehension** when students read *Nights of the Pufflings*.

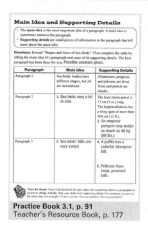

Main Idea and Supporting Details

- The **main idea** is the most important idea of a paragraph. A main idea is sometimes stated in the paragraph.
- **Supporting details** are small pieces of information in the paragraph that tell more about the main idea.

Directions: Reread "Shapes and Sizes of Sea Birds." Then complete the table by telling the main idea of a paragraph and some of its supporting details. The first paragraph has been done for you. Possible answers given.

Paragraph	Main Idea	Supporting Details
Paragraph 1	Sea birds' bodies have different shapes, but all are streamlined.	Albatrosses, penguins, and pelicans are stout. Tern and petrels are slender.
Paragraph 2	1. Sea birds vary a lot in size.	The least storm petrel is 13 cm (5 in.) long. The largest albatross has a wing span of more than 360 cm (12 ft.). 2. An emperor penguin may weigh as much as 40 kg (88 lbs.).
Paragraph 3	3. Sea birds' bills are very varied.	4. A puffin has a colorful, triangular bill. 5. Pelicans have large, pouched bills.

Notes for Home: Your child identified the main ideas and supporting details in paragraphs of an article. **Home Activity:** Help your child write supporting details for a sentence you give to the main idea. For example: *Picnics are fun. (You eat outdoors. You eat good food.)*

Practice Book 3.1, p. 91
Teacher's Resource Book, p. 177

MULTI-AGE CLASSROOM

LOOKING BACK

Grade 2

- Students learn that the topic is who or what the paragraph is about.

- Students recognize that the main idea is the most important idea about the topic.

Grade 3

- Students understand that the main idea of a paragraph is sometimes stated directly.

- Students learn to identify supporting details that tell more about the main idea of a paragraph.

LOOKING AHEAD

Grade 4

- Students can identify the stated or implied main idea.

- Students can state this main idea in their own words.

- Students can use details to support their answers about main ideas.

Comprehension: Main Idea and Supporting Details

Figure 8.3 (continued)

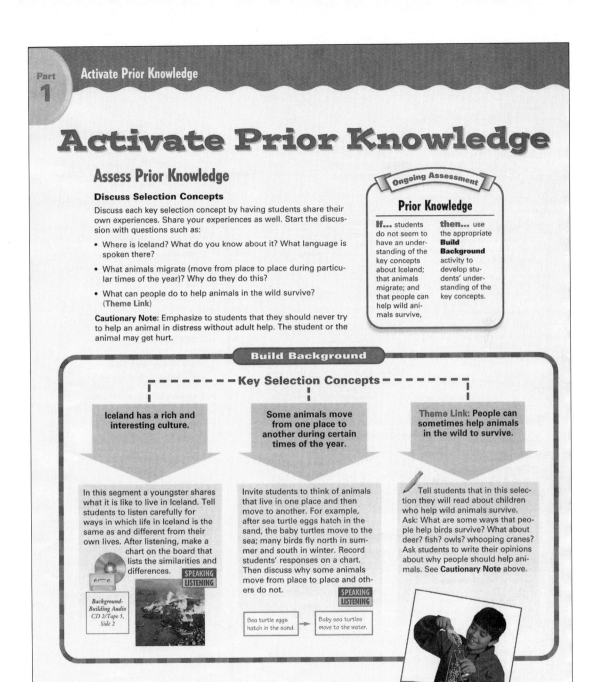

Activate Prior Knowledge

Assess Prior Knowledge

Discuss Selection Concepts

Discuss each key selection concept by having students share their own experiences. Share your experiences as well. Start the discussion with questions such as:

- Where is Iceland? What do you know about it? What language is spoken there?

- What animals migrate (move from place to place during particular times of the year)? Why do they do this?

- What can people do to help animals in the wild survive? (Theme Link)

Cautionary Note: Emphasize to students that they should never try to help an animal in distress without adult help. The student or the animal may get hurt.

Ongoing Assessment

Prior Knowledge

If... students do not seem to have an understanding of the key concepts about Iceland; that animals migrate; and that people can help wild animals survive,

then... use the appropriate **Build Background** activity to develop students' understanding of the key concepts.

Build Background

- - - - - **Key Selection Concepts** - - - - -

Iceland has a rich and interesting culture.

Some animals move from one place to another during certain times of the year.

Theme Link: People can sometimes help animals in the wild to survive.

In this segment a youngster shares what it is like to live in Iceland. Tell students to listen carefully for ways in which life in Iceland is the same as and different from their own lives. After listening, make a chart on the board that lists the similarities and differences. **SPEAKING LISTENING**

Background-Building Audio CD 2/Tape 5, Side 2

Invite students to think of animals that live in one place and then move to another. For example, after sea turtle eggs hatch in the sand, the baby turtles move to the sea; many birds fly north in summer and south in winter. Record students' responses on a chart. Then discuss why some animals move from place to place and others do not. **SPEAKING LISTENING**

| Sea turtle eggs hatch in the sand. | → | Baby sea turtles move to the water. |

Tell students that in this selection they will read about children who help wild animals survive. Ask: What are some ways that people help birds survive? What about deer? fish? owls? whooping cranes? Ask students to write their opinions about why people should help animals. See **Cautionary Note** above.

Figure 8.3 (continued)

Vocabulary

Discuss Word Meanings

Have volunteers read the words. Then lead a discussion of the meanings of the words. You might have students look up words in the glossary to find correct pronunciation and meaning.

Practice Book 3.1, page 92 provides a word knowledge checklist and additional practice with tested selection vocabulary.

If students are already familiar with the Words to Know, you might want to introduce More Words to Know.

Vocabulary

Directions: The first sentence of each pair is a clue. Choose the word from the box that best completes the second sentence. Write the word on the line to the left.

underground   1. A plane flies overhead. A subway travels _____.

cardboard   2. A dress is made of cloth. A box is made of _____.

hatch   3. Kittens are born. Ducklings _____.

Directions: Choose the word from the box that best matches each clue. Write the word in the puzzle.

Across

4. come out from an egg

8. beneath the surface of the ground

9. a very steep slope of rock

10. a body of land surrounded by water

Down

5. stiff, light material used to make cartons and boxes

6. holes dug in the ground by an animal for protection or shelter

7. looking carefully for something

Write a Story

Write a story about rescuing an animal or bird. Use as many vocabulary words as you can. Check that students' stories correctly use included vocabulary words.

Check the Words You Know
___ burrows
___ cardboard
___ cliff
___ hatch
___ island
___ searching
___ underground

Notes for Home: Your child identified and used vocabulary words from *Nights of the Pufflings*. *Home Activity:* Go for a walk with your child. Look for animals together. Talk about ways to help animals and birds survive. Use as many of the vocabulary words as possible.

Practice Book 3.1, p. 92
Teacher's Resource Book, p. 178

Words to Know

✓ **burrows** holes dug in the ground by animals for shelter or protection

✓ **cardboard** stiff material made of layers of paper pressed together

✓ **cliff** a very steep slope of rock or clay

✓ **hatch** to come out from the egg

✓ **island** a body of land surrounded by water

✓ **searching** examining carefully

✓ **underground** beneath the surface of the ground

More Words to Know

confused unable to tell people or things apart

puffin a sea bird of northern waters, having a thick body, large head, and bill of several colors

puffling offspring of a puffin

rescue to save from danger or harm

stranded left in a helpless situation

✓ = Tested Word

For vocabulary and building background strategies to support ESL students, see *Adding English: ESL Teacher's Guide.*

Classify Words

Display Transparency 25 and write the column headings as shown. Write *burrows* in the Word column. Have a volunteer use *burrows* in a sentence. Discuss which column students should check. Point out that *burrows* is both an action and an object (a home for animals). Using the class chart as a model, students can work in pairs to create charts of their own to classify the remaining vocabulary words.

ESL *Especially good for ESL*

Word	Object	Action
burrows	✔	✔
cardboard	✔	
hatch	✔	✔
island	✔	
searching		✔
underground	✔	

Transparency 25

Use Context Clues

See page 216 for a lesson on using context clues to identify and define homophones.

Figure 8.3 (continued)

Vocabulary Strategies

Context Clues: Homophones

Students will

- use context clues to determine the correct meaning of a homophone in a sentence
- develop vocabulary through reading
- use new vocabulary in writing a slogan

Introduction

Ask students to identify any *homophones* (words that sound the same but have different spellings and meanings) they know, such as *see* and *sea*. Explain that good readers look for clues in the words and sentences in a paragraph to help them figure out the meaning of a homophone.

Teach

Have students read Words to Know and think about what each word means. Then ask them to read the paragraph. After reading, point out the word *burrows* and model using context clues to identify the correct meaning of this homophone.

 I know the word b-u-r-r-o-w-s. But I also know that there is another word that sounds the same, but is spelled differently: b-u-r-r-o-s. I read the sentences before and after the one with *burrows*. The writer talks about some birds going underground. These clues help me choose the correct word meaning "holes dug into the ground."

Close and Assess

To see if students can choose the correct meaning of a homophone when they read, write *hole* and *whole*. Ask:

How could you decide that *hole* means "a place in the earth for an animal"?

This page contains vocabulary words to know, a definition of homophone, and a paragraph containing the vocabulary words. Using the vocabulary words, students are asked to create a slogan to motivate people to help rescue birds.

Vocabulary Support

Halla (hat′l lä) Icelandic girl's name

Heimaey (hā′mä ā) Island of Iceland

Lundi (lün′dä) puffin

Arnar Inge (at′när ing′ē) Icelandic boy's name

fisk (fisk) fish

baldusbrá (bal′dèrs brō) flowering plant

lundi pysja (lün′dä pēsh′yär) puffling

Einn-tvier-PRíR (i n-tvâr-thir) 1, 2, 3

216   *Nights of the Pufflings* • Vocabulary Strategies

Figure 8.3 (continued)

Reading Strategies

Preview and Predict

Students should read the title and look at the pictures. Tell students that pufflings are baby puffins. Then ask:

- Does this selection look like it will be realistic or make-believe? Why?
- What can you tell about puffins and pufflings by looking at the pictures?
- What do you expect to learn in this selection?

Set Purposes

Create a K-W-L chart (Transparency 7). Have students list what they **k**now about puffins and what they **w**ant to know. After reading, they can list what they have **l**earned. Model using the chart to set a purpose for reading.

Think ALOUD I know that puffins are black and white birds with reddish beaks. I can tell they live near water. I want to know more about pufflings and how the children in the selection are helping them.

Nights of the Pufflings photographs and text by Bruce McMillan

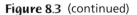
Suggestions for Reading

Small Group

Before reading, tell students that this selection is about some children who help baby birds. Let students preview the illustrations and predict how the children might help the birds.

While reading, use the questions to guide comprehension. Students can read the story in two parts: pages 217–225 and 226–230.

Independent

While they read, have students look for the main ideas in this selection. Suggest that they take notes to separate the main ideas from the supporting details.

Needs-Based/ Intervention

While reading, students can listen to the selection CD or tape and follow along in their books.

Selection Audio CD6/Tape 11, Side 1

After reading, students can use the pictures to retell the story of the birds' adventures and then reread the story.

Response Log

In their Response Logs, students can
- write about experiences they have had with birds
- record questions they have about puffins or Iceland
- jot down ideas for writing a story about puffins
- draw pictures of puffins

Figure 8.3 (continued)

Guiding Comprehension

Drawing Conclusions/Inferential

1 Why is Halla searching the sky?

She is watching for the puffins to return from the sea.

Main Idea and Supporting Details/Inferential

2 What is the main idea on page 219? What are some details that tell more about the main idea?

The main idea is that millions of puffins return to the island. Supporting details:
1. They return to lay eggs and raise chicks;
2. They come ashore only at this time.

Cause and Effect/Literal

3 Why do the puffins return to Halla's island every year?

The puffins come ashore to lay eggs and raise puffin chicks.

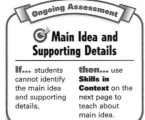

Ongoing Assessment

Main Idea and Supporting Details

If... students cannot identify the main idea and supporting details,	then... use **Skills in Context** on the next page to teach about main idea.

Every day Halla looks from the high cliff down to the sea. She searches for the first puffin of the year. "Lundi" means puffin in Icelandic.

Meeting Diverse Needs

ESL

Use pictures that portray a general idea with several nonessential details that support the main idea. Invite students to point to and name anything they see in each picture. Then display all the pictures and ask: "Which picture is about (main idea)?" Then name an incidental in a picture. Ask: "Is this picture about (detail)?" Repeat this for all the pictures.

Guiding Comprehension Support 2:
Main Idea and Supporting Details

For extra support, see *Adding English: ESL Teacher's Guide.*

218   *Nights of the Pufflings*

Figure 8.3 (continued)

Puffins fill the sky in every direction. They return by the millions after spending the winter at sea. The birds return to lay eggs and raise their young. This is the only time they land.

Skills in Context

Comprehension: Main Idea and Supporting Details

Objective

Students will identify the main idea of a paragraph and find supporting details.

Introduce

Find a short article in a newspaper. Read it to students. Then ask: What is this article about? The main idea is what the writer is trying to tell readers about the topic, for example, "The weather is going to be bad." Have students identify supporting details, such as rain and high wind.

Teach

Model your thinking about the main idea and supporting details of the paragraph on page 219.

Think ALOUD The topic of this paragraph is puffins. The main idea seems to be that there are many puffins—the sky is "speckled" with them. The rest of the paragraph has details that support this main idea: "millions" of birds are returning, and this is the only time that the puffins come to shore.

Close and Assess

To assess students' understanding of main idea, read these three statements to students: Thousands of puffins nest on the shores. Many puffins fly in the sky. Few puffins returned to the island this year.

Then ask:

Which of these does *not* support the main idea of the paragraph on this page? (The last statement does not support the main idea.)

------- tested vocabulary

SKILLS TRACE

Main Idea and Supporting Details

Introduce/Teach	Review/Reteach
TE: 3.1 83	TE: 3.1 89b, 143, 161b, 214-215, **219**, 223, 235a
	PB: 3.1 27, 57, 91, 93
Skills Test, Unit 2	

Figure 8.3 (continued)

Guiding Comprehension

Drawing Conclusions/Inferential

4 Why is it important for the puffins to get their underground nests ready?

Soon the puffins will lay eggs. The eggs will hatch, and the chicks will need a nest in which to live and grow.

Cause and Effect/Inferential

5 Now that it is summer, why do the grown-up puffins need to catch a lot of fish?

They are not feeding only themselves. They are also feeding chicks that have hatched.

Ongoing Assessment

Digraph *ow;* Diphthong *ow*

If... students cannot identify the two sounds of *ow,*

then... use **Skills in Context** on the next page to teach the vowel digraph *ow* and the vowel diphthong *ow.*

Puffins make their underground nests in the same burrows year after year. Halla and her friends watch the birds on the cliffs. Soon the eggs will hatch and the little chicks will grow into pufflings.

☀Meeting Diverse Needs

Intervention

Make an interactive audiotape on which you say words that contain the vowel digraph *ow,* such as *now, brown, down, clown,* and *meow.* Leave adequate time on the tape for students to say them after you. Repeat with words containing the digraph *ow.* Use *grow, burrows, below,* and *blow.* Prompt students to add other words that could fit in the lists.

Phonics Support: Diagraph *ow;* Diphthong *ow*

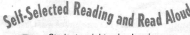

Self-Selected Reading and Read Aloud

Students might enjoy hearing you read another book about puffins, *Puffin's Homecoming: The Story of an Atlantic Puffin,* by Darcie Bailer. (Smithsonian Soundprints, 1994) An Atlantic puffin returns to the place he was born to mate and raise chicks.

220 *Nights of the Pufflings*

Figure 8.3 (continued)

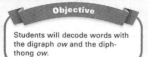

Halla and the puffins both splash in the cold ocean water during the summer. Young puffins ride the waves close to shore, but the older birds fly farther out to sea for better fishing. Adult puffins must catch more fish in the summer to feed their chicks.

——— tested vocabulary

Skills in Context

Phonics: Digraph *ow;* Diphthong *ow*

Objective

Students will decode words with the digraph *ow* and the diphthong *ow.*

Introduce

Ask students to think of words that contain *ow.* As students name words such as *brown* and *blow,* list their responses on the board. Help students identify the sound that *ow* represents in each word.

Teach

Have students reread the second sentence at the top of page 220 and model reading the first *ow* word, *clown.*

Think ALOUD When I see *clown,* I notice *ow* in the middle of the word. I know *ow* can represent /ō/ as in *grow* or /ou/ as in *now.* I try each sound to see which one makes sense in the sentence. When I say the same sound as in *now,* the word *clown* makes sense.

Model the same thinking process for *burrows.*

Close and Assess

To see if students understand how to figure out the sound that *ow* represents in a word, ask:

How would you read the words *below* and *down?* (Try out the two sounds of *ow* as in *now* and *grow* to see which sound gives a word that makes sense.)

Nights of the Pufflings **221**

Figure 8.3 (continued)

Guiding Comprehension

Predicting/Critical

6 **Why do you suppose Arnar Ingi is thinking about getting some cardboard boxes?**

Students are likely to predict that the children are going to use the boxes to help the pufflings in some way.

Main Idea and Supporting Details/ Inferential

7 **What is the most important idea in the first paragraph on page 223? What are some details that tell more about this main idea?**

The most important idea is that only the chicks' parents see them and care for them at this time. Details include that baby puffins never come out; they stay hidden in tunnels of their burrows; and the parents have to carry fish to feed the chicks.

Ongoing Assessment

🎯 Main Idea and Supporting Details

| **If...** students cannot identify the main idea and supporting details in this paragraph, | **then...** use **Skills in Context** on the next page to teach about main idea. |

Drawing Conclusions/Inferential

8 **How does Halla know it is time for the pufflings to come out?**

The flowers (*baldusbrá*) are in full bloom; this is the time of year when the pufflings come out.

The eggs have hatched and puffin parents are bringing fish to feed their young. Although the nights of the pufflings are still weeks away, the children are getting boxes ready.

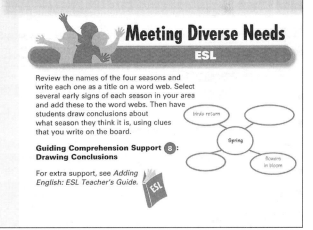

Meeting Diverse Needs
ESL

Review the names of the four seasons and write each one as a title on a word web. Select several early signs of each season in your area and add these to the word webs. Then have students draw conclusions about what season they think it is, using clues that you write on the board.

Guiding Comprehension Support 8:
Drawing Conclusions

For extra support, see *Adding English: ESL Teacher's Guide.*

Figure 8.3 (continued)

Only the puffin parents see their chicks because they are safely tucked away in the dark long tunnels of the burrows. Parents feed their hungry chicks up to 10 times a day. By August the chicks have grown into pufflings. The pufflings will soon fly out into the night.

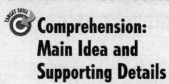

Skills in Context

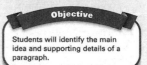 Comprehension: Main Idea and Supporting Details

Objective

Students will identify the main idea and supporting details of a paragraph.

Introduce

Tell students that the topic of a paragraph or article is one or two words that tell what the paragraph or article is about, such as *birds* or *flowers*. Explain that the main idea is the most important idea about the topic. Give an example of a main idea, such as "Adult puffins eat fish from the water." Explain that supporting details for this main idea might tell how, when, or why the adult puffins eat fish from the water.

Teach

Model thinking about the topic, main idea, and supporting details of the first paragraph on page 223.

 Think ALOUD I know the topic is puffin chicks. But after reading the whole paragraph, I decide that the main idea is, "Only the parents see and care for the chicks." That is the most important idea about the chicks. I found these details that support the main idea: "Baby puffins never come out. They stay hidden. Parents feed the chicks."

Close and Assess

To assess students' understanding of main idea, ask:

- What is the main idea of the last paragraph on page 223? (The pufflings are ready to fly.)

- What details support the main idea? (The chicks have grown into pufflings, and Halla knows the wait is over.)

_____ tested vocabulary

SKILLS TRACE

Main Idea and Supporting Details

Introduce/Teach	Review/Reteach
TE: 3.1 83	TE: 3.1 89b, 143, 161b, 214-215, 219, **223**, 235a
	PB: 3.1 27, 57, 91, 93

Skills Test, Unit 2

Figure 8.3 (continued)

Guiding Comprehension

Stop to Check Comprehension

Self-Monitoring

9 What has happened to the puffins so far in the selection?

1. The puffins return to Heimaey Island.

2. The puffins lay eggs and raise their chicks.

3. The pufflings leave their burrows for their first flight to the sea.

4. Some pufflings become confused and crash-land in the village.

Ongoing Assessment

Self-Monitoring

If... students	**then...** use
cannot state the events that have taken place so far,	**Strategies in Context** on the next page to teach a fix-up strategy.

For the next two weeks pufflings will be leaving for their winter at sea. With boxes and flashlights children try to find stray pufflings before the village animals do.

Meeting Diverse Needs

Challenge

Some students can research the geography of Iceland. Others can read articles about pufflings in encyclopedias for information not given in the selection. A third group can reread the text and note things that the Icelandic children did that they have never done. Then regroup students so that each new group has at least one student each from the original groups. Each "expert" can share ideas with the others.

Tiered Assignments

Response Log

Students can imagine that they have just found a lost puffling. In their Response Logs, they can describe how they feel and what they will do.

Figure 8.3 (continued)

Most pufflings leave their burrows and fly off the cliffs during the night and land safely in the water. Some get lost and land in the village. Because they cannot fly from flat ground they try to hide, not only from the animals but also from the cars.

_____ tested vocabulary

Strategies in Context

Self-Question/Fix-Up

Ask:

- When do you need to read a selection slowly? (when the words or ideas in the selection are difficult or new)

- When can you read more quickly? (when the ideas and words are easier to understand)

Explain to students that when they read more slowly or more quickly, they **adjust their reading rate** to better understand what they are reading and to remember what happens.

 Think ALOUD When I started reading this selection, I read quickly. It was not too difficult for me to understand that millions of puffins were coming to land. Later on though, I had to slow down to understand what I was reading.

Students may also want to add to their K-W-L charts new questions they have and facts they have learned.

Predict

Have students check their earlier predictions. Then ask them to predict whether Halla and her friends will be able to help all the stranded pufflings.

Quote for the Day

"It is wise to write on many subjects, to try many topics so that you may find the right and inspiring one."

—Henry David Thoreau
U.S. philosopher and author of *Walden*

Figure 8.3 (continued)

Guiding Comprehension

Drawing Conclusions/Inferential

10 Why does Halla yell, "puffling"?

She is excited to see one.

Sequence/Literal

11 What do the children do after they catch some pufflings?

They put the pufflings in cardboard boxes and take them home. The next day, they take the boxes of pufflings to the beach to send them on their way.

Summarizing/Inferential

12 What are the main points so far?

Each year, the puffins return to Iceland to lay their eggs and raise chicks. Some of the pufflings land in the village after they leave their nests. The children rescue and return them to the sea.

Ongoing Assessment

Summarizing

| **If...** students cannot summarize this part of the selection, | **then...** use **Skills in Context** on the next page to teach about summarizing. |

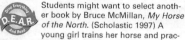

Self-Selected Reading and Read Aloud

Students might want to select another book by Bruce McMillan, *My Horse of the North.* (Scholastic 1997) A young girl trains her horse and practices for the annual sheep round-up in this photo essay. **average** Encourage students to try to read silently for increasing periods of time.

226 *Nights of the Pufflings*

Halla and her friends call to the pufflings as they run up and down the streets picking up lost birds and putting them in cardboard boxes.

Meeting Diverse Needs
Other Ways to Learn

Divide the class into small groups. Select the part of the story in which the author tells about the nights of the pufflings. As one student rereads the account out loud, invite a group to use simple props, like flashlights, boxes, and stuffed animals, to pantomime the actions of the Icelandic children.

Kinesthetic: Sequence

Figure 8.3 (continued)

During the two-week period the children save thousands of birds. Each day they take the rescued pufflings to the sea and set them free.

Skills in Context

REVIEW

Comprehension: Summarizing

> **Objective**
>
> Students will summarize the main events of a selection.

Introduce

Ask students to tell the story of a recent class field trip or a day they spent at the park or at a game. Ask students: Did you tell every detail about the day, or did you choose the most important ideas? Point out that choosing the most important ideas of a story and telling them in a few sentences is called summarizing.

Teach

Have students review the pages of the selection up until this point. Model your thinking about summarizing the most important events:

Think ALOUD **Although there are many details in this selection, I try to narrow them down to just the most important ideas. Here are three important ideas: "Each year, the puffins return to Iceland to lay their eggs and raise chicks. When the pufflings get big enough to leave their nests, some become confused and land in the village. Children of the village then help them get to sea."**

Close and Assess

To decide whether students understand how to summarize, ask them to summarize a familiar movie, television show, book, or story. Summaries should include the most important events and comprise only a few sentences.

SKILLS TRACE	
Summarizing	
Introduce/Teach	Review/Reteach
TE: 3.1 227	TE: 3.1 235b, 266-267, 273, 281, 289a, 299, 305b
	PB: 3.1 97, 111, 113, 127
Skills Test, Unit 3	

Figure 8.3 (continued)

Guiding Comprehension

Stop to Check Comprehension

Self-Monitoring

 13 What happens after some of the pufflings crash-land in the village?

1. The children rescue the pufflings from the dangers of the city.

2. Each night for two weeks, the children collect stranded pufflings and put them in cardboard boxes.

3. In the mornings, the children take the pufflings to the beach and set them free.

Ongoing Assessment

Self-Monitoring

If... students cannot summarize the last few events of the selection,	**then...** use **Strategies in Context** on the next page to teach a fix-up strategy.

Two photos illustrate how a child prepares to release a puffling to the sea.

 ## Meeting Diverse Needs

ESL

Display a three-column chart headed by the numerals 1, 2, 3. Write the words *one, two,* and *three* in the appropriate columns. Then ask students for suggestions for the first three counting numbers in other languages that they know. Finally, add *einn* (in), *tvier* (tvår), and *PRiR* (thir), the Icelandic words for *one, two,* and *three*.

Prior Knowledge Support: Developing Vocabulary

For extra support, see *Adding English: ESL Teacher's Guide.*

Response Log

Students can write about whether or not the children in the selection did something good and important. Encourage students to support their opinions.

Figure 8.3 (continued)

Part
2

The children launch the pufflings by throwing them up in the air with two hands. Their wings flutter and they land safely in the water.

Strategies in Context

Self-Question/Fix-Up

Have students who did not **adjust their reading rate** reread the selection at a slower pace. Then direct students to complete their K-W-L charts.

Check Predictions

Have students discuss the predictions they made at the beginning of the selection. Did this selection tell them what they expected it to? What other things did they learn?

Main Idea and Supporting Details

To check students' understanding of main idea and supporting details, use Practice Book 3.1, page 93.

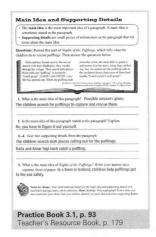

Practice Book 3.1, p. 93
Teacher's Resource Book, p. 179

Figure 8.3 (continued)

336

Guiding Comprehension

Character/Critical

14 How do you think Halla feels as she watches the pufflings leave for their winter at sea?

Halla probably feels a little sad that the nights of the pufflings have ended, but she must feel good that she has done something to help the birds.

Drawing Conclusions/Inferential

15 How did the author's father help the author to become a photographer?

The author's father gave him a camera when the author was a child.

Halla watches as the last of the pufflings and adult puffins swim out to the sea. She says good-bye until next spring.

More About the Author

Bruce McMillan might be best known for his concept books for young readers. Books such as *Dry or Wet?*; *Here a Chick, There a Chick*; *Counting Wildflowers*; and *Time To. . .* use McMillan's photos to demonstrate concepts with clarity and, often, humor.

Quote for the Day

"Once you realize that learning is up to you, you have the right attitude to succeed in school and beyond."

— Tony Bennett, singer

230 *Nights of the Pufflings*

Figure 8.3 (continued)

This is a "Reader Response" page—it contains a discussion question, several comprehension questions, and a related activity to do with a classmate.

Reader Response

Open for Discussion

Personal Response

Set the stage for sharing personal responses by modeling. For example: *I would like to help save the pufflings because I think it is important to help other people or animals who are in need.*

Comprehension Check

Critical Response

1. The adult puffins have been catching more fish. **Inferring**

2. They are excited and concerned about the pufflings. They start looking for the pufflings long before it is time to help them. They work hard to save the pufflings. **Making Judgments**

3. Responses will vary. The pufflings peck the children. An animal that is hurt could hurt the person trying to help it. You might hurt an animal when you try to help it. **Hypothesizing**

4. They rescue thousands of pufflings. ⊙ **Main Idea and Supporting Details**

5. These details support the main idea: pufflings everywhere and helping hands; take rescued pufflings home; send their guests on their way; boxes full of pufflings. ⊙ **Main Idea and Supporting Details**

Selection Test

Selection Test

Directions: Choose the best answer to each item. Mark the space for the answer you have chosen.

Part 1: Vocabulary

Find the answer choice that means about the same as the underlined word in each sentence.

1. Anna stood on a cliff.
   - a very steep hill
   - a large wooden box
   - a kind of step stool
   - the top of a lighthouse

2. Hundreds of chicks will hatch.
   - hunt for food
   - grow wings
   - come out of eggs
   - learn to fly

3. The police are searching for clues.
   - working hard
   - looking carefully
   - flying low
   - calling loudly

4. Some animals live underground.
   - in the trees
   - in the same place
   - a long time
   - beneath the earth's surface

5. Many birds live on that island.
   - small body of land surrounded by water
   - large nest
   - small group of trees
   - bush with red berries

6. These burrows have been here for years.
   - small carts with wheels
   - holes in the ground
   - long-legged birds
   - large pieces of metal

7. Liam found a cardboard box.
   - rock formed from mud that has become hard
   - strong board made of thin layers of wood glued together
   - a bunch of metal threads twisted together
   - stiff material made of layers of paper

Part 2: Comprehension

Use what you know about the selection to answer each item.

8. *Lundi* is the Icelandic word for—
   - clown
   - island
   - puffin
   - chick

9. Who are the "clowns of the sea" mentioned in this selection?
   - the puffins
   - Halla and her friends
   - the children of Heimaey
   - seals and otters

10. Pairs of puffins "talk" to each other by—
    - flapping their wings.
    - taking care of eggs.
    - stamping their feet.
    - tapping their beaks together.

11. How do Halla and her friends know there are chicks in the burrows?
    - They can hear the chicks calling.
    - They can see the chicks.
    - The chicks come out to swim in the ocean.
    - The chicks eat fish that the children put out for them.

12. The children use cardboard boxes to—
    - collect puffin eggs.
    - catch cats in the village.
    - carry pufflings to the beach.
    - sit on when they get tired.

13. What can you tell from this selection about the children of Heimaey Island?
    - They are cruel to animals.
    - They care about nature.
    - They are not very good students.
    - They like to sleep late.

14. What would be another good title for this selection?
    - "Lazy Summer Days on an Island"
    - "The Villages of Iceland"
    - "Puffing Rescue on Heimaey Island"
    - "The Children of Iceland"

15. Which sentence tells what this selection is mostly about?
    - Every summer, Icelandic children work hard to help the pufflings survive.
    - Dogs and cats pose a great danger to pufflings.
    - Puffins make large nests where chicks will be safe all summer.
    - Puffins come ashore to have chicks and then fly out to sea.

Practice Book 3.1, pp. 95-96. • Teacher's Resource Book, pp. 180–181

Come to Iceland

Creative Response

Answers will vary but could include glaciers, hot springs, geysers, volcanoes, rushing rivers, waterfalls, fjords, plateaus, and coastlines.

SOCIAL STUDIES CONNECTION

Reader Response • *Nights of the Pufflings*   **231**

Figure 8.3 (continued)

Comprehension Reteach

Students will
- find the main idea of a paragraph or passage
- learn that supporting details are facts and bits of information that tell more about the main idea

SKILLS TRACE

✔ Main Idea and Supporting Details

Introduce/Teach	Review/Reteach
TE: 3.1 83	TE: 3.1 89b, 143, 161b, 214-215, 219, 223, **235a** PB: 3.1 27, 57, 91, 93

Skills Test, Unit 2

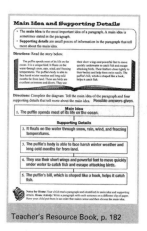

Teacher's Resource Book, p. 182

Main Idea and Supporting Details

Introduce

Write this sentence on the board: *Weekends are fun.* Have students identify the topic of the sentence. Ask: What is this sentence about? (weekends) What does this sentence say about weekends? (They are fun.) Elicit from students examples that would support this statement. Point out to students that their examples of fun weekend activities are supporting details. They support the main idea that weekends are fun.

Teach and Practice

Remind students that the topic is what a paragraph is about. The main idea is the most important idea about a topic. Read with students the paragraph on page 227. Ask them to figure out the topic of this paragraph (pufflings) and the main idea (rescuing pufflings). Tell students that sometimes the main idea is stated in a sentence in the beginning, middle, or end of the paragraph. Sometimes readers have to figure it out. They can do this by thinking about the supporting details, or the small pieces of information that tell about—or support—the main idea. Work with students to fill out Transparency 15, a main idea map.

> Main Idea
>
> Supporting Details

Assign partners different paragraphs in the selection. They can read the paragraphs together to create main idea maps like the one on the transparency. Have partners share their work.

Close and Assess

Review students' main idea maps to see if they
- identify the main idea as the most important idea about a topic
- identify supporting details that support the main idea

Students can practice identifying main idea and supporting details with another selection using page 182 of the Teacher's Resource Book, or they can listen to the Reteach Lesson on the selection audio CD or tape.

Selection Audio CD 6/Tape 11, Side 2

MORE PRACTICE

Figure 8.3 (continued)

REVIEW

Comprehension

Summarizing

Introduce

Ask students: What is a summary? (a brief retelling of the most important ideas in a piece of writing) Remind students that summaries include only the most important ideas and leave out unimportant details. Write sentences such as these on the board: *Halla's friend spies a puffin overhead. Each year, the puffins return to Iceland to lay their eggs and raise chicks.* Ask: Which sentence(s) would need to be included in a summary of the selection? (the second)

Teach and Practice

Review with students each page of the selection and briefly discuss the important events that are happening in the selection. Then write the following sentences on the board.

- Some of the pufflings become confused and land in the village after they leave their nests.
- By ten o'clock, the streets of Heimaey are alive with roaming children.
- The children rescue the pufflings at night and return them to the sea in the morning.
- Halla bids the puffins farewell.

Have students decide which are important ideas and which are less important details. Record their answers in a chart.

Invite students to use the "Important Ideas" as a reference as they create summaries of the selection. They can use their charts to guide them in creating summaries.

Important Ideas	Details
Some of the pufflings become confused and land in the village after they leave their nests.	By ten o'clock, the streets of Heimaey are alive with roaming children.
The children rescue the pufflings at night and return them to the sea in the morning.	Halla bids the puffins farewell.

Close and Assess

Review students' work to see if they

- separate important ideas from details
- use the ideas to write summaries that make sense

Students can practice summarizing with another selection using Practice Book 3.1, page 97, or they can summarize the Big Book, *From Seed to Plant.*

MORE PRACTICE

Objectives

Students will

- produce summaries of text selections
- include only the most important ideas about selections in their summaries

SKILLS TRACE

Summarizing

Introduce/Teach	Review/Reteach
TE: 3.1 227	TE: 3.1 **235b**, 266-267, 273, 281, 289a, 299, 305b
	PB: 3.1 97, 111, 113, 127

Skills Test, Unit 3

Summarizing   REVIEW

Directions: Read the passage. Then read each question about the passage. Choose the best answer to the question. Mark the space for the answer you have chosen.

The Beak of the Puffin

The puffin's beak helps this sea bird in many ways. The beak is like a hook, and it quickly catches and holds fish. A puffin can catch and hold many fish in its beak while it swims underwater.

The puffin's beak also is used as a shovel to dig into the earth to push and pull rocks.

While the puffin's beak is grayish brown most of the year, it grows a bright cover in the spring. The colors of this cover are bright red, blue, and gold. These colorful beaks help draw the attention of a mate.

1. This passage tells about—
   - puffins catching fish.
   - puffins digging in the earth.
   - the colors of the puffin's beak.
   - the ways puffins use their beaks.

2. Which sentence best summarizes the first paragraph?
   - Puffins are seabirds.
   - The puffin's beak helps it catch lots of fish.
   - The puffin's beak is like a hook.
   - The puffin's beak has many uses.

3. Which sentence best summarizes the second paragraph?
   - Puffins dig with their beaks.
   - Puffins' beaks are very strong.
   - Puffins like to dig.
   - The puffin's beak has many uses.

4. Which sentence best summarizes the third paragraph?
   - Puffins' beaks are greyish brown.
   - Brightly-colored beaks help puffins find mates.
   - Puffins have bright colors on their beaks.
   - Puffins' beaks turn red, blue, and gold.

5. Which sentence best summarizes the passage?
   - Puffins dig with their beaks.
   - Puffins' beaks help them to catch lots of fish.
   - The puffin's beak has many uses.
   - The puffin's beak is very strange.

Notes for Home: Your child summarized key ideas in individual paragraphs and a whole passage. *Home Activity:* Talk with your child about the day's activities. Then help your child summarize the conversation in two or three sentences.

Practice Book 3.1, p. 97
Teacher's Resource Book, p. 183

Figure 8.3 (continued)

Writing Descriptive

Descriptive Paragraph

Prompt Write a descriptive paragraph about a favorite animal you have seen in nature. Your descriptions should provide vivid details to help readers imagine what such an animal would be like if they saw it themselves.
Purpose To inform
Audience Classmates

Prewrite

Invite students to recall that the photographs in *Nights of the Pufflings* provide reader's with information about what puffins look like, while the writer gives details about the animal's behavior. Tell students to use all their senses as they picture their chosen animals. Have them create word webs to organize words and phrases that describe how their animals look and act. Mention that good writers include even small details in their descriptions.

Draft

Have students refer to their word webs to draft their descriptions. Tell them they are describing the animal to someone who has never seen it. Encourage them to put the details in an order that creates a clear picture.

Drafting Strategy: Observing Details Point out that in *Nights of the Pufflings*, the author writes about details he

noticed while watching the pufflings. Phrases such as "it's a short wing-flapping trip" and "the birds splash-land safely in the sea below" help the reader get a mental picture of the pufflings flight. Have students imagine what they have observed about their animals. Tell them to include words that will help capture this image on paper.

Revise

Have students reread their descriptions to a partner. Encourage writing partners to ask questions about any part of the description that is unclear. Encourage them to provide more details as needed.

Edit

Have students check their revised paragraphs for spelling, capitalization, and punctuation. Tell them to pay particular attention to the spelling of plural nouns, the capitalization of proper nouns, and the formation of possessive nouns.

Publish

Invite students to draw an illustration to accompany their descriptions. They can gather the descriptions into a class book about animals in nature.

Clowns of the Sea

Puffins are known for their colorful markings, especially on their beaks. In the spring, the triangular-shaped beaks are bright red, vivid blue, and brilliant yellow. The puffin's eyes are also ringed with red, and the black and white birds have bright orange feet. It's no wonder they are sometimes called "clowns of the sea"!

Key Features

Descriptions

- are informative
- use sensory details to create vivid images
- give specific details
- put details in an order that makes sense

Scoring Guide

4 Exemplary
- vivid sense words and images
- ideas clear and focused
- elaboration with strong details
- clear, varied, smooth sentences
- errors do not prevent understanding

3 Competent
- includes sense words and images
- ideas generally clear and focused
- elaboration with three or more details
- most sentences varied and smooth
- errors do not prevent understanding

2 Developing
- some sense words; images may not be clear
- ideas may lack focus and clarity
- elaboration with two or more details
- simple sentences; sometimes awkward
- errors may prevent understanding

1 Emerging
- few or no sense words or images
- ideas lack focus and clarity
- lacks elaboration
- incomplete and/or awkward sentences
- errors may prevent understanding

Figure 8.3 (continued)

Writing Prompts

It's for the Birds

Imagine you are one of the Icelandic children in Nights of the Pufflings. Write a humorous story describing what it is like to stay up late at night trying to catch pufflings.　**easy**

Descriptive Names

Puffins are sometimes called "clowns of the sea" or "parrots of the sea" because of their colorful markings. Find pictures of other birds, and write descriptive nicknames for them.　**average**

Birds of a Feather

Nights of the Pufflings explains how children in Iceland work to rescue pufflings. "Saving the Whooping Crane" tells about efforts to save whooping cranes. How are puffins and whooping cranes alike? How are they different? Write an expository paragraph comparing and contrasting each bird. Teacher's Resource Book page 184 can help students recall details.　**challenge**

Writing Across Texts

Directions: Consider what you learned about puffin and whooping cranes in the selections *Nights of the Pufflings* and "Saving the Whooping Cranes." Think about ways the two birds are alike and different. Read the five statements in the box and use them to complete the table. Write the statements that are true of puffin, whooping cranes, and both birds in the correct place in the table. Add other information you have read to the table.

Statements
- come to Iceland in summer
- come to the United States in winter
- are kinds of birds
- are in danger of becoming extinct
- fly in flocks of millions of birds

Puffins	Whooping Cranes	Puffins and Whooping Cranes
come to Iceland in summer	come to the United States in winter	are kinds of birds
fly in flocks of millions of birds	are in danger of becoming extinct	Additional answers will vary.
Additional answers will vary.	Additional answers will vary.	

Write an Expository Paragraph

Write an expository paragraph that compares and contrasts the birds and their habitats. Use information from each selection to support your paragraph. Write your paragraph on a separate sheet of paper. Paragraphs will vary. Check that students use information from both selections.

Note for Home: Your child compared and contrasted information about two kinds of birds, *Home Activity* As you read a story or article about an animal with your child, discuss ways it is like or unlike another animal you know about.

Teacher's Resource Book, p. 184

Portfolio Encourage students to choose a writing project for their portfolios.

Oral Language

Listening for Details Before students gather their descriptions from the previous page (235c), invite students to read them aloud to their classmates. Make this a guessing game where listeners must guess the animal described before the speaker says the name or shows the picture.

SPEAKING LISTENING Tips

Remind students that listeners should
- ✓ imagine how things look, sound, smell, taste, and feel
- ✓ listen for sense words that describe things
- ✓ listen for details

Speakers should
- ✓ speak clearly
- ✓ maintain eye contact
- ✓ use expression

Weekly Fluency Check

Check for Fluency

Listen to students read aloud something of their own choosing or something you choose. Possible passages from Nights of the Pufflings are

- pp. 218–219, beginning with "Halla searches. . ."
- pp. 222-223, beginning with "Halla's Friend, Arnar. . ."

Improve Fluency: Read with Accuracy

Model or review with students ways to read for accuracy, for example, deciding in advance how names should be pronounced. Pronounce the names and Icelandic words in the selection for students and write them on the board, or students can keep the names in a notebook with phonetic pronunciations. Encourage students to practice the names and difficult words so they can read smoothly.

Figure 8.3 (continued)

Grammar   Quick Review: Possessive Nouns

Objectives

Students will

Day 1 recognize that possessive nouns tell to whom or what something belongs

Day 2 form possessive nouns that use an apostrophe

Day 3 use possessive nouns in sentences

Day 4 distinguish common nouns from proper nouns and recognize capitalization of proper nouns

Day 5 write proper nouns correctly

Grammar: Possessive Nouns   REVIEW

Directions: Write the possessive form of the word in ( ) to complete each sentence.

town's	1. Each spring the (town) children have a special tradition.
tulips'	2. It happens after the (tulips) buds open.
robin's	3. It happens after they hear the first (robin) chirp.
parents'	4. The children, with their (parents) help, clean up the park.
park's	5. One group puts all the litter in the (park) trash cans.
playground's	6. Raul and his friends scrub the (playground) swings and monkey bars.
tables'	7. The whole Li family paints all the picnic (table) tops and benches.
Tina's	8. At the end of the clean up, (Tina) friends are tired.
Raul's	9. (Raul) friends are hot and dirty.
children's	10. The parents are proud of their (children) hard work.

Directions: Use the possessive form of each noun below in a sentence. Write the sentence on the line. Possible answers given.

Yoko   people   cats   Charles   mother

11. Yoko's mother is a veterinarian.
12. She takes care of people's sick animals.
13. She found homes for my two cats' kittens.
14. She put up notices when Charles's dog was lost.
15. Yoko is proud of her mother's work.

Teacher's Resource Book, p. 185

Language Review
See the Language Review activities on page 214f for a daily review of possessive nouns.

Day 1

Revisit Possessive Nouns

Remind students that nouns can show who owns, or possesses, something, as well as name a person, place, thing, or idea. These kinds of nouns are called **possessive nouns**. Show students this chart. Ask them to write the possessive form of each noun.

Nouns	Possessive Form
Iceland	Iceland's
Halla	Halla's
the town	the town's
Stephanie	Stephanie's
Ross	Ross's
the pufflings	the pufflings'
their mothers	their mothers'

Day 2

Write Possessive Nouns

Ask students to read these sentences. Have them choose the possessive noun that correctly completes each sentence.

1. The puffins are coming to _____ island. (Hallas /(Halla's)/ Hallas')

2. The _____ excitement is obvious. (children /(children's)/ childrens')

3. When they are first born, the _____ parents care for them. (pufflings / puffling's /(pufflings'))

For additional practice, have students write the possessive form of the underlined noun.

1. a nest belonging to a <u>puffin</u>	1. the _____ nest (puffin's)
2. boxes belonging to the <u>boys</u>	2. the _____ boxes (boys')
3. the secretary who works in the <u>bank</u>	3. the _____ secretary (bank's)
4. leaves from the <u>flowers</u>	4. the _____ leaves (flowers')

Day 3

Write with Possessives

Have students use these singular and plural possessive nouns to write sentences. When they finish, have them trade papers and edit one another's work, watching carefully for problems with apostrophes. Students can use Teacher's Resource Book page 185 to practice nouns.

parents'
animal's
geese's
puppies'
nurse's
Carlos's

Figure 8.3 (continued)

Common and Proper Nouns

Day 4

Teach Common and Proper Nouns

Explain that nouns such as *girl, park,* and *dog* do not name which girl, which park, or which dog. They are called **common nouns** because they can name any person, place, or thing. The names of particular persons, places, or things are called **proper nouns**. In addition, the names of days, months, and holidays are proper nouns.

Proper nouns begin with capital letters; common nouns do not. In proper nouns of more than one word, the first word and each important word are capitalized, as in *United States of America.*

Show students this word jumble. Have them circle the proper nouns.

When they have finished, have students choose two proper nouns from the jumble and use both in a sentence. Check to be sure they capitalize the proper nouns correctly.

Students can use Teacher's Resource Book page 186 to learn more about common and proper nouns.

boy (February) (Mexican)
(John Smith) (Hayes Middle School)
(Sunday) nation woman
(Lincoln Memorial) lake (Lake Erie)
(Veteran's Day) (Al's Auto Repair)

Grammar: Common and Proper Nouns

Teacher's Resource Book, p. 186

Day 5

Practice Common and Proper Nouns

Remind students that a proper noun (circled) names a particular person, place, or thing. Common nouns (underlined) name *any* person, place, or thing. For example:

My favorite <u>holiday</u> is (Mother's Day) On this <u>day</u>, (Dad) and I serve <u>toast</u>, <u>eggs</u>, and (Krispy Korn) <u>cereal</u> to (Mom). My <u>friends</u> thinks that's great!

Have students review this list of common nouns. Have them write a proper noun alternative for the common noun.

author	(Bruce McMillan)	movie	(Wizard of Oz)
day	(Wednesday)	doctor	(Dr. Sohn)
friend	(Halla)	teacher	(Ms. Svenson)
country	(Iceland)	child	(Arnar Ingi)

For practice with common and proper nouns, ask students to write a short journal entry about a time they took care of an animal, bird, or insect. Remind them to use a combination of common and proper nouns.

Students can use Teacher's Resource Book page 187 for additional practice with common and proper nouns.

Grammar: Common and Proper Nouns

Teacher's Resource Book, p. 187

Figure 8.3 (continued)

Phonics   Digraph *ow*; Diphthong *ow*

Connect to Spelling

Studying words with the vowel digraph *ow* and diphthong *ow* helps students read and spell words in which *ow* stands for various sounds.

Introduce

Display Phonics Songs and Rhymes Chart 10, "An Owl." Play the recording and have the class echo each line as it is sung. Discuss with students the different sounds the letters *ow* can represent. Use *owl* and *low* as examples. Ask a volunteer to read each line and have the class echo. Ask students to look for other words that contain *ow*. Have volunteers underline these words on the chart.

Teach

Have students locate this sentence on page 220 of *Nights of the Pufflings*. These "clowns of the sea" return to the same burrows year after year. You might wish to have students locate the two words in this sentence that contain *ow*. Model for students how you would decode these words if they were unfamiliar to you.

Think ALOUD I see that the second word in the sentence begins with *cl*, like another word I know. The letters *ow* sometimes stand for the sound in the word *cow*. I'll try these sounds together. /cl/ /ou/ /n/ /z/. *Clowns*.

Continue modeling with *burrows* from the same sentence.

For students having difficulty, use the Routine in the side column.

An Owl

I see an owl . . .
He's big and brown . . .
He is full grown . . .
He lives in town . . .

He flies up high . . .
He flies down low . . .
He flies through town . . .
He's wise, you know . . .

I'm kind to owls . . .
I'll tell you how . . .
I show respect . . .
I'll show him now . . .

**Phonics Songs and
Rhymes Chart 10**

*Phonics Songs
and Rhymes
Audio CD 1/
Tape 5, Side 2*

Routine

Blend and Segment Sounds

Practice blending sounds by having students clap their hands when they hear the *ow* sounds.

1. **Say it slowly:** /n/ /ow/. Have students clap their hands as they say /ow/.

2. **Blend it:** Have students blend the sounds together and say the word *now*.

3. **Stand up:** Repeat routine using *flowering* and *clowns*.

For extra practice see the Phonics Workbook, pages 46–48.

Figure 8.3 (continued)

Phonics Practice Activities

Build Words Use phonogram cards *-ow, -own;* letter cards *b, c, d, g, h, l, m, n, t,* and consonant blend cards *bl, cl, fl, gl, pl, sl, br, cr, fr, gr, sn, st, thr.* Ask students to create as many words as they can. Have pairs take turns reading their words aloud.

Phonics Game Use Phonics Activity Mat 5 from the Phonics Kit, or make copies from the Phonics Sourcebook. Instructions for this game using digraphs and dipthongs are on the back of the mat.

For additional practice with the vowel digraph *ow* and diphthong *ow,* use Practice Book 3.1, page 98.

Phonics Reader Students can read *Growing Up in Colonial Times,* which practices digraphs and dipthongs. This selection tells about how colonial children worked and played. After reading, ask them to:

- identify words that contain *ow*
- decode words that contain *ow*
- share this story with a friend

A take-home version of the Phonics Reader is also available.

Close and Assess

Give students another opportunity to differentiate between the sounds *ow* represents. Write *cow* and *grow* on the board and have students copy the words to label the top of a sheet of paper. Read the following words in any order as students record them under the appropriate label. Then let students demonstrate their ability to differentiate between the sounds *ow* represents by sharing their lists and saying the *ow* sound for each word in their lists.

cow	grow
vowels	bowl
gown	throw
shower	mow
down	snow
flower	row

Phonics: Vowel Digraph ow; Diphthong ow

Practice Book p. 3.1, p. 98
Teacher's Resource Book, p. 188

Phonics Reader

Take-Home Reader

Figure 8.3 (continued)

346

Phonics Consonants *j* and *g*, *s* and *c*

Objectives

Students will

- decode words containing *j* and *g* /j/

- decode words containing *s* and *c* /s/

Phonics: Consonants *j* and *g*;
s and c   REVIEW

Directions: Read the sentence. Choose the word that has the same consonant sound as the underlined letter. Mark the space for the answer you have chosen.

1. Not many people have seen Iceland.
   - cookie
   - count
   - place
   - pack

2. It is a long voyage to Iceland.
   - good
   - journey
   - brag
   - gold

3. It would be fun to see some pufflings.
   - safe
   - ocean
   - coat
   - pancake

4. The village children feed the pufflings.
   - triangle
   - ground
   - large
   - ago

5. They try to save the pufflings from cats and dogs.
   - shore
   - candy
   - cousin
   - once

6. Pufflings face other dangers.
   - high
   - just
   - began
   - regret

7. The children race to find the pufflings first.
   - sea
   - catch
   - clowns
   - busy

8. The children search in the dark.
   - teacher
   - distance
   - she
   - capture

9. At last the pufflings fly to the sea.
   - island
   - nose
   - cent
   - country

10. We wish them a safe journey.
    - goodbye
    - guess
    - spring
    - page

Notes for Home: Your child reviewed words with the consonant sounds /j/ spelled *j* and *g* and /s/ spelled *s* and *c*. **Home Activity:** Work with your child to make word pairs by matching words with the same consonant sounds and different letters (homebrown).

Practice Book 3.1, p. 99
Teacher's Resource Book, p. 189

Introduce

Display Phonics Songs and Rhymes Chart 9, "Our Voyage," to review *j* and *g* /j/ and *s* and *c* /s/ sounds. Have volunteers read alternate lines. Ask students to name words with /j/. Then ask them to name words with /s/. Have students circle these words on the chart.

Teach and Practice

Write these two sentences from the selection on the board.

> Hundreds of the pufflings crash-land in the <u>village</u> every night.
> This puffling flutters just a short <u>distance</u>.

Model for students how to figure out an unfamiliar word that has /j/ represented by *g*.

Think ALOUD   When I try to figure out *village,* I look at the letters. The end of the word looks like a word I know—*package.* I remember that sometimes *g* is pronounced /j/, especially if it is followed by an *i* or an *e*. I'll try to say this word using /j/—*village.*

Use this strategy to model how to pronounce *distance.*

Students can use Practice Book 3.1, page 99, for additional practice with consonants *j* and *g* /j/ and *s* and *c* /s/.

Close and Assess

Play a variation of "Simon Says." Students should raise their hands if they hear *c* /k/ as in *cat* or *g* /g/ as in *gas* in the word you read. Their hands should remain on their desks if you say a word containing *c* /s/ or *g* /j/ sound. Read these words aloud: *village, cliff, egg, once, chick, distance, sea, just, get, danger, same, can, Iceland, journey, grab.* (Students will raise hands for *cliff, egg, chick, get, can, grab.* Hands remain on desk for *village, once, distance, sea, danger, just, same, Iceland, journey.*)

For extra practice see the Phonics Workbook pages 49–50.

Figure 8.3 (continued)

Spelling Long *o* and Short *o*

Generalization

Short *o* is often spelled *o*: al*o*ng.
Long *o* can be spelled *o*, *oa*, and *ow*: ag*o*, c*oa*t, l*ow*.

Word List

monster	collar	along
gold	most	ago
Ohio	hello	coat
toast	road	coach
load	grown	low

Pre- and Posttest

To administer pre- and posttest, read the underlined word, read the sentence, and then repeat the underlined word. Guide students in self-correcting their pretests and correcting any misspellings.

Day 1

Pretest

1. Bari drew a red monster.
2. Button your collar.
3. Can we come along?
4. She wore a gold locket.
5. Most birds can fly.
6. It happened long ago.
7. My aunt lives in Ohio.
8. I waved hello to my friend.
9. Wear a coat outside.
10. Is the toast too hot?
11. This road is bumpy.
12. Our team has a coach.
13. Carry this load of books.
14. Have our plants grown?
15. The plane is flying low.

Day 2

Think and Practice

Teacher's Resource Book, p. 190

Day 3

Proofread and Write

Teacher's Resource Book, p. 191

Day 4

Review

Teacher's Resource Book, p. 192

Day 5

Posttest

1. He roared like a monster.
2. My collar is too tight.
3. We went along with her.
4. He has a gold coin.
5. I ate most of my sandwich.
6. She left one hour ago.
7. Ohio is a great state.
8. He greeted them hello.
9. I will wear a coat today.
10. I ate toast for breakfast.
11. Roy lives down this road.
12. Our new coach is here!
13. Wash a load of laundry.
14. I have grown taller.
15. The cat's water is low.

Spelling • *Nights of the Pufflings* 235j

Figure 8.3 (continued)

Genre
Narrative Nonfiction

Discuss the Skill

Discuss the characteristics of narrative nonfiction in *Nights of the Pufflings*.

- The story tells about a true happening. (Children in a village in Iceland help save baby puffins each year.)
- It tells the events in the order in which they happen. (Halla sees her first puffin; millions of puffins return from their winter at sea; the puffins begin making their nests; and so on.)

Revisit the story with students and discuss how the author tells, or narrates, the events in chronological order. Then have partners begin a chart like the one below.

Narrative Nonfiction

Story Title	True Events the Story Tells About
Night of the Pufflings	children helping to save baby puffins in Iceland

Have pairs of students think of other books they have read that are narrative nonfiction. For each book, have them identify real events the book tells about and write them on the chart.

Check for Understanding

Review the charts that students make to see if they can

- distinguish the features of narrative nonfiction
- distinguish between fiction and nonfiction

Reading-Writing Connection
Compare Selections in a Genre Log

Have students record information about narrative nonfiction selections in a genre log.

- Students can list the main events in each selection and note whether the events are told in the order in which they happen.

- Check the logs periodically to see if students understand the concept of narrative nonfiction.

Figure 8.3 (continued)

Research Skills
Card Catalog and Library Database

Discuss the Skill

Tell students: "Imagine that you are writing a report about birds. How will you find books about birds?" Remind students that all libraries use an organizational system to help people locate books easily. Most libraries use a card catalog, a set of drawers containing cards filed in alphabetical order. The cards list information by book title, by book author, and by subject. Tell students that card catalog information is often available in a computerized catalog system or library database.

Gather students around a computer with the school library database and demonstrate how to search by subject by entering *bird* in the subject field.

Have groups of three to four students select a search word that relates to *Nights of the Pufflings (Iceland, sea, puffin)*. Invite a representative from each group to enter the selected search word into the computer. Have students answer these questions:

1. How many items did your search return?
2. What are the call numbers for three of the books?
3. What happens when you enter the title of one of the books or authors in the search field?

Check for Understanding

As students work with the database, check to see that they

- enter words that are appropriate for a database search
- can search by subject, title, and author
- are able to locate the title, author, and call number of a book revealed by a search

For more practice with searching a library database, use Practice Book 3.1, page 100.

> **Research Tip**
>
> Students can also find books using the card catalog. Show them examples of a subject card, a title card, and an author card. Have them use the alphabetized drawers to search for books by subject, title, and author.

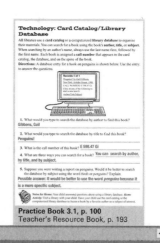

Practice Book 3.1, p. 100
Teacher's Resource Book, p. 193

Figure 8.3 (continued)

Discussion and presentation of background information

Basal manuals often provide background information about concepts and themes found in stories that are intended to activate students' experiential and conceptual backgrounds. Durkin found that none of the teachers reviewed or developed background information for their students.

Presentation and discussion of prereading questions

Rarely did the observed teachers present and discuss questions before their students read a story from their basals. Most manuals present questions to ask students before they read a story for the first time to guide students' reading.

Silent reading of the story

Durkin reported that silent reading was uncommon in the first grade. Although third- and fifth-grade teachers used silent reading more often, they typically ignored the recommendations found in the manuals. Basal manuals often recommend that teachers supervise students' silent reading by questioning them after they have read a few pages or discussing their reading immediately following silent reading of the whole story.

Meaningful oral reading or rereading

Basal manuals do not typically recommend oral reading or rereading of every story assigned to students; however, the observed teachers spent considerable time on oral reading.

Instruction

Today, considerable emphasis is given to instructional procedures that foster comprehension and provide meaningful, supervised skill practice. All teachers, except one fifth-grade teacher, used the manual sections on practice assignments. The focus, however, was on completing written practice assignments rather than using many of the manuals' suggestions for instruction.

Practice assignments

Suggested assignments are often abundant in basal manuals, but manuals seldom suggest that teachers use every one of these. All but one of the observed teachers assigned all of the written practice activities found in the skill-development portions (workbook pages and worksheets). None of these teachers used the manual when giving assignments, and the teachers did not appear to make assignments in terms of students' needs. The teachers also failed to provide students with a purpose for reading, to review the format and directions, to complete practice examples, or to establish a relationship between the assignment and the ability to read.

Provisions for individual differences

With most stories in the basal, manuals include provisions intended to help teachers differentiate their instruction and address the needs of individual students. Durkin found that one third-grade teacher used these recommendations with the whole class, and a first-grade teacher used some of them for her whole class. The other teachers did not use the recommendations in their teaching.

Durkin's findings are limited because they deal with a small number of teachers observed for a short time; however, these findings are no different from those reported in other classroom observation studies (Durkin, 1984). Teachers do not use the suggestions and recommendations in basal reader manuals for two common reasons: (1) they do not have the time to do everything the manual recommends, and (2) they often do not think the manual recommendations are important. Durkin thought teachers should connect these two concerns. That is, if teachers don't have the time to follow all of the recommendations, they should heed those that develop and enhance students' reading abilities. Durkin offers the following advice for using the basal manual to improve the quality of reading instruction:

> Giving more time to new vocabulary, background information, prereading questions, instruction on essential topics, and better but fewer assignments, and . . . spending less time on oral reading and comprehension questions is a possible change that is not likely to promote any more problems than were seen in the classroom. What the different allotment of time may promote, however, is better readers. (p. 744)

Bacharach and Alexander (1986) also found teachers to be selective in using the basal manual. As in the Durkin study, teachers did not give the prereading step the attention it should have in teaching a lesson. Teachers in this study viewed the vocabulary suggestions as most helpful, followed by comprehension instruction, skill instruction, and background and prereading questions. Least helpful were enrichment activities.

Going Beyond the Basal

The overall goal of teaching literacy is to develop students who can (and do) read and write on their own for a variety of reasons. Teachers at every level must be sensitive to a range of instructional goals: mastery of basic skills, facility in using comprehension strategies, development of critical and creative responses to various forms of text, and growth of appreciation and enjoyment of language used in reading and writing. However, the transfer of reading skills and strategies to recreational reading is not automatic: Skills and strategies are mastered through wide reading of literature.

Although one may suspect that mastery of literacy skills automatically leads to increased recreational reading and learning, a study by Blair and Turner (1984) indicates otherwise. As part of a status study of reading interests and attitudes, they assessed the perceptions of middle-school students regarding how well basic reading instructional materials fostered recreational reading. Surprisingly, almost half of the

The hornbook was the earliest form of reading activity that children were to use by themselves. It received its name from the thin layer of horn that was placed over the text to prevent it from becoming dirty. Most hornbooks were in the shape of a paddle and measured about 21/2 by 5 inches. The alphabet, Arabic numerals, and the Lord's Prayer were usually written or printed on a piece of paper. The paper was then pasted onto the paddle and covered with the thin layer of horn. Hornbooks were used in America into the nineteenth century.

From *McGuffey's First Eclectic Reader,* Revised Edition. New York: American Book Company, 1896.

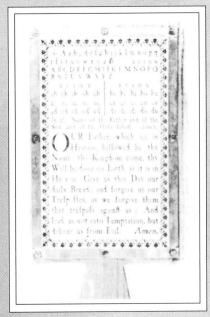

Photo courtesy of The Horn Book, Inc.

From McGuffey's *Eclectic Reader,* published in the mid-1800s, children were taught to read and recite. The readers primarily used an alphabetic-phonetic approach along with a controlled vocabulary. Although the language of the beginning-level readers was choppy and uninteresting, the readers were extremely popular for many years. The story content often was intended to teach religious, moral, and patriotic values.

Dick, Jane, Sally, Spot, Father, Mother, and Puff are familiar to many of us as the characters of a popular reading series used in the mid-1900s. These readers were characterized by controlled vocabularies, near-total emphasis on a narrative style of writing, and stories dealing with middle-class white families living in single-family homes.

"Look here," said Father.
"Look at Mother and me.
Here we come."

Sally said, "Away we go!
Dick and Jane.
Father and Mother.
Tim and me."

"And Spot and Puff," said Dick.
"Away we go!"

From *Fun With Our Family* by Helen M. Robinson et al. Copyright © 1962 by Scott, Foresman and Company. Reprinted by permission.

UPDATE

Today's reading programs are characterized by the use of quality literature as the central component in developing competent readers. This is the case for reading programs utilizing the basal reader as the core, those programs embracing the whole-language philosophy, and literature-based reading programs. Various literacy works are the primary vehicle for developing attitudes, skills, strategies, and understanding in each phase of a complete reading program: developmental reading, application-transfer, independent or recreational reading, content reading, and functional reading. Also, the content of today's basal series represents the multiracial, multicultural, and multiethnic nature of our society.

students thought their regular reading materials neither helped them learn in other school subjects nor develop recreational reading habits.

The findings of this study strongly support the integration of literature into the regular basal program. A common strategy for elementary teachers using a basal is to encourage students to read library books related to a basal story or to bring in copies of the book excerpted in a basal for students to read. This practice integrates literature more fully into the basal reader program.

In addition to individual classroom strategies to implement a literature-based reading approach, the following are strategies for the school environment:

- reading and literature, including **silent sustained reading** (SSR), book fairs, and multimedia projects
- magazines, including opportunities to read a variety of magazines independently, group discussions of various stories, and student oral reports
- reading-related projects, including a literature emphasis based on writing (e.g., plays) and a semester project (e.g., on China or energy)
- careers, including extensive reading and writing about careers and assembly programs on various occupations with guest speakers

As the preceding discussion indicates, basal readers cannot be viewed as the complete reading program. No matter how comprehensive a basal program might appear to be, it must be combined with other materials for students to learn what they need to know. Clements (1991) agrees and suggests "that we go beyond the basal and the workbook to supplement reading programs with extensive reading, enrichment, and follow-up" (p. 59). Clements's undergraduate students compiled the following excellent listing of ways reading teachers can go beyond the basal:

storytelling	letters
menus	recipes
music	cereal boxes
games	read-along cassettes
projects	comic books
filmstrips	computers
plays	puppet shows
language experience	paired reading

INSTRUCTIONAL PROCEDURES

The Language-Experience Approach (LEA)

A valuable supplemental reading approach is the **language-experience approach (LEA).** Regardless of what other materials schools or other teachers may have adopted, most teachers of beginning literacy include teacher-written charts and stories in their literacy programs (Eichenberger & King, 1995). Using student experiences as the content for writing charts and stories is a long-standing practice.

Adjusting Instruction in Beginning Basal Anthologies

Many students with varying exceptionalities have difficulties in learning new words. Some students are extremely weak in the area of auditory discrimination of letter sounds and as such have difficulty in learning letter–sound correspondences (i.e., phonics). Without adjusting instruction for these students, success in beginning reading is threatened. If you desire to use a basal program and capitalize upon its built-in structure and specific skill and strategy development with students lacking some of the necessary readiness abilities to be successful in learning the alphabetic principle, a different approach to individual word learning in conjunction with using the regular basal program may prove to be successful.

A very popular, effective, and time-honored approach to use with students experiencing extreme difficulty in learning words through the usual auditory–visual (AV) method is the Fernald–Keller approach. Harris and Hodges (1995) define this approach as "a technique for learning to identify printed words also called VAKT because it involves looking at a word (visual) while saying it (auditory) and tracing it (kinesthetic, tactile)" (p. 83). This approach enables the reader to learn words through a combination of four senses: seeing the word, hearing the word said, tracing the word with a finger, (i.e., movement), and feeling the word being traced (i.e., touch). The procedure itself is based on a four-stage process (Fernald, 1943), bringing students to the point of identifying unknown words through visual analysis. No phonic analysis techniques are taught in this method, whose outline follows:

Stage 1: The teacher writes a new word on paper and pronounces it for the student. The student then traces the word and pronounces the word by syllables until it can be written from memory. The word is then used in a short language experience story for practice.

Stage 2: The student reaches this stage when words can be learned without tracing. The teacher still writes the word for the student. New words are used in experience stories and kept in a file for practice.

Stage 3: The student has reached this stage when the word can be written by looking at it and having the teacher pronounce it. The teacher no longer writes the word for the student but does continue to pronounce it.

Stage 4: The student should now be able to recognize new words by comparing them to similar words that have been learned. No longer must the student write a word to remember it. Some students may need considerable teacher assistance to note the similarities between known and new words. The major focus of this stage is on visual analysis of words by syllables and reading in a variety of materials.

Inclusion Strategies

While this approach has proved to be successful on a one-to-one basis, disadvantages include the heavy time commitment and the approach's reliance on visual learning of new words that come from the student's experience. Dr. Louis Cooper of the University of Connecticut devised a modification of the Fernald-Keller method that can be successfully implemented by classroom teachers using a published basal program. The Cooper method (1964) recommends that words to be learned come from the first readers in the basal program, that book reading be introduced from the outset, and that the inclusion of both structural and phonic analyses eventually replace sight-word learning. An outline of the Cooper method is as follows:

1. Select the basal reader program.
2. Find the child's instructional level by means of an informal reading inventory. (**Note:** It is assumed here that if this procedure is indicated, the child's instructional level will not be more than primer level and probably will be lower.)
3. Assess the child's recognition of the total list of words in the first preprimer and make a list of those words that are not known. These become the words to be taught as the book is read.
4. Teach these words to the child, using the appropriate stage of Fernald-Keller and have the child read them in the contextual setting of the book.
5. Practice these words, both in context and isolation.
6. Repeat steps 3, 4, and 5 with the second preprimer, third preprimer, primer, and so on, moving from one stage to another as the child is able to do so.
7. Parallel the early stages with additional visual discrimination training and auditory discrimination training.
8. At some point in the sequence of stages, depending on the readiness of the child, introduce a systematic program of word-analysis skills, which will eventually replace all sight techniques.

The implementation of Cooper's method to word learning used in conjunction with the regular basal anthologies may be a viable alternative for teaching students with varying exceptionalities beginning reading in the regular classroom. Students are using the same materials as their classmates with the same advantages of reading high-quality literature with specific instruction and structured practice activities. Thus, the same materials are used, but instruction in word learning is *adjusted* to meet students' needs.

Throughout the years, modifications and extensions have placed renewed emphasis on this procedure (Combs, 1996). The LEA is used predominately with primary-grade children but is also adaptable for slower learners of all ages and for ESL students. Hall (1981) summarized the rationale and philosophy of the language-experience approach.

The language-experience approach for teaching literacy, Hall said, is based on the relationship of language to the learner's experiences as the core from which language communication radiates. Language-experience literacy is viewed as a communication process closely related to communication in speaking and listening. The approach uses students' oral language and experiences to create personal reading and writing sources. This approach integrates the teaching of literacy with all of the language arts; as students listen, speak, write, and read about their personal experiences and ideas, their speech determines the language patterns of their reading materials, and their experiences determine the content. The language-experience approach assumes that literacy has the most meaning to students when the materials being read are expressed in their language and are rooted in their experiences.

Features of the LEA

Although the language-experience approach has many variations, teachers should understand some basic features when using this approach. They include the following:

- a shared experience for the students
- shared talk about the experience
- decisions about the written product, including a group chart or story or individual student stories
- shared reading of the charts or stories by the students
- follow-up activities
- group-experience charts and stories

Group-experience charts and stories are means of capturing students' interest by tying their personal experiences to their literacy activities. The charts and stories, which tell about shared activities, are prepared cooperatively by the teacher and the class. They are often extensions of earlier and less difficult experiences, wherein the teacher wrote single words, short sentences, days of the week, names of the months, the seasons, and the dates of students' birthdays and holidays on the chalkboard. Group-experience charts and stories provide practice and application in a number of developmental areas closely related to literacy, including the following:

- using oral language in group planning prior to a trip and in recounting the experience after a trip
- giving and taking ideas as the experience is discussed
- sharpening sensory acuity, particularly visual and auditory, while on excursions
- developing and expanding print-related concepts, such as directionality (left to right), space between letters and words, punctuation, capital letters, and the relationships between oral and written language
- expanding concepts and vocabulary

- learning words as wholes in meaningful contexts, thus building a sight vocabulary based on one's language
- focusing on reading and writing as a process of constructing meaning
- reading and writing about one's own experiences

In preparing group-experience charts and stories, the teacher should plan a meaningful shared experience, such as taking a field trip, viewing a film or filmstrip, hearing a story, reacting to a picture, observing an experiment, or participating in a class or school activity. Let us assume that the teacher arranges a trip to a nearby farm. This teacher organizes the necessary transportation and visits the farm in advance to determine specifically what students will experience. As a result of the visit, this teacher identifies what students need to know to benefit from the experience. Several days of instruction help prepare students for their visit.

Following the trip to the farm, the teacher guides the students through a discussion and sharing of the highlights of their experiences. This discussion serves to get all of the students involved and attending to the task to follow—writing the experience chart. After each student's response, the teacher writes it on the chalkboard or on large poster paper. Students are encouraged to respond and to discuss their response. The group-composed chart follows:

<u>Our Trip to the Farm</u>

We went to Mr. Johnson's dairy farm.

We saw lots of cows.

We saw a machine that milks the cows.

The cows' heads are put in bars.

In Mr. Johnson's big barn, he milks five cows at once.

After the teacher and children read the completed chart, the teacher may ask a student to point out (1) the line that tells what kind of farm they visited, (2) the line that tells the name of the owner of the farm, (3) his or her favorite or most exciting event, and so forth.

The same chart may be used in other ways. The teacher may duplicate each line in the chart on a strip of heavy paper, hand a sentence to a student, and ask him or her to find this line on the chart. The teacher may print individual words on oaktag or cardboard, hold them up, and ask a student to point out that particular word on the chart. The teacher may prepare word cards for a particular line, hand them to a student in mixed order, and ask him or her to arrange them in proper order to correspond with the line on the chart. A group-experience chart can be used with a class as a whole and also with various groups of students. After its use with a unit, the teacher may refer to it when certain words used on the chart arise in other contexts and activities.

Individual experience stories

Children enjoy talking about their experiences, particularly about incidents that involve them, their families, their pets, special events, and the like. One of the best ways to take advantage of such motivation is to write individual experience stories.

These language productions are usually brief, ranging from one to several sentences about one incident. In the early stages of literacy, students usually dictate the stories and the teacher usually transcribes them. Because these brief stories relate to students' own experiences, they encourage involvement in literacy. The stories are always meaningful and should be written using words that parallel students' own language usage.

Expansions and Variations of the Language-Experience Approach

In addition to the features and uses of LEA mentioned earlier, teachers can use this instructional approach in a variety of ways. Reimer (1983) suggests several ways to expand and vary the use of the LEA; these are presented in the following paragraphs.

Direct and indirect discourse

Use different-colored pens to identify different speakers when recording a group experience story. Students can identify who said what by noting the color of the writing. The teacher should use the same color consistently for each individual so that the class can associate that color with a particular student. As a variation, use a photograph of each student and attach a discourse balloon to help everyone understand who contributed what to a group story. Later, write these stories with the youngsters and replace the color or picture with the words, "May said," or "Benny said," to help students understand how these words function in direct discourse. Teach indirect discourse by removing the punctuation marks and introducing the word *that* (as in "Sue said *that* the horse is big.").

Various forms of writing

Use group LEA to introduce different forms of writing. Demonstrate a science experiment and have the group tell what happened, have students report a shared experience by responding to reporters' questions (who, what, where, when, why, and how), or have students learn about letter writing by composing a group letter.

Shape stories

Guide children to write stories about an experience that is represented by a shape—a fish, clown, car, dog, and so on. As children dictate the story, write it on paper cut into that particular shape.

Written dialogue

This procedure works well with many youngsters at all elementary levels. Rather than talking with students, exchange notes. These notes may range from extremely simple phrases ("Good job!") to paragraphs. Match the complexity of the notes to the students' abilities to read and respond in writing. This variation of LEA helps students to understand the relationships between oral and written language and realize that written language must make sense to the reader.

The concept of language experience has been extended far beyond the group chart and writing individual stories. Today, the term *language experience* applies to practically every type of self-expression through language and every experience that involves manipulation of language.

The role of teachers has undergone considerable change also. Teachers now assume responsibilities far beyond those of scribes who write down stories that students tell. Teachers still reinforce students' egos by writing personal stories, but by using additional language stimuli, they also help students expand their concepts and improve their language proficiency.

Language activities that promote both learning about language and using language as a tool for further learning are becoming major features of instruction (Dole, 1984). Students write poetry, read poetry, solve riddles, and make up some of their own. Working with homonyms, they learn that different spellings may have the same pronunciation. Working with homographs, students learn that words may be spelled the same but have different meanings and pronunciations. They learn about relationships through analogies, combining sentences, and arranging sentences into larger units. In working with language, students learn that a word may have dozens of meanings, that plurals take many forms, that new words are constantly added to our language, and that over time, the meanings of words change.

Language experience is, thus, experiencing language. The teacher's role is to help children understand that:

Writing a word is an achievement
Writing a story is a larger achievement
Combining stories into a book is quite a production.

Saying something one way is an achievement
Saying it another way and noting what you did the second time permits you
   to control language!

When you can control language
you can mold words like clay
   mix words like paints
   use words to draw pictures.

The next step is to let children try it. Let them tell or write the answer to the following question:

How many ways can a leaf fall?

"Down" you say.
Surely there's another way.
   A leaf can

> just fall—
>> fall gracefully
>
> glide—
>> glide like a glider
>>
>> glide and swerve
>
> sail—
>> sail like a rudderless ship
>>
>> sail like it had a mind of its own
>
> dip—
>> dip and glide
>>
>> dip and rise and bank gracefully to a landing
>
> dance—
>> complete its solo dance
>>
>> dance with the wind
>>
>> fall with no map to guide it—
>>
>> map its own course
>>
>> try many detours
>>
>> twist slowly in the wind.

How many ways can a leaf fall that we didn't write today?

"No other way," you say?

Don't you think leaves like to play?

> playfully! (of course)
>> If in a hurry?
>
> plummet
>> with memories of summer?
>
> reluctantly

Any procedure has both merits and limitations, and this is true of the language-experience approach to teaching reading. The major strengths of experience charts and stories have already been discussed. Relying too heavily on teacher-written materials may have drawbacks of its own, including the following:

- Difficulty in controlling the vocabulary—too many words may be introduced at one time.
- Not enough repetition of basic sight words to ensure mastery.
- When used exclusively as a method, too much of a burden on the teacher, demanding too much time and too high a level of training.
- Difficulty in adapting this type of instruction to the needs of all students.
- Encouragement of memorization rather than mastery of sight words.

- The strengths and weaknesses of the experience method are a factor of the teacher's application and are not inherent in the method itself. Under certain conditions, overemphasis, misuse, or lack of understanding may cancel out all the advantages of the method. The language-experience approach is vulnerable when used as the total reading program. Most teachers prefer to use the approach as a supplement to other materials and instructional procedures (see Figure 8.4).

Language-experience activities can enhance basal reading instruction and vice versa. Aspects of LEA can be used to do the following:

- Provide for both individual and group reading instruction.
- Allow for practice, transfer, and application of word-identification and comprehension skills and strategies in meaningful context.
- Build on and emphasize students' life and language experiences.
- Emphasize the relationship between oral and written language to help students understand that reading and writing are constructing meaning.
- Engage students in meaningful instruction based on their own interests.
- Encourage vocabulary development by having students try new words and use these new words in meaningful context.
- Develop better writers and children who will experiment with writing. (Rupley & Blair, 1989)

As emphasized throughout this text, the processes of reading and writing development are complementary. LEA is a wonderful springboard for both processes. Karnowski (1989) proposes linking the process-writing approach and LEA by combining process-writing steps (i.e., prewriting discussion, actual writing, revising, and publishing) in a modified language-experience approach. Karnowski explains: "By using a modified LEA in which students decide what topics to explore, what ideas to include, and what modifications to make, young readers and writers begin to realize the work and the job of becoming published authors" (p. 465).

USE OF TECHNOLOGY IN LITERACY INSTRUCTION

Every school district in our country is using computers in one way or another. Computers are also becoming more and more a part of literacy instruction in our classrooms. In many schools, students interact with computers in all phases of learning. There is no escaping the Web—students are surfing the Internet and checking their e-mail. Students (i.e., "surfers") browse the Internet for information on a variety of subjects both at home and at school. Any display of literacy approaches, materials, and activities today includes myriad computer applications, so a key concern is how schools and teachers are using the computer's marvelous capabilities. Like other tools, computers can help teachers and students. Anderson and Speck (2001) explained that classroom teachers can use computers in the areas of word processing, technology or electronic texts, publishing students' work, integrating the Internet into the

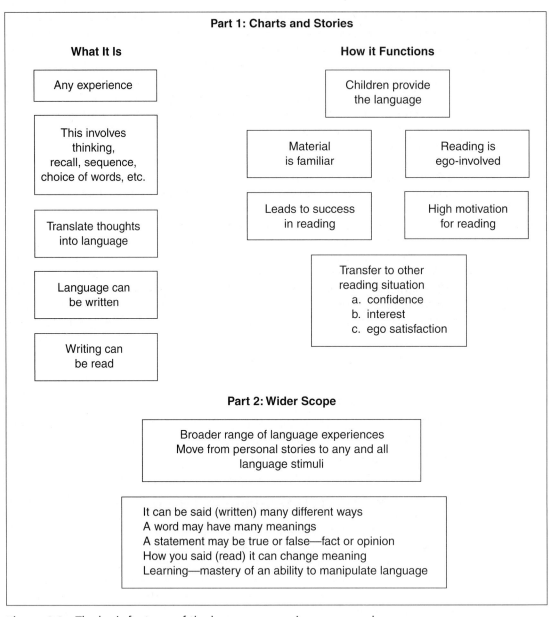

Figure 8.4   The basic features of the language-experience approach.

curriculum, researching information on-line, using databases and spreadsheeets for studying topics, and identifying and using various sites for a variety of instructional and management materials. The challenge is to harness the computer's power and versatility to provide interesting and meaningful learning. While acknowledging the potential support computer technology can provide for reading instruction, Snow, et al. (1998) of the Committee on the Prevention of Reading Difficulties in Young Children cite the unequal distribution of computers between rich and poor schools and computer program implementation difficulties. Additionally, the authors issue a precaution regarding computer technology by stating "it is still only a promise by any large-scale measure of effectiveness to address reading instruction" (p. 265).

The first thing teachers should realize is that computers cannot replace good teaching. Second, computers may or may not assist individual teachers in achieving their instructional goals. Third, computers can certainly supplement books but computers cannot replace them. The advantages to using the computer to aid in teaching literacy are many. Teachers must always consider the possible uses of technology in relation to students' learning needs. If computers are used properly, they have enormous potential to increase literacy levels. Conversely, if computers are not used in relation to student needs and offer little opportunity for students to interact meaningfully with various texts, literacy levels can adversely be affected. Among the advantages of using computer-based instruction in literacy instruction are the abilities to do the following:

increase the motivational levels of students

present information in a variety of formats

give immediate feedback

tailor individual practice and reinforcement

promote personal awareness of one's own learning needs

increase student involvement with text

explore a wealth of narrative and expository writing

integrate reading with the content subjects

Futurists see classrooms in which students interact with computers in all phases of learning: They read and write and hold sophisticated conversations with the computers at all levels of thinking. In today's classrooms, most of the computer usage in reading is in the form of **computer-assisted instruction (CAI)** (Heinich, Molenda, Russell, & Smaldino, 1999). Harris and Hodges (1995) defined computer-assisted instruction as "an automated learning program presented step by step by a computer with responses from the learner evaluated and indicated as correct or not, and with options for the learner to follow" (p. 39–40).

Software Programs

CAI software comes in a variety of modes, for example, drill-and-practice exercises, tutorial dialogues, simulations, learning games, and creative writing. Drill-and-practice programs are very popular, but they are also the most unimaginative of the computer applications. In essence, many of the programs are merely electronic workbook exercises. However, such applications have good potential for helping students practice and reinforcing basic word-identification and comprehension skills in terms of individual student needs. Although many educators have criticized the quality of the programs, it is hoped that the quality will improve as teachers become more involved in software development.

The typical sequence in a drill-and-practice program is (1) presentation of a question, (2) student response, and (3) computer response (usually, "correct," "incorrect," or "let's try again"). The cycle then begins again. The student receives very little, if any, explanation of the task. Drill-and-practice programs allow students to practice skills independently and provide the practice necessary to make basic skills automatic. Some programs even give teachers a report of student tries per item and an analysis of student performance on particular skills. With quality software, these programs can be most beneficial for both teacher and students in carrying out the independent practice step of the direct-instruction format.

Tutorial dialogues are more sophisticated than drill-and-practice programs. The computer provides more explanation of a drill and reteaches, if necessary. Instead of just providing feedback of "correct" or "incorrect," these programs give students more detailed explanations. If a student response is incorrect, an explanation appears along with more examples similar to the one missed. If the student responds correctly, the computer branches to more difficult material.

Simulations are programs that allow students to role-play an experience. In a typical program, the computer displays an experiment or hypothetical situation, and the student responds with new information as needed. The computer then displays the new results.

In reading and writing, a variety of learning games provide interesting practice in reading skills (Fox & Mitchell, 2000). Many of these games reinforce spelling and vocabulary development. The instructional cycles are similar to those of the drill-and-practice programs.

New uses of computers are continually being developed and tested. One such application integrates reading and writing through word-processing programs. This application allows students to type a story or any text and to edit the text by inserting words, deleting words, or rearranging paragraphs and sentences. This application is popular with writers in all fields, but its use at the elementary level is only beginning to grow. In beginning reading, as part of the language-experience approach, a teacher can type a student's story and play back the story in print and voice. Also, literature books are now available in a personalized format. Hefty Publishing Company produces software to personalize books for children. The student's name, the name of their town, and that of their friends and relatives can be woven into the fabric of the story. Creating books for individual children adds to student motivation and involvement. The student himself or herself can become the star of the story, so repeated readings of a story are never a chore.

Another new use of computers involves classroom teachers actually utilizing software programs as tools in the teaching-learning process (Blair, 1998). While the literature is saturated with articles on topics such as recent advances in multimedia computer technology and new software packages, the literature is not plentiful in the area of actually using computers in teaching new literacy skills and strategies to students and assessing student learning. Whether one is interested in any of the basic teaching components such as background and motivation, step-by-step explanation, modeling or demonstration of the lesson objective, guided practice, independent practice or review, various computer software programs can parallel a teacher's efforts to help engage students in meaningful learning. Emphasizing the tremendous advantages that computers bring to word recognition and vocabulary teaching and learning, Fox and Mitchell (2000) stated:

> Software and Internet sites with color, animation, and audio clips invite students to use such modalities to interact with the sights and sounds of language. Sound reinforces, extends, or confirms the letter and sound relationships of our English language. Also, in combining the sight of words with the sound of words, technology gives students opportunities to develop their reading vocabulary and to practice reading words in context. When sight and sound are coupled with immediate feedback, students know right away if they have applied a skill or strategy successfully. When you set a purpose for using technology to support skill development in your classroom and identify the content students need to learn, technology is a powerful teaching tool that goes far beyond drill-and-practice exercises in paper-and-pencil workbooks. (pp. 42–43)

Bowman (1998) conducted one study on the effectiveness of the computer as a tool in the teaching-learning process. Low-achieving urban third graders participated in a three-month after-school program "*CyberHood Kidz.*" As part of the instructional cycle, tutors utilized *PrintShop* software to support the teaching of word identification, especially phonic generalizations. Other elements of the program included practice with commercial electronic reading programs with feedback and continuous progress reports and a World Wide Web-based project pairing students with other students from a nearby state to complete writing projects together. Preliminary findings indicated students' reading performance improved by one grade level for the three-month program with additional improvement in computer skills.

CIERA researcher Nichole Pinkard (1999) conducted an interesting investigation using culturally responsive software with African American children. Utilizing two computer-based learning environments (*Rappin' Reader* and *Say Say Oh Playmate*), small groups of early beginning readers made substantial gains in basic sight vocabulary. The software programs capitalized on the children's language, prior knowledge, cultural background, and interests in the early literacy instruction.

In addition to CAI, a growing application of the computer in teaching reading is computer-managed instruction (CMI). In CMI, computers administer diagnostic tests, score the tests, record and store the results, and prescribe appropriate instruction. Computer-managed instruction offers excellent possibilities for aiding teachers in these areas.

Computer-Based Multimedia

The combination of the computer with audio and visual media has generated a new approach to multimedia learning. A new focus of computer technology is to develop multimedia software that allows students the ability to interact with text at their own pace. Hypertext, which is a particular type of computer application, is nonlinear text which is linked to other texts. Applied to combining other media, the term *hypermedia* is defined as "computer software that uses elements of text, graphics, video, and audio and is connected in such a way that the user can easily move within the information" (Heinich et al., 1999). The authors cite the following advantages of hypermediaware:

Engrossing	The opportunity for deep involvement can capture and hold student interest.
Multisensory	The incorporation of sounds and images along with text expands the channels to the mind.
Connections	By using "hot buttons" students can connect ideas from different media sources, for example, connecting the sound of a foghorn with the word "lighthouse."
Individualized	Web structure allows users to navigate through the information according to their interests and to build their own unique mental structures based on their exploration.
Teacher and student creation	Software allows teachers and students to easily create their own hypermedia files; student projects can become opportunities for collaborative work. (p. 263)

A key ingredient to the success of computer-based multimedia is the amount of interaction generated by the teacher, the student, and the computer. Applications of hypertext and hypermedia in the language arts area include literature-based software, which allows students to interact with stories, make responses to characters, hypothesize future events, and write their reactions. Interactive computer books are now available with sound effects and wonderful graphics. The CD-ROM (compact disc-read-only memory) format is often utilized for interactive computer books and has the capacity to store not only text and graphics but also audio, animation, and photographs. One of the most popular children's book series of all times, Little Golden Books, is now available on CD-ROM interactive software. Powerhouse Entertainment and Golden Books Family Entertainment in 1996 produced 24 interactive books, including *The Sailor Dog, Right's Animal Farm,* and *The Little Red Caboose.* New CD-ROM literature offerings have 3-D graphics, animated sequences, different levels of educational and creative activities, and automated "read to me" functions for beginning readers.

Multimedia, interactive computer books have the potential to promote active learning.

Chu (1995) reported a study utilizing interactive computer books with three first-grade boys. Findings indicated that students demonstrated high interest in reading the computer books. Chu used literature-based hypertext software developed by Discis Knowledge Research, Inc. The computer books used by Chu in her study were *The Tale of Peter Rabbitt* by Beatrix Potter, *Scary Poems for Rotten Kids* by Sean O'Huigin, *The Paper Bag Princess* by Robert Munsch, *Cinderella* by Charles Perrault, and *Benjamin Bunny* by Beatrix Potter. In summarizing the positive results in her study, Chu (1995) noted the following:

> The three readers have benefited from their hands-on experience with computer books. They talked, moved about, and made contrasts and comparisons between story events, characters, and real life experiences. They were active learners, not passive recipients of information. (p. 364)

An exciting computer application is Apple Early Language Connections (1992). This is a literature-based multisensory language arts program for kindergarten through grade 2 featuring an array of hardware, software, books, and audiotapes. More than 200 literature books are available on the Macintosh computer, which brings the stories to life. Students can progress at their own rate and interact with each story using various senses. The quality literature is thematic in nature, and the units contain lesson plans with literature, music, math, art, and science activities. Valmont and Wepner (2000) reported on current practices with technology and the use of electronic books in the classroom. The authors cited the following additional interactive software programs utilized in many elementary schools: *Kid Pix Studio Deluxe, AppleWorks, Storybook Weaver, Word Munchers Deluxe, The PrintShop Deluxe, WiggleWorks Plus,* and *HyperStudio.* Speaking to the benefits of these programs they stated:

> These programs are used with students to read stories, write stories, add artwork to their original stories, and produce presentations to share with other students. CD-ROMs are available in some classrooms and libraries so that students can read and listen to stories such as *Arthur's Teacher Trouble* and *Odell Down Under.* Many multimedia software packages in classrooms promote reading, writing, and listening. Speaking is fostered in students' efforts to present to teachers and other students that which they have created with the help of a computer. (p. 14)

Software Evaluation

The ultimate success or failure of computer-assisted instruction depends on two conditions: (1) the quality of the educational software (the programs containing the steps and procedures for the computer to follow) and (2) the ability to use the computer to meet instructional goals. Software programs for elementary reading are proliferating. A quick glance at any magazine rack indicates that this market is growing more competitive. In fact, teachers attempting to select a few reading programs among the hundreds on the market may easily begin to feel confused. "Which program is best?" is the wrong question. The correct question is "Which program will best match my students' learning needs?"

Just as effective teachers select other supplemental materials in relation to student needs, so too must they select computer programs. Underlying this concern is determining the quality of the programs. Do the steps in a lesson and the related procedures follow the tenets of effective instruction? Does the software allow students to interact with the computer? Unfortunately, a majority of software programs offer poor rather than good instruction. Yet, remember that many current programs are written by computer experts, not educators. Many of today's programs purport to teach a skill but do not fulfill this expectation. Also, although software production is expanding at an unbelievable rate, software development is still in its infancy. If teachers eventually have greater influence on software development, the quality will improve.

Remember, the best hardware (the computer) is only as good as the software the teacher selects. Demand quality software for your students. The cardinal rule in software evaluation is: Never buy or use a program until you try it for yourself. This allows you to experience how user-friendly it is, as well as whether directions are clear, help is easy to obtain, you can control the pacing, and you can enter and exit easily. A trial run can help you evaluate these and other important aspects of the program. Figure 8.5 should help you evaluate reading software by examining the program's ease of use, instructional design, content accuracy, and special features.

	Good	Adequate	Poor

Type of Program
_____ Drill and practice
_____ Tutorial
_____ Simulation
_____ Learning game

Ease of Use
Clear directions
Exit capabilities
Control of pacing
Provision for help

Instructional Design
Clear objectives
Introductory explanations of skills
Sample exercises
A number of practice exercises
Immediate and varied feedback
Branching capability
Built-in assessment of progress
Monitoring of student responses
Corrections made by reteaching,
    giving clues, or explaining skill
Summary statements
Program length
Appropriate difficulty level

Content Accuracy
Direct correspondence between
    lesson objectives and lesson
    procedures
Accuracy
Procedures reflecting what a reader
    has to do in the process of reading
Correct sequence in presenting skill

Special Features
Animation
Speech
Music
Laser videodiscs
Touch screen
Graphics
Audio
Color

Figure 8.5   Literacy software evaluation guide.

371

In addition to actually running through the software program and systematically using an evaluation form, you must have your students try out the program. Their perceptions of the effectiveness of a program are most crucial—after all, they are the ones who will need to spend their time completing the program.

Instructional Principles

In addition to quality software, the effectiveness of CAI ultimately depends on its proper implementation. While teachers do not need to learn new teaching techniques, they do need to apply sound educational principles to integrate CAI into the total reading program. Teachers should consider the following principles as they begin to make decisions regarding the use of computers in the classroom:

- Teachers must devote considerable time to planning CAI applications in their classrooms.
- Students should have a great degree of control and interaction with the computer.
- Teachers should use CAI only with students who respond positively to it.
- Teachers should hold weekly conferences with all students to review their progress.
- Managing use of the computer should not inordinately disrupt normal teaching routines.
- Teachers should introduce students to the computer by explaining how and why they will use it in their class.
- Teachers should always share a program's objectives with students.
- Teachers should be certain to use software that corresponds to their instructional goals.
- Teachers should monitor student involvement to ensure a high degree of time on task.
- Teachers should vary the use of CAI so that students will not get bored doing the same thing each time they work with the computer.
- Teachers should never view CAI as being more than one part of the total reading program.
- When appropriate, teachers should assign students to work in pairs on a computer.
- Teachers should use CAI lessons in a logical sequence.
- Teachers should always evaluate the application of CAI after examining test results, observing the students, and obtaining student evaluations.

SUMMARY

Effective teachers of literacy know how to use a variety of materials and instructional approaches to teach literacy and to match students' needs. Two major approaches to teaching literacy are basal readers and literature-based reading. While each approach has its own unique characteristics, effective teachers integrate various aspects of the different approaches to reflect their students' learning needs.

The basal reader program was highlighted in this chapter. By far the most popular approach in our schools today, this approach incorporates much of the current research on the reading process, reading comprehension, and teaching reading. Modern basals also stress an integrated language arts curriculum with an emphasis on quality literature. Even with the multitude of materials in a basal program, however, no basal program should be viewed as complete; rather, the teacher must supplement it with a variety of materials to satisfy student needs. Effective teachers use a blend of instructional activities to fulfill the major components of a complete reading program, including developmental reading, application transfer, independent or recreational reading, content reading, and functional reading.

In addition to the two major approaches, supplemental reading approaches abound to help in teaching reading. Two significant supplemental approaches discussed in this chapter were LEA and computer-assisted instruction.

Besides understanding the characteristics and assumptions of each of these approaches, teachers should develop a critical questioning attitude in implementing them. Because all approaches have strengths and weaknesses, teachers must become thoroughly familiar with the features of an approach and how they address students' needs. Approaches and materials should be viewed as aids in the teaching of reading, because the teacher—not the approaches and materials—teaches reading. Adapting approaches and materials to learner needs is absolutely necessary for successful literacy instruction.

YOUR POINT OF VIEW

Discussion Questions

1. Why are basal readers viewed as representative of the eclectic method?
2. Why must teachers modify some features of a basal manual regardless of students' literacy capabilities?
3. Which of the features of the basal reader lesson example (DRA) would Durkin's findings suggest deserves the most attention from teachers?

Take a Stand For or Against

1. Someday reading researchers will find one reading approach that will work with all students.
2. All reading instructional materials that follow the structures and patterns of English usage can be said to be linguistic.
3. The time it takes for teachers to integrate the features of the language-experience approach with basal readers is not worth the effort.
4. Teachers who do not use the basic recommendations of a basal manual are probably better than are teachers who use such recommendations blindly.

Field-Based Assignments

1. **Building Background Knowledge.** As you know, recent research on comprehension has highlighted the utmost importance of prior knowledge to understanding new ideas. Even with this strong finding, researchers such as Durkin have noted that few teachers do indeed develop prior knowledge in introducing a story even though teacher's manuals give explicit directions in this area. In your classroom, teach a story and concentrate on reviewing students' prior knowledge and developing background knowledge. Develop your prereading section in detail. Write down the specific questions you will ask your students that will review and highlight what students already know about the topic, what background experiences students may have relating to the story, and how you will help your students make connections regarding what they already know to new upcoming information in the story.

2. **Collaborative Basal Reader Evaluation.** Using your college's materials curriculum lab or public school resources, obtain a copy of a student reader, teacher's manual, and any other materials connected with the basal program used at the school in which you are completing your field experiences. Arrange yourselves in groups of four. Each of you are to choose two of the following eight topics common to most published reading programs:

   - Comprehension lessons on skills and strategies
   - Word-identification lessons on skills and strategies
   - Content reading/study skills and strategies
   - Reading and writing instruction
   - Vocabulary development
   - Testing materials
   - Workbook and practice materials
   - Directed reading lessons

   Prepare a written report on your two areas using the questions below as departure points (and others depending on your particular published program). Meet as a group and share your findings. If possible, share your group report with the entire class.

   > How is your area covered and presented to students? (Provide a brief overview of essential components.)
   >
   > What specific types of materials and/or teaching strategies are utilized to fulfill your area? (Provide examples to show your classmates exactly how the area in question is taught.)
   >
   > In your opinion, does your area provide a balance between direct or explicit instruction and practice in authentic materials? (Provide an example supporting your opinion.)
   >
   > Are there provisions made for students needing additional help? What are they?

Are there recommendations made that you feel are unimportant and should be omitted? What are they?

Are there recommendations made that you feel should be modified in some way to improve the instruction or process? What are they?

Portfolio Entry

Because children are different in a multitude of ways, there is no one miracle approach to the teaching of reading that is successful with all children. Given this reality, it is imperative for effective teachers of reading to know a variety of approaches. Recall the quote by Pescosolido in Chapter 2 regarding effective teaching: "Just being a 'nice' person doesn't a teacher of reading make, but a nice person doing some important things in terms of the reading process results in good teaching and good learning." Respond to the following two questions:

What does this quote mean to you in relation to the implementation of different approaches to literacy?

What are the key areas of concern and emphasis a teacher should focus on regardless of the approach being used in the school or classroom?

Write a one-page typed entry in your portfolio responding to these two questions.

BIBLIOGRAPHY

Anderson, R. C., Hiebert, E. H., Scott, J. A., & Wilkinson, I. A. G. (1985). *Becoming a nation of readers: The report of the Commission on Reading*. Washington, DC: The National Institute of Education.

Anderson, R. S., & Speck, B. W. (2001). *Using technology in K–8 literacy classrooms*. Upper Saddle River, NJ: Merrill/Prentice Hall.

Apple Early Language Connections. (1992). Cupertino, CA: Apple Computer, Inc.

Bacharach, N., & Alexander, P. (1986). Basal reader manuals: What do teachers think of them and how do they use them? *Reading Psychology, 7,* 163–172.

Blair, T. R. (1998). Computers as teaching tools in the elementary school literacy program: Differential control of activities and learning outcomes. In U. Piromruen (Ed.), *Asian Language and Literacy Conference on information technology and its effects on literacy in Asia* (pp. 75–90). Bangkok, Thailand.

Blair, T. R., & Turner, E. (1984). Skills instruction and independent learning. *Middle School Journal, 16,* 6–7.

Bowman, J. (1998). Technology, tutoring, and improved reading. In *English update* (Winter 1998). Albany, NY: University of Albany, SUNY.

Center for the Study of Reading. (1986). *A guide to selecting basal reading programs.* Urbana, IL: Center for the Study of Reading, University of Illinois.

Chu, M-L. L. (1995). Reader response to interactive computer books: Examining literary responses in a nontraditional reading setting. *Reading Research and Instruction, 34,* 352–366.

Clements, N. E. (1991). Maximizing time on task: Supplementing basals and workbooks. In R. A. Thompson (Ed.), *Classroom reading instruction.* Dubuque, IA: Kendall/Hunt.

Combs, M. (1996). *Developing competent readers and writers in the primary grades.* Upper Saddle River, NJ: Merrill/Prentice Hall.

Cooper, J. L. (1964). An adaptation of the Fernald-Keller approach to teaching an initial reading vocabulary to children with severe reading disabilities. *The Australian Journal on the Education of Backward Children, 10,* 131–145.

Dole, J. A. (Spring 1984). Beginning reading: More than talk written down. *Reading Horizons, 24,* 161–166.

Durkin, D. (1984). Is there a match between what elementary teachers do and what the basal reader manuals recommend? *The Reading Teacher, 37,* 734–744.

Durkin, D. (1993). *Teaching them to read* (6th ed.). Boston: Allyn & Bacon.

Eichenberger, C. J., & King, J. R. (1995). Two teacher roles in language: Scaffold-builder and gatekeeper. *Reading Research and Instruction, 35,* 64–84.

Farstrup, A. E. (1999). Multiple methods of beginning reading instruction. A position statement of the International Reading Association, Newark, DE.

Fernald, G. M. (1943). Remedial techniques in basic school subjects. New York: McGraw-Hill.

Fox, B. J., & Mitchell, M. J. (2000). Using technology to support word recognition, spelling, and vocabulary acquisition. In S. B. Wepner, W. J. Valmont, & R. Thurlow (Eds.), *Linking literacy and technology.* Newark, DE: International Reading Association.

Greenlinger-Harless, C. S. (1987). A new cross-referenced index to U.S. reading series, grades K–8. *The Reading Teacher, 41,* 293–303.

Hall, M. (1981). *Teaching reading as a language experience* (3rd ed.). Upper Saddle River, NJ: Merrill/Prentice Hall.

Harris, T. L., & Hodges, R. E. (Eds.). (1995). *The literacy dictionary.* Newark, DE: International Reading Association.

Heinich, R., Molenda, M., Russell, J. D., & Smaldino, S. E. (1999). *Instructional media and technologies for learning* (6th ed.). Upper Saddle River, NJ: Merrill/Prentice Hall.

Hoffman, J. V., & McCarthey, S. J. (1995). The new basals: How are they different? National Reading Research Center. *The Reading Teacher, 49,* 72–75.

Hoffman, J. V., McCarthey, S. J., Elliott, B., Bayles, D. L., Price, D. P., Ferree, A., & Abbott, J. A. (1998). The literature-based basals in first-grade classrooms: Savior, satan, or same-old, same-old? *Reading Research Quarterly, 33,* 168–197.

Karnowski, L. (1989). Using LEA with process writing. *The Reading Teacher, 42,* 462–465.

Osborn, J. (1984). Workbooks that accompany basal programs. In G. G. Duffy, L. R. Roehler, & J. Mason (Eds.), *Comprehension instruction: Perspectives and suggestions* (pp. 163–186). New York: Longman.

Piernek, F. T. (1979). Using basal guidebooks—The ideal integrated lesson plan. *The Reading Teacher, 33,* 167–172.

Pinkard, N. (1999). *Learning to read in culturally responsive computer environments.* (CIERA Rep. No. 1-004). Ann Arbor, MI: CIERA/University of Michigan.

Reimer, B. L. (1983). Recipes for language experience stories. *The Reading Teacher, 37,* 396–404.

Reutzel, D. R. (1985). Reconciling schema theory and the basal reading lesson. *The Reading Teacher, 39,* 194–197.

Roller, C. (1999). Multiple methods of beginning reading instruction. A position statement of the International Reading Association, Newark, DE.

Rupley, W. H., & Blair, T. R. (1989). *Reading diagnosis and remediation: Classroom and clinic* (3rd ed.). Upper Saddle River, NJ: Merrill/Prentice Hall.

Snow, C. E., Burns, M. S., & Griffin, P. (Eds.). (1998). *Preventing reading difficulties in young children.* Washington, DC: National Academy Press.

Spiegel, D. L. (1998). Silver bullets, babies, and bath water: Literature response groups in a balanced literacy program. *The Reading Teacher, 52,* 114–124.

Stauffer, R., (1975). *Directing the reading-thinking process.* New York: Harper & Row.

Valmont, W. J., & Wepner, S. B. (2000). Using technology to support literacy learning. In S. B. Wepner, W. J. Valmont, & R. Thurlow (Eds.), *Linking literacy and technology.* Newark, DE: International Reading Association.

Wiggins, R. A. (1994). Large group lesson/small group follow-up: Flexible grouping in a basal reading program. *The Reading Teacher, 47,* 450–460.

9

Literature-Based Reading Programs

Donna E. Norton

Chapter Outline

For the Reader

Literature-based reading programs promote the fun and joy of reading, enrich students' lives, provide material that is inspiring, interesting, and informative, and increase reading ability.

In the literature-based view, reading is not the acquisition of a set of isolated skills. Instead, reading is the ability to read all types of literature with understanding, appreciation, and enjoyment. In this viewpoint, literature can be used to support the reading curriculum, to teach or reinforce reading skills, and to introduce students to a wide variety of good and enjoyable books.

Key Ideas

- Developing an understanding of and appreciation for literature requires that teachers help students recognize the literary elements and the ways that authors use those elements to create exciting and credible stories.

- In the reading program, the use of literature should develop in students an understanding of literature and an appreciation for it.

- Teachers can develop reading capabilities through the use of literature.

- Literature-based reading programs include objectives related to understanding and appreciating the different literary genres and elements.

- Strategies for teaching reading through literature include using predictable books, analyzing plot structures, semantic mapping, and modeling.

LITERATURE-BASED READING PROGRAMS

Literature may support the basal reading curriculum or it may be the core of the total reading program. When teachers use literature to support the reading curriculum, they identify reading skills taught in the basal approach and assign literature selections that reinforce those skills. As a result, students see that the major goal of the reading program is to understand, appreciate, and enjoy, not merely to complete workbook pages.

Programs in which teachers use literature as the core of the reading and language arts curriculum are multiplying rapidly (Norton, 1992, 1997). These programs frequently identify books according to core literature, extended literature, and recreational literature. **Core literature** includes books that should be taught in the classroom. With close reading and intensive consideration, they are likely to be important stimuli for writing and discussion. **Extended literature** includes works that teachers may assign to individual students or small groups of students as homework or supplemental classwork. Recreational-motivational literature includes works for students to select for individual, leisure-time reading from classrooms, schools, and community libraries. This literature-based curriculum uses the primary sources of the literature (as opposed to anthologies). This approach promotes literacy, developing an understanding of and appreciation for literature.

Whether a total literature approach or a support for the basal reading curriculum is used, teachers must be aware that use of literature in the reading curriculum should develop understanding of literature and an appreciation for it. To choose literature that motivates students to read and that stimulates an appreciation for literature requires knowledge about literature, awareness of students' interests, and knowledge about instructional approaches that stimulate interest and appreciation. Ruddell (1992) argues that motivation is extremely important. He states, "Creating high reader motivation depends on the teacher's understanding of the student and his or her intimate knowledge of literature selections. The development of high reader motivation depends heavily on the teacher's ability to connect the student with the literary work by using student background knowledge and personal interests that are directly relevant to the content, language form and style, and format and illustrations of the literary work" (p. 616). Likewise, to teach reading through literature requires knowledge about appropriate literature and instructional approaches that encourage the broad development of reading skills as well as the understanding of literary elements used by the authors of literature.

In addition to reading for goals such as the main idea, important details, and cause-and-effect relationships, we can emphasize the strengths of good literature by encouraging students to develop understanding and appreciation for characterization, setting, conflict, plot, theme, author's style, and point of view. Within the author's style are such complex areas as symbolism, metaphor, simile, personification, allegory, and allusion. In addition, genre has specific reading and writing demands. Thus, folklore, fantasy, poetry, realistic fiction, historical fiction, biography, autobiography, and informational literature have unique reading requirements.

This chapter emphasizes the selection of literature, the development of an understanding of and appreciation for literature, and the instructional strategies that focus on the strengths of literature. It highlights approaches that encourage oral and written interactions with literature and that inspire readers to develop excitement about what they read.

The Literature and Reading Connection

Sawyer (1987) reviews studies that support literature-based reading curriculums. He argues that we can no longer separate learning to read and reading to learn, because the two are interwoven. Sawyer contends that the story structures chosen to teach reading are important because the structures themselves teach the rules of narrative organization.

Sadoski, Willson, and Norton (1996) found that a literature and composition approach improved both reading and writing abilities. Allison and Watson (1994) discovered that the earlier parents read to their children, the higher the children's emergent reading level was at the end of kindergarten.

Studies show that using literature, whether it is read to students or by students, improves reading comprehension, develops understanding of story structures, and increases appreciation of reading and literature. For example, Feitelson, Rita, and Goldstein (1986) report that first-grade students who listened to and discussed literature for 20 minutes each day outperformed comparable groups in decoding, reading comprehension, and active use of language. Feitelson et al. attribute the success to the adults who helped the students interpret the literature, understand the language that was unfamiliar to them, enrich their information bases, increase their knowledge about various story structures, encounter various literary devices, and extend their attention spans. Norton and McNamara (1987) report that a literature-based reading program that uses modeling and emphasizes cognitive processes and story structures significantly increases reading comprehension and improves attitudes toward reading by students in the fifth through eighth grades.

Educators who use and recommend literature-based reading instruction emphasize the dynamic nature of the environment and the desirability of both understanding of and appreciation for literature. For example, Taxel (1988) describes the literature-based classroom "as fluid and dynamic . . . a place where educators see literature as central to the curriculum, not as an occasional bit of enrichment undertaken when the real work is completed" (p. 74). May (1987) describes a literature-based program in which understanding and enjoyment are the major goals.

Five (1988) uses brief lessons that focus on such literary elements as characterization, setting, flashbacks, and book selection. Following each lesson, students read related literature, discuss the books, and complete writing activities. Five emphasizes that the program dramatically increases independent reading, peer discussions of literature, and student evaluation of such concerns as believable characters and effective language and dialogue.

When the storm was over they explored the island. When they weren't looking, they fell into an enormous hole. They tried to get out but the owner came in (which was the Zerc)!

He was mad because he thought they wanted his food. They tried to stab the Zerc but he was to strong. Ulysses thought up a plan, but it did not work. So a man got the Zerc's attention, and Ulysses tied a rope around the Zerc's legs and he fell!

When Ulysses was climbing out of the hole, he said, "Did you have a nice trip Zerc?" He then kept on climbing.

When they got out, they started to look for a tall, straight tree. Ulysses told a man to go to the ship to get the ax. When he came back with the ax, Ulysses chopped down the tree. When he chopped down the tree, the whole crew carried it back to the ship. When they got back to the ship, they sewed a sheet on it for a sail. Then they put it over the hole where the old hollow mast was. After they got that done, they pushed the Pensaro in the water.

One way of furthering children's literature appreciation is to have children create original stories based on stories they have read.
Source: Excerpt from *Ulysses Fights the Zerc* used with permission of Ian King.

Reading research provides strong rationales for teaching literature and guidelines for how to teach it. Early and Ericson (1988) identify nine findings to consider when developing a literature-based curriculum. First, readers use their knowledge of texts and contextual cues to create meaning during reading. (Schema theory also suggests that successful readers use their knowledge of various kinds of texts, the world, and contextual cues to create meaning.) Literature provides one of the best sources for acquiring and reinforcing this knowledge. Second, readers learn to read by reading. This implies that students need many opportunities to read a variety of literature. Third, readers need to experience whole texts to increase understanding. Literature is an obvious choice for encouraging students to develop meaning from longer texts.

Fourth, good readers understand when their reading makes sense, are aware when their reading processes break down, and use a variety of corrective strategies. Different genres and literary elements encourage students to use a variety of reading strategies. Fifth, readers improve their comprehension if teachers use such techniques as modeling, direct explanation, and questioning. These strategies work especially well with literature. Sixth, good readers use cues in the text and their prior knowledge to make predictions.

Seventh, students benefit from direct teaching of strategies for reading literature. Literary discussions can focus on many details in literature, such as characterization, setting, plot, and theme. Eighth, students need help in looking for details to use in making inferences. Ninth, the range of students' reading achievement grows wider at each successive grade level. Consequently, a wide variety of literature helps meet this variety of needs.

SELECTING LITERATURE

When selecting the literature for a school curriculum, teachers should consider students' development, reading abilities, listening abilities, and interests as well as literary standards, curricular needs, and genre and cultural balance. It is beyond the scope of this chapter to cover the vast amount of information usually covered in children's literature courses. Instead, the chapter provides a brief review of the sources and criteria that you may use to help you select and evaluate literature.

Sources

Major children's literature texts are the best sources to use to help you select literature that meets the needs of your students. For example, Norton's *Through the Eyes of A Child: An Introduction to Children's Literature* (1999) provides evaluative criteria, recommendations for literature, and classroom applications for picture books, traditional literature, fantasy, poetry, contemporary realistic fiction, historical fiction, multicultural books, biography, and informational literature. The books discussed range from those for younger children to those for students through the middle school. Norton's *The Impact of Literature-Based Reading* (1992) suggests books and strategies that may be used with the books. *Children's Literature* (1993) by Huck, Hepler, and Hickman contains chapters on the major literature genres. Sutherland and Arbuthnot's *Children and Books* (1991) discusses the major authors who write in each of the genres.

Literature journals are fine sources for current books as well as for specialized lists. *Booklist, Horn Book, School Library Journal,* and *Publishers Weekly* include reviews. They star reviews of books that the editors believe are of exceptional quality. *Booklist* also publishes specialty lists of books. *School Library Journal* publishes a "best books" list for each year as well as lists of specific subjects. Other helpful journals include *The Reading Teacher, Language Arts,* and *The New Advocate.* "Children's Choices" is published each year in *The Reading Teacher.* The journal *Book Links,* a publication of the American Library Association, is also extremely helpful when selecting books that are related to specific type of literature, theme, or author.

Award-winning books and classics, whether they are read to or by students, are of special interest in reading programs. These books encourage students and teachers to explore and discuss selections considered the best in their fields. For example, the Caldecott Medal and Honor Awards, presented since 1938, are awarded annually to the illustrators of the most distinguished books published in the United States. The Newbery Medal and Honor Awards, presented since 1922, are awarded annually for the most distinguished contributions to children's literature published in the United States. The Children's Book Award, presented since 1975, is awarded by the International Reading Association to a children's author whose work shows unusual promise. These and additional awards are listed on pages A-3–A-10, Appendix B, in Norton's *Through the Eyes of A Child: An Introduction to Children's Literature* (1999).

Many of the older award-winning books are now considered classics. Many other books, however, were published before the awards were given. According to Rudman and Pearce (1988), **classics** are extraordinary books that last beyond their authors' lives and continue to delight and reach the minds and hearts of readers for many generations. The folktales of the Brothers Grimm and Charles Perrault, the picture books of Kate Greenaway *(A Apple Pie)* and Robert McCloskey (1941) *(Make Way for Ducklings)*, the fantasies of A. A. Milne (1926) (the "Pooh" books) and E. B. White *(Charlotte's Web),* the poetry of Edward Lear *(Book of Nonsense),* the realistic fiction of Frances Hodgson Burnett *(The Secret Garden)* and the historical fiction of Esther Forbes *(Johnny Tremain)* and Laura Ingalls Wilder (1932) (the "Little House" series) deserve to be shared with all students. These books and other noteworthy classics have been identified by the Children's Literature Association as touchstones in children's literature. These books are considered so good that they should be used to evaluate all literature. A list of "Touchstone Books" is available from the Children's Literature Association, publisher of *Children's Literature Association Quarterly.* Breckenridge (1988) compiled a list of modern classics in 1988. These lists offer many good examples of children's literature. They include books that teachers and students should read, discuss, and evaluate.

Evaluation Criteria

The various book sources emphasize different and valuable aspects of evaluation. Teachers must be aware of how books are evaluated when they read book reviews and choose literature from those reviews. Older students may also use these different criteria when they discuss or write about books.

Alleen Pace Nilsen and Kenneth L. Donelson (2001) warn, however, that adults add another element when evaluating literature:

> We should caution that books are selected as "the best" on the basis of many different criteria, and one person's best is not necessarily yours or that of the young people with whom you work. We hope that you will read many books, so that you can recommend them not because you saw them on a list, but because you enjoyed them and believe they will appeal to a particular student. (p. 11)

Award-winning books and classics encourage students and teachers to explore and discuss selections considered to be the best in their fields.

Reading and discussing the facts of literature are obviously easier than analyzing the literary or sociological aspects. A good literature program enables students to go beyond the factual level. Reading and discussing good children's literature increases one's awareness, enables one to discover the techniques an author uses to create a believable plot or memorable characterizations, and provides standards for comparison.

This section refers to the literary elements that students should understand and appreciate. It briefly reviews the literary elements of plot, characterization, setting, theme, style, and point of view.

Plot

The plot of a story is the plan of action or sequence of events. A plot must have a beginning, a middle, and an end. A good plot allows students to become involved in the action, feel the conflict developing, recognize the climax, and respond to a satisfactory ending. The plots in most books for younger children follow a chronological, or sequential, order of the character's life, whether the story occurs over a day, several days, or a longer period. Cumulative action, such as that found in "The House That

Jack Built," is popular in books for younger students, as the actions and characters are mentioned again when new action or new characters are introduced. Books for older students sometimes use flashbacks in addition to chronological order.

Excitement in the plot occurs when characters experience struggles or overcome conflict. The major types of conflict found in children's literature include person against person, person against society, person against nature, and person against self. With believable conflict, the readers understand the conflicting circumstances. For example, in *Hatchet* (1987), Paulsen describes nature in such a way that readers visualize the power and the danger. We know that the main character is in a life-or-death struggle and that he must learn about nature if he is to survive alone in the Canadian wilderness.

Many books for more advanced readers develop person-against-self conflicts and person-against-society conflicts. In Curtis's *The Watsons Go to Birmingham—1963* (1995) the plot develops as the characters face person-against-society conflicts in Alabama and then face the conflicts within themselves. In books such as Bat-Ami's *Two Suns in the Sky* (1999) the main character must overcome anti-Semitic attitudes of a society in this story about Jewish refugees.

Characterization

Believable characters, especially in books for older students, should be three dimensional—characters with pasts, futures, hopes, fears, parents, and siblings. Most memorable characters develop throughout the course of the story. To develop the many sides of a character, an author can reveal the character's strengths and weaknesses directly or by describing the character's thoughts, showing the character in action, and recording the character's dialogues. Characters such as Burnett's Mary Lennox in *The Secret Garden* (1911) are memorable because, like real people, they are neither all good nor all bad. Like real people, they must overcome believable problems as they progress through life.

Contemporary characters such as the heroine in Fenner's *Yolonda's Genuis* (1995) frequently relate more closely to modern problems. The author develops vivid characterization for both a bright fifth grader and her slower younger brother, Andrew. The author develops a heroine whose actions show both her intelligence and her respect for her younger brother's musical ability. Her ability to retaliate against those who torment her brother leaves little doubt about her attitude.

Picture-story books may also be valuable sources for strong characterizations. Gilliland's biography *Steamboat! The Story of Captain Blanche Leathers* (2000) develops the life of the country's first female steamboat captain. Fantasy picture-story books such as Falconer's *Olivia* (2000) develop independent characters. In this humorous book a young pig tries to accomplish everything that she imagines.

Setting

Setting is where the story takes place. It identifies the time as past, present, or future. Whether the setting is developed through illustrations or text, it must provide details that reinforce the plot and characterization. Setting in historical fiction is especially important, because the details must be true to the time period. In science fiction and fantasy, the author must provide enough detail to make the readers believe in a world that is yet to materialize or in a place that is impossible from what we know of our world, as in Pullman's *The Golden Compass* (1996), or J. K. Rowling's *Harry Potter and the Goblet of Fire* (2000). As in Brown's *Shadow* (1982), the setting may create both an antagonist and a detailed fantasy world, and the setting may create the mood of a story. As in Sperry's *Call It Courage* (1940), setting may create the antagonist. As in Freedman's *Lincoln: A Photobiography* (1987) and Cushman's *The Midwife's Apprentice* (1995), setting may create the historical background. Finally, as in Burnett's *The Secret Garden* (1911), setting may create a symbolic location for human growth and healing as well as natural growth.

Nonfictional information books are also excellent sources for developing understanding of setting. For example, the detailed illustrations in Millard's *A Street Through Time: A 12,000-Year Walk Through History* (1998) allow viewers to identify many aspects of life as it would appear in the same setting beginning with 10,000 B.C. and progressing into a modern town.

Theme

Theme is the central idea that ties the plot, characterizations, and setting together into a meaningful whole. The theme is frequently the authors' purpose for writing the story, the message. Authors of books for younger children frequently state the theme, while authors of books for older students usually imply the theme through characterizations and conflict resolution. A memorable theme usually relates to the reader's needs. For example, Grifalconi's *Darkness and the Butterfly* (1987) develops two themes: (1) it is all right to experience fears and (2) we can and must overcome our fears. In *Walk Two Moons*, a book for older readers, Creech (1994) uses mysterious messages to formulate her themes.

Style

Style is an author's choice and arrangement of words to create plot, characterizations, setting, and theme. The sounds may appeal to the senses. The word choices and sentence lengths may create a leisurely or frightening mood. Figurative language may allow us to visualize concepts in new ways. Symbolism, such as that found in Voigt's *Dicey's Song* (1982), may allow us to understand characterization and appreciate a well-crafted novel. Effective style is usually most noticeable when reading a book orally. For example, in *Homeless Bird* (2000) Gloria Whelan uses similes, metaphors, and symbolism to enhance characterization, plot, and theme in this National Book Award winner set in India.

Point of view

Authors choose a viewpoint to use when they tell a story, including the details they describe and the judgments they make. Frye, Baker, and Perkins (1985) state, "The narrator, or teller of the story, may stand within the story or outside it, narrating as it occurs, shortly after, or much later, providing in each instance a different narrative perspective in space and time" (p. 302). Consequently, the same story would change drastically if told from another **point of view.** For example, Potter's *The Tale of Peter Rabbit* (1902) would certainly change if told from the viewpoint of Mr. McGregor.

By tracing how Richard Peck uses Mary Alice's changing point of view toward her grandmother in *A Year Down Yonder* (2000) we understand the importance of point of view. We understand how Mary Alice goes from someone who fears her grandmother and does not want to be with her, to someone who understands and respects her grandmother's actions, beliefs, and values. Peck develops a plot that focuses on Mary Alice's respect for her feisty grandmother. By the end of the book, we as readers care about both Mary Alice and her grandmother and what will happen to them.

Authors may use first person, which allows them to speak through the "I" of one of the characters; an objective point of view, which lets actions speak for themselves; an omniscient point of view, which allows the author to tell the story in third person and be all-knowing about the characters; or a limited omniscient point of view, which allows the author to concentrate on one character but to still be all-knowing about other characters. First-person narratives are frequently used in books for younger students, such as in the various "Ramona" stories. Books for older students frequently use the omniscient or limited omniscient point of view. Whatever point of view is used, it should be consistent.

DEVELOPING LITERARY ENJOYMENT AND APPRECIATION

One of the primary goals of any reading program is to develop readers who turn to literature for both pleasure and knowledge. Providing many opportunities for students to listen to, read, and discuss literature entices them to love and appreciate books. This section focuses on activities that are beneficial to the reading teacher who is trying to increase enjoyment of reading: (1) oral reading to students (2) recreational reading groups and (3) reader-response groups.

Oral Reading to Students

Reading to students develops understanding of various story structures, increases knowledge of language patterns, expands vocabularies, and introduces genres of literature that students might not read independently (see Chapters 3 and 4). Consequently, the book selected for reading aloud should be worthy of the time spent by both the reader and the listeners. Children's ages, attention spans, and levels of reading ability are important considerations. The books chosen should increase students' appreciation of outstanding literature. The numerous easy-to-read books should usually be left for younger students to read independently.

Brown (1999) emphasizes that because younger children's listening level is greater than their reading level "reading aloud can build background knowledge, teach new words, and provide a positive role model. It also hooks children on quality literature, demonstrates the pleasures involved in the process, and motivates them to read alone" (p. 520).

Reading aloud should not end in the lower elementary grades. Older students also benefit from being exposed to literature too difficult for them to read independently. Nilsen and Donelson (2001) make a strong case for reading aloud to older students. They emphasize the importance of oral reading of such genres as poetry, drama, and fiction. They state, "If students are to learn how to read poetry or drama, it will come from English teachers comfortable with their own oral reading" (p. 358). Books such as Esther Forbes's *Johnny Tremain* (1943) and Kenneth Grahame's *The Wind in the Willows* (1908) should not be missed because the language is too difficult for students to read.

After selecting a book, the teacher should read it silently to understand the story, identify the sequence of events, recognize the mood, identify any concepts or vocabulary that may cause problems, decide how to introduce the story, and consider the appropriate type of discussion. Next, the teacher should read the book aloud to himself or herself in order to practice pronunciation, pacing, and voice characterization. Teachers should *never* read stories aloud to an audience before reading the stories themselves.

Lamme (1976) provides the following observations concerning effective oral reading to students:

1. Child involvement, including predicting what will happen next and filling in missing words, is the most influential factor during oral reading.
2. Eye contact between the reader and the audience is essential.
3. Adults who read with expression are more effective than those who use a monotonous tone.
4. Good oral readers put variety into their voices; pitch should be neither too high nor too low, and volume should be neither too loud nor too soft.
5. Readers who point to meaningful words or pictures in a book as they read are better than those who merely read the story and show the pictures.
6. Knowing the story, without needing to read the text verbatim, is more effective than straight reading.
7. Readers who select picture books large enough for the students to see and appealing enough to hold their interest or elicit their comments are most effective.
8. Grouping students so that all can see the pictures and hear the story is important.
9. Adults who highlight the words and language of the story by making the rhymes apparent, discussing unusual vocabulary words, and emphasizing any repetition are better readers.

It is impossible to have an effective oral reading experience without adequate preparation. Also notice that many factors, such as highlighting the language of the story and encouraging students to predict what will happen next, are related to important reading skills.

Recreational Reading Groups

Reading widely and frequently encourages literary appreciation and reinforces the development of reading skills. Reading activities based on literature help students synthesize information from several sources, clarify their developing literary skills, and share revelations about their discoveries. Uninterrupted sustained silent reading (USSR) and **recreational reading groups** encourage the reading of literature.

Recreational reading groups are especially appropriate for literature-based reading programs because they encourage discussion of books. The criteria of selection allow discussions that relate to specific objectives for the reading groups.

If students select their own materials, divide the class into about three groups, with a leader designated for each group. Have students bring their books to one of the three circles, read silently for about 30 minutes, and then tell something interesting about their books. During the first experience, it is advisable to form one group in which you model independent reading behavior and begin telling something about the book. Later, you may move from group to group. By placing competent readers next to less efficient readers, you encourage students to get help with unknown words. The reading groups may contain different students each time, or the groups may remain together until their books are finished.

If the groups are formed according to topic, literary genre, or characteristics of literature, leave them together until the subject has been thoroughly explored. Focus discussions on that element of the literature, the authors' development of the element, and what students liked or did not like about the authors' development. Focus groups should provide opportunities to reinforce specific reading skills or to explore topics of interest.

For example, form a group around personification. Choose literature from picture storybooks, poetry, and longer novels, depending on the students' interests and reading levels. Choices of literature may include picture storybooks, such as Anthony Browne's *Gorilla* (1983), Virginia Lee Burton's *The Little House* (1942), Ian Falconer's *Olivia* (2000), Emily Arnold McCully's *School* (1987) (a wordless book in which personification is interpreted through the illustrations), and Margery Williams' *The Velveteen Rabbit* (1958); poetry, such as Stephen Dunning's *Reflections on a Gift of Watermelon Pickle . . .* (1967), Jamake Highwater's *Moonsong Lullaby* (1981), and Henry Wadsworth Longfellow's *Hiawatha* (1893); and longer novels, such as W. J. Corbett's *The Song of Pentecost* (1983), Kenneth Grahame's *The Wind in the Willows* (1908), Brian Jacques's *Redwall* (1986), Robert Lawson's *Rabbit Hill* (1944), and E. B. White's *Charlotte's Web* (1952).

If personification is the focus, have students look for and discuss evidence of personification by identifying how the authors personify animals, nature, and objects; by discussing the meaning of personification; and by deciding on the appropriateness of the personified images for the story.

If symbolism is being studied, have students discuss the symbolism in books such as Frances Hodgson Burnett's *The Secret Garden* (1911), Sid Fleischman's *The Whipping Boy* (1986), Sharon Bell Mathis's *The Hundred Penny Box* (1975), and Cynthia

Recreational reading groups are especially appropriate for literature-based reading programs.

Voigt's *Dicey's Song* (1982). Other effective literary topics include characterization, setting, conflict, theme, point of view, and style. Focus discussions on specific literary characteristics that are also important reading objectives. Focusing on specific genres of literature helps students broaden their reading interests and increase their understandings of the characteristics of folklore, fantasy, poetry, realistic fiction, historical fiction, biography, and nonfiction.

Topics for recreational reading groups are as varied as the students' interests and the available literature. Humorous literature, animal stories, space science, stories by specific authors, and stories about children who are the same ages as the class are just a few. Focus the reading and discussion on such topics as how the author develops humorous stories and the effectiveness of the techniques, and how the readers respond to the humor in the stories. Looking at the various books of one author or poet is interesting. Authors such as Maurice Sendak, Dr. Seuss, Russell Hoban, and Tomie de Paola have written numerous stories for younger students. Likewise, authors such as Betsy Byars, Beverly Cleary, Helen Creswell, and Marguerite Henry have written many stories for middle elementary students. Authors such as Lloyd Alexander, John Christopher, Susan Cooper, Jean Craighead George, Virginia Hamilton, Madeleine

L'Engle, Scott O'Dell, Katherine Paterson, J. K. Rowling, and Cynthia Voigt have written numerous stories for older elementary and middle school students. Ideas for lessons on these topics are found in Norton's *The Impact of Literature-Based Reading* (1992). Norton's *Through the Eyes of a Child: An Introduction to Children's Literature* (1999) and *Multicultural Children's Literature: Through the Eyes of Many Children* (2001) provide sources for identifying literature according to genre, literary elements, and authors.

Reader-Response Groups

Numerous reading and language arts authorities discuss the advantages of allowing children to become involved with reader-response approaches to literature. Spiegel (1998) states that most response-based approaches are accomplished through sustained silent reading in which children are self-paced and usually include responding in writing to what has been read and then through peer discussions. Spiegel summarizes research that supports the following outcomes: readers develop ownership in what they read; they make personal connections with literature; they develop appreciation for multiple interpretations of what they read; they move to higher levels of thinking and richer understanding of literature; and they increase their repertoire of ways to respond to literature.

Leggo (1997) describes a reader-response approach to poetry that he uses with older students. First, Leggo has students listen to and read the poem and then write their initial responses to the poem. He states:

> Writing the responses is important because it gives students a chance to articulate reactions that are still mostly unformed, and because their written texts are now additional texts to be engaged in discussion. The important realization at this stage is that students are not searching for meaning. They are involved in a process of producing meaning out of their own reactions. There follows a further time of reflection and writing. Students then share their written texts with the texts of two or three others in the class. Next they articulate still further responses to the poem. What is the student responding to in the poem? The answer is anything: the shape of the poem, the stanzaic structure, the use of punctuation and capitalization, the length of the lines, the title, the spatial gaps, the words (known and unknown), relationships to personal experiences, intertextual references, the music, pictures of the imagination, the emotions, the characters, and/or the narratives. (p. 32)

Leggo stresses that students need directions as they begin to look for certain characteristics of poetry. You may find the discussions of and the listings for poetry presented in Chapter 8 "Poetry" (Norton, 1999) to be useful for this activity. Recent poetry collections by Jack Prelutsky such as *The Gargoyle on the Roof* (1999) and *The Dragons Are Singing Tonight* (1993) are especially appealing to children. The poetry of Shel Silverstein allows readers to respond to humorous situations. Poets such as Robert Frost, Aileen Fisher, Byrd Bayor, and Paul Fleischman write nature poems. African American poetry such as the poems written by Langston Huges and Native American poetry such as the poems found in *The Serpent's Tongue: Prose, Poetry, and Art of the New Mexico Pueblos* edited by Nancy Wood (1997) provide opportunities to respond to the poetry from multicultural sources.

DEVELOPING READING SKILLS THROUGH LITERATURE

Literature and literature-related activities are important for improving and developing reading skills. Predictable books help students predict language and plot structures. Studying literature and developing semantic maps to accompany literature improve vocabulary.

Using Predictable Books

Books that encourage students to predict language and plot structures are recommended for teaching reading and language skills to younger students. Books with repetitive language and plot development may be used for readiness or beginning reading. Predictable books are frequently introduced for oral-language activities and then used for reading activities. Tompkins and Weber (1983) and McCracken and McCracken (1986) have developed guidelines for this sequence.

Tompkins and Weber describe the following five-step teaching strategy to direct students' attention to repetitive and predictable features of a book:

1. The teacher reads the title orally, shows the cover illustration, and asks students what they believe the story is about.
2. The teacher reads through the first set of repetitions, stopping where the second set of repetitions begins and asking students to predict what will happen next or what a character will say.
3. The teacher asks students to explain why they made their specific predictions.
4. The teacher reads the next set of repetitive patterns to allow students to confirm or reject their predictions.
5. The teacher continues reading the selection, repeating steps 2, 3, and 4.

For example, to use this technique with Mem Fox's cumulative tale *Hattie and the Fox* (1987), read the title, pointing to each word. Point to the cover illustration and ask students what they think the story will be about. Through discussion, encourage the students to predict that Hattie is a hen because a hen's picture is on the cover, that the story is about a fox and a hen because the word *fox* is in the title, and that the story includes a confrontation between the fox and the hen because we know from other stories that the fox and hen are usually enemies. Expand the predictions by recalling other stories that give hints to the possible characterizations of fox and hen, such as "The Cock and the Mouse and the Little Red Hen" (a folktale found in Anne Rockwell's *The Three Bears and 15 Other Stories,* 1975). To help confirm these initial predictions, turn to the title page within the text. On this page, a fox is lurking behind a tree.

During the second step, read the first three pages of the text. These pages introduce the main character, a big black hen named Hattie, the beginning of a cumulative description of the hidden fox, and the repetitive responses of the various farm animals. Read the beginning of the fourth page of the text, "And Hattie said, . . ." Stop here and ask students what they think Hattie will say. Tell the students to look at the illustrations because the illustrator is providing hints about what Hattie will say. Turn the page and ask the students to predict the responses of the goose, pig, sheep, horse, and cow.

During the third step, ask students to provide reasons for their predictions. They should notice that the illustrator helps with the predictions by showing only a hidden nose in the first series of illustrations and increasing the view to a nose and eyes in the second series. Likewise, if students have had frequent experiences with repetitive text, they will expect that the animals will use the same language during the second series.

Next, read the text to allow students to confirm or reject their predictions. Continue the process, as with each repetition Hattie sees a little more of the fox's body. Students enjoy this book, because they quickly catch on to the cumulative action and the repetitive responses of the animals. They easily predict the conclusion, in which the fox acts in a predictable manner and the animals change their complacent responses.

Hattie and the Fox is equally successful with the beginning reading approach recommended by McCracken and McCracken (1986). After reading a predictable book several times to students, they encourage students to join in the reading. They use pictures to help the students follow the sequence. Then, they introduce the students to the text by printing the repetitive portion on the chalkboard or word cards in a pocket chart. They point to the words as the students say the lines.

Next, the students match the words on the word chart or chalkboard with a second, identical set of word cards. If the words form a refrain, they either place the whole refrain on the chart while the students match the words by placing identical words on top of the cards, or they create the first line of the refrain while the students produce the next lines. They repeat this activity several times to provide many opportunities for students to read the text.

Finally, they place the story on phrase cards in the pocket chart, then have the children match the phrases to pictures that represent each phrase. They continue this type of activity as the students build and rebuild the entire story, providing many opportunities for individual and group reading practice.

Additional books that may be used for these activities, because they contain either predictable plots or repetitive language, include the following:

- Bryon Barton   *The Wee Little Woman* (1995)
- Arnold Lobel   *A Rose in My Garden* (cumulative illustrations reinforce this cumulative poem) (1984)
- Jonathan London   *Fireflies, Fireflies, Light My Way* (1996)
- John Ivimey   *The Complete Story of Three Blind Mice* (1987)

Increasing Vocabulary Knowledge Through Literature

Reading or listening to literature encourages vocabulary development and expands vocabulary comprehension. Through literature, students discover the impact of carefully selected words. Many of the vocabulary techniques developed elsewhere in this text are equally effective with literature.

Picture books that contain extensive details or that provide motivational excitement are excellent sources for oral or written vocabulary expansion. Students may examine pictures and describe objects, animals, colors, shapes, and actions. Two books by Chris Van Allsburg are very successful with students in first through fifth grades. *The Z Was Zapped* (1987) encourages interaction between the reader and the text by presenting the alphabet in the form of a 26-act play. In each act, a letter is treated to an action that begins with that specific sound.

For example, introducing the play, the letter *A* is bombarded with falling rock. The reader must look carefully at the page to develop a script to accompany the first act. Prediction enters into the discussion, because readers must turn the page before they discover that the author describes Act 1 as "The *A* was in an avalanche." The readers can then compare their titles with the one identified by the author and consider how to change their scripts and alter their vocabularies if they consider the author's title. They can ask, What words describe an avalanche? What words emphasize the causes of an avalanche? What words tell where an avalanche takes place? What words detail the consequences of an avalanche on an unsuspecting letter?

Van Allsburg's almost wordless book, *The Mysteries of Harris Burdick* (1984), presents 14 full-page illustrations, a title, and a one-line caption to accompany each illustration. In the introduction to the book, Van Allsburg asks readers to provide the missing stories. Teachers report that the illustrations contain enough elements of mystery and fantasy to motivate excellent oral and written stories.

Concept books enhance categorizing vocabulary according to specific functions. For example, Anne Rockwell's *First Comes Spring* (1985) may be used to categorize vocabulary related to clothes, work, play, and environmental characteristics that accompany each season of the year. Janet and Allan Ahlberg's *The Baby's Catalogue* (1982) may be used to classify vocabulary according to such categories as breakfast, toys, shopping, pets, gardens, and games. Brian Floca's *Five Trucks* (1999) shows various vehicles found at an airport. Books such as Tana Hoban's *Shapes, Shapes, Shapes* (1986), and *So Many Circles, So Many Squares* (1998) stimulate identifying and categorizing vocabulary according to shapes. Hutchins's *What Game Shall We Play?* (1990), and Noll's *Watch Where You Go* (1990) foster categorizing vocabulary according to spatial concepts such as *above, behind,* and *under.* Emberley's *Let's Go: A Book in Two Languages* (1993) may be used to categorize vocabulary in both English and Spanish around topics such as seasons, the zoo, and airports.

Older students benefit from responding to wordless books that have geographical, historical, or literary connections. For example, John Goodall's *The Story of a Main Street* (1987) depicts changes over time. Detailed illustrations in *The Story of a Main Street* trace the evolution of an English street from medieval, to Elizabethan, to Restoration, to Georgian, to Regency, to Victorian, to Edwardian, and to current times. Describing the architecture, costumes, customs, trade, or transportation, students may compare similarities and differences across periods as well as increase their technical vocabularies.

Mitsumasa Anno's detailed wordless books contain literary, historical, and geographical details. Some are in the correct time and place, while others are not;

therefore, students must search the illustrations for literary, artistic, and historical details. The detailed drawings in *Anno's Britain* (1982), *Anno's Italy* (1980), *Anno's Flea Market* (1984), and *Anno's USA* (1982) encourage extensive vocabulary development; analysis of time and place; and application of literary, artistic, and historical knowledge.

Semantic mapping or webbing procedures, identified as effective for vocabulary development by Toms-Bronowski (1983) and Johnson and Pearson (1984), are especially effective when used with literature. Semantic mapping can help students identify words with similar meanings, expand a precise vocabulary, understand multiple meanings for words, develop concepts, and perceive relationships among words and ideas.

Semantic Mapping and Vocabulary Development

To use a semantic-mapping approach to increase vocabulary development, first read the literature selection and identify vocabulary words or concepts that are crucial to understanding that book. Next, draw a web on the board with the title of the book in the center of the web (see Figure 9.1). On the arms extending from the center, place the important words from the story. During a brainstorming session, have students add words, such as synonyms and definitions that expand their comprehension of the key words. Complete this activity as a prereading vocabulary introduction, an exploration to discover students' previous knowledge, or an introduction to important information.

Use the same web to build students' understandings of each vocabulary word. Have them consider the meaning developed by the author, select the term that is closest to that developed in the story, add new words or even phrases gained from the story, and use the vocabulary word identified in the web to increase their story comprehension. Vocabulary webs are appropriate at any grade level and may accompany books either read by students or to them (see Chapter 6).

The following is an example of how to conduct this activity with upper elementary students reading a legend, Selina Hastings's *Sir Gawain and the Loathly Lady* (1981). On the chalkboard, draw a web similar to that shown in Figure 9.1. Place the title of the book in the center of the web. Extend the vocabulary words *knight, armour, charger, challenge, foe, enchantment, loathly, honor, bargain,* and *quest* from the center. During the prereading activity, introduce these vocabulary words and have students define them or identify synonyms. Next, have students read the literature. Finally, have them add vocabulary terms to the web and identify the best meanings for the vocabulary within the context of the literature.

DEVELOPING UNDERSTANDING OF LITERARY ELEMENTS

Reading literature with understanding and appreciation requires readers to recognize various literary elements and the ways that authors use those elements to create exciting and credible stories. This section describes some of the techniques teachers may use to develop understanding of the literary elements.

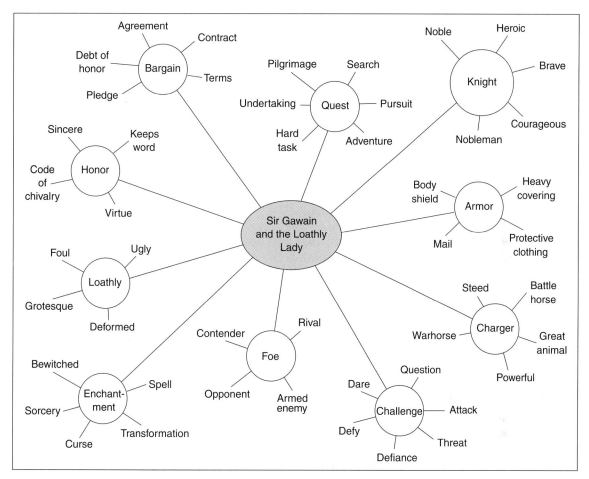

Figure 9.1 Vocabulary web for a literature selection.

Semantic Mapping

Semantic mapping or webbing is effective for identifying the literary elements in a book and extending discussions around those literary elements. Prior to the webbing experience, introduce and discuss the literary elements of setting, characterization, conflict, plot, and theme by reading and discussing folktales with the students. Tales such as "The Three Little Pigs" and "Cinderella" are good for this introduction because the good and bad characters, the conflict, and the theme are easy to recognize.

For the first webbing activity around literary elements, demonstrate the technique to the entire group. On the board, draw a web around the title of the story, with the literary elements extending from the center. As you read the story, have students listen for the various categories. After you complete the story, lead a discussion encouraging students to fill in the various categories on the web or only one element. If necessary, reread sections to help students identify the specific element(s) and choose appropriate wording for the web.

After demonstrating this activity several times, let the students try the webbing approach with other types of literature or with more complex literature. Either read the literature to the students or have them read it themselves. Have students develop their own webs before you lead the discussion or have them develop the webs concurrently with the discussion. If students developed their own webs beforehand, have them add to the webs during the discussion to focus their attention on the task and involve them in the discussion.

The lesson plan shown in Figure 9.2 was developed for and taught in the upper elementary grades (Norton & Norton, 1999). The lesson plan demonstrates the development of a lesson for webbing literary elements using Avi's *The True Confessions of Charlotte Doyle* (1990) (see Figure 9.3).

Activities such as those outlined in the previous lesson plan encourage higher thought processes, analysis of text, synthesis of ideas, understanding of literary elements, and comprehension of story structures. The activities encourage interaction among the students and the text and among the students and the teacher. As students expand their ability to identify and analyze various literary characteristics, they may add new insights to the literature discussion. Additional literary webs are found in Norton's *Through the Eyes of a Child* (1999), *The Effective Teaching of Language Arts* (1997), *The Impact of Literature-Based Reading* (1992), and *Multicultural Children's Literature: Through the Eyes of Many Children* (2001).

Purpose:	**1.** To develop an understanding of the integrated nature of literary elements in a book
	2. To develop a literary web that includes setting, characterization, conflicts, and themes
	3. To discuss the importance of each of the literary elements in a book
	4. To write journal entries that could be the background for the book
Materials:	Avi's *The True Confessions of Charlotte Doyle* (1990), 1991 Newbery Honor Award Winner
Grade level:	Upper elementary, middle school
Book summary:	*The True Confessions of Charlotte Doyle* is a historical fiction novel set in 1832 aboard the *Seahawk* as it sails from England to America. The only passenger on the ship, 13-year-old Charlotte Doyle, is caught between the cruelty of the captain and the mutinous actions of the crew. Details develop the historical accuracy of the time period and a carefully constructed plot creates considerable action as the heroine faces and overcomes charges of murder on the high seas. The heroine shares with the readers the information that she would not have been able to re-create her story if she had not kept a detailed journal of her experiences.

Figure 9.2   Webbing literary elements.

| Procedures: | 1. | Introduce the book by reading and discussing the introduction, "An Important Warning." Ask the students to think about what the author is revealing about the story and the character in the first paragraph: "Not every thirteen-year-old girl is accused of murder, brought to trial, and found guilty. But I was just such a girl, and my story is worth relating even if it did happen years ago. Be warned, however, this is no *Story of a Bad Boy,* no *What Katy Did.* If strong ideas and action offend you, read no more. Find another companion to share your idle hours. For my part I intend to tell the truth as I lived it" (p. 1). Also, ask the students to respond to the impact of this first paragraph on readers. |

To introduce the setting for the book, show and discuss pictures of smaller merchant sailing ships that would have crossed the Atlantic in 1832. You can also discuss the author's references to the two books in the first paragraph. For example, *The Story of a Bad Boy* was written by Thomas Bailey Aldrich in 1870. The types of exploits described in the book are common for Victorian heroes during the late 1800s: boys practiced the "manly arts," formed clubs, and played pranks. These activities are very different from the exploits of Charlotte Doyle. Students can compare what they believe Charlotte's exploits will be with those of *The Story of a Bad Boy.*

2. Place a literary elements web on the board (see Figure 9.3). As you write *setting, characterization, conflicts,* and *themes* on the board, ask the students to consider what they might expect to find under each element in this book after they listen to and discuss the introduction. Ask the students to fill in the details on the web as they either listen to or read the book *The True Confessions of Charlotte Doyle.* After the web is completed, discuss the interactions and importance of each of the details under the literary elements. Figure 9.3 is a partial example of a resulting literary web.

3. After completing the web, ask students to consider the importance of the journal entries in the following quote: "Keeping that journal then is what enables me to relate now in perfect detail everything that transpired during that fateful voyage across the Atlantic Ocean in the summer of 1832" (p. 3). Ask the students to select one of the chapters in *The True Confessions of Charlotte Doyle* and to write the journal entry that motivated the writing of and provided the details for the incidents described in the chapter.

4. Another writing activity may be developed around point of view. Ask students to consider and discuss why they think Avi wrote this story from Charlotte Doyle's point of view. Ask them to look again at the web to identify each of the instances on the web in which the heroine's point of view is extremely important in developing the various literary elements. Then, ask the students to consider how the story might change if told through the point of view of Captain Jaggery, Zachariah, or one of the other crew members. They could also choose to write a response to Charlotte Doyle's journal from the point of view of her father.

Figure 9.2 (continued)

Source: From *Language Arts Activities for Children* (4th ed., pp. 261–263) by D. Norton and S. E. Norton, 1999, Upper Saddle River, NJ: Merrill/Prentice Hall. Copyright 1999 by Pearson Education. Reprinted by permission of Pearson Education, Inc., Upper Saddle River, NJ 07458.

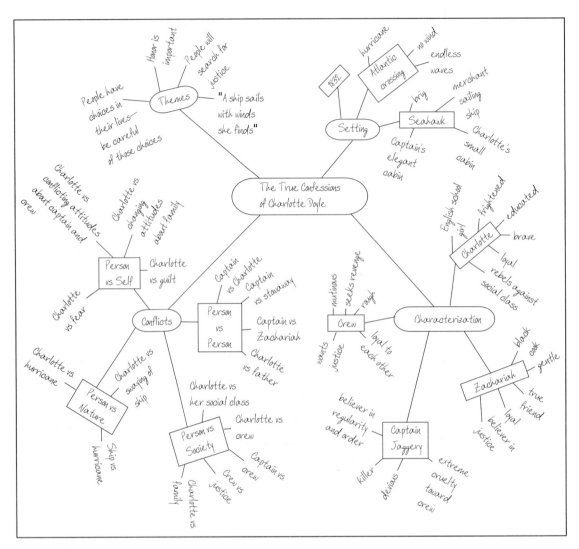

Figure 9.3   Literary elements web.

Plot Structures

As noted, a story must have a beginning, a middle, and an end. Diagrams of plot structure help students understand plot development and the inherent conflicts. Two plot structures are especially important in children's literature: (1) those with external conflict and (2) those with person-versus-self conflict.

Most plots in stories for younger students follow a structure that introduces the characters and conflict at the beginning of the story, increases the conflict until a climax, identifies the turning point, and ends the conflict. This structure is usually

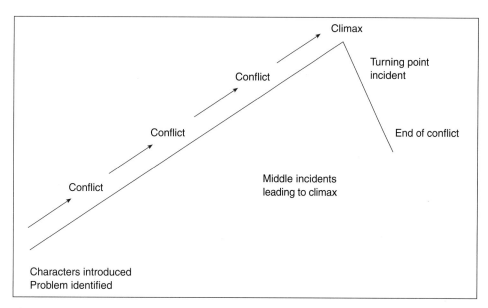

Figure 9.4 Plot structure for external conflict.

found when the main character faces external forces. You can help your students recognize and understand this structure by diagramming the key incidents from such a story. Figure 9.4 diagrams a structure with such external conflict. Using this structure, Figure 9.5 diagrams the plot structure of *Sir Gawain and the Loathly Lady.*

In a second plot structure, the conflict is basically within the main character (see Figure 9.6). Cohen (1985) states that person-versus-self stories follow a structure that introduces the character and conflict, follows the conflict within the character, moves to a climax (the point at which the character realizes the problem and accepts it), and concludes when the character finally achieves peace. Figure 9.7 applies this person-versus-self structure to Marion Dane Bauer's *On My Honor* (1986), a contemporary realistic fiction story.

Modeling Literary Analysis

Modeling is one of the most important strategies to use when developing students' comprehension of literature (Dole, Duffy, Roehler, & Pearson, 1991). Researchers Roehler and Duffy (1984) and Gordon (1985) developed an instructional approach that places the teacher in an interactive role with the students. In this approach, the teacher analyzes literary concepts before expecting the students to accomplish a similar task. The modeling helps students understand important cognitive processes. As the modeling progresses, the approach proceeds from total teacher modeling, to gradual student interaction, to total student analysis. This section considers how to use modeling when developing students' literary understanding.

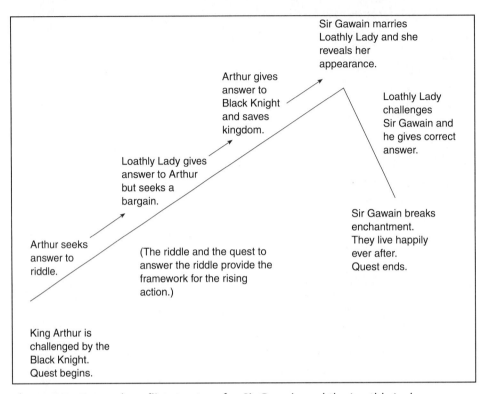

Figure 9.5 External conflict structure for *Sir Gawain and the Loathly Lady.*

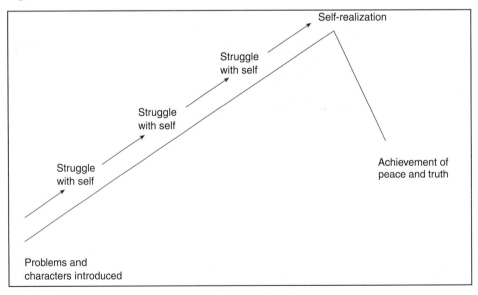

Figure 9.6 Plot structure for person-versus-self conflict.

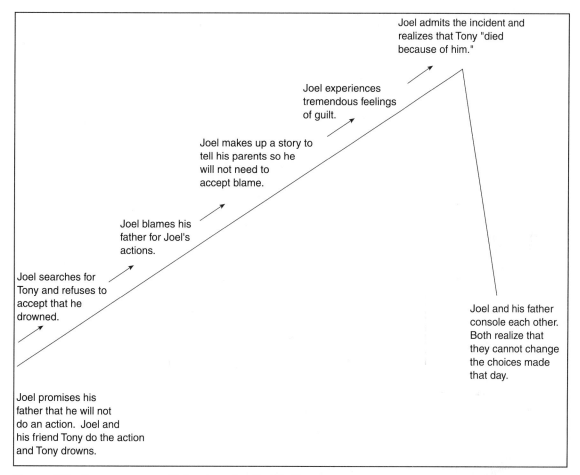

Joel admits the incident and realizes that Tony "died because of him."

Joel experiences tremendous feelings of guilt.

Joel makes up a story to tell his parents so he will not need to accept blame.

Joel blames his father for Joel's actions.

Joel searches for Tony and refuses to accept that he drowned.

Joel and his father console each other. Both realize that they cannot change the choices made that day.

Joel promises his father that he will not do an action. Joel and his friend Tony do the action and Tony drowns.

Figure 9.7 Person-versus-self structure for *On My Honor.*

Modeling is especially effective when developing understanding of literature, because the longer literature texts encourage a synthesis of ideas and provide more opportunity for teachers and students to draw evidence. The reasoning stage of literary analysis encourages teachers and students to think about some of the more difficult aspects of the literature and to draw on their previous experiences. Modeling is especially effective with complex tasks, such as inferring characterization, identifying theme, and speculating about allusions and symbolism.

Teachers who are developing and teaching modeling lessons should follow the recommendations for effective modeling identified by Dole and colleagues (1991):

1. Modeling that provides explicit, unambiguous information is more effective than modeling that provides vague or jumbled information.

2. Modeling that demonstrates flexible adjustment to text cues is more effective than modeling that emphasizes rigid rules.

3. If teachers merely ask questions without explaining the reasoning employed to answer those questions, many students will have difficulty understanding how the questions were answered.

If students do not understand how the questions were answered, they will not gain control of the process associated with answering the questions. Consequently, the process suffers.

Gordon (1985) uses a five-step approach to help students understand important cognitive processes associated with comprehension of text. First, the teacher identifies the skill to be taught, analyzes the requirements for effective reasoning within that skill, identifies text samples that require the skill, and identifies questions to stimulate the students to use that skill or thought process. During this preparatory phase, the teacher also considers how to introduce the skill to students.

Second, the teacher completely models the strategy by reading the text, asking a question, answering the question, citing evidence that supports the answer, and then verbally following the reasoning process used to acquire the answer.

Third, the teacher involves the students in citing the evidence. During this step, the teacher reads the text, asks a question, and answers it. Then the teacher asks the students to cite evidence for the answer. Finally, the teacher leads a discussion that explores the reasoning. The strategy is more clear to students if they make notes concerning the various parts.

Fourth, the teacher involves the students in answering the question. During this step, the teacher reads the text and asks a question; the students answer the question; the teacher cites the evidence; and then the teacher leads a discussion that explores the reasoning process.

Fifth, students have primary responsibility during most of the strategy. The teacher reads the text and asks a question, but the students answer the question, cite the evidence that supports the question, and explain the reasoning involved in reaching their answers.

This approach is especially effective with children's literature in which the author uses inferences to develop characterization; uses figurative language to create mood, suggest characterization, or enhance conflict; uses conflict and interactions among characters to develop theme; or uses historical settings to develop background, create an antagonist, or develop person versus society conflicts, because such literary concepts are difficult for students to understand. Books that contain these characteristics stimulate exciting discussions as students recognize the author's techniques and discover the impact of well-developed literature.

Teachers may model with picture storybooks that are completed in one lesson or with books that take several days to complete. Modeling is especially effective when the teacher identifies techniques used by an author and then demonstrates how to read and understand the techniques. Modeling may introduce a book that the students will read later. In this way, the modeling stimulates interest in the literature and encourages students to read with understanding and appreciation.

Consider how to use modeling to introduce the understanding of figurative language in Rudolf Frank's *No Hero for the Kaiser* (1986). In this historical fiction book for older students, Frank uses figurative language to depict the wartime setting, enhance characterization, clarify the conflict, and suggest theme.

In step 1, identify a skill, such as inferring the author's meaning from figurative language. Analyze the requirements for effective inferences, which follow:

- To identify nonliteral comparisons.
- To realize that figurative language is meant to clarify and enlighten by developing new relationships.
- To identify the similarities or differences between two things.
- To go beyond the information the author provides in the text.
- To use clues from the text to hypothesize about the relationships between figurative language and setting, characterization, conflict, and theme.
- To use background knowledge gained from other experiences.

Then identify text examples of figurative language. For example, similes appear on pages 2, 12, 44, and 46 of *No Hero for the Kaiser.* Many more similes are in the text, but these few should produce interesting modeling and discussions. Contrasts appear on pages 45, 46, and 65. Symbolism appears on pages 2 (plum tree), 18 (Wild Goat), and 59 (Lance Corporal Poodle). Allusions to Napoleon appear on pages 42 and 49–51. Allusions to a myth about the skull of an African sultan that supposedly influenced the beginning of World War I appear on pages 21 and 70–71. Note that students may have comprehension problems in these areas.

In step 2, introduce the text. Review the place by identifying Germany, Russia, and Poland on a map. Discuss these places, the students' knowledge of the historical time (1914–1918), the seasons, and the fact that war causes desolation and destruction. Review figurative language, such as similes, contrasts, symbolism, and allusions, using examples. For example, be sure that the students know that a simile is a direct comparison in which the author uses *like, as,* or *as if.*

Begin reading, stopping on page 2 to emphasize and discuss the meaning of the similes in this passage:

> The distant thud of cannon came closer, like a thunderstorm brewing. And as if the storm had already broken, women, boys, girls, and soldiers began to rush around in confusion; trumpets sounded, and suddenly the Russians had swept out of the village like the wind. Now they were firing down from the low hills into the village. It sounded like the high-pitched whine of mosquitoes as they fly past your ear looking for a place to settle and bite: zzzzzz—a thin, sharp noise, full of malice. (p. 2)

Ask an inferential question or questions, such as "What is the author telling us about the setting in the Polish village?" "What is the author telling us about war?" "How does the author's use of simile increase your ability to visualize the setting and the war that will follow?" "Do you believe that these are good comparisons?" and "Why or why not?"

Answer the question or questions. Tell the students, "The town is, or will be, the setting for a noisy and destructive battle. Soldiers who once enjoyed the town are running to take their places on the battlefield. People in the town are also running. The author tells us that war is terrible and destructive. The author's use of similes helps us hear the battle, see the movement, and feel the danger. I believe that the similes are good comparisons."

Cite evidence for your answers. Say, for example, "The author describes the normal activity and appearance of the town and describes changes. The sound of cannon is compared to a thunderstorm. The rapidly advancing Russian soldiers are compared to wind sweeping through the town. The sound of bullets is compared to the whine of mosquitoes."

Explore your own reasoning process. For example, "The author describes the village and then shows what happens to it when two forces are about to fight. I know from my own experience that a thunderstorm and a cannon sound alike. I also know from my experience and from other reading that a thunderstorm can bring destruction in the form of lightning and high winds. I believe that this is a good comparison for an approaching battle. I can close my eyes and see and hear the battle.

"I also know from experience that when wind sweeps through the streets, it moves everything in front of it. I can close my eyes and see people rushing away from the army as it sweeps through town without thinking of the consequences of its actions. In this way, the army is also like the wind.

"I also know that bullets and mosquitoes sound somewhat alike. I know that mosquitoes have a nasty bite. When the author uses expressions such as "sly malice," I think that he is saying that the bullets are much worse than mosquitoes.

"The author also may be saying that mosquitoes and bullets are alike in another way. They both hit innocent victims. I believe from these comparisons that the author is telling us that war is terrible for all people, including innocent bystanders." Notice that this last statement may also encourage a discussion about what the students believe to be the theme of the book.

Continue the modeling approach, using other examples, until the students can provide evidence for their answers and can rationalize them. Encourage discussion and varied viewpoints. This approach helps students check their reasoning and does not suggest that there is only one correct answer. In fact, modeling lessons usually broaden rather than narrow the students' answers.

Asking students to jot down their answers, their evidence, and their reasoning before discussion encourages them to focus on the task, interact during the discussion, and develop their thought processes. Additional good subjects for modeling and discussion include the following:

- *Additional similes,* such as, "What does the author mean when he states, 'Like huge wolves the four cannons of the Seventh Battery went into the field' ?" (from page 46).

- *Contrasts* of the peaceful and war meanings for words and phrases, such as *bullseye* (from page 45) and *in the fields* (from pages 45–46). Ask, "What is the author saying when he uses these comparisons?" and "How does the author use these comparisons to reinforce the antiwar theme of the book?" Encourage the students to cite evidence that supports their answers and to describe the reasoning they used to reach their answers.
- *Symbolism.* Model and discuss the significance of symbolism for things and names. Ask, for example, "What does the symbolism of the plum tree (on page 18) reveal about the author's attitude toward war?" "What does the author's symbolism of Wild Goat (on page 54) and White Raven (on page 18) reveal about the characterization of the two German officers?" and "What is the author telling us about war when he names the dog Lance Corporal Poodle on page 59?"
- *Allusions.* Model and discuss the author's choice of allusions to Napoleon (see pages 42 and 49–51), the skull of the African sultan (see pages 21 and 70–71), and the Flood (see page 56).

SUMMARY

Discussion strategies that encourage students to respond to and interact with literature are especially effective. This chapter develops several of these strategies, including semantic mapping of literary elements and vocabulary, plot structuring for conflicts outside or within a character, and modeling of the thought processes associated with analyzing literary elements.

Choosing literature that motivates students to read and stimulates an appreciation of literature requires knowledge about literature and an awareness of the students' interests. Likewise, teaching literature requires knowledge about literature and instructional approaches that encourage the broad development of reading skills. In addition to developing literary understanding and appreciation, literature-based programs encourage students to realize the importance of literature as a mirror of human experience, be able to gain insights from their involvement with literature, become aware of writers who represent diverse backgrounds and traditions, become familiar with past and present masterpieces of literature, develop effective ways of discussing and writing about various forms of literature, appreciate the rhythms and beauty of the language in literature, and develop lifelong reading habits.

As students expand their abilities to read literature for understanding, appreciation, and enjoyment, they are confronted with such terms as *plot, characterization, setting, theme, style,* and *point of view.* Literary enjoyment and appreciation are enhanced through oral reading to students and recreational reading groups. Reading skills are strengthened through literature using predictable books, increasing vocabulary knowledge, and developing understanding of literary elements.

YOUR POINT OF VIEW

Discussion Questions

1. Identify the reading objectives stated in a unit of a basal reading series. Develop a list of literature selections that would reinforce and strengthen those objectives. Share your rationales for choosing the books.
2. Assume that you will be teaching a literature-based program at a specific grade level. What are the literature selections that you consider important for that grade? Take into consideration the quality of the literature, the appropriateness of the literature for the grade level, and the reading objectives that you want to teach. Develop a core list of books. Give your reasons for selecting the books.
3. Assume that you will be using recreational reading groups to enhance students' enjoyment of literature. Develop a list of books that follow a genre approach, an author approach, or a literary elements approach. Try one of the recreational reading groups in your college reading class. Analyze the responses of the class. What types of information did they share? Did you want to read any of the books discussed by other members of the group? Now, what do you believe are the strengths of recreational reading groups?

Take a Stand For or Against

1. Some reading authorities want literature to supplement the basal reading curriculum. In contrast, other reading authorities want literature to form the total reading curriculum. Consider the advantages and disadvantages of each approach. Share your responses with your class.
2. Several groups have identified the literature selections that should be the core of the school literature program. Read and analyze several of these lists, such as *Recommended Readings in Literature: Kindergarten Through Grade Eight* (1986) and "Education Secretary Bennett's Suggested Reading List for Elementary-School Pupils" (1988). What is your opinion of each list? Are there books that should be added or deleted? Is there a core of books that every educated person should read? Why or why not?

BIBLIOGRAPHY

Ahlberg, J., & Ahlberg, A. (1982). *The baby's catalogue*. Boston: Little, Brown & Co.

Allison, D., & Watson, J. A. (1994). The significance of adult storybook reading styles on the development of young children's emergent reading. *Reading Research and Instruction, 34,* 57–72.

Anno, M. (1980). *Anno's Italy*. Ontario, Canada: Collins.

Anno, M. (1982). *Anno's Britain*. New York: Philomel.

Anno, M. (1982). *Anno's USA*. New York: Philomel.

Anno, M. (1984). *Anno's flea market*. London: Bodlet Head.

Avi. (1990). *The true confessions of Charlotte Doyle.* New York: Orchard.

Barton, B. (1995). *The wee little woman.* New York: HarperCollins.

Bat-Ami, M. (1999). *Two suns in the sky.* Miami, FL: Front Street/Cricket.

Bauer, M. D. (1986). *On my honor.* New York: Clarion.

Breckenridge, K. (April 1988). Modern classics. *School Library Journal, 34,* 42–43.

Brown, J. (1999). Critical questions. *The Reading Teacher, 52,* 520–521.

Brown, M. (1982). *Shadow.* New York: Charles Scribner's Sons.

Browne, A. (1983). *Gorilla.* New York: Watts.

Burnett, F. H. (1911). *The secret garden.* New York: J. B. Lippincott Co.

Burton, V. L. (1942). *The little house.* Boston: Houghton Mifflin Co.

Cohen, C. L. (August 1985). The quest in children's literature. *School Library Journal, 31,* 28–29.

Corbett, W. J. (1983). *The song of Pentecost.* New York: E. P. Dutton.

Creech, S. (1994). *Walk two moons.* New York: HarperCollins.

Curtis, C. P. (1995). *The Watsons go to Birmingham—1963.* New York: Delacorte.

Cushman, K. (1995). *The midwife's apprentice.* New York: Clarion.

Dole, J., Duffy, G., Roehler, L., & Pearson, P. D. (1991). Moving from the old to the new: Research on reading comprehension instruction. *Review of Educational Research, 61,* 239–264.

Dunning, S., Lueders, E., & Smith, H. (Eds.) (1967). *Reflections on a gift of watermelon pickle. . . .* New York: Lothrop, Lee & Shepard.

Early, M., & Ericson, B. (1988). The act of reading. In B. F. Nelms (Ed.), *Literature in the classroom: Readers, texts, and contexts.* (pp. 31–44). Urbana, IL: National Council of Teachers of English.

Education Secretary Bennett's suggested reading list for elementary-school pupils (September 1988). *The Chronicle of Higher Education,* B3.

Emberley, R. (1993). *Let's go: A book in two languages.* Boston: Little, Brown & Co.

Falconer, I. (2000). *Olivia.* New York: Simon & Schuster.

Feitelson, D., Rita, B., & Goldstein, Z. (1986). Effects of listening to series stories on first graders' comprehension and use of language. *Research in the Teaching of English, 20,* 339–355.

Fenner, C. (1995). *Yolonda's genius.* New York: McElderry.

Five, C. L. (1988). From workbook to workshop: Increasing children's involvement in the reading process. *The New Advocate, 1,* 92–102.

Fleischman, S. (1986). *The whipping boy.* New York: Greenwillow.

Floca, B. (1999). *Five trucks.* New York: Dorling Kindersley.

Forbes, E. (1943). *Johnny Tremain.* Boston: Houghton Mifflin Co.

Fox, M. (1987). *Hattie and the fox.* New York: Bradbury.

Frank, R. (1986). *No hero for the Kaiser.* New York: Lothrop, Lee & Shepard.

Freedman, G. (1987). *Lincoln: A photobiography.* New York: Clarion.

Frye, N., Baker, S., & Perkins, G. (1985). *The Harper handbook of literature.* New York: Harper & Row.

Gilliland, J. H. (2000). *Steamboat! The story of Captain Blanche Leathers.* New York: Dorling Kindersley.

Goodall, J. (1987). *The story of a Main Street.* Upper Saddle River, NJ: Merrill/Prentice Hall.

Gordon, C. (1985). Modeling inference awareness across the curriculum. *Journal of Reading, 28,* 444–447.

Grahame, K. (1908). *The wind in the willows.* New York: Charles Scribner's Sons.

Greenaway, K. (1979). *A apple pie.* Secaucus, NJ: Castle Books.

Grifalconi, A. (1987). *Darkness and the butterfly.* Boston: Little, Brown.

Hastings, S. (1981). *Sir Gawain and the loathly lady.* New York: Lothrop, Lee & Shepard.

Highwater, J. (1981). *Moonsong lullaby.* New York: Lothrop, Lee & Shepard.

Hoban, T. (1986). *Shapes, shapes, shapes.* New York: Greenwillow.

Hoban, T. (1998). *So many circles, so many squares.* New York: Greenwillow.

Huck, C., Hepler, S., & Hickman, J. (1993). *Children's literature.* Orlando: Harcourt Brace Jovanovich.

Hutchins, P. (1990). *What game shall we play?* New York: Greenwillow.

Ivimey, J. (1987). *The complete story of three blind mice.* New York: Clarion.

Jacques, B. (1986). *Redwall.* New York: Philomel.

Johnson, D., & Pearson, P. D. (1984). *Teaching reading vocabulary.* New York: Holt, Rinehart & Winston.

Lamme, L. (1976). Reading aloud to young children. *Language Arts, 53,* 886–888.

Lawson, R. (1944). *Rabbit hill.* New York: Viking Press.

Leggo, C. (1997). *Teaching to wonder: Responding to poetry in the secondary classroom.* Vancouver: Pacific Educational Press.

Lobel, A. (1984). *A rose in my garden.* New York: Greenwillow.

London, J. (1996). *Fireflies, fireflies, light my way.* Illustrated by Linda Messier. New York: Viking.

Longfellow, H. W. (1893). *Hiawatha.* New York: E. P. Dutton.

Mathis, S. B. (1975). *The hundred penny box.* New York: Viking Press.

May, J. P. (1987). Creating a schoolwide literature program: A case study. *Children's Literature Association Quarterly, 12,* 135–137.

McCloskey, R. (1941). *Make way for ducklings.* New York: Viking Press.

McCracken, R., & McCracken, M. (1986). *Stories, songs, and poetry to teach reading and writing: Literacy through language.* Chicago: American Library Association.

McCully, E. A. (1987). *School.* New York: Harper & Row.

Millard, A. (1998). *A street through time: A 12,000-year walk through history.* New York: Dorling Kindersley.

Milne, A. A. (1926). *Winnie-the-pooh.* New York: E. P. Dutton.

Nilsen, A. P., & Donelson, K. L. (2001). *Literature for today's young adults* (6th ed.). New York: Longman.

Noll, S. (1990). *Watch where you go.* New York: Greenwillow.

Norton, D. E. (1992). *The impact of literature-based reading.* Upper Saddle River, NJ: Merrill/Prentice Hall.

Norton, D. E. (1997). *The effective teaching of language arts* (5th ed.). Upper Saddle River, NJ: Merrill/Prentice Hall.

Norton, D. E. (1999). *Through the eyes of a child: An introduction to children's literature* (5th ed.). Upper Saddle River, NJ: Merrill/Prentice Hall.

Norton, D. E. (2001). *Multicultural children's literature: Through the eyes of many children.* Upper Saddle River, NJ: Merrill/Prentice Hall.

Norton, D. E., & McNamara, J. (1987). *An evaluation of the BISD/TAMU multiethnic reading program.* College Station, TX: Texas A&M University, research report.

Norton, D. E., & Norton, S. E. (1999). *Language arts activities for children* (4th ed.). Upper Saddle River, NJ: Merrill/Prentice Hall.

Paulsen, G. (1987). *Hatchet.* New York: Bradbury.

Peck, R. (2000). *A year down yonder.* New York: Dial.

Potter, B. (1902). *The tale of Peter Rabbit.* New York: Warne.

Prelutsky, J. (1993). *The dragons are singing tonight.* New York: Greenwillow.

Prelutsky, J. (1999). *The gargoyle on the roof.* New York: Greenwillow.

Pullman, P. (1996). *The golden compass.* New York: Knopf.

Rockwell, A. (1975). *The three bears and 15 other stories.* New York: Crowell.

Rockwell, A. (1985). *First comes spring.* New York: Crowell.

Roehler, L., & Duffy, G. (1984). Direct explanation of the comprehension process. In G. Durry, L. Roehler, & J. Mason (Eds.), *Comprehension instruction.* New York: Longman.

Rowling, J. K. (2000). *Harry Potter and the goblet of fire.* New York: Scholastic.

Ruddell, R. (1992). A whole language and literature perspective: Creating a meaning-making instructional environment. *Language Arts, 69,* 612–620.

Rudman, M., & Pearce, A. (1988). *For the love of reading:* A parent's guide to encouraging young readers from infancy through age 5. Mount Vernon, NY: Consumers Union.

Sadoski, M., Willson, V., & Norton, D. (1996). The relative contributions of research-based composition activities to writing improvement in grades 1–8. *Research in the teaching of English.*

Sawyer, W. (1987). Literature and literacy: A review of research. *Language Arts, 64,* 33–39.

Sperry, A. (1940). *Call it courage.* Upper Saddle River, NJ: Prentice Hall.

Spiegel, D. L. (1998). Reader response approaches and growth of readers. *Language Arts, 76,* 41–48.

Sutherland, Z., & Arbuthnot, M. H. (1991). *Children and books.* New York: HarperCollins.

Taxel, J. (1988). Notes from the editor. *The New Advocate, 1,* 73–74.

Tompkins, G., & Weber, M. (1983). What will happen next? Using predictable books with young children. *The Reading Teacher, 36,* 498–502.

Toms-Bronowski, S. (1983). An investigation of the effectiveness of selected vocabulary teaching strategies with intermediate grade level students. *Dissertation Abstracts International.*

Van Allsburg, C. (1984). *The mysteries of Harris Burdick.* Boston: Houghton Mifflin Co.

Van Allsburg, C. (1987). *The z was zapped.* Boston: Houghton Mifflin Co.

Voigt, C. (1982). *Dicey's song.* New York: Atheneum.

Whelan, G. (2000). *Homeless bird.* New York: HarperCollins.

White, E. B. (1952). *Charlotte's web.* New York: Harper & Row.

Wilder, L. I. (1932). *The little house in the big woods.* New York: Harper & Row.

Williams, M. (1958). *The velveteen rabbit.* Garden City, NJ: Doubleday & Co.

Wood, N. (Ed.). (1997). *The serpent's tongue: Prose, poetry, and art of the New Mexico pueblos.* New York: Dutton.

CHAPTER 10

Content-Area Reading

Chapter Outline

Major Goals and Trends in Content Reading

> Content-Oriented Literature
>
> Integrating Writing in the Content Areas
>
> Integrating Comprehension Strategies
>
> Primary-Grade Emphasis

Expository Text

> Organizational Structures
>
> Readability

Components of Content Reading

> Vocabulary Development
>
> Studying Strategies
>
> Reading and Study Skills
>
> Collecting, Analyzing, and Criticizing Data

For the Reader

You might logically assume that concentration on providing excellent instruction in the various word-identification and comprehension skills and strategies will automatically produce mature, flexible readers. Such is not the case. Early in the reading program, children are expected to read content material successfully and to locate and synthesize information. Although you could make a case for more than one neglected area in a school's curriculum, the area of reading in content subjects is probably the most important. Think of your own background for a moment and answer the following questions:

Were you explicitly taught how to understand text written in an expository style?

Were you explicitly taught how to study in your content subjects (such as math, science, and social studies)?

Were you explicitly taught how to locate and synthesize information from an almanac, an encyclopedia, and an atlas?

Were you explicitly taught how to interpret various maps, graphs, charts, and diagrams?

Notice the key word **explicitly** in the preceding statements. Many content-reading strategies receive only passing mention in our schools. However, everyone needs explicit/direct planned instruction and practice to meet the challenge of content material and to read in order to learn throughout life.

In each For the Reader section of this text, we ask you to preview the chapter before plunging into reading. We are attempting to change your reading habits by ensuring that you take advantage of the organization of most textbooks. By now, you have probably realized the importance of previewing what you are about to read. This is but one aspect of content reading that we recommend you directly teach in your classes. This chapter presents content-area strategies along with recommended teaching procedures.

Key Ideas

- The ability to read well in narrative text does not ensure the ability to read well in a subject area.

- Students must apply specific strategies and skills to comprehend expository text.

- How successfully a student reads content material depends on the text, the student, and the teacher.

- The major components of content reading include vocabulary development, studying strategies, reading and study skills, and strategies for collecting, analyzing, and criticizing data.

- Teachers should strive to tailor their instruction in the content areas to the needs of their students.

MAJOR GOALS AND TRENDS IN CONTENT READING

The major goal of content-area reading instruction is to teach students the attitudes, skills, and strategies that will enable them to become independent learners. While this goal has always been of paramount importance, its fulfillment has not been achieved and it is a continuing concern for literacy educators. With the new emphases on constructing meaning in text and integrating reading instruction with the other language arts across all curricular areas, the following are growing trends in the content-reading area: content-oriented literature, integrating writing in the content areas, integrating comprehension strategies, and primary-grade emphasis.

Content-Oriented Literature

The world of literature serves many purposes, including that of a rich source of information on content-oriented themes. Students should be exposed not only to narrative literature but also to expository literature (Camp, 2000). Whether the topic is history, different cultures, animals, science, environmental concerns, or mathematics, quality literature not only will help students understand content, but also will stimulate their interest and active engagement, promote reading as a lifelong activity, aid in developing reading fluency, and promote application of reading-comprehension strategies. Incorporating good expository literature, including picture books, into the content areas is an excellent means for reinforcing all of the language processes—reading, writing, listening, and speaking—across the curriculum (Farris & Fuhler, 1994). Choosing a number of expository books at various difficulty levels dealing with a particular topic is another way of meeting the varied needs of students in any classroom.

Integrating Writing in the Content Areas

As stressed throughout the text, reading comprehension improves when the writing and reading processes are combined. Reading and writing simultaneously interact to make content learning more enjoyable and understandable. Both basal and literature-based programs are beginning to capitalize on this supportive relationship.

Typically, content material is more difficult for students to comprehend, primarily because of its presentation of difficult concepts, the technical vocabulary, and the different text structures of expository writing. Combining various writing assignments—whether before, during, or after content-reading instruction—can help improve students' basic understanding of ideas, inferences to be drawn from the text, and creative reactions to topics under study. This trend also must be viewed and implemented from a language arts perspective, which occurs in content instruction throughout all grades. Walmsley and Allington (1995) spoke directly to the importance of integrating the language arts, including writing into the content areas:

> Since one of the major purposes of learning to read is to gain access to the knowledge contained within books and other reading material, and because knowledge of the topic of a book (i.e., prior knowledge) is such an important component of the

Opening students to the world through good literature should be a goal of content-reading instruction at every grade level.

act of reading itself, we feel that the language arts curriculum should not be separated from the content areas (e.g., literature, history, science, music, art, health). These are among the most important domains from which topics for reading and writing can be drawn, and literacy activities within these areas should be considered as integral, not peripheral, components of the language arts curriculum. (p. 31)

Integrating Comprehension Strategies

With the explosion of knowledge on how readers actively and strategically interact with text, content-reading instruction now emphasizes the learning and application of this new knowledge. Intricately related to the last two trends, content reading is viewed more as a prime area for students to learn and apply various comprehension and studying strategies and reading-study skills. They need those same skills to become successful readers of expository text. In many cases, literature and writing assignments can be the vehicles to accomplish these worthwhile goals.

The regular reading program can teach many skills and strategies, but students must apply them to content subjects to comprehend content material. Reading-comprehension and studying strategies and specific reading-study skills also must be taught directly during the content instructional period. Most importantly, students need ample teacher assistance in terms of initial instruction, explanation, clarification, guidance, and ongoing instruction in content-area activities to become strategic, independent learners. Hadaway and Young (1994) recommended using various graphic aids such as time lines, maps, flowcharts, graphs, and Venn diagrams to help build and review background knowledge and teach difficult concepts. Students need to see content reading-study skills and strategies applied to everyday materials they encounter in their own lives (Richardson & Morgan, 2000).

Primary-Grade Emphasis

Traditionally, formal content-area reading instruction was limited mainly to the intermediate, middle, and high school levels. This was true despite the age-old adage that every teacher should be a reading teacher and despite the descriptions of a complete reading program as including broad areas of the instructional curriculum, an independent or recreational program, and skill and strategy development in the content areas at all grade levels. A much-needed emphasis is now occurring at the primary level. Olson and Gee (1991) reported on content instruction in the primary grades and the problems that students at this level experience with expository text. The authors surveyed primary-grade teachers regarding recommended content-reading practices and strategies. They reported that "70% of the teachers found content texts more difficult than stories" (p. 300). The six highest rated practices of the teachers were "previewing concepts and vocabulary, using concrete manipulatives to develop concepts, requiring retellings, developing summaries, visualizing information, and brainstorming" (p. 300). Based on these results and recent research, Olson and Gee (1991) recommended that primary teachers use the following instructional strategies in teaching content reading:

- semantic mapping
- K-W-L: What I know, What I want to learn, What I learned
- concrete manipulatives and experiences
- expository paragraph frames
- group summarizing
- visual imagery

This primary-grade emphasis on content-reading instruction again reflects the developmental nature of learning to read, as discussed in Chapter 1 along with Chall's Stages of Reading Development.

EXPOSITORY TEXT

Content reading ability is the degree to which a student can adequately comprehend and retain content or expository text. An adequate instructional and independent reading program does not ensure successful readers in content material.

Success in the regular literacy program does not automatically spell success in reading for content. Success in understanding any new content requires teachers to teach students necessary strategies and skills.

Students frequently struggle with content materials. A lack of knowledge about **expository text** is a chief reason for this difficulty (Cheek, Flippo, & Lindsey, 1997). More specific reasons include a lack of direct instruction in studying strategies and research skills, the difficulty of many content materials in terms of vocabulary and concepts, and inadequate transfer of skills from the basic reading program to content areas. In essence, students' general reading ability often does not predict how well they will do in various content areas. Evidence of this is not new, although its ramifications for instruction are still under investigation (Leal & Moss, 1999; Shores, 1943).

Camp (2000) presents an effective teaching technique to overcome the difficulty factors associated with content books. The teaching technique "Twin Texts" involves pairing fiction and nonfiction books on the same topic for instruction. The story structure of the fiction book is many times easier for students to comprehend. After first reading the fictional book on a topic and having an understanding of the material, the nonfiction book on the same topic is used to provide a deeper understanding. The author recommends that teachers use popular interactive teaching strategies such as K-W-L, graphic organizers, and DR-TA with both texts to increase student learning and motivation. Highlighting the advantages of this technique, Camp stated:

> Most students are familiar with the format of fiction trade books and with the way a story "sounds." It is often less difficult for teachers to teach content material using those familiar story structures. The many outstanding informational books now available for children can make content material come alive. Many of them use the conversational tone similar to that of fiction books. The use of Twin Texts is a viable method for both teaching and learning critical reading and thinking skills. (p. 400)

Organizational Structures

Students are generally more familiar with narrative writing, because most stories follow this organizational structure. Yet, students increasingly are expected to read and understand material presented in content textbooks. Most content texts are written in an expository style. While narrative materials follow a traditional story structure (including setting, theme, plot, and resolution), expository writing is organized differently. This structure is more compact, detailed, and explanatory in nature.

Meyer and Freedle (1984) identify five common expository text structures: (1) description, (2) collection, (3) causation, (4) problem-solution, and (5) comparison. Figure 10.1 describes each type of structure identified by Meyer and Freedle, giving a sample passage and clue words.

As a teacher of reading, you must realize that your students will not be familiar with these expository text structures. As a result, they probably will have trouble learning material presented in content subjects. Recent research supports a long-held belief that how well a text is written and how successfully readers recognize writing patterns affect student understanding (Tierney & Readence, 2000).

Readence, Bean, and Baldwin (1998) recommend an interactive technique for teaching text structure to students. The technique involves three steps: (1) *modeling*—using the think-aloud technique and showing students how a particular structure type is organized, (2) *recognition*—walking students through a particular text structure and ensuring that students can explain how a paragraph is organized, and (3) *production*—showing students a graphic organizer of a text and then asking students to produce or compose a particular text structure on their own through writing a passage themselves.

Readability

A possible explanation for problems in content subjects is the increased difficulty of the materials to be read. **Readability** is the approximate difficulty level of written material. The concept of readability is important for all teachers. Teachers should strive to match a book's readability with the students' instructional level. Students tend to learn the most from material that is neither too easy nor too difficult. Readability

STRUCTURE	DESCRIPTION*	SAMPLE PASSAGE	CLUE WORDS
Description	Specifies something about a topic or presents an attribute or setting for a topic.	The Summer Olympic Games are the biggest entertainment spectacles of modern times. Every four years they offer two weeks of non-stop pageantry and competition.	
Collection	A number of descriptions (specifics, attributes, or settings) presented together.	The Summer Olympics have so many different things to offer. First, there are many kinds of events: big shows like the opening and closing ceremonies, pure competitions like the races and games, and events that are partly artistic and partly competitive like the subjectively scored diving and gymnastics contests. There are old things and new things, like the classic track and field events staged in 1984 in the same stadium where they were held in 1932, and the almost bizarre sport of synchronized swimming, first presented in 1984.	*First, second, third, next, finally*
Causation	Elements grouped in time sequence (before and after) with a causative relationship (the earlier causes the later) specified.	There are several reasons why so many people attend the Olympic Games or watch them on television. The first Olympics were held in Greece more than 2,000 years ago. As a result of hearing the name "Olympics," seeing the torch and flame, and being reminded in ways of the ancient games, people feel that they are escaping the ordinariness of daily life. People like to identify with someone else's individual sacrifice and accomplishment, and thus an athlete's or even a team's hard-earned, well-deserved victory becomes a nation's victory. There are national medal counts and people watch so that they can see how their country is doing. Since the Olympics are staged only every four years and maybe only in a particular country once in a lifetime, people flock to even obscure events in order to be able to say "I was there."	*so that, thus, because of, as a result of, since, and so, in order to*

*Descriptions adapted from Meyer and Freedle, 1984, pp. 121–24.

continued

Figure 10.1 Expository text structures with sample passages and clue words.

STRUCTURE	DESCRIPTION*	SAMPLE PASSAGE	CLUE WORDS
Problem/solution	Includes a causative relation (between a problem and its causes) and a solution set, one element of which can break the link between the problem and its antecedent cause.	One problem with the modern Olympics is that they have gotten so big and so expensive to operate. A city or country often loses a lot of money by staging the games. A stadium, pools, and playing fields are built for the many events and housing is built for the athletes, but it is all used for only two weeks. In 1984, Los Angeles solved these problems by charging companies for permission to be official sponsors and by using many buildings that were already there. Companies like McDonald's paid a lot of money to be part of the Olympics. The Coliseum, where the 1932 Games were held, was used again and many colleges and universities in the area became playing and living sites.	*a problem is, a solution is, haved solved this problem by*
Comparison	Contains no element of time sequence or causality; organizes elements on the basis of their similarities and differences.	The modern Summer Olympics are really very unlike the ancient Olympic Games. Individual events are different. For example, there were no swimming races in the ancient Games, but there were chariot races. There were no women contestants and everyone competed in the nude. Of course the ancient and modern Olympics are also alike in many ways. Some events are the same, like the javelin and discus throws. Some people say that cheating, professionalism, and nationalism in the modern Games are a disgrace to the ancient Olympic tradition. But according to ancient Greek writers, there were many cases of cheating, nationalism, and professionalism in their Olympics too.	*different from, same as, alike similar to, resemble*

Figure 10.1 (continued)

Source: From L. M. McGee and D. J. Richgels, "Teaching Expository Text Structure to Elementary Students," *The Reading Teacher, 38* (April 1985), pp. 741–742. Reprinted with permission of the authors and the International Reading Association. Copyright by the International Reading Association. All rights reserved.

depends on factors inherent in the text (e.g., sentence structure, organizational pattern, physical presentation of the material, and vocabulary), the reader (knowledge of text structures, interest in the subject, and prior knowledge of a topic), and the teacher (the presentation). To provide effective instruction, teachers must judge the readability level of material.

Many readability formulas are available to judge difficulty of traditional text factors. Fry's readability formula (see Figure 10.2) is based on word and sentence length and is quick to use. Remember, however, that any readability formula will yield only an approximate, not an exact, level of difficulty. Indeed, using different readability formulas on the same material can yield different results. Remember, too, that readability varies within a given text.

Teachers should use a combination of a formula, personal knowledge of their students, and an informal appraisal of text characteristics to assess the suitability of a particular text. Zakaluk and Samuels (1988) recommend a broader method of predicting text difficulty, by collecting and assessing information about outside-the-head and inside-the-head factors. Outside-the-head factors include the traditional text factors of word difficulty, sentence length, and adjunct aids (such as study questions). Inside-the-head factors include facility in word recognition and knowledge of the topic.

In contrast to providing a designation of grade level for readability, the Cloze procedure for content material may indicate students' abilities to read a particular text. The Cloze procedure yields information indicating whether the material matches a student's instructional, independent, or frustration reading level. (See Chapter 11 for a description of the Cloze procedure.) This procedure can be used with a large group and can quickly indicate class and individual capabilities for reading a particular content text.

A new trend in the assessment of text difficulty, given the current use of literature and expository trade books for instruction, is the use of qualitative assessment. Chall, Bissex, Conard, and Harris-Sharples (1996) developed a qualitative method utilizing a matching procedure whereby one matches a text to a passage already scaled for comprehension difficulty. The scaled passages are in the major content areas of literature, science, and social studies. The authors state the advantages of the qualitative method below.

1. Offers and easy-to-use method for judging the difficulty of written texts, relying on qualitative judgments rather than on counting text features.
2. Presents to writers, teachers, and parents exemplars from literature, social studies, and science that can be read with comprehension at specific levels of proficiency.
3. Describes and illustrates changes in vocabulary, syntax, concepts, structure, and other features in materials that range in difficulty from a first grade level to a college graduate level.
4. Provides a reliable and valid method for estimating difficulty which compares favorably with expert teacher judgment of difficulty, student judgment of difficulty, and student reading comprehension. It also compares favorably with classic readability score—and at a fraction of the time.

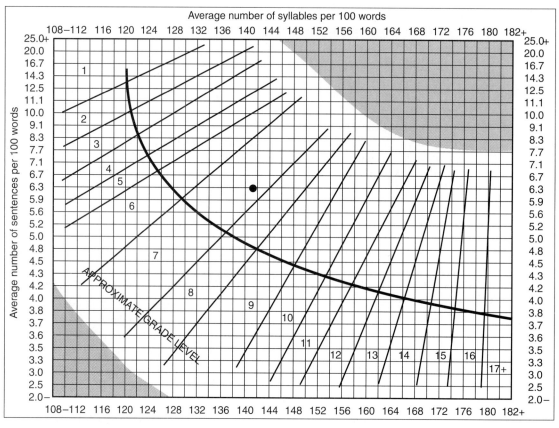

Figure 10.2   Graph for estimating readability—extended. (Note: This "extended graph" does not outmode or render the earlier (1968) version inoperative or inaccurate; it is an extension.)

5. The scales provide an easy-to-use introduction to reading development for beginning teachers, parents, and others interested in reading development from its beginnings to its most mature forms. (p. 4)

COMPONENTS OF CONTENT READING

Formal education has many goals, one of which is to help students become increasingly independent within the framework of the school setting. To achieve such independence, learners must master a number of related language skills. One important cluster of skills determines success in content reading. In schools dominated by basic skills, instruction often gives content skills mere lip service. Although current educational trends emphasize teaching basic skills and administering tests to show that a student is literate, teachers also need to emphasize skills that enable learners to acquire information on their own.

Expanded Directions for Working Readability Graph

1. Randomly select three sample passages and count out exactly 100 words each, beginning with the beginning of a sentence. Do count proper nouns, initializations, and numerals.

2. Count the number of sentences in the hundred words, estimating length of the fraction of the last sentence to the nearest one tenth.

3. Count the total number of syllables in the 100-word passage. If you don't have a hand counter available, an easy way is to simply put a mark above every syllable in each word, then when you get to the end of the passage, count the number of marks and add to 100. Small calculators can also be used as counters by pushing numeral 1, then pushing the + sign for each word or syllable when counting.

4. Enter on the graph the *average* sentence length and *average* number of syllables; plot dot where the two lines intersect. Area where dot is plotted will give you the approximate grade level.

5. If a great deal of variability is found in syllable count or sentence count, putting more samples into the average is desirable.

6. A word is defined as a group of symbols with a space on either side; thus, *Joe, IRA, 1945,* and *&* are each one word.

7. A syllable is defined as a phonetic syllable. Generally, there are as many syllables as vowel sounds. For example, *stopped* is one syllable and *wanted* is two syllables. When counting syllables for numerals and initializations, count one syllable for each symbol. For example, *1945* is four syllables, *IRA* is three syllables, and *&* is one syllable.

Figure 10.2   (continued)

Source: By Edward Fry. Reprinted from *The Journal of Reading,* December 1977. Reproduction permitted. No copyright.

The major components of teaching content reading are: (1) vocabulary development, (2) specific skills and strategies needed to read a chapter in a content subject, (3) study skills instruction, and (4) skills and strategies required for collecting, analyzing, and criticizing data.

Vocabulary Development

Curriculum materials in content subjects confront readers with an ever-increasing number of unknown and relatively difficult words and concepts. Students must know many new, more-difficult connotations for familiar words and must understand a large number of idiomatic and figurative expressions. The amount of required reading suddenly increases, and students must read and comprehend at a faster rate. They must also develop the flexibility to adjust their rate to both the difficulty level and the purpose.

Because of the rigid control of vocabulary in beginning reading materials, teachers frequently fail to arouse and maintain students' interest in content materials.

Encouraging parents to read content books with their children promotes comprehension, vocabulary growth, and fosters positive attitudes.

Content textbooks introduce so many difficult words and concepts that many students are frustrated and lost. In addition, content vocabulary differs from vocabulary in regular reading lessons in important ways. Armbruster and Nagy (1992) report that unlike vocabulary in regular reading lessons, content vocabulary is absolutely crucial for comprehension, usually represents unfamiliar concepts, and is usually related to other content vocabulary in the same chapter.

Understanding the meaning of specialized content words and concepts requires planned, systematic instruction. Nagy (1988), summarizing research on vocabulary development, concludes that effective vocabulary instruction to improve comprehension includes three properties: (1) integration (relating new words with known concepts and experiences), (2) repetition (sufficient practice to know words quickly while reading), and (3) meaningful use (interesting practice that results in the ability to use new words properly).

For integrating new words with known concepts and experiences in content reading, various visual aids (e.g., diagrams, flowcharts, outlines, maps, and time lines) are particularly useful. Semantic mapping (Johnson & Pearson, 1984) is a popular visual technique for showing how words relate to one another. To design a semantic map, lead a brainstorming session around a particular word or topic. After listing all the words that come to mind relating to the key word or topic on the

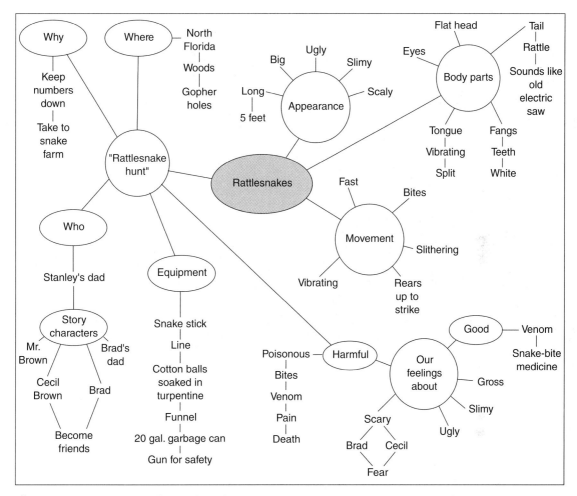

Figure 10.3 Group map for rattlesnakes.

Source: From J. E. Heimlich and S. D. Pittleman, *Semantic Mapping: Classroom Applications* (Newark, DE: International Reading Association, 1986), p. 28. Reprinted with permission of the authors and the International Reading Association. Copyright by the International Reading Association. All rights reserved.

board, group the words into meaningful categories. Finally, draw a semantic map and use it as a vehicle for discussion both before and after reading a portion of text. Figure 10.3 is a semantic map completed by sixth graders before reading a story about rattlesnakes (Heimlich & Pittleman, 1986).

Meaningful content-area reading requires students to understand new concepts continually, because this type of reading presents more difficulties per reading unit than does primary reading. One of the major problems in reading is the gap between students' store of meanings and the demands of the content reading matter. In addition, content reading contains many idiomatic expressions, abstract and figurative terms, and new connotations for familiar words. In the primary grades, even though they occur less frequently, the teacher's editions accompanying basal reader series point out these expressions. Workbooks provide instruction supplementing the reader series.

The shift to separate textbooks in the content areas reduces the emphasis on helping students with meaning difficulties—just when they need the most help. Teachers find that many students do not understand concepts even after the material has been assigned and covered in class. The following are examples of difficult concepts from fourth- and fifth-grade geography, science, and mathematics books:

- The native city is backward and ugly.
- Now, as in ancient times, the Mediterranean is a great connecting highway.
- The people who lived in fixed settlements made far greater progress than the nomads.
- Gradually the continent was opened. Another jewel had been added to the British crown.
- Business and industry were paralyzed.
- A belt of irrigated land stretches almost all the way along the coast.
- The shrinking world and new inventions have made this possible.
- Almost every farmer grows some cash crops besides food for his family.
- Ornithologists have examined the crops of many birds to find out what kind of food they eat.
- We can use a ruler to subtract fractions.

Studying Strategies

Understanding expository text depends largely upon knowledge and application of comprehension strategies to fulfill one's purpose in reading. Good readers, who are aware of what they are doing during their reading, can apply specific strategies and can monitor their progress.

Metacognition

The Literacy Dictionary (Harris & Hodges, 1995) defines **metacognition** as "awareness and knowledge of one's mental processes such that one can monitor, regulate, and direct them to a desired goal" (p. 153). Metacognitive awareness applied specifically to reading is "knowing when what one is reading makes sense by monitoring and controlling one's own comprehension" (p. 153). Good readers generate and monitor purposeful reading of text. In fulfillment of this purposeful reading, metacognition involves not only appropriate reading strategies but also awareness and control of these strategies while reading.

To comprehend content material, students must learn and strategically apply various studying strategies before, during, and after reading. Successful readers are strategic; that is, they know various reading strategies, consciously apply these reading strategies to the particular text at hand, and monitor their comprehension as they read. Conversely, poor readers are not strategic readers. Paris, Lipson, and Wilson (1994) state, "A large body of evidence reveals that poor readers do not skim, scan, reread, integrate information, plan ahead, take notes, make inferences, and so forth as often as skilled readers" (p. 795). Yet, students can become strategic readers through meaningful instruction and practice.

Before reading, include the following strategies:

- Review prior knowledge on the topic.
- Relate the new chapter to previous chapters.
- Relate the new material to personal experiences.
- Discuss key vocabulary and concepts.
- Read the introduction to create a proper mind-set.
- Predict what will be included in the text.
- Establish an overall purpose for reading the text.
- Review the pattern of the text to be read.

Teachers can accomplish the preceding strategies in various ways, including the following:

- *Explicit/direct instruction and thinking aloud.* Walk the students through an appropriate strategy by explaining it point-by-point or by modeling it. Following the direct explanation or modeling, afford sufficient practice in the strategy.
- *The advance organizer.* Provide students with a short written summary and highlight new vocabulary and concepts, background information, and main ideas. Advance organizers help students establish a correct mind-set before reading and aid them in establishing purposes for reading.
- *The structured overview.* This is similar to the advance organizer. Present a structured overview containing the key ideas of the chapter and their relationships in a visual format (usually a flowchart or a hierarchy, spoke, or pie chart). Discuss the key vocabulary words in the chapter before students read silently.
- *Semantic mapping.* This is a visual way to expand vocabulary knowledge and to show relationships among ideas (Heimlich & Pittleman, 1986). Used before reading, semantic mapping teaches new words and introduces relationships developed in the content chapter.

During reading, include the following strategies:

- Turn bold-print headings into questions to guide reading.
- Answer bold-print questions before moving on to the next section.
- Reread parts of the text that cannot be remembered (indicated by not being able to answer bold-print questions).
- Find the author's pattern.

Teachers can accomplish the preceding reading strategies in various ways. These include the following:

- *Study guides.* Study guides provide students with chapter questions to answer while reading and purposes for reading. The questions asked should balance literal, interpretive, and critical comprehension.
- *Explicit/direct instruction and thinking aloud.* Show students how to turn bold-print heads into questions using reporters' questions *(who, what, where, when, why* and *how).* If students cannot recall an answer after reading a section, explain to them that they should reread the section to answer their purpose-setting questions.

    ### *After reading, include the following strategies:*

- Check comprehension by answering the end-of-chapter questions.
- Assess the information conveyed and predict what will happen next.
- Summarize key points.
- Look back or reread parts of the text to understand particular points.

Teachers can accomplish the preceding postreading strategies in various ways. These include the following:

- *Study guides.* Lead a discussion of questions in the study guide.
- *Questioning and discussion.* Following silent reading, ask students to answer their purpose-setting questions. Ask a variety of comprehension questions at different levels of thinking.
- *Semantic map and/or structure overview.* Rework the map or structured overview utilized in the "before reading" step.
- *Cooperative grouping.* Design discussion or assignment groups, grouping students of different ability levels. Have each group complete the end-of-chapter activity together.

Writing to learn

Reading and writing are interdependent. As we have emphasized, reading is best learned through integration with the other language arts. Just as reading and writing are complementary and effective in the regular reading program, the combination yields impressive results in the content areas (Alvermann & Phelps, 1998). In the content areas, writing to learn should be an integral part of the instructional program. Combining reading and writing makes students more aware of text structure and helps them understand ideas better. Anderson (1984) states, "Writing . . . is a way to improve students' schemata, or structured knowledge of subjects encountered in the content areas . . . [and is] fundamental to comprehending, learning, and remembering concepts in stories and texts" (p. 243).

Writing should be an integral part of content-reading instruction beginning in kindergarten. Using shared experiences, student-dictated language-experience charts can be springboards for content learning and writing development. For example,

Study skills and being able to read content text with a specific purpose were important in the early 1800s. The partial page shown is from Daniel Adam's *Geography of the World*, 1830. Students reading the text were directed to questions the teacher would ask by the use of a superior *q*. Students were directed to ask themselves questions for each of the *q* symbols and come up with the appropriate answers.

GEOGRAPHY.

☞ The "Interrogative system" of teaching, has now become very general in almost every branch of school education. The introduction may be traced to the Scholar's Arithmetic, in 1801, many years before the appearance of Goldsmith and of Guy in our country. A further improvement in this system is here attempted, and instead of printing the question at length, which necessarily swells the book, a character (ᵍ) is introduced, intimating both to the Instructer, and the pupil, that a question is required, and this character is invariably placed BEFORE the word or words intended to ask the question, and to which the answer, FOUND BY READING THE SENTENCE, is to be a direct reply. For example, take the first sentence; the character is placed before the words "certain knowledge;" the question then is, Had the ancients any certain knowledge of the figure of the earth? The answer, from reading the sentence, is evident, No; or, They had not. Where the construction of the sentence suggests no particular form put the quest   What is said

THE WORLD.

THE ancients had no ᵍcertain knowledge of the figure of the earth. But later discoveries, both by astronomy and navigation, demonstrate the world we inhabit to be a large opaque globe or ball, nearly eight thousand ᵍmiles in diameter. In proof of this it is only necessary to notice, that various navigators have actually sailed around it. Of these, the ᵍfirst was Sir Francis Drake, who in 1580 completed the circumnavigation of the globe, after an absence of two years, ten months, and twenty days, from England, his native land.

Reprinted from *Old Textbooks* by John Nietz by permission of the University of Pittsburgh Press.

UPDATE

The superior *q* was in vogue more than 260 years ago, and today, the whole area of promoting a self-questioning, self-monitoring attitude while one reads is once again in style. Today, the new cognitive view of reading stresses interactive reading through the development of strategies students use themselves to understand, reason, and reflect on ideas in the text. As students make sense of the text, one strategy emphasized today is student-generated questions. Teachers of reading need to teach students specific ways to generate their own questions before, during, and after reading. Examples of questioning strategies recommended today include QAR, K-W-L, and reciprocal teaching.

students can summarize their understanding of content through writing (even invented spelling), illustrate their writing, and make individual or class books.

Teachers can integrate writing into content instruction in a number of ways. It is probably best to think of creative ways to incorporate writing during the prereading or postreading phases of a lesson. During the prereading portion, instruct students to write about a particular topic after reviewing their prior knowledge or brainstorming about their past experiences. Following guided silent reading, have students write to fulfill a number of purposes: to summarize main ideas, to classify information, to compare and contrast, and to predict future consequences.

Different approaches for different abilities

Invariably, classrooms use one content textbook for each subject and grade. This practice presents problems in accommodating differing student abilities. Because many students cannot read successfully in a particular text, teachers should understand the concept of readability and know how to measure a text's difficulty level. Teachers should teach and model reading and study skills to help students understand expository text. Finally, teachers should know various ways to tailor instruction to students who are unable to read a required text. Alternative instructional approaches that move away from reliance on a single text include providing different assignments, using multilevel content materials, providing meaningful oral reading, using educational media resources including literature, newspapers, magazines, and environmental print (such as brochures, advertisements, and junk mail), conducting small-group instruction, assigning library books of various difficulty levels for a particular topic, and incorporating the arts in instruction.

SQ3R

In addition to individual studying strategies, many students profit from learning a specific approach to reading content chapters. Reading a content chapter resembles following a road map: Students must learn how to get from point A to point B in the shortest, most meaningful way. The best-known systematized procedure for reading content chapters is SQ3R. Babineau (1997) developed an effective technique of teaching SQ3R along with cooperative learning groups.

This procedure applies many skills and strategies. In fact, many of the previously discussed studying strategies are part of SQ3R. Developed by Robinson (1961), **SQ3R** stands for "survey, question, read, recite, and review." Students need direct instruction and a great deal of practice in each step of the procedure.

Survey encourages students to get an overall picture of the chapter before reading it by looking at the title, introduction, main headings, illustrations, and end-of-chapter questions. *Question* helps students read with a purpose by turning each bold heading into questions. *Read* asks students to read each chapter section and to answer each purpose-setting question, keeping in mind the chapter organization and visual aids. *Recite* involves stopping periodically to answer the purpose-setting questions in one's own words. Students are encouraged to take notes during silent reading. *Review* instructs students to check their memory by reviewing their notes and reciting major points under each heading.

The steps we have asked you to follow so far in the text are a modification of this procedure. We recommend teaching the following method and practicing it with students.

1. Read the introduction.
2. Survey all visual aids in the chapter and read each bold heading.
3. Read the summary.
4. Study the questions at the end of the chapter.
5. Return to the beginning of the chapter and read.

Combination Strategies

In addition to teaching specific prereading, during reading, and postreading strategies, classroom teachers can promote metacognition and increased comprehension by teaching various combination strategy techniques. Certainly, the previously discussed guided reading plan and the directed reading-thinking activity (DR-TA) can be most effective applied in the content areas. The elements of the prereading step in guided reading (motivation, reviewing prior knowledge, background information, vocabulary, and purpose setting) help students read purposefully and learn specific content. Similar in purpose to guided reading, the directed reading-thinking activity directs students' thinking about the text to be read (Haggard, 1988; Stauffer, 1975). In the first step of the DR-TA, teachers introduce students to the material to be read and help them set their own purposes for reading by predicting what they think will be covered. Three additional combination teaching techniques to promote strategic comprehension are K-W-L, reciprocal teaching, and collaborative strategic reading (CSR). Each technique is explained in the following sections.

K-W-L

The K-W-L instructional strategy (Ogle, 1986) is designed to capitalize on students' knowledge of a topic before reading and to promote more active, strategic reading of text. The letters *K, W,* and *L* stand for the instructional steps of "assessing what I *Know,* determining what I *Want* to know, and checking what I *Learned* from my reading." Students use a worksheet to record their own responses to the three areas as the lesson progresses. In the first step, K, the teacher brainstorms with students what the students already know about the topic at hand. Next, the teacher helps students group what they know into categories. In the second step, W, the teacher guides the students to generate questions the students would like answered in their reading. In the last step, L, students write down what they learned from their reading. A sample K-W-L is presented in Figure 10.4.

Hurricanes		
K **(Known)**	**W** **(Want to know)**	**L** **(Learned)**
They are dangerous. They change directions. They bring rain and wind. You must get away from beaches. The eye is the center of the storm.	What is a category III storm? What is the difference between a tropical hurricane watch and a hurricane warning? What do you do during a hurricane if you are at home?	A category III storm has winds of 111–130 mph and a storm surge of 9–12 ft. A hurricane watch is an announcement for specific areas that hurricane conditions pose a threat to a coastal area. A hurricane warning is an announcement that winds of 74 mph or higher are expected in a specific coastal area within 24 hours. During a hurricane, stay indoors, stay away from windows and glass doors, and fill water containers with a week's supply of water.

Categories of Information

Types of hurricanes: _____

Terms to know: _____

Things to do: _____

Figure 10.4   Sample K-W-L worksheet on hurricanes.

Reciprocal teaching

Reciprocal teaching (Palincsar & Brown, 1986) is an effective technique to foster strategic reading that combines four separate strategies in a unique way. The technique involves the teacher initially modeling all of the cognitive strategies, followed by the students themselves gradually taking control over executing each strategy. The four strategies used in reciprocal teaching are:

- Predicting what the text will be about and thus setting purposes for reading
- Following silent reading of the text, asking questions about what was read and answering them
- Summarizing the text
- Clarifying any difficult parts or ideas by rereading portions of the text

After reading a portion of a story or chapter, the teacher models each of the four comprehension tasks to students. When students feel comfortable with the four tasks, the students themselves become the teacher and gradually assume full responsibility in subsequent stories or chapters. The teacher monitors the students' performance and provides feedback and encouragement.

Collaborative strategic reading

Collaborative strategic reading (CSR) (Klinger & Vaughn, 1999) is comprehension strategy designed to be used with expository text. This technique has proven to be effective with all students including students learning English as a second language. CSR combines grouping students in mixed ability cooperative groups and applying the following four strategies to reading text: (1) before reading strategy of reviewing prior knowledge and setting purposes (called "preview"), (2) monitoring one's reading during reading by using various fix-up strategies (called "click and clunk"), (3) stating the main ideas during reading (called "get the gist"), and (4) summarizing the text and generating questions to be answered (called "after reading"). The steps in CSR are:

1. The teacher explicitly teaches the four comprehension strategies to the entire class and models how the strategies are applied in reading.
2. Students gradually learn how to apply the four strategies and assume responsibility for using them.
3. Students are assigned to mixed-ability cooperative groups (four to five students).
4. Each student has a specified role in the group to ensure participation and collaboration—leader, clunk expert, gist expert, announcer, or encourager.
5. Students read the text and use "cue cards" that focus on the before reading, during reading, and after reading strategies while reading (see Figure 10.5).
6. The teacher acts as a facilitator by monitoring each group's progress.
7. Students record their ideas related to the four strategies in "CSR learning logs."
8. Follow-up activities (i.e., games, Venn diagrams, asking questions, and using dictionaries) are encouraged to enhance the learning of new vocabulary and important concepts.

Reading and Study Skills

Every instructional level presents its own challenges to teachers. The emphasis on separate textbooks in the various subject areas is a chief source of instructional problems. These books call for a high level of independent reading ability and special facility in a number of reading and study skills. Following is a listing of some of the major reading and **study skills** needed for comprehension in the various content subjects.

In math, the ability to

1. Use a slow and deliberate reading rate.
2. Master technical vocabulary and symbols.
3. Follow directions.

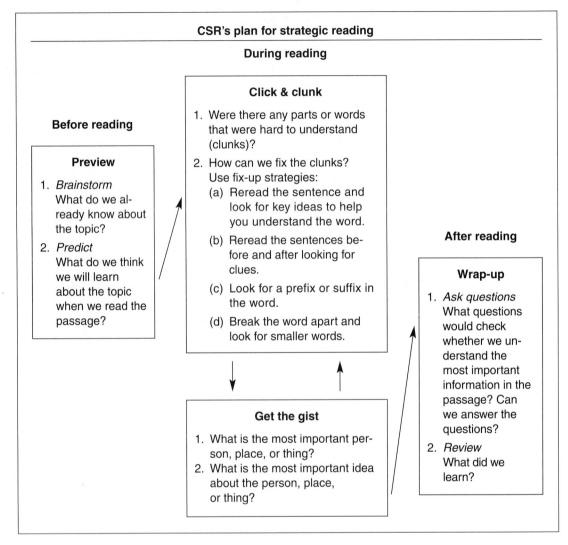

Figure 10.5   CSR's plan for strategic reading.

Source: From J. K. Klinger and S. Vaughn, "Promoting Reading Comprehension, Content Learning, and English Acquisition through Collaborative Strategic Reading (CSR)," *The Reading Teacher, 52* (April 1999), p. 740. Reprinted with permission of the authors and the International Reading Association. Copyright by the International Reading Association. All rights reserved.

In social studies, the ability to

1. Follow ideas and events in sequence.
2. Read maps, tables, time lines, and graphs.
3. Outline main ideas.
4. Follow directions.

5. Master a specialized vocabulary.
6. Use reference materials.
7. Identify and use the author's organizational pattern.
8. Summarize key ideas.
9. Identify propaganda techniques.
10. Identify facts versus opinions.

In science, the ability to

1. Follow sequence.
2. Follow directions.
3. Classify details and main ideas.
4. Interpret graphic material visually.
5. Identify and use the author's organizational pattern.
6. Master a specialized vocabulary.
7. Summarize key ideas.

Teachers and other educators constantly stress teaching various facets of reading concurrently with subject matter. Even in departmentalized schools, with one teacher responsible for social studies, another for science, another for mathematics, and so forth, the importance of integrating reading and the content subjects emerges in the slogan "Every teacher is a teacher of reading."

New teaching materials are helping both teacher and students meet the demands of content reading. For example, new basal programs integrate content knowledge, strategies, and skills into their total program. New basal teacher's manuals include lesson suggestions for teachers as well as practice materials in a variety of forms, including both narrative and expository literature.

The nature of reading materials and the great difference in students' instructional needs make it logical and perhaps even essential to relate some reading instruction to social studies, science, literature, mathematics, and other subject areas. This very point was emphasized in *Becoming a Nation of Readers* (Anderson, Hiebert, Scott, & Wilkinson, 1985). The authors state, "The most logical place for instruction in most reading and thinking strategies is in social studies and science rather than in separate lessons about reading. The reason is that the strategies are useful mainly when the student is grappling with important but unfamiliar content" (p. 73).

Each reading skill applied in a content area should be taught in a systematic, direct fashion. Teachers must not assume that students already know and can apply various reading skills in content areas.

A major problem undermining mastery of reading and study skills is insufficient attention to these skills in both teaching and practice. To properly emphasize teaching of reading and study skills, teachers should use the explicit/direct instructional model and practice these skills primarily in the content areas. Instruction in connection with content subjects has many advantages, including a text organization, a functional setting, and motivation. Figure 10.6 presents a lesson on sequence of events using explicit/direct instruction.

Intended Learning Outcome
Students will list events described in a newspaper article in sequential order.

Past Learning
Students understand that being able to arrange events and ideas in sequential order closely relates to the ability to comprehend a story.

Students are aware that events occurring in sequential order can be related to each other to bring meaning to a story.

Building Background
Review the importance of sequencing events in a story. List two or three events on the chalkboard that are from a story with which students are familiar. Ask students to identify additional events by telling you what key words and phrases helped them know when things happened in the story. Call on various students to give their answers. Write the responses on the chalkboard and discuss common key words and phrases that students were able to recall. These responses might include the following:

then	last
now	event
today	after a while
first	the next day
second	only yesterday

Increase students' engagement and attention by telling them that these key words and phrases will help them complete the activity at the end of this lesson. Describe briefly what that activity will be and stress the idea that you know they will be successful with the task.

Teacher-Directed Instruction
Provide students with a written list of questions that they should focus on as they read the story you will provide. Display a newspaper article on the overhead projector and have students read it silently. After reading, engage students in a discussion by asking such questions as the following:

> What is the first thing that happened in this story?
>
> Which events in this news story are the important ones to list in order?
>
> How could we summarize in sequential order the events that occurred?

Remind them that these questions focus on a sequence of events and set their purpose for reading. Discuss the students' responses, then write them in sentence form on the chalkboard and number them.

Independent Student Practice
Allow each student to choose one of two or three newspaper articles that you have selected for this seat-work activity. Carefully select articles that emphasize sequential order. Instruct students to read the newspaper article and write in numerical order the major events as they happened. After all the students have completed the activity, they can compare their lists.

Ongoing Diagnosis
Evaluate students' ability to sequence events of the newspaper article. Discuss with students why they identified specific events for sequencing.

Modifying Instruction
This activity can be extended, using the same procedure, by providing students with two or more articles to sequence. Difficulty level depends on the selection of reading material. To maximize students' success, the material should clearly contain events that can be sequenced and the content of the articles should contain information with which students are familiar.

Figure 10.6 Explicit/direct instruction lesson.

Source: From *Teaching Reading: Diagnosis, Direct Instruction, and Practice,* Second Edition, by W. H. Rupley & T. R. Blair, 1990, Upper Saddle River, NJ: Merrill/Prentice Hall. Copyright 1990 by Pearson Education. Reprinted by permission of Pearson Education, Inc., Upper Saddle River, NJ 07458.

Transfer

Student difficulty in content materials may result from the absence of interesting, varied practice. Furthermore, students do not automatically transfer skills to content materials. For example, students taught how to interpret a diagram in science require additional practice in a variety of situations before they can transfer this skill to their reading of mathematics or social studies materials. Following are examples of ways to encourage transferring the skill of interpreting a diagram:

- Bring in supplemental materials containing diagrams of topics already studied. Ask students appropriate questions about each diagram, or allow individuals to assume the role of the teacher and explain the diagram to the rest of the class.
- Have students make their own diagram on a topic of their choice. Make certain each diagram is labeled properly. Ask students to construct a series of questions concerning their diagrams.

Teachers can use numerous kinds of meaningful practice to promote transfer of a particular skill. Teachers must be aware of this need and provide the necessary time and opportunity to ensure the transfer.

Collecting, Analyzing, and Criticizing Data

To find answers in varied reading materials, students must understand and use all available aids. In other words, knowing how to use a book is a prerequisite for intelligent use of supplementary reading materials in the subject areas or in any unit of work. In the intermediate grades, study skills grow more important, reflecting the nature and variety of the materials used and the fact that supervision is not always readily available. Although development of study skills requires reading ability, this ability in itself does not ensure that students have mastered the study skills.

During the past few years, the availability of books, computers, professional journals, and other printed matter has expanded tremendously. The past three decades have seen such a dramatic advance in knowledge that this period has been labeled the "knowledge explosion." Competency in any given field has taken on new meaning, and educational methods, of necessity, have changed radically to adapt to this new challenge.

No single textbook or even series of texts can completely cover a subject. The time lag between research, publication, and the adoption of textbooks causes inadequacies in even the most recent texts. To address this situation, good teachers have always provided supplementary reading materials. Today, however, providing a wide array of supplementary materials is not only desirable, but necessary. Thus, learners need study skills more now than ever, but the school's respect for these skills and its ability to teach them effectively have declined.

Inclusion Strategies

Strategies for Students with Visual and Hearing Impairments

As you know, success in the regular reading program does not automatically spell success in reading in the content areas. This is true for all students. However, teachers must make adjustments for students with special needs in the content areas. The content subjects of mathematics, science, and social studies pose literacy difficulties especially for students with visual and hearing disabilities. When possible, pair students with and without impairments to work together on an assignment. In addition to using the instructional techniques described in this chapter to meet students' needs, one must be conscious of the physical environment of the classroom itself. Seating students with special needs near the chalkboard, computer, overhead screen, or activity centers and near doors will provide for easy movement and help eliminate physical barriers for completing assignments. Audiotaping of content chapters is beneficial for students with visual impairments, as well as using the many visual formats discussed throughout this text, including pictures, videotapes, semantic maps, webs, K-W-L worksheets, time lines, graphs, diagrams, and charts. Also, captioned films and filmstrips aid students with hearing impairments. Multimedia CD-ROM computer programs are effective with all students, especially students with special needs. In addition, the use of the overhead projector can be beneficial for all students. Teachers can put outlines of chapters, write pre-, during-, and after-reading questions, and write page-by-page study guides on overhead transparencies. Use verbal directions and explanations for students with visual impairments as you interact with the class. Realia (i.e., actual objects) and hands-on activities are especially helpful. For example, in social studies, the use of braille globes, maps, and atlases and models of landforms to promote the use of the tactile mode of learning is effective for students with visual impairments. In introducing science vocabulary and concepts, use objects that students can hold and manipulate. In both science and mathematics, the use of manipulatives to reinforce concepts is effective. Your goal of improving all your students' literacy abilities is greatly enhanced when you are sensitive to the needs of exceptional students and adapt your instruction to meet student needs.

Using books

In teaching any study skill, the teacher at each grade level must build on what students already know. To do this, first the teacher must determine each student's ability level. A good place to begin is with the textbook adopted for a given course. Teachers can assess their students' ability to understand the text and their knowledge of specific study skills and their application.

Exercises that foster such growth are easy to devise. The major concern is how to use exercise materials in relation to the goals to be achieved. Some important learnings deal with the mechanics of learning—how to use a card catalog, where to look in an encyclopedia, when an appendix or glossary might be useful, and what is likely to be found in an appendix or glossary.

Written exercises are often used to help students understand the function of an index, table of contents, or appendix. It is common to find students who can work out correct solutions to workbook problems consisting of sample lines from an index but who still do not know how to get help from a real index. One of the best ways to teach children how to use a book effectively is to design a learning situation around a textbook they will be using throughout the year. A social studies, health, or other text can provide ample opportunities for teaching the functions of the table of contents, charts, indexes, and appendices. The text the student is using will give him or her something concrete to return to when in doubt. Skills learned in using one text should transfer more readily to books in other areas, provided there is teacher direction and guidance.

Teachers frequently fail to detect student deficiencies in using a table of contents, index, glossary, and appendix, so they do not teach these skills. Too often, they assume that these basic skills have been taught or are being taught elsewhere. For example, as an outcome of an inservice program, one group of teachers agreed to build a one-page testing and teaching exercise consisting of 15 to 20 questions to measure students' skills in using the parts of a book. The exercise was to be specifically applicable to the textbook the students were using in one of their courses. Although students had used the books for nearly 3 months, few were able to complete the exercise perfectly. The teachers discovered glaring deficiencies and individual differences in students' ability to use these reader aids. In one class, students took from 6 to 22 minutes to do the "book-mining" exercise, with some students unable to complete the task.

Exercises such as that presented in Figure 10.7 may be used initially with an entire class and can serve as diagnostic instruments. Observant teachers will note which students have difficulty and what their problems are. Those findings should help them teach small groups and individual students the skills they need along with general concepts. This exercise was constructed for use with a sixth-grade social studies text.

The exercise shown in Figure 10.7 teaches a number of facts about the book. Question 1 takes the readers to the table of contents and requires them to associate their home state with part of a larger geographical region of the United States. Question 2 calls attention to a 16-page atlas; the next question focuses on a second, highly specialized table of contents dealing exclusively with maps.

Questions 4 through 8 deal with areas in which the index may be helpful. The reader must locate pictures using key words and must be prepared to look under different headings. Topics may be listed as subheads under a more general heading. Questions 9 through 11 deal with information about pronunciation and meanings of difficult words and emphasize that these aids are divided between the index and glossary.

Students sometimes fail to realize that most reference books and textbooks include a number of reader aids. Lack of familiarity with or inclination to use these aids inhibits students from optimizing their use of books. Although students need these skills, they do not always recognize their value.

HOW TO USE A BOOK

1. The region in which we live is discussed under the heading _____

_____.

2. The last 16 pages in the book are called an *atlas.* Looking at these pages, can you define *atlas?* _____

_____

_____

3. On what page can you find a listing of all maps, graphs, and diagrams found in the book? _____

4. Does the book contain a picture of Wonder Lake? How did you go about answering this question? _____

5. Is there a picture of the Grand Coulee Dam in the text? _____

_____

6. Under what heading must you look to find it? _____

_____

7. In the index, there is a main heading entitled "Exploration." What six subheadings are found under it? _____

_____

_____

8. The book contains a double-page map called "Main Air Routes in the U.S." There is no "Main Air Routes" heading in the index. How can you find this map? _____

_____

_____

9. There are two sections of the book that provide the pronunciation of difficult words. These are _____ and _____.

10. The pronunciation of the following words is provided in the _____.

_____. In the blank spaces, show the pronunciation and page number where the word is found.

Shoshone _____ Page _____

Commanche _____ Page _____

Fort Duquesne _____ Page _____

11. A particular page contains the definition of difficult words used throughout the book. That page is called the _____.

Figure 10.7 A study skill assignment and diagnostic test.

AID	INFORMATION
Title Page	The main title and possibly a subtitle. (The latter may set forth the limitations and narrow the topic.) The name of the author and where the book was published.
Table of Contents	Chapter titles possibly followed by the major topics discussed in each chapter. Is the book divided into major parts (I, II, III)? What are these? The length of the chapters gives a hint to thoroughness of the treatment.
Preface	To whom does the author address the book? What is the author's stated purpose? What new features does the author stress? What unique features does the author believe are found in the book?
List of Illustrations	The title, item, and page where it can be found.
Index	The major topics in alphabetical order; minor topics under each heading; key phrases, cross-references, photographs, drawings, charts, and tables.
Glossary	Difficult or specialized terms are presented in alphabetical order with a definition.
Appendix	An organized body of facts related to the subject under consideration. For example, in a geography book the appendix may give the areas of states or nations, populations, state and national capitals, the extent of manufacturing, exports, imports, and mineral deposits.

Figure 10.8   Typical book aids for the reader.

One purpose may require students to skim the table of contents, while another demands that they read it critically. Comparing different books discloses that a table of contents may consist exclusively of chapter titles, similar to an outline composed of nothing but major topics. In some books, chapter titles precede a number of topics in their discussion order. Students may note that this is essentially a modified index containing only major headings in chronological order. In contrast, the index is in alphabetical order, dealing with narrower topics and cutting across chapters.

Every student should learn that (1) parts of the book are deliberately designed as aids, (2) these are valuable and are used profitably by efficient readers, and (3) the different parts of a book have definite purposes. Efficient readers decide instantly where to go for specific types of help. To do so, they must know what type of information each section contains, where the various aids are, and how to use each effectively. Once learned, this knowledge can be transferred and applied to any book. Figure 10.8 is an abbreviated treatment of what a reader might expect to gain from the aids found in most books.

Using the library

Effective use of library resources may well be one of the most underrated and undertaught skills in the entire school program. The library is where students read and receive guidance in both the use of books and research techniques. Students at all grade levels need the experience of frequent contact with a good school library.

Some teachers use the library effectively themselves but do not assume responsibility for teaching students to do so. On the other hand, a number of teachers make little personal use of library facilities.

At one school we visited, the librarian and principal believed that a substantial portion of the teaching staff seldom used the library for personal reasons. They also found that students seemed less inclined to turn to the library for these teachers' classes. The school incorporated a one-hour library unit into its total inservice program. Teachers were each relieved of their regularly scheduled duties to spend an hour in conference with the librarian. The librarian discussed and pointed out resources directly related to the teachers' various subjects, locating pamphlets, bound volumes, pertinent books, government documents, current magazines, and the like. The librarian also suggested ways to help the faculty members and students. The attitudes of a number of the teachers changed markedly after this experience. Some teachers visited the library more frequently, spent more time there, and checked out more materials. In addition, students in these teachers' courses began to use the library much more effectively.

It is generally conceded that teaching library usage is difficult in a classroom setting removed from the library materials themselves. However, students can learn important points about the library prior to a library visit. Several teachers in one school built a model card catalog drawer using a box for 3-by-5-inch index cards and compiled approximately 100 author cards ranging from *A* through *Z*. The teachers used this model in various classrooms, particularly in working with individual students who were not yet competent in using the card catalog. Another useful teaching device was a library checklist that teachers and the librarian devised. The list consisted of 8 or 10 specific tasks for the students to perform with teacher direction. Examples included the following:

1. Find the book *King of the Wind* by Marguerite Henry.

2. **a.** Who is the author of the book *A Child's History of Art?* _____

   _____

   b. What is the call number of this book? _____

   c. Fill out a library card for this book. _____

3. Where are the bound volumes of *My Weekly Reader* located? _____

   _____

These items provided guided practice in using title and author cards, locating books and journals on the shelves, and filling out library request cards properly. Other tasks covered specific information about the library.

To use this checklist technique effectively, small groups or individual students go to the library at specific times. The librarian briefly demonstrates and explains how to use certain facilities in the library. Each student then receives a checklist of tasks, which the librarian reviews briefly to ensure that students understand them. Such tasks should vary according to grade level and individual student needs.

Using technology

Most elementary schools have computer access for students to search various topics on-line and to use electronic reference works. To know and be able to efficiently use the skills of gathering appropriate information, organizing it, and evaluating its content—whether with real books or on the computer—requires explicit, sequential instruction and practice beginning in the primary grades. Computer software programs labeled databases, which are programs that allow for information storage and retrieval, permit students to perform research projects involving a host of comprehension and reference strategies. Collecting and analyzing information requires students to be able to use the Internet, encyclopedia, maps, thesauruses, and other sources of information. Many libraries have computer databases for searching topics (as opposed to the traditional card catalog) and, of course, electronic reference works such as encyclopedias and thesauruses are available on the Internet. The following Internet sites offer on-line reference materials themselves and an array of instructional suggestions for teaching and using reference skills and the synthesizing process:

http://www.cord.edu/dept/curric/researchprocess.htm
Research Process for Elementary Students
A site from Concordia College in Minnesota that directs students and parents on how to research effectively. Includes a sample bibliography form and sample ways to research topics.

http://www.thesaurus.com/Thesaurus.com
Resource for finding the definitions and synonyms of words. Also provides games and writing resources.

http://www.iss.stthomas.edu/studyguides/Study Guides and Strategies
Site for teachers, parents, and students. Provides information on ways to improve and apply study and test-taking skills. Also includes assessment and motivation techniques.

http://www.factmonster.com/Fact Monster
This site includes information on facts from across the board. Includes a search engine to help you find what you need. Includes information that you could attain from an atlas, an almanac, a dictionary, or encyclopedia. Teacher and student friendly. Includes a section for students to take polls, play games, and research subjects.

http://www.yahooligans.com/content/ka/Yahooligans! The Web Guide for Kids
Site for helping students find interesting information about a subject. Includes a guide for parents and teachers to help narrow down searches.

http://sunsite.berkeley.edu/KidsClick!/KidsClick!
A web search tool for kids, made by librarians.

http://www.EnchantedLearning.com/Dictionary.html
Little Explorers by Enchanted Learning Software
An on-line dictionary/encyclopedia for primary students. Allows students to study a specific topic with ease and excitement. Contains many pictures and colorful images that are easy to follow and understand.

http://school.discovery.com/schrockguide/reference.html
Kathy Schrock's Guide for Educators
Includes information on how students can research as well as how to present their research in the form of papers and projects.

http://www.ipl.org/youth/
The Internet Public Library Youth Division

http://www.night.net/kids/Not Just for Kids!!
A site for primary students looking for information about a certain topic.

http://www.geocities.com/EnchantedForest/Tower/1217/
4th and 5th Grade Student Research Resources
Site listing links to help students and teachers find effective ways to study, write essays, structuring essays, transitions, thesis statements, and editing tips.

http://www.hatboro-horsham.org/officeofelementaryeducation/
Elem_Curriculum_Guides/Elem_Curriculum_Guide_Studyskl.htm
A collection of study skills and how teachers can incorporate them into their classroom and assignments.

http://www.itools.com/research-it/Research-It!!
A list of research tools including dictionaries, a thesaurus, and geographical tools.

SUMMARY

Content reading presents many challenges to both students and teachers. To be successful in reading content materials, readers must know the characteristics and demands of expository text. To maximize student understanding, teachers must understand the concept of readability and factors that determine the difficulty of content material. To facilitate successful reading of expository text, teachers should actively teach and guide student involvement in (1) content-reading vocabulary, (2) studying strategies to employ before, during, and after reading, (3) reading and study skills, and (4) skills and strategies for collecting, analyzing, and criticizing data. Skills in these four areas should be taught in a direct fashion integrated into the curriculum. Following instruction, an abundance of varied and interesting practice will help ensure that students transfer these skills automatically to expository text.

YOUR POINT OF VIEW

Discussion Questions

1. Why is it possible that certain students may be proficient readers in science and also be incompetent readers in social studies?
2. The statement "Every teacher should be a teacher of reading" was first made more than 50 years ago. Why do you think it has not become a reality?
3. With regard to the studying strategies discussed in the chapter, how do teacher and student behaviors change before, during, and after reading strategies?

Take a Stand For or Against

1. Reading skills pertinent to specific content areas should be exclusively taught by content teachers.
2. The organizational structure of classrooms prohibits individualized instruction in the content areas.

Field-Based Assignments

1. Read the article by Hadaway and Young, "Content Literacy and Language Learning: Instructional Decisions," in *The Reading Teacher* (Volume 47, pp. 522–527, 1994). Design a Venn diagram, an H-map, or card sort for use in your classroom. Following your lesson, critique and reflect on its usefulness with one of your classmates.
2. Using the following questions, interview six students concerning their exposure to content reading instruction. Summarize your findings and share them with the class.
   Have you been taught

   - a study skill method for reading a content chapter in science or social studies?
   - the different types of maps, charts, and graphs?
   - how to use an index, atlas, and encyclopedia?
   - how to outline a chapter?
   - how to summarize a chapter?
   - how to skim a chapter for main ideas?
   - how to scan a chapter for a specific fact?

Portfolio Entry

Reflect on how you were taught social studies and science in your elementary school years. Compare your recollections with the way in which social studies and science are taught today and described in this chapter. What are the similarities and differences? Is it easier to teach these content areas today? Why or why not? Write your findings and feelings for your portfolio.

BIBLIOGRAPHY

Alvermann, D. E., & Phelps, S. F. (1998). *Content reading and literacy* (2nd ed.). Boston: Allyn & Bacon.

Anderson, R. C. (1984). Role of the reader's schema in comprehension, learning, and memory. In R. C. Anderson, J. Osborn, & R. J. Tierney (Eds.), *Learning to read in American schools: Basal readers and content texts.* (pp. 243–257). Hillsdale, NJ: Lawrence Erlbaum Associates.

Anderson, R. C., Hiebert, E. H., Scott, J. A., & Wilkinson, I. (1985). *Becoming a nation of readers: The report of the Commission on Reading.* Washington, DC: National Institute of Education.

Armbruster, B. B., & Nagy, W. E. (1992). Vocabulary in content area lessons. *The Reading Teacher, 45,* 550–551.

Babineau, T. L. (1997). Teaching the SQ3R procedure with cooperative learning. In R. F. Flippo, (Ed.), *Reading assessment and instruction: A qualitative approach* (pp. 284–285). Orlando, FL: Holt, Rinehart & Winston.

Camp, D. (2000). It takes two: Teaching with twin texts of fact and fiction. *The Reading Teacher, 53,* 400–408.

Chall, J. S., Bissex, G. L., Conard, S. S., & Harris-Sharples, S. (1996). *Qualitative assessment of text difficulty: A practical guide for teachers and writers.* Cambridge, MA: Brookline Books.

Cheek, E. H., Flippo, R. F., & Lindsey, J. D. (1997). *Reading for success in elementary schools.* Dubuque, IA: Brown & Benchmark.

Farris, P. J., & Fuhler, C. J. (1994). Developing social studies concepts through picture books. *The Reading Teacher, 47,* 380–387.

Hadaway, N. L., & Young, T. A. (1994). Content literacy and language learning: Instructional decisions. *The Reading Teacher, 47,* 522–527.

Haggard, M. R. (1988). Developing critical thinking with the directed reading-thinking activity. *The Reading Teacher, 41,* 526–535.

Harris, T. L., & Hodges, R. E. (Eds.). 1995. *The literacy dictionary.* Newark, DE: International Reading Association.

Heimlich, J. E., & Pittleman, S. D. (1986). *Semantic mapping: Classroom applications.* Newark, DE: International Reading Association.

Johnson, D. D., & Pearson, P. D. (1984). *Teaching reading vocabulary* (2nd ed.). New York: Holt, Rinehart & Winston.

Klinger, J. K., & Vaughn, S. (1999). Promoting reading comprehension, content learning, and English acquisition through Collaborative Strategic Reading (CSR). *The Reading Teacher, 52,* 738–747.

Leal, D., & Moss, B. (1999). Encounters with information text: Perceptions and insights from four gifted readers. *Reading Horizons, 40,* 15–22.

Meyer, B. J. F., & Freedle, R. O. (1984). Effects of discourse type of recall. *American Educational Research Journal, 21,* 121–143.

Nagy, W. E. (1988). *Teaching vocabulary to improve reading comprehension.* Urbana, IL: ERIC Clearinghouse on Reading and Communication Skills and Newark, DE: International Reading Association.

Ogle, D. M. (1986). K-W-L: A teaching model that develops active reading of expository text. *The Reading Teacher, 39,* 564–570.

Olson, M. W., and Gee, T. C. (1991). Content reading instruction in the primary grades: Perceptions and strategies. *The Reading Teacher, 45,* 298–307.

Palincsar, A. S., & Brown, A. L. (1984). Reciprocal teaching of comprehension-fostering and comprehension-monitoring activities. *Cognition and Instruction I,* 117–175.

Palincsar, A. S., & Brown, A. L. (1986). Interactive teaching to promote independent learning from text. *The Reading Teacher, 39,* 771–777.

Paris, S. G., Lipson, M. Y., & Wilson, K. K. (1994). Becoming a strategic reader. In R. B. Ruddell, M. R. Ruddell, & H. Singer (Eds.), *Theoretical models and process of reading* (4th ed., pp. 788–810). Newark, DE: International Reading Association.

Readence, J. E., Bean, T. W., & Baldwin, R. S. (1998). *Content area reading: An integrated approach.* Dubuque, IA: Kendall/Hunt.

Richardson, J. S., & Morgan, R. F. (2000). *Reading to learn in the content areas* (4th ed.). Belmont, CA: Wadworth.

Robinson, F. P. (1961). *Effective study* (rev. ed.). New York: Harper & Row.

Shores, J. (1943). Skills related to the ability to read history and science. *Journal of Educational Research, 36,* 584–594.

Stauffer, R. (1975). *Directing the reading-thinking process.* New York: Harper & Row.

Tierney, R. J., & Readence, J. E. (2000). *Reading strategies and practices: A compendium* (5th ed.). Boston: Allyn & Bacon.

Walmsley, S. A., & Allington, R. L. (1995). Redefining and reforming instructional support programs for at-risk students. In R. L. Allington & S. A. Walmsley (Eds.), *No quick fix: Rethinking literacy programs in America's schools* (pp. 19–44). New York: Teachers College Press.

Zakaluk, B. L., & Samuels, S. J. (1988). Toward a new approach to predicting text comprehensibility. In B. L. Zakaluk & S. J. Samuels (Eds.), *Readability: Its past, present, and future.* Newark, DE: International Reading Association.

11

Literacy Assessment

Chapter Outline

Meeting Individual Needs
    Differentiated Instruction
    Forms of Assessment

Standardized Tests
    Typical Features
    Norm-Referenced Tests
    Criterion-Referenced Tests
    Diagnostic Tests
    Cautions About Standardized Tests

Informal Assessment
    Teacher Observation/Kid Watching
    Assessment Materials That Accompany
    Published Reading Materials
    Informal Reading Inventories
    Running Records
    Cloze Procedure
    Authentic Assessment/Performance-Based
    Assessment
    Rubrics
    Anecdotal Records
    Response Journals
    Portfolios

For the Reader

The primary purpose for the use of literacy assessment is to obtain information about students' reading and writing abilities in order to design and improve the quality of literacy instruction. In practice, however, some schools and teachers believe that testing programs per se have little educational value. Sometimes testing becomes an end in itself rather than a basis for instruction. In some communities, a metal filing cabinet with a folder for each student represents evidence of good practices. This phenomenon suggests that some teachers have forgotten that assessment alone has no beneficial effect on students. The importance of assessment is to help design instruction based on students' literacy needs. As you read this chapter, focus on how to assess students' reading and writing and how to use this information in planning and evaluating your instruction.

Key Ideas

- Ongoing assessment of students' literacy development is used to adjust instruction to meet students' needs.

- Students' reading and writing abilities can be assessed through the use of (1) norm-referenced tests, (2) criterion-referenced tests, (3) placement tests, (4) informal reading inventories (IRIs), (5) teacher-developed procedures, and (6) authentic assessment.

- Standardized reading tests only sample students' reading (and sometimes writing) behaviors and provide only a small piece of a much larger picture.

- Informal and teacher-developed procedures are valuable because they use assessment strategies that are in line with the classroom instruction.

- An effective reading teacher interacts with students as they engage in reading and writing to assess the processes the students use.

MEETING INDIVIDUAL NEEDS

It is important to remember that assessment alone cannot change the profile of the learner, but it can have a direct affect on the method of instructional delivery. The (International Reading Association, 1994) point out that the fundamental purpose of assessment is to improve teaching and learning. Ongoing assessment of students' reading and writing development forms the foundation for planning both reading and writing instruction and determining its effectiveness. Information about students' literacy strengths and weaknesses allows teachers to select instructional strategies and materials in relation to students' needs. The key here is not simply gathering information about students' reading and writing, but determining how to use the information to optimize growth for each student (Ivey & Broaddus, 2000).

Assessment is a combination of procedures and strategies that is intended to provide the teacher with a sample of students' reading and writing that will form the foundation for instruction. The importance of understanding that there are many pieces to assessment is necessary because many states are requiring assessment of reading in the early grades. For example, Texas and Arkansas require that schools select and use assessment instruments to determine students' capabilities in areas such as phonemic awareness, alphabetic knowledge, phonics, and reading comprehension. Texas and Arkansas provide a list of recommended assessment instruments and encourage the schools to select from that list; however, schools may either select different assessment instruments or develop their own. There is a movement nationwide to legislate assessment and tests in reading and use the results to make decisions about student retention and school funding. Teachers must continue to be effective and ensure that they help students to do well on such assessments and tests (Worthy & Hoffman, 2000). Therefore, assessment in reading and writing should be an ongoing and integral part of teaching reading and writing that informs the students and the teacher about the quality and effectiveness of the instructional program.

Differentiated Instruction

Students at any given grade level show great differences in their literacy skills and abilities. Some of them read and write at a level considerably below their grade-level placement, while others have advanced literacy capabilities. Figure 11.1 illustrates the overlap between grades and the range of abilities found at the primary level.

These facts, which apply to practically every classroom, emphasize the need for differentiated instruction. One criterion that distinguishes excellent literacy programs from others is the degree to which they accommodate individual needs. Teachers must be alert to differences among students in order to follow sound teaching principles. Use of a variety of assessments can help teachers determine needs and plan instruction for students whose needs vary considerably. Assessment should be ongoing, because students change rapidly. An assessment conducted in Septem-

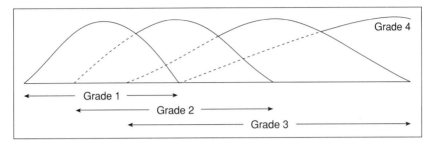

Figure 11.1 Graphic representation of reading abilities in the primary grades. Note that the range of abilities increases at each succeeding grade level.

ber may be followed by a student having a breakthrough in some vital skill or by a failure to understand some new step in reading and writing. In either case, the earlier assessment is obsolete.

Forms of Assessment

Assessment of literacy strengths and weaknesses can take a variety of forms, including standardized tests, informal tests, observation, portfolios, and interaction with learning tasks and activities. However, the most prevalent form of assessment stems from the daily instruction delivered in the classroom. During this informal on-the-spot assessment, the teacher reflects and evaluates how the lesson was received by the students and makes the appropriate adjustments for the next lesson.

STANDARDIZED TESTS

Assessment comes in many different forms, has many different purposes, and is used at many different levels. Standardized tests are one of the most formal measures of assessment and serve several educational purposes, which may not always be clear to the classroom teacher.

Standardized tests sample students' reading in a controlled, systematic fashion. Procedures for administering, scoring, and interpreting each test are determined under controlled experimental conditions. These procedures are usually explained in a manual accompanying the test.

Essentially, schools use two types of commercially published standardized reading tests: (1) norm-referenced tests and (2) criterion-referenced tests. Both may feature similar types of test items, but each serves a different purpose and has a different interpretation. **Norm-referenced tests** are used to compare a student's performance with that of a representative sample (the norming group) of students. **Criterion-referenced tests** compare a student's performance with established benchmarks or criteria that have been identified as abilities that students are to achieve.

Commercially printed standardized tests fall into two classes: (1) those designed for group administration and (2) those designed to be administered individually. Both give credit for acceptable responses and determine the student's score by correct responses, lack of errors, and rate of reading.

Typical Features

Commercially published standardized tests usually provide a manual of directions for administering, scoring, and interpreting them. Information contained in the manual generally includes (1) an overview, (2) directions for administering, (3) directions for scoring, (4) a description of the types of scores, (5) procedures for using the results, and (6) information on development, national norms, reliability, validity, and other technical aspects.

Read the administrator's manual carefully to ensure that you understand fully each important aspect of administering, scoring, and interpreting the test. Failure to administer the test according to the manual can seriously jeopardize the validity of the test results. A valid test is one that measures what it purports to measure. In addition to studying the manual carefully, it is a good idea to take the test yourself. This allows you to become familiar with what the students must do when taking the test. Furthermore, by giving close attention to individual test items, you can determine how well the test fits the class based on past reading instruction. If the items do not accurately reflect past reading instruction, then the test lacks content validity and the results have little value in making decisions about students' reading and writing.

Most standardized tests have a template or scoring key to facilitate rapid, accurate hand-scoring of answer sheets. This can be very beneficial to the teacher who wants to use the results of the standardized test to help plan instruction for individual students. By scoring the test by hand, the teacher has useful information about the questions asked as well as the reading strengths and weaknesses of individual students. A large number of norm-referenced test publishers also provide computer scoring services for their test users.

Although computer scoring frees the teacher from spending time scoring each student's test, the teacher often must wait for the results. The teacher thus cannot immediately use the test results to plan and implement reading instruction.

Reliability

The consistency with which a test measures reading skills is referred to as its **reliability.** A reliable test provides a stable sample of students' reading performance. For example, if test X was administered to a student in September, you would expect that administering the test 2 or 3 weeks later would result in a similar score. If the student's score was 80 on the first administration and 15 on the second administration, however, then it is impossible to decide which score accurately reflects the student's reading ability. Such a test would be highly unreliable because it does not consistently sample students' reading skills.

Test reliability is generally reported in the administrator's manual and is expressed as a coefficient of reliability. Tests with reliability coefficients of .80 or above are considered highly reliable. Test X presented in the earlier example would have a low coefficient of reliability. Reliability is one important feature to consider when selecting or interpreting students' reading performance on standardized tests. If the test does not report reliability, you can assume that it has low reliability and should select another form of assessment to use. High reliability does not ensure, however, that a test is also valid.

Validity

As noted earlier, a valid test measures what it purports to measure. As with reliability, the administrator's manual also discusses the validity of a standardized test. Several different types of validity are important to consider in relation to the intended use of the test results, including content validity and criterion-related validity.

Content validity means that the test items are an accurate sampling of reading-instruction content and the behavioral changes under consideration. A test may be called a reading test, and the test items may be easily identified as measuring reading skills, but the test still may not have content validity. Content validity means that the test measures the same aspects of reading that students had an opportunity to learn in the instructional program. This is why it is extremely important for the teacher to examine the test beforehand in order to determine whether the test has content validity.

If the results from a test are used to predict future reading performance or estimate current performance in a reading task (i.e., mastery or lack of mastery in reading skill areas), then criterion-related validity is extremely important. Criterion-related validity is especially crucial in early reading when scores are used to predict the likelihood of success in later reading tasks. The administrator's manual for these tests specifies criterion-related validity as a coefficient of correlation between performance on the early reading test and other standardized tests measuring later reading ability. The higher the validity coefficient, the better the early reading test predicts later reading performance.

Norm-Referenced Tests

Norm-referenced tests compare the performance of an individual or individuals with the performance of a norming group. The norming group generally consists of a large sample of students who are representative of the national school population. These students take the test, and their performance determines the test's national norms. Following this, each student's raw score (total number of correct responses) on the test is compared to the norming data. It is important for teachers to examine the norming information in the administrator's manual to make sure the norming population is representative of the class being assessed.

Several types of norms compare an individual's relative standing to a defined variable. Norming information found in the administrator's manual is based on the test's national norms. Similar norms, however, can be developed locally for a school district, school, or individual classroom. Most standardized norm-referenced tests provide for the conversion of a student's raw score to a percentile rank, stanine, and grade-level equivalent.

Ongoing assessment of students' reading and writing development form the foundation for effective instruction.

Percentile ranks

Percentile ranks range from 1 to 99 and indicate the percentage of students in the norming group that scored at or below a given score. For example, if a raw score of 62 is equal to a percentile rank of 80, this means that the student did as well as or better than 80 percent of the individuals in the norming group. A percentile rank of 50 represents the median, or middle score, and indicates average performance.

Stanines

Stanines also indicate a student's relative standing in comparison to other students in the norming group. As the term implies, stanines range from a low of 1 to a high of 9. Stanines 1 through 3 usually indicate below-average performance, 4 through 6 average performance, and 7 through 9 above-average performance. Stanines represent a range of scores rather than a specific score. For example, a raw score of 28 at the 77th percentile and a raw score of 31 at the 88th percentile could be equivalent to stanine 7. Stanines represent units that are approximately equal; a difference between stanines 5 and 7 is about the same as the difference between stanines 3 and 5. Because of this, stanines can help in comparing a student's performance across various sections of a test and are better at determining student gains than percentiles are.

Grade-level equivalents

Grade-level equivalents of raw scores on a norm-referenced test indicate a student's performance in relation to the average score for the grade level of the norming group. Grade-level scores are reported by school grade and tenths of the school year. A grade-level equivalent of 4.0 indicates that a student's raw score equals the score of the average fourth grader in the norming population.

A grade-level equivalent is not necessarily the same as the level at which a student should be reading. A fourth grader who scored a grade-level equivalent of 6.0 on a recently administered standardized test should not be given sixth-grade work. Instead, these results indicate that this fourth grader scored the same on the fourth-grade test as a sixth grader would have on the same test. Likewise, a fourth grader who received a grade equivalent of 2.0 probably should not be instructed at the second-grade level; instead, it should be noted that this fourth grader did as well on this test as a second grader taking the same test. In the former example, the grade equivalent suggests that this student is above average. In the latter example, the grade equivalent indicates that this student may be a low achiever for his or her grade. Grade-level equivalents can often be very confusing to both parents and students who do not understand the definition of these scores.

Criterion-Referenced Tests

Criterion-referenced tests (CRTs) are designed to measure students' mastery of specific reading skills. Rather than comparing a student's performance to that of the norming group, CRTs view performance in relation to mastery level of one or more skills. These skills are usually stated as performance, or behavioral, objectives; for example, "The student will identify correctly the order of events found in short reading passages."

CRTs include several items for each reading benchmark or objective. A student's response to these items is evaluated in terms of the number of correct items for each benchmark or objective. Evaluation typically compares the student's performance to established criteria. For example, if 20 items test an objective, a student who scores 16 or more correct may have mastered the skill or demonstrated acquisition of the benchmark; 12 to 15 correct answers might indicate that review is needed; and fewer than 12 correct items could indicate a need for reteaching the skill. Some criterion-referenced tests use only one criterion of performance to indicate a level of competence: 15 out of 20 similar items correct may mean mastery, but fewer than 15 correct is lack of mastery. The criterion for mastery can be established by the teacher, the district, the state, or the testing company.

Diagnostic Tests

In addition to standardized achievement tests that contain reading subtests, standardized diagnostic reading tests are available for classroom use. These tests help teachers sample specific reading strengths and weaknesses in a variety of areas. Diagnostic tests often have more subtests than achievement tests do. They also test items related to specific reading behaviors. The number of subtests included on diagnostic reading tests varies; however, most of them have from 5 to 10.

Many standardized tests can provide information about students' reading. All norm-referenced achievement batteries designed to test elementary students contain reading subtests. These tests usually provide a vocabulary score, a comprehension score, and a total reading score (the average of vocabulary and comprehension). Many criterion-referenced reading tests include subtests that focus on specific aspects of word identification and comprehension. With so many different reading tests, it is no surprise that many measure virtually the same aspects of reading. Nevertheless, tests vary significantly in what they measure, their intended level of difficulty, the care that went into their construction, and their ease of administration. Each of these factors influences two important attributes of reading tests: (1) how consistently they measure reading skills and (2) how well they actually measure the skills that they supposedly measure.

Cautions About Standardized Tests

Standardized tests have been criticized because they do not reflect all of the skills and capabilities associated with literacy, are often assumed to accurately measure students' learning, and provide little information about students' problem-solving capabilities and learning processes (Tompkins, 2001). Students bring much more to a reading task than a standardized test can sample. Nonetheless, many school districts and states require the administration of standardized tests for reading and writing.

Standardized tests sample only students' literacy in relation to the tasks (identifying words in context, selecting word definitions) and do not provide a broad view of how well an individual reads. Teachers should view results from standardized tests as only one part of a much larger picture of a student's literacy. Also, test results provide little meaningful information that teachers can use to improve the quality of their literacy instruction and better address the needs of individual students. The shortcomings of standardized tests were recently noted by Early (1992/1993): "The need to know how children are doing persists—with teachers, with parents, with the children themselves—but recently gained knowledge of the reading process convinces us that standardized tests fail to measure those processes accurately, wholly, or diagnostically" (p. 306). Even with these noted weaknesses, standardized tests continue to play a major role in our evaluation of our schools. As stated earlier, assessment is used at many different levels, and while the information provided on standardized tests may not be of particular importance to the classroom teacher or the students, it is of high value to school districts and state officials who are examining the success and failure rates of schools. Information gained at the state level can help teachers continue their professional development and increase funds to schools that are not reaching the same criteria that other schools are, though they are often within the same district.

INFORMAL ASSESSMENT

Conventional literacy tests examine the products of a student's performance (such as instructional level, specific skill strengths and weaknesses, and national, state, or local ranking), not the processes a reader and writer employs. Yet certain strategic processes characterize effective reading and writing.

Teacher and student interaction can provide a wealth of assessment information.

The discrepancy between our knowledge of effective reading and writing and the prevailing assessment procedures has prompted many experts to recommend changes in how we assess literacy. The *Standards for the Assessment of Reading and Writing* (1994) indicate that the most productive way to assess students' reading and writing processes is when teachers observe and interact with students as they read and write. As teachers interact with students, they evaluate the ways in which the students construct meaning, and they are able to intervene in order to provide scaffolding support or suggestions when the students appear to have difficulty.

While our knowledge of various reading strategies has dramatically improved in the last 20 years, effective teachers have always known the value of simultaneous assessment and instruction. In interacting with students, effective teachers assess each student's reading strategies. In doing so, they look at the student's use of prior knowledge, story structure, headings, self-questioning, and purpose setting. They also look at how the student understands main ideas, summarizes key points, infers relationships, and rereads parts for clarification. This is called process-oriented assessment.

Effective classroom reading teachers modify existing informal tests to accentuate the processes of reading rather than the products. They may add expository passages to the traditional narrative or expand the passage length to more realistically assess a student's reading skills and abilities. Before reading, they may informally assess prior knowledge by asking questions and initiating a discussion with the student.

After reading, they may ask questions, encourage retellings, and promote discussion to assess summarizing or inferencing abilities. Additionally, teachers may assess metacognition by asking students how they make sense of what they read.

Teacher Observation/Kid Watching

One of the most powerful assessment tool is keen teacher observation, which has also been referred to as kid watching. Effective kid watchers know what to look and listen for and then translate this information into instructional decisions to improve students' facility in interacting with text. Observations are often the first step in informal on-the-spot assessment. Teachers use observation to interpret whether students are listening and understanding what they are learning. They use observation to help detect distractions and avoid complications that could interrupt learning. Some teachers use checklists (see Figure 11.2) that serve as guides to help them focus on observing stimuli that will best enable them to make accurate assessments.

Walker (2000) addresses this quality of assessment during instruction to emphasize the reflective and self-monitoring attitude of effective teachers. Diagnostic teachers assess while they teach. They evaluate children's use of strategies in a specific context for varying reading purposes. Questions such as "Do students use both text-based (bottom-up) processing and reader-based (top-down) processing when they read?" and "When a reading task for the students is modified, do they gain more understanding and control of their reading process?" help diagnostic teachers think about what students already know and how they can guide students to a more integrated understanding of the reading process.

The power of watching kids is that it helps teachers to pinpoint students' strengths and weaknesses in a variety of literacy tasks and use such information to plan appropriate instruction. Standardized tests are limited in helping the teacher identify students' literacy strengths and weaknesses. Furthermore, standardized tests alone cannot accurately assess students' literacy and the effectiveness of literacy instruction. Effective teachers combine observation with a variety of informal assessment procedures. Informal assessment of students' literacy can include materials that accompany reading instructional materials, informal reading inventories, performance-based assessment, portfolios, observation, interviews, and interaction with students.

Assessment Materials That Accompany Published Reading Materials

A large number of published reading materials contain student assessment materials. The main purposes of these materials are to (1) facilitate assignment at the appropriate level of difficulty in the materials, (2) determine whether students have progressed in their reading development, and (3) identify some reading strengths and weaknesses. In comparison with norm-referenced standardized tests, assessment materials do not compare students' performance with that of students at a grade level in a wide geographic area.

Name _____ Age _____ Grade _____ Date _____

School _____ Teacher _____

Examiner _____

I. *Word Analysis*
  A. Knows names of letters
    Needs work with: _____ Yes No
  B. Attacks initial sound of words
    Deficiencies noted: _____ Yes No
  C. Can substitute initial letter sounds
    Further drill needed: _____ Yes No
  D. Can sound out initial blends and digraphs
    Deficiencies noted: _____ Yes No
  E. If root word is known, can solve words
    formed by adding prefixes and suffixes _____ Yes No

II. *Sight Words* (check if applicable)
  _____ Knows a word one time, misses it later
  _____ Guesses at unknown words
      _____ Errors frequently do not change intended meaning
      _____ Errors indicate not reading for meaning
  _____ Frequently adds words
      _____ Errors frequently do not change intended meaning
      _____ Errors indicate not reading for meaning
  _____ Omits words
      _____ Errors frequently do not change intended meaning
      _____ Errors indicate not reading for meaning

III. *Reading Habits Noted*
  _____ Reads word-by-word   _____ Loses place frequently
  _____ Phrasing inadequate   _____ Does not utilize punctuation
  _____ Poor intonation   _____ Lacks persistence

Explain: _____

_____

IV. *Sustained Reading* (basal, textbook, trade book)
  (Do quantitative and qualitative analysis using techniques presented earlier.)

	Grade Level	Approx. Number of Running Words	Number of Errors
1.			
2.			

Errors noted (example): Said *lied* for *lying*; *banged* for *bumped*; *stuck* for *start* (corrected)

Needed help with: *clown, stomach, curious, squeal*

Read with some hesitation, not smoothly, etc.

continued

Figure 11.2   Reading observation checklist.

	Excellent	Average	Below Average
V. Comprehension			
Recall of facts	_____	_____	_____
Recognizes main ideas	_____	_____	_____
Draws inferences	_____	_____	_____
Maintains sequence of events	_____	_____	_____
Understands humor	_____	_____	_____
Interprets figurative expressions	_____	_____	_____
VI. Reading Skills			
Relates with audience	_____	_____	_____
Enunciation	_____	_____	_____
Adequate volume	_____	_____	_____
Reads with intonation	_____	_____	_____
Phrases for meaning	_____	_____	_____
VII. Behaviors Related to Reading			
Attitude toward reading	_____	_____	_____
Self-confidence	_____	_____	_____
Background knowledge	_____	_____	_____
Language facility	_____	_____	_____
Originality of expression	_____	_____	_____
Range of vocabulary	_____	_____	_____
Stock of concepts	_____	_____	_____
Variety of sentence patterns	_____	_____	_____

VIII. Other Comments _____

_____
_____
_____
_____
_____
_____
_____
_____
_____
_____
_____
_____

Figure 11.2   (continued)

Many assessment materials provide criteria, or benchmarks, to assist the teacher in identifying whether students have acquired various aspects of reading. Unlike standardized criterion-referenced tests, benchmarks are presented only to assist the teacher in evaluating students' performances. Placement tests can help you to make decisions about students' placement in a particular level of a literature series, but they also can help you to evaluate students' progress in the materials.

Assessment materials are content specific; that is, they assess students' progress in terms of the reading materials for which the assessments were developed. You should, however, evaluate and review them carefully to ensure that they closely match what is taught. Also, pay careful attention to the number of items and the descriptions of benchmarks to ensure that they adequately sample the area of reading identified. Some assessment materials that accompany reading materials are attempting to incorporate more of the features of reading reflecting current thinking.

Informal Reading Inventories

One of the more helpful tools one can use in the classroom to assess students' reading strengths and weaknesses is the informal reading inventory (IRI). Essentially, IRIs take three forms: (1) commercially published, (2) accompanying reading series, and (3) teacher prepared. Regardless of the type of inventory you choose, its major purposes are to establish students' reading levels and to identify their reading strengths and weaknesses. The typical IRI consists of graded word lists, graded reading passages (often both narrative and expository), and comprehension questions.

Graded word lists consist of 10 to 20 words for each grade level represented in the IRI. Most commercially published and reading series IRIs have graded word lists for preprimer through sixth grade. A student's performance on the graded word list provides the teacher with information for placement in the graded passages, sight vocabulary strengths and weaknesses, and word-identification strategies used to decode and identify words presented in isolation.

Graded reading passages are series of passages, usually ranging in reading difficulty from preprimer or primer through eighth or ninth grade. Performance on the passages can provide insights about a reader's strategies in using context, attention to meaning, identification of unknown words, reading interests, and different levels of reading competence.

Comprehension questions consist of 5 to 10 questions for each graded reading passage. The questions typically cover vocabulary, main idea, inference, literal meaning, cause and effect, and sequence. The questions are intended to identify students' reading-comprehension competence. Some IRIs also have features to evaluate the children's retelling of the passages that they read.

Most commercial IRIs have at least two equivalent forms. Either form may be administered orally or silently. A student's performance on the oral administration of the IRI can identify his or her independent, instructional, frustration, and listening-capacity reading-competence levels. At the independent level, the student can read materials without any assistance. The instructional level is the teaching level at which students can read materials successfully with teacher guidance. At the frustration level, materials become too difficult and, as a result, frustrating for the students. The listening-capacity level indicates what students can understand when material is read aloud to them. It is identified by evaluating responses to the comprehension questions for grade-level passages that are read aloud to students.

Reading the passages aloud and responding to comprehension questions orally allows identification of instructional, independent, and frustration levels for both word recognition and comprehension. Silent reading of the passages identifies the same reading-competence levels, but only for comprehension.

Administration

Administering an informal reading inventory is easy. You should follow some basic guidelines, however, to ensure that the oral reading accurately samples a student's reading. The following paragraphs outline the procedures to follow when administering an IRI.

1. Prior to administering the IRI, become thoroughly familiar with the coding system used to record students' deviations from the text as they read passages orally. Figure 11.3 presents a coding system that you can use to note such deviations. It is strongly recommended that you practice using the coding system and also tape-record the student's oral reading to ensure accurate coding of miscues. The importance of using the described coding system is that other teachers who examine your IRI will know what they are looking at.

2. To administer the IRI, select an area that is free of distractions. Establish a relaxed atmosphere to minimize student anxiety. Tell the student that the IRI is not a test and that he or she is going to read aloud some words and stories and answer some questions about each story. Also, it is extremely important to explain that you will be doing some writing as the student reads the story, because many students become highly anxious when the teacher begins to write. Introduce the student to the tape recorder and let the student record his or her name, the date, and something about himself or herself. Play back what is recorded to check for proper settings. This procedure usually eliminates the novelty of the tape recorder and prevents it from becoming a distraction.

3. Select the graded word list that is two levels below the student's current grade level (word lists for the student should be typed on separate note cards) and ask the student to read the list of words aloud. Some teachers use a flash and untimed measure to determine word recognition automaticity as well as word-attack skills. Encourage the student to read each word, even if the student is not sure of a word's pronunciation. This provides some indication of the student's word-identification strategies. The teacher should write the word as the student phonetically pronounces it.

If the student makes a miscue on this first word list, drop to an easier list until there are no miscues. Continue administering more difficult word lists and noting the student's miscues by using the coding system. Stop administering the word lists when the student's miscues reach the maximum number suggested in the teacher's manual. If you use teacher-prepared graded word lists, stop administering the lists when the student's miscues reach 25% or greater.

4. The highest graded word list on which the student makes no miscues is the entry level for the oral reading passages. For example, if a student read from graded

Type of Miscue	How to Mark	Example
Omission: Word, several words, or punctuation is omitted.	Circle (◯) the word(s), part of the word, or punctuation omitted.	The large (black) dog jumped (high) into the air and grab(bed) the ball.
Substitution: Real word is substituted for text word.	Draw a line through the word substituted and write the substituted word above the text word.	*huge* *leaped* The ~~large~~ black dog ~~jumped~~ high *bait* into the air and grabbed the ~~ball~~.
Insertion: Word is inserted in the passage text.	Use a caret (∧) to indicate where word was inserted and write the word.	The large black dog jumped high *big* into he air and grabbed the ∧ball.
Unknown or Aided Words: Word or words are pronounced for the reader.	Place a letter "P" over the word pronounced for the reader.	*P* The large black dog jumped high into the air and grabbed the ball.
Transposition: Order of words in the text is transposed.	Use a curved mark (‿) over and under the words transposed.	The ⁀black╲large⁀ dog jumped high into the air and grabbed the ball.
Repetition: Phrase or several words are repeated. Count as one miscue.	Place an "R" with lines extending in both directions over the words repeated.	The large black dog jumped high ———— R ———— into the air and grabbed the ball.
Mispronunciation: Word is pronounced incorrectly.	Write the phonetic spelling above the word or use diacritical markings to indicate the pronunciation.	*largé* *jumptéd* The large black dog jumped high into the air and grabbed the ball.
Self-correction: Miscue is self-corrected by the reader. Important to note, but do not count as a miscue.	Place a check mark (✓) above the miscue.	✓ *jumpted* ✓ The large black dog jumped high into the air and grabbed the ball.

Figure 11.3   Marking system for recording oral reading miscues.

word lists 1 through 6 and made no miscues on list 4 but missed several on list 5, then the teacher should begin administering the oral reading passage at level 4. Before a student begins the oral reading passages, provide a reminder that he or she is going to be reading a story aloud and that after reading the story you will ask some questions about it. Some published IRIs have motivation or overview statements for each passage that you are to read to the student just before beginning oral reading of the passage. The manuals may encourage you to ask the student to make predictions about what they are to read. These may provide insight into the student's reading interests and background knowledge. As the student reads, record the miscues on the teacher's corresponding passage. Because many students rapidly read the passage or make many mistakes, it is the recommendation of this text that the teacher use a tape recorder so he or she can go back and listen to the reading passage at a convenient time.

Once the student has read the passage, remove it and ask the student to provide you with a retelling of the story. This step provides the teacher with another measure of comprehension. During the retelling, the teacher judges the student's comprehension based on the retelling. After the student has completed the retelling, ask the student the comprehension questions that were not addressed during the retelling. If necessary, you may restate the questions. If the student responds to the questions correctly, indicate this with a check beside the question. If the student responds incorrectly or only partially, write the response beneath the appropriate question. The student need not respond to each question on the question sheet, but he or she should answer correctly to get credit.

5. Continue having the student read subsequent passages and answer comprehension questions until you identify a frustration level for either word recognition or comprehension, or both (see Figure 11.4).

6. To assess the student's silent reading capabilities, the teacher begins the silent reading passages at the highest instructional level that the child read during the oral reading. During this informal assessment, the student reads the passage silently and then responds to comprehension questions asked by the teacher. Many teachers time the student as he or she reads the passage to get information about the student's reading rate. It is important to use the silent reading assessment in order to accurately judge the student's reading comprehension. Comprehension difficulties that were noted during oral reading may not be noticed during silent reading because the student may not feel as pressured to decode accurately aloud to the teacher. Some manuals encourage teachers to assess silent reading first and then proceed to the oral reading of the same passage. This method provides the student with practice before reading the passage out loud.

7. To identify the student's capacity or potential reading level, have him or her begin reading at the level above the passage that produced frustration. Again, set purposes by telling the student to listen carefully as you read the story aloud and that he or she will answer some questions after hearing the story. Stop administering passages when the student answers less than 75% of the comprehension questions correctly. The highest level at which the student answered 75% of the questions correctly is the capacity level.

Interpretation

Use both quantitative and qualitative analysis to interpret a student's performance on an IRI. Counting the number of scorable miscues in each passage and the

Reading Competency Level	Betts's Criteria		Powell's Differentiated Criteria					
	Word Recognition	Comprehension	Word Recognition in terms of grade-level difficulty of passage being read:			Comprehension in terms of grade-level difficulty of passage being read:		
			PP–2	3–5	6+	PP–2	3–5	6+
Independent	1 miscue per 100 words (99% accuracy)	90% or greater accuracy	94% + accuracy	96% + accuracy	97% + accuracy	81% + accuracy	86% + accuracy	91% + accuracy
Instructional	5 miscues per 100 words (95% accuracy)	75%–89% accuracy	87–93% accuracy	92–95% accuracy	94–96% accuracy	55–80% accuracy	60–85% accuracy	65–90% accuracy
Frustration	10+ miscues per 100 words (less than 90% accuracy)	less than 50% accuracy	86% or less accuracy	91% or less accuracy	93% or less accuracy	54% or less accuracy	59% or less accuracy	64% or less accuracy
Capacity or Potential	at least 75% accuracy		at least 75% accuracy for all levels					

Figure 11.4 Criteria for determining reading-competence levels from student performance on an IRI.

number of incorrect comprehension questions for each passage and determining reading competence levels are the bases of a quantitative analysis. Figure 11.4 presents two sets of criteria for determining reading-competence levels. Betts's (1946) criteria for independent, instructional, and frustration levels apply to all passages, regardless of difficulty (Woods & Moe, 1999). Powell's (1976) criteria take into account the passage's level of difficulty and permit more miscues below the sixth-grade level.

When both criteria are applied to a student's performance in word recognition and comprehension, Betts's criteria usually place the student at a lower competency level. Remember that reading tasks should be at a level of difficulty that maximizes students' chances of success yet should not be so easy that students lose interest. Therefore, teachers could apply both sets of criteria to students' performance. If they yield a noticeable difference in competency levels, it might be best to assign students reading materials with a difficulty between the two competency levels rather than at either extreme. This increases the likelihood that the reading task is at an appropriate difficulty level. If a student's actual reading performance suggests that the task is either too easy or too difficult, however, then move the student up or down to the appropriate level.

Most published IRIs have forms for analyzing results (see Figure 11.5) and forms for summarizing students' performance (see Figure 11.6). A summary sheet enables you to identify reading levels and tally both oral reading miscues and comprehension difficulties. Also, such sheets consider the types of oral reading responses a student makes. Qualitative analysis of miscues (see Figure 11.7) provides insights into the reading strategies that students use in their reading. Specific reading strengths and weaknesses become more evident as miscues are qualitatively analyzed for several orally read passages.

Running Records

Two important components of the informal reading inventory are word recognition and fluency. Automatic recognition of words contributes to fluent reading, which enables students to give their attention to comprehending what they read. Reading with appropriate speed, feeling, expression, and phrasing represent fluency. Teachers can assess students' word recognition and reading fluency by using running records. Also, running records can provide insights about the difficulty level of reading materials, assess the reading progress of individual children, and be used on a regular basis.

Running records are easy to use and are similar to the qualitative analyses done with an IRI. The teacher selects a 100- to 150-word passage that is to be read by the child. The text can be either narrative text or informational text that the teacher has available in the classroom. After selecting the text, the teacher listens to the child read it and records the child's reading. As the child reads, the teacher records the

FORM C, LEVEL 4 — Reader's Passages page 31

Prior Knowledge/Prediction

☐ Read the title and predict what the story is about. *A sick pony.*
 Q: What do you know about a sick pony?
 SR: I don't know. I've never been on a pony.

☐ Read the first two sentences and add more to your prediction.
 A boy is really worried about his pony. The pony's sick.

Prior Knowledge
☐ a lot
☐ some
☑ none

A Sick Pony

	A Sick Pony	O	I	S	A	Rp	Rv
1	Jody was so/worried that he didn't even want to eat. He had stayed						
2	*Grab / Grahil* ... *cold* in the barn all day/to take care of his sick pony, Gabilan. The pony's/condition		/	/	/		
3	*breath* was growing worse as/his/breathing grew louder and harder.			/			
4	*night* ... *horse SC* At nightfall, Jody/brought a blanket from the house so he could sleep/				/		
5	*wind SC* near/Gabilan. In the middle of the night/the wind whipped around the barn						
6	and blew the door open.						
7	At dawn Jody awakened to the banging of the barn door. Gabilan						
8	*follow* ... *up / buzz SC* was gone! In/alarm he ran from the barn following the pony's tracks.		/		/		
9	Looking upward he saw buzzards, the birds of/death, flying overhead.				/		

The text is continued on the next page.

Cueing Systems

LINE #	Miscue	Grapho-phonically Similar (I M F) (word level)	Syntactically Acceptable / Unacceptable (sentence level)	Semantic Change in Meaning (CM) / No Change in Meaning (NCM) (sentence level)
2	cold	I	A	CM
3	breath*	IM	A	*slight* CM
4	night*	IM	A	*slight* CM
8	follow*	IM	A	CM
9	up*	I	A	NCM
10	clear*	IM	U	CM
11	anger	IF	U	CM
12	printed	IF	A	CM

* *Note the omissions of word endings.*

The cueing system grid is continued on the next page.

continued

Figure 11.5 IRI form for student-teacher response sheet.

Note: This passage is a retelling from the novel, *Tuned Out,* by Maia Wojciechowska.

Cueing Systems

	Miscue	Graphophonically Similar I M F (word level)	Syntactically Acceptable Unacceptable (sentence level)	Semantic Change in Meaning (CM) No Change in Meaning (NCM) (sentence level)
L I N E #				

Summary

☑ Most, ☐ few, ☐ no   miscues were graphophonically similar to the word in the passage.

☐ Most, ☐ few, ☐ no   miscues were syntactically matched.

☐ Most, ☑ few, ☐ no   miscues maintained the author's meaning.

☑ The self-corrections demonstrate that the reader monitors the meaning.

Form C, Level 4

	O	I	S	A	Rp	Rv
1						
0			/			
1						/
1			/			
1	/					
2			/			

clear
Jody stood still, then ran to the top of a small hill. In a clearing below, he

anger
saw something that filled his heart with anger and hate. A buzzard/was

printed
perched on his dying pony's head.

TOTALS

Number of miscues 16   Number of self-corrections 3

Fluency: Does the reader . . . .

☐ read smoothly?   ☑ word-by-word?   ☐ read words in meaningful phrases?

☐ use pitch, stress, and intonation to convey the meaning of a text?

☑ repeat words and phrases because he or she is monitoring the meaning (self-correcting)?   *some*

☑ repeat words and phrases because he or she is just trying to sound out the words?

☑ use punctuation to divide the text into units of meaning?   *Some W/R difficulties are beginning to interfere.*

☐ ignore the punctuation?

Rating Scale
1 = clearly labored, disfluent reading, very slow pace
2 = slow and choppy reading/slow pace   2.5   3 = poor phrasing/intonation/reasonable pace
     4 = fairly fluent reading/good pace

Figure 11.5 (continued)

Source: From *Analytical Reading Inventory* (6th ed., pp. 42–43) by M. L. Woods & A. J. Moe, 1999, Upper Saddle River, NJ: Merrill/Prentice Hall. Copyright 1999 by Pearson Education. Reprinted by permission of Pearson Education, Inc., Upper Saddle River, NJ 07458.

STUDENT SUMMARY RECORD

Student_____ Grade _____ Sex _____ Age _____
(yrs. and mos.)

School _____ Administered by _____ Date _____

Level	Word Lists	Graded Passages			Reading Levels
	Form _____ % correct	Form _____ Word Recognition	Form _____ Comprehension	Form _____ Listening	**Narrative Passages**
Primer					Independent _____ Instructional _____
Level 1					Frustration _____
Level 2					Listening _____
Level 3					
Level 4					**Expository Passages**
Level 5					Science / Social Studies
Level 6					At grade level / At grade level
Level 7					WR. Comp. / WR. Comp.
Level 8					Other level _____ / Other level _____
Level 9					WR. Comp. / WR. Comp.

OVERVIEW OF READING BEHAVIORS

1. <u>Predictions</u>
☐ Reader most often made a logical prediction from the title.

☐ Reader most often made a logical prediction from the first two sentences.

2. <u>Reader had prior knowledge of</u>
☐ many passages

☐ some passages

☐ few passages

3. <u>Types of Oral Reading Miscues</u>
☐ Omissions ☐ Insertions
☐ Substitutions ☐ Aided words
☐ Repetitions ☐ Reversals

<u>Reader Self-Corrects</u>
☐ a lot ☐ sometimes ☐ seldom

4. <u>Fluency Analysis</u>
1 = labored, disfluent reading/very slow pace
2 = slow and choppy reading/slow pace
3 = poor phrasing/intonation/reasonable pace
4 = fairly fluent reading/good pace

_____ independent
_____ instructional
_____ frustration

5. <u>Cueing Systems: Miscue Analysis</u>
Graphophonic Similarities
☐ Initial ☐ Medial ☐ Final

Syntactic: Most miscues were
☐ acceptable ☐ unacceptable

Semantic: Most miscues caused
☐ ch. in meaning ☐ no ch. in meaning

6. <u>Retelling Analysis: The reader most often</u> retold
☐ many details, logical order
☐ some details, some order
☐ few details, disorder

<u>Reader most often summarizes</u>
☐ adequately ☐ not adequately

7. <u>Comprehension Questions Analysis</u>
The examiner
☐ asked few ☐ asked many

<u>Reader's Strength(s)</u>
☐ Retells In Fact (RIF)
☐ Puts Information Together (PIT)
☐ Combines Author and Reader (CAR)
☐ Evaluates and Substantiates (EAS)

<u>Reader Text Relationship (RTR)</u>
<u>Reader responds adequately</u>
☐ From the Text ☐ From Head to Text

8. <u>Emotional Status at Various Reading Levels</u>
Reader was — relaxed/confident —
slightly nervous — stressed/little confidence

Independent Level _____

Instructional Level _____

Frustration Level _____

Listening Level _____

Figure 11.6 An informal reading inventory (IRI) student record summary sheet.

Source: From *Analytical Reading Inventory* (6th ed., p. 75) by M. L. Woods & A. J. Moe, 1999, Upper Saddle River, NJ: Merrill/Prentice Hall. Copyright 1999 by Pearson Education. Reprinted by permission of Pearson Education, Inc., Upper Saddle River, NJ 07458.

Case Study: Description
of Reading Behaviors Across Levels

Narrative Passages, Form C

Level 2, "The Busy Road"

◆ Prior Knowledge/Prediction

Jenny's predictions were focused and based on a lot of prior knowledge.

◆ Miscues: Substitutions

At this level, it was evident that she was searching for meaning as she read. For example, she self-corrected some miscues (*nose* for *noise*, *scar* for *scared*), showing that she was attending to the meaning, using context clues to select the correct word. Even though the miscue count was 6, and even though most miscues changed the meaning within the sentence, her overall grasp of the meaning was accurate, causing the word recognition score to be high instructional.

◆ Fluency

Even though Jenny's reading appeared somewhat choppy, she did group many of the words in meaningful phrases. In some instances, intonation was used to convey the meaning of the text. Some repetitions were made because she was sounding out the words. Punctuation was effectively used to divide the text into units of meaning. At this level, her reading was fairly fluent and maintained a good pace.

◆ Comprehension

The retelling was very thorough and reflected all the story elements, Jenny used complete, well-structured sentences and in some instances used the author's exact words. Responses to the comprehension questions were accurate.

◆ Emotional Status

Jenny was confident and relaxed.

◆ Summary: Word Recognition = high instructional   Comprehension = independent
Overall = independent

Level 3, "Belonging to the Club"

◆ Prior Knowledge/Prediction

Jenny had some background knowledge about club membership; however, the miscue in the first two sentences (*Triggers* for *Tigers*) caused her to lose the chance for a meaningful prediction.

◆ Miscues

Jenny continued to self-correct. She made some word substitutions that were close choices (*be in* for *belonging*, *ask* for *agree*, *soon* for *suddenly*), which shows that she was continuing to search for meaning, but she did not self-correct these miscues. The Cueing Systems Miscue Analysis shows that her strength is using the initial portion of the word, but that medial and final portions are often not attended to.

Figure 11.7   Description of reading behaviors for a student's reading of narrative passages from an IRI.
Source: From *Analytical Reading Inventory* (6th ed., p. 57–58) by M. L. Woods & A. J. Moe, 1999, Upper Saddle River, NJ: Merrill/Prentice Hall. Copyright 1999 by Pearson Education. Reprinted by permission of Pearson Education, Inc., Upper Saddle River, NJ 07458.

◆ Fluency

The reading was choppier than at Level 2, but many of the words were still grouped into meaningful phrases. In some cases, intonation was used to convey the meaning. Some words or phrases were repeated because Jenny was attempting to self-correct. Most of the time punctuation was used effectively.

◆ Comprehension

Despite the fact that the number of miscues increased, Jenny retold much of the story; however, some important information was omitted (e.g., Jack was new to the neighborhood). In addition, her failure to correct the word *Triggers* for *Tigers* caused her to miss an important concept in the story (the connection between the yellow and black paint and the name of the club). The responses to some of the comprehension questions didn't contain enough information.

◆ Emotional Status

She did not have the same confidence as she did reading Level 2. Her posture became more slumped and her breathing less relaxed, yet she persisted with determination.

◆ Summary: Word Recognition = instructional   Comprehension = instructional   Overall = instructional

Level 4, "A Sick Pony"

◆ Prior Knowledge/Prediction

Jenny's prediction expanded after reading the first two sentences, but it was limited because she had little prior knowledge about ponies.

◆ Miscues

The number of miscues increased considerably. Substitutions and repetitions comprised the majority of miscues. Only three self-corrections were made, indicating that Jenny was less able to use context clues and was more confounded by word recognition difficulties. At this level she used both initial and medial portions of the words, but for the most part the miscues changed the meaning. Two miscues, *breath* for *breathing* and *night* for *nightfall,* caused a slight change in meaning. Other miscues (5) were totally inaccurate, such as *cold* for *condition.* A pattern emerged with substitutions; the final portion of words were dropped (*breath* for *breathing, night* for *nightfall, follow* for *following,* and *up* for *upward*). For the first time, the examiner aided a word.

◆ Fluency

The reading was word-by-word. Although Jenny repeated some words in an attempt to clarify the meaning, most repetitions were made in an effort to sound out words. The use of intonation to convey meaning was less evident at this level. For the most part, punctuation was used to divide the text into units of meaning. Some word recognition difficulties began to interfere.

◆ Comprehension

Jenny's retelling was scanty and poorly organized. Responses to most comprehension questions were incorrect.

◆ Emotional Status

Jenny did not look like or sound like a confident reader. She showed physical signs of stress— her hands were tightly fisted, and her breathing became short and choppy. Sometimes she appeared confused. She was reluctant to take any risks such as making meaningful word substitutions. During the retelling her voice reflected a tentative quality as if she were asking for verification, *and the barn door started banging?*

◆ Summary: Word Recognition = frustration   Comprehension = frustration   Overall = frustration

Figure 11.7   (continued)

Silent Reading Level 4, Form B, "The Small Colt"

◆ Prior Knowledge/Prediction

The prediction was inaccurate, and Jenny didn't even know the meaning of the word *colt*.

◆ Silent Reading Behavior

Jenny read through the text rapidly. It looked like she was running from line to line in a fast manner without careful attention to the text.

◆ Comprehension

The retelling was scanty, and incorrect responses were given to most of the comprehension questions.

◆ Emotional Status

She seemed more relaxed than with the oral reading at Level 4. When responding to the retelling and the questions, her voice had the same tentative, question-mark quality.

◆ Summary: Word Recognition = N/A   Comprehension = frustration   Overall = frustration

Level 5, "A Woman Race Car Driver" (Listening Level)

◆ Prior Knowledge/Prediction

Jenny's prediction was adequate, and she had prior knowledge about women race car drivers.

◆ Comprehension

Even though the retelling was not comprehensive, Jenny's responses to the comprehension questions showed that she remembered a lot of the story.

◆ Emotional Status

Jenny retold in a confident manner. Her responses to the comprehension questions were given in a more relaxed, direct manner. Her voice conveyed more certainty. Her body straightened, and her hands relaxed.

◆ Summary: Word Recognition = N/A   Comprehension = instructional   Overall = instructional

Expository Passages, Forms S and SS

Science, Level 4, "A Comet"

◆ Prior Knowledge/Prediction

The prediction was weak, and Jenny had little prior knowledge about comets.

◆ Miscues

The miscues were primarily omissions, substitutions, and repetitions. There was only one self-correction. The analysis of the substitutions showed that Jenny relied mostly on the use of initial consonants and blends as a key strategy to pronounce the words. Toward the end of the passage, she was so frustrated that it was necessary to aid three words.

◆ Fluency

Jenny's reading was clearly labored and disfluent, with a very slow pace.

Figure 11.7   (continued)

◆   Comprehension

The retelling was scanty. The retelling contained the same information as the prediction. There was no new information from the text. Most comprehension question responses were incorrect.

◆   Emotional Status

Jenny showed all the obvious signs of frustration.

◆   Summary: Word Recognition = frustration   Comprehension = frustration   Overall = frustration

Social Studies, Level 4, "French Explorers in North America"

◆   Prior Knowledge/Prediction

The prediction was inadequate, and she had no prior knowledge about French explorers.

◆   Miscues

The miscues were so numerous that Jenny was unable to complete the passage. She made sixteen miscues in the first paragraph and asked for help with so many words that it was necessary to stop the session.

◆   Fluency

Jenny's reading was not fluent.

◆   Comprehension

Jenny did not complete the passage.

◆   Emotional Status

Jenny showed all the obvious signs of frustration.

◆   Summary: Word Recognition = incomplete   Comprehension = incomplete   Overall = frustration

Figure 11.7   (continued)

reading by making checks (✔) for each word read correctly and records miscues as read on either a blank sheet of paper:

Text	Running Record
The wildest pony in the West was the son of the Black Mustang. The cowboys and vaqueros who tried to capture him named him Pegasus.	✔ ✔ ✔ ✔ ✔ ✔ is ✔ ✔ ✔ ✔ ✔ ✔ ✔ ✔ TP ✔ ✔ ✔ catch it ✔ ✔ TP

or on a duplicate copy of the text being read:

Text Running Record

✔   ✔   ✔ ✔ ✔   is   ✔ ✔ ✔
The wildest pony in the West was the son of
✔ ✔   ✔   ✔   ✔   ✔
the Black Mustang. The cowboys and
TP   ✔ ✔ ✔   catch it   ✔
vaqueros who tried to capture him named
✔   TP
him Pegasus.

Many teachers find it easier to make a duplicate copy to record the child's reading, particularly when informational text is being read.

When the running record has been completed, the percentage of words read correctly is calculated. Similar to the Cloze procedure, the teacher uses the percentage of correct words to determine if the text is too difficult, too easy, or at an appropriate instructional level. A high success rate in recognizing words of 95% or more indicates that the text is at an independent level, a success rate of 90% indicates that the text is at the instructional level, and a success rate below 90% is the student's frustration level.

Miscues can be analyzed qualitatively to gain insights about students' reading. Questions that can guide the qualitative analysis are:

- Did the miscue change the meaning of the text?
- Did the reader self-correct or attempt to self-correct miscues?
- Was there a pattern to the meaning miscues in terms of parts of speech, tense, or setting?
- Did mispronunciation miscues indicate an attempt to use a word recognition capability, such as phonics or structural analysis?
- Were there mispronunciation miscues of a particular type, such as multisyllabic words or irregular words?

Answering questions such as these, enables the teacher to begin looking at children's running records to gain insights into their oral reading and reading fluency capabilities. In addition to examining the miscues, attention should also be given to children's reading performance, such as appropriate speed, feeling, expression, and phrasing.

Cloze Procedure

The Cloze procedure is an informal diagnostic procedure that helps identify reading levels and provides information about a reader's ability to deal with the content and structure of the information presented—syntax, word meanings, and story grammar. A Cloze test is typically constructed by selecting a freestanding written passage approximately 250 to 300 words long and deleting every fifth word. The first and last sentences are left intact; the first deletion is the fifth word in the second sentence. Every fifth word after this is deleted throughout the passage. Each deleted word is replaced with a line of uniform length, as illustrated in the following example:

Jake saw the two horses just south of the timber ridge over by Clear Lake. He and Rusty had _____ hunting these Mustangs for _____ last two days. Yesterday _____ horse ran away and _____ gone for several hours.

_____ time that Jake lost _____ searching for the runaway _____ had made him think they would not _____ the wild horses. (The deleted words are **been, the, Rusty's, was, The, while, horse, seriously,** and *catch*.)

The words deleted from a passage may be any part of speech. The basic rule is to delete the fifth word regardless of its function in the sentence.

Administering and scoring a Cloze test for determining reading levels are simple, straightforward procedures. Instruct students to read the passage and write in the blank the word that was deleted. Then score each of the responses as either correct or incorrect. Only the exact word is considered a correct response. Determine the percentage of correct responses by dividing the total correct replacements by the number of deleted words (e.g., 30 words correctly replaced divided by 50 words deleted would be a 60% correct replacement). Compare the percentage of correct word placement with this scale: 61% or more correct replacements for the independent reading level, 41% to 60% correct for the instructional level, and less than 40% correct for the frustration level (Rankin & Culhane, 1969).

Determining reading levels using the criterion of exact word replacement is intended to help you decide whether students can handle the content and language structure of various reading materials, such as science, social studies, and math texts. You can better understand a reader's use of syntax, semantics, and reasoning by qualitatively looking at incorrect word choices. If incorrect choices are syntactically correct (the same part of speech), the student may be analyzing words preceding and following the deletion in an attempt to supply a meaningful response. Semantically correct word choices may indicate that the reader understood the meaning but chose a different word from the author's. If the words are both syntactically and semantically correct, then the reader is revealing meaning and applying a knowledge of language.

Cloze testing is an informal assessment strategy that is neither time-consuming nor difficult. Interpreting the responses may prove more valuable in securing information about a student's reading level than simply identifying the level. Many teachers use the Cloze procedure as a prereading activity in order to determine the students' background knowledge for the content. If the majority of the students perform at the instructional level, the teacher may decide to spend time developing students' prior knowledge before actually beginning the unit, or the teacher may decide to bring in additional resources about the subject at varying readability levels.

Just as with all forms of informal assessment, the teacher may decide to modify the Cloze procedure to make it more appropriate for diverse learners. A fifth-word deletion may be too difficult for some students, so you may wish to delete every eighth or tenth word.

A modification of the Cloze procedure is the maze procedure. Rather than supplying the deleted word, the student selects a word from a vertical array. The Cloze procedure is essentially a recall task, whereas the maze procedure is a recognition task. Selective identification of words allows you to determine a student's attention to context and understanding of language. Obviously, in using this or any idea incorporated into informal assessment, you must fit the levels of the students involved. Following is an example of the maze procedure.

paddled
The boy swam his boat across the large lake.
leaned

swimming
   searching for a good fishing spot. He saw a small
moved

                                    water.
cove with tree limbs hanging over the ice.
                              case.

Authentic Assessment/Performance-Based Assessment

Observing, interacting, and interviewing are authentic or performance-based assessment procedures that provide information beyond basic skills development. Whether you use the term authentic assessment, *alternative assessment,* or *performance-based assessment,* you are still using a form of assessment that no longer views assessment as the endpoint to learning. Instead, assessment is viewed as an integral part of teaching (Reichel, 1994). Authentic forms of assessment enable the teacher to gather information specific to instruction and to students' progress while they are engaged in meaningful reading and writing tasks. Assessing for instruction provides teachers with the opportunity to gain useful information about students' world knowledge; attitudes towards reading, writing, and content area; and strategies used to gain meaning from text.

One of the simplest and most-used authentic assessment procedures might consist of having a student read aloud a short selection from a book to determine whether he or she can identify the words and construct meaning for that particular book. Such an informal assessment procedure can yield important information about the student's word-recognition strategies and comprehension. In addition, such interaction focuses on real literature that engages the student over longer passages of sustained reading than standardized tests generally contain.

Another form of authentic assessment is interviewing. Interviewing students about their reading and writing can provide teachers with valuable insights and help students become more aware of their own literacy interests, reading and writing strategies, and progress (McKenna & Kear, 1990). Examples of questions that teachers can use when interviewing students include the following:

1. What do you think makes a good reader? What do you think makes a good writer? (These questions indicate how the student conceptualizes reading and writing.)
2. If you were to read a story about (any chosen topic), what kinds of information do you think you would find in the story?
3. When you come to a word you don't know, how do you figure it out? Show me in a story how you would figure out a word you did not know.
4. Let's look at the list of books that you have read. Which ones were your favorites? Which books did you find hard to read? Which book(s) would you like to read again and again? Why?

Teachers of literacy have long realized the value of gathering informal assessment information on individual students. Such information is needed to adequately plan an instructional program that meets each student's needs.

Photo courtesy of Anne M. Hyland, Bexley, Ohio Schools; photographer, Arthur Burt, Inc.

UPDATE

In addition to the teacher's gathering informal assessment information on individual students for planning instruction, students are also becoming active participants in the assessment process. Portfolios are expandable folders for each student that can include a variety of literacy learning indicators. For example, students often select their best works to include in their portfolios. Actively involving students in the assessment process makes them more aware of their own learning and causes them to reflect on their own learning in positive ways.

Presidental Biography
GRADE SHEET

1. **DESCRIBE YOUR PRESIDENT. (Remember to elaborate!)**

   - What did your president look like? **(2 points)**   2
   - Tell what your president's nickname was, if he had one. **(1 point)**   1
   - What is the most famous thing your president is known for? **(2 points)**   2

   5 points possible   **Total points earned:** 5

2. **PROVIDE DETAILS ABOUT YOUR PRESIDENT'S CHILDHOOD.**

   - birthday **(2 points)**   2
   - parents' names/jobs **(1 point)**   1
   - place of birth **(2 points)**   2
   - brothers/sisters **(1 point)**   1
   - tell about an interesting event that happened as a child/teen **(4 points)**   4

   10 points possible   **Total points earned:** 10

3. **WHAT JOBS DID YOUR PRESIDENT HAVE BEFORE BECOMING PRESIDENT?**

   - Did you list the jobs and add interesting details about at least one job? 5

   5 points possible   **Total points earned:** 5

4. **TELL WHAT MADE YOUR PRESIDENT INTERESTED IN POLITICS/WHY YOUR PRESIDENT RAN FOR OFFICE.**

   - Did you attempt to give a reason based on your research? 2

   2 points possible   **Total points earned:** 2

5. **OF WHICH POLITICAL PARTY WAS YOUR PRESIDENT A MEMBER?**

   - Did you explain some things that the political party believed in at the time? (This is called a party's **platform**.) 2

   3 points possible   **Total points earned:** 2

Figure 11.8 Example of a teacher-developed rubric for reading research.

5. What do you enjoy most about writing? What do you not enjoy about writing? What makes writing fun or easy for you?
6. What makes understanding some stories easy for you?
7. If you have to read a science book to discuss in class, what do you think this means? Tell me how you would read a science book so we can later talk about it.
8. What do you like to write about the most? Why?
9. What does the title of a story or book tell you?
10. If we had a new student entering our class who did not know what it meant to read, how would you describe reading to that student?

6. **ANSWER THESE QUESTIONS ABOUT HIS PRESIDENCY:**

- During which years was he President? **(5 points)**   5
- Who was his vice-president? **(4 points)**   4
- Did most people like him as President? Give reasons. **(4 points)**   4
- What were the **most important** things he did during his presidency? **(15 points)**   15
- What was the country like while he was President? **(3 points)**   3
- What happened to end his presidency? **(4 points)**
  (died, defeated, couldn't run)   0

35 points possible   **Total points earned:**   31

7. **WHAT DID YOUR PRESIDENT DO AFTER HE LEFT OFFICE?**   10
   OR
   TELL HOW YOUR PRESIDENT DIED IN OFFICE.

10 points possible   **Total points earned:**   10

8. **TELL ABOUT THE PRESIDENT'S FAMILY.**

- Tell about his wife (wives) if he was married. **(5 points)**   5
- Tell about his children. **(5 points)**   5
- (OPTIONAL) Tell about the President's pets.
- (OPTIONAL) If you can, tell an interesting fact about his family.

10 points possible (+ bonus)   **Total points earned:**   10

9. **TELL HOW YOUR PRESIDENT DIED.**   5
   (Skip this if your president is still alive).

5 points possible (5 credit if still alive)   **Total points earned:**   5

10. **TELL WHAT YOU ADMIRE ABOUT YOUR PRESIDENT.**   5
    (This is your opinion, and you won't find this in a book.)

5 points possible   **Total points earned:**   5

11. **MECHANICS/GRAMMAR**

- Were most words spelled correctly?   **(2 points)**   2
- Were all sentences capitalized?   **(2 points)**   2
- Did all sentences have end marks?   **(2 points)**   2
- Was your handwriting or typing neat and clean?   **(2 points)**   2

10 points possible   **Total points earned:**   10

Total Score: 95

COMMENTS: _____

Matt, you wrote a very well-written,
informative report. Thank you for working
so hard on this!

Figure 11.8 (continued)

Source: From Susan O'Neill, fourth-grade teacher, Rock Prairie Elementary School, College Station, TX.

Insights for both the teacher and students can be gained from such interviews about perceptions of reading and writing, strategies used for both reading and writing, and growth and development in literacy.

It has also been determined by teachers that asking students about their writing and reading miscues can shed some light on the thought processes used by the students. Asking a child why he or she pronounced a word a certain way forces the child to analyze his or her own miscues. Audiotaping students while they read orally and having them go back and critically listen to themselves read while the teacher leads them in discussion about their reading performance is also a beneficial interviewing technique.

Rubrics

Rubrics are a form of authentic, performance-based assessment that guides both students and teacher. Rubrics can be used for assessment in both reading and writing. A benefit of using rubrics is that they can focus on a stated learning outcome or benchmark (uses punctuation correctly), represent a broad area of proficiency (writing a cohesive piece), and provide a road map or guide for synthesis of learning (integration of multiple ways to represent learning). A major advantage of using rubrics as either a learning situation or as an assessment procedure is that students develop skills for thinking about and reflecting on their learning that transfer to new learning situations (Skillings & Ferrell, 2000). The rubric presented in Figure 11.8 was developed by Susan O'Neill, a fourth-grade teacher, to guide and evaluate stu-

Very best level 3	Okay level 2	Not so good level 1
• Choose a character	• Choose a character	• Choose a character
• Write four things the character did	• Write two to three things the character did	• Write one thing the character did
• Write two reasons for character's actions	• Write one reason for character's actions	• No reason given for the character's actions
• Illustrate character in appropriate setting with at least three details	• Illustrate character in appropriate setting with at least two details	• Illustration wrong for setting—few details
• Complete sentences	• Most sentences are complete	• Some sentences not complete
• Proper heading	• Heading complete	• Heading incomplete
• Neatly done	• Not as neat	• Paper is messy

Figure 11.9   Structured character rubric.

Source: From M. J. Skillings and R. Ferrell, "Student-Generated Rubrics: Bring Students into the Assessment Process," *The Reading Teacher, 53* (2000), pp. 452–455. Reprinted with permission of the authors and the International Reading Association. Copyright by the International Reading Association. All rights reserved.

dents' reading research on Presidents of the United States. The features that are associated with each part of the students' research and writing are clearly identified for the students before (used as a purpose-setting introduction), during (to guide and assist in researching and writing), and after (specific feedback about how the final report was evaluated).

Additional advantages for students and the teacher include:

- Assessment is objective, consistent, and focused on valued learning outcomes.
- Evaluation of the work, project, or participation is made clear to the students.
- Feedback is provided about the effectiveness of the teacher's instruction.
- Criteria identified by the teacher are explicit and aligned with instruction.
- Confidence for the students is increased because they are aware of the standards they are to meet and the knowledge associated with the learning concepts.

Students can actively play a role in both developing and expanding rubrics based on an identified set of criteria. For example, Figure 11.9 is a teacher-developed rubric that is structured for instruction and assessment of students' understanding of story characters. The students provided input and expanded the rubric application to a broader range of reading and writing activities (see Figure 11.10).

Anecdotal Records

Observation checklists can be helpful when teachers are focusing on features of reading and writing for a number of students. Anecdotal records, however, provide more detail, allow for variations among students, and recognize the range in literacy capabilities within a classroom. As noted by Rhodes and Nathenson-Mejia

3 Very best level	2 Okay level	1 Not so good level
• Shows clear understanding • Shows creativity • Illustrations colored with details • Correct spelling • Done on time • Neatly done • Proper heading	• Some understanding • A little creativity • A few colors & details • Some spelling errors • Done on time—1 day late • Not neatest work • Proper heading	• Not so clear understanding • Little or no creativity • Little coloring & details • Many spelling errors • More than 1 day late • Sloppy work • May have proper heading

Figure 11.10 Expanded rubric.

Source: From M. J. Skillings and R. Ferrell, "Student-Generated Rubrics: Bring Students into the Assessment Process," *The Reading Teacher, 53* (2000), pp. 452–455. Reprinted with permission of the authors and the International Reading Association. Copyright by the International Reading Association. All rights reserved.

(1992), "What is focused on and recorded depends upon the teacher, the student, and the context, not on predetermined items on a checklist" (pp. 502–503).

Guidelines for writing anecdotal records (Rhodes & Nathenson-Mejia, 1992) include the following steps: (1) describe the event or product rather than just recording the general impression, (2) focus on rich descriptions rather than evaluations, and (3) relate the anecdote to information known about the child. The following example illustrates these features:

Showed Mary how to skip a word that she didn't know in her reading as a way to figure out its meaning. She was reading a book about experiments for children and didn't know the meaning of *absorbed.*

She grasped the idea quickly and read two sentences beyond the word and noted excitedly that the word must mean the liquid went from the glass up to the petals of the flower. Encouraged her to do this with other words that she might not know the meaning of.

Anecdotal records can be used effectively with individual students as well as with small groups. Teachers can identify students for whom anecdotal information would be beneficial. For example, anecdotal records might help in trying to determine what is contributing to a student's disruptive behavior at the writing center, or why Jason is unwilling to edit his writing, or how well Mary is using context to figure out the meaning of unknown words.

Analysis of anecdotal records often reveals patterns of both difficulty and success for students. Teachers using anecdotal records for assessment have noted why certain organizational schemes (e.g., paired reading, interest groups, peer editing) were successful or unsuccessful, how students used or failed to use strategies for reading informational text, how certain instructional features (e.g., time allotted for an activity, modeling, scaffolding, feedback) enhanced and facilitated students' learning, and how much growth students have experienced over a period of time. One of the most important features of anecdotal records is that their use makes teachers more aware of their interaction with their students and the effects of their instruction on students' learning.

Response Journals

Although all forms of student writing can be used in assessment, response journals are of important value because they integrate reading and writing. **Response journals** are written responses, between the student and teacher or between students, to a learning experience and to the written responses of others. Response journals encourage students to think about how and what they read, and how their reading develops through writing. This form of reflection encourages students to take a more active role in the reading and evaluation process. As students write about their reading, it becomes more personal. They are encouraged to connect what they are reading with past experiences, monitor their comprehension, and ask questions left unclear by the text. Through reading the teacher's responses, students become more

Inclusion Strategies

Meeting Students' Literacy Needs

Assessment is an essential component of every classroom literacy program. The value of assessment is increasing as we include children with special needs in regular classrooms. Effective teachers of reading employ a variety of informal assessment procedures, as evidenced by the following description of Joan Thrumond's assessment of Brett's delayed literacy acquisition.

Mrs. Thrumond used a variety of informal assessment procedures with Brett. She administered an IRI, observed literacy behavior in a variety of contexts, and focused on construction of meaning. Mrs. Thrumond's qualitative analysis of Brett's miscues resulted in the following:

> Brett relies heavily on a limited sight vocabulary to recognize words. He guessed at many words using the initial letter as a cue to identification. He recognized few words on sight and would not attempt to identify words that did not offer him initial-letter cues (this could account for the large number of teacher-pronounced words on the IRI). It appears that Brett has minimal strategies for recognizing and identifying words. He does not appear concerned with whether or not his guesses make sense in the context of the sentence or the text. There were no regressions or self-corrections noted in his reading.

Brett had minimal success in both answering comprehension questions and retelling the stories he had read. This came as no surprise to Joan, however; she had anticipated that Brett would construct little meaning from what he read. He appeared to have no idea that we read to get meaning. When he was asked to describe reading, Brett used examples that related to identifying words, completing school-related tasks, and performing a difficult task.

---

conscious of their reading strategies and development. With the advancement of technology, many response journals today are conducted via the Internet by the use of electronic mail. These technological advancements can allow the teacher to respond to several journals at the same time and facilitate interaction among students.

Students' responses can disclose what they are understanding about what they read, their attitudes and motivation toward what they read, and the strategies they use when reading. Response journals will help teachers better understand four areas of students' reading: comprehension, reading processes, knowledge of literature, and engagement in reading.

Wollman-Bonilla (1991) summarized the assessment information teachers obtain in these four areas:

Inclusion Strategies

Meeting Students' Literacy Needs (continued)

Synthesizing assessment information gained from the IRI (word recognition, comprehension, and strategies), observation, and the interview, Mrs. Thrumond felt that Brett had a limited sight vocabulary, lacked strategies for recognizing words, thought reading was a school task only, and experienced difficulty in using context as an aid in identifying words that made sense in reading. She reflected on Brett's strengths and weaknesses and identified the following instructional procedures to meet his needs.

- Read books about camping and the outdoors to Brett. Use selected text from them to illustrate that reading is getting meaning by discussing story content with him. Use Brett's knowledge and enjoyment of the outdoors to form the basis for writing activities.
- Guide and encourage Brett to talk about camping and outdoor activities for language experience stories. Direct and guide him in selecting words from the stories to include in his word bank.
- Provide concrete examples of application of sight words in the meaningful context of trade books and language experience stories.
- Construct meaningful phrases and sentences from words from Brett's word bank. Develop games in which he and other students take turns using words selected from the word bank that make sense in a given context.
- Complete several practice examples for independent activities before Brett completes the activity independently.
- Use prompts and cues to maximize his chance of success in responding to instructional demands in discussion situations.
- Focus instruction on his strengths and emphasize the relationship of words he recognized to words he is to learn. Structure instruction in small, highly related steps.
- Provide many opportunities for teacher-supported practice and reinforcement of new words and strategies to real reading situations.
- Use sincere feedback and verbal praise to focus on his success during learning activities.

- *Comprehension:* Students' responses can reveal their understanding of characters, setting, story events, and resolutions, which are the major components of story grammar. Wollman-Bonilla says, "Responses can illuminate the reason for comprehension problems and the type of instructional guidance [that is needed] " (p. 57).
- *Reading processes:* Information about linguistic cues (graphophonic, syntactic, and semantic) that students use can be their responses.
  "I didn't know what repetition meant. But after I read that Mark said, 'I'm going to do it again, and again, and again, until I can do it,' I figured out what it meant." Other

All forms of student writing can be used in assessment.

responses—such as *"I like the way she* (the author) *told what kind of day it was (bright, cheery, and everything seemed to sparkle). It made me think that everything was going to turn out okay for Sara"*—indicate that students are forming hypotheses as they read.

- *Knowledge of literature:* Students' knowledge of literature (e.g., language, foreshadowing, irony) helps them to predict what the text will be about. For example, Billy wrote in his journal, *"I knew Jake was going to get lost when just before the big snowstorm he lost his compass."*

- *Engagement in reading:* Indicators of students' engagement are questioning, relating the text to their own lives, sharing opinions, and demonstrating feelings and emotions. Examples of engagement are *"I began to cry when . . ."* *"I know how Cassie feels because . . ."* and *"I didn't like the part where. . . ."*

Teachers' responses to students' journals can reinforce the use of strategies; motivate continued reading; model grammar, spelling, and punctuation; and communicate the value of reading and writing (see Figure 11.11). In addition, students can be active participants in their own assessment (Santa, 1995). They can use self-evaluation forms to focus on areas related to their reading. The questions used for interviews can form the core for such self-evaluations for older students (e.g., "When I come to a

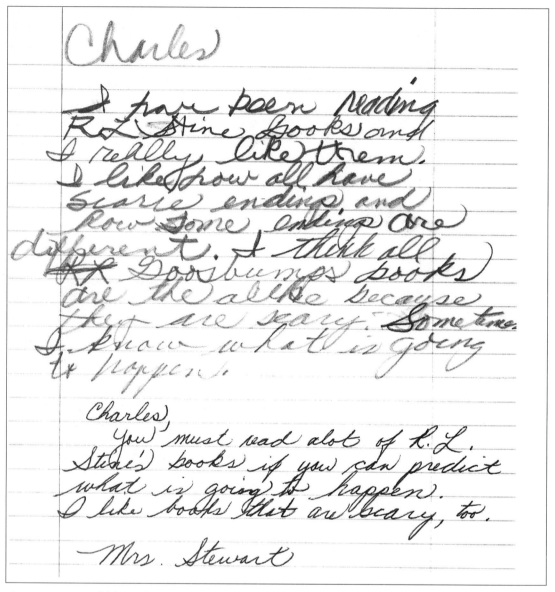

Charles

I have been reading R.L. Stine books and I really like them. I like how all have scarie endings and how some endings are different. I think all ~~R.L.~~ Goosbumps books are the alike because they are scary. ~~Sometime~~ I know what is going to happen.

Charles,
You must read alot of R.L. Stine's books if you can predict what is going to happen. I like books that are scary, too.

Mrs. Stewart

Figure 11.11 A fifth grader's entry in his response journal about reading *Goosebump* books. Notice that Mrs. Stewart commented on his ability to predict based on knowledge of the books' language structure and context.

word I don't know I figure it out by _____ "). Younger students can respond to similar questions to those on reading experience inventories by circling *yes* or *no* or by circling a happy or sad face. Anecdotal records can summarize students' response journals over time. Teachers can share this information with the students, their parents, and administrators to illustrate students' reading and writing development.

Another way to evaluate students' learning through their writing is through the use of admit slips and exit slips. These slips of paper administered to students as they enter or exit the classroom are brief comments written by the students that address students' reactions to what they are studying in class. Students are asked to respond to questions such as the following:

What is your favorite thing about this class?

What is the most valuable thing you learned from this assignment?

What was your least favorite part of this assignment?

What problems did you encounter in the text?

This simple form of assessment allows the teacher to gain insight into each student's learning processes and attitudes toward learning. Admit and exit slips also allow the students some control in the direction of their learning and allow them to evaluate the method of instruction as well as their own learning styles.

Portfolios

Teachers have long recognized the value of keeping samples of students' work in reading and writing as a means of assessment. In the past, however, these samples were often based solely on skill activities and, occasionally, creative writing. Literacy portfolios are a type of performance-based assessment—they represent students' engagement with real literacy tasks (e.g., reading books, writing letters, creative writing, response journals, diaries). A portfolio also can contain many of the assessment features presented earlier, such as anecdotal records, experience inventories, observation records, and conference notes (Tierney, Carter, & Desai, 1991).

Portfolios are expandable file folders, binders, or boxes created and decorated by each student that include a variety of indicators of learning to help students, teachers, administrators, and parents understand literacy growth and development. These selected collections of student work and records of performance collected across diverse contexts over time demonstrate the advancement of student learning (Wolf & Siu-Runyan, 1996). For portfolios to be useful, they should be kept in an easily accessible place for students and teachers, and both students and teachers should contribute to them regularly and use the contents for planning subsequent learning (Valencia, 1990).

What should be included in a student's portfolio?

Any item that the student deems important and shows development and growth of the student's learning over time should be included in the portfolio. A portfolio is a repository of a student's thoughts, ideas, and language-related growth and materials. Because many portfolios are working portfolios, students often include original pieces, thoughts, and inspirations. These pieces should reflect a student's work and growth in the creation process. The best portfolio pieces represent the integration among all learning and are constantly evolving to illustrate lifelong learning.

How often should portfolios be used?

Portfolios are used on a daily basis and become the focal point for student and teacher interactions and discussion. Students should have access to their portfolios at all times and should be encouraged to assess their working portfolios on the basis of need. Because student-teacher discussion is a key element in the success of the portfolio assessment, teachers should regularly talk with students about their developing processes as language users. Teachers and students should also discuss student attitudes and interests related to reading, writing, and thinking through the use of their portfolios.

According to Wolf and Siu-Runyan (1996), portfolios should meet the following criteria:

1. Portfolios should be selective. They should include a selection of information gathered for specific purposes. These purposes can include self-assessment, documentation of student learning, guidance for teacher instruction, and communication among parents, teachers, and students. Portfolios also can be used to provide administrators and policy makers with information about the school district's instructional program.

2. Portfolios should be a collection of students' work and progress. The essential element of all portfolios is the students' work. This can include student writing, reading journals, collaborative projects, and artistic creations.

3. Portfolios should contain diverse information. When students' portfolios include diverse information, the teacher is able to see each students' full range of talents and interests.

4. Portfolios should show development over time. One of the differences between standardized tests and portfolios is that standardized tests provide the teacher only with black-and-white snapshots of students' performance, while portfolios are more like color movies that show events over time.

5. Portfolios should be reflective. Student portfolio reflection allows students to assess their own learning experiences and become more evaluative of their work. Reflections in portfolios often take the form of written comments focusing on the quality of the work and the revision processes that were used in improving the portfolio piece. Reflection can be in the form of drawings and graphs as well as other types of student and teacher reflection.

6. Portfolios should be collaborative. Because learning is not viewed as a solitary process, portfolios should include the interactions of others. The interaction of one's peers, parents, and teachers should play a significant factor in the portfolio process. When students discuss their ideas with others, they deepen their ability to reflect on their own work from more than one perspective.

7. The goal of portfolios is to advance student learning. The advancement of student learning must be the overall objective of portfolio development.

The form of a portfolio can vary greatly, depending upon its purpose. Wolf and Siu-Runyan (1996) identified three distinct portfolio models. These three models are the ownership portfolio, the feedback portfolio, and the accountability portfolio. Ownership portfolios contain samples of student's work and self-assessment. Students choose which examples of their work to add to their portfolios. Often, the teacher may wish to help students select the examples by discussing with each child the features of the selection and reasons for including it in the portfolio. The major advantage of having students select their own examples for ownership portfolios is that it actively involves them in the process and makes them more aware of their own learning. The teacher can use students' portfolios to engage them in discussions about why they included a particular sample, how they have grown in their learning, what they liked and disliked in books they read, the quality of their writing, and their use of reading and writing strategies. Ownership portfolios provide students with the opportunity to take an active and responsible role in their own learning.

The feedback portfolio, coconstructed by the student and the teacher, includes comprehensive collections of student work and teacher records. These portfolios not only include student work and reflection, but also include anecdotal records about student learning, observations, interviews, response journal entries, activity work, and responses to discussion, as well as peer and parent feedback. These portfolios provide students, parents, and teachers with information about students' learning strengths and weaknesses. They are extremely useful in assisting teachers in designing effective instruction based around student learning styles and needs as well as assessing students' learning growth. This type of portfolio is also valuable in communicating with parents about their child's use of effective learning strategies.

An accountability portfolio includes selective collections of student work, teacher records, and standardized assessments selected by both student and teacher according to structured guidelines. Accountability portfolios are used primarily to evaluate student achievement for accountability and for program evaluation.

Portfolios can be extremely useful in instructional decisions because they provide a broad sampling of students' literacy development over extended periods, in a variety of tasks, and in different contexts. These features are important for several reasons. First, multiple samples of students' reading and writing help better explain individual students' learning of these complex processes. Second, by collecting current information about their students, teachers can better understand how their students regularly perform classroom tasks (Winograd & Jones, 1992).

A discussion of some of the basic assessment purposes (Defina, 1992; Engel, 1994) of portfolios follows. Teachers need to determine which of the basic purposes are appropriate for their students and their instructional goals.

- *Monitoring students' growth over time.* Contents of students' portfolios will provide information about how much they have learned in specific areas, such as descriptive writing, use of reading strategies, and so forth.
- *Examining students' understandings about process.* Students going back to learning activities and products will help provide the teacher with insights into their understanding that a completed product (a piece of writing) requires careful deliberation, revision, and rethinking.
- *Creating opportunities for students' self-evaluation.* Portfolio contents readily identify students' literacy strengths and weaknesses, which helps teachers address individual student needs.
- *Observing growth of culturally and linguistically diverse students.* Diverse students' performance on standardized tests typically does not accurately reflect their literacy capabilities. Portfolios do, however, allow teachers to determine better students' growth and development in relation to literacy tasks occurring in the classroom.
- *Observing students' language development.* Because portfolios contain samples that represent students' actual language use, they can help teachers evaluate students' language comprehension and development.
- *Evaluating and developing a literacy curriculum.* Teachers can revise the curriculum based on students' learning in relation to what they know, what they have learned, and what they need to know.
- *Determining the effectiveness of literacy instruction.* The teacher can analyze items in portfolios to determine what is effective with individual students, groups of students, and the class.

Although portfolio assessment can be extremely beneficial for both teachers and students, some obstacles hinder its successful use in an elementary school. Portfolios will work successfully only if they have (1) schoolwide support, particularly from the principal, (2) no competition from other forms of assessment, such as skills tests, which can result in teachers becoming frustrated, (3) self-reliance on the part of the teacher, and (4) valid teacher judgments (Dewitz, Carr, Palm, & Spencer, 1992).

SUMMARY

Students' literacy abilities, interests, and development in any given classroom reflect a wide range. Assessment is necessary to differentiate instruction, which, in turn, is essential for a sound literacy program. In effective literacy instruction, ongoing assessment provides the blueprint for instruction.

Formal assessment generally involves the use of standardized tests. Unfortunately, many of the standardized tests do not accurately reflect all of our knowledge about the reading and writing processes. Assessment of students' learning should include a combination of procedures that reflect what we know about literacy and the use of literacy skills in meaningful reading and writing situations.

Meaningful assessment is ongoing and includes a variety of informal procedures, such as anecdotal records, informal reading inventories, portfolios, and teacher observation. Any time students engage in a literacy activity or event—reading, writing, and editing, to name a few—they provide the teacher with clues about their instructional needs and literacy growth.

YOUR POINT OF VIEW

Discussion Questions

1. You have just gotten your first teaching position. You are teaching fourth grade and it is the third week of school. You suspect that Dee cannot read the social studies text that has been adopted for class use. You wish to verify or refute this suspicion. What assessment procedures would you use? How would you interpret the assessment information?

2. A new student has enrolled in your classroom and you want to plan the student's reading instruction. What assessment procedures would you use if no information is available from the student's former school?

Take a Stand For or Against

1. Informal assessment procedures can yield as much information about an individual student's reading as can standardized tests.

2. Authentic assessment is better than any type of assessment strategy or procedure that a teacher could use.

Field-Based Assignments

1. Administer an informal reading inventory to a child in the classroom in which you are working. Conduct a qualitative analysis of the child's performance on the IRI. Interview the child using the questions suggested in this chapter. Record the child's responses and discuss them with the child. Compare the results of your IRI analysis with the child's performance in class.

2. Request to look at several teachers' examples of how they use portfolio assessment in their literacy program. Using the information about different types of portfolio entries presented in the chapter, identify the types being used by these teachers. Discuss with one or two children the entries they chose to include in their portfolios and why they selected those pieces.

Portfolio Entry

Draw a chart of how you would begin assessment in your own classroom and what steps would emanate from that beginning. Reflect on what you would do, what information you would gain for instructional planning, and your rationale for using different types of literacy assessment.

BIBLIOGRAPHY

Betts, E. A. (1946). *Foundations of reading instruction.* New York: American Book Co.

Defina, A. A. (1992). *Portfolio assessment.* New York: Scholastic Professional Books.

Dewitz, P., Carr, E. M., Palm, K. N., & Spencer, M. (1992). The validity and utility of portfolio assessment. In C. Kinzer & D. Leu (Eds.), *Literacy research, theory, and practice: Views from many perspectives* (pp. 153–159). Chicago: National Reading Conference.

Early, M. (1992/93). What ever happened to . . . ? *The Reading Teacher, 46,* 302–309.

Engel, B. S. (1994). Portfolio assessment and the new paradigm: New instruments and new places. *Educational Forum, 59,* 22–27.

International Reading Association and National Council of Teachers of English. (1994). *Standards for the assessment of reading and writing.* Author.

Ivey, G., & Broaddus, K. (2000). Tailoring the fit: Reading instruction and middle school readers. *The Reading Teacher, 54,* 68–78.

McKenna, M., & Kear, D. (1990). Measuring attitude toward reading: A new tool for teachers. *The Reading Teacher, 43,* 626–639.

Powell, W. R. (1976). Informal reading inventories: Points of view. Speech presented at the annual meeting of the College Reading Association, Miami.

Rankin, E., & Culhane, J. (1969). Comparable Cloze and multiple choice comprehension test scores. *Journal of Reading, 13,* 193–198.

Reichel, A. G. (1994). Performance assessment: Five practical approaches. *Science and Children, 22,* 21–25.

Rhodes, L. K., & Nathenson-Mejia, S. (1992). Anecdotal records: A powerful tool for ongoing literacy assessment. *The Reading Teacher, 45,* 502–511.

Santa, C. M. (1995). Assessment: Students lead their own parent conferences. *Teaching PreK–8, 25,* 92–94.

Skillings, M. J., & Ferrell, R. (2000). Student-generated rubrics: Bring students into the assessment process. *The Reading Teacher, 53,* 452–455.

Tierney, R., Carter, M., & Desai, L. (1991). *Portfolio assessment in reading-writing classrooms.* Norwood, MA: Christopher-Gordon.

Tompkins, G. E. (2001). *Literacy for the 21st century* (2nd ed.). Upper Saddle River, NJ: Merrill/Prentice Hall.

Valencia, S. (1990). A portfolio approach to classroom reading assessment: The whys, whats, and hows. *The Reading Teacher, 43,* 338–341.

Walker, B. J. (2000). *Diagnostic teaching of reading: Techniques for instruction and assessment* (4th ed.). Upper Saddle River, NJ: Merrill/Prentice Hall.

Winograd, P., & Jones, D. L. (1992). The use of portfolios in performance assessment. In J. Craig (Ed.), *New directions for education reform: Performance assessment* (pp. 37–50). Western Kentucky University.

Wolf, K., & Siu-Runyan, Y. (1996). Portfolio purposes and possibilities. *Journal of Adolescent and Adult Literacy, 40,* 30–37.

Wollman-Bonilla, J. (1991). *Response journals.* New York: Scholastic Professional Books.

Woods, M. L., & Moe, A. J. (1999). *Analytical reading inventory* (6th ed.). Upper Saddle River, NJ: Merrill/Prentice Hall.

Worthy, J., & Hoffman, J. V. (2000). Critical questions: The press to test. *The Reading Teacher, 53,* 596–598.

12

Classroom Management and Organization

Chapter Outline

For the Reader

Do you recall your first experience with a large group of students in a classroom? If you have not yet started to teach, do you worry about how you will handle a large group of children? In either case, you can contemplate some of the demands and constraints of a classroom. Your perceived notions of assessment teaching—pretesting, setting objectives, teaching, allowing for student practice, using a variety of materials, reinforcing abilities in a variety of situations, and posttesting—must operate in the context of a class of 20 to 35 children.

As you know, students within any group differ in a variety of ways. Within the context of the classroom, you must strive to accommodate these individual differences. Effective reading teachers understand the organizational conditions found in their teaching situations and use various grouping procedures to maximize student learning.

This chapter discusses the various options teachers have in teaching a large group of children. Current research suggests a strong relationship between classroom management and student achievement; therefore, meeting the demands of the classroom setting will provide rewards for both you and your students.

Key Ideas

- Effective classroom management and organization correlate with increased student achievement.

- Teachers of reading must be adept at planning and organizing their classrooms.

- Effective teachers are successful managers; they are aware of the total classroom environment and practice preventative measures to maintain a good learning environment.

- Small-group instruction promotes more interaction, discussion, and learning than does whole-class instruction.

- Cooperative grouping promotes peer tutoring, encouragement, and achievement.

- An individualized reading approach uses the principles of seeking, self-selection, and self-pacing.

- Implementing effective reading instruction in a class requires careful planning of materials, instruction, and time to meet the needs of individual students.

THE IMPORTANCE OF CLASSROOM MANAGEMENT

A history of U.S. education dealing primarily with classroom practices would be, in essence, a history of the attempts to deal with student differences. All of the principles, techniques, approaches, materials, and assessment tools of effective teachers contribute to the instruction of students. The plural *students* is key in the previous sentence; effective teaching of reading includes organizing and maintaining a classroom environment for 20 to 35 students that maximizes their learning. Effective classroom management and organization correlate with increased student achievement. Evertson, Emmer, and Worsham (2000) underscore the importance of effective classroom management in stating:

> Students entering the nation's schools come with such widely diverse backgrounds, capabilities, interests, and skills that meeting their needs and finding appropriate learning activities require a great deal of care and skill. Because one of the first and most basic tasks for teachers is to develop smoothly running classroom communities where students are highly involved in worthwhile activities that support their learning establishing an effective classroom management system is a first priority. (p. xi)

The preceding quote underscores the interdependence of instructional and managerial concerns. A teacher can employ the best reading techniques and materials but be unsuccessful as a result of poor classroom management. The reverse can also happen; a teacher may implement management techniques for conditions conducive to learning but not provide differentiated instruction. Often, new teachers are judged by their ability to manage a classroom effectively. In addition, studies of new and experienced teachers indicate that classroom management is one of the most difficult and stressful elements in teaching (Lasley, 1987).

PREVENTATIVE CLASSROOM MANAGEMENT

The literature on teacher effectiveness indicates that effective classrooms are well managed and feature large amounts of quality time, that is, periods when students are actively engaged with the teacher or materials (Blair and Jones, 1998). Poor management of students, reading groups, and activities usually translates into little quality engaged time. Effective classroom managers devote considerable time to preventative classroom management. As Good and Brophy (1987) succinctly state, "The key to success lies in the things the teacher does ahead of time to create a good learning environment and a low potential for trouble" (p. 177).

Effective classroom managers (1) prepare and plan, (2) manage group instruction, and (3) monitor student progress. At the beginning of the school year, successful teachers devote the time and energy necessary for getting to know their students, setting instructional goals, and making sure that the students know what is expected of them. Successful teachers also plan their lessons in advance, break their lessons down into small, concise parts for presentation, and plan a variety of activities to keep students engaged in learning. Effective teachers invest time and energy

Preventative classroom management includes having all plans and materials ready to use well in advance of the actual lesson.

into planning. As a result, they have fewer disruptions and are more productive during the reading class.

Grouping students by itself does not automatically boost student achievement. The quality of student and teacher interaction during grouping is the key. The successful teacher manages group instruction by maintaining quality learning time. Berliner and Casanova (1996) summarize what researchers know about good classroom managers:

> In short, from the opening bell to the end of the day, the better classroom managers are thinking ahead. While maintaining a pleasant classroom atmosphere, these teachers keep planning how to organize, manage, and control activities in order to facilitate instruction. They also insure that the instructional program is interesting and that the goals of the program are achievable by most students. Management is

much easier when the curriculum is interesting and success in it is possible. So the best managers of classrooms also were excellent in designing instruction. (p. 35)

Kounin (1970) identified group management techniques of effective teachers. His findings relate to both planning the groups of students and actually conducting group discussion. Blair and Jones (1998) reported on the six qualities of successful managers that Kounin identified:

1. With-it-ness is a teacher's ability to be continuously aware of what's going on in the classroom and to communicate this awareness to students.
2. Overlapping is a teacher's ability to do more than one thing at a time in the classroom without getting frustrated.
3. Smoothness of transition is the ability to go from one activity to another or one part of a lesson to another without wasted time and/or undue delay.
4. Momentum is the teacher's ability to pace lessons.
5. Group alerting is the teacher's ability to keep students' attention during lessons.
6. Accountability is the teacher's ability to know how well students are learning. (p. 67)

Monitoring students during group work entails (1) interacting directly with students or checking on student progress during seatwork and (2) using physical proximity or task-related comments to ensure that the students are working productively. Monitoring students helps you realize how well your students are understanding the activity; it also serves to maintain student engagement. Monitoring can help prevent, or at least minimize, potential management problems.

Following are practical suggestions by Blair and Jones (1998) to implement the preventative classroom management areas. Consider the following suggestions in your preparation before the school year begins:

- Collect as much assessment data on students as possible.
- Decide on classroom behavior rules and procedures that are not negotiable with students. These rules may concern tardiness, dismissal, hall passes, makeup work, homework, and so forth.
- Decide how you will explain classroom behavior standards, your expectations concerning assignments, and classroom procedures.
- Organize and arrange instructional materials for easy access or distribution.
- Plan the seating arrangement to ensure a smooth transition of movement from one activity to another. When teaching, you should be able to see the whole class.
- List your rules and procedures on the chalkboard or on a bulletin board. Communicate to students the consequences of improper behavior. (pp. 65–66)

Consider the following suggestions in your preparation to teach a lesson:

- Have all materials ready to use well in advance of the actual lesson.
- Decide on how and when you and the students will use the materials.

- Know when you will distribute materials.
- Highlight times when students will be moving around the room, planning ahead for smooth transitions.
- Plan how you will handle seatwork assignments—including giving directions, collecting finished products, and providing activities for students who finish early—and how you will monitor the students' attention to assignments. (p. 66)

Consider the following suggestions while teaching a lesson:

- Be sensitive to the timing of your explanation. Notice cues from students that indicate interest or lack of interest.
- Do not dwell too long on a topic or a response, but do not leave a question hanging.
- Anticipate problems and handle any misbehavior as quickly and positively as possible.
- Move around the room. (p. 67)

Consider the following suggestions in monitoring student progress:

- Have students show their work to you.
- Have students demonstrate any particular skill or knowledge.
- Ask students directly how they are proceeding.
- Provide meaningful praise.
- Monitor seatwork by walking around the room and stopping to work with individuals.
- Give explicit directions for seatwork assignments. Go over the first two or three examples of any assignment to be certain that students understand the task.
- Be sensitive to signs of confusion, such as unnecessary movement or talking, puzzlement, or an incorrect response to an easy question. (p. 68–69)

GROUPING FOR INSTRUCTION

Grouping students to achieve instructional goals facilitates literacy learning. Grouping for instruction was formerly done more for administrative convenience than anything else. Research supports the use of grouping to increase direct instruction and the amount of engaged time in the classroom. Yet, grouping per se is ineffective if it fails to account for individual needs. The effective teacher uses flexible grouping plans, depending upon the instructional goal. The key is how well various grouping procedures permit the teacher to teach what students need to know. Grouping makes learning with and from one another possible. Researchers at the National Reading Research Center "demonstrated that a carefully orchestrated classroom environment that enables and encourages children to talk and interact socially in multiple literacy-related events (e.g., storybook reading, reading and writing workshops, class sharing times) allows them opportunities to learn about language as they are using it for real, communicative purposes." (Baumann & Duffy, 1997, p. 12).

Teachers must plan and organize their classrooms according to the particular learning goals they have established for their students. Teachers can choose from three basic grouping procedures: (1) whole groups, (2) small groups, and (3) individual learning. At various times, every classroom should incorporate all types of groups.

Large Groups

Large-group or whole-class instruction is appropriate at times in any classroom. When all children need to learn certain skills, large-group instruction is a more efficient use of both teacher and student time. This grouping is appropriate for storytelling, working on art activities related to a story, and teaching various study skills (such as SQ3R; skimming; scanning; reading maps, graphs, diagrams, and charts; using reference books; and using the library effectively).

Small Groups

Small-group instruction is certainly not new. However, various forms of small-group instruction are becoming more and more popular in today's classrooms. As discussed in Chapters 2 and 5, small-group instruction is a factor associated with high levels of student engagement and learning in recent research (Taylor, Pearson, Clark, & Walpole, 1999). Under the umbrella of small groups, skill or special-needs groups, paired or partner groups, interest groups, research groups, and cooperative learning groups are being practiced and studied in classrooms across the country. With learning to read and write an active process in which students need numerous opportunities to construct meanings, more learning results from more classroom interaction than passively listening to a teacher in a large-group setting or reading a book alone. Furthermore, because students are different in so many ways, whole-class grouping does not provide for adapting a lesson's objective to each student's learning needs, nor does it provide the corrective feedback that comes from personalized instruction in small groups. Researchers at the National Reading Research Center (Alvermann et al., 1996) reported that middle and high school students preferred small-group to whole-class discussions. Students felt they had more opportunities to talk and were more willing to take risks and share their ideas in small-group discussions. Newman (1992) points out the advantages of small groups:

- With appropriate tasks and enough flexibility in use of time and resources, small groups afford all students the opportunity to work with knowledge actively—through writing, talking, and dramatization.
- Small groups increase opportunities for feedback on individual work from peers and from the teacher, who can circulate throughout the class and give sustained attention to specific groups and students.
- Small groups offer a motivational boost, because they situate learning in a social setting that many students find more satisfying than working alone.

- In addition to cognitive objectives, small groups offer opportunities to pursue affective and social goals such as building student respect for individual and cultural diversity and developing cooperative social skills. (p. 2)

Likewise, Faltis (2001) reports that small-group learning is advantageous to second-language learners. He lists the benefits for second-language learners in small groups to include increased exposure to meaningful discussion, opportunities for practicing the language, peer interaction that provides a practice ground for students to try out new words and expressions, and increased opportunities for enjoyable, authentic interactions.

Paired/Peer Groups

Pairing two students together to read a story or learn and practice a reading skill or strategy has long been an effective classroom arrangement. Students of similar ability or students of differing abilities can be paired together. In a study by Benton, Belk, and Holifield (1994), high-achieving students were paired with low-achieving students in the fourth grade for all reading activities. Results indicated that the paired reading arrangement motivated children to read more. It was further observed that all the students enjoyed the sharing of a good story with a partner.

Leal (1993) reported on the benefits of peer-group discussions of all types of text. Nine groups of six students in grades 1, 3, and 5 were read a storybook, an informational book, and an informational storybook. Three benefits identified from the collaborative talks about the three types of text were (1) students' assuming responsibility for the discussion, sharing their background of experiences with other students, (2) the opportunities for peer tutoring and collaboration, and (3) the opportunity for a genuine audience of one's peers for discussion topics. In commenting on the positive outcomes of the collaborative talks, Leal states, "When children are provided opportunities to share their own ideas with peers, many good things can happen" (pp. 114–115).

Evertson, Emmer, and Worsham (2000) provide the following additional strategies for using student–student interaction:

- Students work in pairs, reading and listening to each other read. "Reading with a buddy" can be part of contract work.
- Certain students are assigned as monitors to help other students when the teacher is busy with group or individual instruction.
- When the teacher is busy with small-group instruction, students who need help are encouraged to get assistance from another student before interrupting the teacher.
- Group leaders are assigned to each learning station to answer questions and set up materials.
- A capable, mature student is assigned as a helper for another student who needs frequent assistance. The helper's responsibilities are to answer questions and explain directions.
- Students may be permitted to help or seek help from a neighbor on some seatwork activities. (p. 208)

Skill Groups

This type of grouping should depend on assessment of students' specific strengths and weaknesses. Such grouping brings together a small number of students for a specific purpose. Once the skill is mastered, the group is disbanded. Skill groups formed on the basis of students' needs include those for specific word-skill instruction (e.g., sounds represented by consonants) and those for specific comprehension instruction (e.g., inferring character traits).

Interest Groups

Groups also may be formed based on a common interest. If group members are on different instructional reading levels, cooperation among members can increase motivation and self-satisfaction. Many activities lend themselves to interest grouping. Students who read books by the same author can research that author's life or style of writing, compare stories, or complete artwork related to his books. Students who are interested in a particular subject can come together and read various books on their instructional level and prepare a group report. Others can listen to a recorded story or watch a filmstrip about a particular topic together.

Research Groups

Grouping students together to research a particular topic is similar to interest grouping. With research grouping, students collect, organize, and synthesize information from a variety of sources and produce a final product (e.g., an oral report, a written report, an art activity, or a play). Topics may include, for example, life in the local community 50 years ago, how electric lights work, exploration and settlement of the West, the growth and change of the South, John F. Kennedy, the Supreme Court, Albert Einstein, hurricanes and tornadoes, how our circulatory system works, or the United Nations.

Cooperative Groups

Cooperative learning is rapidly becoming one of the most popular teaching techniques throughout the country. Cooperative learning involves placing students in small groups to work together in completing learning assignments. Cooperative grouping is enormously popular, and justifiably so. Research on teaching and learning supports the use of cooperative learning (Putnam, 1997). With the great range of differences in today's classrooms, cooperative grouping places students into small, heterogeneous groups. This type of grouping mixes ability levels of students. Combining a fast, moderate, and slow reader encourages peer tutoring. These groups have the potential to increase students' academic engaged time and achievement by promoting active learning, with students talking and working together rather than passively listening. Being active in the learning process and having the support of peers, students have opportunities to explain what they are learning, apply and

Cooperative learning groups promote active learning with students talking and working together.

strengthen their critical-thinking and problem-solving skills, discuss the pros and cons of an idea, receive help in learning the lesson objective, and give support to other members of the group. The major requirement of cooperative groups is that individual members have a vested interest in ensuring that other members learn. In contrast to traditional groups that pit one student against another, cooperative learning fosters combining energies of students toward a common goal. Skill, interest, and research groups can be arranged to promote cooperative learning. Johnson and Johnson (1990) completed extensive research on the use of cooperative groups in elementary and secondary classrooms. Their research has supported the overall finding that students working together with other students will generate positive effects. The authors summarize the positive benefits of cooperative learning as follows:

> Cooperative learning experiences, compared with competitive and individualistic ones, promote higher achievement, greater motivation, more positive interpersonal relations among students (regardless of differences in ability, ethnic background, handicap, or sex), more positive attitudes toward the subject area and teacher, greater self-esteem and psychological health, more accurate perspective taking, and greater social skills. Employability and career success largely depend on a person's ability to work cooperatively with others. (p. 4)

In addition, Johnson and Johnson feel that cooperation among students positively affects critical thinking and metacognition. In cooperative groups, students have multiple opportunities to orally summarize, explain, teach, and elaborate on ideas and receive feedback from their peers to improve their reasoning (Johnson & Johnson, 1989).

Although no one set of guidelines ensures successful implementation of cooperative grouping, the following steps can help teachers initiate cooperative groups:

1. Specify the instructional objectives.
2. Provide an explicit or direct explanation of the lesson objective with guided practice to the whole class.
3. Select the group size most appropriate for the lesson.
4. Assign students to heterogeneous groups.
5. Arrange the classroom so that group members are close together and the groups are as far apart as possible.
6. Provide appropriate materials.
7. Explain the task and the cooperative goal structure.
8. Observe student-student interaction.
9. Intervene as a consultant to help the group solve its problems in working together effectively and to help the group learn the interpersonal and group skills necessary for cooperating, or check that all members are learning the material.
10. Evaluate the group products, using a criterion-referenced evaluation system.

An interesting spin-off involving literature-based reading, interest groups, and cooperative learning groups is the use of literature study groups (Keegan & Shrake, 1991). Heterogeneous groups meet three times during the week to discuss a particular novel that each group selected to read. Students interact with each other on various levels and complete different tasks, including writing their reactions to the novel in literature logs. The group's discussion is taped and the teacher critiques it and provides valuable feedback. Citing students' resulting enthusiasm and excitement for reading, Keegan and Shrake (1991) "are convinced that literature study groups offer a framework for allowing children opportunities to discover what they know, to extend their thinking, and to develop strategies that will make them life-long readers" (p. 547).

Cooperative learning is the basis for a highly effective elementary school literacy program entitled "Roots and Wings" (Slavin, Madden, Dolan, & Wasik, 1994), a part of the overall program called "Success For All," which is a delivery program with a focus on prevention and early intervention. Currently in place nationwide at 200 elementary schools and 59 districts, in areas with high rates of poverty, this literacy program integrates reading with writing and is based on cooperative learning groups. "Roots and Wings" promotes a balanced approach to reading development combining various approaches and integrating phonics and meaning-centered reading of whole stories. In describing the cooperative aspects of the program, Slavin et al. (1994) note that children "are placed in cooperative learning groups, where they read to one another and work together to find the main elements of stories. They learn to support one another's reading and to challenge one another to explain and justify their understanding" (p. 12). Evaluations of this program have found positive effects on reading achievement, especially reading comprehension.

Another reading and writing program for grades 2 through 8 using cooperative grouping is "Cooperative Integrated Reading and Composition" (CIRC) (Madden, Stevens, & Slavin, 1988; Slavin, 1994). In this program, teachers use literature or basal reader stories for completing guided reading activities, direct/explicit instruction in reading comprehension, and writing/language arts activities. Students work in heterogeneous learning teams.

Underlying Slavin's Student Team Learning methods are not only students working together and being responsible for their classmates' learning as well as their own but also achieving team goals and team success. Speaking of this importance, Slavin (1994) stated:

> Research on cooperative learning methods has indicated that team rewards and individual accountability are essential elements for producing basic skills achievement. It is not enough to simply tell students to work together; they must have a reason to take one another's achievement seriously. Research further indicates that if students are rewarded for doing better than they have in the past, they will be more motivated to achieve than if they are rewarded based on their performance in comparison to others, because rewards for improvement make success neither too difficult nor too easy for students to achieve. (p. 2)

Ability Groups

Grouping students on the basis of previous learning in order to satisfy instructional needs is a long-standing practice in our schools. Ability grouping is an accurate description when it refers to present rather than potential achievement. It was (and still is) sometimes used to imply intellectual capacity, however. When this occurs, the grouping suggests a final judgment rather than an initial step in ongoing diagnosis.

Certain other widespread but indefensible practices have resulted in criticism of ability grouping. Once groups are established, often their composition changes very little. Also, student mobility among groups does not follow any performance criteria. Often, the high, medium, and low groups all inexplicably follow the same procedures—all read, or attempt to read, the same book(s) and attempt to cover the same amount of material. Without differentiation of instruction, the grouping is assumed to be a ritual unrelated to instructional strategy. Special care must be exercised in using ability and cooperative groupings. Although ability grouping helpfully narrows the range of ability a teacher has to deal with in a class, the possible negative effects often outweigh this initial potential advantage. Other negative practices sometimes associated with ability grouping include the teacher's inadvertently treating groups differently according to whether they are labelled of high, middle, or low ability; that is, the teacher may give more time, attention, smiles, physical contact, comprehension instruction, and wait-time, as well as higher-cognitive-level questions to high-ability groups. Research by Allington (1983) also indicates that students in low-ability groups often receive less beneficial instruction than students in other groups. He notes that children with reading difficulties actually read less than advanced students and have fewer opportunities to be engaged with real stories. If grouping by ability is used, it is wise to employ other types of grouping as well. It is crucial that teachers be aware of the possible negative effects of ability grouping and guard against them to ensure each student a quality education.

It is realistic to assume that grouping is inherently neither good nor bad. Practices within any type of grouping may either enhance student growth or become meaningless and even harmful educational rituals. Grouping students on the basis of instructional needs can, however, provide the framework for an alert teacher to develop meaningful, differentiated instruction. Grouping can narrow the range of differences and reading problems that face a teacher during a given instructional period. As a result, teachers can focus on particular short-term goals for specific students.

Practical considerations should always influence group management. Attempting to work with five or six groups, for example, may result in instructional time blocks that are too small to be effective. Two groups may produce too heterogeneous a collection of students in both groups. Such problems emphasize that grouping practices should be flexible.

In *Becoming a Nation of Readers* (1985), Anderson, Hiebert, Scott, and Wilkinson concluded that "grouping by ability may slow the progress of low-ability students" (p. 92). To improve the instruction provided to low-ability groups, the authors suggest "switching group assignments periodically, using criteria other than ability for group assignment, and maybe, increasing the time devoted to the whole classroom" (p. 92).

The basal reader is a systematic, coordinated, sequential anthology of stories and related materials designed to teach reading. The effective implementation of the basal reader approach relies heavily on grouping students by ability. Although ability grouping narrows the range of ability a teacher has to deal with in a class, the possible negative effects often outweigh this initial potential advantage. In response to the possible negative effects of the basal and as a way to keep and to enhance the basal as the main program, Wiggins (1994) proposed an adaptation of the traditional grouping by ability using the basal reader. Wiggins's flexible "Large Group Lesson/Small Group Follow-up" approach to using basal materials included presenting a main lesson to the whole class followed by small-group instruction based on need. Students were placed in the same basal reader and instruction was adjusted to meet student needs. While initial findings were positive, it is important to note that this arrangement did not include students reading below grade level. However, the potential of this innovative practice in providing for a balanced reading program is promising. Highlighting the advantages of this flexible grouping plan, Wiggins stated:

> This type of organization for instruction frees the teacher to circulate throughout the room providing more student-teacher interaction. This should contribute to more effective classroom management, an increased use of classroom learning centers, more independent reading and, ultimately, a greater sense of responsibility and independence on the part of the students. Most important, this arrangement puts the responsibility for instructional decision making back into the hands of the classroom teacher. (p. 456)

Teaming with the Special Education Teacher to Achieve the Correct Balance

Professionals in every field work together. Effective literacy teachers realize that they are members of a team, acknowledge the expertise of other professionals, and seek their advice or help when necessary. It is common today for regular classroom teachers and special education teachers to collaboratively plan for the education of students with special needs. Classroom teachers realize that they will not be able to solve all problems by themselves. While the same principles of effective instruction apply to all students, both teachers need to pool their resources together in designing and devising accommodations for students with special needs. It may be helpful to return to Chapter 1 and review the major content strands of an elementary school reading curriculum of word recognition, word meaning, comprehension, reading study skills, recreational reading, and literature and the major program areas of a complete reading program of developmental reading, application-transfer, recreational reading, content reading, and functional reading. With respect to these areas, how can you as a classroom teacher ensure that all your students will receive the best instruction possible? What must you do in order to deliver a balanced literacy program to all students? Effective teachers believe that all their students will be successful in reading, assume personal responsibility for the progress of their students, and believe in their ability to provide instruction to meet the varied needs of all their students. Yet you must realize that no simple recipe is available for effective instruction in all situations with all students. Effective teachers work together with the special education teachers to combine different grouping and management plans, teaching strategies, and approaches to literacy to meet the needs of all students. In discussing the importance of the teaming process, noted special education experts Ysseldyke and Algozzine (1995) report that, by doing the following, teachers can accommodate diversity in the classroom:

- varying the amounts of instruction on the basis of individual student capabilities.
- using modified instructional approaches, materials, and procedures to enable students to master content at paces suited to their individual capabilities and interests.
- monitoring pupil progress and providing students with immediate feedback. Instruction is then adapted on the basis of student performance.
- teaching students to monitor their own performance and identify modifications they need in order to make satisfactory progress.
- providing students with opportunities to make choices and decisions about their learning objectives.
- using peer teaching, in which students assist one another in mastering subject matter content. (p. 116)

ORGANIZING A CLASS FOR INSTRUCTION

Implementing reading instruction in a class requires careful orchestration of time, materials, and instruction to satisfy the needs of individual children. Based on assessment data, teachers must make several decisions regarding student instructional levels, their specific skill development needs, materials to use, and types of grouping to improve learning. A visitor to a typical classroom will readily see that a reading class can be organized many ways. No one way is the only correct one. The guiding principle in deciding how to organize reading instruction should be how best to accommodate students' needs in reading.

Effective teachers use different types of groups at different times to achieve desired results. Flexibility in using groups is a key, because students are different and their needs continually change. They need a careful blend of teacher-directed and independent activities for their reading ability to improve. Figures 12.1 and 12.2 suggest possible ways to organize a class for reading instruction using two or three reading groups. Although many other combinations are possible, these figures should help you visualize the decisions a teacher must make when organizing instruction. Each day's reading lesson includes both teacher-directed and independent activities. The schedules offer one possible way to distribute components of the guided

	Monday	Tuesday	Wednesday	Thursday	Friday
Group 1	**Teacher Directed** Guided Reading: Prereading Silent Reading	**Teacher Directed Postreading:** Comprehension Check Meaningful Oral Rereading Specific Skill Lesson	**Student Independent Work** Supplemental Activities Activity: Kit and/or Practice Activities	**Student Independent Work** Free Reading	**Teacher Directed** Special Needs Grouping and
Group 2	**Student Independent Work** Supplemental Activities	**Student Independent Work** Free Reading	**Teacher Directed** Guided Reading Prereading Silent Reading	**Teacher Directed Postreading:** Comprehension Check Meaningful Oral Rereading Specific Skill Lesson	**Student Independent Work** Supplemental Activities

Figure 12.1 Suggested schedule for two reading groups.

	Monday	Tuesday	Wednesday	Thursday	Friday
Group 1	**Teacher Directed** Guided Reading: Prereading Silent Reading	**Teacher Directed** Postreading: Comprehension Check Meaningful Oral Rereading Specific Skill Lesson **Student Independent Work** Practice Activity	**Student Independent Work** Supplemental Activities	**Student Independent Work** Supplemental Activities Free Reading	**Teacher Directed** Special Needs Grouping
Group 2	**Student Independent Work** Supplemental Activities **Teacher Directed** Guided Reading: Prereading Silent Reading	**Student Independent Work** Free Reading **Teacher Directed** Postreading Comprehension Check	**Student Independent Work** Practice Activities **Teacher Directed** Meaningful Oral Rereading Specific Skill Lesson	**Student Independent Work** Practice Activities	and
Group 3	**Student Independent Work** Supplemental Activities	**Student Independent Work** Supplemental Activities	**Teacher Directed** Guided Reading: Prereading Silent Reading	**Teacher Directed** Postreading: Comprehension Check Meaningful Oral Rereading Specific Skill Lesson	**Student Independent Work** Supplemental Activities

Figure 12.2 Suggested schedule for three reading groups.

reading plan throughout a week. The organization gives students a balance of instructional and independent activities.

Regardless of group membership, differences among students always exist. Therefore, teachers need to plan time for special-needs grouping. Teachers can use this time to provide instruction to students lacking in particular skills (e.g., dictionary skills, study skills, and skills with vowel sounds). Once students in a special-needs group learn the targeted skill or skills, the group is disbanded.

In looking at the suggested time schedules, it is important to remember that various reading activities (both teacher-directed and student independent work) are simultaneous. What the suggested schedules do not show are the preplanning efforts to ensure (1) the success of the teacher-directed and student independent activities and (2) the smooth transition from one activity to another to avoid wasting instructional time. These efforts depend on several considerations:

1. Grouping of any type should consider the students' needs.
2. Groups should be flexible—different types should be used for different purposes, permitting students to move to other groups if they progress.
3. Groups should be task-oriented.
4. Groups should permit students to work with the teacher as much as possible.
5. Groups should be structured to keep each group working productively, even while completing activities on their own.

The last consideration is critical. Although maintaining a high level of academic engaged time with students may be easier in a teacher-directed activity, guaranteeing that students will complete activities on their own is another matter. Success in this area requires explaining clearly what students are to do and how to do it before moving to another group, circulating around the room at times to monitor seatwork and to give feedback to students in different groups, explaining in advance what students are to do if they finish an assignment early, and preparing all materials ahead of time to ensure a smooth, systematic transition when moving from one group to another (Evertson, Emmer, & Worsham, 2000).

ALTERNATIVE MANAGEMENT APPROACHES

Part of organizing the classroom for instruction is providing for individual differences among learners. As noted, finding ways to differentiate instruction is a top priority in education. This is a justifiable preoccupation, because success in this endeavor is the key to effective school programs.

The Ungraded School

The term *ungraded* signifies an administrative-instructional organization that deemphasizes or suspends grade-level structure and emphasizes continuous student progress. It is one approach for dealing with student differences. Attempts at un-

Effective classroom managers utilize a variety of grouping plans to keep students actively engaged in instructional activities.

grading have been most successful at the beginning instructional levels. Thus, much of the literature focuses on the ungraded primary school, embracing the first 3 years of formal schooling.

The ungraded primary school has a highly structured curriculum that accommodates a wide range of student achievement. All tasks are placed within a series of levels arranged in ascending order of difficulty. Students move through the sequence at their own pace. As they master one level, they move on to the next, thus making continuous progress. At the end of a year's instruction, each student is located somewhere on an identified skills continuum. The next year's instruction begins at this point.

Although instruction in the conventional grade-level system is geared to the average, experience tells us that students do not cluster closely around an achievement mean. Differences in achievement are marked, and they increase with instruction. The ungraded primary school starts from the premise that each student should progress at his or her own rate, and the instructional program centers on each student's need at the moment. This is accomplished by breaking the primary years into a number of units of accomplishment, or levels of competency. As students achieve competency at one level, they start working at the next level.

Teachers in the program determine the number of levels and the skills for students to master at each level.

Some of the educational advantages believed to be inherent in the ungraded primary plan include the following:

- It is easier to accommodate students' reading growth if you do not consider grade-level norms the first year.
- Failure and frustration in reading are less likely if comparison and promotion are deemphasized.
- Teachers often stay with the same group of students for 2 years or longer. This gives them an opportunity to know their students better. They are less likely to push students beyond their ability during the first year, because they expect to work with them the next year.
- Students always work at the level on which they need instruction; consequently, they are not likely to miss some facet of instruction when they are absent for several days.
- The slower learner does not repeat the first or second grade but may take 4 years to move up from the primary level.
- The ungraded plan is flexible, allowing students to cover learning phases rapidly when they are capable of doing so and giving them more time when they need it.
- Bright students do not skip a grade; they simply go through the entire primary curriculum at a faster rate.

No grouping method automatically solves all instructional problems. If a school shifts to the ungraded plan without understanding the goals to be achieved, any potential benefits are not likely to be realized. If teachers or parents continue to think in terms of a grade-level system, the plan is doomed from the start. On the other hand, if they consider the plan's philosophy sound and believe the chief reason for adopting it is to foster growth in students' reading abilities, any problems that do arise will be surmountable.

The Integrated Unit

The integrated-unit approach has a long history of successful classroom use. Although it can be considered a method of instruction, this chapter discusses it because of its classroom management aspects. Units provide many ways for coping with individual differences, differentiating instruction, and grouping students for specific short- and long-term activities.

This approach provides teachers with so many options that it has a wide array of names, including *resource units, teaching units, activity-centered instruction, core approach,* and *survey units.* Teachers can integrate reading instruction and related language skills in numerous learning activities, all focusing on a specific curricular theme.

In developing an integrated unit, teachers may discover that the first important task is finding materials at various levels. The references available vary from school

Integrated units can and should include many hands-on experiences.

to school. Basal readers at all levels can serve for such a unit, as can subject-matter texts. Functional resources can provide materials on many topics, and the school and public libraries can be sources of books on special topics.

The teacher can devise a unit for any subject area. It can span a few days, during which students attempt to find the answer to a particular question, or it may extend over several weeks and end in some type of class project. The product might be a play, a school program, or a science fair with many individual and committee projects. Although the unit approach is not new, it is consistent with the aims of modern curriculum planning. Unit study can help avoid the tendency toward fragmentation of the curriculum into isolated, seemingly unrelated parts.

Units lend themselves to two types of major emphasis. The first builds students' experiences around a specific topic, such as How We Get Our Food. Experiences might include visits to various types of farms, a cannery, a cold storage plant, a meat packing plant, a dairy, and a bakery. Students may plant and care for a garden or window box. The second major emphasis is broad reading. The early elementary grades will probably emphasize the experience approach, while the intermediate grades will shift to reading. These two methods are extremely compatible; when combined properly, they undoubtedly make for a better total learning situation.

Advantages

The potential advantages of the integrated-unit approach are numerous. Actual benefits of its use vary according to such factors as the teacher's skill, the students' reading ability and work habits, and the amount of supplementary reading material available. Following are some of the more frequently mentioned advantages of the integrated-unit approach:

- The unit serves as the framework for shaping learning experiences into larger, more meaningful wholes. The unit permits more than the superficial study of a topic and encourages application of skills in broadly varied reading.
- Units can be used in any curricular area.
- Students learn that reading is the key to learning about all subjects and not just an operation performed in the basal reader and accompanying workbooks.
- The unit approach can and should include a great variety of experiences related to reading, such as excursions, field trips, and small-group participation, in working on various facets of the topic.
- Units structure the learning situation to make reading more varied, more meaningful, and more interesting.
- Units permit readers of widely different abilities to work on different facets of the same project. Reading materials at many levels of difficulty can be used, and students need not be directly compared as readers.
- The unit approach gives teachers flexibility and freedom to work with an individual or group engaged in some reading activity at its own level. The reader with problems and the accelerated reader can work independently and successfully on something that is challenging.
- Units aid independent reading and help foster independence in research reading.

A unit on weather for a fifth-grade class may be used as an illustration. The teacher arouses the interest of the class through an assignment to watch weather reports on television, to find interesting pictures of weather stations, and to discuss in class stories dealing with weather. Out of this grows the decision to have a study unit on weather. Under the teacher's direction, students work cooperatively in identifying objectives, finding questions to be answered, and working on individual projects within the unit's limits.

Objectives of the unit on weather include the following:

- To learn ways in which weather helps or harms people.
- To learn what causes various types of weather and changes of seasons.
- To learn the causes and effects of rainfall, temperature, and fog.
- To become familiar with the instruments used in measuring or predicting weather changes.

Questions to be answered include the following:

- How is a thermometer constructed and how does it work?
- What is fog?

- What causes hail?
- What is lightning? Why is it followed by thunder?
- Why do we have seasons such as winter and summer?
- Why are some parts of Earth always hot and others always cold?
- Why is there very little rainfall in one part of a country and a great deal in another part?
- Why is it important for people to be able to predict the weather?
- What is a barometer? How does it work?
- What is humidity?

Activities or projects, both individual and group, include the following:

- Keeping a daily record of temperature. Recording temperatures registered in cities in different parts of the country.
- Preparing charts and graphs illustrating some aspect of weather, including average rainfall for different states and countries, the relationship between rainfall and the type of crops raised in a particular area, and the effect of rainfall on population density.
- Preparing maps showing occurrences of tornadoes, hurricanes, and floods during the past decade.
- Explaining and demonstrating a thermometer and barometer.
- Researching the work of the U.S. Weather Bureau in predicting weather.
- Studying the effects of weather on human dress, shelter, and diet.
- Measuring rainfall during a rain.
- Obtaining pictures illustrating any facet or effect of weather, such as floods, erosion, storms on land and sea, barren deserts, and permanent snow.

For the culminating activity, the class decides to have a weather fair. They display all individual and group projects, including posters, graphs, charts, picture series, student-made instruments for measuring weather, and written projects. Parents are invited to visit the class on a particular afternoon, and other classes in the school see the displays at certain times that day. Students explain their projects and derive a great deal of satisfaction from this culminating activity.

This well-planned unit provides a variety of purposeful learning experiences. The teacher structures activities so that all facets of the curriculum receive attention.

Mathematics

In the intermediate grades, a lack of understanding of the problems to be solved is more of a stumbling block in mathematics than is a lack of computational skills. Failure to read problems critically results in hazy understanding. In unit work, math problems emerge from the learner's immediate experiences. Problems such as finding the average rainfall, average temperature, or total foodstuffs raised are related to larger goals and become meaningful. The need for accurate measurement becomes apparent in building a barometer or measuring rainfall.

Health

One particular topic, how weather affects our health, almost becomes a unit within a unit. The entire class participates, with students writing a brief account of anything they find in their reading that pertains to the topic. The teacher has a few references for students who need help in finding material. The health lesson also becomes a lesson in communication skills as students work on their written assignments. Students also practice their oral language skills as they report their findings to the class.

Social studies

The discussion on health leads into social studies topics. A discussion of diet in relation to health leads to questions and discussion of how weather affects diet or production of foodstuffs. A discussion of the economic value of climate logically follows. The class discusses climate's relationship to certain natural resources, such as forestry, deposits of coal, and petroleum. The relationships among rainfall, temperature, winds, forests, and the types of crops are discussed. Methods of cultivation and crop rotation are studied in relation to land erosion.

Science

This unit essentially is a science unit. It emphasizes how scientists predict and track the weather and the scientific instruments they use in the process. Studying the thermometer and barometer raises many scientific principles and questions, such as the principles of expansion, gravity, and pressure, and the questions of whether mercury is a metal, why it is used in the instruments, and how heat causes a thermometer to work.

Spelling

Students learn many words incidentally as they print them on their posters or charts. The teacher assigns new words as part of the unit (such as *weather, thermometer, mercury, rainfall, temperature, erosion,* and *bureau*).

Reading

Reading provides the vehicle for all of the other curricular activities. The unit stresses that students are getting information for health, geography, and science. The reading is purposeful. Neither the reading nor the teaching of it is the compulsive let's-get-this-workbook-page-finished approach. The teacher keeps in mind the principles of teaching reading, being particularly careful to provide a variety of supplementary materials at many grade levels.

Using the integrated unit method in no way restricts the teacher in developing students' reading skills. In fact, once the teacher has completed preliminary planning, he or she has as much time and opportunity to help individual students or small groups as with conventional lessons.

Most unit work introduces a heavy vocabulary load, so the class must spend time on vocabulary development. As different students read and ask for help with unknown words, the teacher can prepare several lists of new words to be studied during the course of the unit. One such list might be taken from the more difficult sources and used exclusively with the advanced reading group. Vocabulary exercises for average readers and those experiencing problems can include easier words. Many new and unknown words can help in teaching phonic analysis and stressing the importance of contextual clues in solving meaning difficulties.

INDIVIDUALIZED READING

A movement? A method? A classroom organization? A philosophy of instruction? The term individualized reading has different meanings for different users, but it has enjoyed wide acceptance and use in our schools for many years. Paradoxically, its greatest potential strengths and weaknesses stem from the same factors. It has no concise definition, and no blueprint exists for making it work. Its success depends upon creative responses. However, its drawback is its inability to prevent teachers from developing nonproductive rituals.

Practices

Individualized reading rejects the lockstep instruction that tends to become standardized within the framework of the graded system and traditional graded materials. The success or failure of an individualized program rests almost exclusively with the teacher, which is one of the reasons why individualized reading is so difficult to define.

Over the years, a number of practices have become associated with individualized reading. These include students' self-selection of materials, self-pacing in reading, individual student conferences with the teacher, and emphasis on record keeping by the teacher, student, or both. One other notable characteristic is the need for a wide variety of reading material in each classroom. This becomes mandatory if students are to select books that they are interested in and can read.

Seeking, self-selection, and self-pacing

Willard C. Olson's writing (1949, 1959) is frequently cited as the basis for the emphasis on seeking, self-selection, and self-pacing. Although these concepts are not new to education, the individualized reading movement has given them a new emphasis in reading instruction. The principle underlying the advocacy of self-selection is psychologically sound. Because individual differences among students in a given classroom are tremendous, the teacher cannot assume that one basal series or a single text will address all their needs.

The success of self-selection depends on several factors. First, students must have some interests they wish to explore further. This helps motivate them in the reading situation. Second, the available materials must fit their interests and ability to read independently. When these conditions are met, students should seek out the materials fitting their needs, interests, and reading levels. If they select wisely, their reading ability should grow.

Carried to extremes, this idea of individualized reading minimizes the teacher's role in guiding students to materials, so that self-selection almost becomes a fetish. Teachers should not assume that students, when permitted to do so, will select materials they can read. While that may be true in a number of cases, it is not an inevitable law of child behavior.

Students' self-selection is often limited by the fact that teachers have previously chosen the 100 or 200 books found in the classroom from among thousands available. Individualized reading and self-selection do not preclude teachers from recommending books or guiding students toward certain materials, but this type of guidance does call for a high level of teacher competency. The teacher must know students' interests, their reading abilities, and the difficulty level of materials if their suggestions are to help students grow.

Economy in the teacher-learning situation must also be considered. If, after a period of seeking, students have not made a selection and settled down to reading, they may not yet be ready for self-selection. Thus, with many students, self-selection can safely be tempered with guidance.

Teacher-student conferences

The teacher-student conference is one of the major features of individualized reading. It is also potentially one of its great strengths. The conference is a brief session in which teachers give their undivided attention to one student. The primary goal of the conference is to assure children that they have an appreciative audience.

The chief value of the conference is that it involves students in the reading process. For the conference to be most effective, however, teachers must be more than listeners. In addition to being appreciative audiences, teachers must assume some responsibility for helping students develop values and self-understanding, goals often best achieved through judicious questioning. The conference provides a means by which teachers can learn important facts about students' psychological needs and how they fulfill these needs. Discussing reading with a respectful adult helps give students insights into their own problems and discover how others have handled such difficulties.

The conference serves as a catalyst for teacher-student rapport. For some students, the teacher's positive response to their reading is a stronger motivation than the act of reading itself. A skillful, sympathetic teacher can provide this extrinsic reward while slowly moving the student toward accepting reading as its own reward.

In the case of a reader who needs little encouragement to read, a brief exchange between the teacher and student may suffice on some occasions. A word of praise, a question about whether there are still a number of books in the classroom that the student wishes to read, and an offer of help when needed may be adequate. Because the sharing conference is primarily a confidence-building experience, some students obviously will need more attention than others. Some continually avoid a conference because they consider reading a threat rather than a pleasure. These students need constant encouragement and praise for their accomplishments.

Record keeping

Record keeping received considerable attention in the early descriptions of individualized reading. This activity generally had little or nothing to do with actual diagnosis of reading needs. Rather, records seemed to emphasize the number of books read and to offer proof that the system was working. In some cases, this feature became dominant, with students reading primarily to add titles to their lists. Also, it tended to invite comparisons of achievement, the opposite intention of individualized reading. Over the years, attention to this activity has diminished.

Problems

The idea of students reading independently, selecting what they wish to read, and reading at their own pace strikes some critics as quite idealistic. To keep this philosophy from becoming unrealistic, teachers must expend a great deal of effort in classroom management. Over the years, teachers have voiced a number of concerns, including the following:

- What types of materials are needed?
- How does one initiate an individualized program?
- When and how is ongoing diagnosis achieved?
- How is provision made for teaching the necessary reading skills?
- When the teacher is involved in teacher-student conferences, what are the other students doing? How do these students get "instant help" for their reading problems?

How the teacher handles these and other issues determines the success or failure of an individualized program.

Materials

A reading program embracing self-selection and self-pacing and tailored to individual students' interests cannot function in a learning environment that does not include a wide selection of reading materials. This is not a special problem limited to individualized reading. Every classroom and school should meet this requirement, regardless of the methodological approach or program.

Although it is difficult to say how many books are adequate, a minimum figure frequently mentioned is approximately 100 different trade book titles per classroom. These 100 books also should be changed throughout the year. Factors to consider include grade level, students' interests and abilities, class size, whether books can be rotated with other classrooms, whether the school supports a central library, and whether the same materials are used extensively in other subject areas, such as social studies and science, in preparing units. Trade books are not the only source of materials, although they are likely to be the major source. Classrooms should contain electronic books, magazines, newspapers, various reading kits, functional materials and other reading materials students might choose. Reading materials should cover many areas, such as biography, science, sports, exploration, hobbies, fairy tales, medicine, space, poetry, humor, adventure, myth, and travel.

Starting a program

All elementary teachers are likely to be doing some things that fit logically under the heading of individualization. Any of the formal aspects of individualized reading, such as self-selection or individual conferences, can be used with one student, a small group, or an entire class. Obviously, the latter approach presents the most problems; therefore, perhaps you should start with one of the alternatives.

Prior to any conference, assemble a number of books on a reading table. Include a number of new books and books that you think will appeal to the student or students involved. Begin by calling together five or six students. Explain that they will be selecting their own books to read at their desks during the reading period. At the end of the group conference, tell the group members that after selecting the books they wish to read, they are to go to their desks and read their selections silently. Also tell students that they may keep the books at their desks until they are finished.

Within a day or two, have students meet again in the individualized group. Explain that each student is to schedule a conference with you to tell you something about the book and to read a part of the book to you that was particularly interesting. Individuals are to tell you when they are ready for a conference.

Providing for assessment

Individualized reading is an approach that by its very nature calls for considerable assessment if students are to progress smoothly in reading. Some may not be able to achieve in an individualized setting without ongoing assessment. No assessment techniques are associated exclusively with individualized reading. Yet, by its very nature, individualized reading lends itself to performance-based or authentic assessment procedures. Anecdotal records, collecting samples of work, conferencing, and portfolios are examples of ways to monitor students' growth in literacy.

Teaching reading skills and strategies

The early individualized movement was in part a reaction against reading instruction that stressed skills at the expense of the total reading process. In some classrooms, all students received the same instruction, worked on the same skill-building exercises, and read the same materials. When these practices were prevalent, one could argue that instruction was predetermined rather than based on students' needs and abilities. Such uniform practices inevitably caused some students to become bored with reading instruction.

Unfortunately, the attack on uniform skills instruction for all spread to the teaching of skills themselves. Actually, skills teaching was not explicitly rejected, but this facet of individualized reading instruction was neglected. In recent years, most proponents of individualized reading have accepted the importance of direct instruction on skills and strategies. How and when the program incorporates this instruction remain open to question, however. Two common responses are to

(1) teach some skills and strategies in the teacher-student conference and (2) teach other skills and strategies as students need them.

The first answer represents an inefficient procedure, unless the student participating in the conference is the only one in the class who can profit from the instruction. Any reading skill that can justifiably be taught to the entire class should be taught to everyone. Students who learned with the first presentation should be doing something else when the teacher makes subsequent presentations to students who did not learn.

The basic validity of the second response (teach skills and strategies when they are needed) cannot be faulted, but it can be both vague and difficult to implement when each student in the class is reading a different book. Differentiating skills instruction need not assume that no two students or groups can profit from the same instruction. This extreme position is simply the opposite of the idea that all students in a class can profit from the same amount of time spent with the same book. Diagnosis is the best way to identify what is appropriate instruction.

Basic skills can include dozens of abilities. The major concerns for the elementary teacher include word identification, knowledge of word meanings, and application of reading skills in meaningful context.

Meaningful class activities

Individualized reading calls for a high degree of planning and subtle directing. The following brief listing of activities is only illustrative. The tasks are not identified by grade level, because many may be adapted to various levels. The listing includes class, group, and individual activities covering skill development, recreational reading, reading in curricular areas, and creative activities.

1. Self-selection of books or other reading materials. This may include browsing and sampling. Selection is followed by independent reading of materials.
2. Conducting library or Internet research for an individual or group report. Such an activity may relate to a unit in some other subject.
3. Planning creative writing experiences to include original stories, poems, letters to a classmate who is in the hospital or who has moved away, invitations to parents to visit school, or a riddle composition to be read to the class during a period set aside for such activities.
4. Preparing artwork such as
   a. drawing or pasting pictures in a picture dictionary.
   b. drawing a picture to accompany a student-dictated, teacher-written story.
   c. preparing posters or book covers to illustrate the key point in a book or story the student has read.
5. Using practice materials to develop particular skills such as
   a. a dictionary exercise that follows an introduction of a skill, for example, alphabetizing by initial letter or by two or more letters, use of guide words, pronunciation guides, or syllabication.
   b. word-analysis skills, for example, associating sounds with graphic symbols, noting compound words, abbreviations, and the like.

The use of research groups in individualized reading programs is an excellent means to intregrate literacy skills and strategies in the content areas.

    c. study skills involving effective use of parts of a book, such as the index, table of contents, glossary, or appendix.

    d. study skills involving effective use of the library card catalog or reference materials.

6. Using an appropriate filmstrip with the entire class, a smaller group, or two students.

7. Teaching and testing word meanings.

    a. Workbook pages or teacher-prepared seatwork.

    b. Vocabulary building cards or notebooks in which students write one or more common meanings for new or unknown words that they come across in their reading.

    c. Activities in which students write as many sentences as possible, using a different connotation for words listed by the teacher, for example, *light*—light in weight, light in color, light the fire, light on his feet, her eyes lighted up, and lighthearted.

8. Making a tape recording of a story. A group of four to six students may each read the part of one character. Students may do practice reading and actual recording in the rear of the classroom or in any available space in the building.

9. Testing or assessment activities. The entire class or any size of group may take a standardized test (or reading subtest), tests that accompany basal series, informal or teacher-made tests. These should be scored and studied for assessment information.

Applications

The basic tenets of individualized reading—seeking, self-selection, and self-pacing—form a basis for any successful reading program. Every reading program should be individualized in the sense that it addresses students' individual needs.

Grouping students to achieve instructional goals is part of individualizing instruction. As discussed, grouping students for particular purposes can result in improved achievement scores. This is the essence of individualized instruction. It is particularly satisfying to note that instruction can be individualized in many ways, depending on the teacher, the program, and the students.

Effective teachers use assessment procedures and teacher-student conferences. Using individual teacher-student conferences in every reading program is perhaps the greatest contribution of individualized reading. With conferences, teachers can personalize their teaching, diagnose student strengths and weaknesses, teach necessary skills, and prescribe individual assignments.

Teachers at every grade level, in all reading programs, should promote independent reading habits. Student self-selection and self-pacing can be integrated with the basal reading program, giving teachers and students some measure of flexibility but still retaining the structure inherent in the basal system. Students can have some freedom in choosing particular stories, and the teacher can assign workbook and reinforcement activities to fit individual needs.

Moreover, the essential elements of individualized reading closely resemble the literature-based reading program (see Chapter 9). This literary approach uses various types of literature to teach reading skills and strategies and stimulate reading as a leisure-time activity.

SUMMARY

Effective reading teachers are proficient in providing and maintaining conditions conducive to learning. These teachers practice preventative managerial strategies to reduce the likelihood of trouble and to maintain student engagement in reading activities.

Key elements of classroom management include planning reading activities, managing group instruction, and monitoring student progress. Students can be grouped several ways. Options of maximizing student involvement include flexible use of the whole group, small groups, and individual learning. Small groups can be arranged according to ability, skill, need, interest, or a research topic. Peer, or paired, grouping also is effective.

Cooperative learning groups benefit all students and promote active learning. Alternative approaches to classroom management include the ungraded school, integrated-unit teaching, and individualized reading. Grouping itself is not the most important factor in learning, however. The real concerns are accommodating individual differences and increasing the degree of students' time engaged in selected tasks.

YOUR POINT OF VIEW

Discussion Questions

1. Is it possible to overemphasize a concern for classroom management?
2. What are the disadvantages of cooperative grouping?
3. What are the major advantages and disadvantages of the unit approach? The ungraded school? Individualized reading?
4. A major feature of individualized reading is the student-teacher conference. What are some important features to consider before, during, and after such a conference?

Take a Stand For or Against

1. Being proficient in classroom management is not as important in kindergarten and grade 1 as it is in grade 6.
2. Teachers tend to view their students in terms of their placement level.
3. Ability grouping reduces the opportunities for students to learn from one another.
4. The present structure of the classroom environment prohibits cooperative learning groups.

Field-Based Assignments

1. Interview your supervising teacher regarding classroom management and discipline during the reading period. Use the following questions as a starting point and discuss the responses with your teacher. Share your findings with a small group of your peers and classmates.

   What are the four or five most common management or discipline problems you experience in the reading class?

   What do you usually do to resolve these problems?

   How can I prepare to be an effective classroom manager in teaching reading?

2. One major problem teachers have is maintaining student engagement in reading and writing activities while working with another group of students.

Interview as many teachers and administrators as you can regarding possible solutions to this perennial dilemma. Share your findings with other members of the class in a collaborative group, discuss your findings together, and present a group summary of what teachers do to resolve this issue to the whole class.

Portfolio Entry

The advantages and disadvantages of grouping students for instruction were discussed in this chapter. Research has indicated that in many instances, students having difficulties in learning to read are simply not involved in the learning process as much as other students are. These students are called on less often, receive less praise, and receive less actual instruction from the teacher. Obviously, students falling behind in reading need more instruction, more praise, and involvement in the reading class. As a prospective teacher, it is important that you are aware of your expectations and provide ways to ensure that all students are receiving instructional programs that meet their needs. What can you do as a beginning teacher to ensure that all your students (even those who are falling behind in reading) receive a top-notch education in your class? Write a response in your portfolio to this question listing specific things you intend to do in your classroom that will ensure that **all** students will have your attention and be totally involved in the teaching-learning process.

BIBLIOGRAPHY

Allington, R. L. (1983). The reading instruction provided to readers of differing reading abilities. *Elementary School Journal, 82,* 548–559.

Alvermann, D. E., Weaver, D., Hinchman, K. A., Moore, D. W., Phelps, S. F., Thrash, E. C., & Zalewski, P. (1996). *Middle- and high-school students' perceptions of how they experience text-based discussions: A multicase study.* No. 36. Athens, GA: University of Georgia, National Reading Research Center.

Anderson, R. C., Hiebert, E. H., Scott, J. A., & Wilkinson, I. A. G. (1985). *Becoming a nation of readers: The report of the Commission on Reading.* Washington, DC: The National Institute of Education.

Baumann, J. F., & Duffy, A. M. (1997). *Engaged reading for pleasure and learning: A report from the National Reading Research Center.* Athens, GA: National Reading Research Center.

Benton, G., Belk, J., & Holifield, S. (1994). Increased student motivation through paired reading. *Balanced Reading Instruction, 1,* 16–20.

Berliner, D., & Casanova, U. (1996). *Putting research to work in your school.* Arlington Heights, IL: Skylight Professional Development.

Blair, T. R., & Jones, D. L. (1998). *Preparing for student teaching in a pluralistic classroom.* Boston: Allyn & Bacon.

Evertson, C., Emmer, E. T., & Worsham, M. E. (2000). *Classroom management for elementary teachers* (5th ed.). Boston: Allyn & Bacon.

Faltis, C. J. (2001). *Joinfostering: Teaching and learning in multilingual classrooms* (3rd ed.). Upper Saddle River, NJ: Merrill/Prentice Hall.

Good, T. L., & Brophy, J. E. (1987). *Looking in classrooms* (4th ed.). New York: Harper & Row.

Johnson, D. W., & Johnson, R. T. (1989). *Collaboration and cognition.* Minneapolis, MN: Cooperative Learning Center, University of Minnesota.

Johnson, D. W., & Johnson, R. T. (1990). Cooperative learning and achievement. In Shlomo Sharan (Ed.), *Cooperative learning: Theory and research* (pp. 22–37). New York: Praeger.

Keegan, S., & Shrake, K. (1991). Literature study groups: An alternative to ability grouping. *The Reading Teacher, 44,* 542–547.

Kounin, J. S. (1970). *Discipline and group management in classrooms.* New York: Holt, Rinehart & Winston.

Lasley, T. J. (1987). Classroom Management. *The Educational Forum, 51,* 285–298.

Leal, D. J. (1993). The power of literary peer-group discussions: How children collaboratively negotiate meaning. *The Reading Teacher, 47,* 114–120.

Madden, S., Stevens, R., & Slavin, R. (1988). *Cooperative integrated reading and composition (CIRC).* Baltimore, MD: Center for Social Organization of Schools, Johns Hopkins University.

Newman, F. M. (1992). *Issues in restructuring schools: Making small groups productive.* Madison, WI: Center on Organization and Restructuring of Schools, School of Education, Wisconsin Center for Education Research, University of Wisconsin–Madison.

Olson, W. (1949). *Child development.* Boston: D. C. Heath Co.

Olson, W. (1959). Seeking, self-selection, and pacing in the use of books by children. In J. Veatch (Ed.), *Individualizing your reading program.* New York: G. P. Putnam's Sons.

Putnam, J. (1997). *Cooperative learning in diverse classrooms.* Upper Saddle River, NJ: Merrill/Prentice Hall.

Slavin, R. E. (1994). *A practical guide to cooperative learning.* Boston: Allyn & Bacon.

Slavin, R. E., Madden, N. A., Dolan, L. J., & Wasik, B. A. (1994). Roots and wings: Inspiring academic excellence. *Educational Leadership,* 10–14.

Taylor, B. M., Pearson, P. D., Clark, K., & Walpole, S. (1999). *Beating the odds in teaching all children to read: Lessons from effective schools and exemplary teachers.* Center for the Improvement of Early Reading Achievement (CIERA Rep. No. 2-006). Ann Arbor, MI: University of Michigan School of Education.

Wiggins, R. A. (1994). Large group lesson/small group follow-up: Flexible grouping in a basal reading program. *The Reading Teacher, 47,* 450–460.

Ysseldyke, J. E., & Algozzine, B. (1995). *Special education: A practical approach for teachers.* Boston: Houghton Mifflin.

13

Focus on All Learners

William Dee Nichols
Viola E. Florez

Chapter Outline

For the Reader

Every classroom is composed of individuals of varying intellectual ability, social or cultural background, language ability, and physical attributes. Today, more than ever, all teachers should be prepared to deal effectively with diversity. Since the evolution of P.L. 94-142 into the Individuals With Disabilities Act (IDEA), the focus has switched off of the disability and onto the individual. More and more students who were once enrolled in special education classes are now included in the regular classroom. This chapter focuses attention on culturally and linguistically diverse students as well as students with special needs. Although such students are certainly receiving considerable attention in professional journals, newspapers, magazines, and school programs, it is important to remember that all children have specific needs and that literacy instruction should consider these needs. This separate chapter on the topic of diverse learners highlights the important aspect of teaching reading in today's schools and focuses its attention on the classroom teacher rather than specialty teachers.

Key Ideas

- Student differences must be a primary consideration in effective literacy instruction.

- Culturally and linguistically diverse students and students with special needs require an education based on their educational needs rather than on clinical or diagnostic labels.

- Teachers must be knowledgeable of and sensitive to the dialects and languages of the students they instruct.

- P.L. 94-142, the Individuals With Disabilities Education Act, mandates a free and appropriate education for all children with special needs and encourages the teacher to consider the individual rather than the disability.

- An Individualized Education Plan (IEP) must be developed and maintained for all students with learning disabilities.

ACCEPTING DIFFERENCES

Today's teachers must be well prepared in **culturally responsive instruction** in order to teach reading to a student population having great diversity in cultures, backgrounds, interest in social learning, linguistic and reading abilities, and reading styles. To teach such a wide range of students effectively, the teacher must be knowledgeable in current theories and research about how children learn to process verbal information including how they learn language, how they learn to read, and how they learn to use printed material for a variety of purposes. The effective teacher must also know how to plan, implement, and evaluate a growing variety of approaches to teaching reading, using many kinds of reading materials, with the intention of integrating reading with all areas of the curriculum.

Knowledge of each student's background and learner characteristics is necessary for effective instruction. Teachers must remember that all students are individuals who require educational modifications based on their needs. The diagnostic teaching procedures previously recommended for regular classroom instruction also apply to students who are culturally and linguistically diverse, disabled, or gifted. Teachers must understand cultural diversity, however, to diagnose accurately a student's strengths and weaknesses. (McGill-Franzen, 2000).

CULTURAL AND LINGUISTIC DIVERSITY

In Chapter 3 we discussed the term *culturally and linguistically diverse,* which refers to students whose culture and language or dialect differ from those of the school. The term refers to individuals from diverse ethnic and racial backgrounds, including Native American, Mexican American, Puerto Rican, Asian, and African American (Norton, 2001). The culture of many of these students, while different from that upon which much of the U.S. educational system is based, is neither inadequate nor deficient; rather, the problem often lies in the instructional practices of the classroom teacher. Instructional practice that bases its expectations, delivery, and curricular content on the norms of the mainstream population is insufficient for students of culturally and linguistically diverse backgrounds (Banks, 1994; Cushner, McClelland, & Safford, 1996).

Students from culturally and linguistically different backgrounds often experience a mismatch between home and school expectations (Faltis, 1997; Nieto, 1996). This cultural discontinuity often results in a misunderstanding between teachers and students in the classroom. Thus, to ensure equal educational opportunities for all students, teachers' literacy instruction must be transformed so that all students have an equal chance to succeed.

Chapter 3 included instructional recommendations and guidelines for working with culturally and linguistically diverse students. These guidelines and recommendations can apply to all students, but they are crucial when teaching linguistically and culturally diverse students. Knowledge and application of these guidelines within the instructional approaches and strategies presented in this chapter can better serve the literacy needs of culturally and linguistically diverse students. An important instructional feature is the interrelatedness of the language arts (speaking, listening, reading, and writing) coupled with children's literature. Literature provides students with additional vocabulary and ideas to enhance their knowledge base of English (Bieger, 1996; Norton, 2001).

EARLY READING APPROACHES FOR CULTURALLY AND LINGUISTICALLY DIVERSE STUDENTS

When culturally and linguistically diverse students enter school, a major challenge for teachers is meeting the unique needs of each child. Many children bring with them experiences and socialized patterns of behavior that have not traditionally been valued in public school contexts. (Banks & Banks, 1997). The growing and changing demographics in classrooms throughout the United States requires that educators develop and construct culturally responsive instruction (Delpit, 1995; Ladson-Billings, 1994). Two potential solutions are obvious: (1) providing experiences the children need in order to cope with the tasks that they face in school and (2) altering the curriculum in order to accommodate their needs. Teachers need to take care when altering the curriculum not to stereotype and create a segregated curriculum that weakens the educational program (Guild, 1994).

Although culturally and linguistically diverse students are on the same continuum as other children, they often have experiences that are different from the mainstream. For example, insufficient emergent literacy experiences and exposure to literature from their own culture or from traditional American literature may inhibit their early success in early literacy instruction. Sometimes even well-structured early reading activities fail with these students because they need additional or different activities. These students demand a rethinking of early reading activities to use their strengths and concentrate on eliminating their weaknesses. Banks (1994) suggests that instead of adding units or special topics to the curriculum or discussing the different cultural heroes, teachers need to transform their curriculum so students interact with content from a variety of cultural perspectives.

Culturally responsive reading instruction bridges the gap between the school and the world of the student. Culturally responsive instruction is consistent with the values of the students' own culture aimed at ensuring academic learning (Au, 1993). This type of reading instruction encourages teachers to adapt their instruction to meet the learning needs of all students.

Reading instruction provides the foundation for school development in all content area subjects and subsequent learning experiences. Students who belong to historically marginalized groups (i.e., African American, Hispanic American, Asian American, and Native American) are rarely included in research paradigms that describe and assess the academic impact of reading instruction from a cultural perspective. While the field is persistent in documenting how these groups fall behind their European American counterparts, it does little to assess the academic growth and development from a culturally contextualized perspective (Nichols, Rupley, Webb-Johnson, & Tlusty, 2001).

While literature patterns have begun to change, instruction in schools has been slower in implementing such changes in materials chosen by teachers. What is most promising about multicultural school reform, however, is its potential for impacting all children and youth. If educators are to strive toward successful academic reading outcomes for "all" children, it may be important to develop instructional strategies that empower all children to prosper. Exposure to a variety of reading experiences will enrich the lives of everyone.

The early reading and writing approaches discussed in this section attempt to redefine early literacy activities in terms of the needs of culturally and linguistically diverse learners. Their philosophy and techniques differ, but all share the goal of maximizing the probability of success in reading and writing development.

Academic Early Reading Intervention

Perhaps the most radical procedures for helping culturally and linguistically diverse students get off to a successful start in literacy instruction are found in academic early reading programs. Some of these programs concentrate on the explicit/direct teaching of specific language and reading skills. This is a teaching strategy in which the teacher presents stimuli designed to elicit specific language responses. Integrating specific language activities that encourage student involvement is critical for early intervention of language development, especially for students who have limited opportunities to experience literacy outside of the classroom. A wide range of literature-based activities (see the "Basal Reader Approach" and "Literature-Based Reading Approach" sections in this chapter) combined with such a program can enrich students' early reading experiences. Figure 13.1 illustrates some of the goals and explicit/direct instruction techniques for teaching specific language skills. These skill activities should not be considered the sole focus of this program. Skills can be taught throughout the school day by engaging students in meaningful language that focuses on acquisition of each goal. For example, Ms. Chavez, a second-grade teacher, purposefully engages in conversation with various culturally diverse students. Ms. Chavez explains that the focus of the lesson is to use the magazines placed on their desks to individually create a collage of words that they have been learning from their thematic unit on Arctic Animals. The teacher walks over to the desk of a Latino student and engages him in a conversation to incorporate meaningful language related to the collage instructions. She asks, "Miquel, I noticed that you do not have a pair of scissors. Where are the scissors in the classroom?" Miquel is encouraged to respond in a language manner that describes where the scissors are. Miquel answers, "The scissors are on the big table, Ms. Chavez."

While the primary focus of the lesson is vocabulary development using functional text, the secondary purpose is to engage students in meaningful language exchanges.

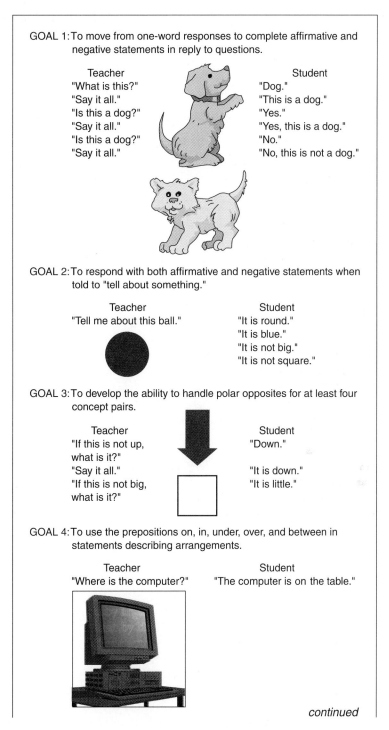

GOAL 1: To move from one-word responses to complete affirmative and negative statements in reply to questions.

Teacher	Student
"What is this?"	"Dog."
"Say it all."	"This is a dog."
"Is this a dog?"	"Yes."
"Say it all."	"Yes, this is a dog."
"Is this a dog?"	"No."
"Say it all."	"No, this is not a dog."

GOAL 2: To respond with both affirmative and negative statements when told to "tell about something."

Teacher	Student
"Tell me about this ball."	"It is round."
	"It is blue."
	"It is not big."
	"It is not square."

GOAL 3: To develop the ability to handle polar opposites for at least four concept pairs.

Teacher	Student
"If this is not up, what is it?"	"Down."
"Say it all."	"It is down."
"If this is not big, what is it?"	"It is little."

GOAL 4: To use the prepositions on, in, under, over, and between in statements describing arrangements.

Teacher	Student
"Where is the computer?"	"The computer is on the table."

continued

Figure 13.1 A procedure for teaching specific language skills.

"Where is the long line?" "The long line is over the short line."

"Where is the number 2?" "The number 2 is between the numbers 1 and 3."

1 2 3

GOAL 5: To name positives and negatives for at least four classes.

Teacher	Student
"Tell me something that is clothing."	"A hat is clothing."
	"A chair is not clothing."
"Tell me something that is food."	"An apple is food."
	"A pencil is not food."

GOAL 6: To perform simple "if-then" deductions.

Teacher	Student
"If the circle is big, what else do you know about it?"	"It is red."

Teacher	Student
"If the circle is little, what else do you know about it?"	"It is black."

GOAL 7: To use not in deductions.

Teacher	Student
"If the circle is red, what else do you know about it?"	"It is not little."
"If the circle is black, what else do you know about it?"	"It is not big."

Figure 13.1 (continued)

Inclusion Strategies

The Beginning Reading Program

Many educators feel that bilingual or bicultural students who also have **limited-English proficiency (LEP)** need to understand and speak English before they can begin to read it (Brisbois, 1995). Other educators feel that it is not necessary for LEP students to master the oral language before they are introduced to the written form (Gonzales, 1994). Even though the research seems to be divided on whether students need to proficiently speak the English language before they can read it, the majority of the research seems to be in agreement that **English as a second language (ESL)** students will learn to read better if the initial reading instruction is in their native language (Allen, 1994). Gonzales (1994) and Brisbois (1995) determined that students can learn to read in their native language and English at the same time if teachers use strategies that are mutually reinforcing and provide adequate vocabulary instruction in both languages. Some strategies that have been successful for developing reading skills for LEP students are discussed in the following sections.

In the alphabet learning phase of the program, children familiarize themselves with the letter names of the alphabet through identity and position statements. The child is taught first to spell words by letter sounds (*cat*) and is then presented clusters of words that follow the same spelling pattern (such as *cat, fat, hat,* and *bat*). As students become more aware of the patterns found in word families, they develop a metacognitive awareness of orthographic features of words that enables them to increase their word recognition skills. Word meanings are reinforced by yes–no questions of lexical terms.

Brisbois (1995) discusses the importance of vocabulary instruction and word recognition instruction in the second language. Word recognition begins with the production of isolated words in the clarification of meaning as related to the learner.

Ms. Chavez prints the word *cat* on the chalkboard. As she points to the word, she explains to the class the rule, "This is a word." She then follows this statement with an identity statement, "This is the word *cat.*" She encourages the students to respond with complete identity statements. Ms. Chavez begins by asking questions such as, "Is this the word *dog?*"

Ina raises her hand and responds, "That's *cat,* not *dog.*"

Ms. Chavez responds by recognizing Ina's correct answer but encourages Ina and other students to respond to the answer by using complete identity statements. "Good job, Ina. That's correct. Could you answer the question with the sentence structure that I suggested earlier?"

Ina answers, "Okay. No, that is not the word *dog.* That is the word *cat.*"

Ms. Chavez responds, "That's exactly right, Ina!"

Gestures illustrate action words. Students are invited to suggest other words they wish to learn. If no one volunteers, the teacher supplies another word. Students should be encouraged to use instrumental language with other children. By providing directions to their peers they will be expanding their own language.

Word-placement exercises teach visual discrimination of word forms and word meanings.

> Ms. Chavez labels objects with five-by-eight-inch cards and identifies them: "This card has a word on it. This is the word *toy*." Five or more words are identified in this way, and Ms. Chavez places one word card on the proper object. Students are asked, "This is the word what?" (*desk*) "So where does it belong?" (*On the desk*). Each child has a turn at naming and placing a word. The class then identifies these words on the chalkboard. The rule "If all the letters are the same, the words are the same" is taught.

Word-identification exercises can help students to acquire a sight vocabulary useful for developing simple sentences. As students learn to recognize their own names, they then receive instruction on recognizing other children's names. New sets of words (such as *is not* and *big*) can be added to construct sentences. Meaning is stressed in sentence reading by having students answer questions about their reading.

Ms. Chavez implemented this approach during her literacy instruction. "Now that we've completed the reading about Joe, here are some questions I want you to think about. First, could someone tell me this? Is Joe big?"

Amy, a Native American student, answers, "No, he's not."

Ms. Chavez responds to Amy, "That's correct. Can you tell me a little more about Joe using the words we have covered in our vocabulary list?"

Amy tries again this time answering; "Joe is not big."

Ms. Chavez then asks the rest of the class, "Is Joe little?"

Rashim raises his hand and responds, "Yes, Joe is little." After students progress with such basic tasks, they then apply their capabilities to read from teacher-prepared booklets.

A beginning reading program can serve as an extension of the language development program. It can be designed to help students become familiar with letter names, associate pictures visually with their naming words, recognize and produce rhyming words, and learn and use a limited number of sight words. Cognitive embedded tasks can help relate these activities to real-life experiences (Nichols, Rupley, Webb-Johnson, & Tlusty, 2001).

APPROACHES TO TEACHING READING AND WRITING TO CULTURALLY AND LINGUISTICALLY DIVERSE STUDENTS

Several approaches can provide reading instruction to students who speak a nonstandard dialect or a primary language other than English. Teachers must have an awareness of the students' cultural background and the linguistic features of their language. They must realize that a multicultural education is based upon the "fundamental belief that all people should be respected regardless of age, race, gender, economic class, religion, or physical or mental ability" (Bieger, 1996, p. 308). One way to demonstrate respect is to use the student's own language and cultural experiences to facilitate reading.

The Language-Experience Approach

A frequently used approach for introducing and teaching literacy to linguistically diverse students is the language-experience approach (LEA). The language-experience approach has several advantages. First, by using the student's oral language, the reading material reflects the student's syntax and sentence structures, eliminating much of the comprehension difficulty caused by using other beginning reading materials. Another advantage is vocabulary usage. Words used in constructing the reading materials come from the student's language and experiential backgrounds. These words reflect meaningful content for the student, facilitating the student's construction of meaning. The student's own oral vocabulary is often larger than the student's sight vocabulary, which allows the student to read words they ordinarily would not recognize in traditional reading approaches. Students who have experienced difficulty in the past in traditional reading approaches experience success at reading stories created from their own language and experiences. This newfound success in reading is often extremely motivational to the beginning reader and produces a positive attitude toward reading. An additional advantage is the incorporation of writing in the creating of individual—and group—experience stories.

While using the LEA, it is important to use the student's own language. Attempts to correct grammatical miscues and dialectical differences defeats the purpose of the language-experience approach. In order for the student to benefit from the LEA, it must be consistent with the student's spoken language. As the teacher makes authentic assessment of the student's instruction, the teacher may want to focus on syntactic miscues as a reading skill for future lessons. These skills may be taught in the context of the LEA, but the purpose of the LEA is to teach the student to read and in order to do this the story must be transcribed in the student's authentic form.

The advantages of the language-experience approach multiply when an individual story is dictated. However, when a group story is dictated, the vocabulary and syntax both may exceed an individual student's abilities. Teachers, therefore, should encourage group discussion to help linguistically diverse students construct meaning for group-dictated stories.

Teachers may wish either to incorporate the language-experience approach into their reading programs or to use it as the primary instructional program. Because of the flexibility of the LEA, it can easily be combined with other approaches. Another possibility is to begin reading instruction with the language-experience approach and then gradually introduce a literature-based approach. Stahl (1990) states that there is research evidence to support the use of an LEA for students who do not yet understand the purpose of reading or who lack exposure to printed literature. Stahl

LEA integrates reading, writing, listening, and speaking abilities.

states that for beginning readers in kindergarten, the use of an LEA approach can have positive gains; however, as students progress through the phases of reading development, he feels that a larger emphasis needs to be placed on direct instruction in the areas of decoding, which are typically found in basal reader programs.

An instructional aide or parent volunteer can facilitate implementation of the LEA. An aide or volunteer can record and copy stories, make word cards and follow-up practice materials, read and reread stories with students, create an LEA classroom library, and follow up with practice activities for students who otherwise might not succeed in reading.

An Integrated Language Approach

Many schools are stressing natural acquisition of second languages and building on each student's linguistic strengths. Integrated language instruction incorporates literature to develop and enhance students' knowledge base. The approach also integrates language with all other aspects of language teaching, such as content-area instruction in science or social studies.

In an integrated classroom, students engage in reading for enjoyment and to gather information. Teachers are available to give students the help they need at a particular time, but the guidance the teacher provides enables students to become problem solvers and to seek other resources to help solve problems. Students sharing their work with others and communicating their accomplishments orally or in written form are major goals of an integrated classroom. In an integrated classroom students learn from relevant, meaningful instructional materials. Students have the opportunity to learn all of the necessary reading skills, but the reading materials are student-centered and the teacher functions as the facilitator of learning.

Literature-based instruction for culturally and linguistically diverse students can feature stories from various cultures and languages displayed around the classroom; writings of students covering the walls like ribboned wallpaper; portfolios showing drafts of creative writing pieces, such as journals of all kinds, letters, and poetry; and field notes of student activities. ESL students should be able to use literature that reflects their language and culture. Bieger (1996) encourages teachers to develop lessons using traditional literature to help provide a multicultural education to all students. Because myths, legends, and folktales reflect the values of people from around the world, these forms of literature are encouraged for teachers to use when working with culturally and linguistically diverse learners. Integrated language instruction values all languages, and students become literate in their own language and ultimately in English.

Because children develop language naturally, teachers must create classrooms where students can interact with others and experiment with language. Similarly, second-language learners need to construct their own meanings rather than memorize text or reiterate others' thoughts. Bilingual and English language programs should use a wide variety of instructional activities designed to encourage student interaction. These can be literature-based activities that focus on developing various language and literacy skills: reading, writing, listening, and speaking. Using thematic units to teach language is an excellent way to introduce meaning that interconnects with students' lives. These units may incorporate stories that include everyday language events. Developing language through stories in the primary language and in the students' second language is important to cognitive development. Using literature to help students become literate and educated in their own language while adding another language builds students' self-concepts and encourages a positive attitude toward learning. An acceptance of each student's culture and language is a major principle of second-language teaching.

Teaching language to bilingual and second-language learners suggests that students naturally construct new meanings from whole to part of the whole. The parts—for example, the specific skills of reading and writing—must be broken down by the learner, not the teacher, and learned as needed within the context of real books and stories and writing activities (Poplin, 1992). An integrated approach in a bilingual classroom should emphasize early literacy teaching of skills as a whole and within context, such as literature stories to promote meaningful literacy. Emphasizing teaching language with meaning will prevent instruction in isolated skills. Skill instruction separate from the primary literacy activities can be irrelevant and not make any sense to the student. Teachers must integrate language with real situations to stimulate a positive language-learning attitude.

Stressing meaning within context and students' experiences facilitates reading comprehension. Engaging all of the modes of language as they interact in learning settings helps students acquire language skills. Teachers must understand all of the factors that influence students' work in teaching reading and writing to second-language learners. The match between what is being taught and what is being comprehended is especially critical for the second-language learner. When students are working in their primary language, a mismatch is unlikely to occur, but occasionally it does. When that happens, the student will attempt to understand meaning in various ways. Because the mental mismatch often reflects a student's cultural or linguistic background, integrating literature to supplement instruction is often recommended. A connection must be made between what the reader knows and what is being read or heard for the reader to comprehend it.

Predictable reading materials offer another way to develop bilingual language literacy skills. Patterned books have stories with predictable features such as rhyming and repeated phrases or refrains that promote language development (Norton, 2001). Patterned books frequently contain pictures that may facilitate story comprehension. The predictable patterns immediately involve beginning second-language readers in a literacy event in their first or second language. Books with patterned structure can provide modeling as a reading strategy, challenge students' current level of linguistic competence, and provide assistance in comprehending difficult concepts. Comprehension through the repetition of a simple sentence pattern can motivate second-language learners to continue trying to learn to read. The process is important for developmental purposes and teaches students to use contextual and syntactic features of the text to identify the repeated words or phrases. A popular patterned book is Bill Martin's *Brown Bear, Brown Bear, What Do You See?* (1970). The fully illustrated story repeats simple patterns that second-language learners can use to begin the reading process. Students become familiar with the story and language patterns and soon begin to create their own text with their own illustrations. In the early stages of second-language acquisition, the use of the first and second language is critical for conceptual development. Later, as the second-language proficiency develops, the student will focus on learning English. Patterned books' most important function is to offer immediate access to meaningful, enjoyable literacy experiences that facilitate lifelong reading.

The language-experience approach should be a major component of an integrated language approach for teaching reading and writing to linguistically diverse students. In addition to the LEA, teachers should use materials from a variety of sources. The following materials have been recommended for integrated programs in Spanish language classrooms: (1) poetry and stories from Spanish language basal readers, (2) Spanish language trade books, (3) Spanish language resource books, (4) Spanish language newspapers, newsletters, comics, and magazines, (5) Spanish language publications from government and health agencies, (6) telephone books, cookbooks, and television guides in Spanish, (7) books and stories written in Spanish by members of the Hispanic community, and (8) stories written by the students themselves. In addition to these sources, Norton (2001) has compiled a list of sources for alternatives to Spanish language basals. An abbreviated list is presented in Figure 13.2. In a recent article, Godina (1996) discusses the cognitive dissonance that many Mexican American students feel. In order for bicultural students to see a connection between what they learn at school and their daily life encounters, schools must include a larger multicultural selection of literature in their curriculum.

An integrated approach to teaching encourages production of student-generated stories (Freppon, 1995). The stories help develop students' self-concepts simply by the creation of their own works. The language-experience approach and a process approach to writing offer students an excellent way of developing skills that integrate cooperation—fostering story writing and peer interaction strategies for language and content learning (Godina, 1996). Promoting story writing by second-language learners will create a literate classroom with students enthusiastic about reading and writing. Allowing students to read and write every day about their own experiences enhances literacy skills and the desire to learn. Positive literacy experiences involving reading promote students who learn to enjoy reading and begin to seek out more information to accomplish classroom tasks in the early grades.

The Literature-Based Reading Approach: Integrating Multiethnic Literature

Diverse cultural literature is one means to move closer toward becoming a nation that is accepting and tolerant of all cultures. For our country to develop an understanding and acceptance of others, we will have to become educated about the cultural heritage of many groups. One of the most effective ways to accomplish this task is to incorporate multiethnic and multicultural literature into our classrooms. Multiethnic literature helps students discover the intricacies of a language, as well as the people's history and culture (Bieger, 1996; Godina, 1996). In addition, when students read literature they encounter a multitude of characters that are both similar to and different from themselves. Each character of a story is driven by certain emotions and must deal with the problems and joys of life in various ways. How the heroes and heroines react and cope provides students with insights and information well beyond their own personal experiences.

According to Banks (1994) there are four levels that teachers can use to integrate ethnic content into the curriculum. The lowest levels of integration are the "contributions approach" and the "ethnic additive approach." Teachers who use the contributions approach have their students read only about the contributions of ethnic groups such as reading about ethnic holidays, heroes, and customs. The ethnic additive approach does add content, concepts, and themes that reflect diverse cultures, but it does not integrate it into the existing curriculum. Instead, it may become a unit that is taught for a month out of the year and then forgotten. Teachers

BIBLIOGRAPHY

"Americas Award" by The Consortium of Latin American Studies Programs. *School Library Journal* 45 (August 1999): 38–39.

Barrera, Rosalinda B. "Latina and Latino Researchers Interact on Issues Related to Literacy Learning: Conversations." *Reading Research Quarterly,* 34 (April/May/June 1999): 217–230.

Bierhorst, John, translated by. *History and Mythology of the Aztecs: The Codex Chimalpopoca.* Tucson: University of Arizona Press, 1998.

Finazzo, Denise Ann. *All for the Children: MIticultural Essentials of Literature.* Albany, N.Y.: Delmar, 1997.

Freidel, David, Linda Schele, and Joy Parker. *Maya Cosmos: Three Thousand Years on the Shaman's Path.* New York: Morrow, 1993.

Griego y Maestas, Jose, and Rudolfo A. Anaya. *Cuentos: Tales from the Hispanic Southwest.* Santa Fe: The Museum of New Mexico Press, 1980.

Hearne, Betsy. "The Big Picture." *The Bulletin,* 51, (April 1998): 271–272.

Helms, Cynthia Newman, edited by. *Diego Rivera. A Retrospective.* Founders Society, Detroit Institute of Arts, 1986.

Lodge, Sally. "Spanish-Language Publishing for Kids in the U.S. Picks Up Speed." *Publishers Weekly* (August 25, 1997): 48–49.

Miller, Mary, and Karl Taube. *The Gods and Symbols of Ancient Mexico and the Maya: An Illustrated Dictionary of Mesoamerican Religion.* New York: Thames and Hudson, 1993.

Moll, Luis. "Latina and Latino Researchers Interact on Issues Related to Literacy Learning: Conversations." *Reading Research Quarterly,* 34 (April/May/June 1999): 217–230.

Moseley, Michael. *The Incas and Their Ancestors: The Archaeology of Peru.* New York: Thames and Hudson, 1992.

National Association of Hispanic and Latino Studies. National Conference. February 21–26, 2000, Houston, Texas.

Norton, Donna E. *The Effective Teaching of Language Arts,* 5th ed. Upper Saddle River, N.J.: Merrill/Prentice Hall, 1997.

_____ . *Through the Eyes of a Child: An Introduction to Children's Literature,* 5th ed. Upper Saddle River, N.J.: Merrill/Prentice Hall, 1999.

Publishers Weekly. "Review of Sid Fleischman's *Bandit Moon.*" (August 3, 1998): 86.

Rochman, Hazel. *Against Borders: Promoting Books for a Multicultural World.* Chicago: American Library Association, 1993.

School Library Journal. "Review of Sid Fleischman's *Bandit Moon.*" (August 3, 1998): 86.

Silva-Diaz, Maria Cecilia. "Rites of Initiation in Recent Latin American Narratives." *Bookbird* 35 (Summer 1997): 21–26.

Vargas, Lucila, and Bruce DePyssler. "Using Media Literacy to Explore Stereotypes of Mexican Immigrants." *Social Education,* 62 (November/December 1998): 407–412.

CHILDREN'S AND YOUNG ADULT LITERATURE REFERENCES

Abelove, Joan. *Go and Come Back,* DK, 1998 (I: 14+ R: 6). Set in a Peruvian jungle, the story is told by a cultural anthropologist.

Alarcon, Francisco X. *From the Bellybutton of the Moon and Other Summer Poems.* Illustrated by Maya Christina Gonzalez. Children's Press, 1998 (I: all). A collection of poems written in Spanish and English.

Anaya, Rudolfo. *Maya's Children: The Story of La Llorona.* Illustrated by Maria Baca. Hyperion, 1997 (I: 5–9 R: 4). The tale of the crying woman who wanders through the night.

Ancona, George. *Barrio: José's Neighborhood.* Harcourt Brace, 1998 (I: 6+ R: 4). Photographic compositions enhance a story set in the Mission District of San Francisco.

Figure 13.2 Resources for multicultural children's literature.

Anzaldua, Gloria. *Prietita and the Ghost Woman.* Children's Press, 1996 (I: 5–8 R: 5). A girl searches for herbs.

Atkin, S. Beth, edited by. *Voices from the Fields: Children of Migrant Farmworkers Tell Their Stories.* Little, Brown, 1993 (I: 10 +). The text includes interviews with nine children.

Beals, Carleton. *Stories Told by the Aztecs: Before the Spaniards Came.* Illustrated by Charles Pickard. Abelard, 1970 (I: 10+ R: 7). o. p.* A collection of tales has footnotes and a bibliography.

Behrens, June. *Fiesta!* Photographs by Scott Taylor. Children's Press, 1978 (I: 5–8 R: 4). This book contains photographs of the Cinco Mayo fiesta.

Bernardo, Anilú. *Jumping Off to Freedom.* Pinata, 1996 (I: 10+ R: 5). A boy and his father flee from Cuba on a raft.

Bertrand, Diane Gonzales. *Sip, Slurp, Soup. Soup/Caldo, Caldo, Caldo.* Illustrated by Alex Pardo De-Langa. Pinata, 1977 (I: 4–7). Four children watch as soup is prepared.

Blackmore, Vivien. *Why Corn Is Golden: Stories About Plants.* Illustrated by Susana Martinez-Ostos. Little, Brown, 1984 (I: all R: 5). This book contains folklore about corn.

Brimmer, Larry Dane. *A Migrant Family.* Lerner, 1992 (I: all). The text and photographs describe the life of Mexican American migrant workers in California.

Brown, Tricia. *Hello, Amigos!* Photographs by Fran Ortiz. Holt, Rinehart & Winston, 1986 (I: 3–8 R: 3). Photographs tell the story of a boy on his sixth birthday.

Carling, Amelia Lau. *Mama and Papa Have a Store.* Dial, 1998 (I: 3–8 R: 4). A Chinese family have a store in Guatemala City.

Carlson, Lori Marie, selected by. *Sol a Sol* Holt, 1998 (I: all). A collection of bilingual poems.

Cherry, Lynn, and Mark J. Plotkin. *The Shaman's Apprentice: A Tale of the Amazon Rain Forest.* Harcourt Brace, 1998 (I: 6–8 R: 4). A boy learns the importance of the shaman's wisdom.

Cisneros, Sandra. *The House on Mango Street.* Arte Publico, 1983 (I: 12+ R: 7). A girl records her feelings about her world.

Cockcroft, James. *Diego Rivera.* Chelsea House, 1991 (I: 10+ R: 6). A biography of the artist written for adolescent readers.

Cozzen, Judy, edited by. *Kids Explore America's Hispanic Heritage.* John Muir, 1992 (I: all). This is a report of a school project.

Delacre, Lulu. *Arroz con Leche: Popular Songs and Rhymes from Latin America.* Scholastic, 1989 (I: all). This text includes a variety of songs and poems.

dePaola, Tomie. *The Lady of Guadalupe.* Holiday House, 1980 (I: 8+ R: 6). This is a traditional Mexican tale.

DeSpain, Pleasant. *The Dancing Turtle: A Folktale from Brazil.* Illustrated by David Boston, August House, 1998 (I: 5–8 R: 4). An animal uses its wits.

Dorros, Arrthur. *Radio Man: A Story in English and Spanish.* HarperCollins, 1993 (I: 6–10). This book focuses on migrant farm workers.

Dorson, Mercedes, and Jeanne Wilmot. *Tales from the Rain Forest: Myths and Legends from the Amazonian Indians of Brazil.* Ecco, 1997 (I: 8+ R: 7). A collection of folktales.

Ehlert, Lois. *Cuckoo: A Mexican Folktale.* Translated in Spanish by Gloria de Argon Andujar. Harcourt Brace, 1997 (I: 4–8). A *pourquoi* tale.

Emberly, Rebecca. *Lets Go: A Book in Two Languages.* Little, Brown, 1993 (I: 4–8). A picture dictionary of concepts related to places children might go.

_____ . *My Day: A Book in Two Languages.* Little, Brown, 1993 (I: 4–8). A picture dictionary of concepts related to daytime activities.

_____ . *My House: A Book in Two Languages.* Little Brown, 1990 (I: 4–8). A picture dictionary shows captioned illustrations of things found in the house.

Figure 13.2 (continued)

_____ . *Taking a Walk: A Book in Two Languages.* Little, Brown, 1990 (I: 4–8). A picture dictionary showing items a child sees while on a walk.

Ets, Marie Hall, and Aurora Labastida. *Nine Days to Christmas: A Story of Mexico.* Illustrated by Marie Hall Ets. Viking, 1959 (I: 5–8 R: 3). Ceci is going to have her first Posada with her owl piñata.

Fleischman, Sid. *Bandit's Moon.* Illustrated by Jos A. Smith. Greenwillow, 1998 (I: 8+ R: 5). Historical fiction set in the time of the California Gold Rush.

Fritz, Jean, Katherine Paterson, Patricia McKissack, Fredrick McKissack, Margaret Mahy, and Jake Highwater. *The World in 1492.* Illustrated by Stefano Vitale. Holt, 1992 (I: 8+). The section "The Americas in 1492," written by Jamake Highwater, includes information about the Aztecs and the Incas.

Garza, Carmen Lomas. *Family Pictures.* Children's Book, 1990 (I: 4–8). The illustrations and text in English and Spanish show family scenes.

Geeslin, Campbell. *On Ramon's Farm: Five Tales of Mexico.* Illustrated by Petra Mathers. Atheneum, 1998 (I: 4–8). A collection of five stories.

Gerson, Mary-Joan. *People of the Corn: A Mayan Story.* Illustrated by C. Golembe. Little, Brown, 1995 (I: all). The illustrations are based on Mayan art.

Gonzalez, Ralfka, and Ana Ruiz. *My First Book of Proverbs.* Children's Book, 1995 (I: all). A collection of sayings in English and Spanish.

Greger, C. Shana. *The Fifth and Final Sun: An Ancient Myth of the Sun's Origin.* Houghton Mifflin, 1994 (I: 8+ R: 5). A myth about the creation of the sun.

Griego y Maestas, Jose, and Rudolfo A. Anaya. *Cuentos: Tales from the Hispanic Southwest.* Illustrated by Jaime Valdez. Museum of New Mexico, 1980 (I: 9+ R: 5). This is a collection of tales.

Griego, Margot C. *Tortillitas para Mama and Other Spanish Nursery Rhymes.* Illustrated by Barbara Cooney. Holt, Rinehart & Winston, 1981 (I: 3–7). Nursery rhymes appear in Spanish and English.

Hausman, Gerald. *Doctor Bird: Three Lookin' Up Tales from Jamaica.* Illustrated by Ashley Wolff. Philomel, 1998 (I: 3–8 R: 3). These tales show how the national bird of Jamaica interacts with animals.

Herrera, Juan Felipe. *Calling the Doves.* Illustrated by Elly Simmons. Children's Press, 1995 (I: all R: 5). The story of an immigrant family.

Jaffe, Nina. *The Golden Flower: A Taino Myth from Puerto Rico.* Simon & Schuster, 1996 (I: all). A creation tale shows how vegetation came to the land.

Jiménez, Franciso. *La Mariposa.* Illustrated by Simon Silva. Houghton Mifflin, 1998 (I: 8+ R: 5) The son of immigrant workers has difficulty in school.

Kalnay, Francis. *Chucaro: Wild Pony of the Pampa.* Harcourt, Brace, 1958 (I: 8+). Winner of the 1959 Newbery Honor.

Keister, Douglas. *Fernando's Gift.* Sierra Club, 1995 (I: 6+). Text and photographs show the life of a young boy who lives in the rain forest of Costa Rica.

Kroll, Virginia. *Butterfly Boy.* Illustrated by Gerardo Suzan. Boyds Mills, 1997 (I: 5–8 R: 4). A boy tries to ensure the return of the butterflies.

Martinez, Victor. *Parrot in the Oven: Mi Vida.* HarperCollins, 1996 (I: 12+ R: 6). A Mexican American family struggles against poverty.

McCaughrean, Geraldine. *The Bronze Cauldron: Myths and Legends of the World.* Illustrated by Bee Willey. (I: 8+ R: 4). Includes a Mayan myth.

Meltzer, Milton. *The Hispanic Americans.* Photographs by Morrie Camhi and Catherine Noren. Crowell, 1982 (I: 9–12 R: 6). Puerto Ricans, Chicanos, and Cubans have influenced the United States.

Mora, Pat. *The Race of Toad and Deer.* Orchard, 1995 (I: all). An adaptation of a fable.

Myers, Walter Dean. *Scorpions.* Harper & Rowe, 1998 (I: 11+ R: 5). A boy has difficulties with a gang.

Ober, Hal. *How Music Came to the World.* Houghton Mifflin, 1994 (I: all R: 4). This is an Aztec myth.

Orozco, Jose-Luis. *Ten Little Fingers and Other Play Rhymes and Action Songs from Latin America.* Illustrated by Elisa Kleven. Dutton, 1997 (I: 4+). Music and words in Spanish and English.

Figure 13.2   (continued)

Paulsen, Gary. *The Crossing*. Doubleday, 1987 (I: 12+ R: 6). The harsh realities of a border town are developed as a boy longs to cross into the United States.

_____. *Sisters Hermana*. Harcourt Brace, 1993 (I: 12+ R: 6). Two girls, one Mexican and one Anglo, discover that they have many similarities.

Peña, Sylvia, edited by. *Tun-ta-ca-tun: More Stories and Poems in English and Spanish for Children*. Illustrated by Narciso Peña. Arte Publico Press, 1986 (I: all). The collection of poems and stories are written for children from preschool to older levels.

Politi, Leo. *Pedro, the Angel of Olvera Street*. Scribner's, 1946 (I: 5–8 R: 4). Winner of the 1947 Newbery Honor.

_____. *Song of the Swallows*, Scribner's, 1949 (I: 5–8 R: 4). Juan lives in Capistrano, California.

Prago, Albert. *Strangers in Their Own Land: A History of Mexican-Americans*. Four Winds, 1973 (I: 10+ R: 7). This book traces both the history and the difficulties of Mexican Americans.

Reeve, Kirk. *Lolo and Red-Legs*. Rising Moon, 1998 (I: 8+ R: 5). An eleven-year-old boy has adventures after he captures a tarantula.

Reinhard, Johan. *Discovering the Inca Ice Maiden: My Adventures on Ampato*. National Geographic, 1998 (I: 8+ R: 4). Photographs show the discovery.

Rohmer, Harriet, and Mary Anchondo. *How We Came to the Fifth World*. Children's Book Press, 1988 (I: all R: 5). This is an Aztec version of creation.

Rosenberg, Joe. *¡Aplauso!*. Pinata, 1995 (I: all). Hispanic children's plays.

Saenz, Benjamin Alire. *A Gift from Papa Diego*. Illustrated by Geronimo Garcia. Cinco Puntos, 1998 (I: 7+). A story in English and Spanish about a boy's love for his grandfather.

San Souci, Robert D. *Cendrillon: A Caribbean Cinderella*. Illustrated by Brian Pinkney. Simon & Schuster, 1998 (I: all). Creole words are included in this variant.

Schaefer, Jack. *Old Ramon*. Houghton Mifflin, 1960 (I: 8+ R: 5). Winner of the 1961 Newbery Honor.

Slate, Joseph. *The Secret Stars*. Illustrated by Felipe Davalos. Cavendish, 1998 (I: 6–8 R: 4). Set in New Mexico, the text focuses on the Three Kings.

Sola, Michele. *Angela Weaves a Dream: The Story of a Young Maya Artist*. Photographs by Jeffrey Jay Foxx. Hyperion, 1997 (I: 8+ R: 5). Photographs show the weaving process and symbols in designs.

Soto, Gary. *Baseball in April and Other Stories*. Harcourt Brace Jovanovich, 1990 (I: 11+ R: 6).

Swann, Brian. *Touching the Distance: Native American Riddle-Poems*. Illustrated by Maria Rendon. Harcourt Brace, 1998 (I: all). Riddles are written in the form of poems.

Tashlik, Phyllis, edited by. *Hispanic, Female and Young: An Anthology*. Arte Publico, 1993 (I: 12+). This is both an anthology of stories and a collection of interviews conducted by a group of students.

Turner, Robyn Montana. *Frida Kahlo: Portraits of Women Artists for Children*. Little, Brown, 1993 (I: all). A biography of a great Mexican artist.

Van Laan, Nancy, retold by. *The Magic Bean Tree: A Legend from Argentina*. Illustrated by Beatriz Vidal. Houghton Mifflin, 1998 (I: 4–8 R: 4). The people are saved from drought.

Vidal, Beatriz. *The Legend of El Dorado: A Latin American Tale*. Knopf, 1991 (I: all R: 5). The treasures of the gilded man are believed to be at the bottom of Lake Guatavita.

Volkmer, Jane Anne, retold by. *Song of Chirimia—A Guatemalan Folktale*. Carolrhoda, 1990 (I: 6–10 R: 5). A Mayan folktale in English and Spanish tells how a man tries to win the hand of a Mayan princess.

Wisniewski, David. *Rain Player*. Clarion, 1991 (I: 5–8 R: 5). Paper constructions enhance this Mayan tale.

I = Interest age range
R = Readability by grade level
o. p. = Books that are out of print but too good to eliminate.

Figure 13.2 (continued)

Source: From *Multicultural Children's Literature: Through the Eyes of Many Children,* by D. Norton, 2001, Upper Saddle River, NJ: Merrill/Prentice Hall. Copyright 2001 by Pearson Education. Reprinted by permission of Pearson Education, Inc., Upper Saddle River, NJ 07458.

should be encouraged to use the two highest levels of multicultural integration ("transformation approach" and "social action approach") when designing curriculum. Use of the transformation approach completely reconstructs the curriculum in order to allow students to view concerns, themes, problems, and concepts from the perspective of diverse groups. This is not a unit that lasts a month, but instead it is a commitment to culturally responsive instruction throughout the whole year. The highest form of cultural integration is the social action approach. During this approach teachers select literature that allows students to identify social problems and concerns and to read about how the main character made decisions and took action to solve the problem. Through the modeling of the character's actions students learn how to identify and resolve problems related to cultural differences.

Teachers can integrate a social action approach into their curriculum by using literature-based reading instruction. Integrating multiethnic literature into a school curriculum for second-language learners helps students realize that all ethnic groups have roots in the past and a strong heritage that is a part of their culture (Bieger, 1996). Knowing about others from a similar culture encourages a sense of pride that builds a positive self-concept for students. They may discover by reading that others from their own culture made significant contributions to society. Students encountering multiethnic literature as a part of their reading curriculum benefit academically and learn the social values and behaviors of people in society (Bieger, 1996; Godina, 1996).

Existing reading programs can easily integrate multiethnic literature for explicit reading instruction. Teachers can share stories both orally and in written form, and instruction can coordinate language arts exercises such as vocabulary, comprehension, writing, and language development in both the first and second languages. The use of literature is an excellent way to increase cultural awareness, build vocabulary and language, develop comprehension skills, and provide writing opportunities. Multiethnic literature can provide teaching opportunities for creating lessons on figurative language, examining the story's symbolism, and integrating context with idiomatic expressions. Such explorations help students understand meaning and enhance the development of language while stimulating interest in reading.

Using instructional strategies that create a culturally affirming perspective in the classroom to support reading instruction can be effective with culturally diverse learners. Examples of such strategies that can be implemented in K–8 reading environments where students may be experiencing difficulty with critical reading comprehension skills are Inventionisation and Footsteps in the Hall of Fame (Nichols, Rupley, Webb-Johnson, & Tlusty, 2001).

Inventionisation uses yearlong thematic units as its foundation of discovery in order to create a transformative approach that focuses on all cultures' contributions to scientific inquiry. Inventionisation begins by having students read biographies of African Americans, Asian Americans, Hispanic Americans, and Native Americans who are often not included in instructional delivery that involves the work and inventions of Thomas Edison, Alexander Graham Bell, and Benjamin Franklin. Sharing with students the contributions of individuals like Lewis Latimer, who worked initially as a chief draftsman for Edison and Bell, provides an excellent foundation for discussions of the time period, inventions, and the critical reading skills necessary to assist in building a knowledge base. Sharing the diversity of people who have contributed to making our society more efficient and convenient can also be used as a vehicle to promote critical reading skills. Studying, for example, the development of the contact lens, the bing cherry, the polio vaccine, blood plasma, government, and marital property rights will open the world of discovery from an Asian, European, African, Native, and Hispanic American perspective, while providing students the opportunity to engage in critical reading. Informational text such as *African-American Inventors* by Sullivan, Haskins, and Haskins (1998) can be extremely beneficial while planning for Inventionisation units.

Footsteps in the Hall of Fame is a social action approach that examines the leadership of all Americans who contributed to the development of the United States regardless of their cultural heritage. Genres of biography and historical fiction can become the foundation of critical reading development during this type of activity. Study of people and periods from a sociopolitical and personal perspective allows students the opportunity to study the historical period and its people. Opportunities for generating gender consciousness can also be explored as all students are provided exposure to research and the study of men and women who are also culturally diverse at different time periods throughout our history. This culturally responsive activity can also be framed from an interdisciplinary perspective so that collaboration among teachers, parents, and students is a targeted goal in reading development. As students learn about each aspect of a person's life they earn footsteps into the Hall of Fame that highlights their development as a reading scholar of the period and of the person. Other projects can evolve from this initial reading activity to highlight a variety of language arts within the classroom context (i.e., drama, writing, oratory, and media presentations) (Nichols, Rupley, Webb-Johnson, & Tlusty, 2001).

The Oral Reading Approach

A reading approach developed for linguistically diverse students that is popular in New Zealand and the South Pacific stresses high interest in reading through the use of short stories with natural language and some vocabulary control for repetition. Norton (2001) believes that books that include repetitive language are excellent for oral reading. The teacher reads the story to the group, then the teacher and students chorally reread the story in unison. They discuss the story and read it once again. In this approach, the teacher selects individual words and phrases and emphasizes choral reading (all or several students reading in unison). Research has noted significant results in comprehension and word recognition for students with limited-English proficiency who were taught with this method.

Choral reading has also been used successfully in promoting language learning for linguistically diverse students. Implementing choral reading for second-language learners begins with identifying poems and adapting them for students.

Poems should cover familiar topics that students can relate to. For second-language learners, the poems should contain a lot of action and allow lines to be added to help clarify vocabulary and emphasize meaning.

After the poem has been selected and adapted, McCauley and McCauley (1992) suggest the following general procedure:

1. Give a quick, interesting introduction. Focus on getting students involved in talking about the poem.
2. Read the poem aloud to students. Use expression, sound effects, and movements that the poem could represent.
3. Make copies of the poem available to the students.
4. Read the poem again to the students as they follow along.
5. Read the poem with the students slowly at first, and gradually increase the speed of reading. Appropriate movements and sound effects also should be included.
6. Give lines to the students when they feel comfortable with the words and movements. Students who want solo lines may be given them.
7. Practice reading the poem with assigned parts.
8. Recognize a job well done with applause, verbal praise, or both.

An example (McCauley & McCauley, 1992) of how movement and drama are added to "Jack and Jill" is presented next. This acting-out part of choral reading is very important for second-language learners, because it aids in construction of meaning and helps text become more meaningful for them.

(Boys, as they stand)	Jack
(Girls, as they stand)	and Jill
(All, walking)	went up the hill
	to fetch a pail of water
(Boys)	Jack fell down and broke his crown
	Ouch! (Hold head)
(Girls)	And Jill came tumbling after.
	(Lean toward boys, hand gesture—i.e., hand on side of cheek—as if worried about Jack's fate, and say)
	Are you all right, Jack?
(Boys)	(While rubbing head)
	Yeah.
(Girls)	(While wiping forehead in relief)
	Whew!

Choral reading can be done with the whole class and ensures success for linguistically diverse students. It promotes positive attitudes toward both second-language acquisition and reading.

The Basal Reader Approach

Basal reading programs are still used throughout the United States, and teachers of linguistically diverse students often choose to use them to teach reading. However, teachers should be aware of special considerations when using basal readers as the main method for teaching reading, especially to linguistically diverse students. Among these considerations are (1) special attention to developing background concepts and vocabulary in depth before reading, (2) skillful questioning during silent reading to identify and clear up misunderstandings and to enhance the students' comprehension, and (3) specific emphasis on listening to the language rather than on oral reading. These three considerations are important to all reading approaches and should be considered when developing any reading plan. Linguistically diverse students often worry about having to read orally, so they may not concentrate on the language they hear, particularly in group situations. Keeping in mind the special instructional considerations, teachers may find that linguistically diverse students can progress with their classmates in a basal reading program.

Today, many of the basal series have integrated a literature approach to teaching reading and have become more sensitive to teaching reading skills in the context of the literature (Eldredge, Reutzel, & Hollingsworth, 1996). They have also shifted their design to include more guided reading approaches, flexible grouping, and leveled texts. Most series also include multicultural extensions to go along with focus text. Most current basal reader programs include supplemental literature selections to be used in conjunction with basal readers. Some individuals (Delpit, 1991) have indicated that culturally and linguistically diverse students may need a bridge from the basal series to a more process-focused literature-based program. Combining features of explicit/direct instruction with literature of the home culture of students from diverse backgrounds may also benefit students.

The features of an integrated basal reading program include the following:

1. Literacy centers within each classroom that provide students with access to a variety of books and literacy materials. Include in the centers multiple genres of children's literature, comfortable seating, and manipulatives (felt stories, roll movies, and taped stories).

2. Teacher-guided activities that help students understand what they could do and should do. Include in these activities use of modeling and scaffolding, the use of the directed reading-thinking activity (DR-TA), and retellings using both books and props (felt stories, puppets, and roll movies).

3. Independent reading and writing periods to allow students to choose between working alone or with others, and to select from a variety of activities ranging from retelling to dramatizing stories.

Morrow's (1992) study showed that students from diverse backgrounds had improved literacy achievement when they used an integrated basal approach. Concerns about whether students from diverse backgrounds would benefit from integrating the basal reader approach with a literature-based approach were unfounded. Components of the program that might account for its success were teachers demonstrating, facilitating, and participating in literature activities with high expectations for their students. In addition, integrated basal programs should feature literature that reflects the various cultural backgrounds found in the classrooms.

The Dual-Language Reading Approach

Many bilingual programs provide reading instruction in the students' primary language as well as in standard English (e.g., Spanish and English). Gonzales (1994) found this to be an effective approach to reading instruction. Many of the bilingual programs in the southwestern United States teach reading with Spanish basal programs.

Research (Weber, 1991) indicates that some instructional practices in and beliefs about teaching reading may be counterproductive to reading and language development of linguistically diverse students. Many programs use only phonics to teach reading to students with limited-English proficiency (as demonstrated by many Spanish basal reading programs). Teachers of linguistically diverse students often think that a phonics approach is the only way to teach reading to second-language learners. One need only observe readers both inside and outside a classroom to confirm that this is not so. If children's concept knowledge in their first language is limited, this inhibits their realization that print represents meaningful language (Neuman & Koskinen, 1992). Instruction that focuses only on decoding words in English limits students' opportunities to realize that reading conveys meaning.

Second-language learners benefit from reading programs that incorporate a range of contexts, both social and functional, in which reading begins and develops. Adapting several reading approaches can help linguistically diverse students become effective, efficient users of written English.

The **dual-language reading approach** makes use of native language and literacy skills to strengthen the reading process of speakers whose English is limited. Primary language reading materials, trade books, basal texts, and other instructional materials help strengthen bilingual reading programs. In addition, reading activities develop cognitive structures, vocabulary, comprehension strategies, and higher cognitive levels. This focus is important for a smooth transition from first-language to second-language reading.

EXPANDING AND DEVELOPING MEANING VOCABULARY

Linguistically diverse students need to develop a large base of immediately recognizable words for fluent reading (Brisbois, 1995). They come to school already knowing words related to logos, advertisements, and print in their environment. They see print everywhere (at home, on television, while shopping, and along highways, to mention a few) that can serve as a foundation for developing language-experience stories, writing stories, and learning other words.

Another approach that enables linguistically diverse students to acquire vocabulary in the second language is simply through the process of reading. This would suggest that a literature-based approach, an integrated language approach, or features of either combined with a basal reader approach would be more successful in expanding vocabulary than would learning words in isolation.

Teachers can choose words from the students' language-experience stories, discussions of stories read, writing activities, and environmental print. Words selected for the students should be familiar ones. Choral reading, which was presented earlier, can also enhance and expand second-language learners' vocabulary. Students are more likely to recognize a word in print when they can recognize either how the word functions or what it represents.

SPECIAL STUDENTS

Addressing individual student needs in reading instruction has always been an enormous task. Providing appropriate reading instruction for the individual needs of students within a large group demands many long hours of planning and hard work by teachers. Today, with the implementation of the Individuals With Disabilities Act (IDEA), teachers are adapting their classrooms to accommodate individual needs and to provide appropriate education for students with special needs (Rupley & Nichols, 1998).

Special students are those who have unique needs. Included among this group are students who are physically disabled, emotionally disabled, learning disabled, and gifted. Special students may or may not have learning difficulties; however, they often require special teaching. Such teaching is intended to ensure that special students are successful learners.

Mainstreaming

In 1975, Public Law 94-142 (Education for All Handicapped Children Act) was passed. This was one of the most significant developments in U.S. education. This law affected the placement of students with disabilities into the public schools. It allowed for students with disabilities to be mainstreamed into regular classrooms. Children with disabilities must be placed in the "least restrictive environment," which is interpreted, in many cases, to be the same environment as that for regular students. This trend to educate children with disabilities in the closest possible proximity to the regular classroom in which the child can succeed is often referred to as **mainstreaming.** Lewis and Doorlag (1999) define mainstreaming as:

> The inclusion of special students in the general educational process. Students are considered mainstreamed if they spend any part of the school day with general education class peers. In a typical mainstreaming program, special students in general education classrooms participate in instructional and social activities side by side with their classmates. Often they receive additional instruction and support from a special educator such as a resource teacher. That instruction may take place within the general education classroom or outside of it in a setting such as a resource room. (p. 4)

Addressing individual student needs in literacy has always been an important consideration.

A critical concern for a classroom teacher is, Who is going to be placed in my classroom? P.L. 94-142 defines students with disabilities as those who are mentally retarded, hard of hearing, deaf, speech impaired, other health impaired, deaf-blind, multihandicapped, seriously emotionally disturbed, orthopedically impaired, visually impaired, or having specific learning disabilities, who because of those impairments need special education and related services (Sec. 121 a. 530-121 a., 534). Given these components, how might a mainstreamed classroom operate? Johnson (1987) provides the following description:

> Exceptional students spend most of the day in regular classrooms, leaving occasionally to go to a resource room or resource center for educational assessments, individual tutoring, or small group instruction, or to pick up and deliver assignments prepared by the resource teacher but completed in the regular classroom. The resource teacher and the regular classroom teacher, working as a team, may schedule a student to use the resource center for a few minutes or several hours, depending on the student's learning needs. The regular classroom teacher and the resource teacher share responsibility for the learning and socialization of the exceptional students, and both take an active instructional role. The exceptional students spend more than half the day in regular classes. While the regular classroom teacher is responsible for grades and report cards, she will usually consult with the resource teacher in giving exceptional students grades. (p. 425)

Inclusion

In 1990 P.L. 94-142 was amended in ways that reflected a more sensitive approach to individual strengths of students rather than highlighting their disability. The provisions and changes to the terminology of P. L. 94-142 that led to the Individuals With Disabilities Act (IDEA) reflected a more sensitive approach to the individual (First & Curcio, 1993).

As part of the concern for the individual, mainstreaming in general has been reexamined. Students who have typically been mainstreamed into regular classrooms are often involved in many pullout programs like Chapter I. This fragmentation of the school day has caused some concern for the individual and raised the question, Is this the best instructional setting for the child with special needs? Educators have turned to inclusion for the answer to this question. **Inclusion** means that students with special needs are assigned to regular classrooms for the full instructional day and are allowed to participate in all school activities and functions. This type of inclusive atmosphere requires adequate support systems. IDEA requires that classrooms must be made physically accessible to accommodate all students with special needs. In addition to the physical setting, provisions need to be made for additional personnel, staff development, and technical assistance. This may mean that in addition to the regular classroom teacher, a special education teacher will be made available to coteach the entire class. It is important that the special education teacher be involved in the instruction of the whole class.

For inclusion to work, teachers need to create a classroom atmosphere in which differences are addressed up front and accepted by everyone in the class. The students in the class are as much responsible for the success of inclusion as are the classroom and special education teachers. One way to ensure student involvement in the inclusion process is to use cooperative groups as an instructional method. By allowing students to work cooperatively in groups, all students share in the contributions to the learning process and are more likely to develop a positive attitude toward individual differences.

The success of students placed in the least restrictive environment depends on the cooperation of teachers, administrators, specialized personnel, and parents. In essence, however, an individual teacher's ability to accommodate all students in the regular classroom determines the success or failure of such efforts. Implications for reading teachers are clear—they must employ a variety of instructional and organizational techniques to suit a wide range of student abilities and encourage the constructive interaction of special students with regular students. Teachers should use the following guidelines, adapted from Mohr (1995), when teaching literacy to special students who exhibit learning difficulties:

1. Observe the students in authentic settings. Assess the students' learning strengths, styles and differences, and the conditions of any disability or differences that may interfere with learning.
2. Teach to a student's strengths while remediating weaknesses and developing compensation skills. Do not allow the disability to become a barrier to learning.
3. Restructure a task when a student cannot master it. Change the way the task is presented or change the method of response.
4. Check understanding of the content material or directions by following up with a specific question. Avoid asking, "Do you understand?"
5. Repeat or rephrase what is being said in the classroom by varying the vocabulary and the mode of presentation or method of instruction.
6. Give both oral and written directions and provide both visual and auditory cues for directions and instructions.
7. Be aware of auditory and visual distractions in the classroom. Even subtle ones can be very distracting to some students, such as sitting near the window or a pencil sharpener.
8. Provide help through peer teaching or the buddy system. Provide reinforcement for newly learned or previously learned skills by allowing the student with differences to become a peer tutor to another student who is just beginning to learn a skill.
9. Include all students in the classroom activities and projects. Minimize the differences and maximize the similarities during classroom participation.
10. Match a student's learning style with appropriate selection of methods and materials. Use learning styles and strengths of all learners in the classroom as tools for planning instruction.
11. Evaluate students by their individual performance without lowering the standards for the class. Investigate evaluation alternatives to ensure success and not failure.
12. Manage behavior positively, consistently, and assertively. Set limits, structure consequences, and follow through! The use of logical consequences, natural reinforcers, contingency contracting, praise, encouragement, and recognition will help structure success for all students. Some students with disabilities and learning differences may need differential discipline considerations.

The preceding guidelines suggest that most children with learning difficulties are not in need of specialized techniques, but simply good instruction. Indeed, the similarities among special children and so-called normal children are greater than the differences. Labeling children (emotionally disturbed, mentally retarded, learning disabled, and so forth) tells teachers next to nothing about how to develop an appropriate instructional program. A positive aspect of the Individuals With Disabilities Act (IDEA) is that it shifts the focus away from use of labels (which are usually negative and counterproductive) and toward consideration of students' educational needs.

No mystique should surround the teaching of special children. These students, like all students, require instruction that emphasizes present achievement level, determination of student strengths and weaknesses, and appropriate approaches and materials. Many students carrying a label have been misdiagnosed and misplaced for years in school systems. Instruction should be based on student needs, not labels. Teachers can avoid the negative effects of labeling students by simply viewing these children as different. After all, nothing is more basic in teaching than learning how to deal with differences in individual students. Next time you come across a label, such as *dyslexic,* instead of saying "Oh no, how can I work with someone who is dyslexic?" try saying "Dyslexic—so what! What do I need to do to help this child learn to his or her fullest potential?"

The Individualized Education Plan

The vehicle for providing the most appropriate educational program for many special students is an **individualized education plan (IEP).** An IEP is a written plan for each special child, detailing that child's educational program. In accordance with the Individuals With Disabilities Act (IDEA), the IEP must include the following:

- The student's present achievement level, including the student's strengths, weaknesses, and learning styles.
- A statement of annual goals.
- A listing of long-range and short-term instructional objectives that include the materials, strategies, and assessment measures to indicate mastery of the objectives.
- A statement detailing specific special educational services to be provided to the student and the extent to which the student will participate in the regular classroom.
- The classroom accommodations that need to be made in order to provide general teaching techniques and subject matter modifications to enable the child to learn to his or her potential.
- Identification of the person(s) (or agents) responsible for teaching each objective.
- Project data for the beginning of program services and the anticipated duration of the services.

The IEP is an educational program that the multidisciplinary team, which includes the school, teachers, children, and parents, develop jointly (see Figure 13.3). Because many children with disabilities spend part or most of the

Unified School District

Individualized Education Program

Student: <u>Marty Glick</u>   DOB: <u>8/5/90</u>

School: <u>Hudson Elementary</u>   Grade <u>5</u>

Placement: <u>General Education Classroom</u>   Disability Classification: <u>LD</u>

Date of IEP Meeting: <u>12/17/2000</u>   Notification to Family: <u>11/28/2000</u>

Date of Initiation of Services: <u>1/3/2001</u>   Review date: <u>1/3/2002</u>

Dominant Language of Student: <u>English</u>

PRESENT LEVEL OF PERFORMANCE IN THE GENERAL EDUCATION CURRICULUM ACADEMIC/EDUCATIONAL ACHIEVEMENT

Mathematics

Marty's strongest areas include geometry, measurement, time, and money. He has difficulty with multiplication, division, fractions, and word problems. He especially had difficulty solving problems that contained nonessential information.

Reading

Marty's reading is characterized by weaknesses in word recognition, oral reading, and comprehension. Marty had difficulty with the passages that were written at a third-grade level. His oral reading of the passages revealed difficulties sounding out words and a reliance on contextual cues. He had particular problems with comprehension questions related to large amounts of information and interpreting abstractions.

Written Language

Marty's writing portfolio reveals that he has many ideas to write about in a broad range of genres. However, Marty avoids using prewriting tools such as semantic webs or outlines to organize his thoughts. Consequently, his stories don't usually follow a chronological sequence, and his reports do not fully develop the topic. He uses a variety of sentence patterns but frequently ignores the need for punctuation. Marty has difficulty editing his own work but will make mechanical changes pointed out by the teacher. He rarely revises the content or organization of his writing in a substantial manner. Marty's teacher has observed that Marty enjoys working on the computer and performs better on writing tasks when he uses a talking word processor.

SOCIAL DEVELOPMENT

Level of Social Development

Marty shows attention difficulties when attempting some academic tasks. He has a good sense of humor and seems to relate fairly well to his peers.

Interest Inventory

Marty likes working with peers and using computers. He prefers projects to tests. He likes working with his hands and fixing things.

Physical Development

Marty is physically healthy and has no difficulties with his hearing and vision. He has had no major illnesses or surgeries, and he is not taking any medications.

Figure 13.3   Sample IEP.

Behavioral Development

A functional assessment of Marty's classroom behavior indicates that Marty is frequently off-task and has difficulty completing his assignments. He often works on assignments for a short period of time and then works on another assignment, engages in an off-task activity such as playing with objects, leaves his work area, or seeks attention from his teacher or his peers. His behavior also appears to be affected by other activities in the classroom, the placement of his work area near certain students, and the type and difficulty of the activity.

RELATED SERVICES

Service	Frequency	Location
Group counseling	Once/week	Social worker's office

SUPPLEMENTARY AIDS AND SERVICES

Service	Frequency	Location
Collaboration teacher	2 hours/day	General education classroom
Paraprofessional	3 hours/day	General education classroom

PROGRAM MODIFICATION AND SUPPORT FOR SCHOOL PERSONNEL

Marty and his teacher will receive the services of a collaborative teacher and a paraeducator. Marty's teacher will be given time to meet with the collaboration teacher, who also will modify materials, locate resources, administer assessments, and coteach lessons. Marty's teacher also will receive training related to differentiated instruction, classroom management, and assessment alternatives and accommodations.

EXTENT OF PARTICIPATION IN GENERAL EDUCATION PROGRAMS AND WITH PEERS WITHOUT DISABILITIES

Marty will remain in his fifth-grade classroom full-time. The collaboration teacher and the paraeducator will provide direct service to Marty in the general education classroom.

RATIONALE FOR PLACEMENT

It is anticipated that Marty's educational needs can best be met in the general education classroom. He will benefit from being exposed to the general education curriculum with the additional assistance of the collaboration teacher and the paraeducator. The use of testing modifications and computers with talking word processors also should help Marty benefit from his general education program. Marty's social skills and self-concept also will be improved by exposure to his general education peers. Counseling will provide him with the prosocial skills necessary to interact with his peers and complete his work.

ANNUAL GOALS AND SHORT-TERM OBJECTIVES

Annual Goal: Marty will read, write, listen, and speak for information and understanding. (State Learning Standard 1 for English Language Arts)

Figure 13.3 (continued)

Short-Term Objectives and Evaluation Criteria   **Evaluation Procedures**

1. Given the choice of a narrative trade book at his instructional level, Marty will be able to retell the story, including major characters, the setting, and major events of the plot sequence.   Teacher-made story grammar checklist

2. Given a passage from his social studies or science textbook, Marty will develop three questions that require inferential or critical thinking.   Teacher evaluation of student response

3. Using a prewriting structure to organize his ideas, Marty will write a paragraph describing a process that shows logical development and has a minimum of five sentences.   Writing rubric

Annual Goal: Marty will read, write, listen, and speak for literary response and expression. (State Learning Standard 2 for English Language Arts)

Short-Term Objectives and Evaluation Criteria   **Evaluation Procedures**

1. After choosing a favorite poem to read to his peers, Marty will memorize it and recite it with fluency and intonation.   Peer and teacher feedback

2. Given the choice of texts with multi-syllabic words, Marty will read with 90% accuracy.   Teacher analysis of running record

3. Given a choice of biographies. Marty will reflect upon the events and experiences which relate to his own life.   Teacher evaluation of dialogue journal

Annual Goal: Marty will understand mathematics and become mathematically confident by communicating and reasoning mathematically. (State Learning Standard 3 for Mathematics, Science, and Technology)

Short-Term Objectives and Evaluation Criteria   **Evaluation Procedures**

1. Given a one-step word problem with a distractor, Marty will write the relevant information and operation needed to solve it 90 percent of the time.   Teacher-made worksheet

2. Given the task of writing five one-step word problems with a distractor, Marty will write four that are clear enough for his classmates to solve.   Teacher evaluation of student response

Annual Goal: Marty will demonstrate mastery of the foundation skills and competencies essential for success in the workplace. (State Learning Standard 3a for Career Development and Occupational Studies)

Short-Term Objectives and Evaluation Criteria   **Evaluation Procedures**

1. When working independently on an academic task, Marty will improve his time on task by 100 percent.   Self-recording

2. When working in small groups, Marty will listen to peers and take turns speaking 80 percent of the time.   Teacher observation or group evaluation

Figure 13.3 (continued)

TRANSITION PROGRAM

Marty is very interested in and skilled at working with his hands to make and fix things. In addition to using these skills as part of the educational program, Marty will participate in a career awareness program designed to explore his career interests.

This program will expose Marty to a variety of careers and allow him to experience work settings and meet professionals who are involved in careers related to Marty's interests. This program also will aid Marty in understanding his learning style, strengths and weaknesses, interests, and preferences.

Annual Goal: Marty will be knowledgeable about the world of work, explore career options, and relate personal skills, aptitudes, and abilities to future career decisions. (State Learning Standard 1 for Career Development and Occupational Studies)

Short-Term Objectives and Evaluation Criteria	Evaluation Procedures
1. Marty will identify three careers in which he may be interested and explain why he is interested in each one.	Self-report
2. Marty will research and explain the training and experiential requirements for the three careers he has identified.	Interview
3. Marty will evaluate his skills and characteristics with respect to these careers by identifying his related strengths and needs.	Self-report
4. Marty will follow and observe individuals involved in these three careers as they perform their jobs.	Student-maintained log

ASSISTIVE TECHNOLOGY AND COMMUNICATION NEEDS

Marty will be given a computer and talking word processing system with word prediction capabilities and a talking calculator to assist him with classroom activities and tests.

PARTICIPATION IN STATEWIDE AND DISTRICTWIDE ASSESSMENTS, AS WELL AS TESTING ACCOMMODATIONS AND ALTERNATIVES

Marty will participate in all statewide and districtwide assessments. He will take these tests individually in a separate location, with extended time and breaks every 30 minutes. Tests that last for more than 2 hours will be administered over several days, with no more than 2 hours of testing each day. Marty will be allowed to use a computer with a talking word processing program and word prediction capabilities. For math tests that do not involve mental computation, he will be allowed to use a talking calculator.

When possible and appropriate, Marty will demonstrate his mastery of classroom content through projects and cooperative learning activities rather than teacher-made tests. When Marty must take teacher-made tests, they will be administered in a separate location by his collaboration teacher with extended time limits. A mastery level grading system will be employed.

METHOD AND FREQUENCY OF COMMUNICATION WITH FAMILY

Marty's family will be regularly informed through IEP progress reports, curriculum-based assessments, and Marty's general education report cards. In addition, feedback on Marty's performance and progress will be shared with his family through quarterly scheduled family-teacher meetings, results of state and district assessments, and portfolio reviews.

Figure 13.3   (continued)

Committee Participants	Relationship/Role
Ms. Rachel Tupper	5th grade teacher
Mr. Terry Feaster	Special Ed. teacher
Mr. Kris Brady	Sp. Ed. administrator
Ms. Jeessica Amatura	Educational evaluator

Signatures(s)

If family members were not members of the committee, please indicate:

I agree with the Individualized Education Program   _____
I disagree with the Individualized Education Program   _____

Harry Glick, Agnes Glick
Parent/Guardian Signature

I participated in this meeting. I agree with the goals and services of the Individualized Educational Program.

Marty Glick
Student's Signature

Figure 13.3   (continued)

Source: From *Creating Inclusive Classrooms: Effective and Reflective Practices* (4th ed., pp. 41–44) by S. J. Salend, 2001, Upper Saddle River, NJ: Merrill/Prentice Hall. Copyright 2001 by Pearson Education. Reprinted by permission of Pearson Education, Inc., Upper Saddle River, NJ 07458.

day in the regular classroom, the classroom teacher must be involved in developing the IEP. As shown in Figure 13.3, the basic ingredients of an IEP are not new—they are essentially those of a good teaching plan (pretest objectives, teaching to those objectives, and the posttest). It is important to avoid thinking of inclusion (or least restrictive environment) as separate or different from the basic principles associated with any good learning environment. The principles of a quality learning environment include all aspects of an IEP, and thus the process of equal education for all children (see Figure 13.4). Although many problems remain unsettled regarding the implementation of P.L. 94-142, cooperative interaction among teachers, students, parents, specialized personnel, and administrators in placing every individual in a setting in which that individual may succeed will yield benefits for all students.

Attention-Deficit Hyperactivity Disorder

In today's classrooms, many children are described as having difficulty staying on task and maintaining attention. Some of these children are diagnosed with attention-deficit hyperactivity disorder (ADHD). This disorder is the most frequently occurring disorder affecting our school-age children (Rupley & Nichols, 1998). According

SPECIAL CONSIDERATIONS FOR STUDENTS WITH MEDICAL NEEDS

The IEPs for students with medical needs should identify and address their unique needs and be developed collaboratively with medical professionals. Therefore, IEPs for these students should contain a health plan and include:

- the findings of medical and therapy evaluations
- appropriate health-related goals
- suggestions for placement, related services and supports, scheduling, and classroom adaptations
- medical treatments and medication requirements including potential side effects
- equipment requirements
- vocational, social, and psychosocial needs
- training for students so that they can perform or direct others to perform specialized health care procedures
- training for professionals and families
- procedures for dealing with emergencies (American Federation of Teachers, 1993: Heller, et al., 2000; Hill, 1999; Phelps, 1995; Prendergast, 1995)

SPECIAL CONSIDERATIONS FOR STUDENTS WITH SENSORY IMPAIRMENTS

The IEPs for students with sensory impairments can address their unique needs and focus on helping them succeed in the LRE. Therefore, IEPs for these students should address:

- the skills and instructional strategies necessary to develop reading and writing
- the skills and technological devices needed to access information
- orientation and mobility instruction
- socialization skills
- transitional, recreational, and career education needs (Heumann & Hehir, 1995)

SPECIAL CONSIDERATIONS FOR STUDENTS FROM LINGUISTICALLY AND CULTURALLY DIVERSE BACKGROUNDS

The IEPs for students from diverse backgrounds should give teachers additional information to guide the educational program for these students. IEPs for these students should include:

- a summary of assessment results, including the student's language skills in her or his native language and English and in social and academic interactions, as well as information about the student's life outside of school
- the language(s) of instruction matched to specific goals and objectives
- the goals and objectives related to maintaining the student's native language and cultural identity and learning English
- teaching strategies relating to the student's linguistic ability, academic skill, cultural and socioeconomic background, and learning style
- teaching materials and curricula that address the student's linguistic and cultural background
- motivation strategies and reinforcers that are compatible with the student's cultural and experiential background
- related services that reflect the student's educational, medical, psychological, linguistic, and cultural needs
- Bilingual and culturally sensitive educators, paraeducators, community volunteers, and other district resources available to meet the student's needs (Garcia & Malkin, 1993; Ortiz, 1997; Ortiz & Wilkinson, 1989)

Figure 13.4   Special considerations in designing IEPs.

Source: From *Creating Inclusive Classrooms: Effective and Reflective Practices* (4th ed., p. 45) by S. J. Salend, 2001, Upper Saddle River, NJ: Merrill/Prentice Hall. Copyright 2001 by Pearson Education. Reprinted by permission of Pearson Education, Inc., Upper Saddle River, NJ 07458.

to Fowler (1994) **attention-deficit hyperactivity disorder (ADHD)** is a syndrome in which the learner is characterized by having serious and persistent difficulties in the following three areas:

1. attention span
2. impulse control
3. hyperactivity

Students with ADHD in the past were often referred to as having hyperkinesis, a minimal brain disorder, hyperactivity, or a learning disability. Even though ADHD may be a relatively new term, the disorder has been found in the medical literature for more than 100 years (Fowler, 1994). The American Psychiatric Association (1994) has stated that in order for a child to be diagnosed with attention-deficit hyperactivity disorder, the child must display for 6 months or more at least 8 of the following 14 characteristics prior to the age of 7:

1. Fidgets, squirms, or seems restless.
2. Has difficulty remaining seated.
3. Is easily distracted.
4. Has difficulty awaiting turn.
5. Blurts out answers.
6. Has difficulty following instructions.
7. Has difficulty sustaining attention.
8. Shifts from one uncompleted task to another.
9. Has difficulty playing quietly.
10. Talks excessively.
11. Interrupts or intrudes on others.
12. Does not seem to listen.
13. Often loses things necessary for tasks.
14. Frequently engages in dangerous actions.

Obviously, children displaying these characteristics may demonstrate difficulties in the areas of learning to read and write. To help treat this condition, doctors often prescribe stimulants such as Ritalin to help reduce hyperactivity and improve the student's ability to focus, work, and learn. According to Neuwirth (1994) the use of medication has sparked quite a debate. Many of the critics argue that medication is often prescribed unnecessarily and that some students on medication often experience weight loss, grow at slower rates, and have difficulty with their sleep patterns. On the other hand, many children with ADHD have been helped tremendously by proper medication. If doctors carefully monitor a child's height, weight, and overall development, the use of medication to help control ADHD appears to be extremely beneficial to the student, and the positive results far outweigh the potential side effects.

While the use of medication is one way to help manage the behavior of the ADHD child, teachers can also provide behavioral support by creating an environment conducive to academic performance. Such an environment is crucial for literacy instruction because students need to devote full attention to comprehending, writing, and learning from meaningful text. Teachers who follow the recommendations presented in the *Diagnostic and Statistical Manual of Mental Disorders* (American Psychiatric Association, 1994) will better facilitate ADHD students' learning.

1. Seat students with ADHD near the teacher's desk, but include them as part of the regular class seating.
2. Place ADHD students up front with their backs to the rest of the class to keep other students out of view.
3. Surround students with ADHD with good role models, preferably students whom they view as significant others. Encourage peer tutoring and cooperative/collaborative learning.
4. Avoid distracting stimuli. Try not to place students with ADHD near air conditioners, high-traffic areas, heaters, doors, or windows.
5. Children with ADHD do not handle change well, so avoid transitions, physical relocation (monitor them closely on field trips), changes in schedule, and disruptions.
6. Be creative! Produce a stimuli-reduced study area. Let all students have access to this area so the student with ADHD will not feel different.
7. Encourage parents to set up appropriate study space at home, with set times and routines established for study, parental review of completed homework, and periodic notebook and/or bookbag organization.

In addition to these environmental features, teachers can also help ADHD students by doing the following:

1. Maintain eye contact during verbal instruction.
2. Make directions clear and concise and be consistent with daily instructions.
3. Simplify complex directions and avoid multiple commands.
4. Make sure students comprehend the instructions before beginning the task.
5. Repeat instructions in a calm, positive manner if needed.
6. Help the students feel comfortable with seeking assistance (most children with ADHD will not ask for help).
7. Gradually reduce scaffolding, but keep in mind that these students may need more scaffolding for a longer period of time than the average child.
8. Require a daily assignment notebook if necessary.

Teachers who are willing to modify their instruction to meet the needs of the ADHD child will help these students realize their potential and allow them to experience success that may have seemed unattainable in the past.

Gifted Students

A renewed thrust in the public schools is the development of programs for **gifted students.** The U.S. Office of Education identified six areas of giftedness: (1) general intellectual ability, (2) specific academic aptitude, (3) creativity, (4) leadership ability,

(5) ability in the visual or performing arts, and (6) psychomotor ability. Gifted students may demonstrate capability of exceptional performance in only one or two areas.

With specific reference to reading abilities, Shaughnessy, Siegel, and Stanley (1994) and Dooley (1993) noted that gifted students' cognitive skills are advanced beyond the activities and materials normally provided for students at their age and grade level. Gifted students may demonstrate some or all of the following characteristics:

1. A rich, well-developed vocabulary and interest in words.
2. Early reading ability prior to entering school.
3. An advanced linguistic ability in sentence construction, expression of ideas, and listening vocabulary.
4. An interest in library books and reading in a variety of topic areas.
5. An early interest in learning to write and in writing creative stories.
6. Frequent use of information sources, such as the dictionary, encyclopedia, and information texts, to explore ideas and areas of interest.
7. An enhanced ability in the area of critical thinking.
8. An inquisitive nature to learn.
9. Comprehension abilities at early grade levels that exceed the literal level and demonstrate an understanding of the relationship of ideas.
10. Well-developed reading skills and abilities by the end of first grade.

Identifying gifted children and designing a reading and writing curriculum to accommodate their learning needs should be accomplished through a variety of formal and informal assessment procedures. Standardized achievement tests, intelligence tests, creativity measures, actual student performance in the reading program, peer nomination procedures, and parent and teacher observations are avenues to employ for this purpose. Also, giftedness is not reserved for any one group or class of children. Teachers should not be preoccupied with ethnicity or social characteristics when identifying the gifted and talented. When identifying giftedness in children who speak a language other than English it is important to employ informal and first language assessment procedures.

For too long, gifted children were expected to be silent and follow along with the regular curriculum designed for less-able students. Today's reading teachers and program administrators realize that gifted children have unique needs, as do all students, and require differentiated instructional programs, practice, and support. Gifted readers are not all the same; each has unique strengths and weaknesses. As such, gifted readers need the same diagnostically based instruction afforded all learners (Shaughnessy et al., 1994). Indeed, many gifted children are "disabled" readers when their performance is compared to their potential. Gifted children require an instructional program that reflects their needs.

Meeting the needs of the gifted reader in the classroom

There are several avenues available to meet gifted readers' needs in the classroom. One way to enhance the gifted student's reading performance is to make use of curriculum compacting (Dooley, 1993). Curriculum compacting assures student mastery of basic skills at a proficient rate to make time for enrichment and acceleration. To make use of curriculum compacting, the teacher must develop an assessment measure that will allow him or her to identify those skills and content areas that the student has already mastered for the next reading unit. Once the skills and content have been identified as already mastered, the teacher does not have to provide instructional activities in those areas. This allows the teacher to concentrate on undeveloped skills and content and provide additional enrichment activities without losing any instructional time. This form of instruction allows the gifted student to progress through reading materials at an appropriate pace.

Two other instructional approaches for the gifted child are content and process modification (Dooley, 1993). Content modifications enable the gifted reader to read more complex and in-depth selections. The selections that the gifted student reads can be related to the same theme, topic, or genre of the regular classroom instruction. For example, if students were studying World War II, all students might be encouraged to read *The Diary of Anne Frank* during reading instruction. In addition to *The Diary of Anne Frank,* the gifted child might also read *Zlata's Diary* so that the child has the opportunity to make connections between the way Jewish people of Nazi Germany suffered and the way the Bosnians of Sarajevo suffered. These types of content modifications allow gifted students more control over their academic content.

Process modifications require students to use higher level processes to become critical readers, and to enhance their abilities to make judgments about the authenticity, accuracy, and validity of what they read. Several ways to help all students become more creative and critical readers is by effective questioning strategies, use of reading guides, and the integration of writing with reading. Integrating writing and reading to promote the development of critical thinking can be accomplished by teaching writing as a thinking process (Jampole, Konopak, Readence, & Moser, 1991). Developing writing skills as a logical thinking process enables gifted students to refine, synthesize, and elaborate upon their understanding of a particular topic.

Application in the classroom and observation support instructional practices such as compacting the curriculum, modifying content, and modifying process; however, many teachers do not use these approaches. One underlying reason for this lack of implementation may be teachers' concerns for efficient classroom management. Teachers may ask themselves how can I organize and plan for a high percentage of academically engaged time for my diverse students? Dooley (1993) responds to this question by arguing that curriculum compacting should be done to assess every child, and that by determining the needs of your students, it actually frees up time for enrichment activities. She feels that much of the instructional time in the classroom is wasted because many of the students have already mastered the skills and content being taught. She also feels that by taking advantage of content and process modifications, the teacher is not adding more work to the instructional day but actually enhancing the content being taught.

Whereas the reading curriculum goals are the same for gifted readers as for all readers, many individuals (Lewis & Doorlag, 1999) think the reading program should be differentiated in terms of content covered, methods taught, and pacing of instruction for gifted readers. A wide variety of literature should be used to tap gifted students' abilities and interests.

Gifted students learn material faster than other learners and may require less practice and fewer application activities. Providing such differentiated instruction requires diagnosis of students' strengths and weaknesses. To provide the decisive and most effective lessons for gifted students the teacher must consider their abilities, needs, and interests. Once again, this should not be considered an extra burden to the teacher. Instead, it should be considered part of the daily instructional practice that the teacher uses with all students.

SUMMARY

The ability to deal effectively with student diversity is crucial to teaching reading. Teachers must address the needs of culturally and linguistically diverse students as well as students with special needs in the regular classroom. The ability of teachers to handle differences effectively translates into instructional practices that provide for each student's self-respect and that lead all students to feel secure in the classroom.

Creating opportunities for success for students with limited proficiency in English requires an understanding of nonstandard dialects, characteristics of foreign languages spoken by the students in the classroom, and students' cultural values. Although speaking a nonstandard dialect or a primary language other than English can present problems in learning to read, a sensitive and knowledgeable teacher minimizes these problems.

Teachers can adapt reading instruction to the needs of speakers whose English proficiency is limited. The language-experience approach, an integrated approach, oral reading approach, basal reader approach, and dual-language reading approach can be useful in addressing the needs of culturally and linguistically diverse students.

Students who have special needs are increasingly taught in the least restrictive environment, which often means the regular classroom. Mainstreaming and inclusion provide the most appropriate education for each student in the least restrictive setting. Inclusion considers the educational needs of students rather than their clinical labels. A key ingredient of the legislative mandate for mainstreaming is the development of an individualized education plan (IEP) for each student with disabilities. The regular classroom teacher's total involvement in the team process is foremost in the successful implementation of the IEP. All students would benefit from the same individual approach to learning that students with special needs must receive.

ADHD is one of the most common mental disorders among children, and on the average, at least one child in every classroom in the United States needs help with this disorder. While at times this disorder can be frustrating and disruptive to the classroom teacher, there are effective environmental and instructional strategies that the teacher can take advantage of to ensure a successful learning climate for the child with attention-deficit hyperactivity disorder. This is particularly important because many students with ADHD are also academically gifted.

Reading curricular goals are the same for gifted students as for all readers. Accommodating the needs of the gifted learner is best accomplished by modifying the content, methodology, and instruction for gifted readers. A wide variety of theme literatures can be used to tap gifted students' abilities and interests. Availability of books ranging from award-winning literature to popular serials is a primary ingredient in creating the successful literacy experience for gifted readers.

YOUR POINT OF VIEW

Discussion Questions

1. Brainstorm: List ways teachers can help limited-English-speaking students feel more secure in the classroom environment.
2. Inclusion of children with special needs into the regular classroom should produce a better learning environment for all students. However, inclusion can also make matters worse instead of making them better. What are possible reasons for this occurrence?

Take a Stand For or Against

1. Of all the factors that influence academic achievement in the school, the dialects or language behaviors of the culturally and linguistically diverse students are the most important.
2. An IEP should be required for all students.

Field-Based Assignments

1. Good teachers are constantly making adaptations to their lessons to meet individual students' learning styles and needs. Good teachers realize that the content must be taught, but they find ways to teach the content and still provide instruction that is at a level at which each child will be successful yet challenged at the same time. While you are working in the classroom, keep a reflectional journal on how the classroom teacher made modifications to work with students of diverse needs. Work with the teacher as lesson plans are developed and ask the teacher to think aloud while planning lessons that will be used with diverse learners.
2. When you have the opportunity to observe teachers providing instruction for diverse learners, take time to notice the way they use the classroom environment to provide effective instruction. See if the classroom teacher is taking advantage of collaborative instruction, environmental print, learning

centers, and seating arrangements that would be beneficial to students with diverse learning styles and needs. If you do not notice the teacher taking advantage of environmental features while working with diverse learners, develop a plan that would make better use of the classroom environment to provide effective instruction for students with special needs.

Portfolio Entry

Working with diverse learners can be challenging and rewarding at the same time. Create a list that addresses concerns you have about working with diverse learners. Be sure to utilize the information discussed in the text as well as outside references while composing your list. After you have compiled your list of concerns, develop a plan that will enable you to overcome your concerns and provide you with the joyous rewards of working with diverse learners.

BIBLIOGRAPHY

Allen, V. (1994). Selecting materials for the reading instruction of ESL children. In K. Spangenburg & R. Pritchard (Eds.), *Kids come in all languages: Reading instruction for ESL students* (pp. 108–131). Newark, DE: International Reading Association.

American Psychiatric Association. (1994). *Diagnostic and statistical manual of mental disorders* (4th ed.) (DSM-III-R). Washington, DC: Author.

Au, K. (1993). *Literacy instruction in multicultural settings.* Orlando, FL: Harcourt Brace College Publishers.

Banks, J. A. (1994). Transforming the mainstream curriculum. *Educational Leadership, 51,* 4–8.

Banks, J. A., & Banks, C. A. (1997). *Multicultural education: Issues and perspectives* (3rd ed.). Needham Heights, MA: Allyn & Bacon.

Bieger, E. M. (1996). Promoting multicultural education through a literature-based approach. *The Reading Teacher, 49,* 308–312.

Brisbois, J. E. (1995). Connections between first- and second-language learners. *Journal of Reading Behavior, 27,* 565–584.

Cushner, K., McClelland, A., & Safford, P. (1996). *Human diversity in education: An integrative approach* (2nd ed.). New York: McGraw Hill.

Delpit, L. D. (1991). A conversation with Lisa Delpit. *Language Arts, 68,* 541–547.

Delpit, L. D. (1995). *Other people's children.* New York: New Press.

Dooley, C. (1993). The challenge: Meeting the needs of gifted readers. *The Reading Teacher, 46,* 546–551.

Eldredge, J. L., Reutzel, R. D., & Hollingsworth, P. M. (1996). Comparing the effectiveness of two oral reading practices: Round-robin reading and the shared book experiences. *Journal of Literacy Research, 28,* 201–225.

Faltis, C. (1997). *Joinfostering: Adapting teaching for the multicultural classroom.* Upper Saddle River, NJ: Merrill/Prentice Hall.

Filipovic, Z. (1994). *Zlata's diary.* New York: Penguin Books.

First, P., & Curcio, J. (1993). *Individuals with disabilities: Implementing the newest laws.* Newburg Park, CA: Corwin Press.

Fowler, M. (1994). *Attention-deficit/hyperactivity disorder.* National Information Center for Children and Youth with Disabilities. (ERIC Accession No. ED 378 729) Washington, DC.

Frank, A. (1958). *Anne Frank: the diary of a young girl.* New York: Doubleday.

Freppon, P. A. (1995). Low-income children's literacy interpretations in a skills-based and a whole-language classroom. *Journal of Reading Behavior, 27,* 505–533.

Godina, H. (1996). The canonical debate—implementing multicultural literature and perspectives. *Journal of Adolescent & Adult Literacy, 39,* 544–549.

Gonzales, P. (1994). Second language literacy. *Illinois Reading Council Journal, 22,* 13–16.

Guild, P. (1994). The culture/learning style connection. *Educational Leadership, 51,* 16–21.

Jampole, E. S., Konopak, B. C., Readence, J. E., & Moser, B. E. (1991). Using mental imagery to enhance gifted elementary students' creative writing. *Reading Psychology, 12,* 183–198.

Johnson, D. W. (1987). *Educational psychology.* Englewood Cliffs, NJ: Prentice Hall.

Ladson-Billings, G. (1994). *The dream keepers: Successful teachers of African American children.* San Francisco, CA: Jossey Bass.

Lewis, R. B., & Doorlag, D. H. (1999). *Teaching special students in general education classrooms* (5th ed.). Upper Saddle River, NJ: Merrill/Prentice Hall.

Martin, B. (1970). *Brown bear, brown bear, what do you see?* New York: Holt, Rinehart and Winston.

McCauley, J. K., & McCauley, D. S. (1992). Using choral reading to promote language learning for ESL students. *The Reading Teacher, 45,* 526–535.

McGill-Franzen, A. (2000). How will diversity affect literacy in the next millennium? *Reading Research Quarterly, 35,* 550–551.

Mohr, L. L. (1995). *Teaching diverse learners in inclusive settings: Steps for adapting instruction.* Paper presented at the Council for Exceptional Children Annual Convention, Indianapolis, IN.

Morrow, L. M. (1992). The impact of a literature-based program on literacy achievement, use of literature, and attitudes of children from minority backgrounds. *Reading Research Quarterly, 27,* 250–275.

Neuman, S. B., & Koskinen, P. (1992). Captioned television as comprehensible input: Effects of incidental word learning from context for language minority students. *Reading Research Quarterly, 27,* 94–106.

Neuwirth, S. (1994). *Attention deficit hyperactivity disorder: Decade of the brain.* National Institute of Mental Health, Washington, DC: U.S. Government Printing Office. (ERIC Clearinghouse No. ED 386 011)

Nichols, W. D., Rupley, W. H., Webb-Johnson, G., & Tlusty, G. (2001). Teacher's role in providing culturally responsive literacy instruction. *Reading Horizons, 41,* 1–18.

Nieto, S. (1996). *Affirming diversity* (2nd ed.). New York: Longman Publishers.

Norton, D. E. (2001). *Multicultural children's literature: Through the eyes of many children.* Upper Saddle River, NJ: Merrill/Prentice Hall.

Poplin, C. E. (1992). Making our whole-language bilingual classrooms also liberatory. In J. V. Tinajero & A. F. Ada (Eds.), *The power of two languages: Literacy and biliteracy for Spanish-speaking students* (pp. 58–61). New York: Macmillan/McGraw-Hill.

Rupley, W. H., & Nichols, W. D. (1998). Academic diversity: Reading instruction for students with special needs. *Reading Horizons, 38,* 246–256.

Salend, S. J. (2001). *Creating inclusive classrooms: Effective and reflective practices* (4th ed.). Upper Saddle River, NJ: Merrill/Prentice Hall.

Shaughnessy, M. F., Siegel, J., & Stanley, N. V. (1994). *Gifted and reading.* Albuquerque, NM: U.S. Information Analyses. (ERIC Accession No. ED 368 145)

Stahl, L. A. (1990). Riding the pendulum: A rejoinder to Schickedanz and McGee and Lomax. *Review of Educational Research, 60,* 141–151.

Sullivan, O., Haskins, J., & Haskins, J. (1998). *African American inventors.* Brookfield, CN: The Millbrook Press.

Weber, R. M. (1991). Linguistic diversity and reading in American society. In R. Barr, M. L. Kamil, P. Mosenthal, & P. D. Pearson (Eds.), *Handbook of reading research* (Vol. 2, pp. 97–119). New York: Longman.

Appendix

Text leveling for kindergarten through grade 2 basal stories from five basal reading series

Publisher	Basal title	Story title	Author	Level
Scholastic	Express Yourself	Animals A to Z	D. McPhail	A
Scholastic	Beginning Literacy	In the City	S. Pasternac	A
Scholastic	Beginning Literacy	Let's Get the Rhythm	A. Miranda	A
Houghton Mifflin	Welcome	Moonbear's Books	F. Asch	A
Houghton Mifflin	Welcome	The Hen Sat	K. Lewis	A
Silver Burdett Ginn	Readables	Who's in the Show	S. Long	A
Silver Burdett Ginn	Readables	Our Saturday Clothes	S. Costigan	A
Silver Burdett Ginn	Readables	A Day in the Park	V. Tripp	A
Silver Burdett Ginn	Readables	Spring is Here	T. Gomi	A
Silver Burdett Ginn	Readables	Make a Line	S. Long	A
Silver Burdett Ginn	Readables	All By Myself	S. Costigan	A
Silver Burdett Ginn	Readables	Moving Time	A. Miranda	A
Silver Burdett Ginn	Readables	Jimmyjammy Had a Hat	I. Cumpiano	A
Silver Burdett Ginn	Readables	The Baker's Cake	A. Miranda	A
Silver Burdett Ginn	Readables	My Five Senses	M. Miller	A
Silver Burdett Ginn	Readables	Peaches	V. Tripp	A
Silver Burdett Ginn	Readables	How to Get to Harry's House	M. Banks	A
Silver Burdett Ginn	Readables	You Can Ride	A. Koss	A
Silver Burdett Ginn	Readables	What Am I?	S. Costigan	A
Silver Burdett Ginn	Readables	What's Up?	L. Nuzzolo	A
Silver Burdett Ginn	Literature Works Collection 1/2	Little Elephant	T. Hoban & M. Ford	A

Source: From P. C. Fawson & R. D. Reutzel, "But I Only Have a Basal: Implementing Guided Reading in the Early Grades," *The Reading Teacher, 54* (September 2000), pp. 89–95. Reprinted with permission of the authors and the International Reading Association. Copyright by the International Reading Association. All rights reserved.

Publisher	Basal title	Story title	Author	Level
Scholastic	Join In	My River	S. Halpern	A
Silver Burdett Ginn	Literature Works Collection 1/2			
Scott Foresman	Under My Hat	So Can I	A. Ahlberg	A
Scott Foresman	Hurry, Furry Feet	When the Elephant Walks	K. Kasza	B
Harcourt Brace	Picture Perfect	I Went Walking	S. Williams	B
Scholastic	Information Finders	Fish Faces	N. Wu	B
Scholastic	Literacy Place Book	Louis Builds a House	L. Pfanner	B
Houghton Mifflin	Welcome	One Red Rooster	K. Carroll	B
Houghton Mifflin	Welcome	Wake Up!	M. Menschell	B
Houghton Mifflin	Hello	Listen to the Desert	P. Mora	B
Houghton Mifflin	Hello	BUGS!	P. McKissack	B
Houghton Mifflin	Share	My Friends	T. Gomi	B
Silver Burdett Ginn	Literature Works Collection 1/1			
Houghton Mifflin	Welcome	Annie, Bea, and Chi Chi Delores	D. Maurer	B
Scholastic	Hello!	When This Box Is Full	P. Lillie	B
Houghton Mifflin	Welcome			
Silver Burdett Ginn	Readables	Quick as a Cricket	A. Wood	B
Scholastic	I Spy	Flower Garden	E. Bunting	B
Silver Burdett Ginn	Readables			
Houghton Mifflin	Share			
Silver Burdett Ginn	Readables	Together	G.E. Lyon	B
Silver Burdett Ginn	Readables	An Egg Is an Egg	N. Weiss	B
Silver Burdett Ginn	Readables	Sing a Song of People	L. Lenski	B
Silver Burdett Ginn	Readables	Come and See	M. Banks	B
Silver Burdett Ginn	Literature Works Collection 1/1	What Do You Like	M. Grejniec	B
Silver Burdett Ginn	Literature Works Collection 1/1	Faces	S. Rotner	B
Silver Burdett Ginn	Literature Works Collection 1/3	It Looked Like Spilt Milk	C.G. Shaw	B
Harcourt Brace	Picture Perfect	Five Little Rabbits	K. Butler	C
Harcourt Brace	Picture Perfect	Down on the Farm	R. Lascaro	C
Harcourt Brace	Picture Perfect	What I See	H. Keller	C
Scholastic	Beginning Literacy	I Love Mud, and Mud Loves Me	V. Stephens	C
Houghton Mifflin	Welcome	Pumpkin, Pumpkin	J. Titherington	C
Houghton Mifflin	Welcome	Snuffy, Fluffy, and the Mice	P. Sturges	C
Silver Burdett Ginn	Readables	Down by the Bay	N.B. Westcott	C
Silver Burdett Ginn	Readables	One Funny Day	D.A. Dodds	C
Silver Burdett Ginn	Readables	Abuela's Big Bed	I. Cumpiano	C
Silver Burdett Ginn	Readables	On the Go	A. Morris	C
Scholastic	Team Spirit	Growing Vegetable Soup	L. Ehlert	C

Publisher	Basal title	Story title	Author	Level
Silver Burdett Ginn	Literature Works Collection 1/2	Good-Night Owl	P. Hutchins	C
Silver Burdett Ginn	Literature Works Collection 1/2	I Am Eyes: Ni Macho	L. Ward	C
Silver Burdett Ginn	Literature Works Collection 1/3	Eek! There's a Mouse in the House	W.H. Yee	C
Silver Burdett Ginn	Literature Works Collection 1/3	George Shrinks	W. Joyce	C
Silver Burdett Ginn	Literature Works Collection 2/1	Nature Spy	S. Rotner & K. Kreisler	C
Houghton Mifflin	Be A Nature Detective			
Scott Foresman	Under My Hat	One Gorilla	A. Morozumi	C
Scott Foresman	Hurry, Furry Feet	Sitting in My Box	D. Lillegard	C
Scott Foresman	Hurry, Furry Feet	Old Hat, New Hat	S. Berenstain & J. Berenstain	C
Harcourt Brace	Big Dreams!	Cloudy Day, Sunny Day	D. Crews	D
Scholastic	Hello!	The Chick and the Duckling	M. Ginsburg	D
Harcourt Brace	Big Dreams!			
Houghton Mifflin	Welcome			
Silver Burdett Ginn	Literature Works Collection 1/1			
Harcourt Brace	Big Dreams!	Big Brown Bear	D. McPhail	D
Harcourt Brace	Picture Perfect	Sometimes	K. Baker	D
Scholastic	Imagine That!	In the Attic	H. Oram	D
Scholastic	Express Yourself	Crocodile Beat	G. Jorgensen	D
Scholastic	Express Yourself	City Sounds	J. Marzollo	D
Houghton Mifflin	Hello	Citybook	S. Rotner & K. Kreisler	D
Houghton Mifflin	Discover	My Best Shoes	M. Burton	D
Silver Burdett Ginn	Readables	Good-Bye Hello	B.S. Hazen	D
Silver Burdett Ginn	Readables	What Is the Sun?	R. Lindbergh	D
Silver Burdett Ginn	Readables	Music in the Night	E. Wilson	D
Silver Burdett Ginn	Literature Works Collection 1/3	The Wind and the Sun	T. dePaola	D
Silver Burdett Ginn	Literature Works Collection 1/3	Rain Talk	M. Serfozo	D
Silver Burdett Ginn	Literature Works Collection 1/3	When Summer Comes	R. Maass	D
Scott Foresman	My Favorite Foodles	Hello, Mouse!	L. Hayward	D
Scott Foresman	The Big Blank Piece of Paper	Pete Pats Pigs	Dr. Seuss	E
Scott Foresman	Once Upon a Hippo	Two Chinese Rhymes	Traditional Poetry	E
Scott Foresman	Once Upon a Hippo	There's a Hole in the Bucket	N.B. Westcott	E

Publisher	Basal title	Story title	Author	Level
Harcourt Brace	Warm Friends	And I Mean It, Stanley	C. Bonsall	E
Harcourt Brace	Big Dreams!	Later Rover	H. Ziefert	E
Harcourt Brace	Big Dreams!	Catch Me If You Can!	B. Most	E
Harcourt Brace	Warm Friends	Best of Friends	L. Leedy	E
Harcourt Brace	Big Dreams!	Moving Day	A. Brandon	E
Harcourt Brace	Warm Friends	Making Friends, Keeping Friends	E. Davis	E
Harcourt Brace	Warm Friends	The Shoe Town	J. Stevens	E
Houghton Mifflin	Hello	The Foot Book	Dr. Seuss	E
Scott Foresman	Hurry, Furry Feet			
Houghton Mifflin	Be a Nature Detective	Where Does the Trail Lead?	B. Albert	E
Houghton Mifflin	Surprise	If the Dinosaurs Came Back	B. Most	E
Houghton Mifflin	Share	The Doorbell Rang	P. Hutchins	E
Houghton Mifflin	Share	The Little Red Hen	B. Barton	E
Harcourt Brace	Full Sails			
Scott Foresman	Our Singing Planet	My Mom Travels a Lot	C.F. Bauer	F
Scott Foresman	Our Singing Planet	"Pardon?" Said the Giraffe	C. West	F
Scott Foresman	A Canary With Hiccups	Brave Dog	C. Rylant	F
Scott Foresman	A Canary With Hiccups	Two Greedy Bears	M. Ginsburg	F
Scott Foresman	Once Upon a Hippo	Jimmy Lee Did It	P. Cummings	F
Harcourt Brace	Warm Friends	Rex and Lilly Playtime	L. Krasny	F
Harcourt Brace	Warm Friends	Hattie the Fox	M. Fox	F
Scholastic	Express Yourself	Duckat	G. Gordon	F
Scholastic	Imagine That!	Starring First Grade	M. Cohen	F
Scholastic	Information Finders	Daniel's Dinosaurs	M. Carmine	F
Scholastic	Imagine That!	The Night Sky	A. Pernick	F
Houghton Mifflin	Discover	Swimmy	L. Lionni	F
Houghton Mifflin	Surprise	Con Mi Hermano/With My Brother	E. Roe	F
Houghton Mifflin	Discover	One of Three	A. Johnson	F
Houghton Mifflin	Be A Nature Detective	Animal Tracks	A. Dorros	F
Houghton Mifflin	Discover	Something From Nothing	P. Gilman	F
Houghton Mifflin	Share	The Itsy Bitsy Spider	I. Trapani	F
Scholastic	I Spy	The Very Hungry Caterpillar	E. Carle	F
Houghton Mifflin	Hello	The Lady With the Alligator Purse	N. Westcott	F
Scott Foresman	Our Singing Planet	Tommy Meng San	B.Y. Louie & D. Louie	G
Scott Foresman	A Canary With Hiccups	A Healthy Day	P. Showers	G
Scott Foresman	A Canary With Hiccups	Eat Up, Gemma	S. Hayes	G

Publisher	Basal title	Story title	Author	Level
Scott Foresman	Once Upon a Hippo	Hot Hippo	M. Hadithi	G
Scott Foresman	The Big Blank Piece of Paper	Pigericks	A. Lobel	G
Harcourt Brace	Full Sails	Wonderful Worms	L. Glaser	G
Harcourt Brace	Full Sails	Henny Penny	S. Butler	G
Harcourt Brace	Full Sails	Little Lumpty	M. Imai	G
Harcourt Brace	Full Sails	The Wild Woods	S. James	G
Harcourt Brace	Out of the Blue	This Is the Way We Go to School	E Baer	G
Harcourt Brace	Living Colors	Shoes From Grandpa	M. Fox	G
Harcourt Brace	Out of the Blue	Matthew and Tilly	R. Jones	G
Silver Burdett Ginn	Literature Works Collection 2/1			
Scholastic	Hometowns	It Takes a Village	J. Cowen-Fletcher	G
Houghton Mifflin	Surprise	There's an Alligator Under My Bed	M. Mayer	G
Houghton Mifflin	Be A Nature Detective	What Lives in a Shell?	K. Zoehfeld	G
Houghton Mifflin	Discover	Fishy Facts	I. Chermayeff	G
Houghton Mifflin	Getting Started	Three Cheers for Tacky	H. Lester	G
Silver Burdett Ginn	Readables	Rhyme Me a World		G
Silver Burdett Ginn	Literature Works Collection 1/4	The Leaving Morning	A. Johnson	G
Harcourt Brace	Full Sails	Jenny's Journey	S. Sampton	H
Harcourt Brace	All Smiles	Dreams	E. Keats	H
Harcourt Brace	Living Colors	The Sun, the Wind, and the Rain	L. Peters	H
Harcourt Brace	Out of the Blue	Max Found Two Sticks	Pinkney	H
Scholastic	Super Solvers	Pigsty	M. Teague	H
Scholastic	Information Finders	The Listening Walk	P. Showers	H
Scholastic	Hometowns	A Special Trade	S. Wittman	H
Scholastic	Super Solvers	The Paper Crane	M. Bang	H
Scholastic	Information Finders	Creatures at My Feet	C. David	H
Scholastic	Literacy Place Book	The Three Little Pigs	G. Bishop	H
Scholastic	Beginning Literacy	What Do You Do With a Kangaroo?	M. Mayer	H
Scholastic	Super Solvers	Belling the Cat	E. Rice	H
Scholastic	Literacy Place Book	Five Live Bongos	G. Lyon	H
Scholastic	Imagine That!	Moondance	F. Asch	H
Houghton Mifflin	That's Incredible!	The Day Jimmy's Boa Ate the Wash	T. Noble	H
Houghton Mifflin	Share	A Color Of His Own	L. Lionni	H
Houghton Mifflin	Surprise	If You Give a Moose a Muffin	L. Numeroff	H
Houghton Mifflin	Discover	A Mother For Choco	K. Kasza	H
Houghton Mifflin	Discover	Enzo the Wonderfish	C. Wilcox	H

Publisher	Basal title	Story title	Author	Level
Houghton Mifflin	Good Friends	My First American Friend	S. Jin	H
Houghton Mifflin	Surprise	The Tug of War	V. Ellis	H
Silver Burdett Ginn	Literature Works Collection 2/1	Little Nino's Pizzeria	K. Barbour	H
Silver Burdett Ginn	Literature Works Collection 2/1	Home in the Sky	J. Baker	H
Silver Burdett Ginn	Literature Works Collection 2/1	Dear Mr. Blueberry	S. James	H
Silver Burdett Ginn	Literature Works Collection 2/1	Julius	A. Johnson	H
Harcourt Brace	All Smiles			
Houghton Mifflin	Pet Show Today!			
Scott Foresman	My Favorite Foodles	From Seeds to Zucchinis	L. Delacre	H
Scott Foresman	My Favorite Foodles	The Great, Big, Enormous Turnip	A. Tolstoy	H
Scott Foresman	Happy Faces	Mouse's Marriage	J. Morimoto	H
Scott Foresman	Our Singing Planet	The Little Red Hen and the Grain of Wheat	S.C. Bryant	I
Scott Foresman	Happy Faces	It's George	M. Cohen	I
Scott Foresman	How to Talk to Bears	Slippery Ice	J. Stevenson	I
Scott Foresman	Why Does Water Wiggle?	The Tortoise and the Hare	J. Stevens	I
Scott Foresman	You Be the Bread and I'll Be the Cheese	Hello Amigos!	T. Brown	I
Scott Foresman	Bathtub Voyages	Dinosaurs on the Road	L. Brown & M. Brown	I
Scott Foresman	The Big Blank Piece of Paper	The Chicken and the Egg	J. Martin	I
Scott Foresman	Once Upon a Hippo	Rosa and Blanca	J. Hayes	I
Scott Foresman	The Big Blank Piece of Paper	Eddy B. Pigboy	O. Dunrea	I
Scott Foresman	You Be the Bread and I'll Be the Cheese	The Relatives Came	C. Rylant	I
Harcourt Brace	Living Colors			
Harcourt Brace	Full Sails	Frog and Toad Together	A. Lobel	I
Harcourt Brace	Full Sails	Lionel in the Winter	S. Krensky	I
Harcourt Brace	All Smiles	Planets	K. Jackson	I
Harcourt Brace	All Smiles	Geraldine's Baby Brother	H. Keller	I
Harcourt Brace	Living Colors	Too Many Tamales	G. Soto	I
Houghton Mifflin	Family Photos			
Harcourt Brace	Out of the Blue	Coyote	G. McDermott	I
Harcourt Brace	Out of the Blue	Rabbit and Tiger	F. Nicholson	I
Harcourt Brace	Living Colors	The Great Ball Game	J. Bruchac	I

Publisher	Basal title	Story title	Author	Level
Harcourt Brace	All Smiles	The Adventures of Snail at School	J. Stadler	I
Scholastic	Story Studio	The Legend of the Indian Paintbrush	T. dePoala	I
Houghton Mifflin	Tell Me a Tale			
Scholastic	Information Finders	Don't Tease the Guppies	P. Collins	I
Scholastic	Snapshots	Ruby the Copycat	P. Rathmann	I
Houghton Mifflin	Good Friends			
Scholastic	Lights! Camera! Action!	Lights! Camera! Action!	G. Gibbons	I
Scholastic	Lend a Hand	Under the City	S. Kroll	I
Scholastic	Snapshots	George Ancona: Then & Now	G. Ancona	I
Scholastic	Animal World	The Old Ladies Who Liked Cats	C. Greene	I
Scholastic	Lights! Camera! Action!	The Little Pigs' Puppet Book	N. Watson	I
Houghton Mifflin	Pet Show Today!	Arthur's Pet Business	M. Brown	I
Silver Burdett Ginn	Literature Works Collection 1/4			
Silver Burdett Ginn	Literature Works Collection 1/4	Baby Rattlesnake	L. Moroney	I
Scott Foresman	Happy Faces			
Silver Burdett Ginn	Literature Works Collection 1/4	Stone Soup	M. Sharmat	I
Scholastic	Hometowns	Stone Soup	A. Betz	I
Silver Burdett Ginn	Literature Works Collection 1/4	Lazy Lion	M. Hadithi & A. Kennaway	I
Silver Burdett Ginn	Literature Works Collection 1/4	Lizzie and Harold	E. Winthrop	I
Silver Burdett Ginn	Literature Works Collection 2/1	The Letter	A. Lobel	I
Silver Burdett Ginn	Literature Works Collection 2/1	A Birthday Basket for Tia	P. Mora	I
Silver Burdett Ginn	Literature Works Collection 2/1	Truman's Aunt Farm	J.K. Rattigan	I
Scholastic	Super Solvers			
Silver Burdett Ginn	Literature Works Collection 2/1	The Mysterious Tadpole	S. Kellogg	I
Silver Burdett Ginn	Literature Works Collection 2/2	Big Old Bones: A Dinosaur Tale	C. Carrick	I
Scott Foresman	Happy Faces	Mama's Birthday Present	C. Tafolla	J
Scott Foresman	Why Does Water Wiggle?	A Pet for the Goofs	J. Cole & P. Cole	J
Scott Foresman	Bathtub Voyages	The Tub People	P. Conrad	J
Scott Foresman	Why Does Water Wiggle?	Animal Babies	J. Burton	J

Publisher	Basal title	Story title	Author	Level
Scott Foresman	How to Talk to Bears	Higher on the Door	J. Stevenson	J
Scott Foresman	Bathtub Voyages	My Dog Is Lost!	E. Keats & P. Cherr	J
Scott Foresman	How to Talk to Bears	Gino Bandino	D. Engel	J
Scott Foresman	Bathtub Voyages	Dinosaurs, Dragonflies, & Diamonds	G. Gibbons	J
Scott Foresman	Once Upon a Hippo	Three Up A Tree	J. Marshall	J
Scott Foresman	Why Does Water Wiggle?	The Monkey and the Pea	N. Ryan	J
Scott Foresman	The Big Blank Piece of Paper	The Story	A. Lobel	J
Scott Foresman	The Big Blank Piece of Paper	Regina's Big Mistake	M. Moss	J
Scott Foresman	Once Upon a Hippo	About Jimmy Lee	P. Cummings	J
Scott Foresman	You Be the Bread and I'll Be the Cheese	The Mother's Day Sandwich	J. Wynot	J
Scott Foresman	The Big Blank Piece of Paper	Do-It-Yourself Experiments	G. Penrose	J
Harcourt Brace	All Smiles	New Shoes for Silvia	J. Hurwitz	J
Harcourt Brace	Out of the Blue	Anansi and the Talking Melon	E. Kimmel	J
Harcourt Brace	Out of the Blue	Six-Dinner Sid	I. Moore	J
Harcourt Brace	Out of the Blue	Nine-in-One, Grr! Grr!	C. Spagnoli	J
Harcourt Brace	Out of the Blue	Dinosaurs Alive and Well!	L. Brown & M. Brown	J
Harcourt Brace	Out of the Blue	Emily and Alice Again	J. Champion	J
Harcourt Brace	Out of the Blue	Mr. Putter & Tabby Pour the Tea	C. Rylant	J
Harcourt Brace	All Smiles	Henry and Mudge in the Green Time	C. Rylant	J
Harcourt Brace	Living Colors	Annie's Gifts	A. Medearis	J
Harcourt Brace	Living Colors	Shooting Stars	F. Branley	J
Harcourt Brace	Living Colors	Grandfather's Dream	H. Keller	J
Harcourt Brace	Living Colors	The Night of the Stars	D. Guitierrez	J
Scholastic	Super Solvers	Marti and the Mango	D. Moreton	J
Scholastic	Snapshots	Amazing Grace	M. Hoffman	J
Scholastic	Super Solvers	The Code King	B. Lewis	J
Scholastic	Information Finders	The Plant Castle	P. Morea	J
Scholastic	Lights! Camera! Action!	Circus Girl	M. Garland	J
Scholastic	Snapshots	Ronald Morgan Goes to Bat	P. Giff	J
Scholastic	Lights! Camera! Action!	The Swallow's Gift	L. Curry	J
Scholastic	Story Studio	Abuelo and the Three Bears	J. Tello	J
Scholastic	Story Studio	The Treasure Hunt	A. Medearis	J
Scholastic	Hometowns	The Snow Glory	C. Rylant	J

Publisher	Basal title	Story title	Author	Level
Scholastic	Story Studio	Red Riding Hood	J. Marshall	J
Scholastic	Lend a Hand	Follow the Drinking Gourd	J. Winter	J
Scholastic	Lights! Camera! Action!	The Bremen Town Musicians	H. Wilhelm	J
Scholastic	Story Studio	Little Grunt and the Big Egg	T. dePaola	J
Scholastic	Hometowns	Maps and Journeys	K. Petty & J. Wood	J
Houghton Mifflin	That's Incredible!	What Happened to Patrick's Dinosaurs?	C. Carrick	J
Silver Burdett Ginn	Literature Works Collection 2/1	Abuela	A. Dorros	J
Harcourt Brace	Out of the Blue			
Silver Burdett Ginn	Literature Works Collection 2/2	Fossils Tell of Long Ago	Aliki	J
Silver Burdett Ginn	Literature Works Collection 2/2	The Littlest Dinosaurs	B. Most	J
Silver Burdett Ginn	Literature Works Collection 2/2	The Bossy Gallito	L. Gonzalez	J
Silver Burdett Ginn	Literature Works Collection 2/2	Two of Everything	L.T. Hong	J
Houghton Mifflin	Tell Me a Tale			
Silver Burdett Ginn	Literature Works Collection 2/2	Aunt Flossie's Hats	E.F. Howard	J
Silver Burdett Ginn	Literature Works Collection 2/2	Will You Please Feed Our Cat	J. Stevenson	J
Scott Foresman	The Big Blank Piece of Paper	Emma's Dragon Hunt	C. Stock	K
Scott Foresman	Bathtub Voyages	Plant of the Grown-Ups	G. Gedatus	K
Scott Foresman	How to Talk to Bears	Minnie the Mambo Mosquito	C. Tafolla	K
Scott Foresman	How to Talk to Bears	Nessa's Fish	N. Luenn	K
Scott Foresman	Why Does Water Wiggle?	Buffy's Orange Leash	S. Golder & L. Memling	K
Scott Foresman	Why Does Water Wiggle?	My Dog and the Green Sock Mystery	D. Adler	K
Scott Foresman	Why Does Water Wiggle?	Tomas and the Library Lady	P. Mora	K
Scott Foresman	You Be the Bread and I'll Be the Cheese	Amelia Bedelia Helps Out	P. Parrish	K
Scott Foresman	Why Does Water Wiggle?	The Big Fish Who Wasn't So Big	J. Lester	K
Scott Foresman	You Be the Bread and I'll Be the Cheese	Molly the Brave and Me	J. O'Connor	K
Harcourt Brace	Living Colors	The Little Painter of Sabana Grande	P. Markun	K

Publisher	Basal title	Story title	Author	Level
Scholastic	Lend a Hand			
Harcourt Brace	Living Colors	Postcards From Pluto	L. Leedy	K
Scholastic	Lend a Hand	Halmoni and the Picnic	S. Choi	K
Scholastic	Lend a Hand	Fire Fighters	R. Maass	K
Scholastic	Story Studio	The Real Author	M. Cohen	K
Scholastic	Lights! Camera! Action!	Music, Music For Everyone	V. Williams	K
Scholastic	Animal World	Ibis: A True Whale Story	Himmelman	K
Scholastic	Animal World	When the Monkeys Came Back	K. Franklin	K
Scholastic	Lend a Hand	The Many Lives of Benjamin Franklin	Aliki	K
Scholastic	Animal World	Will We Miss Them?	A. Wright	K
Houghton Mifflin	Good Friends	What Kind of Baby-sitter Is This?	D. Johnson	K
Houghton Mifflin	Family Photos	A Chair For My Mother	V. Williams	K
Houghton Mifflin	Family Photos	Now One Foot, Now the Other	T. dePaola	K
Houghton Mifflin	That's Incredible!	An Octopus Is Amazing	P. Lauber	K
Houghton Mifflin	Good Friends	Watch Out, Ronald Morgan!	P. Giff	K
Silver Burdett Ginn	Literature Works Collection 2/2	Aesop's Fables	T. dePaola	K
Silver Burdett Ginn	Literature Works Collection 2/2	Soon, Annala	R. Levinson	K
Scott Foresman	Bathtub Voyages	The Lost Lake	A. Say	L
Scott Foresman	How to Talk to Bears	Soccer Sam	J. Marzollo	L
Harcourt Brace	Living Colors	Willie's Not the Hugging Kind	J. Barrett	L
Scholastic	Animal World	Kid Heroes of the Environment	C. Dee	L
Scholastic	Animal World	Balto: The Dog Who Saved Nome	M. Davidson	L

Glossary

academic engaged time (time on task) classroom time in which students are actually attending to the valued learning.

academic learning time (ALT) classroom time in which students are actually attending to the work at hand with a high success rate (80% or above).

affixes prefixes, suffixes, and inflectional endings.

analytic phonics a phonic approach using letter-sound relationships by referring to words already known to identify a new phonic element.

assessment procedures used by teachers to identify students' literacy strengths and weaknesses in planning and executing instruction to meet the students' needs.

attention-deficit hyperactivity disorder (ADHD) a disorder in which some students are often more frequently impulsive, fidgety, distracted, impatient, uncooperative, interruptive, and lack the ability to pay attention than children with the same mental age.

auditory discrimination the ability to recognize the differences in speech sounds within words.

automaticity the ability to decode words with minimal effort.

balanced literacy program the use of a variety of teaching approaches, strategies, and materials to teach students what they need to know.

basal reader "a collection of student texts and workbooks, teacher's manuals, and supplemental materials for developing reading and sometimes writing instruction used chiefly in the elementary and middle school grades" (Harris & Hodges, 1995).

big books books with large pictures and print that children in group settings can easily see. The stories often use predictable, repetitive language and pictures.

classics extraordinary books that last beyond their authors' lives and continue to attract readers.

computer-assisted instruction (CAI) instruction that interacts with a microcomputer.

content reading ability the degree to which a student can adequately comprehend and retain content or expository information.

contextual analysis a word-identification strategy that helps students figure out the meanings of words by how they are used in the context of sentences or passages.

contextualized language use keeping language in context, such as reading and writing full texts rather than excerpts.

contextual knowledge word knowledge derived from context.

core literature books that should be taught in the classroom through close reading and intensive consideration. These books can serve as important stimuli for writing and discussion.

culturally and linguistically diverse learners students whose culture as well as language or dialect differ from those of the school.

culturally responsive instruction teaching that is consistent with the values of the students' own culture and aimed at improving academic learning.

decontextualized language use the basis for literacy, requiring developing language awareness.

definitional knowledge word knowledge based upon a definition from a dictionary or glossary.

dialects the ways people speak in different parts of the country or in specific cultures.

directed reading activity (DRA) an organized, sequenced strategy for teaching a reading selection. Typical steps include motivation, vocabulary, silent reading, comprehension checking, purposeful oral reading, skill development, and enrichment activities.

directed reading-thinking activity (DR-TA)   an organized, sequenced strategy for teaching a reading selection that focuses on reading as a thinking process. Three overall steps include readiness and prediction, active reading, and reaction (Stauffer, 1975).

dual-language reading approach   a reading approach that provides reading instruction in the primary language of the students as well as in standard English.

emergent literacy   children's reading and writing behaviors that occur before and develop into conventional literacy.

English as a second language (ESL)   an instructional program developed for teaching English to students who live in an English-speaking community, but come from homes where English is not the spoken or native language.

environmental print   print in the environment, such as store names, menus, and signs, that has meaning to children.

experiential and conceptual backgrounds   readers' experiences that are both concrete and abstract (knowledge), as well as their reasoning abilities in using this knowledge. This is also known as background knowledge.

explicit/direct instruction   systematic teaching in which the teacher models and demonstrates learning and gradually turns the responsibility for learning over to the student. This teaching method emphasizes students' understanding of the "when" and "why" of utilizing various capabilities and strategies.

expository text   the text structure found in content books, including (1) description, (2) collection, (3) causation, (4) problem-solution, and (5) comparison.

extended literature   works that teachers may assign to individuals or small groups as homework or supplemental class work.

functions of written language   to inform, entertain, and direct.

gifted students   students identified to have high-performance abilities and capabilities based on mental age and creativity.

grapheme-phoneme relationships   the relationships between written letters and letter combinations and the sounds they represent.

homonyms   words that sound alike but are spelled differently.

inclusion   students with disabilities are assigned to regular classrooms for the whole day and are allowed to participate in all school activities.

individualized education plan (IEP)   a plan of education that details the educational program for each student who has a learning disability. The school, student, and parents jointly develop an IEP and are often referred to as the multidisciplinary team.

inferential questions   questions that combine background knowledge and text information to make predictions about story content.

interactive theory of reading   the theory that readers use information from the text, their experiential and conceptual backgrounds, and the context in which reading occurs to arrive at meaning.

language-experience approach (LEA)   the approach for teaching reading that is built on children's experiences. Children dictate their experiences and the teacher writes them down or the children write their own stories as the basis for instruction.

limited-English proficiency (LEP) students   students who lack sufficient English language skills to achieve in a regular classroom setting. These students need special linguistic instruction in order to have the opportunity to achieve in the regular classroom setting.

literacy   the ability to read and write proficiently.

literal questions   questions based on information explicitly stated in the text.

literature-based reading program   a program that emphasizes the ability to read all types of literature with understanding, appreciation, and enjoyment.

mainstreaming the least restrictive school environment, which has been interpreted to mean the regular classroom. Students who are mainstreamed move in and out of the regular classroom in order to receive special instruction.

meaning vocabulary words whose meanings and concepts are represented by words already understood.

mediated instruction intervention or guidance that another person (such as a peer, parent, or teacher) provides in the teaching-learning process.

metacognition awareness and control of one's cognitive functioning while reading.

modeling demonstration of strategies and behaviors to enhance their conceptualization.

opportunity to learn allotment of time and exposure to instruction.

oral language the language abilities of speaking and listening.

paired reading one student reads aloud as another follows along in the text.

phonemic awareness understanding that spoken words are represented by units of sounds or can be separated into speech sounds.

phonics the teaching of reading in a manner that stresses symbol-sound relationships.

point of view the viewpoint that authors choose when they tell a story, including the details they describe and the judgements they make.

polysemous words words having different meanings (such as *air* in *air* ball and "to *air* one's views").

predictable books books in which students can grasp easily what the author is going to say next. Such books use much repetition of content, language, and illustrations.

readability the approximate difficulty level of written material.

readers' theater a performance of literature (e.g., a story, poetry, a play, or a picture book) that is read aloud in an interpretative manner.

reading the active process of constructing meaning from written text in relation to the experiences and knowledge of the reader.

reading log a short-term writing activity that supports student discussion or reflection on ideas found in literature that they have read.

recreational reading groups students grouped on the basis of their interests to discuss the same book, books by the same author, or books with similar characteristics.

response journals written letters or dialogues that students share with each other and/or their teacher on a regular basis.

scaffolds "forms of support provided by the teacher (or another student) to help students bridge the gap between current abilities and the intended goal (Rosenshine & Meister, 1992).

schema the background knowledge structure for an idea, object, or word meaning.

schemata the meaningful organization of knowledge based on one's experiences. We have schemata for places, events, and roles.

schema theory of reading the theory that reading involves many different levels of analysis at the same time but at different levels.

semantic clues a contextual-analysis strategy using the meanings of known words in a sentence or passage to identify an unknown word.

semantics the meaning features of language.

shared reading students see the text as it is read aloud to them—usually from big books—and are invited to read aloud.

sight vocabulary words that a reader knows and comprehends instantly.

skill learning that is specific in nature and amenable to behavioral objectives.

slots attributes of a schema that must be recognized for a reader to activate that schema.

SQ3R a systematized study procedure for reading content chapters. *SQ3R* stands for "survey, question, read, recite, and review."

sustained silent reading (SSR) a scheduled period of silent reading in the classroom. During this time, both teacher and students may read a book or any form of print without interruption.

story schema   readers' mental representation of story parts and their relationships. Story schema is also referred to as story grammar and story structure.

strategic learning   learning that is less specific than skill learning and represents higher-level cognitive thinking that is used in interacting with text information.

structural analysis   a word-identification strategy that focuses on visual or structural patterns and meanings that change as a result of adding inflectional endings, prefixes, and suffixes and combining root words.

study skills   a general term for those techniques and strategies that help a person read or listen for specific purposes with the intent to remember; commonly, following directions, locating, selecting, organizing, and retaining information, interpreting typographic and graphic aids, and reading flexibility.

style   an author's choice and arrangement of words to create plot, characterizations, and setting together in a meaningful whole.

syllabication   the division of a word into its basic units of pronunciation.

syntactic clues   a contextual-analysis strategy using the knowledge of word order in a language to identify an unknown word.

syntax   the word order or grammar of a language.

synthetic phonics   a phonic approach beginning with instruction on individual sounds.

thematic units   integrating content (e.g., of science, math, and social studies) and using literacy to facilitate children's learning of important concepts and ideas.

theme   the central idea that ties the plot, characterizations, and setting together in a meaningful whole.

visual discrimination   the ability to note visual similarities and differences, particularly in letters and words (e.g., the difference between *b* and *g* and the difference between *bat* and *bit*).

whole language   a style of reading instruction based on the idea that students learn best when literacy is naturally connected to their oral language.

whole-word approach   a word-identification strategy that focuses on learning words as wholes rather than by any form of analysis.

word identification   the process of arriving at the pronunciation of a word, given the printed letter representations (also known as decoding).

Index